7/89

Child of Paradise

HARVARD FILM STUDIES

Pierre Renoir and Jean-Louis Barrault in the
final sequence of *Les Enfants du paradis*

Child of Paradise

MARCEL CARNÉ
AND THE
GOLDEN AGE OF
FRENCH CINEMA

Edward Baron Turk

HARVARD UNIVERSITY PRESS
Cambridge, Massachusetts
London, England · 1989

Publication of this book has been aided by a grant from
the Foreign Languages and Literatures Section of the School
of Humanities and Social Science at the Massachusetts
Institute of Technology.

This book is printed on acid-free paper, and its binding materials
have been chosen for strength and durability.

Library of Congress Cataloging-in-Publication Data

Turk, Edward Baron.
    Child of paradise : Marcel Carné and the golden age of French
cinema / Edward Baron Turk.
    p.   cm.—(Harvard film studies)
    Filmography: p.
    Bibliography: p.
    Includes index.
    ISBN 0-674-11460-4 (alk. paper)
    1. Carné, Marcel. 2. Motion picture producers and directors—
France—Biography. I. Title. II. Series
PN1998.3.C37T87 1989   88-17558
791.43'0233'0924—dc19   CIP

*In memory of my father and
my brother Richard*

*In honor of my mother and
my brother Alan*

Contents

Acknowledgments

First and foremost I thank Elfrida Filippi of the Bureau du Cinéma, Ministère des Affaires Etrangères, Paris, for facilitating my access to films and people in France. I am also grateful for the good will of the French Cultural Services of Boston and Cambridge: to Cultural Attaché Véronique Marteau and her predecessors Bernard Genton and Xavier North, I express deep thanks; for her unflagging interest in my project, I am beholden to their administrative assistant, Marie-Françoise Saddier-Paquette.

Support for preparing this book came in part from a *bourse de séjour d'études* granted me in 1985 by the Ministère des Affaires Etrangères, Paris. The Massachusetts Institute of Technology provided other significant support: I extend particular gratitude to former Dean of the School of Humanities and Social Science Harold J. Hanham; to his successor, Ann F. Friedlaender; to Associate Dean Emeritus E. Cary Brown; to Professor Claire Kramsch, head of Foreign Languages and Literatures; and to Administrative Officer Karen Bushold and her predecessor Marjorie Lucker. I also thank Administrative Assistants Jack Hayes, Susan Jarczyk, June Al-Khatib, Lynn Mittal, Sarah Brady, Julie Ogletree, Carol Watson, and, most heartily, Chris Pomiecko and Barbara Schulman.

The Cinémathèque Française enabled me to view prints of films unavailable in the United States: to Mary Meerson, Hubert Astier, André Rieupeyrout, and Lucie Lichtig, I extend deep appreciation. For special screenings on this side of the Atlantic, I am grateful for the invaluable help of Armelle Maala at the Audiovisual Services of the French Embassy, New York; of Charles Silver and his associates at the Film Study Center of the Museum of Modern Art, New York; and of Jan Crocker and his staff at the University Film Study Center, Cambridge, Massachusetts.

The French Library in Boston granted me full access to the Carné Archives. I sincerely thank the library's Executive Director Vera Lee, her predecessors Mylo Housen and Jane Stahl, and Chris Szabo and Persheng Sadegh-Vaziri of the library's Médiathèque. I also wish to acknowledge the kindness of Count Arnaud de Vitry d'Avaucourt, Chairman of the Board of the French Library in Boston.

Alain Hardel, Patrick Lepaul, Jean-Rémy Mantion, and Lutz Wenner assisted me in obtaining written sources from France. For further help in acquiring documentation, I am indebted to André Heinrich and Ralph Vitello. I also thank Philippe Demange, Director of the Victorine Studios, Nice, and Jacques François, President of the Société des Arts de Tourrettes-sur-Loup. For assistance in tracking down sources in this country, I salute Thomas J. Kiely and the Interlibrary Loan staff of the MIT Libraries.

Numerous members of the French film community agreed to share thoughts and memories with me. I thank Arletty, Jean-Louis Barrault, Fernand Bernardi, Tania Busselier, Margot Capelier, Christian-Jaque, Gilles Kohler, Madame Jacques Prévert, Pierre Prévert, Claude Renoir, Paule Sengissen, and Alexander Trauner for their time and interest. My exchanges with François Truffaut were especially profitable. I owe an immense debt of gratitude to Roland Lesaffre for his generosity of spirit. Above all I thank Marcel Carné for many hours of lively conversation in January 1980, May 1981, June and July 1983, and September and October 1985.

The response of those who read an embryonic version of this work helped to shape my subsequent endeavor. In this regard I offer warm thanks to Professors Catherine Chvany, Robert E. Jones, Margery Resnick, and Peter H. Smith of MIT, Professor Charles Affron of New York University, and Professor Emeritus Warren French of Indiana and Purdue Universities. John R. Pearson, Jr., also read portions of that prior version, and his perceptions were enlightening. Work on my present text profited from discussions and correspondence with François Garçon, André Heinrich, and Jacques Siclier, and from a reading by Evelyn Ehrlich of drafts of chapters 9 and 11. I am grateful to Professor Peter S. Donaldson for advice on illustrations.

Annette Insdorf is responsible for my having discovered the worthiness of writing about filmmakers. Louis J. Iandoli alerted me to the circumspection required when relating an artist's life to his works. David E. Lapin scrutinized each word of nearly each draft of this book and urged me relentlessly to do better. Philip D. Cobb furnished constant moral support. Barry G. MacMillan helped me to cope with self-doubt. To all these friends, I express enduring affection. To those who facilitated this book's production at Harvard University Press, I signal genuine appreciation.

If you live in France . . . and you have written one
good book, or painted one good picture, or directed
one outstanding film fifty years ago and nothing else
since, you are still recognized and honored accordingly.
People take their hats off and call you *maître*. They do
not forget. In Hollywood—in Hollywood, you're as
good as your last picture.

ERICH VON STROHEIM

Why [is] it that I [am] always being honored and
celebrated abroad, while in the country that is my
own, in which I was born, I encounter only attacks,
sarcasms, and even disdain from those who claim to
love an Art to which I have devoted my life?

MARCEL CARNÉ

Be beautiful! and be sad!

CHARLES BAUDELAIRE

Prologue:
Fortune and Critics' Eyes

On May 14, 1980, Marcel Carné became the first French film director to occupy a seat in France's Academy of Fine Arts. The event generated ironic touches that escaped neither Carné nor his confreres. Rooted in the era of Richelieu, Mazarin, and Colbert, the Academy is a monument to French elitism. Carné, the self-educated son of a cabinetmaker, declared himself "a child of the people." Having long outgrown his legendary taste for extravagance, Carné insisted that the installation ceremony take place not in the grand hall ordinarily used for formal occasions but in a modest room designed for working sessions. The day's incongruities became most apparent when Carné, as is customary, was called upon to eulogize his predecessor, the art historian Count Arnauld Doria, a military leader of noble lineage. A pacifist whose professed politics have always inclined to the left, Carné could only point jokingly to "the impressive gap that separates me from my illustrious predecessor."

Carné had at first been unreceptive to the idea of a seat in the Academy, since throughout his career he has found himself at odds with the French government's policies toward the arts. Yet Carné came to realize that his election was more than a personal tribute. It represented a legitimation of the cinema by France's arts establishment. As he declared to his fellow Academicians, "It would be impossible not to acknowledge that by calling upon me to sit with you and take part in your work, you have honored, through me, all of French cinema." [1]

Indeed, Marcel Carné has come to symbolize an era which the popular imagination refers to nostalgically as the Golden Age of French cinema. Generally thought of as extending from 1930 to 1939 but arguably lasting through World War II, this was the period when France recaptured the creative vitality and critical prestige it had relinquished almost completely to the American film industry by 1914. At least four directors dominated the Golden Age: Jacques Feyder, René Clair, Jean Renoir, and Carné. The Golden Age also embraced figures as diverse as Jean Vigo, Marcel L'Herbier, Sacha Guitry, Marcel Pagnol, and Julien Duvivier. Not until the New Wave (1958–62) would a constellation of French filmmakers again display such imposing and influential creative powers.

Carné is careful not to overestimate the extent of high achievement during this period: "It is claimed that France had an astonishing density of 'genius directors.' Actually there were not that many. About five or six of us, who directed almost one film per year, and each one was anticipated with impatience and curiosity." Yet he, too, speaks of the era in heroic, almost mystical terms: "Above all, the cinema was our religion. We would partake of the sacrament by making a film: the director and those around him moved in a kind of trance. I had the best team the cinema will probably ever see: Prévert, Trauner, Kosma, Schüfftan, to name just a few. They all moved with me. We dug deep. We were not afraid of risks . . . Ambition must not be confused with *arrivisme*. We had the former, and that requires no excuse." [2]

The current tendency of the French press to dub Carné "the exemplary man of 'the Golden Age' of French cinema" [3] is not without explanation. The only surviving member of this legendary group of directors, Carné is still a presence in French cultural affairs. Clair's film career ended in 1965, Renoir's in 1969. Carné completed his latest movie, *La Bible*, in 1977, and he has plans for several more. The fact that most critics judge his later work to be hopelessly outdated simply reinforces the association of Carné with times past and strengthens his mystique as a sole survivor. [4]

The import of Carné's longevity can be appreciated in contrast with the brief life and career of Jean Vigo (b. 1905). Both men were once considered to be filmdom's wonder boys. But Vigo died in 1934, when Carné was still an apprentice to Feyder. This premature death consecrated an image of Vigo as the cinema's Rimbaud: a short period of intense brilliance suddenly extinguished left unresolved the question of what might have been produced had Vigo continued to create. Carné's lengthy career has made him more like the cinema's Jacques-Louis David. As in the case of David, Carné's creative gifts have not matured with age. Yet in witnessing the director's period of decline, the general public has become all the more willing to mythologize Carné's years of unmistakable strength.

The natural association of Carné and the Golden Age is reinforced by the period's salient aesthetic features. The Golden Age was known for its literate film scenarios and dialogue. But Feyder, Clair, and to a certain extent Renoir all produced major works during the era of silents. Only

Carné came to the profession after the shift to talkies. The Golden Age is also recognized as the great period of French realism. Yet Clair and Vigo were leaders of the avant-garde's quest in the 1920s for "pure cinema," or a cinema completely distinct from the codes of written poetry, theater, and the representational novel; their talent for self-conscious, abstract tricks is plainly visible in their narrative films of the 1930s. Carné's concept of filmmaking was shaped principally by Feyder, and it reflected the latter's adherence to an ideal of directorial unobtrusiveness and to precepts of realism that, while eminently cinematic, had clear links with literature.

One further reason for the popular image of Marcel Carné as the French Golden Age director par excellence is his allegiance to France throughout his career. Feyder directed at various times in Germany, Hollywood, and England before retiring to Switzerland during World War II. Clair worked in England and, during much of the war, in America, returning to France from Hollywood only after the Liberation. Renoir, too, spent the 1940s in Hollywood, where he became an American citizen; and although he returned to France after directing *The River* (1950) in India, Renoir chose to spend his final years in Beverly Hills. By contrast, Carné has never worked abroad. He chose not to exile himself during the war—a fact which many have construed as an accommodation to the Nazi Occupation. He declined Alexander Korda's offer to direct in London when the war ended. With the exception of three weeks of location shooting in New York for *Trois Chambres à Manhattan* (1965) and several months of preparation and shooting for *La Bible* in Sicily and Israel, Carné has remained wedded to *la douce France*. Of the directors belonging to the Golden Age pantheon, he is the only one no country but France can lay claim to.[5]

The facts that explain the perception of Carné as the central Golden Age figure also account for the reality of his postwar decline. Longevity has worked to the advantage of certain filmmakers, such as Ford, Buñuel, and Kurosawa. But it is rare that a director can sustain the level of excellence Carné achieved in the late 1930s and early 1940s with works like *Le Quai des Brumes*, *Le Jour se lève*, and *Les Enfants du paradis*. Further, Carné's entry into the profession at a time when rules of film narrative seemed firmly established enabled him to produce polished pictures at the outset of his career; he never had to grapple with the basic assumptions of film language, as had Clair and Renoir, and as would Truffaut and Godard. He was therefore conditioned to cling to principles of film aesthetics even when these no longer proved fashionable. Finally, Carné's professional insularism, which allowed him to work repeatedly with perhaps the best creative and technical crew ever assembled in France, foreclosed the possible rejuvenation of his practice through interaction with filmmakers in other countries. Ironically, Carné's special brand of team production might have made him more at ease in America than were Renoir and Clair, whose more idiosyncratic manners of self-expression were not particularly suited to Hollywood's system of creative collaboration.

Between 1937 and 1945 Carné directed six works that have become part of France's cultural patrimony: *Drôle de Drame*, *Le Quai des Brumes*, *Hôtel du Nord*, *Le Jour se lève*, *Les Visiteurs du soir*, and *Les Enfants du paradis*. The artistic merit of these films is widely acknowledged. Their interest, however, is not solely aesthetic. Taken together, these works constitute a unique document on the manner in which art responds to social and political events—in this case, to the period in French history that witnessed the Popular Front, the Front's demise, France's fall to Germany, and the Occupation. Carné's early achievements, and his later failures, tell us as much about the state and spirit of France as about the art of French film.

In recent years Carné has become something of a French national institution. In 1975 the cabinetmaker's son was guest of honor at a luncheon held at the Elysée Palace by President Valéry Giscard d'Estaing—the first time a French head of state bestowed such a tribute on a film director. In 1978 France's Academy of Cinema Arts and Techniques designated *Les Enfants du paradis* the best French film in the history of talking pictures.[6] In recognition of this distinction Carné was awarded in 1979 a special César (the French equivalent of the Oscar) that was dubbed hyperbolically "the César of Césars." In the same year the French Library in Boston inaugurated Les Salles Carné, the first permanent public exhibition and repository for a French filmmaker's archives in the United States.[7] In October 1985 President François Mitterand granted Carné the insignia of Commander of the Legion of Honor.

Yet Carné's professional destiny has not been a happy one. His sizable creative output since *Les Enfants du paradis*—fourteen films, to date— has been subject to a degree of general neglect unprecedented for a director with the critical standing Carné once enjoyed. The French government's grantmaking agencies have refused Carné all but the most meager support for his films-in-preparation. Since 1961 none of his pictures has been distributed theatrically in the United States. In fact, until the opening of Les Salles Carné in Boston, many American cinephiles were unaware that Marcel Carné is still alive. As the headline of a 1982 piece in

Le Figaro put it, Marcel Carné has become "the honored hobo of French culture."[8] Awards and retrospectives acknowledge ceaselessly the man's early accomplishments. But Carné's recent attempts to direct have consistently miscarried.

Carné's fall from critical grace has been especially dramatic. Since at least 1947 his worth as a motion-picture artist has been challenged and disputed. Critics writing in the 1950s for *Cahiers du Cinéma* fueled the controversy. Hoping to foster a break with the "tradition of quality" then dominating French film production, these astute, like-minded writers deplored the reliance of successful directors such as René Clément, Henri-Georges Clouzot, and Jean Delannoy upon cinematic concepts and values that were much like those which Marcel Carné had espoused in the 1930s and 1940s. By extolling directors whose freer spirits and less schematized approaches to filmmaking were distinct from Carné's, such as Max Ophuls, Jean Cocteau, and Jean-Pierre Melville, and by lionizing Jean Renoir, with whom they felt complete empathy, the *Cahiers* critics skewed French film history in a manner clearly unfavorable to Carné.

Critical equanimity requires the passage of time. The special César awarded to Carné in 1979 probably bespeaks a more balanced view of film history. Coming two decades after the first efforts by directors Godard, Truffaut, and Resnais to dislocate feature-film tradition, the award suggests the ease with which the film industry is now able to acknowledge the contribution of a man who virtually embodies one tradition of French classical filmmaking. But why is Marcel Carné a central figure in French film history? What accounts for the extraordinary esteem and the intense disfavor which the man and his works have elicited at various points in time? How have his controversial wartime activities and even his sexual orientation promoted this ambivalence? These are questions, among others, which my exploration of Carné's career and films will address.

A critical biography of Marcel Carné offers an opportunity to examine the interaction of personal, social, and historical factors in the creation of cinematic art. Fundamental issues must be raised about authorship in film and about film's capacity to speak to—or ignore—the needs of particular segments of society at particular times. The enterprise calls for a probe into the so-called Golden Age of French cinema and an attempt to discern the realities behind the myth. A biography of Marcel Carné also necessitates a disinterested review of the abundant clichés surrounding the man and his career. It especially demands addressing two crucial subjects which commentators over the decades have avoided: his politics and his sexuality. Critics' reticence constitutes a disservice not only to Carné but to film history as well.

In this book I will note the early influences on Carné the boy and Carné the apprentice filmmaker. I will assess his alliance with scenarist Jacques Prévert to determine why this collaboration bore extraordinary results. I will highlight the images, themes, patterns, and techniques that one generally associates with "the Carné touch." I will examine the best of Carné's films as projections of France's moods in moments of social crisis and political flux, and the worst as repetitions of directorial habits too ingrained to allow for flexibility and change. I will explore how a private mythology, deriving from Carné's personal needs and frustrations, has imbued his entire oeuvre. I will outline a psychodynamic entailing the relations between masochism and primal scene experience and engendering much of what I consider specific to Carné's filmmaking practice and aesthetic. I will present many of France's finest actors as they sometimes yield to the requirements of a script and director and sometimes exert an individual force that transcends all prescriptions. I will compare Carné's work with that of other Golden Age directors, especially Jean Renoir's. I will examine the changing criteria for assessing cinematic value during a fifty-year period in France. Above all, I will show the obstinacy with which one man has sought—despite a father's opposition, French censors, Nazi officials, mistrustful producers, vituperous critics, and the New Wave—to create the films he believes in.

The story of Marcel Carné is not simply an account of triumph and decline, of the expulsion from paradise of one of its more talented children. It is also the story of an individual's unremitting effort to reinstate past glories and recapture a remnant of that lost paradise. Carné has made a call for "constructive, impartial, and honest" analysis of his films and career.[9] No artist can ask for anything more, and no commentator should strive for anything less.

PART I

The Novice

CHAPTER 1

Intimations of Eden

Marcel Carné enjoys maintaining a veil around his private life. For many years he refused even to admit that his year of birth was 1906. This evasiveness resulted from an incident that occurred in 1938, when the producer of *Hôtel du Nord* cited Carné's youth as sufficient reason to demand that the film's preliminary budget be trimmed. An indignant Carné vowed never to reveal his age publicly, and to the dismay of early film historians, it is a vow he kept.

Carné's cunning has received considerable attention. In Christian-Jaque's documentary *Carné, l'homme à la caméra* (1985), Jean-Louis Barrault comments that Carné "can be secretive and difficult. He likes to observe but dislikes being watched. He approaches the images he wants to capture on film with feline patience. Like a cat, he can turn around and scratch whoever tries to stroke his back . . . There is no one image of Marcel Carné. There are hundreds, thousands. His contradictions must be accounted for without his help, his truths must be wrenched from him, his insincerities must be held in check."[1]

Carné is not, at least on the surface, the ill-humored, aloof being which the cat analogy suggests. He is affable among company and garrulous, almost to a fault, in conversation. He is nonetheless a master at turning aside inquiries into his personal life and tastes. One can open to almost any page of Renoir's autobiography, *My Life and My Films*, and find details about what the director likes to eat and drink, the kind of furnishings he enjoys, and whom he prefers to be with after a day's shooting and why. Yet the reader of Carné's copious memoirs, *La Vie à belles dents*,[2] remains at a near loss to discern the man behind the professional. The book provides glimpses into the personalities and the practical problems that Carné confronted in the making of his films. But for all it reveals about the author's feelings, it could very well have been written by an observant bystander.

Both *My Life and My Films* and *La Vie à belles dents* conclude with generalizations about love. Renoir notes, "We must never let ourselves be separated from the beloved, because after a long absence she will have become another person."[3] Carné writes, "What counts, lasts, and sometimes marks a life forever is a rejected friendship or a great love betrayed" (*Vbd*, 490).* Carné's thought appears to be the more revealing, pointing to a loss from which he never recovered. But the statement simply floats: Carné never discloses the facts to which, presumably, it is anchored. Although less dramatic, Renoir's remark takes on real personal depth from the fact that it evokes in Renoir (as he explains in the book's final paragraph) memories of his older cousin, Gabrielle, who taught him as a boy "to see the face behind the mask."

Carné prefers the privacy that masks can ensure. This predilection helps account for his leading aesthetic principle, according to which characters and things are subject to the complete control of a removed, omniscient director—a concept of filmmaking that is at odds with Renoir's more spontaneous and participatory approach. While the relative artistic values of Carné's voyeurism and Renoir's exhibitionism can be judged by the films they engender, it is more difficult to assess the effect of sustained secretiveness on a person's life. Yet Roland Lesaffre, Carné's closest friend, points to the fact that for all his apparent gregariousness, Carné is a lonely man. "Solitude is one of the distinctive traits of Marcel Carné. The man lives alone, despairingly alone. That is why he likes to drown himself in the whirlwind of light and shadows."[4]

Marcel Albert Carné was born in Paris on August 18, 1906.[5] His father, Paul, was a cabinetmaker who worked in the faubourg Saint-Antoine. The family lived in an apartment near the Square des Batignolles in the seventeenth arrondissement, a residential working-class district several blocks west of Montmartre. When Carné's mother, Marie, died at age twenty-five, her only child, Marcel, was five years old. Several years later, the boy was offered an account of her death, and it ran like this: "Your mother was from a Breton family, and had very long, beautiful black hair. One day she washed her hair and it didn't dry well enough. She came down with pneumonia and died." Carné has lived his life with this simple story of his mother's past. It is no less a fairy tale than *Juliette ou la clef des songes* (1951) and *La Merveilleuse Visite* (1974), two of his

---

*All references to *La Vie à belles dents* will be indicated parenthetically in the text by "*Vbd*" followed by a page number.

fantasy films whose subject is the sudden loss of an ideally beloved and beautiful being. Nearly all of Carné's films treat love as an ephemeral experience subject inevitably to pain and loss, and Carné's women are themselves more half-finished statues than fully-drawn presences. It is certain that the premature death of his mother influenced Carné's dark conception of love and women.

Carné confides that he has only two memories of his mother, one light-hearted, the other mournful. He recalls her giving him sugar-coated almonds to distribute to friends at his belated baptism, several months before her death. And he remembers visiting her as she lay dying in a hospital ward; hers was "the second bed to the left as you entered." Throughout Carné's oeuvre, simple acts of generosity (epitomized in Carné's memory by the distribution of candy at his baptism) are rare. When they occur, they are regularly opposed by malevolent destiny (exemplified in Carné's life by the illness and demise of his mother).

Carné senses the importance of his mother's death for his subsequent development, but takes care not to overvalue its effect. Although he was not permitted to attend her funeral, he recollects standing over his mother's grave with his father shortly thereafter: "Frankly, I didn't realize any impact. I didn't understand it. I cannot say that it imbued me with an immense and persistent sense of despair. Of course, scores of books have been written on the effect of a child's losing a mother at an early age. Two wonderful women took my mother's place, and I adored them, especially my grandmother. But I do believe there exists something between a son and a mother that I never knew. Without being overly pretentious, I think this lack resulted, for me, in a kind of emotional hypersensitivity. Yes, it's perhaps that. And it gets stronger with the years."[6]

Carné's father was thirty-one years old when his wife died. Lacking the means to hire someone to care for his son at home, he had the boy accompany him to work—and to play. Marcel soon became acquainted with the "stunning succession" (*Vbd*, 13) of his father's mistresses, often in the setting of tawdry Montmartre bordellos. Scandalized by the father's lack of restraint and the boy's early introduction to the realm of adult pleasures, Marcel's paternal grandmother and his maiden aunt Marguerite decided to take responsibility for raising him. From this time on, Carné's father was indifferent to the boy. Although he still lived in the family's apartment on the rue des Moines, the father chose to spend most of his free time alone and away from home.

The father's aloofness was more than counterbalanced by the grandmother and aunt's indulgence. Carné relates his first experience at the neighborhood movies (speaking of himself in the third person singular):

"At one point the film showed a trunk filled with snakes; the trunk toppled over and the slinky reptiles wriggled and writhed along the ground. For the next three or four nights the child was beset by nightmares: he would suddenly awake and howl. His father rightly forbade him to go again to the cinema. His grandmother secretly slipped him a few coins. The child returned to his new discovery, no longer had nightmares, and already had some vague, undefined dreams" (*Vbd*, 14).

This anecdote is revealing on two scores. First, the horrific image of unconfined serpents reappears in Carné's own dreamlike film, *Les Visiteurs du soir* (1943), and can be viewed as emblematic of a major thrust of Carné's entire work: the unleashing of diabolical forces that seek to destroy beauty and love. Further, the anecdote expresses Carné's initial position vis-à-vis film. It suggests that, at the outset, film signified for Carné a secret pleasure, the transgression of a paternal interdiction, and an expression of complicity between him and a woman who replaced his mother. Surely the aesthetic detachment and guardedness of the adult director is in some measure a consequence of the alluring, potentially dangerous, and decidedly feminine associations which the experience of film held for the boy.

Carné's childhood pastimes gave signs of the future director. Throughout much of his life, Carné has been uncomfortable with his diminutive stature (fig. 1). His notoriously tyrannical comportment on the set is, in part, a compensation for his sense of physical inferiority. Even as a child, Marcel was conscious of his difference from playmates. Rather than retreat, he chose to assume an aggressive leadership posture, taking control over his band of friends as they frisked, sported, and waged war against other boys in the Square des Batignolles (fig. 2). One of these "enemy" boys was a year older than Marcel and very proud of the roller skates that added height to his already tall body. He was Pierre Brasseur, the future actor who would eventually portray characters with oversize egos in three of Carné's films, *Le Quai des Brumes*, *Les Enfants du paradis*, and *Les Portes de la nuit*.

Carné is famous for having filmed dreary cityscapes. A major theme of his oeuvre is the unfulfilled desire to escape from the city and return to nature. If he has treated this theme with a mix of nostalgia and cynicism, it is in some degree the result of the Square des Batignolles' impact on his early sensibilities. One of Paris's prettiest small parks, this wooded *jardin à l'anglaise* was, for Marcel, an enchanted oasis in an otherwise unattractive urban environment. It furnished the child with his first intimations of Eden. But Marcel, precocious and alert, intuited early on that just as the Square was a man-made illusion of a country landscape, so

1   Marcel Albert Carné, ca. 1913

society would require that he camouflage his authentic nature behind acceptable masks. Physical pleasures shared with neighborhood boys in a pseudopastoral setting would of necessity yield to the adult world's pressure to conform.

Carné's boyhood exploits in the Square des Batignolles generated his lifelong ambivalence toward nature: a Romantic longing for communion and a post-Romantic disbelief in the possibility of its realization. This duality helps account for the director's obsession with studio reconstructions of vast slices of reality. By controlling the appearance of things himself, Carné risked sealing out authentic human vitality from his films.

2   The Square des Batignolles: an intimation of Eden

But he also forestalled the personal disappointments which, he learned at a tender age, the real world inevitably provokes.

Also forecasting the aesthetic temper of the adult director is the fact that indoor activities quickly took on greater appeal for the young Carné than did outdoor adventures. One of his earliest amusements was staging slide shows for neighborhood friends with the magic lantern he had persuaded his grandmother to buy for him. (Repeatedly, the women in Carné's life provided primary support for his first leanings toward visual entertainment.) Marcel converted his father's bedroom into a makeshift movie theater. He would close the shutters tight, nail a white tablecloth to the wall, and—after locking the door to ensure a captive audience— present repeatedly one-picture slide spectacles with exotic titles such as *Hunting the Tiger in Central Africa* and *Whale-Fishing in the Waters of Iceland*. The boy was ecstatic, his friends less so (*Vbd*, 15).

Carné's early inclination to play impresario may have expressed a half-conscious longing to be part of the professional world of spectacle. This desire's impetus was curtailed, however, by his father's insistence that his son carry on his own trade of cabinetmaking. Carné acquiesced, and upon graduation from primary school he enrolled in a two-year beginners' wood-carving course. He did not find the lessons distasteful; in fact, he acquired an artisan's habit of mind that remained with him for life: a sense for the slow care required to make a quality product, and an ideal of perfect craftsmanship that products bearing his name would have to exhibit. But clearly Carné's interests did not lie in cabinetmaking.

For years, the boy had been attending Sunday movies with the five *sous* given him weekly by his grandmother and his aunt Marguerite. The diversion eventually became a daily habit. After gulping dinner, Carné would walk miles to find a low-priced movie house that might be showing a film by Chaplin, Lang, or Murnau. He would also seek out the farces, biblical dramas, and dramatic comedies of which Gaumont Studios, under the direction of Louis Feuillade, produced scores throughout the 1920s. At this stage in Carné's life, his tastes were joyfully indiscriminate.

Films were not, however, Carné's sole diversion. Equally seductive to the adolescent Marcel were music-hall revues. Carné recalls his first visit to the Folies Bergère in the company of friends who thought it time for him to enlarge his perspective on life: "At the end of the show, one of them turned to me, wide-mouthed, and said, 'Did you see those girls? Dynamite!' No, I had not especially noted the beauty of the women. I saw them only as a function of the décor of which they were a part. I had eyes only for that enormous machinery, those sumptuous sets, those sparkling costumes, all the glitter which some will call sham but which, for a boy of fifteen, was a dazzling revelation" (*Vbd*, 19–20).

Although a consummate film enthusiast, Carné did not yet fathom the sophisticated tricks required for cinematic illusionmaking. The lavish live show at the Folies Bergère, however, gave the future director of *Les Enfants du paradis* his first inkling that, much like cabinetmaking, creating spectacle is a matter of intricate craftsmanship—but without the constraint of practicality. Moreover, to a lad whose world had been defined primarily by the Square des Batignolles and local Paris movie houses, the shows he began to attend at the Casino de Paris, the Moulin Rouge, and the Music-hall des Champs-Elysées suggested new visions and new styles of life.

The Paris music hall, as integral to *les années folles* as jazz, served in no small measure to soften the unpleasant realities that World War I had etched in the minds of Europeans. Frequently compared to a pagan temple in which a fearsome victim, reality, is immolated on an altar, the stage, the French music hall can also be likened to the world of childhood fantasy which Carné, in a manner more modest and naive, attempted to exploit and control in his exotic magic lantern shows for his friends. As Alain Hardel observes, the music hall "reinvents the lost paradise of childhood, of fantasy and magic . . . In the time of a simple song, [the spectator] is at one with the stage, and the entire theater 'communes' in a hymn to the very act of celebration."[7] *Les Enfants du paradis* is Carné's most elaborate glorification, in a nineteenth-century setting, of the world of theatrical spectacle and its interaction with the spectacle of the real world. But throughout Carné's works, artifice and symbolism predominate over ostensible realism. At least part of this directorial inclination finds its roots in Carné's experience of the music hall.

Carné's indifference to the charms of the showgirls he saw on his first night at the Folies Bergère betokens his lifelong lack of sexual interest in women. Yet in a sense Carné's response was more appropriate and sophisticated than that of his prurient companions. He was reacting not to the real women on stage but to a manufactured, mythologized image of woman which the music hall, along with the contemporary cinema, was working to contrive. The inviting image of the Charleston-dancing flapper that had dominated feminine styles in the early 1920s was now giving way to the more ambiguous and awesome persona of the femme fatale, as incarnated by actresses Garbo, Dietrich, and Harlow on screen, and singers Jane Harnac, Josephine Baker, and Mistinguett on stage. This newer brand of sexuality was a mixture of triumphant sex appeal and prosaic vulgarity, combining arrogance and accessibility, distance and proximity. This view of woman as a removed, inscrutable goddess resonated in Carné's imagination for many years. Along with the nostalgia for his deceased mother, it would influence the director's handling of female characters in all of his films, and contribute especially to his most elusive female creation, Garance in *Les Enfants du paradis*.

The practice of attending at least one film or revue daily could not be maintained on a student's allowance. Carné therefore stopped his wood-carving lessons after one year to work for a bank, a grocery store, and, at age eighteen, an insurance company. Unbeknownst to his family, he was also studying photography and elementary filmmaking two nights a week and every Sunday at the Ecole des Arts et Métiers. Although this experience exposed him to the rudiments of the craft, Carné today puts little trust in the utility of film schools. He believes that the ability to create atmosphere, to lighten or darken a face or detail, is a natural talent that cannot be learned. He is also convinced that firsthand experience with a professional crew is a budding director's finest teacher, and that such opportunities best come about through personal contact with individuals already established in the industry. This was the case in Carné's own development.

In truth, the second most important meeting of Carné's professional life—the most important being his encounter (much later) with Jacques Prévert—occurred in the spring of 1928, under very nonprofessional cir-

3 Autographed photo of Françoise Rosay, 1932; inscription translates as "To Marcel Carné, Affectionate Remembrance"

cumstances. A dinner party at the home of mutual friends found Marcel Carné seated next to actress Françoise Rosay (1891–1974) (fig. 3). Rosay was married to one of the directors Carné most admired, Belgian-born Jacques Feyder (fig. 4). Carné was euphoric. During dinner he monopolized the conversation, speaking only of cinema and directing all his remarks to Rosay, who, to his surprise, listened attentively. Exhibiting the same spirit of complicity and protectiveness that Carné found in his aunt and grandmother, Rosay ended the evening by saying: "You absolutely must see Jacques. Call him at the office . . . No, rather . . . let me speak to him, and you phone me in three days. You'll find my number in the phone book" (*Vbd*, 26).

No artificial love goddess of music-hall fantasy, Rosay was a strong-minded woman who knew how to make things happen. Within less than

4 Autographed photo of Jacques Feyder, 1928; inscription translates as "To Marcel Carné, With all my good will and wishes for success in 'the profession'"

a week, a meeting of the two men took place. Several days later, the destiny of the boy torn between movies and stage revues was decided: Feyder hired Carné as assistant cameraman for his next film comedy, *Les Nouveaux Messieurs*. In fact, Carné worked not as assistant cameraman but as assistant director: Feyder had hired an old but ineffectual friend to be his titular assistant and needed someone with the energy and enthusiasm the young Carné evinced.

What does an assistant director do? This is the question Carné asked himself before appearing for work at Billancourt Studios. As he would soon learn, the job might entail as much as substituting for the director at any stage of a film's production, or as little as running to the canteen to buy him a pack of cigarettes. Carné recalls: "Extremely disoriented, and in a position that is hazily defined, I did my best to be useful. Did Feyder ask for a chair to be moved? I rushed forward and beat the prop man, who was always looking over my shoulder. Did a carpet need to be rolled up, a vase of flowers carried from a table to a chest of drawers? I was there, always there" (*Vbd*, 30).

Carné may have done little of substance, but he observed intently. And after shooting was finished, he watched Feyder take control of the film's editing, thus gleaning the fundamentals of cinematic rhythm and movement. Carné remembers this as one of the happier periods of his youth. He had not only found his métier and the joy of taking part in a collective endeavor. He was also harboring an almost filial closeness toward Jacques Feyder. For the first time in his life, Carné sensed that his individual worth was being recognized by an older man he respected.

This experience was not, however, free from anxiety. Convinced that his genuine father would brand professional filmmaking forbidden fruit, Carné felt obliged to conceal his job with Feyder and pretend to be selling insurance. One day, however, a friend of the family accidentally noticed him working on location behind the Paris Opera. He informed the father, and this led to a definitive confrontation. The elder Carné was outraged, calling the cinema a trade for quacks and down-and-outs. Yet realizing that his son's fate was beyond his control, Paul Carné urged him to do as he pleased—so long as he never came begging for money.

Carné thus became part of a profession that, in France, attracted and accepted mainly sons of upper bourgeois families. Always conscious of his social difference, Carné never renounced or felt ashamed of his roots. Indeed, the distinctiveness of his cinematic practice and vision owes much to his abiding respect for the working classes and, especially, artisans. However, like that of the protagonists in the films he would later direct, Carné's newfound sense of well-being was short-lived. *Les Nouveaux Messieurs* proved highly successful. But months before it premiered, Feyder had departed for Hollywood under a three-year contract with Metro-Goldwyn-Mayer, and Carné had been summoned to the Rhineland for eighteen tedious months of military service.

Upon his return to Paris in 1929, Carné worked as assistant cameraman on *Cagliostro*, a film directed by Richard Oswald. He deemed the experience less than rewarding. Carné's commitment to excellence during the next few years found expression less in filmmaking—he refused all subsequent offers to assist mediocre directors—than in writing about movies. In 1929 the weekly (and later, monthly) film journal *Cinémagazine* organized a competition for amateur critics, with a first prize of two thousand francs. Carné submitted five pieces on contemporary works, including *Les Nouveaux Messieurs*, Lang's *Spione*, L'Herbier's *L'Argent*, Clair's *Les Deux Timides*, and Joris Ivens's first documentary, *The Bridge*. The choice of directors is telling, since each influenced Carné's later development. But if the reviewer extols Lang for the manner in which, in *Spione*, "we *undergo* the facts, without actually *living* them," and Feyder for the tour de force of having "adapted to the [silent] screen a stage play whose entire worth lay in the irony of its dialogue," he is less complimentary to L'Herbier: "The great simplicity of American masterpieces in recent months has made untenable the notion of technique for its own sake. More than ever, technique must be a means to an end, without calling attention to itself. In Marcel L'Herbier's film, however, technique makes itself felt from beginning to end." [8]

Carné won first prize and was hired to write for *Cinémagazine*, with which he published until 1933. He also wrote nonfilm articles for the magazine *Vu*, the era's equivalent of *Paris-Match*. He created waves there with a piece concerning the drawings of mental patients at the Sainte-Anne Asylum: the illustrations he succeeded in getting printed were clearly pornographic. But Carné's prime allegiance was to film, and he was intent on having the public distinguish the good from the bad. When André de Reusse—the publisher of *Hebdo-films*, a trade magazine which Carné edited in 1931—secretly inserted into one issue a devastating piece on Chaplin's *City Lights*, Carné was outraged. Before tendering his letter of resignation, Carné included in the next issue an article praising the film and citing the equally enthusiastic views of other critics. The publisher responded as might be expected, with a virulent attack on Carné, calling him "an atrocious Bolshevik" and "an ungrateful viper whom he [de Reusse] himself had nurtured" (*Vbd*, 36). This was the first of many contradictory political labels that would be attached cavalierly to Carné throughout his long career.

Carné enjoyed the esteem of fellow journalists because he knew filmmaking firsthand. In the early 1930s he joined writer Jean Aurenche and designer Paul Grimault in realizing some of the first advertising films destined for commercial moviehouses. These half-minute dramatic reels had little artistic value, but they gave Carné the chance to break down a script, shoot, and edit—all on his own, but with the counsel of ingenious co-workers. Yet how did the man who never attended a university, nor even a lycée, acquire the writing skills so many admired? Carné explains: "As soon as I started to earn my own money, I had the chance to make friends with some very cultivated people. Whenever they referred to something foreign to me, I'd question them about it. Whatever books they were reading, I'd read. I am totally self-educated. I became an avid reader. I was curious about everything, as I still am today." [9]

As a critic, Carné was often severe in his judgments. But he made clear to his readership that these constituted personal opinions, not absolute truths. Carné also sought to sensitize the public to continuities between contemporary and prior film production. In pieces such as "Retrospective on the American Gangster Film," "War Films," and "Remembrances of Films Past" (in which he supported the new cause of revival repertory exhibition), Carné alerted readers that film, like other arts, had a history.[10] Soon after he started to write for *Cinémagazine*, however, Carné had pangs of bad conscience. He felt it improper to evaluate the films of others when he had not yet proven his own worth as a filmmaker. This recurrent unease incited him to purchase a hand-held camera and a supply of 35mm film stock and to shoot his first movie, a documentary short entitled *Nogent, Eldorado du dimanche*.

Nogent is bound to surprise a viewer who associates Carné's talent with the staid, slow-moving rhythm of films like *Les Visiteurs du soir* and *Les Enfants du paradis*. Its quick cutting and ceaseless variation of camera angling keep the spectator's eye moving constantly about the screen. Bold use of subjective camera recurs throughout, from the lyrical beginning in which the camera is placed in the engineer's compartment of a moving train, to the playful antics of its being positioned on one side of a seesaw, on a moving swing, in the lap of someone gliding down a slide, and upside down to represent the world as seen by a man dangling from suspended metal rings and doing a somersault. *Nogent* conveys the glee of a fledgling filmmaker exploring the possibilities of his medium.

The film is an affectionate tribute to Paris's working classes. It documents the simple pleasures of their Sunday outings to Nogent-sur-Marne, a suburb southeast of Paris. It presents images of sunbathers, bicyclists, and oarsmen; of dancing halls, amusement parks, and outdoor restaurants; of old-timers, youngsters, and babies; of crowds, couples, and loners. In recording a slice of French life from over a half-century ago, *Nogent* arouses nostalgia like that provoked by the tableaux of painters such as Renoir, Sisley, or Pissarro. Carné admits that his love of the Impressionists influenced his choice of subject, his manner of framing, and his lighting effects (*Vbd*, 36). In fact, the film is informed by a nostalgic strain that could have stirred the hearts of even its original spectators in 1929–30. For *Nogent* is, first and foremost, the documentation of a festive ritual of regression.

In its kaleidoscopic formal design, *Nogent* is a variation on the "city symphony" genre. The first and most influential of such nonfiction works was Walter Ruttmann's *Berlin: Die Symphonie einer Grossstadt* (*Berlin: The Symphony of a Big City*, 1927). Inspired in part by the experiments with montage of Russian filmmakers Eisenstein and Vertov, *Berlin* begins with a train transporting workers from the suburbs to the city. It chronicles about twenty hours in the city's life, moving from the early morning quiet of empty streets, through the hysteria of midday, to the more relaxed yet still hectic activity of the evening, and ending with a depiction of the frenetic, neon-lit city late at night. While Ruttmann was interested primarily in the film's structural aspects, his collaborator Carl Mayer conceived of the film as social criticism. Indeed, *Berlin* is a blistering indictment of the dehumanizing effects of cramped and dirty city life.

Nogent, too, begins with a commuter train in motion, and its initial patterns of interlaced telegraph lines and railroad bridges recall those of *Berlin*. Yet *Nogent* is not really a city symphony; it is, rather, a city dweller's hymn to nature. With its locomotive carrying Parisians away from the metropolis, the film launches into a glorification of the countryside's capacity to reinstate workers' health and vitality. Ruttmann's seventy-six-minute work has numerous extended sequences that differ from one another in mood and tone, thereby giving the film its "symphonic" fullness. By comparison, the thematics of the seventeen-minute *Nogent* are considerably more unified. If *Berlin* is a symphony, *Nogent* is a pastoral divertimento.

Carné made *Nogent* with the financial and practical assistance of a would-be actor friend, Michel Sanvoisin. His choice to create a variation on the city symphony genre is due in part to the limited capacity of the camera which he and Sanvoisin were able to purchase. Holding only seven meters of film at one time, the camera could produce a shot no longer than about twenty seconds—hence the practical appeal of creating a rhythmic montage of relatively brief shots. Yet other factors were also at play. Jean Mitry recalls that in 1928–29 Carné identified with a "new wave" of avant-garde filmmakers that included Pierre Chenal, Georges Lacombe, Jean Vigo, and Jean Lods.[11] These young men met regularly for drinks at Le Dôme or La Coupole, where their major preoccupation was to denounce the work of the film establishment, which comprised directors such as Louis Feuillade, Henri Fescourt, and Luitz Morat. At this time French avant-gardists were following the lead of the Soviet school. They were learning, especially from Pudovkin, that as much poetic resonance could be found in a face of the man or woman on the street as in the mechanical objects and cut-out shapes of the abstract films pursued by the earlier avant-garde of the 1920s (perhaps best exemplified by Léger's *Ballet mécanique*, 1924). The tide was also turning away from films like Clair's Dadaist *Entr'acte* (1924), Germaine Dulac's Surrealist *La Coquille et le clergyman* (1928), and Buñuel and Dali's Freudian-inspired experiment in automatism, *Un Chien andalou* (1928). It was moving instead toward a more representational mode of filmmaking, but one which could nonetheless distinguish itself from mainstream commercial fare. Out of this general context sprang Carné's *Nogent*.

Carné asserts that *Nogent* was a response not to Ruttmann's *Berlin* but possibly to Alberto Cavalcanti's dawn-to-dusk portrait of Paris, *Rien que les heures* (1926), which appeared just a few months before Ruttmann's film was released in France.[12] Yet these two films are very different in approach and tone. The moody and mercurial picture of Paris in *Rien que les heures* is replete with cinematic tricks—freeze frames, multiple exposures, superimpositions, split-screen effects, and self-conscious wipes—that give evidence of Cavalcanti's association with the French avant-garde of the mid-1920s. The bravura of *Nogent* results instead from a prodigious accumulation of single, technically straightforward shots. Moreover, Cavalcanti's rubato rhythmic line often allows him time for heavy-handed ironies, whereas Carné's visual tempo remains quick and sharp, and his tone lighthearted.

Equally marked is the distance separating *Nogent* from another resort documentary, Jean Vigo's *A Propos de Nice* (1930). In this brutal social exposé, Vigo and cameraman Boris Kaufman put a way of life on trial, showing that the vulgar pleasures of fashionable society take place inevitably under signs of oppression and death. In clear opposition, *Nogent* discloses a rustic world of joy and desire momentarily disengaged from the shadows of objective history. Where Vigo is aggressively subversive, Carné is gentle and utopian. Where Vigo deconstructs reality, Carné reanimates archetypal mythic patterns.

Read mythopoeically, the very beginning of *Nogent* intimates that the city has become the locus of a fallen, sterile world while Nogent-sur-Marne, the proletariat's Eldorado, is the site of paradise regained. Carné establishes this contrast by intercutting the train's glide through the countryside with a series of lifeless shots depicting a closed factory, vacant steps in front of the Stock Exchange, and rows of black-covered office typewriters so eerie in their stillness that they resemble draped coffins in a potter's field. By highlighting the travelers' switch from stiff and formal suits and dresses to bathing attire and exposed flesh (fig. 5), Carné intensifies the aura of communal return. Like the clothing, the serious cares of civilization dissolve away in Nogent. The sun's rays bounce like diamonds off the headlights of a Renault, making a product of modern technology appear more like an enchanted toy. A wrinkled old-timer recovers juvenile bliss as he slurps his peppermint soda through a straw; middle-aged men mount miniature tricycles; and—above all—the body is freed from inhibitions. Without calling undue attention to itself or to its subjects, Carné's camera records naked babies, muscular oarsmen, awkward bicyclists, a man picking his nose, a woman gathering flowers (fig. 6), and a couple lying in passionate embrace. The Casino du Tremblay alerts its dancers to the availability of "furnished rooms." And a sheet-music vendor singing into her huge megaphone peddles a song entitled "Seduction." (The woman is Carné's aunt Marguerite, playing one of the film's few assigned roles.)

Nogent is timelessness, nature, and sensuality. Nogent is Eden, with Eros at large, and with Carné's camera voyeuristically taking it all in. Perhaps the most significant shot occurs when Carné's low-level, hand-held camera penetrates a grove of shrubs before disclosing, ever so quickly, the couple engaged in amorous activity (fig. 7). This shot betrays the influence of Murnau's use of the camera in the famous marsh scene in *Sunrise* (1927), where the young peasant embraces the city vamp. (Carné, as critic, was among the first in France to comment upon Murnau's directorial technique here.) It establishes what will become a fundamental narrative principle in all of Carné's works: an individual's unwitting intrusion upon a scene of physical intimacy. It also sets forth the self-distancing posture that characterizes Carné's portrayal of male-female relations throughout his oeuvre.

Yet not all is perfect in Carné's populist paradise. *Nogent* is essentially devoid of plot and characters: its protagonist is the town, or rather, the *petit peuple parisien* who collectively bring the town to life on Sundays; and the film's narrative structure is defined simply by the people's arrival, sojourn, and departure. But the film does take on a dramatic sense. Ultimately, shots of accumulating clouds attenuate the prevailing glow, and lengthening shadows are a reminder of time's inexorable sway. The steel cogs, bars, and gratings of the train that transports the workers back to Paris—and which Carné shoots in almost Futuristic fashion—bespeak the supremacy of soulless technology over resilient humanity. Nogent, the town, may stand for Eden at its most pleasurable, but *Nogent*, the film, includes signs of man's fall from grace, of his inevitable expulsion from paradise.

Carné protests the significance for general film history that has sometimes been attached to *Nogent*. Because of its being made on location and having amateurs for its "cast," *Nogent* has been seen by some as a precursor of Italian Neorealism.[13] Carné prefers to view *Nogent* as a

Facing page:

5 A communal return to nature in *Nogent, Eldorado du dimanche*

6 The first idealization of the female figure in the Carné canon: a woman culling flowers in *Nogent*

7 Primal scene in *Nogent*: eroticized scopophilia

simple, sentimental film that had no pretensions save evoking the nostalgic atmosphere of Parisian Sundays spent on the banks of the Marne. Yet within Carné's oeuvre *Nogent* occupies a capital position, for it discloses a primordial conception of the world to which all his later films hark back. Lying beneath the surface of Carné's fictive universe is a primal scenario of humankind's fall and its quest for redemption in a secularized world. From *Jenny* through *La Merveilleuse Visite*, Carné's anguished characters seek ceaselessly to break from the claustrophobia of their physical and spiritual environment and return to an earthly paradise. Never does the fulfillment of that quest come so close to being realized as in *Nogent*. Like the Square des Batignolles in Carné's private mythology, Nogent-sur-Marne, or rather the resonance of timelessness, communality, and uninhibited sensuality which the town acquires in the film, is the artistic symbol for that which has been lost and that which Carné's film heroes seek to reinstate.

It is remarkable that *Nogent*—a purported documentary made seven years before Carné collaborated with poet-scenarist Jacques Prévert—elicits considerations pertaining to symbol and reality. Especially in his work with Prévert, Carné has generally been recognized as the leader of poetic realism, a school whose defining characteristic may best be described as the tension between "the drive toward realism and an impulse to transcend or essentialize reality." [14] André Bazin was among the first to address this particularity in Carné's fiction films: "We can see how Carné's realism tends toward the poetic transposition of a setting, while remaining meticulously true to life. It does not do this by modifying it in a formal and pictorial way, like German expressionism, but by releasing its inherent poetry, by constraining it to reveal its secret links with drama. It is in this sense that we can talk of Marcel Carné's 'poetic realism,' which distinguishes his work from the much more objective realism of [René] Clément or [Georges] Rouquier. In getting right away from German expressionism's tendency to visibly transpose its setting, Carné was able to integrate it perfectly with his poetic message . . . Whether it be psychological [the characters] . . . or material [the setting] . . . the art of Carné and his colleagues is to make reality fulfil itself in terms of reality, before insinuating symbolic values. As if poetry only began to glow precisely when the action appears to be identified with the most life-like details." [15]

Although *Nogent* is Carné's only movie shot exclusively outdoors and on location, the release of symbolic values that characterizes Carné's later studio efforts is already operating. In this regard, one element of the film's "poetry" deserves special attention. While *Nogent* has no characters in a conventional sense of the word, it contains one figure who

8 *Nogent*'s blind accordionist

stands out from the rest. Carné could have chosen to end his film with the shots of the commuter train rushing back to Paris. Such an ending would have underscored the privileged, mythic quality of time and space in Nogent as disengaged from defined, real-world coordinates. But Carné goes further, and concludes with the shot of a seated, blind accordionist illumined by the rays of the setting sun (fig. 8). This is an intriguing image, because both blindness and musicianship recur many times in Carné's later films, where they are often associated with destiny. Of course, blind accordionists playing outdoors are a common real-life occurrence: they can be found in other films of the period that represent or suggest the texture of open-air activities, such as Vigo's *A Propos de Nice* and Clair's *Sous Les Toits de Paris*. It is nonetheless tempting to examine the symbolic resonance of *Nogent*'s blind musician. He might represent fate and the inevitability of the Parisians' return to "civilization." He might also stand for a genuine, permanent denizen of paradise, recalling—because of the sunlight shining off his instrument—the archangel with fiery sword positioned at the east side of the Garden of Eden. But in a film that is essentially a visual celebration of physical movement, and one that employs principles of rhythmic patterns with musical associations, the sedentary and blind accordionist might best be seen as an allusion to the filmmaker himself.

A rare instance of self-reference in Carné's oeuvre, this figure prompts us to apprehend the elusive Marcel Carné as a director whose personal vision draws upon, fosters, yet exists apart from the ordinary pleasures of the masses. Indeed, the image of a blind musician provides us with an emblem of Carné's cinematic career. For Carné's art is not concerned with the mundanely visible or the objectively real. Its aim, on the contrary, is to illuminate the invisible.

Nogent was exhibited for two months at the Studio des Ursulines and, to Carné's surprise, the press greeted it enthusiastically, calling it "intelligent and sensitive," and its maker "a beginner in possession of his gifts." [16] But for decades *Nogent* suffered the fate of most documentary shorts: it was rarely screened. Common wisdom held that the negative and all existing prints had been destroyed during the war. In fact, the picture did circulate among various *ciné-clubs*, including the Cinémathèque Française. [17] Moreover, Carné had an excellent print hidden away in a closet at home. When a representative of the journal *L'Avant-Scène Cinéma* discovered this fact in the late 1960s, he managed to convince the director to allow a screening at a Sunday afternoon film society. The film was judged to be a great rediscovery, and *L'Avant-Scène Cinéma* agreed to distribute it. But without Carné's authorization a soundtrack was added. Carné protests such insolence, deeming it typical of the way he has been treated in recent years. The result, however, is far from unsatisfactory. A well-synchronized score by composer Bernard Gérard mirrors the shots' visual rhythms and punctuates each cut with *bal-musette* melodies played by an accordion and an occasional violin. It provides a fine aural accompaniment to the lively yet nostalgic tone of Carné's first independent endeavor.

CHAPTER 2

Monsieur Feyder's Protégé

René Clair was among those who viewed *Nogent* at the Studio des Ursulines. Extremely impressed, he hired Carné to serve as his second assistant director on *Sous Les Toits de Paris* (*Under the Roofs of Paris*,
1930). This was Clair's first sound film, and it would become the first
classic of the sound era in France. Although Carné's contributions to the
picture were meager, his experience with Clair helped to solidify his own
views on filmmaking, especially with respect to sound. Carné is convinced that moviemaking is essentially a visual art. The priority he extends to the visual over the verbal (his literate scripts notwithstanding)
and the frequent bows he makes in his works to silent film technique
(contributing to the oft-perceived dated quality of his oeuvre) are due in
no small measure to René Clair and the unique manner in which Clair
responded to the crisis precipitated by the introduction of talkies.

The Paris release of *The Jazz Singer* in January 1929 forced a complete
reevaluation of the technical and artistic premises of the cinema. Clair
himself sums up the situation, recalling that "while most intellectuals
and artists were frightened at the danger threatening not only an art, but
also a universal medium of expression, an alchemy of images, the industrialists and businessmen favored a novelty that held out the promise of
bigger profits."[1] Indeed, sound required a technological revamping for
which the French were not prepared. Hollywood (Paramount) and Germany (Tobis Klangfilm) seized the occasion to wage patent wars on
French soil, and the result was lucrative for both sides. By the end of
1929, Paramount's Jesse Lasky and Walter Wanger had purchased studios outside Paris at Joinville-le-Pont and equipped them with Western
Electric's ground projection sound system. Tobis built a large studio at
another Paris suburb, Epinay-sur-Seine, where it installed its Tri-Ergon
optical sound system. Although theater owners converted to sound cau-
tiously, foreign investment in French production and exhibition—thanks

especially to the enormous capital provided by Paramount—resuscitated a collapsing market.[2]

Not all filmmakers were fearful of sound. Veteran silent director Henri Fescourt declared that the innovative technique would lead to "new means of expression" if film artists, without wounded vanity, could "make a clean sweep of all that the theater and the cinema has taught us." Jean Grémillon understood that talkies had the potential for widening immeasurably "the cinema's capacity for portraying direct action." Perhaps most ecstatic was Abel Gance: "Talking pictures and synchronous sound are completely changing the commercial and artistic horizons of the cinema. I deliberately exclude film dialogue from the future of the cinema, but I view with passion the grand visual and aural symphony which, thanks to synchronization, will have captured universal movement and sound, and will offer them to our wonderstruck ears and eyes like a magnificent and divine gift." [2]

Gance's remarks point to the distinction between a talking picture (*un film parlant*) and a sound film (*un film sonore*). While there was near-unanimous approval of the latter—that is, the use of music and sounds in film—the former was controversial. The debate was heightened by the positions of dramatists such as Sacha Guitry and Marcel Pagnol. Talkies, they proclaimed, were the long-awaited means of "canning" stage plays. The astounding screen success of Pagnol's *Marius* (directed by Alexander Korda, 1931) and *Fanny* (directed by Marc Allégret, 1932) exacerbated the fears of those who felt that motion pictures would either revert to the stilted stage-bound productions made by the Film d'Art in the early part of the century, or simply record popular and anodyne boulevard plays.

Clair shared these apprehensions, but his stance was complex and ambivalent. At times he deplored the potential of talking movies to destroy the charm that the cinema derives from its unreal nature, and he asserted that sound could be useful only as a musical accompaniment to newsreels and educational films. At other times he allowed the possibility that words could be added to images without renouncing the virtues of the silent cinema. He imagined, for example, a film in which a spoken text would take the place of written titles, but in which words would remain the servant of the image, intervening only as a supporting means of expression: "It would be a brief, neutral text for which no visual aspect would have to be sacrificed. All that is required for this kind of compromise is a bit of intelligence and good will." [3]

Sous Les Toits de Paris is the demonstration of Clair's proposal. The story of a street singer who falls in love with a girl he espies among the crowd and then loses to his best friend, it is anchored throughout to concrete images that lend themselves to visual rather than verbal render-ings. Natural speech is kept to a minimum, and is often obfuscated by competing noises; dialogue is ignored, as when two characters complete an argument behind a glass panel door, preventing their words from being heard by the audience. Marcel Carné's films, especially those scripted by Jacques Prévert, have often been criticized for their distract-ing wordiness. Yet key moments of *Jenny*, *Le Quai des Brumes*, *Hôtel du Nord*, and *Les Enfants du paradis* minimize or even eliminate dialogue. Carné's penchant for such scenes is rooted in the example of Clair and *Sous Les Toits de Paris*.

Carné's experience as Clair's second assistant was less than satisfying. He did little more than monitor continuity, keeping a written record of the details in each shot in order to match them appropriately with later shots of the same scene. Although an essential service in the making of a picture, continuity is more a secretarial than a directorial task. More-over, Carné felt much the outsider, since most of the film's technicians and actors had worked with Clair previously. When he remarked one day that a particular scene being shot reminded him of one in an earlier movie, Clair and his coterie were struck with silence, as if Carné had just committed lese majesty. From that moment on, he became the company's whipping boy and an object of ridicule. To his intense disappointment, Carné's name was omitted from the film's credits. But what displeased Carné most was Clair's lack of passion during the act of direction: "I've often thought with regret about the 'incommunicability' (though the word itself was not yet in fashion) that existed between Clair and me. I understood it better the day I read a statement of his saying that once his screenplay was finished, its realization mattered little to him. That's pre-cisely what was missing on the set. I did not find that passionate love of the profession, of which Feyder was the living incarnation" (*Vbd*, 38).

Carné nonetheless admired certain of Clair's traits, especially his sen-sitivity to the charms of the Parisian working classes. *Sous Les Toits de Paris* was the first of the 1930s "populist" films. This genre, to which Renoir, Duvivier, and Carné would make contributions, sought to depict the *petit peuple* and their daily life. In a celebrated critical piece, "When Will the Camera Get Out into the Street?" (1933), the future director of *Hôtel du Nord* praised the populist thrust in several Clair pictures: "You call it populism. And so what? The word no more than the thing fright-ens us. To describe the simple life of the small folk, to render sympathetic their hard existence—isn't that worthier than refabricating the dim, overheated ambience of chic dancing halls filled with fictitious aristo-crats, or those nightclubs which the cinema has depicted without end?"[4]

Clair's mobile camerawork also found favor with Carné. In an article written for *Cinémagazine* in 1929, entitled "The Camera, a Character in the Story," Carné addressed the aesthetic problems posed by the introduction of sound and the necessity of immobilizing the noisy camera in a soundproof booth. Carné concluded that talkies must be pursued, but not at the expense of camera movement. In a tribute to the silent director most responsible for demonstrating the potential of a moving camera, he wrote of F. W. Murnau's *The Last Laugh* (1924): "Placed on a dolly, the camera glided, ascended, hovered, and weaved everywhere that the plot required. No longer conventionally shackled to a tripod, it took part in the action, it became a character in the story. No longer did we have the sense of actors stationed in front of the lens, but of a lens that unexpectedly took them by surprise."[5] The same could be said of Clair's early silent works, such as *Paris qui dort* (*The Crazy Ray*, 1923) and *Un Chapeau de paille d'Italie* (*An Italian Straw Hat*, 1927), two films whose comic chase scenes in the manner of Mack Sennett are undisguised tributes to the joy of cinematic movement. *Sous Les Toits de Paris* lacks this exuberance. But the frequent lilt of the camerawork in Clair's first sound film confirmed for Carné that Clair was not going to sacrifice to sound that which both men believed to be fundamental to film art: images in motion.

Clair's fastidiousness served as a model for the meticulous attention Carné came to devote in his own films to formal order and balance. Clair was also the source of Carné's conception of the director as ultimate decisionmaker, obliging actors and technicians to conform to a preconceived view of the total film which he alone holds. Yet Clair's cinematic style is very removed from Carné's. "The Clair touch" bespeaks an upper-bourgeois background and fine education. It is characterized by verbal wit and ironic distance, by easy grace and elegance. Like the comic theater of Marivaux (and Clair has been called the most eighteenth-century of Gallic filmmakers), Clair's cinema retains the tone of rational discourse: "If it is going to touch us emotionally, it will do so through the filter of our intelligence."[6] For Clair, the cinema was a refined, light-hearted game. For Carné, it would become a serious, often ponderous expression of human anguish. In Clair's work, style seems to take precedence over content. In the best of Carné's, the two are indissociable. In Clair, fantasy and reality are continually juxtaposed. In Carné, the two intermesh. If the characters of both directors seem lacking in human warmth, it is for different reasons. Clair's are like marionettes in a comic dance, for which the director visibly pulls the strings; they belong to the world of operetta. Carné's are like awesome embodiments of abstract principles regulated by an invisible Fate; they move in the realm of tragedy. Clair is a director of surfaces; Carné, of depths.

Both Carné and Clair have been subject to critical disfavor over the years. If Clair has suffered less, it is not only because the quality of his oeuvre is more even than that of Carné's, it is also because Clair's work, its finish and polish notwithstanding, never had the ambition and scope of Carné's. Clair's sound films are superlative *divertissements*. As such they allow us the choice of either indulging in their charms or ignoring them altogether. Many of Carné's films—from *Les Visiteurs du soir* to *Juliette ou la clef des songes*—were conceived as monuments. Whether or not they chime with current tastes, they command attention as grandiose undertakings in the history of French film.

One further result of Carné's work on *Sous Les Toits de Paris* was the crystallization of his view that the reality which the cinema was meant to capture has nothing to do with a simple choice between on-location shooting and studio reconstruction. In the words of the man who directed *Nogent* but would become France's most renowned (and, for some, most notorious) practitioner of exclusive studio shooting: "René Clair's Paris—so true, right, stirring, and tangible—is in fact a Paris made of wood and stucco, and reconstructed at Epinay. But Clair's talent is so great, his gift of observation so subtle, that he manages to give us— within an artificial setting and with the help of characters miraculously taken from real life—an interpretation of life more lifelike than life itself. If it is true that we'd swear to have met on the streets, in the course of our daily existence, the various characters in *Sous Les Toits de Paris* and *Quatorze Juillet*, it is also true that we'd swear, as we wander among Paris neighborhoods, that we've come smack up against the streets imagined by [set designer Lazare] Meerson . . . Though we know they are artificial through and through, they move us by their flagrant authenticity, perhaps even more than if Clair and company had actually gone out to the spots where the action supposedly takes place." [7]

Without the advances in scenic design and technique that Russianborn Lazare Meerson (1900–1938) brought to French film in the late 1920s and early 1930s (such as the use of iron, glass, cement, and oil paint on a large scale), the "poetic realism" of Carné's films, with its dependence on new standards of detail and authenticity, would have been impossible. It is therefore no small matter that while Carné was assisting Clair on *Sous Les Toits de Paris*, a twenty-one-year-old Hungarian was learning his trade from Meerson. His name was Alexander

Trauner, and he would eventually become Carné's most longstanding co-worker, designing each of Carné's films from *Drôle de Drame* (1937) through *Juliette ou la clef des songes* (1951).

In 1933 Feyder returned from Hollywood frustrated by the commercialism of a film industry which Erich von Stroheim had recently dubbed "the Sausage Machine." When the story department of Metro-Goldwyn-Mayer rejected as too sophisticated his proposed adaptation of Pirandello's play *As You Desire Me*, Feyder was more than eager to abandon Culver City for his adopted homeland, where, he believed, fantasy and personal directorial preferences could enjoy freer reign. France was, in fact, more accommodating to Feyder's creative instincts. His three most intriguing sound films—*Le Grand Jeu* (1933), *Pension Mimosas* (1934), and *La Kermesse héroïque* (1935)—were produced in the period immediately following his return, and their boldness bespeaks Feyder's disillusionment with Hollywood. Many of his silent films—*L'Atlantide* (1921), *Crainquebille* (1922), *Carmen* (1926), and *Thérèse Raquin* (1927)—had been adaptations of classic literary texts; the new works, on the other hand, had original screenplays written by Feyder himself in collaboration with one of France's most gifted screenwriters, Belgian-born Charles Spaak (b. 1903). Their sets were designed by Lazare Meerson, and—to the joy of a certain disenchanted movie critic—they all featured Marcel Carné as assistant director.

Carné's idolatry of "Monsieur Feyder"—as the latter insisted on being called, even by intimates—had taken hold in 1928 during the shooting of *Les Nouveaux Messieurs*. Carné was attracted not only by Feyder's talent but by the director's aristocratic bearing, which contrasted with his own short and chubby physique and with his father's rough, working-class manner: "Tall, slim, graceful, dressed with refined elegance . . . His breeding, allure, and the look of his eyes made me think immediately of a greyhound" (*Vbd*, 26). Carné's work on *Les Nouveaux Messieurs* had triggered a definitive estrangement from his father, and Feyder assumed, in Carné's mind, the role of a father substitute. Carné remembers the euphoria he experienced when Feyder allowed him to observe the editing of *Les Nouveaux Messieurs*: "From that moment on, I never left his side. Every day I'd go to the apartment on the rue de l'Université in which he and Françoise Rosay lived until their deaths. From there we'd head for the cutting room at Billancourt . . . Of course, I wasn't paid. But so what! I had been saving my pennies. Sometimes Feyder invited me to dine at Chez Francis on the Place de l'Alma. We would chat endlessly, often beyond the last metro. Unable to afford a taxi, I'd traverse all of Paris by foot in order to reach the Batignolles. I was happy as a king" (*Vbd*, 31).

These warm recollections were tempered by the sternness with which Feyder treated his protégé during the later period of apprenticeship. One scene in *Le Grand Jeu* required Rosay to burn a packet of letters. Carné had been assigned the task of collecting used envelopes. With typical gusto he amassed enough for at least ten takes. Hoping to impress Feyder with his industriousness and attention to detail, Carné made sure to display the result of his efforts to members of the company who, he believed, would speak well of him to Feyder. They did, but the outcome was not as expected. Unknown to Carné, Feyder ordered the third and fourth takes of the burning to be printed. Yet he deliberately shot the scene not four, not even ten, but eighteen times. And when his assistant had no more envelopes to supply, he turned to him and said: "So, Monsieur Carné, that's what you call your triumph? Not even competent enough to gather a few envelopes to shoot this wretched little scene. I do not congratulate you!"

With time, Carné put an end to what he calls Feyder's "sadomasochistic jokes" by masking with feigned indifference his devotion to the man. He eventually came to understand that Feyder, sensing in him a potential rival, needed to assert his authority. Yet following the letter incident, Carné rushed from the set to an empty dressing room and wept. Seconds later, Rosay came to console him, detailing her husband's ruse. When Carné asked for an explanation, she could only whisper: "Look, that's the way Jacques is. He has to hurt those he loves" (*Vbd*, 46–47).

Rosay's maternal instincts found a willing surrogate son in Carné. (The eldest of her three sons was ten years younger than Carné.) As an emotional buffer between him and Feyder, Rosay offered the kind of support which, in Carné's childhood, his aunt and grandmother had provided vis-à-vis his father. Whenever one of Carné's rushes was screened, Rosay's shouts of praise would counter Feyder's silent sang-froid; if Carné needed advice on how to deal with her husband, she shared with him her well-tried devices. Yet Rosay's kindness actually heightened Carné's frustration at not being able to elicit similar warmth from the person he most revered.

One incident confirms the extent to which Carné imagined this ersatz family as his own. En route from Casablanca to Marrakech for the on-location shooting of *Le Grand Jeu*, the company, minus Feyder and Rosay, decided to stop for refreshment at an isolated inn. To their surprise, they discovered the presence of Feyder and actress Gina Manès, who had played Joséphine in Gance's *Napoléon* and the title role in Feyder's

Thérèse Raquin. Manès claimed to be on a needed retreat, and Feyder maintained that he had simply stopped there by chance. Carné divined the reality of things: "I suddenly understood why he had chosen Morocco over Algeria or Tunisia . . . Instantly I recalled a letter which the star of *Thérèse Raquin* had written several years earlier to Feyder, and which he showed me one day, proud as a schoolboy who receives his first love letter and wants everyone to know it . . . With a profusion of details which even the most daring of today's films avoid—at least until now—the actress spoke about a certain dinner party at which hands did not remain inactive under the table. Reading the letter, I blushed, and felt admiration. But finally I felt cruel disappointment. How could a man I esteemed so fervently give in to such pranks? As you can see, I was still, if not pure, at least very young" (*Vbd*, 43–44).

In boyhood Carné witnessed his father's relations with prostitutes; if the widower Carné was being unfaithful, it was not to a real woman but to the memory of an idealized mother with long black hair who died of pneumonia. At age twenty-seven Carné learned that his mentor was being unfaithful to the one woman who brought him motherlike affection. It is impossible to assert the precise effect of these episodes on Carné the man or on Carné the filmmaker. But two things are certain. First, Carné's Morocco anecdote adumbrates the dramatic situation central to all of his films: one character's intrusion into the scene of a couple's intimacy. Second, for all his feeling for Rosay and the sense of complicity he shared with her, and for all his regret over the tarnished image of Feyder, of whose sarcasm and abuse he remained the butt, Carné never divested himself of an overvalued conception of his adopted father. Even the dandyism and fickleness he cultivated in his private life were derivations of his mentor's personal style (fig. 9). Many years after Feyder's death, scenarist Didier Decoin asked Carné why, given all the unflattering stories told about Feyder's treatment of his protégé, he nonetheless always spoke of Feyder "with great feeling in his voice and a tender smile on his lips." Carné's sole, irrational response was: "That may be. But he was Feyder!" (*Vbd*, 65).

Carné did not dwell on the interpersonal intricacies of his apprenticeship to Feyder. He was too busy acquiring the skills needed for directing films. Feyder taught Carné to mistrust theories of the cinema and to work directly from his heart and mind. He provided a model of meticulousness, craftsmanship, and self-confidence on the set. He demonstrated that sophisticated technique need not call attention to itself. He showed Carné how to work sympathetically with great actors and release from them a maximum of expression. Above all, he taught his disciple that a

9   Portrait of the apprentice director, ca. 1934

film director must strive to compose images with the same preoccupation for clarity of expression found in the old masters of painting.

Carné's apprenticeship culminated with his work on *La Kermesse héroïque* (*Carnival in Flanders*). Following a dispute with his production manager, Feyder delegated the latter's responsibilities to his now-seasoned assistant director. Thereupon Carné served both as Feyder's creative assistant and as the managerial agent responsible for organizing the day's work, for bringing together actors and extras, and for assuring the availability of props. Carné has acknowledged that physical stamina is essential for a long career in moviemaking. *La Kermesse héroïque* more than put his fortitude to the test. Holding two positions, Carné actually had to perform each one twice, since Feyder was shooting, simultaneously, a German-language version of the film with an entirely different cast, save Rosay.

La Kermesse héroïque is arguably the most dazzling period film made in France between Gance's *Napoléon* and Carné's *Les Enfants du paradis*. It depicts a town in early seventeenth-century Flanders on the day when a detachment of Spanish soldiers is expected to arrive and play havoc with the inhabitants' lives and property. The city fathers cower in fright, but the townswomen—led by the burgomaster's wife (Rosay)—decide to welcome the troop with open arms. By means of feasts and flirtations, they ensure the town's survival, and also inject touches of excitement into their ordinarily humdrum existences.

The film has the look of sixteenth- and seventeenth-century Dutch and Flemish canvases come to life. Inspired by Breughel, Hals, and Vermeer, the director and his designer sought to emulate the mix of intimate themes and visual robustness found in the pictures of these artists. For the exterior sets, Meerson succeeded in building, within a limited space, a kind of synthesis of a Flemish town. As Léon Barsacq notes, "It is a reflection of Bruges, but Bruges interpreted by the camera lens." [8] Similarly, Trauner's reconstruction of the Boulevard du Temple eight years later for *Les Enfants du paradis* would be a reflection of nineteenth-century Paris as interpreted by Carné's camera lens. In fact, the designers of both films employed a similar technique to give their sets the illusion of greater depth: by using scale models for the long shots of roofs and silhouetted buildings, they were able to create an impression of a cityscape extending indefinitely.

La Kermesse héroïque was a harbinger of Carné's subsequent career in one further respect. Like many of his films, it contains a political dimension that lends itself to interpretations which do not necessarily conform to the authors' intentions. Consciously, Feyder and Spaak conceived their scenario as a whimsical farce to offset the emotional heaviness of *Pension Mimosas*. Yet wittingly or not, they produced a script with a political subtext that evoked issues relating to national oppression and the relative virtues of pacifism, organized resistance, and collaboration. When the film opened in Feyder's native Belgium, many were offended by its depiction of the town's notables as cowards and pompous fools. Others saw the picture as an allegory of the German Occupation of Belgium in World War I and an apology for the collaboration of anti-French Flemish nationalists. Writing in Paris for *La Flèche*, Henri Jeanson called the movie "Nazi-inspired." [9] His view was reinforced when *Die Klugen Frauen* (as the German-language version was entitled) premiered in Berlin on January 15, 1936. Present among the audience was Dr. Joseph Goebbels, who was ecstatic about this film produced by Tobis. Under Goebbels's auspices *Die Klugen Frauen* represented Germany at the Venice festival, where it won the prize for best direction. Not surprisingly the same Minister of Propaganda soon banned all screenings in Germany of another film scripted by Charles Spaak, Renoir's *La Grande Illusion* (1937). For just as *La Kermesse héroïque* could be read as a defense of collaboration, so *La Grande Illusion* might be considered "a last sincere, but already hopeless, appeal to the Germans not to go to war again." [10]

Is *La Kermesse héroïque*—the film Carné admired more than all others for which he was assistant director—a sympathetic depiction of collaboration, or is it a subtle satire of the accommodating spirit of the bourgeoisie? There is no sure answer. But the question is pertinent because Carné, too, would eventually be charged with having fostered the cause of collaboration, specifically, the German Occupation of France in the 1940s. Writing in 1971, Barthélemy Amengual underscores rather compellingly the defeatist thrust of Feyder's picture. He concludes that irrespective of intentions, the film's pacifism "anticipates 'the peace at any price' of the French bourgeoisie under Daladier and Pétain." [11]

Significantly, it was during his period of apprenticeship to Feyder that Carné developed a political consciousness which inclined unequivocally to the left. In fact, Feyder's patrician and paternalistic attitude toward his crew helped to crystallize Carné's leftist sympathies. Even at the risk of alienating his mentor, Carné readily interceded when he perceived the director as abusing the good will of his technicians.

Carné never joined the Communist Party. But by 1934 he had become a member of the Association of Revolutionary Writers and Artists, a group founded by Paul Vaillant-Couturier, the editor of *L'Humanité* and a leading Communist intellectual. This was a time of great economic uncertainty and political confusion. France was seeking an outlet for her perplexity. The government scandal provoked by the financial adventurer Alexandre Stavisky provided the occasion, bringing radicals and reactionaries to a state of collision. On February 6, 1934, an antigovernment demonstration of reactionaries took place on the Place de la Concorde, opposite the Chamber of Deputies. Defending a regime in which they did not have confidence, the national police were forced to fire on members of the Croix de Feu—an association of war veterans who had been decorated at the front and whose politics were vaguely Nazi-oriented. The result was utter turmoil. The Republic stood, but it was badly shaken: the next day Prime Minister Daladier resigned.

It so happened that Carné was in the gallery of the Chamber of Deputies on the sixth of February. He recalls that "only the pen of the author of the *Rougon-Macquart* [Emile Zola] could describe the atmosphere of panic that reigned in the amphitheater: the feverish confusion of the deputies, the disorder of their reason, and the hatred each of the factions in the Assembly felt toward one another" (*Vbd*, 55). When the Assembly adjourned, Carné found the Place de la Concorde empty. With typical bulldoggedness, he decided to walk home—despite the urgings of the police to avoid crossing the Place. By the time he reached the faubourg Saint-Honoré, Carné found himself in the midst of a clash between police and rightist demonstrators. Within seconds he was struck down by a policeman's bludgeon.

It is less this incident than its interpretation by Feyder that has stayed with Carné. The apprentice was forced to miss work the following day. When he returned, the conservative Feyder had already presumed a scenario of his own, and quipped, "So, you've been helping the national police? Do you really think it's right to have Frenchmen shooting at Frenchmen?" Two days later the Communist Party held its own demonstration near the Gare de l'Est, where nine men were killed. The following day Feyder tried to justify the police action. Carné simply looked at Feyder and said, "Do you really think it's right to have Frenchmen shooting at other Frenchmen?" He recalls: "But I had hardly uttered these words when I realized a fundamental truth: politics is a distorting mirror, and everything depends upon the point of view you decide to take. Those whom you call 'rioters' will be considered by others as demonstrating their disgust for the erosion of basic principles. And if it is your side demonstrating for the love of threatened liberty, you can be sure that you'll never allow your opponent to use the term 'rioters' to describe that situation" (*Vbd*, first edition, 58; eliminated from the second edition).

Although these thoughts may in fact represent the young Carné's perceptions, they suggest an attitude that comes with experience. From *Le Quai des Brumes* to *Le Jour se lève*, from *Les Jeunes Loups* (1967) and *Les Assassins de l'ordre* (1970) to his recent efforts to create an audiovisual spectacle on the history of Versailles, Carné has been labeled variously as pro-Communist, pro-Fascist, pro-populist, and pro-royalist. His manner of confronting these allegations has ranged from public expressions of indignation to extended periods of private exasperation. To say the least, these multiple labels are simplifications that cannot account for the complex relations between Carné's political affinities and his films.

The knowledge and craftsmanship required for Carné to undertake a film on his own—his sense of methodic mise en scène, his firm direction of actors, and his almost Neoclassic concern for a film's formal balance— were obtained from Clair and Feyder. But numerous aspects of Carné's work, and especially those most often associated with "the Carné touch," such as the slow-paced shots, the gloomy décors, and the pressure placed on objects to release transcendent meaning, find their roots less in Carné's experience as an apprentice than in his appreciation of the German silent cinema: "As a boy, I loved Expressionist films. When I did my military service in the Rhineland, I'd try to leave the barracks every day to see films, most of which were in German. My greatest passion was for Murnau and Lang, who influenced me greatly. My 'plastic language' derives from them, not from Feyder. This is evident in *Le Quai des Brumes* and *Le Jour se lève*, although the latter is not without traces of Sternberg."[12]

The German director to whose sensibilities Carné felt closest was F. W. Murnau, and the Murnau film Carné most admired was *Der letzte Mann* (*The Last Laugh*, 1924). Made at a time when German production had moved completely to studio reconstructions, this portrait of a hotel porter's spiritual and psychological breakdown exemplifies the cinematic application of Max Reinhardt's notion of *Kammerspiele*, or chamber plays designed for an intimate theater. In many respects, *Kammerspielfilme* anticipated the dramaturgy and atmosphere of Carné's dark trilogy, *Le Quai des Brumes*, *Hôtel du Nord*, and *Le Jour se lève*. They were concise, intimate psychological dramas characterized by a unity of time, place, and action. Their bleak settings often reflected the subconscious of their characters. And objects in these films seemed to take on a life of their own. In studying *The Last Laugh*, Carné observed how shooting through glass and catching reflected light on opalescent surfaces, oilskin raincoats, and wet city streets could create an atmosphere of human dread. He learned how a closed system of poetic correspondences can be established through slow camera movements and varied angling, thereby amplifying the significance of individual gestures and details. Above all, he observed how the inorganic world, although invested with transcendental meaning, could sustain an impression of objective reality.

In 1931 the forty-three-year-old Murnau was killed in a car crash in California. His former assistant, Frank Hansen, declared on that occasion that Murnau had brought to the cinema "a culture, a knowledge of production, a sense of artistic beauty and lighting which . . . have known no equal."[13] In terms of craftsmanship and pictorial beauty, it can be argued that Carné was Murnau's principal successor. But perhaps more important, the world of Murnau's films—from *Nosferatu* through *The Last Laugh* to *Sunrise*—is suffused with an anxiety that floats about characters with the same relentlessness found in Carné's. Also common to the Murnau and Carné oeuvres is a persistent displacement of spectator interest from woman's body to man's: both *Faust* (1926) and *Les Enfants du paradis*, for example, jostle dominant codes of gender identification and sexual orientation.[14] It is precisely in *human* vision and sensibility that Carné is F. W. Murnau's spiritual heir.

Indeed, a crucial difference separates Murnau's aesthetic from Carné's. In Murnau, camera movement constantly implies the presence of a world beyond the cinematic frame: filmic space is fluid, imbalanced, and incomplete. This dynamic visual sense contrasts with the more static compositional tendency of the other principal German influence on Carné, Fritz Lang. Following a formulation outlined by Leo Braudy, we may view Murnau (along with Renoir, Ophuls, Mizoguchi, and Rossellini) as an essentially "open" filmmaker, whereas Lang and Carné (along with Eisenstein and Hitchcock) are eminently "closed" ones.[15] A closed-film style lends itself to expressing a sense of humankind's inescapable limits (as in *Le Jour se lève*); characters and objects are manipulated by outside forces—ultimately, by the director himself (as in *Le Quai des Brumes*); through deadly coincidences and the entrapment of innocent bystanders, characters come to perceive the world as chaotic, even though it is actually very much under control (as in *Les Portes de la nuit*); the closed film is akin to ritual (*Les Enfants du paradis*), allegory (*Les Visiteurs du soir*), and fantasy (*La Merveilleuse Visite*); finally, the aesthetic motion of a closed film can be defined as an effort to get as far as possible into the invisible heart of things, where all connections become clear—a project emblematized, as we have seen, by Carné's blind accordionist in *Nogent*.

Open and closed are distinctions rather than absolute differences. Yet they describe two approaches to moviemaking that, at least until the 1950s, were mutually exclusive. Perceiving Carné as France's most tenacious closed filmmaker will help us understand why he, unlike Jean Renoir, could not survive the changing mood and values of the 1950s—the period when young directors, in the wake of technical and cultural changes, self-consciously sought to make open and closed styles commingle. Carné's films uncompromisingly fit together with perfect balance and equilibrium, with impeccable clarity and propriety. They emerge from Carné's private need to restore a semblance of paradise lost and from his professional wish to belong to and maintain a tradition of quality established by Murnau, Lang, Clair, and—especially—Monsieur Feyder.

CHAPTER 3

Carné and Jacques Prévert

Carné's creative powers were best energized through interaction with the imaginative strengths of his finest co-workers. Of these, none was more influential than Jacques Prévert (1900–1977) (fig. 10). Prévert was arguably France's most imposing Golden Age scriptwriter. He was also a gifted poet and, in accordance with his view that all of life's activities share in the same creative spirit, he claimed to find "no difference between writing a book, working on a film, or taking a walk." [1] His writing for the cinema is therefore as much a part of the history of poetic expression as it is of the history of cinema. In the words of novelist-scenarist Henri-François Rey, "He was the first poet able to shout, sob, and laugh by means of the camera." [2]

In truth, Prévert's collaboration with film directors as diverse as Pierre Prévert (Jacques's younger brother), Jean Renoir, Jean Grémillon, Christian-Jaque, André Cayatte, and Paul Grimault brought forth a corpus of scripts whose thought and imagery evince the same exuberance of emotion and richness of invention found in his verse writings. "One very willingly says 'a film by Jacques Prévert,'" notes critic Guy Jacob, "because there is a profound unity among all his films, irrespective of the different styles of the directors he worked for." [3] Jacob's view requires an important qualification. With the possible exceptions of Renoir's *Le Crime de Monsieur Lange* (1936) and Grémillon's *Lumière d'été* (1943), Prévert's most accomplished and enduring screen work was written for Carné. Although these films are unmistakably "Prévertian," the darker resonances of their themes and the more tamed and mannered quality of their style set the Carné scripts decidedly apart from the rest of the Prévert canon.

Many believe that the quality of films like *Le Quai des Brumes, Le Jour se lève,* and *Les Enfants du paradis* results from Prévert's contributions more than from Carné's—especially in light of the fact that the

10   Jacques Prévert (left) with Carné, ca. 1939

films Carné directed without Prévert's dialogue or screenplays are, in general, of lesser distinction.[4] This view implies that Prévert was the principal creative force behind these pictures, and that Carné was simply the script's handmaiden. I would contend that the nature of the Carné-Prévert collaboration cannot be defined in terms of one partner's submission to or eclipse by the other. The distinctive character of a Carné-Prévert film results, instead, from the clash of two strong creative forces, from the interaction of two incompatible visions. To trivialize either man's contribution in an effort to ascribe primary responsibility to one or the other is to falsify the dialectic process of their filmmaking.

Carné and Prévert met for the first time one January morning in 1936. Carné had been hired to direct Françoise Rosay in a gangster film based on a potboiler by Pierre Rocher, *Prison de velours* (*Velvet Prison*), and he was searching for a scenarist to adapt this work. Although Carné found Rocher's novel overly melodramatic, the novice was in no position to argue with the film's producer, Albert Pinkéwitch, who viewed excessive sentiment as a guarantee of box-office success. Carné responded to the dilemma in inspired fashion. Why not choose a screenwriter, he reasoned, whose temperament is utterly different from that which seems required by this dime novel? Prévert's name readily came to mind. Three years earlier Carné had seen a performance of his antimilitarist farce, *La Bataille de Fontenoy*. Carné was convinced that the writer responsible for the Surreal and anarchistic touches in that play would be able to breathe life into Rocher's story of frustrated passions. To Carné's surprise, Pinkéwitch found the choice of scenarist unobjectionable. In fact, Prévert had recently written an inoffensive script directed by Jean Stelli which Pinkéwitch had backed. The challenge still facing Carné, however, was to persuade Prévert that a project based on material as mediocre as Rocher's novel was worth pursuing.

Their meeting took place at the Edouard VII movie theater. When Carné arrived, he found that Prévert was not alone: seated beside him was Jean Renoir, who had come to examine the print of *Le Crime de Monsieur Lange* which was being screened in the theater that night. Prévert greeted Carné warmly, while Renoir simply muttered some words that Carné did not catch. The immediate absence of sympathy which the future director of *La Règle du jeu* demonstrated for the future director of *Les Enfants du paradis* is perhaps as prophetic as the inability of Carné to comprehend Renoir's remarks. Nonetheless, the slight unease which Renoir's presence instilled in Carné was more than counterbalanced by the screening of the film. As Carné listened to the easy modulation of Prévert's dialogue from moments of tenderness to cruelty, and from cruelty to humor, he was certain that Prévert was the perfect choice.

The following day the two men met at a café, and after reading a twelve-page summary of *Prison de velours*, Prévert assured Carné that together they could rise above what he, too, viewed as a deadly plot. With little fanfare—but with the absolute self-confidence that characterized all their work together—the association of Marcel Carné and Jacques Prévert had come into being. Within weeks the two men transformed *Prison de velours* into a screenplay entitled *Jenny*.

Six years older than Carné, Prévert brought considerable experience to the partnership. By 1925, the house he shared with actor-producer Marcel Duhamel and painter Yves Tanguy on the rue du Château in Montparnasse had become a meeting place for leading figures of the Surrealist movement, including André Breton, Robert Desnos, Michel Leiris, and Raymond Queneau. Yet in 1928—the year he collaborated with his brother Pierre on their first short film, *Souvenirs de Paris*—Prévert was excluded from the group, ostensibly for having written a farce which

Breton, the movement's acknowledged leader, judged to be tasteless. Prévert retaliated two years later with a lampoon against Breton entitled *Un Cadavre*, co-written with Desnos, Leiris, and Georges Bataille. If by this time Prévert was sure of one thing, it was his status as a marginal even among marginals. Accordingly, his preferred haunt became Les Deux Magots, the café at Saint-Germain-des-Prés that served as unofficial headquarters for heretical Communists, dissident Surrealists, and anticommercial filmmakers.

Prévert's leftist politics were especially central to his art during the period in which he wrote plays, sketches, and monologues for the Groupe Octobre, an actors' collective created in 1932 to dramatize social issues for proletarian audiences at factories and workers' rallies. In 1933, on the very day Hitler was appointed Chancellor of Germany, Prévert wrote a satirical sketch entitled *L'Avènement d'Hitler* (*Hitler's Arrival*); the Groupe performed it the next evening, with Prévert himself playing the caricatured Nazi leader. The Groupe won first prize at Moscow's 1933 International Congress Olympiad of Workers' Theaters with *La Bataille de Fontenoy*. Although it disbanded in 1936 because of financial problems, the Groupe Octobre's members sustained strong ties. Indeed, many of Prévert's closest friends in the Groupe—Raymond Bussières, Jacques Brunius, Fabien Loris, Sylvia Bataille, Henri Cartier-Bresson—performed in films written by Prévert for Renoir and Carné. For Marcel Carné, who was very much a loner, the association with Prévert had one immediate effect: it brought him in touch with numerous talented people who—unlike the majority of those who worked for Clair and Feyder—perceived themselves as occupying the fringes of the creative arts establishment.

Although not collected until 1945 in *Paroles*, Prévert's poems appeared steadily throughout the 1930s. Some were published, some were placed in drawers, others were distributed to friends via handwritten copies or word of mouth, and still others were scrawled on paper tablecloths—and put out with the garbage. Prévert's early film efforts, too, experienced varied destinies. In 1932 he wrote the screenplay for Pierre Prévert's *L'Affaire est dans le sac*, a burlesque that tells of a bored millionaire who decides to marry off his daughter to the man who succeeds in amusing him. Shot in eight days, this forty-seven-minute satire so outraged Pathé Distributors that the film was denied a single commercial showing and all prints were ordered to be destroyed. Fortunately, the master negative remained intact, and the farce is now generally deemed one of the more engaging French avant-garde films. Without restraining his taste for whimsy and controversy, Prévert proceeded to write six feature-length pictures, including Autant-Lara's *Ciboulette* (1933), a parody of the operetta by Reynaldo Hahn; Allégret's *L'Hôtel du Libre Echange* (1934), from the Feydeau farce; Autant-Lara's English-made dramatic fantasy, *My Partner Mr. Davis* (1934); and Renoir's homage to the spirit of the Popular Front, *Le Crime de Monsieur Lange* (1936). Also in 1936, producer Pierre Braunberger asked Prévert to compose additional scenes for Renoir's unfinished *Une Partie de campagne*. Prévert did so, adding new situations and characters, including a homosexual baker to be played by Michel Simon, but Prévert's scenes were never filmed.

Carné felt an instant affinity toward his more seasoned associate. This might be explained by their shared heritage: Prévert was a Breton on his father's side, as was Carné on his mother's. More important was each man's identification with the common Parisian. (Prévert was born in the Paris suburb of Neuilly-sur-Seine.) As Carné reminisced in his 1980 speech to the Academy: "Both born of the working class, both educated at the school of life, we shared the same window on the world, we liked the same authors and artists and ignored the others. We had no choice but to get along well together."[5] To the extent that like background engenders like ideology, Prévert and Carné were compatible. Antibourgeois, antiecclesiastic, and antimilitarist, they perceived themselves as defenders of the working classes against the rich. They viewed honesty, courage, and brotherly affection as virtues peculiar to the proletariat. With unembarrassed sentiment, they shared a view of the *milieu populaire* as a world in which prostitutes and petty criminals were but victims of circumstance and potentially redeemable through a rediscovery of the basic working-class virtues of candor and simplicity.

Yet Carné and Prévert were very different temperamentally. This is perhaps best reflected in the diverging ways in which each envisioned his art and career. Both men admired intelligence while mistrusting intellectuals. They were wary of French filmmakers such as Jean Epstein and Louis Delluc who, like their counterparts in the Russian avant-garde, wedded film practice to theory and doctrine. (The final lines of Prévert's poem "Il ne faut pas . . ." read: "Le monde mental / Ment / Monumentalement," which translate literally as "The mental world / Lies / Monumentally.")[6] Carné, however, was less spontaneous than Prévert, and relied more on forethought and calculation than on instinct and intuition. Family background can account in part for this difference. Prévert came from a close-knit family that adored the movies: his father dreamt of becoming an actor and actively encouraged his sons to fulfill his dream. Carné's unaffectionate father was the reverse of Prévert's: he sneered at the cinema and tried futilely to dissuade his son from pursuing it as a career. Thus,

while the cinema seemed, for the young Prévert, a totally natural undertaking meant to be tackled with zest, it was from the outset a matter of
deception and transgression for Carné. Where Prévert could trust to inspiration, the more guarded Carné was inclined to predetermine the creative act through disciplined rumination.

Similarly, the convivial Prévert had no difficulty in displaying—in art
as in life—emotions of friendship, love, scorn, and dislike. Carné, in
contrast, felt awkward about baring his feelings as well as those of the
characters in his films. Perhaps because Prévert was so much at ease with
himself, he was unconcerned with fame. Actually turning timid among
strangers, Prévert preferred never to give interviews, which he considered
the most contrived mode of human contact. Carné, however, was something of a dandy who, very early in his career, constructed a public mask
that thrived on celebrity.[7]

It would be excessive to assert that Carné saw Prévert as the kindly
father figure whom the young director sought out but never attained in
Clair and Feyder. Yet part of Prévert's appeal did reside in his caring,
familial manner. When he was six years old, Prévert dissuaded his father,
André, from committing suicide. From then on, the intensity of the father's affection for Jacques was equaled only by that of Jacques for his
brother Pierre (b. 1906). Not surprisingly, relations between Carné and
Pierre Prévert were always strained: Pierre was convinced that Jacques's
ebullient temper was better suited to working with him than with the
finicky maker of Le Quai des Brumes, and Carné envied the authentic
brotherly love that Pierre shared with Jacques. But Jacques Prévert's capacity for tenderness and love was not limited to family. Henri-François
Rey recalls the impact of Prévert's charisma during the dispiriting winter
of 1943: "Every day we had to go from hotel to hotel, from meetings
with Carné, Pierre Laroche, Trauner and Kosma (who were in hiding),
Pierre Brasseur and almost all the old pals from the Groupe Octobre . . .
Each one had his own existence, but in fact each was stirred, each could
truly express himself only thanks to the extraordinary poetic power, or
rather the 'presence,' of Jacques Prévert."[8]

One speaks commonly of "the Carné team" in describing the more or
less constant group of colleagues who worked on Carné's early films. In
point of fact, the team was composed of Prévert's associates, not Carné's,
and although it was under the direction and employ of Carné, the team
felt itself as belonging emotionally to Prévert. Consequently, the Prévert
band evoked ambivalent feelings in Carné. On one hand, it served as a
kind of belated surrogate for the family unity which Carné lacked as a
child: "I had the best team the cinema will probably ever see: Prévert,

Trauner, Kosma, Schüfftan, just to name a few. They all moved with me." [9] On the other, Carné remained an outsider even here, never enjoying the personal allegiance which the team felt for one another and for Prévert. The team members respected Carné as the coordinator of their talents, but they were friends of Jacques Prévert, whom they loved as a brother.

It is tempting to view Prévert as the healthy partner and Carné as the neurotic. Gérard Guillot lends support to such a position when he asserts that "Jacques Prévert has nothing to repress: without anguish, he knows only healthy anger. He has no complexes to work out; he has only well-defined and justified dislikes; he is tortured neither by regrets, rancor, guilt, bitterness, or sense of loss. He likes only *la belle vie*." [10] However, given Prévert's chain-smoking and protracted bouts of alcoholism, it is unlikely that the writer actually conformed to Guillot's idealized sketch. Likewise, care must be taken not to attribute psychological categories to Carné that are contradicted by facts, one of which is that Carné is today a well-adjusted octogenarian. In the late 1930s, however, Carné was less at ease with his social self than Prévert was with his.

Both men took freedom as the main value of life, especially the freedom to love whenever and whomever they chose. But where the heterosexual Prévert could fight for freedom in love with the same unmuffled voice used to decry social and political injustice, Carné felt obliged to conceal his private feelings from a society basically intolerant of homoerotic emotions. Carné admired and envied Prévert's forthrightness. Prévert sympathized with Carné's need to dissemble. Therein lay the nub of their attraction to one another: Carné served as a constant reminder to Prévert of how social masks repress natural instinct, and Prévert provided Carné with a voice to articulate, through metaphor, his own frustration and outrage.

Scenarist Didier Decoin (who co-wrote Carné's *La Merveilleuse Visite*, 1974) employs a conjugal image to describe the Carné-Prévert association. He proposes that Prévert saw himself as "the father (or the conceiver)" of his characters, while Carné "played the powerful, primordial role of mother, with the mission of engendering, giving existence to the characters." [11] Decoin's metaphor is accurate inasmuch as the screenwriter's active participation in the project ceased as soon as he turned over a finished screenplay to Carné. The film's "gestation" period then took place under Carné's absolute authority. Decoin's image must not, however, be read to mean that Prévert, like some aloof father (Carné's, for instance), was indifferent to the fate of his offspring. Nor should it imply that Carné's professional demeanor was characterized by feminine or maternal qualities of tenderness and warmth. On the contrary, it was Prévert who provided much of the spiritual nourishment of actors and crew, often visiting the studios to engage in funmaking with his friends; but it was Carné who attended to the ruder exigencies of getting the film made.

Carné was in no way insensitive to Prévert's view of love as a second innocence, as the only paradise available to humankind, as the sole form of eternity within one's reach. ("Thousands of years and thousands more / Would not suffice / To describe / That little second of eternity / Which transpired when you kissed me," wrote Prévert in "Le Jardin.")[12] Nor was he indifferent to Prévert's conviction that love, as a means of liberation from established custom, is situated beyond good and evil, beyond transgression and atonement. But Prévert placed emphasis on the emancipation of women as a prerequisite for the emotional fulfillment of men. Throughout his verse as well as his scripts, Prévert attributes a nearly beatific status to children, birds, hobos, flowers, and—that rarest of breeds—uninhibited men and women in love. Although Carné understands masculine eroticism well, he is more removed from the allure, needs, and frustrations of women. In the world of Prévert, however, "all women, all feminine beings, girls or lovers, mothers or prostitutes, women who sacrifice themselves, young wives or orphans, little working-class girls or women of the world, are physically beautiful, well built, agreeable to view, to desire, to caress."[13] Thus, according to Guillot, directors such as Renoir and Grémillon, whose personal lives included full relations with women, were better suited than Carné to transform Prévert's female figures into screen presences. Even the small female roles in, for example, *Le Crime de Monsieur Lange*, such as Valentine (played by Florelle) and Edith (Sylvia Bataille), breathe, to quote Jacques Siclier, "not only the love that comes from the flesh (lovingly contemplated by the director's camera) but that love which comes instinctively from the heart and timidly from the secret regions of the soul."[14]

It is highly debatable whether experiencing physical intimacy is necessary before a director can depict convincingly a member of the opposite sex. But it is certain that where Renoir and Grémillon highlighted the sensuality of Prévert's women, Carné tended to either reduce them to banal sweethearts or mythologize them into awesome sorceresses.

For Carné, the basic components of love were suffering, separation, and loss. Although Carné's pessimism is surely linked to the early death of his mother and to the social stresses that accompany homosexuality, Carné's doomed protagonist-lovers are not simply projections of the director's emotional anxieties. Undeniably, Prévert fashioned his Carné screenplays to conform more closely to the darker and brooding views of the man for whom he was writing. In fact, along with Queneau, Man Ray, and Aragon, Prévert had been one of the few members of the Surrealist group to repudiate André Breton's homophobic declarations.[15] But the Carné-Prévert films are not about homosexual experience recast in heterosexual terms; they are films that treat universal themes of life, love, and social destiny. Moreover, the pessimism of the pre-1940 Carné-Prévert works is symptomatic of a climate of expectancy and fear that pervaded France in the years preceding its fall to Germany—a disquietude shared and expressed by other directors and scriptwriters. It is nonetheless certain that where, for example, Renoir in *La Règle du jeu* (1939) articulates his sense of moral decay and imminent disaster without sacrificing a surface level of comic exuberance and irony, humorless films like *Le Quai des Brumes* (1938) and *Le Jour se lève* (1939) exhibit "the hollowness, the sadness, the profound despair of Carné." [16]

Carné's fierce adherence to the view of a shooting script as a finished blueprint is one of the more salient features of his artistic practice, and it contrasts decidedly with the attitude of his most formidable colleague, Jean Renoir. For the latter, a shooting script has nothing definitive about it but is, rather, a simple starting point for filming. During the shooting of *Le Crime de Monsieur Lange*, for instance, Renoir insisted that Prévert be present on the set, anticipating that much of the dialogue and even complete scenes would be modified in the course of production. Renoir explains: "He [Prévert] came every day, very agreeably; and constantly I said to him, 'Well *mon vieux*, there we must improvise.' And the film was improvised like all my films, but with the constant cooperation of Prévert. I am sure that it would be impossible in this film to know the origins of the ideas, if it were Jacques or I who found this or that. Practically, we found everything together." [17]

Carné, on the contrary, puts no faith in improvisation. He allows that "sometimes a quick change on the set seems called for," but he is suspicious of such changes and their "unforeseen, harmful consequences." Because he conceives each film in its entirety before shooting, he maintains that "what might seem to an actor or a technician like a good change while filming one scene will not necessarily work for the movie as a whole." [18] Consequently, Carné prefers to rehearse a shot unsparingly until the words and gestures of his actors, as well as the mise en scène and camerawork of his shot, correspond absolutely to a preconceived notion which he alone envisions. Not surprisingly, Carné's directorial posture in the studio borders on the tyrannical: his temper tantrums when his ideal of perfection is not achieved are legion and legendary.

Possibly, Carné's inflexibility on the set derives from the real need, while making his first films, to impose his personality on actors and technicians who, off the set, felt united by Prévert's presence rather than his own. More certainly at play is the closed-film aesthetic which Carné inherited from Clair, Feyder, and Lang. Carné exemplifies the paradox, common among closed-film directors (one thinks especially of Hitchcock and Lang), according to which the praxis of an ideologically liberal director is decidedly autocratic. Carné does not indulge the whims of his actors because, in the closed-film scheme of things, his actors are no different from objects: they are destined to be manipulated by the director and to mean solely what it has been preestablished that they ought to mean. The actress Arletty, who feels genuine affection for Carné and believes that his ironhandedness on the set "was pure show," compares the director to conductor Herbert von Karajan, because "like von Karajan, he treats his shooting scripts like musical scores which he conducts entirely from memory . . . We felt secure with him because he knew exactly what the final product was supposed to look like." [19]

It does not follow that Carné, to quote Truffaut's celebrated snub, simply "renders in images films created by Jacques Prévert." [20] Certainly, Prévert had the primary responsibility for inventing and developing story and dialogue. Moreover, because he began to write only after Carné—with his scenarist's advice—had chosen a film's principal actors, Prévert was able to tailor situations and dialogue to the personae, talents, speech patterns, and idiosyncrasies of the players. Prévert thus contributed, at least in part, to such production elements as acting tone and facial gesture that are more often perceived as resulting from directorial choices. But in point of fact, the writing of Prévert's screenplays for Carné was not a solitary undertaking: there was constant consultation between scenarist and director. Although Carné never penned a line of Prévert's scenarios, the director's criticisms, suggestions, and outright demands were a decisive factor in defining their content and shape.

According to Carné, who today refers to Prévert as his co-author, "there were never any shouts between us. Debates yes; but disputes never." Prévert understood, Carné continues, "that to force a director to do a scene in a manner not to his liking engenders a mediocre result. If I didn't succeed in making him share my views, he would say, without at all being vexed: 'I don't agree with you, but it's your film.' And he would write the scene the way I wanted it, knowing that it wasn't to satisfy my ego, and that if the next time I found that he was right, I'd bend his way just as easily as he did to me." [21]

Had Prévert not had the gift of thinking and writing cinematically,

Carné would probably have been less successful in making the leap from word to image. But however overdetermined and anticipatory Prévert's words may have been, the execution of that leap from paper to celluloid, the transformation of written text into a living sequence of sounds and images, in other words, the core of the filmmaking process—lighting, angling, composition, texture, sound, narrative pace, rhythm, and so forth—all this fell to director Carné.

The tug between Prévert's optimistic iconoclasm and Carné's grim fatalism is perhaps most manifest in the contrast between the friskiness, the verbal charge, the often throbbing rhythms of Prévert's dialogue, and the restrained, overcautious mise en scène and camera movements of Carné's traditionalist direction. Prévert's verbal style represents a rebellion against conventional language and an affirmation of the poet's capacity to reanimate empty expressions of everyday discourse; turning commonplaces, well-worn metaphors, and pseudopopular clichés back against themselves, Prévert transforms them into freshly minted conceits. His favored device of listing words in apparently random order (best exemplified by the poem "Inventaire" but informing many moments of Prévert's screen work, too) is a variant of the Surrealists' effort to liberate images stored in the unconscious through the technique of "automatic writing."[22] Nothing is further from Prévert's toying with the seemingly accidental and nonrational in language than Carné's staid visual aesthetic. Prévert's ability to wring eloquence by its neck so that his characters appear to pronounce words that spring directly from the heart corresponds to a fundamental confidence in humankind. Carné's hyperformalism and icy classicism correspond, in turn, to feelings of anxiety, disillusion, and deprivation.

Prévert was a poet of the sun: in "Fête" (included in his collection *Spectacle*), he describes his moment of conception in his mother's womb as "the sunshine of life" (*le soleil de la vie*). Carné was a tragedian of darkness who never found compensation for his lack of what Prévert, in the same poem, experienced as "the fireworks burst between my parents" (*un feu d'artifice entre mes parents*).[23] But if Prévert was the sun and Carné the shadows, Prévert saw in Carné doubts and anxieties lurking in his own being, just as Carné discerned in Prévert the possibility of living life with fullness and joy. As unlikely as their "marriage" may have been, it resulted, from *Jenny* through *Les Portes de la nuit*, in the creation of a melancholy fictional world in which desire is realized ephemerally and sensibilities remain forever wounded.

CHAPTER 4

Framing an Identity

Carné is a master of disguise. Just as he has attempted to conceal the date of his birth, so has he tried to obscure the genesis of his first feature. For years, film historians have agreed that the project to film *Jenny* fell to Carné virtually by chance. Pierre Leprohon, for example, relates that "in 1936 Jacques Feyder was supposed to make *Jenny*. Called to London [to shoot *Knight Without Armour* for Alexander Korda], he entrusted the direction to Marcel Carné, who at last succeeded in making his first full-length picture. Françoise Rosay had been slated as the film's star, and it was she who insisted, in the absence of her husband, that the mise en scène be consigned to Carné." [1]

Carné's version of the story is quite different. As he tells it, Rosay had promised during the shooting of *La Kermesse héroïque* to work without pay on the first film directed by her husband's protégé. Exploiting this advantage, Carné succeeded in meeting producer Albert Pinkéwitch, who agreed to entrust Carné with the making of a feature. A Jewish emigré with personal links to the Rothschilds, Pinkéwitch had, in the director's words, "a marked weakness for gangster stories." Although Carné was not stirred by "the sordid aspect" of gangster plots, he realized how infrequent it was for assistants to leap to full director status. After some hesitation, he "finally agreed and accepted to adapt, *faute de mieux*," Pierre Rocher's *Prison de velours* (*Vbd*, 69).

Carné thus proposes that the project to film *Jenny* was designed, from the outset, by and for him. He takes special care in *La Vie à belles dents* to detail his assembling of much of the film's creative and technical crew, especially his selection of Prévert as scenarist (*Vbd*, 76). Carné does not reveal, however, precisely who chose *Prison de velours* as the text to adapt, although the implication is that Feyder had nothing to do with the matter. It is as if the director—to recall Didier Decoin's metaphor—were demanding retroactive recognition for more than the gestation or "motherly" functions typically attributed to him by critics. In fact, RAC, the production company represented by Pinkéwitch, insisted initially that Feyder be hired to serve as the film's "supervisor." Carné balked, claiming with good sense that if the film turned out well, credit would go to Feyder. His wishes were respected, and Feyder appeared on the set only twice—each time simply to join his wife for a dinner appointment. On the second occasion, when Feyder asked to see some rushes and then joked that Rosay "looked like Raimu in drag," Pinkéwitch—already sensitive to Carné's requirements and temper tantrums—insisted that Feyder not step foot in the studio again. Feyder acquiesced, but resented his disciple's arrogance.

Carné's pluck also enabled him to neutralize the annoying presence of Jean Stelli, the production company's "technical director." Stelli hoped that Carné would flounder and that he, Stelli, could come to the aid of a misguided RAC. But Carné did succeed, and with considerable flair. Albert Préjean, who played the male lead, recalls: "Carné was a little nervous, which is quite normal for a first film. But at the end of five or six days I took him aside, put my hand on his shoulder, and said, 'Don't worry. I've rarely seen a director like you. You have a true gift, and a great career ahead of you.'"[2] Jean-Louis Barrault remembers: "His meticulousness in setting up shots was so excessive that many of us actors became a bit irritated. After all, what did we care about framing and lighting and so forth? But Marcel knew the craft better than we. He knew what worked and what didn't."[3] One of Carné's later co-workers, cinematographer Claude Renoir (b. 1913), observes: "There are two kinds of directors. Those who know nothing about film technique and those who know exactly what they are doing. Carné was of the second ilk, which is why, I think, he became a great director."[4]

In truth, the making of *Jenny* was a kind of ritual trial that required Carné to display a fully formed professional personality to those who preferred to think of him as Feyder's boy. Ambivalence accompanied this rite, since Feyder had come closest to representing the father Carné yearned for. But this very ambivalence elucidates further the authoritarian persona which the diminutive, cherublike Carné adopted. To give the impression of total autonomy, the twenty-nine-year-old director carried Feyder's traits of vigor, firmness, and impertinence to an extreme. Carné has always been, in the words of Claude Renoir, "an anxiety-prone worrywart": "He feels absolute fright each time he has to shoot in new surroundings. To deal with his fears, he would terrorize his crew, scolding them for some imagined error, and then dismiss them for the day in order to spend hours alone, coming to terms with every inch of the new set, of which he then became the master." [5] Unable to share his insecurities with others, Carné framed for himself, beginning with the direction of *Jenny*, a professional identity that bordered on the dictatorial. The tyro was alerting the French film industry that—to play upon the famous line about Napoleon by Victor Hugo (the director's favorite poet)—"Already Carné could be seen emerging from Marcel."

Jenny is an unabashed tearjerker which, today, evokes titters as well as tears. Its convoluted plot centers on the aging Jenny (Rosay), who runs a Paris nightclub frequented by gamblers, gangsters, tycoons, and demimondaines. When her strait-laced daughter, Dany (Lisette Lanvin), a concert pianist, returns to France after six years abroad, Jenny tries to spare her the shame which, the mother is sure, knowledge of her profession would bring. Although sequestered in the respectable suburb of Boulogne-sur-Seine, Dany discovers Jenny's secret life. Almost simultaneously, she falls in love with Lucien (Albert Préjean), a young, unemployed auto racer whom her mother has been supporting lavishly and loves despairingly. With neither one aware of the other's relation to Jenny, Dany and Lucien make plans to flee France and start new lives together; but their dream nearly collapses. Jenny has alienated the affection of her middle-aged suitor, Benoît (Charles Vanel), who attends to Jenny's financial affairs. When one of Benoît's cronies, the humpbacked Dromadaire (Jean-Louis Barrault), is insulted by Lucien, Benoît takes revenge on his young rival, while Jenny—self-denying through and through—borrows a large sum from Benoît in order to pay anonymously for Lucien's hospital fees. By the film's end, Dany and Lucien's love is sealed and Jenny loses both daughter and lover. Worn and heartbroken, she resigns herself to an ill-starred destiny as proprietress of the Club Jenny—described ironically in the film's final words as "the gayest spot in all of Paris."

Jenny's fateful coincidences, crisscrossed lovers, and intersecting subplots are hallmarks of the screenplays Prévert wrote for Carné. Like a Greek chorus reflecting upon the drama, one of *Jenny*'s secondary characters, Madame Vrack, remarks: "Life is funny . . . It always has people entering and exiting; arrivals and departures, departures and arrivals." Vrack's observation anticipates a similar statement by Lacenaire in *Les Enfants du paradis*: claiming to write a melodrama involving "two young things who love each other, lose each other, find each other and lose each other again," the would-be dramatist summarizes neatly the main narrative line in *Les Enfants du paradis*'s intricate plot. But with its emphasis on feminine psychology, *Jenny* falls into a category that sets it apart from the subsequent Carné-Prévert efforts: it is a "woman's film." With the story revolving around a mother's embarrassment over her station in life, *Jenny* bears comparison with contemporaneous American pictures, particularly *Imitation of Life* (1934) and *Stella Dallas* (1937).

Yet *Jenny* is very much a part of French film tradition, sharing traits with scores of sentimental tales of the 1930s. Among the first of the French sound melodramas was Henri Duvernois's *Faubourg Montmartre* (1931), which finds *Jenny*'s Charles Vanel in a story about two sisters, one who yields to the temptation of prostitution, the other who resists. In Anatole Litvak's *Coeur de lilas* (1931), Jean Gabin is a gangster saved from the police through the self-sacrifice of an adoring woman to whom he is indifferent. The adaptations of Pagnol's *Marius* (1931) and *Fanny* (1932) depict an abandoned mother-to-be who marries an older man she does not love. Along with other specimens of the genre, these films all treat one individual's struggle against middle-class morality, with the latter generally winning out.

Such pictures have fruitfully been viewed as embodiments of "bourgeois ideology": they ignore class struggle without at all ignoring the class differences their plots turn on.[6] Rather than question the causes of their protagonists' plights, these films portray the consequences of those causes in beings incapable of either accepting or overcoming them—hence the pathetic quality surrounding film melodrama's plethora of impossible love affairs, the protagonists' internalized, self-destructive guilt for having transgressed society's taboos, and, above all, the pervasiveness of fatalism and despair. Certain French melodramas of the early 1930s did try to address social issues through satire—for example, Litvak's *Cette Vieille Canaille* and Dréville's *Trois pour cent*, both made in 1933. But even in these films, attention falls principally on the predicament of individuals, not on modified social structures.

Although Carné and Prévert, after *Jenny*, never abandon the plot conventions of melodrama, they enrich them by privileging evocative objects over action, and delicate imagery over bald sentiment. Nonetheless, the dominant tone of their work is continuous with the fatalism found in *Jenny*. From *Le Quai des Brumes* through *Le Jour se lève* and *Les Portes de la nuit*, Carné and Prévert portray heroic attempts by individuals to defend themselves against social injustice. Yet alternatives that might effectively do away with injustice are rarely presented. This absence of positive alternatives is partly a reflection of the general climate in Europe immediately preceding World War II. It also testifies to the impact which Carné—the more morose, frustrated, and alienated partner—had on his scenarist. Only months prior to writing *Jenny*, Prévert scripted Renoir's *Le Crime de Monsieur Lange*, in which interpersonal drama yields not only to a critique of capitalism but to a demonstrated solution: the co-operative enterprise system. With Carné, Prévert seemed to embrace a philosophy which the character Dromadaire enunciates in *Jenny* when he muses, "At bottom, when you're at the bottom, it's best to remain at the bottom."

Prévert enlivened the plot of Rocher's *Prison de velours* by populating his screenplay with a gallery of original supporting characters. Perhaps the most intriguing is the sadistic hunchback, Dromadaire. Was this role conceived for Barrault? The actor responds: "I don't know. Prévert and I knew each other very well and saw one another every day. I had been close with Jacques even during his Surrealist period . . . Jacques knew that I liked to jostle the public. We belonged to a little tribe that thrived *en famille* at Saint-Germain-des-Prés. It was a *douce anarchie*. Yes, we were a band of inoffensive anarchists."[7] Dromadaire, however, is anything but inoffensive. Showing no trace of the nobility of spirit found in later Prévert-Barrault creations (William Kramps in *Drôle de Drame* and Baptiste in *Les Enfants du paradis*), he looks forward to the pathetic loveless villains of *Le Quai des Brumes* (Michel Simon's Zabel) and *Les Portes de la nuit* (Saturnin Fabre's Sénéchal). Dromadaire's jealousy of Lucien's good looks ("He's too well-built . . . I'd love to see him limping or lose an eye") turns to frenzied joy near the film's end, as he repeatedly jabs the torso of his fallen victim.

Equally unsettling is Jenny's assistant manager, Madame Vrack, whose Cassandra-like declarations announce the fortune-telling figures in *Les Enfants du paradis*, *Les Portes de la nuit*, and post-Prévert films as well, such as *Juliette ou la clef des songes*. Dragging about a huge feather boa, this jaded and regularly inebriated woman (played by Margo Lion) is amused equally by weddings and funerals. In typical Prévert fashion, she mouths nostalgic, incoherent dialogue about a dead lover, a child ("I, too, once had a daughter . . . or perhaps a son . . . I can't remember"), and peace of mind known long ago in South America. Dreaming of the simple life, Madame Vrack wallows in tawdriness and decadence, her lethargy reinforcing the film's fatalism.

The character of L'Albinos (played by Robert Le Vigan) allows Prévert to vent more vigorous disdain for capitalist morality. Inspired by the international armaments contractor Sir Basil Zaharoff (1850–1936), this lecherous industrialist appears only at night (hence his name) and reduces to cash transactions all that is most precious to Prévert: love, beauty, and women. For L'Albinos, the Club Jenny is "a paradise" in which each female conquest is "a flower." His failed effort to seduce the most innocent of Jenny's employees, Florence (Sylvia Bataille), leads to an abortive attempt to molest Dany, which results in his being beaten up by Lucien. The confrontation marks the plot's turning point: it provokes Lucien's decision to stop being supported by Jenny. This accounts for his defensiveness when, hours later, another Prévert "type"—the fortune-telling tramp—observes that Lucien's smooth palm is that of an idler. For Prévert, hard labor breeds virtue; luxuriance spawns vice.

One other eccentric of particular note is Lucien's buddy, Xavier (Roland Toutain), nicknamed "the Marquis." Described in the shooting script as having a "more refined" bearing than Lucien, Xavier is a fun-loving fop who bears intense affection for his friend. The announcement of Lucien's marriage to Dany rouses enough jealousy ("Don't be an idiot . . . All of this for that girl!") to make Xavier temporarily switch alliances and join Benoît's crowd. He laments to Dromadaire: "Friendship is a very rare thing. I guess friends exist . . . but I've become very skeptical . . . A woman. What's she worth? She comes and goes . . . pfft . . . she goes and it's over . . . but friendship!"

Friendship is a theme dear to Carné. In *La Vie à belles dents* he writes: "It is hard to speak of friendship. Unlike love, it is a chaste feeling that often lies hidden deep within and can only be expressed through acts. Love can be sung and glorified, but friendship, never or rarely. The verb 'to love' can be conjugated in all tenses, but no French verb exists for friendship. And certainly it's better that way" (*Vbd*, 437). Carné's inability to express male friendship on screen other than through obliqueness and indirection is a key to understanding his films and career. Clearly, there is no homosexuality in *Jenny*. But within its world of casual trysts, *coups de foudre*, and broken hearts, Xavier's constancy of feeling for Lucien sets him apart. (He does have one encounter with an unknown woman, but it occurs when he is drunk.) Xavier's last words in the film, when he is reconciled with his friend, include the line "I am what I am" (*Je suis comme je suis*)—the title of the song Prévert wrote as Garance's declaration of emotional liberation in *Les Enfants du paradis*. Like Garance, Xavier is prepared to assert his difference and live life accordingly.

To read the Xavier-Lucien rapport as an allusive portrayal of homoeroticism is to acknowledge the complexity of the Carné-Prévert collaboration. Prévert was sympathetic to homosexual emotion. He viewed it as compatible with the Surrealist project of scoffing at bourgeois mores. In wistful deference to Freud's belief in humankind's naturally polymorphous sexuality, Prévert often insisted to friends, "I am a man; I am a woman; I am plural." But the essential view of Prévertian love as seen in *Jenny* is found neither in Xavier nor in the title heroine, but in the two strangers who meet by chance in the night, Lucien and Dany. Exemplifying Breton's notion of *amour fou*, their love is violent, total, and indifferent to calculation and fear. For Prévert, a man and woman in love possess the power to return to a remembered earthly paradise. For Carné, Eden is always the unrealizable goal of solitary dreamers. Prévert's granting of a certain nobility to the Xavier-Lucien rapport—which subsists despite Lucien's projected marriage—dignifies an alternative to conventional views of emotional fulfillment. It constitutes, one might say, a gesture of regard for Carné and for homosexuality.

This is not the first time that the homoerotic surfaces in Carné's oeuvre. In *Nogent* the amateur Carné focuses considerably more interest on men than on women (fig. 11). The directness and candor with which he glorifies the male body in athletic activity—his shots of scantily clad crew racers display particular verve—underscores, by contrast, the caution and covert quality which male physicality assumes in his subsequent and more public works. But even in *Nogent* Carné suggests a view of the single male as defeated. Near the film's start, two young men eye two young women; near the film's end, we see these four again as two couples walking hand in hand: but within the foreground of the final shot that catches them, Carné momentarily includes one of his handsome rower-athletes walking alone with head bent (fig. 12). The athlete's forlornness is remarkably akin to the estrangement and despondency projected by Rosay in the closing frames of *Jenny* (fig. 13). In both instances we discern sure marks of the Carné imprint.

The director's signature is also visible in *Jenny*'s first shot. From an extreme close-up of a chalk-drawn pavement effigy of King Edward VIII, Carné's camera tilts up, slowly pulls back, and then pans gracefully right to hold on Dany's British suitor, who is waiting for her amid a crowd outside a London concert hall. This is the prototype of the lilting establishing shots that begin and close, with near-perfect symmetry, *Hôtel du Nord*, *Les Enfants du paradis*, *Thérèse Raquin*, and *La Bible*. Clair's *Sous Les Toits de Paris* furnishes an antecedent for this elegant framing device. But in Carné's filmic universe, unlike the more fluid one of Clair, initial shots that sweep across expanses of space before coming to rest on major protagonists accentuate the cramped physical and spiritual environment in which characters find themselves for the remainder of the picture. Carné's technical flourishes are occasional aberrations from a style characterized by sober camera movement and simple editing. While implying that exuberance and boundless opportunity may exist, the fluent opening shot of *Jenny* comes to rest on a confined realm where human experience is regulated by predetermining forces.

Spurned by her suitor because he regards her lower social status as incompatible with his own, Dany remarks, "How absurd and sad . . . clearly our fortunes are not the same." The play on the double meaning of "fortune" (wealth and fate) is a typical Prévert conceit: its effect is to decry the emotional strains fostered by undue attention to status. As Dany and her boyfriend separate, leaving the screen frame at opposite ends, a hand-pushed tea merchant's cart abruptly enters from left foreground and passes horizontally in front of them. Because peddlery signifies trade for profit, and because the motif's first occurrence is associated with the theme of social differences, it is tempting to view the tea merchant's cart as, above all, an extension of Prévert's denunciation of capitalism. But the motif of a pushed or horse-drawn cart reappears in Carné's non-Prévert films as well, including *Hôtel du Nord*, *Le Pays d'où je viens*, and *La Merveilleuse Visite*, where it invariably presages an end to happiness.

The momentary presence of the teacart in *Jenny* reveals how objects in Carné's world take on significance through repetition, variation, and conjunction with other objects. During the shot in which the teacart punctuates the lovers' separation, the camera pulls back to reveal, frame left, a street singer and, frame right, a harmonium player perched on one end of the cart. Thus the association of economics with fate is complemented and enriched by an association of music with destiny—a symbolic relationship prefigured in *Nogent*'s blind accordionist and embellished in subsequent films (for example, Jéricho in *Les Enfants du paradis* blows a trumpet; Destin in *Les Portes de la nuit* plays a harmonica; an accordionist reappears in *Juliette ou la clef des songes*; the angel in *La Merveilleuse Visite* plays a violin). The music motif is literally superimposed upon still another of Carné's favorite symbols for fate, a young child: when the transition from the first scene (London) to the rest of the film (Paris) occurs through a visual and audio overlap, the lyrics of the English love song (warbled to the harmonium's accompaniment) give way to the identical song sung in French by a Paris street urchin (accompanied by an accordion). Visually and aurally, Carné informs us that the

Facing page:

11   A rower in *Nogent:* the glorification of male physicality

12   A single man in a heterosexist milieu

13   Estrangement and despondency: Françoise Rosay at the end of *Jenny*

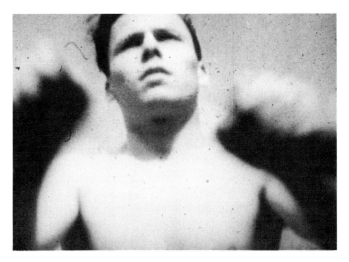

imaginary leap across the Channel in no way undoes the constants of his world—in which loneliness and disillusionment are most poignantly articulated by lost children of paradise.

Jenny is a film about illusion and disenchantment, blindness and vision. A daughter discovers her mother's secret life, and a mother learns that the man she adores has become her daughter's lover. In both cases a childlike faith in the purity of a beloved one—of Jenny in Dany's eyes, and Lucien in Jenny's—is destroyed: the "gods" have fallen. In this regard the film's initial allusion to King Edward VIII holds more than topical interest. Jenny's family crisis virtually echoes that of the English royal family—that mythologized version of familial perfection which was proving in 1937 that it, too, could become tainted through common, mortal emotion. But more important is how Carné treats the theme of disenchantment cinematically.

The first stage of Dany's illumination occurs as she leafs through a magazine and accidentally espies an advertisement for her mother's club. This moment is captured through an extreme close-up that reveals the words: "CHEZ JENNY: In a discreet setting, from midnight to dawn, come discover the most beautiful girls in Paris ... 85, rue Spontini." Dany rushes off to the cabaret. Standing in a lounge adjacent to the main room, she stealthily pulls back a black-velvet curtain divider, disclosing to the camera only the left half of her face. A rapid series of subjective close-ups then conveys the spasmodic movement of Dany's left eye as she contemplates animated tableaux of couples in lascivious frolic. These are interspersed with cuts back to Dany's astonished face. Her most severe expression of pain follows the shot in which she sees her mother carousing with a client (fig. 14).

This is the pivotal moment of the film's plot. Remarkably, it is not written into the shooting script, which specifies that Dany, who "stands near the curtain," simply overhears her mother's voice.[8] Carné's conversion of Dany's moment of revelation from an auditory to a visual one is particularly significant. The most recurrent dramatic situation in Carné's oeuvre involves the intrusion by a third party on a couple in amorous embrace. In all such instances a barrier—typically a door, but just as often a drape or curtain—gives way to disclose what appears to the eyes of the interloper as a scandalous event. For Dany, the climactic experience results in the deflation of her overvalued image of her mother, and this episode is generative of the prevailing vision in the Carné canon: a nostalgia for lost innocence. This dramatic nucleus of Carné's complete

14 Dany (Lisette Lanvin) traumatized by the sight of her mother's apparent licentiousness

works is akin to the scenario Freud called *Urszene*, or primal scene, in which a child inadvertently observes its parents having sexual relations. For Freud, this traumatic event produces anguish, denial, and frustrated desire in the child, and is constitutive of human personality. For Carné— who lost his mother at age five, witnessed his father's liaisons with Montmartre whores, and may plausibly be identified, as we have seen, with a *blind* accordionist—the primal scene concept helps to explain the persistence in his works of the theme of return to a site of pristine communion between men and their surroundings, as epitomized by Nogent and as evoked by Carné's memories of boyhood camaraderie in the Square des Batignolles.

Immediately following Dany's instant of illumination, L'Albinos attempts to molest her. But the valiant Lucien comes to her rescue and accepts Dany's request to be taken "anywhere." Anywhere turns out to be the banks of the Ourcq Canal and a tiny café in a Paris suburb. In narrative terms, the contours of an elemental plot are defined: the primal glance guarantees an end to innocence, but a parcel of paradise can be reinstated through the intercession of genuine love. Cinematically, a distinct change in atmosphere takes place. Until Dany's moment of enlightenment, she moved in a space filled with white leather furniture, plush carpeting, and laminated walls draped with silk and velvet. As of her liaison with Lucien, studio sets give way to a series of on-location out-door scenes that are an index of Dany and Lucien's regeneration. In one, Lucien playfully runs after Dany in a public garden reminiscent of the Square des Batignolles. Enhanced by Kosma's airy music (strings, piano, and flute), the sunlit landscape takes on the quality of a Pointillist paint-ing and recalls *Nogent* as well as Renoir's *Une Partie de campagne*. While these scenes contrast with the artificiality of the studio-shot sequences, they are also, curiously, the only ones that employ music in its most con-ventional manner, to reinforce sentiment; elsewhere, music emanates from sources directly portrayed in the story (principally, the perform-ances in Jenny's cabaret). Nonetheless, the brief park scene is the last truly pastoral moment in Carné's oeuvre. Uninhibited play amid lush greenery henceforth becomes the fragile dream of weary urbanites.

The Carné-Prévert vision is perhaps most palpable in the pale and misty early-morning shots of Dany and Lucien walking aimlessly about the bridges and cobblestone walks that span the banks of the Ourcq Canal. The dialogue is quintessential Prévert: she recollects the fragrant mimosa she knew as a girl on Belle-Ile; he recalls his years in reform school on the same island; together they marvel at how at last they feel "fresh," "simple," and "happy." The episode is extremely wordy. But rather than being a congenial wedding of Prévert's words to Carné's im-ages, the scene emphasizes the fundamental antagonism between the two. As Dany and Lucien engage in revery about beauty and escape to faraway lands, Carné frames them entrapped within an ugly, industrial-ized setting. That is not to deny that the setting takes on a poetic quality of its own. But it is a visual poetry of asphalt and steel, of imprisonment and claustrophobia, which undercuts the Romantic aspirations ex-pressed by the words. The medium two-shot of Lucien and Dany leaning over the railing of a footbridge discloses a set-up Carné will repeat many times. It signals his personal view of love as the precarious union of two lost souls.

In the film's final sequence Jenny learns from the lips of her lover the name of his new love. Jenny's first impulse is to shut her eyes, as if not to acknowledge the truth she has heard. But Carné insists upon the junction of revelation and sight. Positioning Jenny at the far end of Lucien's hos-pital ward—in an exact reversal of the cabaret scene—he has Jenny watch, with her right eye masked by the fur collar of her coat, as Lucien and Dany kiss tenderly (fig. 15). In the cabaret, Dany saw Eden trans-formed into Sodom. In the same voyeuristic pose, Jenny now views the two remnants of earthly bliss, Dany and Lucien, from whom she is com-pletely severed.

15   Jenny (Françoise Rosay) devastated at the sight of her lover and her
      daughter embracing

After leaving the hospital, Jenny crosses a railway bridge and is envel-
oped by smoke rising from a locomotive (see fig. 13). The contrast between her plodding gait and the passing traffic gives expression to Jenny's
alienation; the whir of cars and the piercing train whistle are external
echoes of the news still reverberating in her head; and the encompassing
smoke is the sign of Jenny's bewilderment and despair. Reminiscent of
Monet's smoke-laden Gare Saint-Lazare paintings, these closing shots
are a sure prefigurement of Carné's brand of poetic realism, in which
melodramatic sentiment gives way to symbolism and subtle sensation.

It is frequently observed that characters in film melodrama seem tossed
about at the will of some capricious fate; in the words of one critic, such
characters are "always hoping yet always defeated," whereas heroes in
tragedy "consciously assume their destiny."[9] Inasmuch as Jenny gives
signs of the latter, she announces the tragic heroism found in at least
three Carné-Prévert men: *Le Quai des Brumes*'s Jean, *Le Jour se lève*'s
François, and *Les Enfants du paradis*'s Lacenaire. Indeed, with the exception of *Jenny*, Carné's films focus on male protagonists. Although they
generally depict younger and older men struggling for the love of a
woman, most female characters are either stereotyped or weakly devel-

oped. Lisette Lanvin's Dany is the first example of the pretty, bland in-génue who, despite her romantic adventures, evokes minimal interest. Rosay's Jenny is itself, until the final moments, a caricature of the en-amored matron whose flamboyant dress and exaggerated gestures poorly mask her age. But if *Jenny* transcends its far-fetched plot, it is due to the believability which Rosay brings to her role. Affected and extravagant, she never becomes camp.

The seriousness and sincerity of Rosay and, by implication, Carné de-mand emphasis: first, because the role of the alluring mature woman is repeated in many Carné-Prévert works, culminating in Garance of *Les Enfants du paradis*; second, because Rosay was the wife of Carné's most important father figure, Jacques Feyder. I have suggested that the making of *Jenny* was a symbolic test of Carné's manhood. The fact that this required intimate professional contact with his mentor's wife added a decidedly Oedipal resonance to the enterprise. The extent to which Carné's direction of the film allowed him to play out unconscious fanta-sies and conflicts is undeterminable. Yet on the manifest level of story, *Jenny*'s plot—an older woman's discovery that her young lover is her future son-in-law—is a variation on the classic Oedipus schema. It is also an echo of *Pension Mimosas* (1934), the film Feyder directed with Carné's assistance, in which Rosay portrays a modern Phaedra fallen in love with her adopted son. Carné viewed Rosay as a replacement for the mother he lost as a boy. (Prévert, on the contrary, was not fond of Rosay and often mocked her grande-dame standoffishness.) But to propose a hidden identity between Carné and Lucien would be misguided. Lucien's success in disengaging himself from Jenny's overbearing sway suggests an Oedipal triumph of sorts. However, the distinctly negative overtones that surround Lucien's moralizing, his facilitation of Dany's separation from her mother, and his callousness toward Xavier (a better candidate in any search for a Carné surrogate) point instead to Carné's lack of identification with and sympathy for Lucien. Conversely, Carné focuses our sympathy unstintingly on his title heroine. As a woman whose daughter and lover abandon her in the name of social convention, Jenny is the quintessential Carné protagonist—the marginal figure who, much like Carné himself, defies bourgeois morality while remaining its victim. Jenny may be Carné's projection of an idealized mother who, unlike his real father, would have accepted Carné's own unconventionality. Yet be-cause of the suffering which her unconventionality brings upon herself, Jenny is also a figure of Carné. One might propose that through *Jenny*, Carné gave symbolic expression to a desire to fuse a lost parent and an abandoned child.

Melodrama tends to elicit critical condescension because it sacrifices plausibility to excessive sentiment. Yet melodrama can attain the status of a masterwork if, in Mitry's words, "this exaltation [of sentiment] is infused with dreamlike emotion, with the baroque exaggerations of the unconscious, with the most secret and revealing of desires, so that passion takes on a savage but authentic accent." [10] *Jenny* is not a masterpiece. But the implausibilities of plot and motivation found in all succeeding Carné-Prévert works become irrelevant precisely to the degree that Prévert's scenarios turn into Carné's dreamscapes. With the exception of *Les Visiteurs du soir*, Prévert contributed screenplays that purport to deal with the real world. In the hands of Carné, the real world becomes the stage for a kind of primal theater in which subconscious dramas of identity unfold.

Jenny received mixed reviews. Some critics were uneasy about the interpolation of outlandish characters, Surreal dialogue, and settings as unexpected as the Ourcq Canal in a conventional love story. Others took it as a Feyder film with a few bizarre touches added by a brazen disciple. But Alexandre Arnoux, writing in *Les Nouvelles Littéraires*, saw it as "the film event" of autumn 1936: "Carné—remember that name . . . In this first feature one can sense a sensitivity, an assuredness, an understanding of cinema, and an interior strength that holds great promise." Arnoux accurately predicted that Carné would become a first-rate director provided "he be given enough money and freedom." Less sympathetic was right-winger Lucien Rebatet, writing for *L'Action Française* under the pseudonym François Vinneuil. Sensing a genuine Carné-Prévert style, he dubbed it "stale and corny brasserie Baudelairism" and indicted its mood of sad fatalism on political grounds: "I believe Monsieur Carné is 'on the left,' at least for the moment. *Jenny* thus confirms all our suspicions about the depressing influence of Socialist ideology on artists, even when they pretend to make apolitical works." [11]

Film melodrama thrives in periods when a nation's social and economic crises seem so overwhelming that the public finds release in viewing the more modest problems of parents and children, lovers and spouses. To Rebatet's chagrin, *Jenny* was a box-office success. Holding its own in a season that saw Duvivier's *La Belle Equipe*, Litvak's *Mayerling*, Pagnol's *César*, and Renoir's *Le Crime de Monsieur Lange*, *Jenny* grossed seven times its production costs in its initial run. Distributed abroad, it placed third in the foreign-film category of a popularity poll held in 1938 by—of all places—the Japanese cinema journal *Movie Times*. The career of the boy from the Batignolles was off to a very propitious start.

PART II

The Young Master

CHAPTER 5

The Popular Front

Had Carné been less tenacious, his partnership with Prévert might have ended with *Jenny*. Browsing one day at Synops, an organization that specialized in furnishing filmmakers with synopses of potentially adaptable novels, Carné met Commander Edouard Corniglion-Molinier. An aviator friend of André Malraux, Corniglion-Molinier had helped to form the air squadron attached to the International Brigade in its struggle on behalf of the Republican cause in Spain. He had also taken to financing films between expeditions. The commander held Prévert in high esteem. When Carné indicated a desire to work with him again, the producer lent support immediately to what he deemed a winning team.

This sentiment was not shared by Charles David, whom Corniglion-Molinier assigned to serve as production manager for the new undertaking. An English emigré, David had been the force behind the making of Pierre Prévert's *L'Affaire est dans le sac*. He believed Jacques's brother better suited than Carné to direct the proposed adaptation of Storer Clouston's *The Lunatic at Large: His First Offense*, a zany Victorian novel to which David held the rights. David was especially irked by Carné's insistence that Françoise Rosay play the female lead and that Eugen Schüfftan serve as cinematographer. He considered Rosay's financial requirements exorbitant. And he was certain that Schüfftan would spoil the property's inherent lightheartedness through ponderous Expressionistic lighting. David also feared that the intimacy between the formidable Rosay and the young Carné would give the director an unfair edge in day-to-day negotiations. In short, David wanted this picture to be an effort of the old Prévert team, before it had been infiltrated by what he considered to be Feyder hangers-on. But despite David's efforts to obstruct Carné at each step during preproduction, the film—entitled *Drôle de Drame*—remained Carné's. It starred Rosay. It profited from Schüfftan's substantial experience. And Pierre Prévert served only as an assistant director.[1]

Drôle de Drame was a failure at the box office and with the critics, most of whom implicitly validated the view that Jacques's brother would have made a more entertaining picture.[2] But the film found a following among Saint-Germain-des-Prés intellectuals. Herbert Lottman notes wistfully that while the "mindless middle classes" of the Right Bank made a cultural claim to Guitry, Pagnol, and Rogers and Astaire, Left Bank inhabitants declared allegiance to Buñuel, Loy and Powell, and *Drôle de Drame*.[3] Journalist Suzanne Chantal recalls that she saw the film three times and memorized its dialogue, which she then recited with friends who had done likewise. The picture also provided occasion for informal debate about movies as art. To Valéry's declaration that "film is always impersonal," Malraux could reply, using *Drôle de Drame* as evidence, that "a film is the result of a team and reflects the personality of the person who puts together and directs that team."[4]

Lofty thoughts were not on the minds of the spectators who booed and hissed *Drôle de Drame* when it premiered at the Colisée Theater on October 20, 1937. The Colisée had been the site of a similar reception for Vigo's *L'Atalante* in 1934. It would also resound with the hoots and jeers that greeted Renoir's *La Règle du jeu* in 1939. As in the case of these other films, *Drôle de Drame*'s worth did not become generally apparent until its first postwar reissue, in 1951. The picture exhibited, as Jean-Louis Barrault remarks, a kind of "poetry of the absurd" that was ahead of its time and affronted the Cartesian temper of most filmgoers in prewar France.[5] Yet *Drôle de Drame* is very much a product of its time. The picture's odd mix of euphoric irreverence and impassive gloom is an artistic reflection of the fragility attending that brief moment of France's deviation from the road to decline, the Popular Front.

Conceived in the aftermath of Léon Blum's first government (June 4, 1936, to June 21, 1937), *Drôle de Drame* responds to both the optimism and the uncertainty which the Socialist leader's short-lived regime begat. The Popular Front's alliance of progressive parties of the left (Socialists, Radicals, and Communists) had given fresh impetus to the fight against Fascism and economic depression. Its electoral victory in spring 1936 fostered the belief that a popular majority had demonstrated the will to bring about a new start in French life. This perception, however, was deceptive. The Matignon Agreements advanced the cause of the working class. Yet the Communists' refusal to participate in Blum's cabinet, the government's naiveté about practical economics, its decision to slow down the social reforms program, and its nonintervention policy in the Spanish Civil War all had adverse effects. Within months there was an increase in strikes, a renewal of demonstrations, and, inevitably, the return of street violence: in March 1937, seven persons were killed by police in the Place Clichy. After the Senate denied him full power to deal with the outflow-of-gold crisis, Blum resigned. The ramifications were uncertain: "[Blum] would not admit failure. The pretense that the Popular Front still existed—and that economic recovery was under way— was kept up . . . But the arrangements and conventions of the Third Republic were such that the break-up of his government left a greater loss of confidence, a diminished sense of loyalty for the Republic, a loss of direction which prepared the way for the Vichy government three years later." [6]

The cultural impact of the Popular Front can be gauged by the many intellectuals who participated in its birth and development, and by government initiatives to foster education and the popular arts.[7] Although a handful of independent filmmakers directed nonfiction films for the Left, there was no Popular Front cinema per se. Several commercial films made during the Blum regime point to a heightened awareness of the plight of workers. But with the likelihood of war becoming considerable, cinematic expressions of social issues took second place to dramatizations of France's precarious international status—hence the popularity of Félix Gandéra's *Double Crime sur la Ligne Maginot* (1937) and the immense success of the Renoir-Spaak attempt to counter blind nationalism with *La Grande Illusion* (1937).[8]

The French film of this period that explicitly served social ideology was *La Vie est à nous*. A cooperative production conceived by the French Communist Party as propaganda for the 1936 election campaign, *La Vie est à nous* blended documentary footage with staged fictional scenes in an attempt to define contemporary French life and to persuade viewers to join with the Communists in acting for change. More the film's supervisor than its director, Jean Renoir coordinated the efforts of numerous filmmakers, including Jacques Becker, André Zwoboda, Jean-Paul Le Chanois, Henri Cartier-Bresson, Maurice Lime, and Pierre Unik. Renoir was a natural choice for the project. He had attended numerous Communist Party rallies; he had spoken publicly in support of the Popular Front; and he had just completed a work with Prévert and a band of like-minded associates, *Le Crime de Monsieur Lange*, that was distinctly leftist in outlook. As Le Chanois observes, "The fraternity [depicted] in *La Vie est à nous* was not an invention of the scriptwriters, but rather it was precisely that fraternity among us that allowed the realizaton of the film." [9]

Marcel Carné was excluded from that fraternity. On July 14, 1935, he had been asked by the Communists to film the united demonstration of progressive parties that was taking place at the Place de la Bastille. The result was about thirty shots that showed leaders as diverse as Edouard Daladier, Léon Blum, Maurice Thorez, and Edouard Herriot linking arms amid cheering crowds whose banners included the Bolshevik slogan "Peace, Bread, Liberty." Carné submitted this film to Party headquarters, and was never informed to what use it would be put. In midwinter 1936 he was summoned to meet with Party leaders on the rue Lafayette, where he was greeted more with suspicion than with cordiality. Present, among others, were Paul Vaillant-Couturier, Louis Aragon, Maurice Thorez, and André Marty. "A bit intimidated, I didn't know what countenance to assume. Was I to shake each of their hands or simply nod my head? Only Paul Vaillant-Couturier extended his hand . . . If I remember correctly, it was Thorez who spoke. This was what it was about. With the legislative elections of 1936 near at hand, the Central Committee had decided to produce a propaganda film—though that word was not pronounced—showing the life, struggles, and aspirations of the French people. Remembering the shots I had taken for them a few months earlier at the Bastille demonstration, they had thought of me to direct [réaliser] the film" (Vbd, 70). Carné was dumbfounded. Just days before, he had signed his contract to direct Jenny. "I explained as best I could that . . . I could not devote all my time, but that I was nonetheless ready to make myself free every evening no matter how late, and every Sunday as well." Aragon, who had been eyeing him rather sinisterly, interrupted: "There's perhaps another possibility. I met Jean Renoir last week at some mutual friends in Saint-Germain. He seems entirely devoted to our plans. We could perhaps—" Carné nervously interrupted Aragon to express admiration for the director of Toni and to give his assurance that Renoir would make a superb film. This said, he took leave of the awesome company, with only Vaillant-Couturier again extending his hand.

The motivation behind Carné's inclusion of this anecdote in La Vie à belles dents is complex. In part, it reflects his resentment when, after the war, he was blamed for having collaborated with the enemy. His story suggests that it was the Communist Party who rejected him, not vice versa. The incident also underscores Carné's sense of otherness, his sense of not being accepted by either the mainstream or the fringes of the French film industry: no effort was made to include him among the directors who worked on La Vie est à nous, many of whom were as unseasoned as he. Moreover, when Carné viewed the film he discovered that the Bastille demonstration sequence contained "many shots I had recorded." Although the film was always projected without credits, Carné feels he deserved the courtesy of being informed that his work was going to be included. (To this day, most histories and filmographies do not mention Carné's contribution.)[10] Above all, Carné's tale is an indirect jab at Jean Renoir for the lack of civility which he feels the elder director repeatedly evinced toward him.

In *My Life and My Films*, Renoir relates the saga of his efforts to raise money for *La Grande Illusion*: "I touted the manuscript around for three years, visiting the offices of all the French and foreign producers, orthodox or avant-garde. Had it not been for Jean Gabin not one of them would have taken a chance on the film. He accompanied me on numerous occasions, and eventually found a financier who, impressed by his solid confidence in the film, agreed to produce it."[11] Carné believes Renoir sins through omission. *La Vie à belles dents* relates that it was Carné who was responsible for convincing Albert Pinkéwitch, the producer of both *Jenny* and *La Grande Illusion*, to meet with Renoir and Gabin to discuss their proposed prisoner-of-war film. When a first meeting between the director and producer left Pinkéwitch unimpressed, Carné insisted: "Look . . . I don't know what his treatment is about, I haven't read it. All that I can say is that Renoir and Spaak have been dragging their screenplay to producers for three years. If two men of their caliber are dying to bring this topic to the screen, they must have something to say. They may not produce a masterpiece, but they will certainly not make an insipid film. Believe me" (*Vbd*, 78). Carné's admiration for Renoir the filmmaker persists. He regrets, however, that Renoir the man never acknowledged publicly the pressure which he, Carné, exerted in his favor at a time when Renoir was having little box-office success.

Carné does not expect us to believe that he was the *éminence grise* behind *La Grande Illusion*. Rather, he is underscoring his longstanding rancor at having been rebuffed by Renoir, as well as by those who eventually saw themselves as Renoir's spiritual heirs. Carné's feelings of exclusion during the making of *La Vie est à nous*; his perception that there was something forced about the son of a wealthy, celebrated painter being viewed generally as the Popular Front filmmaker par excellence; his regret that Renoir, like Prévert, was able to elicit more confidence among the Communist leadership than he, the son of an artisan—each of these personal frustrations made him all the more pessimistic about the future of France after the fall of the Blum government. Coupled with Prévert's vitriolic iconoclasm, this socially rooted pessimism contributed to *Drôle de Drame*'s distinctly unsettling tone.

Drôle de Drame's narrative is so improbable that even the most outlandish twist of situation and identity seems utterly natural by the film's end. The story springs from the feigned disappearance of Margarett (Françoise Rosay), the wife of a meek London professor of botany named Irwin Molyneux (Michel Simon). Molyneux writes scholarly tracts on subjects like "Mimesis in Mimosa." He is also the author of racy murder novels written under the pen name Felix Chapel. In reality, Molyneux has no talent for fiction and his material comes from Billy-the-Milkman (Jean-Pierre Aumont), a carefree youth in love with the professor's secretary, Eva (Nadine Vogel). Molyneux's pulp literature supports his wife in the comfortable style she demands. It is Margarett's inflated self-esteem that leads to her voluntary disappearance. Confronted with the unexpected visit of Irwin's cousin, the Anglican Bishop of Bedford (Louis Jouvet)—who just that morning delivered a sermon decrying the evil influence of Felix Chapel's novels—Margarett finds herself without cook and butler. (Unwilling to tolerate Margarett's abuse, the servants quit the Molyneux household that very day.) To save face, Margarett pretends to be away visiting sick friends in Brighton, while she is actually preparing dinner in the kitchen. When the suspicious Bedford decides to await her return, Irwin and Margarett flee to a squalid room in London's Chinatown—leaving Bedford to conclude that Molyneux has killed his wife, and leading the plot into a maze of imbroglios and mistaken identities.

The supposed murder captures the attention of the British public. The *Evening Times* asks—of all people—Felix Chapel to write a series of pieces on the sensational affair. Under pressure from his avaricious wife, Molyneux reluctantly accepts the assignment, dons a false beard, and returns home in the guise of Felix Chapel. Thanks to a ruse executed by Billy-the-Milkman (who is himself under suspicion as an accomplice in the alleged murder), the moralizing Bishop believes that he will be Molyneux's next victim. But to retrieve evidence that would expose his dalliance with a Paris showgirl, the Bishop, too, must return to the Molyneux home in ludicrous disguise: as a Scotsman in kilts, knee socks, and sunglasses. While the Bishop's life, unlike his reputation, is only in apparent jeopardy, the threat to Molyneux-Chapel is quite real: for William Kramps (Jean-Louis Barrault), a notorious assassin who specializes in butchering butchers out of his love for animals, is determined to murder the successful novelist whose writings first inspired him to pursue a life of crime. At knifepoint, the terrified Chapel draws on his imagination for the very first time, making Kramps believe not only that he is Molyneux (which of course he is), but that he has poisoned both his wife and Chapel, whose name he has now assumed.

The resulting friendship between the real and would-be murderers is closer than either man realizes, since Kramps has fallen hopelessly in love with a mysterious woman he calls Daisy, but who in reality is Margarett.

Although Margarett is enticed by the charms of this flamboyant suitor whom she does not know to be the infamous killer, her sense of respectability wins out and she, too, returns home to identify herself as alive and well. But because the daft Auntie Mac Phearson (Jeanne Lory) has decided to disown her bumbling nephew Molyneux and leave her property to the dynamic truthseeker Felix Chapel, Margarett insists that her husband continue to masquerade as the writer. In an effort to "normalize" Margarett's collusion with Chapel (as well as take pressure off the Bishop, who is now the prime suspect in the supposed murder of Molyneux), Kramps nobly asserts that it is he who killed Molyneux, having mistaken him for a butcher in the dark of night. "The widow Molyneux" accepts condolences from friends and neighbors; Kramps is carried off to prison, from which he has every intention of escaping; and the phony drama, or *drôle de drame*, comes not so much to a conclusion as to a state of suspension.

With characters assuming multiple roles, making studied exits and entrances, and ever aware of being observed, the texture of *Drôle de Drame* is abundantly theatrical. Distinct from both the movement-in-space aesthetic of René Clair's comedies and the nonstop cascade of gags found in Pierre Prévert's *L'Affaire est dans le sac*, *Drôle de Drame* is a whodunit burlesque in which Carné's tense compositions, slow traveling shots, extreme angling, and nervous close-ups constitute a parody of mystery and thriller film technique.[12] Cinematic self-consciousness is also apparent in the Surrealist-inspired instances of accelerated speed (to portray Molyneux's carnivorous plants at mealtime), masking (to represent the keyhole used to spy on the Bishop), and reverse motion (to capture the journalist Buffington's trancelike leap from a couch). But *Drôle de Drame* also draws upon nonfilmic dramatic traditions. Just as the plot movement of *Les Enfants du paradis* is shaped in large measure by commedia dell'arte scenarios and Shakespeare's *Othello*, so the doubling of characters, disguised identities, and false deaths in *Drôle de Drame* find their roots in the comic theater of classical antiquity and early modern Europe.

Yet *Drôle de Drame* departs from certain generally accepted notions about comic plots. Traditionally, comedy produces a movement from an oppressive society to a more liberated one. This change usually occurs when a plot device brings together a romantic hero and heroine: "What normally happens is that a young man wants a young woman, that his desire is resisted by some opposition, usually paternal, and that near the end of the play some twist in the plot enables the hero to have his will."[13] In *Drôle de Drame*, resolution and liberation do not occur: the destiny of the ingénue, Eva, and her lover, Billy-the-Milkman, is left undetermined; Kramps gives up his short-lived claim to Margarett; and the fate of Molyneux is to remain imprisoned within the fabricated identity of Felix Chapel. A lyrical, liberating moment does take place when a tipsy Molyneux, believing he can frame and take vengeance on the Bishop, glides gently down the staircase to the accompaniment of a descending scale on a xylophone. Divulging the grace and fluency that lie hidden behind actor Michel Simon's ordinarily awkward and massive exterior, the shot exposes the potential for effective action in an otherwise indolent, tame husband. But this instant of triumph and transition vanishes quickly, as the true obstacles to liberation—the scheming Margarett and the dissembling Bishop—remain to uphold society's irrational folly, pride, and hypocrisy.

Classical comedies frequently conclude with the elimination of an irreconcilable character. The arrest of Kramps is a sardonic twist of convention, since it signifies the expulsion of the film's most generous and poetic character. *Drôle de Drame* thus approaches what Frye has termed "the ironic phase" of comedy, in which "the demonic world is never far away." [14] Indeed, the fear of bodily assault and the potential for death loom large throughout. Although critics and historians have regularly relegated *Drôle de Drame* to a marginal position within the Carné oeuvre, closer consideration shows that it overlaps in theme and tone with films deemed more representative. Along with *Le Quai des Brumes*, it is an expression of isolation and alienation. As in *Hôtel du Nord*, the destiny of love is seen as one of detachment and despair. As in *Le Jour se lève*, goodness and beauty are threatened by the evil that exists in society and in other men's hearts.

The film's capacity to provoke viewer unease even at its most comic moments results in large measure from the interplay of diverse acting styles by *Drôle de Drame*'s leading players, all of whom began their careers in the theater (fig. 16). Swiss-born Michel Simon (1895–1975) performed the classics under Georges Pitoëff before coming to Paris and triumphing as the unscrupulous parasite Clo-Clo in Marcel Achard's play *Jean de la lune*. Although the latter was successfully adapted to the screen in 1931, the early movie roles for which Simon is best remembered were all initially box-office disasters: the bank clerk turned jealous killer in Renoir's *La Chienne* (1931); the perverse tramp in Renoir's *Boudu sauvé des eaux* (1932); the grumbling adventurer in Vigo's *L'Atalante* (1934); and Molyneux in *Drôle de Drame*. An eccentric, often scandalous nonconformist offscreen and offstage, Simon established in over 140 pictures a film persona organized around two extremes

16 Cover page of a publicity packet for *Drôle de Drame:* clockwise from top, Françoise Rosay, Jean-Louis Barrault, Louis Jouvet, Jean-Pierre Aumont, Michel Simon

that often adhered in a single role: the misfit who aspires to social harmony and genuine altruism but is helpless in the face of society's order; and the deceiver who, beneath a sympathetic veneer, subverts social goals.[15]

Simon's physicality is the sign of the malaise which his characters share. His corpulent mass, his undulating jowls and triple chin, his raucous Vaudois voice, and the erratic dart of his glassy eyes call so much attention to his body that Simon—much like Charles Laughton—exerts a primal sensual energy that seduces despite the very ugliness of its source. Simon understood the power of his screen magnetism: "This oversize image of your face, these spoken words that are also overblown, create a kind of intimacy between the audience and the actor. The viewer feels every nuance of your glance. He feels and knows them in that special state of receptiveness, that secular mass known as the cinema." [16]

Simon played many "double roles" in his films, including *La Chienne* and Guitry's *La Vie d'un honnête homme* (1952). But in these pictures Simon is a walking contestation of everyday values. As Molyneux—the name itself suggests the French verb *mollir*, "to grow soft and slack"— Simon is less a contester than a victim. He suffers his wife's bullying, his cousin's meddling, William Kramps's determination to kill him, and his own lack of imagination. The artistry of Simon's characterization lies in his compassionate portrayal of Molyneux's attempt to juggle the conflicting roles which circumstance has forced upon him. He stutters; he flubs movements; he precedes each gesture with a split second of bewilderment. Beneath the layers of lies and adipose tissue, we sense a frightened and impotent soul deprived of affection. But rather than teach us something about the complexity of the human condition, the double role of Molyneux-Chapel reduces to two complementary caricatures of the same type: both the timid scholar and the celebrated novelist hide true feelings behind words and actions not really their own. Only in the nostalgic remembrance of a song from his childhood, "Dormez, dormez petit pigeon," does the character appear to experience a semblance of solace. In this regard, Simon's Molyneux is the quintessential Carné personage. Unlike Renoir's Boudu or Père Jules in Vigo's *L'Atalante*, Molyneux is a victim of restraint and repression, confined to social roles he can merely dream of abandoning. Thanks to Simon's ability to make us feel that his own inclinations are being constrained in the very playing of this character, he assists the film in its becoming, ultimately, an indictment of societal constraint.

The most celebrated dialogue in *Drôle de Drame* is spoken during the dinner scene, when the Bishop interrogates the panic-striken Molyneux and, eyeing the blade of his knife, utters the words "Bizarre, bizarre."

MOLYNEUX: What's the matter?

BISHOP: With whom?

MOLYNEUX: Your knife.

BISHOP: What do you mean?

MOLYNEUX: Yes . . . you were looking at your knife and you said . . . "Bizarre, bizarre." So I thought that . . .

BISHOP (*feigning surprise*): I said "Bizarre, bizarre"? How strange! Why should I have said "Bizarre, bizarre"?

MOLYNEUX: I assure you, cousin, you said "Bizarre, bizarre."

BISHOP: I said "Bizarre"? . . . (*he shakes his head*). How bizarre!

The black humor results not from the dialogue but from its delivery by actors whose style and demeanor could not be more opposed than those of Simon and Louis Jouvet (1887–1951). If Simon's Molyneux projects an overripe Brie, Jouvet's Bishop is as brittle as a toothpick. His diction is classically precise. His body is perfectly controlled. And his smile is as insidious as a panther preparing to pounce—which Jouvet actually resembles in his black cleric's habit and dark, slicked-back hair.

Jouvet was a man of the theater who at bottom scorned movies. Viewing film as "a powerful branch grafted to the robust and venerable trunk of the theater," he engaged in it primarily to finance his stage company. Though he played in memorable pictures, Jouvet took pride in declaring, "I have no personal notions about the cinema: it's a technique; what we do in the studio counts for little; the actor becomes only an instrument." [17] His legendary enmity toward Michel Simon took hold when he directed the latter on stage in *Jean de la lune*. It was sustained by the enviable ease with which Simon, unlike Jouvet, was able to move from one medium to the other. Barrault remembers: "Jouvet, who was much less arrogant than people believe and more timid than you'd ever imagine, found it trying to work again with Simon because he was conscious of the latter's fine critical eye. On the other hand, Simon was very sure of himself; he was able to splutter and stammer because that was his manner, whereas the very precise intonations of Jouvet never allowed him to speak unintelligibly—after all, he was a Professor at the Conservatory. At one point, Jouvet did flub a line. 'Cut,' shouted Carné. And as the camera was reloaded and the set touched up, everyone could hear Simon say to Jouvet, 'You made a mistake!' This sally provoked incredible rage in Jouvet, who refused to continue shooting." [18] Fortunately for Carné, this off-camera tension worked to strengthen onscreen characterization.

Jouvet's Bishop of Bedford is something of an extension of the sly priest the actor portrayed in Feyder's *La Kermesse héroïque*. Ironically, that earlier role was conceived for Michel Simon. Carné observes: "Jouvet tonsured, barefoot, and dressed in a sackcloth that kept flapping round his ankles made for a delightful cameo role. But with him, the character of the priest changed. Simon would have depicted a ribald friar in the tradition of Rabelais. Jouvet made one think more of an Inquisition figure. There lay the difference between the two" (*Vbd*, 61). In *Drôle de Drame*, we may think of the Bishop as a "Jouvet" exterior trying to hold "Simon" impulses in check. Bedford's pious verbiage is the mask of a Tartuffe (one of Jouvet's most successful stage roles) whose carnality advertises itself in his lust for Eva, his infatuation with a music-hall celebrity, his twelve children, and the gusto with which he devours Margarett's *canard aux oranges*—taking two helpings to Molyneux's one. Bedford is clearly the villain of the piece. His duplicity is rendered visual each time his reflection is caught by mirrors. And the chromatic music that punctuates most of his appearances reinforces further his projection of insidiousness.

The use of music in *Drôle de Drame* marks an advance over *Jenny*. *Drôle de Drame* is less talky than *Jenny*, and its music often sustains or underscores action when there is no dialogue. It was composed by Maurice Jaubert (1900–1940), the musician who had worked on Vigo's films and several of Clair's, and who, by the time of his death in the Franco-German war, also scored *Le Quai des Brumes*, *Hôtel du Nord*, and *Le Jour se lève*. *Drôle de Drame*'s music is ironic and jocular: suspenseful, scalelike passages accompany ascents and descents of the Molyneux staircase; trumpet blasts and drum rolls occur with each telephone call to Scotland Yard; strains of "Ta Ra Ra Boom-di-ay" frame the film to establish and reiterate its burlesque flavor. The only uninventive use of music is the lilting, romantic waltz superimposed on the scene between Margarett and Kramps in the Chinatown hideaway. Yet its very conventionality is inspired, for it guarantees that we, like Margarett, will not be swept away by the fancifulness of such an improbable idyll.

As portrayed by Rosay, Margarett is incapable of allowing authentic humanity to pierce the mantle of her false decorum. Bound by an obsession to maintain the trappings and illusions of social propriety ("Sustaining one's position, that's what it's all about. Don't forget, Irwin. We have a nice house with servants for which everyone envies us"), Margarett functions as a comic humor, in Ben Jonson's sense of the term. The original screenplay called for Margarett, early in the film, to sit at her piano and sing a light air. The segment was not filmed. Having begun her career in opera, Rosay would probably have executed the tune honorably, even if sung as the scenario prescribes, "with a bit too much affectation." But to allow Margarett to sing would be tantamount to making her partake of the Prévertian feminine mystique: a love of music, flowers, and generosity—all of which Margarett abhors.

In contrast to Simon's amorphousness, Jouvet's angularity, and Rosay's overbearingness, the grace of Jean-Louis Barrault (b. 1910) injects a peculiarly lyric strain into the frenzied world of *Drôle de Drame*. It matters little that Kramps (a character not found in Clouston's novel) is, officially, a lunatic at large. It is insignificant that the woman he falls in love with is taller, broader, and gruffer than he. Barrault is already incarnating, in a comic key, the ardent idealism that will mark his portrayal of Baptiste in *Les Enfants du paradis*. At the climax of his tryst in the dreary hotel room, the shooting script reads:

Reprise of the medium-close shot of Margarett and William. She is still seated; he is at her feet, now seated cross-legged.

WILLIAM KRAMPS (*with a lyric and tender gesture*): Love!

MARGARETT (*dreamily but skeptical*): Love?

She gets up. He gets up.

WILLIAM KRAMPS (*he speaks gently*): Love . . .

Margarett moves away toward the windows. Semi-long shot, then track-in to Margarett raising the curtain.

MARGARETT: Love . . . love . . .

William rushes toward her and enfolds her in his arms, feverishly.

WILLIAM KRAMPS: Love . . . Daisy . . . love . . .

MARGARETT (*dreamily and letting herself go*): Love!

The scene is ludicrous, but Barrault-Kramps convinces through the same outpouring of enthusiasm which he brings to his primary passion—murder.

Kramps's grandeur resides in his (psychotic) capacity to reject entirely and without remorse society's moral hypocrisies. The price paid for such independence is demonstrated in the celebrated lily-pond scene. Margarett has come out of hiding and reenters her home via the greenhouse. Unexpectedly she finds Kramps lounging beside the pond, stark naked. With her sense of propriety surging forth more strongly than ever, the grande dame shrieks as Kramps, in the foreground with his back to the camera, plunges headlong into the pond. Bourgeois morality brings to a definitive end the young man's experience of love.

The scene's boldness bears underscoring. One historian notes, "If we make an exception for the rare precursors, such as Jean-Louis Barrault in Carné's *Drôle de Drame*, it is only around 1965 that the first male, white buttocks appear in a film without anthropological or bodybuilding alibis—first in a semi-comic vein (Forman's *Loves of a Blonde*), then semi-romantic (Zeffirelli's *Romeo and Juliet*), and then quite rawly (Schlesinger's *Midnight Cowboy*)."[19] The attention Carné devoted to the unclad male in *Nogent* has generally gone uncommented upon, but his glorification of male beauty in *La Merveilleuse Visite* (1974) caused embarrassment for many of its first viewers. Carné has also shocked through the depiction of the female body. His shots of Arletty showering nude in *Le Jour se lève* (1939) were cut as of the Occupation. Similarly, shots of the naked lovers swimming underwater in *Les Jeunes Loups* were censored from that picture's release print in 1967.

It was from fear of censorship that Carné made several takes of

17 Margarett's stupefaction at viewing her suitor nude

Kramps's plunge with Barrault wearing bikini briefs. (American prints of *Drôle de Drame* do not show Barrault in the raw.) But what makes the scene so dramatically effective (in both the French and American versions) is the fact that Rosay was not warned that Barrault—who happens to be a nudist in private life—would appear naked in the final take, which was also the final take of the production. This lack of communication between director and actress resulted in a reaction shot that portrayed genuine shock (fig. 17). Carné recalls: "With the scene completed, I approached Rosay, who burst out with indignation, 'You could have spared me that sight!' And leaving me there bewildered, she brusquely turned round and retreated to her dressing room. Already brought out were the champagne and glasses that traditionally celebrate the end of a film's shooting, so I naturally sent an assistant to get Rosay. But with 'that sight' still rankling in her mind, she responded with a very cool refusal" (*Vbd*, 88).

Jenny established that a fundamental schema in Carné is the unexpected sight of a loved one having intimate relations with a third party. The hoax that Carné and Barrault perpetrated on Rosay might be interpreted as a deliberate, albeit unconscious, effort by Carné to implicate her in a real-life "primal scene." In *Drôle de Drame* itself, the inebriated Molyneux almost catches Margarett and William Kramps *in flagrante delicto* in the Limehouse hideaway; but as befits farce, Molyneux is never enlightened about his wife's escapade. Indeed, in a film that excludes authentic intimacy, Carné's primal schema becomes disjointed, with the two moments of privileged spectacle that do occur emphasizing the primacy of repression over desire. First, Margarett's viewing Kramps nude puts an end to their affair: "Oh, don't call me Daisy anymore; it's so vulgar . . . And then, I don't want to hurt you, my friend, but all the same, our social standings are clearly very different." Second, the discovery by all the film's principals that the presumably dead Margarett is hiding in her living-room closet brings the plot to a quick end. In both instances the potential for insight and illumination is thoroughly undone. Margarett refuses to acknowledge the body of the man she has been pretending to love; and the prolonged search for the victim of a crime of passion (which never actually occurred) comes to a halt when the corpus delicti is observed to be alive and well, clothed and closeted. Burlesque takeoffs on Freudian doctrine, these two episodes tell us not only that Mother (Margarett) remains inviolable, but that she is unreceptive to the exhibitionism of Son (Kramps).

I suggested that *Jenny* gave expression to Carné's need to establish intimacy with Rosay, the woman who came closest to being a substitute for the mother Carné lost at age five. *Drôle de Drame* seems to express a contrary need to separate from the maternal figure. Again, the complexity of the Carné-Prévert symbiosis is manifest. William Kramps—the Oedipal drama's usurping son—is very much a Prévert creation in his love of animals and hatred of the bourgeoisie: "You must understand," Kramps explains to Molyneux-Chapel, "that at bottom it's quite logical for me to kill butchers because I am of a very sensitive nature. I've never harmed a fly, I like animals. I have a passion for animals. Whereas those butchers, they kill animals. Hence, I kill butchers . . . And then I take their money." Extra touches of Prévertian irony derive from the fact that Michel Simon, the son of a pork butcher, was a legendary animal lover who kept domesticated monkeys as well as cats and dogs and never accepted a stage or film role in which he would be called upon to make an animal endure pain, and that Barrault at the time was a vegetarian. Indeed, Kramps's love for animals is stronger and far more enduring than his passion for women. Immediately following his *coup de foudre* for Margarett-Daisy ("That's the most beautiful woman I've ever met"), the Chinese hotel proprietor asks if Kramps has known many women. Kramps's response has a distinct Carné ring: "No . . . I've been too busy. I've never had the time. And then, women, they make me uneasy! They intimidate me! . . . But *that* one . . . That one I love!!!"

On one hand, Kramps's excessive, idealized attraction to Daisy prefigures Baptiste's to Garance in *Les Enfants du paradis*. On the other, his readiness to abandon Daisy ("She's really less beautiful than I thought") announces the attitude of that other poet-assassin, the historical character Lacenaire in *Les Enfants du paradis*—who was probably homosexual. In assuming responsibility for having "killed off" Molyneux, Kramps provides a farcical antecedent for Lacenaire's genuine murder of the Count in *Les Enfants du paradis*. In both cases, the woman who has dominated the man's life, but with whom he has not experienced physical intimacy, is liberated from a husband-lover. Each man's willingness to face death takes on an aura of self-abnegation. Kramps thus embodies a fundamental tension of the entire Carné-Prévert oeuvre: a zestful impulse for heterosexual indulgence (Prévert) and a tendency toward disengagement from women altogether (Carné). For all his apparent sadism, Kramps announces the masochistic psychodynamic that becomes progressively more perceptible in the later Carné-Prévert works.

Were it not that the film's caricatured men fare little better than its women, *Drôle de Drame* might be construed as misogynistic. Margarett is the archetypal shrew; Auntie Mac Phearson, the frivolous hysteric; and her dozen children notwithstanding, the Bishop's wife is as frigid as her husband is lustful. The sole uncaricatured female is Molyneux's secretary, Eva. An orphan who abandoned the Salvation Army because she found it too morose ("Too much music, always the same music! It was so sad"), Eva represents the hope for worldly salvation in a society where joy and spontaneity are regularly crushed. Portrayed by twenty-one-year-old Nadine Vogel, Eva stands out as the rare female character in the Carné oeuvre to convey sustained authenticity. In her capacity to escape typology (ironic, since she is a botanist's aide), Eva breathes, pulsates, and is open to sensual experience.

Unfortunately, the expurgated American prints omit the enchanting scenes of Eva and Billy-the-Milkman as they hide from the law in the attic of the Molyneux house. (These scenes recall Jean Breughel's watchtower liaison with the burgomaster's daughter in *La Kermesse héroïque*.) Wearing a top hat, striped shirt, rubber gloves, and satin apron, the twenty-four-year-old Jean-Pierre Aumont seduces Vogel by appealing to romantic logic: "You believe that there are some things one does, and others one does not. That's idiotic! (*He turns to her and grasps her shoulders.*) Look, the other day, I kissed you. It seems that is part of what one does not do (*close shot of her, he continues offscreen*), but since we did it, the fact is that it is done (*she smiles*). And things that have been done, why not do them again (*camera on him*) if they gave us pleasure . . . if they gave you pleasure? (*Close shot of the two of them. They kiss*)."

Aumont had already gained celebrity by creating the role of Oedipus in Cocteau's *La Machine infernale*, directed in 1934 by Aumont's mentor, Louis Jouvet. Cocteau admired Aumont's "youth, command, wildness, arrogance, and moonstruck quality."[20] It is especially the last that Aumont brings to the Carné-Prévert film. But beyond displaying infectious charm, Aumont's Billy—a character not present in Clouston's novel—assures the coherence of *Drôle de Drame* as a political fable. With its entire plot triggered by the unexpected departure of a cook and a butler, *Drôle de Drame* is a demonstration of the bourgeoisie's incapacity to maintain a façade of propriety when the working classes fail to support it. In oversupplying the Molyneux household with free milk, Billy has a facile pretext for wooing Eva. But his milk, the drink of human sustenance, is also a figure of Billy's creative gift: fabricating stories. When Margarett testily sends Billy away at the film's start, she not only deprives her servants of their only release from the tedium of their jobs, she also (unwittingly) destroys the source of her middle-class comfort—her husband's best-selling novels, which are merely transcriptions of Billy's tales. The moral is clear: the survival of the bourgeoisie is dependent upon the unrewarded labors of the proletariat.

Drôle de Drame was shot in the Pathé studios at Joinville-le-Pont. Arguably, its most affecting set is Molyneux's lush greenhouse, a manicured remnant of Eden in a society gone mad. But the décor most indicative of the talents of artistic designer Trauner and cinematographer Schüfftan is the one portraying London's Chinatown (fig. 18). Its somber smokiness suggests the influence of Pabst's adaptation of Brecht and Weill's *Threepenny Opera* (1931). "Absolutely not," Trauner protests. "Pabst and [designer Andrei] Andrejew copied Gustave Doré's nineteenth-century drawings of London image by image. But I knew London's Limehouse district firsthand."[21]

Trauner's emphatic response highlights an essential part of his method, acquired from Meerson and sustained throughout a career that includes films as diverse as Wilder's *The Apartment* (1960), Losey's *Don Giovanni* (1979), and Tavernier's *'Round Midnight* (1985): always to begin a project with thorough documentation of the slice of reality depicted. Yet the sets of *Drôle de Drame*, including the Limehouse, indicate that Trauner favored mood over verisimilitude. After assembling documentation, Trauner "retained only those elements that affected him by their unusual aspects, thereby coming close to the surrealists. With his selections, aided by his own recollections, he composed very personal sets . . . This trans-

18 Alexander Trauner's Limehouse set: exoticism tailored to bourgeois tastes

position, this sublimation of reality, characterizes Trauner's best sets." [22]

Trauner was a natural choice to collaborate with Carné, since both men schematize the real through elaborate artifice. Yet Carné himself has ambivalent feelings about having eschewed realism in *Drôle de Drame*: "I got a bit angry with Trauner concerning the street set [outside the Molyneux house] for which he had reserved a sound stage that was too small. According to him, we could not acquire any other. Clearly the street's background smacks of a painted backdrop and I've been re-proached for it. And of course I am also responsible. I should have used a short-focus lens to make the street look longer; but I was fairly inex-perienced. With this said, the film was not intended to be realistic, and the problem with the set actually helped to emphasize the baroque aspect of the film. The costumes were extravagant, and Schüfftan's lighting was very Expressionistic. They already prefigured *Le Quai des Brumes*." [23]

Carné's equivocal statement, made decades after the film's initial re-lease, points to a moral question that all his works raise and about which

he is extremely sensitive: to what extent is a filmmaker justified in gloss-
ing over social and political realities in favor of formal, aesthetic constructs? As a political apologue, *Drôle de Drame* presents us with representatives of the bourgeoisie (Molyneux and Margarett), the clergy
(the Bishop), the proletariat (Billy), the *Lumpenproletariat* (William
Kramps), aliens (the Chinese), and bloodthirsty street mobs. Yet properly
speaking, *Drôle de Drame* is not a political film. The Carné-Prévert-
Trauner inclusion of the Limehouse underworld serves principally to en-
hance atmosphere. It is a narrative strategy to transport "ordinary"
(bourgeois) individuals momentarily into "extraordinary" (lowlife) surroundings. As in Pabst's *Threepenny Opera*, the romantic aura of the
underworld "rediscovered for a Left-wing bourgeoisie the 'poetry' of
low-life, while social satire acted as a cautionary deposit allowing them
to embark on . . . sentimental and social delusionism."[24] Pabst sacrifices
much of Brecht's concept of alienation. But by turning the beggars' parade at the story's end into an overture to revolt, Pabst remains true to
the Brechtian project of making a theater audience recognize the nature
of the world and then take action to change it. This is not at all the case
with Carné and Prévert. Belonging to that group of Left Bank writers
and artists who assumed ideological postures without significant political consequences, their anticonformist attitudes served, in the harsh
words of Simone de Beauvoir, "above all to justify their inertia."[25]
Rather than being anchored to concrete political analysis or reference,
the Carné-Prévert films operate more on the rarefied—and elitist—level
of archetype and myth.

In one sense, the subject of *Drôle de Drame* is theatricality, or the
tension between appearances and reality, and in this regard the film foreshadows *Les Enfants du paradis*. The parallels are numerous: the Limehouse sequences announce the milieu of Lacenaire and his gangster cronies; like Madame Hermine's boarding house, the Chinatown hotel turns
next-door neighbors into lovers; in his irresistible attraction to a woman
whose name denotes a flower, Kramps anticipates the emotional drama
of Baptiste and Garance. Moreover, at the heart of both films is the
theme of private drama turned public spectacle. This is perhaps best illustrated in *Drôle de Drame* when Inspector Bray addresses the street
throngs from a curtained window in the Molyneux house. Presenting
Margarett, alive and well, to his stunned "audience," the Inspector executes a *coup de théâtre* the equal of Lacenaire's revelation of Baptiste and
Garance in passionate embrace on the terrace of the Grand Théâtre. The
first shot of *Drôle de Drame* is a high-angle crane shot that glides in
toward the bustle of uniformed soldiers, fancy-dressed ladies with para-

sols, and a band of street musicians, before highlighting, indoors, the film's main characters; this is virtually a scaled-down trial run for the lavish opening shots of the Boulevard du Temple.

Yet as social satire *Drôle de Drame* merits comparison with that "precise description of the bourgeoisie of our age" [26] found in Renoir's *La Règle du jeu* (*Rules of the Game*, 1939). In terms of manifest content, Renoir's picture deals with vestiges of France's aristocracy on the brink of World War II; Carné and Prévert's, with the pretensions of the *nouveaux riches* in England circa 1900. But both films criticize the sterility of existence when it is more performed than lived. Both decry the view of society as a stage on which people willingly dissemble, manipulate, conceal, and submerge that which is real and essential. They depart from one another not so much in subject as in spirit.

Inspired by Beaumarchais's charge, as articulated in the preface to *Le Mariage de Figaro*, to "tear off the mask" of the prevailing morals that disguise vice and abuse, Renoir allows his players, despite their theatricality, "the potential freedom of natural responses and personal choices." [27] Wedded to a tradition of farce, Carné and Prévert move only from one stereotype to the next. As Molyneux complains to Margarett at the film's start, "A double life is not a life. I don't call that living." At the end of *La Règle du jeu*, the murder of the aviator André Jurieu extinguishes the sole individual unwilling to assume the insincere attitudes society demands. Jurieu's death actually strengthens the tacit conspiracy of the bourgeois community, which, in the person of the Marquis de La Chesnaye, declares it "a deplorable accident." Nevertheless, this death of a hero is a supreme expression of human reality. Renoir succeeds—albeit for one split second—in puncturing the hermetic view of the world as a successive series of poses and images, a view which the very nature of narrative cinema encourages and which Renoir's cinematic style of the 1930s fought against. In *Drôle de Drame*, the arrest of William Kramps also removes a character who rebels against society's moral pressures. But for all Kramps's straining to play the self-sacrificing lover, no humanity comes through. In accepting the guilt for a murder that never took place, he in fact becomes an accomplice in the bourgeois refusal to confront reality. Through their adroit cover-up of a real event, *La Règle du jeu*'s characters at least concede that reality exists. Locked into an impenetrable world of histrionics, those of *Drôle de Drame* are unable to distinguish the real from the spurious. *La Règle du jeu* tells a tragic story through comedy. *Drôle de Drame* depicts the tragedy of a world relegated to the comic.

Renoir writes that his film was shaped in response to early lessons acquired from his parents and cousin Gabrielle: "We are all 'mystified'—that is to say, fooled, duped, treated as of no account. I had the good fortune to have been taught to see through the trickery in my youth. In *La Règle du jeu*, I passed on what I knew to the public. But this is something that people do not like; the truth makes them feel uncomfortable." [28]

The young Carné was equally aware of how people prefer not to know the truth. He, too, understood the trickery which society's codes insist upon. But unlike Renoir, he did not receive encouragement to express himself openly. Unlike Renoir, he found himself more and more locked beneath the social armor of hypocrisy and illusion. The unrelenting artificiality of *Drôle de Drame* is Carné's statement on the improbability of France's renewing itself after the fall of the Popular Front. It is also an expression of Carné's pessimism about the prospect of breaking out of the moralistic corset that restrains the body politic. The marginal, he is telling us, can engage with society only through disguise, only through recourse to popular "fronts." In a grossly comic mode, *Drôle de Drame* poses the problems of alienation and inauthenticity that are at the center of Carné's works and his being.

Invariably, Carné films end with arresting images. The final moments of *Drôle de Drame* depict the boisterous crowd marching across and out of the screen frame as they accompany in triumph the policemen who escort William Kramps to prison. Only moments before, this same mob invaded Molyneux's home in order to lynch the Bishop, still believed to be Margarett's murderer. A comment on Europe's susceptibility to demagoguery during the interwar period, the readiness of the masses to harass any scapegoat at hand epitomizes Prévert and Carné's "rather clear-sighted awareness of the Fascist peril." [29] Indeed, when representatives of *le peuple* (the beer vendor, the streetsweeper) pay condolences to the "widowed" Margarett, they appear less as compassionate individuals than as social ciphers. But the film's final shot is its most pessimistic. After the throng moves out of the frame, a toddler remains, staring ahead, unmoved (fig. 19). For one brief moment we sense that youth holds the promise of restoring sanity to a world gone berserk. Yet a second later the child's father turns back into the frame and retrieves him, and they walk off hand in hand to join the crowd.

The idea for this pirouette was Carné's and, uncharacteristically, it came to him spontaneously while shooting the scene: "You feel that the father adores the child but nonetheless abandons him for a moment. He's been carried along by the crowd's shouts of 'Death! Death!' without realizing the cruelty of his having abandoned his son." [30] This is a discon-

19 The toddler and his father at the end of *Drôle de Drame:* the ephemerality of innocence

certing end to a film that excludes any glimpse of family life unencumbered by jealousy, greed, and egotism. It underscores the tenuousness of family ties. It asserts the ephemerality of innocence and its helplessness against so-called civilized society. Above all, it anticipates the haunting final scene of *Les Enfants du paradis,* in which the childlike Baptiste is drowned in a sea of indifferent merrymakers as he struggles to reach the woman of his dreams.

At a symposium held at Perpignan in 1971, Carné was asked to comment on the near-obsessive recurrence of children and childlike figures in his films. The director referred immediately to the loss at age five of his mother: "Freud would be able to explain it better than I, but I'm not surprised that there is this regret, this search for childhood, or even feelings which may appear a bit childlike. For example, one speaks of a certain naiveté in *Les Assassins de l'ordre* [made in 1970]. I don't agree. It's a burst of sincerity. But this is perhaps 'naive' for people less sentimental than I ... I agree, there is a search for childhood in my films because at one time I lacked affection and I have been profoundly marked by that."[31]

Child abuse appears in numerous French films of the 1930s, including Duvivier's *Poil de Carotte* (1932), Jean Benoît-Lévy and Marie Epstein's

La Maternelle (1933), and Vigo's *Zéro de conduite* (1933).[32] It did not become a developed theme in Carné's works until 1960 with *Terrain vague*. But it is noteworthy that *Drôle de Drame* was not the film Carné and Prévert wanted to do as their second feature. They had planned, instead, a fictional exposé on the actual retaliation incurred by a group of rambunctious boys who managed to escape from a French reform school. Rejected as too volatile by the same censorship agency that had forbidden commercial distribution of *Zéro de conduite*, the film was to have had the title *L'Ile des enfants perdus* (*The Island of Lost Children*). Surely, the final shot of *Drôle de Drame* is a projection of Carné's sense of himself as an exiled child of paradise. The poignant presence of the little boy points to the fact that for all the political resonance of the films he made both with and without Prévert, personal mythology is a major motivating impulse behind Carné's creativity.

CHAPTER 6

Poetic Realism

Carné's first financial and artistic triumph was *Le Quai des Brumes*.[1] The most popular French film of 1938, it won the Prix Louis Delluc and the Grand Prix National du Cinéma Français, and it shared the Prix Méliès with Renoir's *La Bête humaine*. Four decades later, it placed ninth in the poll taken among film industry professionals to determine "the ten best French films in the history of talking pictures."

In his memoirs Carné claims that the movie might never have materialized were it not for two women who viewed *Drôle de Drame* one afternoon at the Colisée Theater. The first was the wife of Raoul Ploquin, an executive in charge of French productions at the Neubabelsberg studios of the German picture company Universum Film AG (UFA). In the fall of 1937 Ploquin was overseeing the completion of *Gueule d'Amour*, a film directed by Jean Grémillon and starring Jean Gabin, the husband of Madame Ploquin's movie companion. Like Françoise Rosay, Doriane Gabin often attempted to influence her husband's professional activities. When Mesdames Gabin and Ploquin telephoned their spouses in Germany to extol the virtues of *Drôle de Drame*, the men were persuaded to come to Paris the following week, watch the film, and meet the director over dinner at Allard's. As soon as Ploquin flung the anticipated question—did Carné have a property in mind for Gabin?—Carné proposed Pierre Mac Orlan's 1927 novel *Le Quai des Brumes*, an atmospheric evocation of underworld life at the Montmartre café Le Lapin Agile. The dinner party ended with Ploquin and Gabin only vaguely promising to read the book. But the next day both the producer and the actor telephoned. Having spent much of the night reading the novel, they were convinced it would make a good film. During the weeks following, UFA bought the rights to the book and signed Carné and Prévert to adapt the work for eventual production in Germany (*Vbd*, 91–93).

As in his remarks about the origins of *Jenny*, Carné emphasizes his centrality in shaping a project for which women served as catalysts. But several facts put into serious question the accuracy of Carné's account. First, Gabin's interest in *Le Quai des Brumes* had been kindled as early as 1935, when he instructed Denise Tual, his agent and a founding director of Synops, to acquire an option on the book's film rights in his name. Second, Jacques Prévert had signed a contract on August 6, 1937, to provide UFA with a treatment for an adaptation of Mac Orlan's novel no later than August 28. Third, newspapers were announcing as early as September 22 that Carné would be going to Berlin to run screen tests for the female lead in a new Gabin project. These events all occurred prior to *Drôle de Drame*'s release on October 20, 1937.[2]

Carné also claims to have had misgivings about shooting in a German studio. Being monolingual, he feared that working outside France would impede his effectiveness on the set. He describes his first brief experience at Neubabelsberg as having left an impression of German studios as "gigantic and cold, ruled over by a Prussian sense of discipline," and fostering work "devoid of enthusiasm" (*Vbd*, 93). Coming from the Gallic filmmaker most associated with tyrannical posturing, Carné's remark about Prussian discipline suggests a desire to distance himself retroactively from the country that nurtured many of his directorial models— Murnau, Lang, and to some extent Sternberg, all of whom had left Nazi Germany by the early 1930s. Nonetheless, Carné's reluctance to adapt to foreign tongues and cultures is genuine, and helps explain why he remained in France during the Occupation and why he refused offers to work in Great Britain after the war. These later decisions hurt Carné's reputation and career.

But in 1937 Carné's travel anxieties were conveniently allayed when UFA withdrew its support of *Le Quai des Brumes*. Having read Prévert and Carné's synopsis, representatives of Goebbels's Nazi Propaganda Ministry found their story of a French army deserter to be "plutocratic, decadent, [and] negative" (*Vbd*, 94). Refusing on artistic and political grounds to modify their proposal, Carné and Prévert were dismissed by UFA and found themselves free to pursue the project in France. Thanks to Ploquin, Gabin was released temporarily from his contract with UFA. All that was needed was a new producer. As if to corroborate the Nazis' suspicion that the subject was unworthy of German subvention, the project fell to Grégor Rabinovitsch (1889–1953), a Russian Jewish emigré who had been producing in Germany and France since the 1920s.

Carné and Prévert's allegiance to Mac Orlan's book is a matter of shared sensibilities among director, poet, and novelist. Often referred to as France's Liam O'Flaherty, Pierre Mac Orlan (1883–1970) is best remembered for the novels he wrote between the wars, including *Le Chant d'équipage* (1918), *La Cavalière Elsa* (1921), and *La Bandera* (1931). Popularizing a world of urban adventure, these works evoke the exotic underside of Barcelona, Strasbourg, London, and Paris in the early 1900s. They depict army deserters, déclassé artists, pimps, whores, and crooks banding together in an attempt to find refuge from a hostile world. Mac Orlan's two major themes—escape and destiny—are a response to the gruesome forces unleashed by World War I. They are most conspicuous in his myth of the French Legionnaire, the outcast hero hunted by the law and driven toward fatal dangers that test virility and purity of heart. Such picturesque and sentimental depictions held obvious appeal for Prévert and Carné.

Mac Orlan appreciated the cinema. Responding to a poll conducted by René Clair in 1923, he wrote: "For my tastes, the cinema . . . is the only art that can render our era literally in expressionist and simultaneist [*sic*] form, with all its secret rhythms which music has already grasped, but which the art of writing cannot render because language imposes a rigid framework that cannot be dislocated . . . The cinema allows a faithful translation of the psychology of our time."[3] The film version of *Le Quai des Brumes* bears out Mac Orlan's intuition. Although his novel was popular, it is not a major piece of fiction. Carné's film, however, stands as perhaps the most incisive cinematic expression of the "psychology" of France in the late 1930s.

Prévert and Carné made major changes in their adaptation of Mac Orlan's work. The first half of the novel brings together five strangers one snowy evening at Le Lapin Agile, circa 1910; the rest of the book traces the nearly separate fates of these characters, none of whom is especially highlighted. Prévert's script transposes the setting to Le Havre, the time to 1938, and presents a single protagonist entrapped within a close network of secondary characters. The novel spans many months and follows its characters beyond Paris to Versailles, Dijon, and Marseilles. The film's plot unfolds in barely forty-eight hours and never moves beyond Le Havre.

The novel provides a cue for the temporal and spatial concentration that Prévert brought to the movie. In the final chapter, time leaps to 1919 and the major female character, Nelly, has become a celebrated courtesan. Seated in a Paris nightclub, Nelly recalls the gallery of characters she met years before at Le Lapin Agile. Mac Orlan writes: "In her memory, on the reverse side of her gray eyes, images unwind on a white-as-snow screen . . . The Negro orchestra gives rhythms to the unreeling of this film. And the whore herself arranges the images like cards on a table."[4] These references to film projection and editing can be read as implicit encouragement for Prévert's transformation of a loosely constructed novel into a tightly knit screenplay.

Another film-related simile in Mac Orlan's text announces the picture's mood and vision. It occurs immediately after the army deserter puts on civilian clothes: "He sat down at the terrace of a café on the Boulevard de Magenta and looked at life passing before him like a distant film, an animated object, yet nonetheless dead and from which he was totally removed."[5] Expressing alienation and disillusion, this sentence is the source of Jean's first sarcastic words to Nelly in the film: "It's like in the movies; I see you and then I like you; it's love at first sight." Unlike the character in the novel, however, the film's Jean awakens to the potential of life and love, experiencing what he thought could be found only in film fantasies.

Yet in Carné's world, happiness lasts no longer than the experience of images in black-and-white films. Where the dominant mood-setting colors in the novel are the white of fallen snow and the red of human blood, the film exploits the expressiveness of muted light and shade (fig. 20). Again, the novel points in this direction when Mac Orlan writes of his marginal characters, "Dim sources of light would often make their shadows seem more substantial than the very bodies that engendered them."[6] This sentence describes exactly the physical, moral, and spiritual atmosphere of Carné's picture, usually known in English as *Port of Shadows*. It explains why Mac Orlan remarked upon seeing the film: "It's unbelievable. You changed absolutely everything—era, place, and characters; yet the movie contains the complete essence of my book" (*Vbd*, 117).

Like *Jenny*, *Le Quai des Brumes* is a melodrama of thwarted passion and entangled lives. Like *Drôle de Drame*, it is a complicated murder-and-revenge thriller—in a serious mode. Yet *Le Quai des Brumes* eschews the theatrical convolutions of *Jenny* and *Drôle de Drame* in favor of extended sequences that fade into and out of one another with cinematic ease.

Absent without leave from the French army, Jean (Jean Gabin) arrives at Le Havre with the hope of escaping France. A chance encounter with the vagabond Quart Vittel (Raymond Aimos) leads him to temporary shelter in an isolated meeting place run by an eccentric called Panama (Edouard Delmont). Also hiding there is Nelly (Michèle Morgan), who has run away from her guardian, Zabel (Michel Simon), a trinket-shop owner whom Nelly believes to be the murderer of her former boyfriend,

20   Jean (Jean Gabin) walking along the freight docks of Le
      Havre in *Le Quai des Brumes:* a portrait of human
      insubstantiality

Maurice. Jean and Nelly fall instantly in love, and he defends her against
the advances of the gangster Lucien (Pierre Brasseur), who also suspects
Zabel of having murdered Maurice. The suicide of painter Michel Krauss
(Robert Le Vigan) allows Jean to acquire civilian clothes, money, and a
passport, facilitating his departure plans. The urgency of Jean's need to
escape heightens when Maurice's body washes ashore at a spot known
as Le Quai des Brumes and, simultaneously, Jean's discarded military
garments are discovered—making him a suspect in Maurice's murder.
After spending a night with Nelly in a hotel, Jean boards the *Louisiane*,
a freighter headed for Venezuela, but rushes from the ship minutes before
its departure in order to see Nelly once more. Arriving in time to foil
Zabel's attempt to molest Nelly, Jean kills the old man in a fit of rage.
Urged by Nelly to return to the ship, Jean leaves, but he is shot down by
Lucien after taking only a few steps. As Jean dies, Nelly's cry of anguish

is echoed by the whistle of the freighter—seen departing slowly for the sunny "elsewhere" denied to all characters in *Le Quai des Brumes*.

Prévert was fond of saying that a film's plot, much more than that of a novel or a play, requires at least two stories that "overlap and fit perfectly together." [7] *Jenny* and *Drôle de Drame* attest to Prévert's success at depicting the adventures of crisscrossed lovers. But *Le Quai des Brumes* is a more emphatic prefigurement of the consummate Prévert plot, *Les Enfants du paradis*. Like the latter, it portrays one woman as the love object of at least four men—Jean, Lucien, Zabel, and Maurice. Yet if *Le Quai des Brumes* represents an advance over the prior Carné-Prévert films, it is not because of plot construction. On the contrary, twists of plot are subordinate here to the stylized, atmospheric context in which they occur. *Drôle de Drame*'s plot revolves around acts of writing: Molyneux's novels, the Bishop's telegram, the journalists' articles, Auntie Mac Phearson's will. As the plot's catalyst, Billy-the-Milkman—the buoyant storyteller par excellence—may be seen as a figure of Jacques Prévert. The world of *Le Quai des Brumes* is no less artificial than that of *Drôle de Drame*, but its artifice does not depend upon the verbal stuff of lies, false homilies, and self-conscious role-playing. It is built instead on the unreality of studio light and shadow, on the insubstantiality of manufactured smoke and fog. *Le Quai des Brumes* is more a director's film than a scenarist's, exploiting the visual over the verbal, the cinematic over the literary. With *Le Quai des Brumes*, Carné and Prévert found their shared filmic voice—the distinctive blend of words and images that has come to be known as poetic realism.

An image of Carné as seen by Prévert is discernible in the film's most disturbed character, the painter Michel Krauss. In Mac Orlan's novel, the painter's suicide is described as "a half-sentimental, half-literary tragedy of which he was both the author and the hero" [8]—an observation that resonates with the attitude of Lacenaire, the poet-assassin of *Les Enfants du paradis*, who structures his life and death as if they were part of a well-made play. In the film, the painter's distinctiveness is defined not in dramatic but in visual terms. Embittered and disillusioned, Krauss concedes that conventional beauty exists, but he views it as irrelevant to his life and art: "I tried. I painted flowers, young women, children. It was as if I were painting a crime and all that goes with it. I would see evil in a rose . . . What is more simple than a tree? Yet when I paint one, I make everyone uneasy. It's because there is something, someone hidden behind that tree! I am forced to paint the things behind things. For me, a swimmer is already a drowned man."

As an expression of Carné's pessimism, the painter's credo contrasts with Prévert's faith in humanity. Prévert plays on this difference in the vaguely humorous scene in which the ship's doctor convinces Jean to make the voyage to Venezuela. Maintaining naive admiration for the "bohemian" attitudes of artists, the bourgeois doctor asks Jean—who in taking Krauss's passport and clothes has assumed an identity alien to his own personality and experience—for his views on painting:

DOCTOR: Do you like watercolors?

JEAN: Watercolors? Yes, yes.

DOCTOR: Do you do landscapes?

JEAN: Oh, you know, I'm not concerned with theories . . .

DOCTOR: But at least you're not a cubist?

JEAN: A cubist? Oh, no!

DOCTOR: Good for you! Because cubism, well, you know . . . And what kind of painting do you do?

JEAN: Uh, well, uh . . . generally, I paint . . . I paint the things behind things.

DOCTOR: That's very interesting.

JEAN: For example, if . . . if I see a swimmer . . . uh, well, I say to myself immediately, that guy's gonna drown. And so I paint a drowned man.

DOCTOR: Well . . . Well . . . I guess your painting is not very gay! But the important thing is that it is well-painted. I mean, uh . . . the subject really is of little matter.

In showcasing the doctor's narrow-mindedness and Jean's mimicry of aesthetic statements he does not fathom, Prévert—who was a friend of Picasso and Braque—pokes fun at both the detractors and the pseudo-intellectual pundits of experimental art. But in reiterating the painter's position, Prévert also restates what is fundamental to Carné's art and what was in evidence as early as *Nogent*: the effort not to ally with either the avant-garde or conventional representational filmmaking, but to produce poetic realism—that brand of cinema which aims to illuminate the invisible lying within the normally visible world.

The Carné-Krauss connection bears emphasis. Although other commitments prevented him from appearing in the film, Barrault was the original choice to portray Michel Krauss.[9] In fact, Krauss's morbid obsessions are a redirection inward of traits exhibited by earlier Barrault characters: Dromadaire's sadism in *Jenny* and Kramps's homicidal instincts in *Drôle de Drame*. Both Dromadaire and Kramps were un-fulfilled outsiders also identifiable in some measure with Carné. Had Barrault played the painter, he would have strengthened the not insubstantial case for viewing Baptiste in *Les Enfants du paradis* as Prévert's most complete expression of Carné's private conflicts. Be that as it may, the painter in *Le Quai des Brumes* and the mime in *Les Enfants du paradis* stand out as the two Carné-Prévert characters emblematic of nonverbal art.

With hindsight, the casting of Robert Le Vigan (1904–72) as Krauss reinforces the political overtones of the painter's role. By his suicide the painter's vision of life and art takes on special resonance. With the fall of France to Germany, many blamed films with defeatist themes for having promoted the spirit that facilitated the nation's collapse. No film was more excoriated by Vichy moralizers than *Le Quai des Brumes*. No character epitomizes surrender to destiny more than Michel Krauss. Le Vigan was one of France's leading supporting players in the 1930s and 1940s. His emaciated face and small, troubled eyes allowed him to impersonate complex and deranged characters with ease. Typical of his roles were the scheming fabric dealer in Renoir's *Madame Bovary* (1933), Christ (to Gabin's Pontius Pilate) in Duvivier's *Golgotha* (1934), and the crazed thief in Jacques Becker's *Goupi Mains Rouges* (1943). Possessing what one commentator calls "that spark of madness which is easily confused with genius," [10] Le Vigan became paranoid in 1944. During the Occupation he had been a pro-Nazi spokesman. When the Liberation appeared imminent, he fled France—and the sets of *Les Enfants du paradis*, in which he was slated to play Jéricho. After Le Vigan had joined fellow collaborationist Louis-Ferdinand Céline in Sigmaringen, the actor and the writer condemned the Allies and the Russians as well as the Germans, and prophesied with apocalyptic frenzy that Europe would soon suffer a mass invasion of Asians. By 1951 Céline had returned to France and Le Vigan moved to Argentina, where he resided until his death.

Given the reprimands directed at Carné for having remained in France during the war, it is unlikely that he would overemphasize the similarity of outlook between himself and *Le Quai des Brumes*'s painter. Yet the film's Michel Krauss seems clearly a spokesman for the Carné aesthetic, and he embodies the fatalism at the center of Carné's vision. The name Krauss itself suggests German nationality, a point made explicit in Mac Orlan's novel, where the painter (whose name is spelled with one *s*) is unambiguously German. Krauss's aesthetics can conveniently be viewed as separate from both the politics they imply and the real-life activities of the actor who incarnated them. But to do so is to perpetuate the moral indifference Carné was eventually charged with. Nevertheless, a complete view of Krauss's role in the film complicates the issue of moral condemnation. For within the movie's unheroic context, Krauss the suicide is something of a hero: in bequeathing his papers and wardrobe to Jean, he performs a decisive act of generosity that strengthens the prospect of Jean's temporal salvation. Interestingly, Carné justifies his lack of resistance during the Occupation by emphasizing the extent to which he furnished scores of co-professionals with employment needed to survive difficult times. Viewed today, the Carné-Krauss parallel is remarkably—and uncomfortably—sharp.

Pictorially, *Le Quai des Brumes* shows the influence of Josef von Sternberg's silent film *The Docks of New York* (1928). As in Sternberg's moral melodrama, port atmosphere is established through glimpses of net-draped piers, clapboard shacks, and still, dark waters—all drenched in shadows, smoke, and fog, all rendered dreamlike through uneven lighting and chiaroscuro. In both films, principal settings are studio-fabricated with geographic locales authenticated only by brief location shots—of the New York skyline in Sternberg's work and the freight docks of Le Havre in Carné's. In both, documentary realism gives way to symbolic atmospheric constructs.

Conforming to Sternberg's concept of art as "the compression of infinite spiritual power into a confined space,"[11] Schüfftan, Trauner, and Carné utilize light, décor, and minutely observed details to plumb the material world and human countenances. But for Sternberg, pictorial effect animates and enlivens the space separating the camera from its subject and the subject from its background. Sequences in *Les Visiteurs du soir*, *Les Enfants du paradis*, and *Les Portes de la nuit* (a film conceived for Sternberg's icon, Marlene Dietrich) suggest the cluttered, overflowing, multilayered frames of Sternberg's *Shanghai Express* (1934) and *The Scarlet Empress* (1935). But the tendency toward artifice and abstraction that Carné and Sternberg share expresses itself in *Le Quai des Brumes*, *Hôtel du Nord*, and *Le Jour se lève* more through a visual aesthetic of economy than accumulation; more through immobilization than animation; and more through the withholding of light than through an elaboration of the intricate images that lighting can create.

The visual darkness of *Le Quai des Brumes* is unprecedented in French commercial filmmaking. While assisting Clair in the production of *Sous Les Toits de Paris*, Carné helped direct a gangster shoot-out that takes place in almost complete darkness. With sound effects heightened at the expense of visible action, the scene was Clair's tongue-in-cheek statement about the woeful potential of talkies. Carné never toys with his medium.

For him, darkness is the solemn expression of humankind's condition. When the film first appeared in New York, Frank Nugent called it "a lament for the living . . . by a writer who has looked at life through grey-tinted glasses, seeing nothing but its darkness, its sordidness and the futility of those who expect anything more of it." [12] Nugent errs in placing responsibility for the film's gloominess on Prévert; it is due principally to Carné. Further, human dignity asserts itself through simple kindly deeds: at the film's start, Jean jerks the truckdriver's steering wheel to avoid killing a vagabond dog; later, Nelly slips cash into Jean's coat pocket when she learns he has not eaten for days; and Krauss makes sure that his own death will help Jean to escape from danger. Nonetheless, *Le Quai des Brumes* depicts a world of social outcasts in which acts of human kindness are invariably undermined by evil. Love holds the hope for secular salvation—an eminently Prévertian theme. But love is destined for destruction no sooner than it comes into being—the essential view of Carné.

In Renoir, lovers are never oblivious to their social context. In Carné, love encapsulates two strangers within a hostile world. Carné's lovers, much like Sternberg's, retreat from reality into a realm of precarious fantasy. But where fantasy in Sternberg explodes with delirious excess, the sentimental reveries of Carné's couples are muted and tentative, with neither the characters nor the director convinced that these dreams can take hold for even the duration of the film. In the darkest of Renoir's works—for example, *La Chienne* (1931) or *La Nuit du carrefour* (1932)—fateful coincidences take place, but characters determine their consequences. In *Le Quai des Brumes*, characters are reduced to silent acquiescence vis-à-vis a fate that controls them entirely. As in Sternberg, murders, suicides, and assaults serve as "poetic punctuations for lives drifting to their destinations." [13] But where men and women in Sternberg approach their fate with self-conscious grace, Carné's are stricken with a paralysis born of anxiety and incomprehension. They partake of neither the spontaneity of Renoir's nor the self-awareness of Sternberg's.

I have posited that Carné's films deal with the relations between illusion and disenchantment, blindness and enlightenment. In *Jenny* and *Drôle de Drame* this theme is expressed by having characters view momentous acts. Privileged moments of viewing also occur in *Le Quai des Brumes*, but in a movie whose visual texture is overwhelmingly bleak, the possibility of enlightenment and understanding is virtually nonexistent. The picture begins with disks of light moving against a black background. They are soon identifiable as the headlights of the truck that will transport Jean to Le Havre. Nearly identical in form and impact are the opening shots of *Nogent*, in which the commuter train passes through a tunnel completely dark except for scattered lights. But *Nogent* is Carné's most airy film, and its passengers arrive at a bright site of physical and spiritual renewal. In *Le Quai des Brumes*, Jean's destination is a seaport that promises escape but delivers death. In fact, the film is built around vehicles that go nowhere: the truck, shown more at rest than in motion; the carnival bumper cars; the parked auto from which Lucien kills Jean; the huge vessel bound for Venezuela which, from the film's opening credit sequence through Jean's death, is cabled securely to the dock; and the vacant trolley tracks next to which Jean falls dead.[14]

Within this world of extreme stasis, the play of light against darkness signals disorientation and false hope. The truck's headlights blind Jean, but they portend his destiny as surely as if they were stars in an astrological reading, or opening commentary by a Greek chorus. The flickering sign atop the nightclub Au Petit Tabarin; the dark sheen of Le Havre's rain-drenched streets; the dim glow emanating from Panama's shack; the strange shimmer of Nelly's transparent trenchcoat; and the glimmer of her eyes when she begs Jean for a kiss—all attract but ultimately destroy. Chiaroscuro effects also assume narrative force. The cagelike shadows cast by the latticed door of Panama's shack announce Jean's entrapment. Zabel's massive shadow falling on her ethereally lit face literally eclipses the moment of illumination when Nelly discovers evidence that her tutor murdered Maurice. And when Jean and Nelly sit by the carnival merry-go-round, the light emanating from the ride moves steadily from one face to the other, but never falls simultaneously on both. As in the classic shot of the two of them looking languorously from discrete window panes in Panama's back room (fig. 21), the lovers' dreamy talk of a shared future is contradicted by a mise en scène that asserts their fundamental separateness. Bleak visual tone, fastidious arrangements of space, and slow, restrained movements—these are the fundamental components of Carné's "poetic" style.

Le Quai des Brumes displays Carné's gift for structuring light and shadow. In *Des Lumières et des ombres*, a philosophical consideration of lighting in painting and film, cinematographer Henri Alekan distinguishes the opposed effects of focused spotlighting (*lumière unidirectionnelle*) and diffused floodlighting (*lumière multidirectionnelle diffuse*). By generating well-defined shadows, spotlighting—no matter how aesthetic or antinaturalist its intent—anchors objects and characters to an ostensibly real world and thereby renders palpable an "abstract dimension" concerning the world, namely, the inevitable "passage of time." Diffused lighting, by contrast, creates a "psychophysiological climate" in which

21   Love as a precarious union of lost souls: Jean (Jean
      Gabin) and Nelly (Michèle Morgan) in *Le Quai des
      Brumes*

objects and characters, just like the indeterminate sources of light that
preclude their having well-defined shadows, are left "doubtful in an ill-
defined universe, unsituated in time." Alekan, who worked with Carné
on *Drôle de Drame*, *Le Quai des Brumes*, *La Marie du Port*, and *Juliette
ou la clef des songes*, observes that for *Le Quai des Brumes*, Schüfftan
furnished Carné with a unique type of 2,000-watt lamp, no longer manufactured today, that could cast, at once, "a highly directed luminous
flux embedded in a diffused flux," without producing double shadow

effects.[15] In other words, the very tools of cinematography helped to convey the existential perplexity of *Le Quai des Brumes*'s protagonists, caught in a configuration of time and space that is both all too manifest and all too obscure.

At the moment of his soldier's death, Mac Orlan speaks of Jean as perceiving life "through the fog of death."[16] This equation of life, fog, and death defines the prevailing sensibility of Carné and Prévert's film. Carné had hoped to create fog and mist effects as dense as those in Ford's *The Informer* (1935), but he was thwarted by Simon Schiffrin, Rabinovitsch's punctilious production manager. Nonetheless, Carné imbued much of the film with a mist that serves as a metaphor for human isolation, alienation, and lack of clairvoyance. When fog was unavailable— especially for the location dock scenes—Carné conveyed the weightiness of the sky by darkening the top of his film frame. Many of these shots evoke the sad allure of late Vlaminck landscapes. They also suggest the sterile despair given voice in the poems of Baudelaire.

One of the film's most forceful images occurs in the medium-close shot that finds Jean and Nelly sitting dispiritedly on the wharf's edge. With their legs dangling above a muddy, polluted shoreline, the two rootless beings contemplate the objective correlative of the moral muck that ultimately engulfs them. Through fog, darkened skies, and filth, Carné and Schüfftan create a cinematic equivalent for what Baudelaire named "spleen"—that morbid spiritual state in which the soul's aspiration to rise toward the ideal struggles against the grime of the human order. Like Baudelaire's poem "Spleen, IV" ("Quand le ciel bas et lourd pèse comme un couvercle . . ."), *Le Quai des Brumes* evokes "the low and heavy" skies that weigh like "a lid / over the mind tormented by disgust"; the "daylight dingier than the dark"; and a world "where Hope, / defeated, weeps, and the oppressor Dread / plants his black flag on [an] assenting skull."[17]

In numerous ways Carné's sensibility descends from Baudelaire, just as Prévert finds inspiration in Villon and Rimbaud. Yet Baudelaire's persistent assertion of the spirit's need to perpetuate itself is absent from the Carnésian world. In *Les Fleurs du mal*, the poet reconciles horror and beauty into a rich synthesis that retains their antagonisms but makes each one appear as the necessary condition for the existence of the other.[18] Carné's films exhibit a Manichean stance that makes clear distinctions between evil and pristine goodness, condemning the first and sentimentalizing the latter. Carné is fascinated and titillated by the underside of human behavior. But unwilling to follow Baudelaire in embracing and exploring it rawly, Carné ultimately resists it—hence the tremulous elusiveness and indirection, the fanciful evasion and effeteness that make his films veer toward moral priggishness. At their best, Carné's films transmit a sense of Baudelairean spleen. At their worst, they partake of the "corny brasserie Baudelairism" that Lucien Rebatet lamented in his review of *Jenny* in *L'Action Française*.

Carné's prewar cinematic vision and aesthetic is generally known as poetic realism. Truffaut views *Le Quai des Brumes* as "the masterpiece" of this school of filmmaking, which he believes reached its peak with Carné's *Les Portes de la nuit* (1946).[19] The phrase "poetic realism" was first employed by Jean Paulhan, editor of *La Nouvelle Revue Française*, to describe the mix of realism and symbolism in the novels of Marcel Aymé (1902–67). When Pierre Chenal directed a screen adaptation of Aymé's *La Rue sans nom* in 1933, "poetic realism" entered into the vocabulary of film commentators. For Paulhan, the term helped to distinguish Aymé's works from, on one hand, the postwar fantasy novels of such writers as Giraudoux, Ramuz, and Cocteau, and, on the other, the populist writings of Louis Guilloux and Eugène Dabit. Populist novels flourished in the 1930s and reflected Popular Front aspirations. Dignifying the image of the working classes, they depicted efforts to improve daily life in the face of bourgeois assaults. Although never proposing specific means for changing society, populist novels recognized social injustice. Poetic realism blunted populism's social edge. Barely acknowledging class differences, the literature of poetic realism focused on the atmosphere in which human dramas unfold. Social milieu was important not for its political implications but for the mood that its representation might effect. Likewise, words were valued more for their evocative power than for the reality to which they purportedly referred.

Mitry identifies Griffith's *Broken Blossoms* (1919), Sternberg's *Der Blaue Engel* (*The Blue Angel*, 1930), Lang's *M* (1931), and Vigo's *L'Atalante* (1934) as antecedents of cinematic poetic realism. He defines the style as "an attenuated Expressionism inserted within the norms and conditions of immediate reality."[20] Images in these films—like words in Aymé's fiction—take on values independent of their narrative function. Not reproducing reality so much as recreating it, stories in these films are anchored to defined social settings, but aim to convey "essential" human truths that transcend social realities. Poetic realism undervalues a film's direct links with the material world in order to explore the symbolic resonances which the world—when photographed—is capable of releasing. Through condensation, concentration, and delicate blending, these resonances form fields of evocative, connotative correspondences, resulting in the "suggestive magic" that Baudelaire believed must characterize modern poetic art.

Poetic realism is a slippery concept. In one sense, all films must be deemed poetic because of their inherent capacity "to infuse significance into everything they contain, not necessarily high-sounding, specifiable, even symbolic significance, but significance as an indication of *something more*, an invitation to go beyond the face of things to create a narrative in which meaning often impends, frequently coalesces and solidifies, but just as often may vanish." In another sense, all films are realistic inasmuch as "realism is a necessary characteristic that the whole art grapples with, rather than a particular approach that an artist chooses or disdains"; at best, realism in film denotes "a certain range of possibility in artistic construction, which includes subject matter as well as form, history as well as aesthetics." [21]

"Poetic realism" remains the most adequate term to situate Carné within this range. Carné does not contort reality in the theatrical manner of the German Caligarists, nor does he reproduce it in the documentarylike style of Italian Neorealists. His films present us with believable, plausible, compelling worlds that are at once dependent upon and disengaged from the world as it is regularly perceived. His works are strangely familiar not because they present us with either everyday experience or dark dreams, but because they speak to that part of our imagination which turns one into the other. In this respect Carné's universe bears comparison with that of Orson Welles in *The Magnificent Ambersons* (1942) and *The Stranger* (1945). Welles himself noted in 1948: "I am much closer to Carné than to Rossellini. Carné is not a realist, you know. He transfigures reality through his style. What is interesting in Carné is his style, not the reality he represents." [22]

Carné is wary of theorizing about film art. He especially dislikes the term "poetic realism," which he has repudiated on many occasions. At the Perpignan symposium he remarked: "I must say in all sincerity that I don't like the rubric *réalisme poétique*. Calling me a realist doesn't make me happy. It's perhaps precise; but if so, then I can't be very proud of myself. Because in my opinion I have interpreted reality just a little. Even when I make realistic films, I can't help believing that a personal vision was involved. The category I prefer, even if it is pretentious, is Mac Orlan's celebrated phrase, *le fantastique social*. I think that the *fantastique social* is what shapes *Le Quai des Brumes*, which is closer to the fantastic [*le fantastique*] than to a poetic realism [*un réalisme poétique*]." [23]

Rejecting the term *réalisme poétique* on the grounds that it trivializes the extent to which he "interpreted" or poeticized reality, Carné implies that he takes pride in the visionary, escapist aspects of his films. But his proposed substitution, *le fantastique social*, denotes the same two concepts: reality and fantasy. The difference lies in their order. In French, a noun followed by an adjective tends to emphasize the qualifier. Thus, *réalisme poétique* suggests that the prime aesthetic gesture involved is the poeticization of reality—which Carné admits does characterize his filmmaking. *Le fantastique social*, on the contrary, emphasizes the tempering of fantasy by attention to the "real" or social—the precise opposite of what Carné claims he does and of what critics generally mean when they view Carné as the poetic realist par excellence.

Carné's failure to recognize any contradiction in his public disavowals of poetic realism may point to a defensive reaction against those who have criticized his filmmaking as politically indifferent and evasive. In Mac Orlan, *le fantastique social* highlights the *social* over the *fantastique*: it refers to the social evils that led to World War I and that seemed to be fostering the imminence of a second cataclysm. In Carné, and especially in *Le Quai des Brumes*, Europe's social and political crises are sensed but never depicted. By espousing the term associated with Mac Orlan, Carné suggests, without being explicit, that he was as *engagé* as he was *fantaisiste*—which of course is not true. Significantly, Jean Renoir has also been labeled a "poetic realist." [24] But films like *Le Crime de Monsieur Lange*, *Les Bas-Fonds*, and *La Bête humaine* correspond more precisely to Mac Orlan's *fantastique social* than do any of Carné's. Unlike Carné, the Renoir of the 1930s never overvalues fantasy at the expense of social context. Where Renoir's films galvanize viewers' social awareness, Carné's lull and mesmerize.

For all its political disaffection, *Le Quai des Brumes* is a trenchant cinematic expression of France's prewar psyche. It reflects "a period when everyone knew that the wheels of an infernal machine—in Berlin and Rome, but also in London and Paris—were in motion, refusing any 'escape hatch,' and leading to an atrocious conflict in which our nation would be crushed." [25] The film raised political waves even before it went into production. In a letter dated November 15, 1937, the Ministry of War's representative to the Commission de Contrôle insisted that approval of Prévert's treatment be granted only "on condition that page 9 of this resumé [Jean's murder of Zabel] be treated by the director, dialogue writer, and actors with the utmost of tact in order that the soldier

at no time appear naturally predisposed to executing such a filthy deed";
furthermore, the word "deserter" was never to be pronounced, and the
protagonist's abandoned military garb was not "to be thrown in a corner, but folded carefully and placed on a chair." [26] Producer Rabinovitsch
monitored Prévert and Carné's compliance with these demands. Accordingly, the word deserter is never heard and Jean's uniform sits neatly atop
a table. But Carné outwitted Rabinovitsch in the matter of Zabel's death:
he surreptitiously edited in four blows where the producer wanted
only one.

Mainstream French film production of the late 1930s has been viewed
as "a kind of seesaw between the jingoistic ideology of Daladier . . . and
the oily pavements, damp nights, and anarchistic despair of realist
films." [27] The gap separating right- and left-wing sensibilities is especially
palpable in films that depicted the French military. Numerous adventure
romances exploited the mass appeal of the French Foreign Legion. Two
works scripted by Spaak—Feyder's *Le Grand Jeu* (1933) and Duvivier's
La Bandera (1935)—glorified the Legionnaire's bravery and love of
country. Adapted from Mac Orlan's novel and dedicated to General
Franco, *La Bandera* presents Jean Gabin as an escaped murderer who
redeems himself by defending to the death a besieged Moroccan outpost
of the Spanish Foreign Legion. Other celebrations of the Legion included
Christian-Jaque's *Un de la Légion* (1936), starring Fernandel; Jacques de
Baroncelli's *S.O.S. Sahara* (1938), with Charles Vanel and Jean-Pierre
Aumont; and Henri Garat's *Le Chemin de l'honneur* (1939). The political right applauded all of these films.

Less chauvinistic but equally popular were Duvivier's *Pépé le Moko*
(1937) and Grémillon's *Gueule d'amour* (1937). In the former, Gabin
portrays the title character who—much like the hero of *La Bandera*—
escapes to North Africa to elude the French police. But rather than join
the Legion, this sympathetic gangster becomes imprisoned in the Casbah
underworld. Instead of defending his country, he daydreams of Paris.
And his one attempt to escape the Casbah—motivated by his attraction
to a glamorous woman—is crushed by a police ambush at the film's fi-
nale. In *Gueule d'amour*, Gabin is a wayward Algerian cavalry soldier
who commits murder. Set amid the least attractive parts of the French
navy base at Toulon, this UFA-made film subverts thoroughly the image
of the military which the political right sought to maintain.

Le Quai des Brumes's Jean is not a Legionnaire. Wearing the uniform
of the Colonial Infantry, he belongs to the regular national army. However, the places he speaks of—service in "the desert" and duty in Tonkin—suggest Foreign Legion posts. The brisk but gloomy travel music

that accompanies him throughout the film is reminiscent of the official march of the French Foreign Legion. And the character itself—subject to the malignancy of fate, the ineffectiveness of action, and the pervasiveness of fear and solitude—binds this Gabin role to the defeated Legionnaire "types" of *Pépé le Moko* and *Gueule d'amour*. A schism of character and spirit separates *Le Quai des Brumes*'s Jean from the air force officer Gabin portrayed in *La Grande Illusion* (1937), where fate proved more benign, where action produced results, and where brotherhood and solidarity prevailed.

More germane than Jean's precise military status are the antimilitarist sentiments he holds. At the film's start, Jean informs the truckdriver that having spent time in Tonkin, he is acquainted with fog. When the truckdriver asserts that Tonkin never has fog, Jean responds by thumping his finger against his forehead: "No fog? There certainly is. All within *there*." This oblique indictment of the mentality supporting colonialism becomes explicit in the sullen monologue where Jean explains how war normalizes horror: "It's nothing to shoot . . . Like in Africa . . . Like on other guys, you know . . . you shoot and then . . . The guy gives out a shout . . . he puts his hands on his stomach with a funny little look on his face . . . like a kid who stuffed himself too much . . . And then his hands become red . . . And then he falls . . . And you remain all alone . . . You no longer understand anything . . . It's as if reality were slipping away." Jean is not intellectually inclined, as is his namesake in Mac Orlan's novel. But Gabin's intense, understated delivery of these disjointed phrases constitutes a defense of pacifism as eloquent as that of any Saint-Germain-des-Prés pundit. Jean's casual remark about the dog that keeps trailing him—"I don't like beasts who seek out a master"—gives expression to an entire political philosophy.

France's defeatism, or the fatalistic conviction that the country was too weak to defend itself, was partly a result of genuine military inadequacy. Blum had attempted to expedite French rearmament by doubling the arms budget to nearly three billion francs. Before him, Captain Charles de Gaulle wrote a tract entitled *Vers L'Armée de métier* (1934), urging the formation of a professional corps of elite troops that would constitute a quickly maneuverable French army. Yet what Wilfrid Knapp calls "strategic myopia" afflicted both politicians and generals in prewar France.[28] The country had Dewoitine fighters, Somua and B-type tanks, and the Maginot Line. But it had no plans for offensive action. The prevailing myth had it that the French were conditioned to "rallying round the flag and stirring mankind by their powers of resistance and recovery." [29] The truth was that "the frightful cost of Napoleonic *gloire*, the humiliations of the Franco-Prussian conflict, the internecine horrors of the resulting Commune, the costly attritional tactics of the First World War—all combined to produce an excellent defense for a generalized fear of combat." [30]

Until war occurred, the myth of France's readiness was maintained in newspapers, magazines, and newsreels. On March 25, 1938, a Frenchman could read on page one of *Le Temps*: "The characteristics of the French soldier are well-known, and he can be followed across the ages from the heroic fighters of the feudal armies to the companies of the *ancien régime*, and on to the contemporary era. Are they not the characteristics of the French peoples? Love of glory, bravery, vivacity." [31] How disturbing, therefore, was *Le Quai des Brumes. La Grande Illusion*, for all its pacifistic intent, showed French soldiers as honorable men in whom war could arouse the best of human and patriotic instincts. Released in June 1937, Renoir's film was actually a palliative for the crushed hopes of many who were witnessing the demise of the Popular Front. Appearing one year later, *Le Quai des Brumes* is a distinctly post-Front film, with Gabin "not so much a Popular Front character . . . as one who represents the agony and the end of the Front, and the approach of war." [32]

Compared with the evasive postures assumed by other characters in *Le Quai des Brumes*, Jean's unflinching resignation is admirable. The painter Krauss resorts to self-annihilation. Panama retreats to an artificial paradise of denial. Quart Vittel wallows in self-complacency. Among such company Jean evinces courage and dignity. Yet his lassitude and surrender to destiny betoken an attitude that contributed to France's defeat and that neither the prewar nor the Occupation governments wished to acknowledge. Accordingly, Vichy's Commission de Contrôle Cinématographique banned showings of *Le Quai des Brumes* "on moral grounds," and the Centrale Catholique du Cinéma condemned it as "a profoundly demoralizing, somber story . . . with a clearly offensive atmosphere." [33]

When supporters of Pétain and Laval promulgated the fable that "effete" and "decadent" films such as *Pépé le Moko* and *Le Quai des Brumes* were—along with André Gide and paid holidays—responsible for France's fall, Carné responded publicly in the form of a letter addressed not to his assailants but to the cinema itself: "Reflecting well on the matter, whose fault is it? Your own or an era's that carried within itself the germ of death and destruction? . . . As this era's means of expression, you, dear cinema, could only reflect the unease and turmoil that had seized upon the times." [34] To this day Carné insists that although a film can be a barometer of its times, the barometermaker is not responsible for the storm it may forecast.

Le Quai des Brumes reflects France's political climate in one further respect. In a piece written in 1930 for *Cinémagazine*, Carné expressed enthusiasm for Sternberg's uncontrived portrait of organized crime in *Underworld* (1927). He emphasized the grandeur that inheres in the gangster hero's defiance of an often unjust society: "The gangster film allows us to live a new life far from the colorless humdrum of everyday life. We discover a different society with its own laws and traditions of honor. The men who constitute it are like us; and like us, they are not insensitive to the passions of the heart . . . The gangster film brings us a parcel of dream and poetry." [35] This sentimental reaction was not unique. The Argentine writer Jorge Luis Borges recalls that "when there was anything epic about them—I mean Chicago gangsters dying bravely— well, I felt that my eyes were full of tears." [36] Truffaut believes that had Carné pursued his early penchant for American genre movies, he might have eventually made French gangster films to rival, if not surpass, those of Jean-Pierre Melville.[37] By 1938, however, the figure of the gangster as hero had too much in common with Hitler's storm troopers to be palatable to either Carné or Prévert. *Le Quai des Brumes* therefore presents its thugs as unredeemable cowards and its hero as a well-intentioned outsider driven to murder by uncontrollable forces.

In the film, gangsters compete to establish "turf." With no protective agency to which he can appeal, Jean becomes a pawn in the power struggles of individuals and groups to which he has no allegiance and with whom he is associated only minimally. This picture of authority gone bankrupt replicates France's state of crisis following the Blum regime. Between Blum's resignation on June 21, 1937, and the premiere of *Le Quai des Brumes* on May 18, 1938, France witnessed: the rise and fall of two governments headed by Camille Chautemps, the first of which excluded Socialists entirely; the formation of a second Blum government, which, in the course of twenty-seven days, sought first to be a national alliance, failed, and then tried to reconstruct the Popular Front, and failed again; and finally, the third regime of Daladier, which not only excluded Socialists but had four ministers who were openly hostile to the Popular Front. Massive strikes, bombings at the headquarters of union and employer associations, and uncontrolled outflow of capital exacerbated the general sense of chaos, conflict, and conspiracy—a mood which *Le Quai des Brumes*, without any reference to political realities, captures thoroughly.

A splendid metaphoric rendering of France's breakdown is contained

22   The bumper-car scene in *Le Quai des Brumes:*
a metaphoric rendering of France's chaotic politics

in *Le Quai des Brumes*'s bumper-car scene, which is itself a compendium of the film's plot (fig. 22). The scene is part of a carnival sequence which, beneath its veneer of whirling rides, dizzying lights, and boisterous crowds evokes sadness and potential tragedy. The sequence begins with Jean and Nelly posing for a souvenir photo in front of a painted backdrop that depicts the *S.S. Normandy*—an expression of the insubstantiality of their dream of escape. This is followed by the lovers' finding calm behind a row of booths and trailers, where they share a first kiss and where Gabin delivers the film's best-known line: "T'as de beaux yeux tu sais" ("Ya got great eyes, ya know"). A dissolve links this moment to the animated bumper-car scene. Bent on impressing one of his girlfriends, Lucien runs his car wildly, colliding with whoever gets in his way. When he deliberately knocks off a stranger's hat from behind, the stranger turns out to be Jean, who impulsively slaps Lucien, thereby triggering a threat of retaliation. Foreshadowing the film's tragic end—in which Lucien shoots at Jean from within a genuine automobile—the scene plays out on a miniature scale the clash of destinies that constitutes the entire film's subject. When Lucien cries out for vengeance, Carné's camera moves to include in the frame an advertisement for the astrologer's booth. This slight reinforcement of the scene's "metaphysical" weight is a reminder that the fates of lovers and enemies in *Le Quai des*

Brumes are irrevocably star-crossed; that the carefree and innocent amusements remembered by the director of *Nogent* have now turned rancid; and that France itself is on an anarchic bumper-car course that can lead only to collision and humiliation.

Demonstrating a talent for highlighting ennui and anxiety beneath the surface exhilaration of popular entertainments, the carnival sequence stands among Carné's most accomplished footage. The bumper-car scene is especially intriguing because it presents a variant of the "primal scene" at the core of Carné's cinematic and psychological universe. When Lucien discovers that Jean is the man whose hat he has knocked off, his instinct is to run away: an encounter earlier that day had confirmed the soldier's superior strength. As Jean approaches Lucien, Carné cuts to rapid close-ups of Lucien's girlfriend and his closest friend, L'Orphelin, who behold this spectacle with surprise and anticipation. Two more close-ups, first of Lucien and then of Jean, precede the celebrated shot in which Jean (in medium-close shot) slaps Lucien's face (in close-up) (fig. 23). Underscoring the public aspect of Lucien's humiliation, four more close-ups follow: Nelly, with a worried look; Jean, walking out of the frame; and—most important—Lucien's girlfriend, laughing (fig. 24); and L'Orphelin, grinning (fig. 25). Having played the smart aleck, Lucien unwittingly intrudes on Jean and Nelly's privacy.

In *Jenny* and *Drôle de Drame*, such moments (or variants) of privileged viewing contain the potential for insight and growth on the part of the viewer; they allow characters to acknowledge the sexuality of another. In *Le Quai des Brumes*, emphasis falls on the degradation endured by the interloper, who becomes the object of derisive glances. It is as if the child in the archetypal Freudian scenario assumes the consequences of his transgression. The punishment Lucien incurs for having invaded Nelly and Jean's emotional "turf" is tantamount to emasculation.

A figural representation of the Third Republic and its political impotence, the gangster milieu also provides a metaphoric field for expressing concerns about sexual identity. The first interior shot of the gangster nightspot displays two women in evening clothes dancing together. Carné makes light of Rabinovitsch's objections to this detail, recalling that the producer did not claim to find the act "especially filthy," but feared that co-professionals would think him unable to finance even a minimum number of extras (*Vbd*, 97). Carné is too polite in suggesting Rabinovitsch's liberalism, since he describes fully (*Vbd*, 101) the struggle he endured to shoot the painter Krauss in the nude as he walks to his death in the sea. These shots do not appear in the film. In a letter to Carné, Rabinovitsch condemned the rushes as "tasteless" and "thoroughly without artistic merit." [38] But Carné is on the mark in pointing to the necessity of suggesting lesbianism at the film's start. Although visible for only seconds, the dancing female couple draws attention to the gender dynamics that dominate the gangster-film world, in which young punks band together and women exist principally so that men can prove their manhood to one another.

Carlos Clarens has documented the forms of "nonerotic homosexual attachment" and "pervasive misogyny" that gangster films have displayed from *Little Caesar* and *The Public Enemy* through *The Big Combo*.[39] Carné's fascination with the gangster-film cult of machismo is expressed with disarming ingenuousness in his 1930 encomium of the American genre: "No longer do we see bloodless guttersnipes waiting to rob a late-night pedestrian, nor their companions pursuing a profession 'which the police tolerates but morality condemns.' The *heroes* of American gangster films work *with style*. Dressed by the best tailor in town, his hair impeccably groomed . . . today's criminal . . . execute[s] the most reprehensible acts with unparalleled chic and grace. Although each of his gunshots kills a man, the murderer pulls the trigger with such finesse that we are struck less by the result than by the stylishness with which the murder is perpetrated." [40]

Carné outgrew this youthful idolatry. Lucien does not. As portrayed by Pierre Brasseur (1905–72), Lucien—a character not found in Mac Orlan's novel—is obsessed by the myth of masculine image. His exaggerated virile posturing; his frantic shouts of "I am a man! I am a man!"; his jealousy of Jean's affection for Nelly, who despises Lucien; his ignominious shooting of Jean from behind—all cloak his insecurity. Lucien's buddy, L'Orphelin, is a boyish-faced tough whom we first see chewing on a match. In role and allure he announces Avril, Lacenaire's sidekick in *Les Enfants du paradis*. In a sense, the dandy-assassin Lacenaire is an extension of Lucien. But where Lacenaire exhibits extreme self-awareness, Lucien remains an unconscious victim of sexual stereotypes. One of Lacenaire's most villainous acts is his public disclosure of Baptiste and Garance in tender embrace, which he performs with the "chic and grace" Carné celebrated in his *Cinémagazine* piece. Lucien's most dastardly deed is Jean's murder—a perverse, frenzied reaction to his viewing Jean and Nelly kissing each other. Like Xavier in *Jenny* and Adrien in

Facing page:

23 Lucien (Pierre Brasseur) enduring public humiliation as Jean slaps him
24 Lucien's girlfriend (Jenny Burnay) taking pleasure at his degradation
25 Lucien's buddy looking on with vague amusement

Hôtel du Nord, Lacenaire accepts his difference and is at one with himself. Lucien fears difference. In straining to exhibit sameness, he leads a tortured existence.

The mystique of Jean Gabin (1904–76) is best appreciated within the context of masculine image. Like Marlon Brando in the 1950s, the prewar Gabin gave shape to feelings of anger and frustration among his audience. Like the star of *On the Waterfront*, he projected suppressed power through hesitant, inarticulate, almost incoherent speech and through explosive violence. Like Brando, Gabin's acting style contrasted with the polish and finesse of many of his contemporaries—for example, Charles Boyer and Pierre Brasseur. And like Brando, Gabin exuded raw sexual magnetism of a kind that was new to the screen. But where Brando's striving for naturalism betrayed his debt to the Actors' Studio, Gabin was perceived as simply playing himself.

In a poem composed in his honor, Prévert wrote: "The voice of Jean Gabin is true / it's the voice of his glance / the voice of his gestures and his hands." [41] Renoir marveled at "the calm certainty . . . he uses in getting into the skin of a part," and how "he got his greatest effect with the smallest means." [42] Mac Orlan saw Gabin as "an artist who knows how to solve all problems through simplicity: he is calm, very attentive, well balanced. He looks like an international-class goalkeeper in front of the posts." [43] The reference to soccer is not insignificant. The Gabin persona was built on rugged, masculine types—soccer players, railroad workers, tugboat captains, sailors, soldiers, Legionnaires—displaying brute force in shootings, knifings, and fistfights. Projecting what one commentator calls "an image of the undomesticated male (the bull symbol of mythology)," [44] Gabin is the man of action who abhors effeteness. To the painter's philosophizing in *Le Quai des Brumes*, Jean reacts with the outburst: "Oh, *merde!* I've had enough! Enough! Enough! Enough! You spout words! Words! One leads to another and you have pretty phrases. I can't stand pretty phrases. You get it?" In short, Gabin was the "regular guy" whom Duvivier dubbed "the type every Frenchman enjoys drinking a red wine with." [45]

Marcel Carné is not at all a "regular guy"—and this helps explain the pleasure he experienced in becoming associated with Gabin (fig. 26). Renoir describes his own feelings for Gabin in these terms: "I love Gabin and he loves me . . . Our relationship is entirely professional, but I have a feeling that his tastes are pretty much the same as mine." [46] The personal style and tastes of Gabin and Carné were not similar. But the young

26 On the set of *Le Quai des Brumes:* the movie hero Gabin (right) as a source of emotional strength for the director

director elicited a brotherly affection from Gabin much like that which he provoked in Prévert. Gabin's nickname for Renoir was "le Gros" (the Big Fellow)—a reference to Renoir's corpulence. Gabin chose to call Carné, who was himself somewhat overweight, "le Môme" (the Kid). In truth, Carné-the-posturing-tyrant-director felt secure in the presence of Gabin-the-authentic-virile-hero. He recalls with gratitude the numerous times Gabin "intervened to come to my defense" during the making of *Le Quai des Brumes* (*Vbd*, 108).

For all the manliness Gabin projected, Carné understood the extent to which the actor's image was cultivated, if not exactly manufactured. In his famous essay "The Destiny of Jean Gabin,"[47] André Bazin gives the classic interpretation of the Gabin persona as the tragic figure of modern cinema. He also reveals a certain paradox. On one hand, "through the popularity of an actor like Jean Gabin, millions of our contemporaries rediscover themselves." On the other, the Gabin persona exists outside standard conventional values: "But can you see Gabin as a family man?" asks Bazin. The answer, of course, is no, since movie stars do not express everyday values but are projections of what audiences would like to consider as fresh possibilities for themselves. Gabin was the quintessential loner. Despite emotional entanglements with women, the Gabin figure could ignore society's axiom that a man who does not marry puts his masculinity into question. For Carné, who was often obliged to assume poses that squared with conventional notions of manliness, the Gabin persona represented an ideal alliance of nonconformity and public acceptance which Carné himself could never realize.

Not the least intriguing aspect of *Le Quai des Brumes* is the way in which Gabin's composed masculinity gains in authenticity through juxtaposition with Brasseur's impersonation of a ruffian pathetically flaunting his virility. Writing about the film in *The New Republic* in 1939, Otis Ferguson spoke perceptively of Gabin's "projection of strength in immobility" and "his command of the illusion that crossing a room even to get to the men's room has its meaning."[48] The image may be fabricated, but Gabin is not a stereotype. He has, in Ferguson's words, "that perfect eloquence of the thing as perceived, marked down, and brought across to all who have an interest in and hope for the processes of life, as lived." Brasseur's Lucien fails as a human being because his obsession with toughness divorces him from sentiment. Humanity blossoms in Gabin's Jean because of his fragile romance with Nelly.

Jean and Nelly first meet in Panama's back room. The deserter's glazed, weary eyes turn slowly toward the far end of the room where a girl dressed in a dark beret, transparent raincoat, and clutch handbag stands gazing intently out the window. The girl senses the soldier's stare and turns around; her limpid, soulful eyes meet his. This unexpected moment is one of the exquisite encounters in French cinema. In the minutes following, Jean makes clear his view of the sexes: "A man and a woman simply don't understand one another. They speak a different language. They don't even share the same words." Nelly's reply that "maybe they can't understand one another, but they can love one another" is the hypothesis that the film tests and ultimately proves. From the cynic who makes fun of "that little guy with his wings and arrows," Jean is transfigured into a tender lover who whispers to Nelly at the carnival, "I only have to look at you, or hear your voice . . . and I feel like crying."

At the end of *Pépé le Moko*, Gabin attempts to flee the Casbah and join his mistress aboard a ship returning to France. Reaching the gate beyond which lies the port, he is caught in a police ambush and dies just as a siren announces the ship's departure. At the end of *Le Quai des Brumes*, Jean abandons the ship leaving for Venezuela and is shot down on the cobblestone street in front of Nelly's home. As he expires, the ship's siren screeches its departure. Despite the similarity of situation, *Le Quai des Brumes* is not an imitation of the Duvivier-Jeanson film. In the latter, Pépé's love affair is a pretext to gratify the primary desire he has harbored throughout the film: escape. In *Le Quai des Brumes*, the protagonist's desire for escape is brought to fruition but—spontaneously and deliberately—he squelches its reality for the sake of the nobler goal of personal commitment. Immediately following Jean's murder of Zabel, Nelly asks Jean why he returned. With Prévertian simplicity he responds: "I wanted to see you . . . And then I wanted to tell you that . . . at least one time in my life I've been . . . I've been happy in life because of you."

Jean's seeking out Nelly leads to his death. But as an exercise of free will in the name of sentiment, it alters decisively the general Gabin persona of the doomed, instinctive male. Lucien is powerless because he is locked into a stereotype of the rugged he-man: he is an extreme example of the effect of absolute conformity to simplistic sexual values. Jean, on the contrary, acquires genuine strength because he breaks through gender expectations by learning to value tenderness: in allowing feminine- and masculine-associated traits to coexist within himself, he announces the ideal Carné-Prévert being.

Androgyny is an essential component of the Carné oeuvre. Dominique in *Les Visiteurs du soir*, Baptiste in *Les Enfants du paradis*, and the angel in *La Merveilleuse Visite* attest to a breakdown of distinctions grounded in gender. Shots of Nelly in her dark pageboy and plain make-up project an allure similar to that of Arletty disguised as a boy in *Les Visiteurs du soir*. In their first encounter, Jean jokes about Nelly's slender, boyish frame: "You're pretty, I like you. No kidding! You're not stacked, but I like you!" Nelly's trenchcoat, her beret, and her habit of walking with head bent and hands in her pockets are indeed tomboyish variants of Gabin's own uniform and gait.

It is said that Michèle Morgan's costume came about by accident. Exasperated at not being able to meet the needs of a female character so unpretentious as Nelly, costume designer Coco Chanel remarked unkindly, "Why not just give her a raincoat and a beret!"[49] When the seventeen-year-old Morgan (b. 1920) was approached by a casting agent for the role, she was told, "We're looking for a girl different from the rest, neither a blushing rose nor a femme fatale, but a girl with presence and striking eyes."[50] Morgan's screen image of uncontrived femininity was in fact so imposing that many of the film's first viewers compared the new star to the trenchcoated Garbo of *Anna Christie* (1930).

Gabin and Morgan galvanized moviegoers' imaginations. If they became "the most famous and convincing couple in French cinema of the time,"[51] it was partly because they were expressing genuine feeling. Michèle Morgan claims to have difficulty duplicating real-life emotion in her parts: "Is it easier to interpret love when you are *in* love? On the contrary, though this may be a personal quirk, I find it inhibiting."[52] In truth, Morgan and Gabin's real-life love affair did not occur until 1939—after Gabin's separation from his second wife and while they were making their third film together, Grémillon's *Remorques*. (Gabin and Morgan co-starred in two other pictures: Maurice Gleize's *Le Récif de corail*, 1939, and Jean Delannoy's *La Minute de vérité*, 1952.) But during the shooting of *Le Quai des Brumes*, each was infatuated with the other. Morgan recalls that her being the object of Brasseur's flirtatious teasing on the set aroused enough jealousy in Gabin to make his slap in the bumper-car scene far more forceful than necessary: "Brasseur staggered under the shock, went pale, and clenched his fists. 'Cut!' cried Carné. 'Absolutely superb.' The life of the set was resumed; but for that brief moment reality had taken the place of fiction."[53]

Though she may be "the striking example of banality transfigured by three touches of genius,"[54] Michèle Morgan is a star presence in the Hollywood sense of the term. Carné, Schüfftan, and Prévert knew how to direct, light, and write for her. But the creation of a believable sexual field between her and Gabin is an achievement for which Morgan deserves full credit. An agent of destiny, Morgan's Nelly is not a femme fatale: unlike Arletty and Dietrich, the actress has neither the age nor the magnetism to merit that claim. The "genius" which Morgan brings to the film derives instead from her capacity to accept Gabin's prominence as a given, and then bask lovingly in the reflection of his power, his fate, and his sexuality. Just as Gabin was the idealization of Carné's masculine veneer, so Morgan was the projection of his sentimental core. To this day, the actress whom the casting agent required to be "different from the rest" remains Carné's closest female friend.

Legend has it that as of 1936 Gabin arranged for a clause to appear in each of his contracts guaranteeing that his films would include at least one episode of uncontrollable anger. Inadvertently, Prévert lent credence to this canard by writing the cellar scene in which Jean pounds Zabel to death with a brick. As in the murder at the end of *Les Enfants du paradis*, the horrific quality of the moment is both distilled and intensified by

27 A primal intrusion that triggers the killing of a symbolic father:
Zabel (Michel Simon) and Nelly (Michèle Morgan)

Carné's not letting us see the victim. Yet despite its luridness, the atrocity
takes on the character of a spiritual act. With sacred choir music blaring
from the radio upstairs, Jean assumes the role of a Saint George slaying
the dragon in his lair. A variation upon the schema established in *Jenny*,
Jean's wrath is triggered by his unanticipated *viewing* of Zabel's attempt
to molest Nelly (fig. 27). The murder scene partakes, therefore, of the
Oedipal symbology that informs so many of Carné's works. I have observed how *Jenny* and *Drôle de Drame* express conflicting needs concerning maternal figures. With the introduction of a clear-cut paternal figure—Zabel's first scene includes the line "I've got gray hairs, I could be
the father of you all"—*Le Quai des Brumes* enables Carné to play out
another fantasy: the killing of a father.

The catharsis does not, however, sit well. In rough cut, the film included a scene in which Zabel wraps in tarred paper the severed head of
Nelly's former boyfriend, Maurice, and checks it in the coatroom of the
Petit Tabarin, where he proceeds to pontificate about the decline of morals. By decree of the censors, these shots were eliminated—a change that
actually heightens suspense, since Zabel's responsibility for Maurice's
murder remains uncertain for much of the film in its final form. But the

cuts do not weaken the portrayal of Zabel as evil. In the final cellar sequence, Zabel crouches on the staircase and whimpers that he murdered out of love for Nelly. Comparing himself to "a Romeo with the face of a Bluebeard," Zabel attempts to elicit pathos. He fails because his hypocrisy is too well established by this point to modify perceiving him as anything but insidious. Yet for the present-day viewer of *Le Quai des Brumes*, there is something insidious about the way Zabel's insidiousness is portrayed. This has to do neither with plot dynamics nor with Carné's personal psychology, but with social and political resonance.

At the film's start Zabel declares himself "an honorable merchant." Transformed from the butcher in Mac Orlan's novel to a retailer of knickknacks, Zabel is the film's sole representative of the merchant class. He views the world exclusively in terms of barter: "And so I do you a favor, you do me a favor, and it's even money," he declares to Jean while trying to blackmail him. Posing as an exemplar of domestic and religious virtues, Zabel dubs his apartment "the house of the Lord" and prides himself on his taste for Christian sacred music because "it evokes memories in me, and I like to dig deep into my past." Zabel's selfishness and perversity are blatant contradictions of the image he wishes to project. More subtle is Zabel's physical demeanor. Simon's stiff, controlled movements are much like those of Jouvet in *Drôle de Drame*: they are the sign of suppressed instinct. The incessant rubbing together of his pudgy hands suggests nervous lasciviousness. But it is Zabel's unattractive face, high forehead, and dark, untrimmed beard that insinuate something alien to the French identity as incarnated by the blond, blue-eyed Gabin. Zabel's enthusiasm for church music and excessive claims to rootedness and respectability hint at a man of exotic origins trying to "pass" as a Frenchman. His name itself evokes the Semitic, and Mac Orlan's novel specifies it as a shorthand form of "Isabel"—which derives from the Hebrew, meaning "oath of Baal," and denotes worship of false gods.

Le Quai des Brumes is a very exact expression of prewar France. Read as allegory, the political right was able to find an explanation for France's fall in the movie's passive mood. The left interpreted Jean's murder by a demented gangster as prophetic of Fascism's triumph over the uncommitted. The role of Zabel raises one further aspect of French life reflected by the film but gone generally unrecognized: racial pride and national chauvinism. Jean's vilification of Zabel partakes of the rhetoric applied to Jews by extreme Nazi sympathizers: "Listen. One day in Tonkin I saw a repulsive beast, so spineless that just looking at it move made me want to vomit; they call it a scolopendrid. Well, that's what you resemble. Moreover, you have an ugly voice. When you speak, it sounds like old shoes splashing in sludge . . . Every time something good happens, garbage like you comes along to spoil it. Oh, you disgust me!" It is uncertain whether Prévert intended Zabel to represent "the Jewish problem." Surely neither he nor Carné would have espoused the "solution" that Jean undertakes. Yet because Jean is so alluring and Zabel is so repulsive, Carné and Prévert present viewers with a dramatic situation capable of bolstering a climate of intolerance and inhumanity. It is perhaps for this reason that Renoir expressed immediate displeasure with the film by renaming it *Le Cul des Brêmes*—vulgar slang that translates roughly as "the whores' ass"—and calling it "a Fascist film" (*Vbd*, 116, 481). According to Carné, Prévert succeeded in getting Renoir to apologize for this affront. The elder director explained that what he had meant was simply that the film contained "certain characters who could use a Fascist thrashing." Carné failed to appreciate the difference. But Renoir's initial reaction can be understood in reference to Zabel. Michel Simon had starred in two Renoir films that end by celebrating human potential: *La Chienne* and *Boudu sauvé des eaux*. Viewing Simon's character annihilated in a Manichean world of absolute good and evil could not but have offended the director of *La Grande Illusion*.

Ironically, Michel Simon was accused of collaboration after the war, and he blames this on Jean Renoir. In late spring of 1940 Renoir and Simon were shooting *La Tosca* in Rome. On June 10 Mussolini announced that Italy was at war with France. Renoir returned swiftly to southern France, where he succeeded in obtaining an exit visa; before sailing to New York, he traveled to Algeria, Morocco, and Lisbon. Simon—who was perceived by many as a "rightist anarchist"—never forgave Renoir for his "flight" and "betrayal."[55] Supposedly, Renoir had promised to arrange for Simon, too, to come to the United States, but never gave the Swiss-born actor a hint of having remembered his promise. Simon's desire to come to America was less political than professional—he wanted to rejuvenate his career. Simon stayed in Italy during the first half of the war and claims to have been denounced as a Jew and a Communist in Occupied France, where he nonetheless made several films.

As is the case with so many celebrities of the time, a web of circumstance and mixed motivations makes pat conclusions about political allegiances difficult. What is certain is that Simon—the future star of Claude Berri's film on anti-Semitism in Occupied France, *Le Vieil Homme et l'enfant* (*The Two of Us*, 1966)—did not become a pro-Nazi spokesman, as did his colleague Robert Le Vigan. It is also a fact that when Giscard d'Estaing hosted a small but highly publicized luncheon party to honor Carné in February 1975, Michel Simon, Michèle Morgan, and Jean Gabin all accepted the invitation to attend (although an unforeseen professional commitment made it impossible for Gabin to be present); Simone Signoret declined on political grounds; and Arletty—who following the war had been imprisoned because of alleged collaboration—also declined, asserting that all governments, left or right, were of little interest to her. Three months after the event, Michel Simon died in Bry-sur-Marne. In November 1976, Jean Gabin died in Paris. On February 12, 1979, Jean Renoir died in Beverly Hills.

Much like *Casablanca* in this country, *Le Quai des Brumes* holds something of a cult status in French popular culture today. Its nostalgic power derives in large measure from its depiction of love. As Maurice Clavel put it in 1971, the picture evokes an era, perhaps the last, in which *amour* still rhymed with *toujours*: "It was free love's historical moment: before, it lacked freedom; afterwards, it lacked love." [56]

In a strange way *Le Quai des Brumes* is Carné's most personal film and his least. As a maker of images, he reveals his individual style more emphatically and successfully than in any of his prior works. In the visual and technical authority it exerts, *Le Quai des Brumes* is the product of a mature, fully developed artist. As a maker of fictions, Carné succeeds, too, in rendering palpable a scenario of two beings who assert their love despite the odds. But this accomplishment is less the result of Carné's individual talent than of the collective creative force exerted on him by Gabin, Morgan, and Prévert. *Le Quai des Brumes* is a great love story, but its depiction of secure emotion is something Carné did not know firsthand.

CHAPTER 7

"Atmosphere, Atmosphere"

In the fall of 1938, producer Jacques Lucachevitch was negotiating a film to star Annabella (b. 1909), who was then the biggest box-office draw in Europe. Carné did not admire this actress; he especially deplored the awkwardness of her love scenes with Gabin in *La Bandera*. When Lucachevitch asked Carné to consider working with her, the director's reluctance was counterbalanced only by his opinion that Annabella's talents had been put to fine use in Clair's populist romance *Quatorze Juillet*. Carné therefore proposed a similar property which he had wanted to bring to the screen for some time and which he suspected would suit Annabella: Eugène Dabit's novel of popular life along Paris's quai de Jemmapes, *L'Hôtel du Nord* (1929).[1]

Lucachevitch and Annabella responded with enthusiasm. All agreed that the likely candidate to adapt the novel was Jacques Prévert. But Prévert, who did not suffer from the travel anxieties that plagued Carné, was then visiting New York and California. Carné claims (*Vbd*, 122) to have contemplated "for a moment" going to Los Angeles to work on the screenplay with Prévert and to become better acquainted with Annabella, who had recently launched a Hollywood career. However, when Lucachevitch refused to finance the trip, Carné abandoned the idea—a reaction that may point to a deficiency of initiative in Carné's handling of his career, but also suggests an assuredness about his capacity to direct a project without Prévert's assistance. Carné turned to Jean Aurenche (b. 1904), the scenarist with whom he had made advertising shorts in the early 1930s and who would eventually enjoy longstanding collaborations with dialogue writer Pierre Bost and, more recently, director Bertrand Tavernier. Because Aurenche felt competent to compose only the adaptation, not the dialogue, Carné nominated Henri Jeanson (1900–1970) to serve as dialogue writer.

Journalist, boulevard playwright, and scriptwriter, Jeanson was a notorious polemicist who had no qualms about penning devastating reviews in *La Flèche* or *Le Canard enchaîné* of films he himself had worked on. Although his name initially provoked terror in Lucachevitch, the smooth-talking writer succeeded in winning the producer's confidence by suggesting changes in Aurenche's adaptation that would, he insisted, ensure greater audience appeal. Above all, Jeanson proposed the expansion of two secondary characters, a pimp and his whore, whom he already conceived as being played by two of his friends, Louis Jouvet and Arletty.

As early as 1933 Carné had evinced interest in Dabit's novel. In the *Cinémagazine* article "When Will the Camera Get Out into the Street?" he praised *L'Hôtel du Nord* for its depiction of "the hidden soul" of life along the Canal Saint-Martin in Paris's tenth arrondissement. He expressed hope that the cinema would follow the lead of Dabit and fellow populist novelists André Thérive and Bernard Nabonne in depicting the working classes' daily existence. In public life, Dabit (1898–1936) was a spokesman for Communism, disarmament, and the League Against Anti-Semitism. André Gide's travel account of Stalinist Russia, *Retour de l'U.R.S.S.* (1936), is dedicated to Dabit, and it was while accompanying Gide on that trip that the younger writer died, apparently of typhus. Like Gide, Dabit was disillusioned by what he saw in Russia. The final entry in his diary includes the words "the present is as dark and obstructed as the future." [2]

The populist literary movement was an earnest, avowedly middlebrow reaction to the verbal acrobatics of the avant-garde. *L'Hôtel du Nord*— winner of the first Prix Populiste—typifies the genre. A loose collection of sentimental tales about simple people residing in a hotel, the novel is framed by two events that impart a clear-cut social dimension to the work. It begins with Monsieur and Madame Lecouvreur's buying a run-down hotel and transforming it into a decent dwelling for working-class tenants. It ends with the Lecouvreurs' reluctantly selling the hotel to a large company that plans to construct an office building on the site. The closing moments describe the melancholy departure of the tenants, the hotel's demolition, and the sense that years of hard work have been undone by the impersonal forces of big business.

Carné and Aurenche's version is dramatically more tight, but it dilutes the novel's ideological thrust. Pierre (Jean-Pierre Aumont) and Renée (Annabella), determined to end their lives together, rent a room in the Hôtel du Nord. After shooting Renée, Pierre lacks the courage to kill himself. Following another unfinished suicide attempt, Pierre surrenders to the police, even though Renée, who was only wounded, lodges no complaint. While Pierre is in prison, Renée returns to the hotel to work as a waitress. One of the residents, Edmond (Louis Jouvet), is a reformed gangster who tires of his life with the prostitute Raymonde (Arletty). He entices Renée to leave with him for Port Said. Only hours before their ship is scheduled to depart from Marseilles, Renée goes back to Paris to be near the man she loves. Pierre, released from prison, is reunited with Renée. Amid an animated Bastille Day celebration, Edmond returns and is gunned down by an underworld foe. As dawn breaks, the lovers set out, hand in hand, to confront their destinies beyond the confines of the Hôtel du Nord.

Given the controversy surrounding the army deserter in *Le Quai des Brumes*, it is understandable that Carné would not want his next picture to have overt political resonance. Focusing less on genuine working people than on a picturesque *Lumpenproletariat* of criminals, prostitutes, and vagabonds, *Hôtel du Nord* develops the sentimental rather than the political themes of Dabit's novel. The film does make specific reference to a truckdrivers' strike—which allows one of the residents, Kenel, to pursue his affair with the wife of another tenant, the canal lock-keeper Prosper. Pierre and Renée are portrayed allusively as victims of a depressed economy: he is an unemployed draftsman, and she, an underpaid salesgirl in a bakery. "We are killing one another because there is nothing else to do," laments Renée. And in an early sequence, Monsieur Lecouvreur muses: "For me, the most wonderful day of my life was two years ago, when I bought this Hôtel du Nord. Because until then I had always worked for others. I was a cabinetmaker. When I walked in here . . . I said to myself, 'This is yours, just like your watch, it's yours alone,' and I felt like blubbering." Taken almost verbatim from the novel, these words are spoken at the very moment Pierre and Renée attempt suicide—an episode not found in the novel—and convey a measure of social pertinence. But their impact is so oblique as to be nonexistent. Further, in eliminating the opening and closing events of the novel, the hotel's establishment and destruction, Carné and Aurenche do away with the book's most forceful strategy for heightening political awareness.

Carné's retreat from politics to psychology is symptomatic of France's condition in late 1938. Already in a state of internal chaos, the nation was becoming paralyzed vis-à-vis world events. When Hitler's *Anschluss* of Austria occurred in March 1938, France was in a period of transition between the second Chautemps government and the second Blum regime. Hence, it took no official stance on the matter. With right-wingers urging peace at any price, Blum fell, and the subsequent Daladier regime (his third) lacked the stamina to thwart Germany's move on Czechoslovakia, with whom France had maintained an alliance since the 1920s.

Although it made a feeble gesture of manning the Maginot Line in the summer of 1938 (during which *Hôtel du Nord* was shot), France found itself locked into an uneasy peace when, in late September, it took part in the Munich Agreements. It was not without humiliation and embarrassment that, on December 6, 1938 (four days before the premiere of *Hôtel du Nord*), France signed a Franco-German Declaration expressing agreement that relations between the two nations were "of the first importance."

Suzanne Chantal recalls that throughout the crisis Carné thought only of one thing: "finishing his film." [3] Carné himself admits that he viewed the conscription that began in the weeks before Munich principally as a hindrance to his production, depriving him day after day of another grip or gaffer and forcing him to rearrange his shooting schedule—an especially urgent requirement when Jean-Pierre Aumont received a draft notice (*Vbd*, 134). Carné's singlemindedness is telling. It denotes a lifelong obsession with completing a project as initially conceived despite real-world constraints. Equally significant is the parallel between Carné's conversion of the ideological underpinnings of Dabit's novel into psychology and the retrenchment of France from a position of international power and prestige to one of self-centered concern for peace and stability. In this regard *Hôtel du Nord* is a less courageous film than *Le Quai des Brumes*. Rather than comment upon France's paralysis, *Hôtel du Nord* contributes to it. Reducing politics to a matter of the Romantic couple—Pierre and Renée—*Hôtel du Nord* glorifies a Tristan-and-Iseult relationship in which individuals react to the increasing infringement of the outside world by fabricating a universe unto themselves.

The film's disengagement from real time and space is signaled by the symmetry of its first and final shots, among Carné's most elegant and memorable. Coming after a lengthy credit sequence, the first shot starts with a slow pan that follows Pierre and Renée descending a footbridge from screen left to right; as the two characters leave the film frame, the camera moves left, descends, and dollies under the bridge to recapture the lovers as they walk along the bank of the canal, sit on a bench, and stare forlornly into space; still within the same shot, the camera tilts up gradually to reveal the Hôtel du Nord behind them. At the film's close, the shot is repeated in reverse, as the timid couple muster up strength to leave the vicinity of the hotel via the same footbridge, walking from screen right to left. This fastidious framing intimates that the lovers' world has no existence beyond the purview of Carné's camera lens. It suggests that what has transpired between the start and the end belongs more to the rituals of cinema than to historical time and space.

28   Alexander Trauner overseeing the reconstruction of the Canal Saint-
      Martin at Billancourt Studios; behind him (right) stands the façade
      of the Hôtel du Nord

The studio reconstruction of an entire section of Paris's La Villette
district was Carné and Trauner's most flamboyant tour de force before
Les Enfants du paradis (fig. 28). Faithful to the Clair-Meerson tradition
of balancing sweep and detail, the director and the designer produced
the impression of "intimate reality" which Graham Greene, writing on
Hôtel du Nord in 1939, viewed as the special gift of French film.[4] But in
Carné, intimacy always implies enclosure and constriction. The tubular
channels, dams, and crisscrossed footpaths of the canal; the corridors
and compartments of the hotel; the iron beds, barred windows, and
paned interior walls of the hospital; the passageways, catwalks, and
mesh grating of the prison—all contribute to the sense that Carné's characters are caught and caged.
    The picture's most elaborate sequence is the nighttime Bastille Day
street celebration (fig. 29), which required over four hundred extras. This
populist tableau features a *danse du tapis*, in which celebrants join hands
to dance in a circle, except for the few who kneel on a mat and select

29 *Hôtel du Nord*'s Bastille Day celebration: short-lived communality

another to kiss and then replace them. This brief depiction of human warmth and solidarity comes to a standstill, however, when a honking bus—which Carné impetuously rented from Paris's mass transit company—enters the frame from the extreme background, moves toward the camera, and forces the dancers to disperse. Filming this scene was especially difficult. The shooting script called for "a car." Carné's bus, it turned out, was too high to pass under the low-hanging paper garlands, which took two hours of production time to restring. The bus was also out of scale with Trauner's hotel façade; it reached almost to the windows of the second story. The hasty attempt by Carné and cinematographer Armand Thirard to minimize this discrepancy through lens changes was not entirely successful.

This incident became notorious for certain postwar French theorist-critics. Writing in 1954, Claude Mauriac viewed the bus's intrusion as scandalous because it "underscores the inauthenticity of the papier-mâché street and canvas-painted café"; "the raw matter of film . . . being life itself, there is . . . no misconception more serious than shooting scenes that are supposed to take place outdoors on sets (no matter how faithful these may appear)."[5] An anticipatory response to Mauriac can be found in Carné's "When Will the Camera Get Out into the Street?" In that essay the young proponent of on-location filming nonetheless asserted that a studio set can often be more convincing than location shots because "to be lifelike, the set must be thought of *in relation to the story*" (my italics). In his memoirs Carné proposes that the bus episode reflected a sentimental whim to depict what he had remembered fondly from his youth—that on July 14 the streets of Paris belonged to the people: "The buses would only borrow the streets . . . and would have to wait until the dance ended" (*Vbd*, 132). But his 1933 statement is more on the mark, for the bus *as filmed* is an interloper destroying the revelers' communal spirit. Moreover, the cutting between the oversize bus's appearance and Edmond's unexpected return makes the vehicle an omen of the criminal's demise. *In relation to the story*, the sole genuine object in an otherwise artificial milieu becomes the most phantasmagoric. The bus is indeed an intrusion. But it does not point, as Mauriac would have it, to a clash between realism and artifice. Like the miniature bumper cars in *Le Quai des Brumes*, the outsize bus is the index of a collision between nightmare and dream in an imaginative world which, despite its purported naturalism, is a sealed space unto itself.

In this respect the film's most famous bit of comic dialogue has symbolic consequence. At the end of a squabble that occurs when Edmond breaks his vacation plans with Raymonde in order to go fishing alone, the rogue informs his sulking companion: "I need a change of atmosphere. And the atmosphere in question is *you*." Unable to reason with him—or fathom the meaning of his words—Raymonde explodes, unleashing scorn for Edmond's arrogance and, above all, for the pretentious vocabulary he spouts expressly to intimidate her: "This is the first time anyone's treated me like an atmosphere! Well, if I'm an atmosphere, then you . . . you're a rotten dump!" (*un drole de bled!*). Exaggerating the open vowels with all the shrillness her Parisian-accented voice can muster, Raymonde shouts, "At-mos-*phè*-re! At-mos-*phè*-re! Do I have the mug of an at-mos-*phè*-re?" (*Est-ce que j'ai une gueule d'atmosphère?*), and exits with the jibe "Happy fishing . . . and happy atmosphere!" (*Bonne pêche . . . et bonne atmosphère!*).

Carné claims to have wanted to eliminate these lines when he first read Jeanson's script: "I thought it unlikely that a whore would respond quite that way. I nonetheless shot the scene, and Arletty said it with such conviction that I knew it was right."[6] The scene attests to the capacity of two great performers—Arletty and Louis Jouvet—to rise above trivial dialogue, and it demonstrates that Carné, although never favoring improvisation, remained alert to the specific talents of his actors. Above all, this barely understood but intensely felt word—"atmosphere"—expresses a need shared by the main characters in *Hôtel du Nord* as well as in virtually all of Carné's other works: to escape from moral, physical, and spiritual suffocation. As a gesture of self-reference, the cry for atmosphere articulates a desire in Carné's characters to be released from the very cinematic world to which they belong—the overly atmospheric fabrications of an unremittingly closed-style director.

Carné's eagerness to adapt *L'Hôtel du Nord* derived in part from a wish to present on film a social context absent from his previous pictures and vainly sought after in his own life: a warm, close-knit, surrogate family. Carné also saw the enterprise as an expression of sympathy toward Eugène Dabit's parents, the actual hotel proprietors who inspired the book and who were then mourning the death of their son. (The real Hôtel du Nord—whose façade looks just as it does in the film—still stands at 102 quai de Jemmapes [fig. 30].)

To portray Madame Dabit-Lecouvreur, Carné chose one of France's great character actresses, the plump, high-voiced Jane Marken (1895–1976). Projecting a mix of motherliness and sensuality, Marken's 1930s persona was characterized by unselfish giving. Her talents were perhaps best exhibited as the mother in Renoir's *Une Partie de campagne* and the hotelkeeper in *Les Enfants du paradis*. For Carné, Marken was the perfect incarnation of an older female whose sexual exploits—unlike those portrayed by Françoise Rosay—were sincere, direct, and unmenacing. Possibly because of Prévert's absence, but more directly a consequence of Carné's sentimentalism, Marken's sexuality is deemphasized in *Hôtel du Nord*, where she preoccupies herself with lodging and feeding her band of misfits. Among these, none receives more demonstrative maternal attention than the hypersensitive mute orphan named Manolo. A character invented for the film, Manolo is a displaced victim of the Spanish Civil War. He epitomizes Carné's vision of childhood as a period of traumatic loss. Like the blind accordionist in *Nogent*, the depressed painter in *Le Quai des Brumes*, and the languishing mime in *Les Enfants du paradis*, Manolo is a figure of the exiled child of paradise whom the "orphaned" Carné saw himself to be.

Nogent remains the only Carné film to include images of happy family life. At one point in that idyll we discern a small boy cheerfully observing the outdoor activities (fig. 31). Seen in full shot, the boy's image is framed by the dress and trousers of his mother and father, who form a literal backdrop of parental unity and security. All subsequent Carné films dismantle this pristine view: *Jenny* deals with the breakdown of family cohesion; *Drôle de Drame* barely pays attention to children, except for

30 The Hôtel du Nord in 1985, its exterior intact despite
interior renovation

the final shot that reiterates the loss and alienation established in *Jenny*;
the one child in *Le Quai des Brumes* is an unsmiling boy who rides an
empty carousel.

The ebullient opening scene of *Hôtel du Nord* seems to reverse this
trend. It depicts the first-communion celebration of Michèle, who lives
in the hotel with her policeman father, Maltaverne. The scene begins
with a close-up of the party cake, and as Carné's camera tracks backward, the frame becomes filled with food, wine, and chatty guests—all

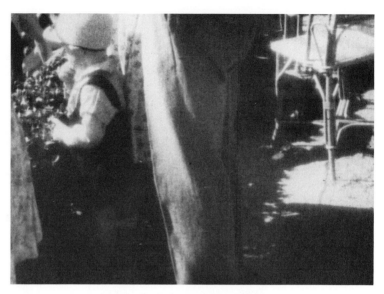

31 A rare instance of family unity: the child framed by his parents in *Nogent*

establishing a Renoir-like mood of carefree camaraderie. Yet the gaiety is undone within seconds. Madame Lecouvreur urges Michèle to bring a piece of cake upstairs to Raymonde, the hotel's courtesan-in-residence. On the first landing, Michèle is accosted by a middle-aged tenant named Mimar (played by Jacques Louvigny, 1880–1951), who unsuccessfully attempts to molest her. When Michèle protests, Mimar silences her with a bribe: "Shut up . . . here's your twenty *sous* . . . You're not being good to your Papa Mimar . . . Damned kid . . . scram!" This is arguably the most unsettling episode in all of Carné's works. In Dabit's novel, Mimar is a Lothario; but his prey is women aged thirty to fifty. In Carné's film, Mimar's sole erotic interest is Michèle, and his pedophilia is all the more disconcerting because of its matter-of-fact presentation. The scene has been cut from most prints now circulating in France. It remains intact, however, in the noncirculating print housed by New York's Museum of Modern Art.

Carne's handling of love scenes between young adults tends to be awkward; he is more adept at directing stylized romances between young men and older women. Yet the chilling credibility of the Mimar-Michèle encounter points to a talent for depicting perversity. Indeed, a pedophilic strain insinuates itself in *Le Quai des Brumes* (Zabel's lust for Nelly), *Le Jour se lève* (Valentin's relations with Françoise), and *La Marie du port*

(Chatelard's affection for Marie). As of *Les Tricheurs*, Carné's films disclose an almost obsessive preoccupation with handsome youths. But save in *Hôtel du Nord*, Carné chose to avoid direct depiction of adult sexual desire for children, preferring instead to attenuate, displace, mask, or sublimate the expression of this and most other controversial erotic activities.

Although generally unacknowledged by commentators, homoerotic inclination is a constant component of Carné's cinematic universe. Not the least of *Hôtel du Nord*'s distinctions is its portrayal of the confectioner Adrien (François Périer, b. 1919), an overtly homosexual twenty-year-old. In Dabit's novel, Adrien does not appear until the thirty-second of the thirty-five chapters. His characterization is cliché: he wears tight clothes, holds his glass with pinkie extended, and attends a costume ball dressed as a gypsy girl. He is also the object of a police investigation. In the film, Adrien appears in the very first interior shot of the hotel, and as the script prescribes, he is "a young man of twenty, rather stylish, but with nothing conspicuous about him" (fig. 32). The note on conspicuousness is telling. It does not signal an attempt to mask or convention-

32   Acceptance of difference: François Périer (seated) as the homosexual youth Adrien in *Hôtel du Nord*, surrounded by André Brunot (Lecouvreur), Jane Marken (Madame Lecouvreur), and Raymone (the maid, Jeanne)

alize Adrien's behavior. On the contrary, because Adrien's difference is recognized and accepted by the hotel's occupants—all marginals themselves—he has no need to assume stereotypic poses. Neither fey nor rugged, Adrien is what he is. He does not advertise his affair with the soldier Fernand. He simply goes about it.

In bringing this portrait to the screen, Carné, Aurenche, and Jeanson exhibited courage. The absolute personal freedom and dignity which Adrien enjoys and which the film takes for granted constitutes a rarity in both European and American cinema, past and present.[7] Never again would Carné be so direct and unmannered in his treatment of homosexuality. But never again would Carné fabricate a refuge so inviting and sheltered. An Eldorado of sorts, the hotel and quay, with its narrow slip of trees and shrubbery, represent an idealized space in which tolerance expunges society's notions of sin, crime, and abnormality.

Manolo, Michèle, and Adrien are not central to *Hôtel du Nord*'s plot, but their dramas reverberate fully with the film's major theme as embodied by Pierre and Renée: the pursuit of lost innocence. According to Carné, Jeanson deliberately "botched" (*Vbd*, 125) the protagonists' dialogue in order to highlight the broad and racy repartee written for Arletty and Jouvet. The love duos of Annabella and Aumont are indeed limp. Preparing to die in the huge bed of room 16 (fig. 33), the lovers whisper:

PIERRE: Renée . . . my love . . . there is still time to say no . . .

RENEE: If I said no . . . we'd be forced to go on living . . . what a burden! . . . and how complicated!

PIERRE: You realize what will happen here, in just a few minutes?

RENEE: Completely . . . I've often thought about it . . . I will stretch out next to you . . . I will place my head on your arm . . . and you will kiss me sweetly . . . like the first time . . . I will close my eyes . . . I will hear the tick-tock of your wristwatch against my ear . . . you will say my name softly. . . and you will shoot me here . . . in the heart . . . Be careful . . . I purposely wore the brooch you gave me so that you would not miss the mark . . . You will immediately close your eyes . . . I don't want you to see me die—and then it is your turn . . .

PIERRE: Renée, my little one . . . .

This languid text supports characterization. Raised in an orphanage and compelled to make her way among the proletariat, Annabella's watery waif is the archetypal Carné ingénue. Dressed in white ankle socks

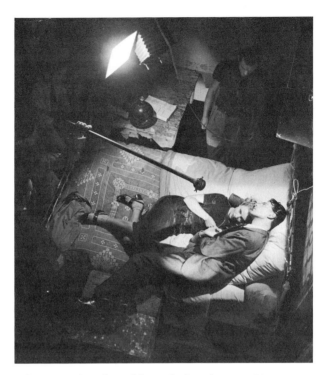

33   Fabricating the ethereal from the banal: preparing to shoot Annabella and Jean-Pierre Aumont in *Hôtel du Nord*

and open-toed shoes, white beret and light cloth coat, Annabella projects the unthreatening girlish persona that Carné was totally at ease with. In the above scene Jeanson underscores the cliché-ridden side of the character, but Carné modulates light and shadow to produce facial close-ups so delicate and ethereal as to make Renée appear heaven-born. As always in Carné, the prosaic, when photographed, releases a beauty that seems at once the height of naturalness and of artifice.

Cocteau has written: "Jean-Pierre Aumont wears a heart of gold on his broad, open face. He is free of shadows and complications."[8] These qualities made Aumont totally inappropriate for *Hôtel du Nord*. In fact, Carné originally wanted the American actor Phillips Holmes to play the film's romantic hero-weakling. Holmes's role as Clyde Griffiths, "the mental and moral coward" in Sternberg's *An American Tragedy* (1931), suggests his suitability for portraying the sullen Pierre and for delivering Jeanson's dainty dialogue. With Aumont assuming the part, Carné had to hold the actor's élan in check. If Aumont's Pierre exerts impact none-theless, it is due, again, to Carné's visuals. In a scene that is almost en-tirely mute, Pierre—believing he has killed Renée yet lacking the courage to destroy himself—escapes from the hotel. Within a lengthy tracking shot that follows him along a dark cobblestone street, Pierre rebuffs the advances of a prostitute, passes shoddy posters advertising soap and Du-bonnet, and comes to a bridge suspended above railroad tracks. Each detail of the shot helps to explain Pierre's emotional state: the debase-ment of love (the prostitute); Pierre's victimization by the economic sys-tem (the posters); and his need to escape (the tracks). This is poetic re-alism at its most dense, with all elements of the setting emitting symbolic value without any distortion of verisimilitude. The scene turns Expres-sionistic when a train, at first represented by a moving light projected on a painted background, prompts Pierre to position himself as if he were about to jump over the bridge. A horse-drawn wagon—Carné's insistent symbol of destiny—next passes in the foreground from left to right and obscures Pierre from the spectator's sight. When the horse disappears, the frame is filled with locomotive smoke, and for one suspenseful mo-ment the viewer wonders whether Pierre has jumped. As the smoke dis-sipates, Pierre reappears intact. This scene expresses remorse, fear, and self-hatred without recourse to verbal discourse. It showcases Carné's nostalgia for the silent German cinema as well as his preference for ef-fecting narrative movement solely through visual means.

Although the full-bloodedness of the whore and her pimp owes much to Jeanson, Carné brings a personal touch to bear upon these characters, too. The director dubs Arletty "the soul" of *Hôtel du Nord* (*Vbd*, 136). She is also its salt. The viewer who comes to this picture only with the experience of *Les Visiteurs du soir* or *Les Enfants du paradis* is bound to be surprised by the vulgarity of Arletty's appearance, speech, and gait (fig. 34). In fact, the composed sensuality Arletty projects in the later films is a deliberate reversal of her prior persona. Arletty began her ca-reer as an actress-singer in the revues and musical comedies that had dazzled Carné in his youth. Portraying naughty soubrettes and flashy streetwalkers, she embodied an easy mix of coquetry and idealism, and had a natural talent for delivering comic dialogue and torch songs with a broad *parigot* accent. It was Arletty's voice that brought her to the attention of moviemakers during the early years of sound film. If the personality of a film star depends as much on the "phonogenic 'grain of the voice'" as on the "photogenic configuration of body and face," Ar-letty had extraordinary "phonogeneity."[9] Her shrill, angular sound—which John Simon once described as "midway between a mountain

34 Arletty as the abused, defiant prostitute in *Hôtel du Nord*

stream and a gin-soaked parrot"[10]—crackles, granulates, grates, and cuts. But throughout the 1930s Arletty's picture career was limited to supporting roles: she had played in twenty-four by the time she made *Hôtel du Nord*. In 1935 she was slated to star in a film, but the prospective producer withdrew, claiming that Arletty (b. 1898) simply was too old and not pretty enough to play a leading lady. Other producers voiced similar views. Trauner explains: "On the stage, she capitalized on her funny and vulgar Parisian speech and gestures. So film directors cast her in similar roles. No one recognized before *Hôtel du Nord* that she also has a deep beauty with character and volume that radiate from inside. People can discover such beauty through the screen because the camera lens sees in a way that is free of the subjective sentiment and preconditioning allied to the human eye."[11] For Arletty, *Hôtel du Nord* stands out as "my first real film. It was only a supporting role, shot in a mere six days, but for me it was worth the fifteen hundred lines of *Cyrano de Bergerac.*" [12] The role also yielded substantial monetary value: after *Hôtel du Nord*, Arletty's salary jumped from 60,000 to 300,000 francs per picture.

Arletty's stagy persona invigorates the *bons mots* which Jeanson wrote specifically for her and Jouvet. At times Arletty sets up retorts for Jouvet; more often she gets the clincher. For example, Edmond's dour "My existence here is no life" provokes Raymonde's glib "And do you think my life is even an existence!" Near the film's start, the fastidious Edmond berates Raymonde for putting a piece of cake near her comb:

EDMOND: Not next to the comb, that cake . . . Moreover, haven't I told you that the proper place for a comb is not on a table next to a jar of jam, that the place for a pot of jam is not next to a curling iron . . . and that I'm tired of seeing you place your face powder next to the toothbrush . . .

RAYMONDE: There's another thing that's not in its place here . . .

EDMOND: What's that?

RAYMONDE: A woman like me next to a guy like you!

A whore with a heart of gold, Raymonde repeatedly excuses Edmond's mental and physical abuse, the latter accounting for the black eye which—along with a tatty fox collar—she sports through much of the film. She befriends the chambermaid, Jeanne, even though she knows that Edmond is sleeping with her. And when Edmond abandons her for Renée, Raymonde takes up with the lock-keeper Prosper (Bernard Blier) not because of attraction to him, not for personal revenge, but out of an instinct to console a man in need: Prosper's wife (Paulette Dubost) has run off with a lover. Near the film's end, in a brief scene with minimal dialogue, Prosper bends to the ground, slips on Raymonde's shoe, and kisses her foot. To all appearances Prosper is serving Raymonde. But it is Raymonde, impassive yet willing, who is serving the emotional and physical needs of Prosper. In this luminous moment we glimpse the "character and volume that radiate from inside" Arletty. The actress who eventually became, to borrow Roger Manvell's term, "the Garbo of France" [13] here projects for several seconds the aura of self-inflicted loneliness that comes to full realization in her portrayal of Garance in *Les Enfants du paradis*.

Jeanson claims that Carné was at first vociferous in his refusal to consider Arletty for the picture. He quotes Carné as having said: "She's impossible! No! I saw her at work in *Pension Mimosas*, and, well, no! Despite Feyder, she was impossible; no! What's more, her voice is not recordable; she tears the track apart. And I dare you to photograph her. Her face just doesn't take to light. She glares under the spotlights. And she doesn't even know how to walk. She moves like a huge flounder!"[14] Carné's account differs (*Vbd*, 125–28). He claims to have wanted Arletty at the outset but to have had some unease, which augmented as Jeanson increased the size of her role. The initial rehearsals of her first scene seem to have justified Carné's apprehensions.

As originally written, Arletty first appears in medium shot, bent over an inhalator; she then rises and removes the towel covering her head, acknowledges the presence of the child who has come to offer her a piece of party cake, and chats with the girl and Jouvet. It is a lengthy shot that requires nuanced gestures, numerous props, and varied vocal registers. With hindsight, the image of Arletty soothing her throat and then disclosing her face is emblematic of the change in persona Carné ultimately effected upon the actress. Yet the director recalls not the inherent symbolism of the situation but the pragmatics of shooting the scene. Carné elaborates: "We had a first run-through. It was catastrophic. Poor Arletty muffed the text, her movements, and the props. We did it again. Then three more times. With the same result. Moreover, Arletty started to get edgy . . . I contemplated filming the scene in fragments, but that would have spoiled the way it was written." Trying to dissemble his own nervousness, Carné asked Arletty to sit down, and then he began to play the scene for her. "And there I was in front of the inhalator, taking in its vapors, with a towel on my head. Putting all that aside, I next went to the other side of the room, lifted the mascara and brush, and did my eyelids . . . then walked back to the other side of the room, and so on. No one laughed, though the scene played by a man gave ample reason. On the contrary, I sensed that everyone was looking on with intensity and fear. When I had finished, Arletty said to me, 'Don't worry, Marcel. I understand.' . . . So we rehearsed again, and this time everything was perfect: text, gestures, props. Everything. And to such a degree that with the rehearsal over, I leapt toward Arletty, locked her in my arms, and kissed her sincerely—even though my effusiveness was mixed with a measure of relief" (*Vbd*, 128).

Louise Brooks has written that "the tragedy of film history is that it is fabricated, falsified by the very people who make film history."[15] It is likely that both Jeanson's and Carné's stories are apocryphal. Arletty claims not to remember the incident related by Carné and insists that "it was very rare for him to play out a role. He left acting to the actors."[16] Perhaps the truth of the matter is less consequential than the impression which the latter-day Carné wishes to give. This anecdote about Arletty provides the only instance of Carné's portraying himself in his reminiscences as demonstratively tender toward a woman: "Such was the start of an affectionate collaboration . . . Not only would Arletty become my favorite actress . . . but she would also be a faithful and dependable friend, although a bit too distant in my opinion" (*Vbd*, 128). Arletty, eight years older than Carné, has remained devoted to him over the years. But the aloofness Carné attributes to her is more plausibly a projection of the distance he himself has steadily kept from her. The anecdote—in which he virtually "becomes" Arletty—can be seen as a belated compensation. Colette remarked that "Arletty admits of no technique that she hasn't invented herself." [17] In other words, Arletty was a natural talent. Naturalness in women intimidated Carné. By curbing Arletty's flamboyance and heightening her inner dignity, Carné eventually refashioned the actress into his ideal woman: an older, enigmatic earth-goddess type who could convey simultaneously the warm fairy-tale allure of his missing mother (Arletty, too, had "long, beautiful black hair") and the safe, cool sexuality of music-hall goddesses.

Carné has often been called a poor director of women. This reproach is not entirely valid. As Carné became surer of his talents, he incorporated, Pygmalion-like, actors and actresses into his scheme of complete control over a film's feel, tone, and atmosphere. Rather than allow a Françoise Rosay or a Michèle Morgan to impose her unique personality, Carné chose to straitjacket actresses according to an idiosyncratic, dualistic vision of women. The result was sometimes near-listless ingénue performances (Annabella, Jacqueline Laurent, Nicole Courcel), sometimes striking depictions of femmes fatales (Arletty, Nathalie Nattier). In both cases, Carné's women arouse a sense of mystery: the underexposed ingénues, because they seem to repress their true selves; the earth goddesses, because their complexity seems so awesome. Carné's women may not correspond to what most viewers would like to see on screen or to how most actresses would like to be directed, but they are unmistakably Carné products.

The most enigmatic character in *Hôtel du Nord*, however, is a man: Louis Jouvet's Edmond. An underworld fugitive evading a pair of ex-convicts whom he once betrayed, Edmond displays an exterior no less austere and deadpan than the Bishop's in *Drôle de Drame*. In the earlier film Jouvet's asceticism was a façade covering a lewd core. Here it is the incrustation grown on a man who has spent life locked into false identities—as Edmond, alias Robert, alias Paulo. Like Gabin's Jean in *Le Quai des Brumes*, Jouvet's Edmond begins to acknowledge his capacity for

natural sentiment. But it is too late. After his abortive departure for
Egypt with Renée, Edmond simply mutters, "Renée, I thank you for having given me, just like that, three days of your life." As if in a trance, he
makes his way past the Bastille Day revelers, ignores Renée's warning that enemies await him, and goes directly to his room. Virtually abet-
ting destiny, he tosses his gun to his former accomplice, who forthwith
kills him.

Edmond fascinates because the motives behind his choice of Renée as
a means of salvation, and then death as the only alternative, are as
opaque as his physical demeanor. His tiring of Raymonde is understandable, his attraction to Renée plausible. But why the radical desire to begin
life anew, to seek out a pristine world, and why specifically with Renée?
The film supplies no complete answers, but its sequence of events provides a clue. Edmond's need for new "atmosphere" is triggered by a version of the Carnésian "primal scene" (notable despite Prévert's absence).
When Pierre shoots Renée, Edmond is in the next apartment developing
negatives. Curious about the noise, he puts his ear to the entryway of
their room, knocks, and then forces the door open (fig. 35). The sight he
beholds is Pierre standing terrified by the window with revolver in hand,
and Renée spread on the bed, moaning softly, her head hanging over the
bedside. For several seconds the two men—viewed singly in a series of
medium-close shots—stare at each other. Finally Edmond whispers, "Go
on . . . skedaddle." Pierre flees, and Edmond walks toward the bed, lifts
Renée's head onto the mattress, and gazes at her. As in corresponding
scenes in *Jenny*, *Drôle de Drame*, and *Le Quai des Brumes*, a third party
has disturbed a couple's intimacy. In this case, however, the interloper
turns into an accomplice. By becoming Renée's suitor and then seeking
out his own death, Edmond fulfills the scenario intended for Pierre. Temporarily internalizing Pierre's being, he exempts the youth from death
and allows the lovers to resume their affair at the film's end. Unexpectedly, Jouvet's Edmond is the first benevolent father figure in the Carné
canon.

Abandoning a whore for an ingénue, Edmond acts out what might
have been an unconscious wish of the son Carné concerning his father:
to have him cease frequenting Montmartre bordellos and remain loyal
to his prematurely dead wife. The making of *Hôtel du Nord* might have
enabled Carné to "resurrect" and refashion the evil father figure killed
in *Le Quai des Brumes* (Zabel). A real-life corollary apparently took
place during the film's shooting. Carné relates that Jouvet, who had been
aloof and condescending toward him on the set of *Drôle de Drame*, now
became "much more cooperative and even cordial . . . Was it the success

35   A primal scene variant: Edmond (Louis Jouvet)
     interrupting the mutual suicide attempt of Pierre (Jean-
     Pierre Aumont) and Renée (Annabella)

of *Le Quai des Brumes* that made him think more highly of me? Perhaps
it was Jeanson's presence, since it is common knowledge that Jouvet did
not appreciate Prévert. I don't know. But his change in attitude was undeniable" (*Vbd*, 130).

Ever conscious of his singularity and supremely self-aware at the moment of his death, Edmond is the quintessential Carné hero. All other
significant characters in *Hôtel du Nord*—Manolo, Michèle, Adrien, Renée, Pierre, Raymonde, and Prosper—partake of Edmond's existential
outsiderdom. Although Carné would have them inhabit an idealized in-
sular space (the hotel) under the aegis of an idealized maternal presence
(Madame Lecouvreur), his characters remain marginal and—with the
possible exception of Adrien—unfulfilled. In this respect *Hôtel du Nord*

is emblematic of Carné's own existential dilemma: the closer the artist comes to attaining his ideal of cinematic perfection, the more the man must acknowledge himself as being divorced from the rest of the world.

Hôtel du Nord is probably the most successful example of 1930s French populist filmmaking. The movie was judged by the contemporary press to be less accomplished than *Le Quai des Brumes*, but its public appeal was enormous. To this day *Hôtel du Nord* is the Carné film which Frenchmen of a certain age look back upon with most affection. The picture's stars, familiar setting, and touching story do not alone account for its wide, receptive audience. Although most moviegoers in the late 1930s did not intellectualize their response, many consciously viewed Carné's films as more than entertainment. They were sensitive to the craftsmanship of Carné's framing and camera movements, the subtlety of his lighting effects, the dexterity of his slow wipes and dissolves, his talent for visual symmetry and rhyme, and the dreamy quality of his realism. Exhibiting a pictorial finish which the working and middle classes could appreciate as evidence of solid achievement, Carné's films allowed even the uneducated to enjoy the special pleasures of "serious" moviemaking.

Today we generously call Carné's style classical; more severely, we dub it academic. In light of the French New Wave and postmodernist film-making, it is impossible to ignore the extent to which the rhetorical and ideological premises of the painterly aestheticism that appealed so thoroughly to the 1930s public hold the potential for locking out from the cinematic experience all traces of real-world vitality. Such is not the case with *Hôtel du Nord*, thanks in large part to Jeanson's having expanded the vigorous, unpredictable relationship of the characters played by Arletty and Jouvet. But if the whore and pimp save the film from ossification, they also prevent it from attaining the exquisite homogeneity of tone and purpose found in *Le Quai des Brumes* and *Le Jour se lève*. The quality of Carné's films always depends upon the temperament of his collaborators and the nature of their working relationship. *Hôtel du Nord* stands out from other early Carné works not simply because it was made without Prévert, but because Prévert's duties were divided between two individuals. The complex but direct relationship between Carné and Prévert gave way to a triangular arrangement in which Carné and Aurenche's original conception was superseded by the work of Jeanson and Aurenche, which was then reinterpreted by Carné. The result is a film whose parts do not coalesce into an integrated whole. For all its "arti-ness," *Hôtel du Nord*—even when assessed by traditionalist standards—seems a work of art *manqué*.

To assert that Carné needed Prévert to achieve unity of tone and seri-ousness of purpose is inexact. *Juliette ou la clef des songes* (1951, scripted by Jacques Viot and Georges Neveux) and *Terrain vague* (1960, written by Henri-François Rey) exhibit as much stylistic consistency and motivated intent as *Le Quai des Brumes*. Yet Prévert's absence accounts for a real loss in *Hôtel du Nord*. Near the film's midpoint, Raymonde packs her suitcase for the trip Edmond has promised to take her on. In the presence of the chambermaid (initially out of view), Raymonde sings the praises of her man:

RAYMONDE: And how he is organized! Traveling with him is a
   dream . . . Once you get him in a railroad station, he's another person entirely . . . He takes care of every little thing . . . He buys you
   oranges and peels them for you. He lights a cigarette and then offers
   it to you . . . Oh is he refined . . . And he explains the countryside on
   the way . . . And the closer you get to the sea, the more tender he
   becomes. Oh, he knows how to travel! With him, you might be in
   third class, but you feel like you're in first . . .

JEANNE: Have you traveled together often?

RAYMONDE: (*pause*) This will be the first time . . .

The motifs (oranges, cigarettes, the sea), the theme (an idyllic escape), and the tone of this passage (self-delusion) are quintessential Prévert. But in Prévert, love's illusions never go unshared. The transcendent power of Prévertian love lies in the creation, however short-lived, of dreams jointly held. In *Hôtel du Nord*, all romantic daydreams are as solitary and un-convincing as Raymonde's. Jeanson once penned, "From the day God placed man in the presence of woman, paradise turned into hell." [18] With Jeanson's cynicism reinforcing Carné's pessimism, *Hôtel du Nord* lacks those precarious but genuine moments of transcendence found in the Carné-Prévert works: the attic episodes with Billy and Eva in *Drôle de Drame*; Jean and Nelly at the fairground in *Le Quai des Brumes*; Fran-çois and Françoise in *Le Jour se lève*'s greenhouse; Baptiste and Garance overlooking Ménilmontant in *Les Enfants du paradis*.

Over the years Carné has disliked Jeanson intensely. He deplores the self-centeredness that made their partnership so quarrelsome. He regrets his own inability to have held in check Jeanson's penchant for spicy *mots d'auteur* when, Carné believes, Jeanson should have been working to animate Annabella's role and not "bury her . . . under hollow and flat verbiage" (*Vbd*, 125). Carné also resents Jeanson's attempt to take credit away from Jean-Louis Barrault for having proposed the subject of *Les Enfants du paradis*. In the preface to Jeanson's posthumous autobiography, Pierre Serval quotes Jeanson: "I was in prison; obviously I couldn't work in movies. But it seems to me—and I'm sure that Jacques Prévert never found out about it—that I gave the idea for *Les Enfants du paradis* to Carné, that I furnished him with materials on the subject, and that he, without any hope of seeing me freed, preferred to work with someone else." [19] Jeanson's assertion is surely false: Maurice Bessy documents the writer's "taste for glorious lies." [20] But the statement reveals the hostility Jeanson felt toward Carné and Prévert, who, less outspoken than himself, managed to work throughout the Occupation.

Indeed, one further reason for Carné's antipathy toward Jeanson is political. Like Carné, Jeanson was a pacifist. In late 1939 he was placed in La Santé Prison by the Daladier regime for an antimilitarist article written before the declaration of war and published in the journal *Solidarité Internationale Antifasciste*. The official charge was formulated as Jeanson's "having cast aspersions on the integrity of the Empire and having attempted to withdraw from this Empire's authority a part of its territory." [21] The territory in question was nothing less than Jeanson himself: refusing to contemplate conscription, he had written: "My body is my own. Private property. Beware. Vicious dog." [22] (Following the Occupation, Arletty would make a similar declaration, designating a specific part of her anatomy.) Jeanson lost his case and was sentenced to five years in prison. Yet his trial was as much a personal triumph as a political defeat. In fervent support came character references from the likes of François Mauriac, Joseph Kessel, and Tristan Bernard, and public testimony from Marcel Achard, Louis Jouvet, and Antoine de Saint-Exupéry—who went AWOL for the sake of his friend. Also seated in the courtroom were friends Alexander Trauner and Pierre Prévert.

When Carné was reprimanded after the war for not having sufficiently resisted the enemy, none of his colleagues in the film or literary world spoke publicly on his behalf. Carné never recovered from that sting.

CHAPTER 8

Strange Defeat

Le Jour se lève, even more than *Le Quai des Brumes,* is the offspring of national crisis, turmoil, and frustration. The film was conceived shortly before Hitler's troops marched into Bohemia-Moravia and was released less than three months prior to the Franco-British declaration of war. The very name of its protagonist, François, imparts an allegorical dimension to the picture, and François's moving plight may well be read as an expression of the state of hopelessness to which the French were succumbing in 1939. As epitomized by its ironic title—in English, *Daybreak* or *A New Dawn Arises*—Carné's fifth feature is in many ways the story of an era's tragic end.

The film's inspiration came from a Montmartre art dealer named Jacques Viot who had an apartment across the hall from Carné's on the rue Caulaincourt. One day Viot presented his neighbor with a three-page synopsis entitled "Le Jour se lève." Carné was stirred by its flashback premise: "I fell in love with it. Not with the plot, which was almost nonexistent . . . but with its manner of construction" (*Vbd,* 140–41). He and Prévert were under contract to do a gangster picture tentatively entitled *Rue des Vertus.* It was slated to star Gabin, with Arletty and Jules Berry in supporting roles. Convinced that *Le Jour se lève* would be more rewarding, Carné persuaded producer Pierre Frogerais to abandon that project. In the following weeks Viot and Prévert moved to the Aigle Noir, a hotel in Fontainebleau, and worked nonstop on the screenplay. Although the screen credits attribute the scenario to Viot and the dialogue to Prévert, Prévert was responsible in large part for both.

Le Jour se lève transforms a cliché gangster-film situation into a complex dramatic structure. A man has just committed murder, barricades himself in his top-floor apartment, and is besieged by the police during an entire night. Three subjective flashbacks constitute the bulk of the movie. They recount major episodes in the life of foundry worker François (Gabin), who falls in love with a demure young girl, Françoise (Jacqueline Laurent), has an affair with a worldly showgirl, Clara (Arletty), and in a fit of rage murders a sinister showman, Valentin (Jules Berry), who has been intimate with both Clara and Françoise. Each flashback is framed by events occurring in the present: the murder and the arrival of the police; the police fusillade; François's harangue to a crowd gathered below in the square; and his suicide one fraction of a second before a gas brigade assaults him. Each is signaled by an elongated dissolve.

Le Jour se lève is a landmark in the history of film narration. François's three flashbacks are first-person narratives that lay bare the workings of a mind bent on suicide. In the words of Jacques Brunius, "Never had the cinema accomplished its destiny so thoroughly: to become a faithful mirror of mental representation, to become the instrument, par excellence, for the objectification of memory." [1]

The dissolves punctuating each flashback's start and end are accompanied by two brief musical themes—a mournful tune played by piccolo and oboe, and a heavy rhythmic motif thumped by bass drum and other percussion instruments. Composed by Jaubert, this obsessive music works to convey the rattle of François's inner voice during the film's passages from objective to subjective reality. *Le Jour se lève* was Jaubert's last picture before his death in the war. It exemplifies a conviction, arrived at late in his career, that film music was meant not to paraphrase action, but to add to it: "The essence of music is . . . rhythm organized temporally. In making it the slave of [dramatic] events or gestures which, by their nature, do not correspond to a defined rhythm but rather to physiological or psychological reactions . . . music is reduced to mere sound." [2]

Carné demonstrated that psychology in film could be structured according to the temporal rhythms which Jaubert saw as belonging more properly to music—hence the austerity of *Le Jour se lève*'s music track. Unlike the melodies Jaubert wrote for Vigo's *L'Atalante*, Duvivier's *Carnet de bal,* and to a lesser extent *Drôle de Drame* and *Le Quai des Brumes*, the score of *Le Jour se lève* resists casual listening by itself. The main body of each flashback (with the exception of the hypersentimental greenhouse sequence in the second flashback) is devoid of offscreen music. Given Carné's success at representing mental processes through visual images, the composer understood that music in these parts of the film would be redundant. If Jaubert's harmonic "language" is guided by a renovated "syntax," [3] the Jaubert-Carné collaboration made silence an essential component of the language of sound film. Indeed, Jaubert's quest to have music "convey the internal rhythm of visual imagery" [4] made him as much a poetic realist as was the director.

Antonioni has compared *Le Jour se lève* to Debussy's Impressionist opera, *Pelléas et Mélisande*.[5] The comparison merits elaboration. It can be posited that Carné is to Golden Age French cinema what the composer of *La Mer* and *Images* is to turn-of-the-century French music: a master of mood. Both men sought to bring greater subtlety and economy of means to their own art forms. Debussy wanted dramatic music not to be "bound to a more or less exact reproduction of nature, but allude . . . to the mysterious correspondences between nature and imagination"[6]— an agenda consonant with Carné's cinematic project. More specifically, *Le Jour se lève* and *Pelléas et Mélisande* present symbolic, dreamlike worlds peopled with ghostly characters and ruled by an irrational fate. In both, action seems pointless, even as the illusion of pointlessness unfolds "within a secretly purposeful dramatic frame."[7] In effect, the musical interludes in Debussy that flow in and out to modulate the delicate mood changes from one scene to the next find their equivalent in the meticulous wipes that connect episodes within each of Carné's flashbacks and the aural-visual dissolves that mark changes between flashbacks and the present. Above all, richness of meaning in both the opera and the film results from the repeated appearance of common objects that generate significance beyond the literal. The poetic prose of dramatist Maurice Maeterlinck, from whose play *Pelléas et Mélisande* is adapted, is as densely imagistic as Prévert's screen dialogue. Yet it, too, remains close in feel to everyday usage.

The figural dimension of quotidian objects in Prévert's poetry and scripts has long been recognized.[8] Although *Le Jour se lève* is a film that is principally about thoughts, nowhere else in the Carné oeuvre is the poetic potential of things more integral to the film. In earlier Carné works, parcels of the material world enjoyed analogical relations with characters' states of being: the locomotive smoke with Jenny's malaise; the mimosa with Molyneux's desire for solace; the muddy shoreline with Jean and Nelly's despair; the iron bridges with Pierre and Renée's sense of entrapment. The success of such half-articulated, half-veiled associations depended in large part on the viewer's sensitivity. In *Le Jour se lève*, correspondences between psyche and matter remain subtle. But because virtually every object in François's room acquires additional meaning from its reappearance in flashbacks, such connections become the movie's very stuff.

Perhaps the most arresting of the film's symbols is the narrow six-story apartment house that towers starkly above the surrounding buildings in what is purportedly a working-class district in Amiens (fig. 36). As the picture progresses, this building becomes an objectification of François's condition: isolated, run-down, and perched precariously beyond the

36 The apartment building in *Le Jour se lève:*
an objectification of the hero's condition

grasp of law and society. The steep high-angle views of the interior stair-case—a maze of banisters and railings—seem to function as an objective correlative for François's bewilderment and the inescapable character of the events he has endured.

To heighten the visual impression of enclosure, Carné required that the set for François's room be constructed from four interlocking and im-movable panels. This meant that Gabin could be filmed pacing from the door to the window opposite, and from the bed (on the left wall) to the chest of drawers (on the right), all within one shot. This is an extreme example of Carné's need—first expressed in the slide shows he ran as a boy in his father's locked bedroom—to create environments in which he can virtually hold captive those participating in his creative endeavors. In the early stages of filming, the fixed décor required the crew to be on the move constantly in order to remain out of camera range. Production became still more trying after the police fusillade. Carné shot this episode only once and with real bullets: "To film the door lock being fired at, my camera was placed about one meter from it, inside the room with the police shooting from outside. Only a few bags of sand piled sixty or seventy centimeters high separated us from the bullets . . . The sound of the fusillade was so strong that one of my assistants lost his hearing for a week" (*Vbd*, 149). Carné insisted that the damaged door and half-shattered windowpanes not be tampered with. For the remainder of the production Gabin and crew had to enter and leave the set via a maze of ladders and catwalks.

Although most of the company found this inconvenience amusing, Gabin was less than enchanted. "Just let me know when your half-assed schemes are over," he reportedly grumbled to Carné (*Vbd*, 150). Of course, what Gabin perceived as madness was method for Carné. But even the punctilious director did not foresee one consequence of the real-bullet fusillade: "With the take completed, I turned toward the interior of the room. I noticed that the spray of bullets had left their impact on the opposite wall. Not only had the wallpaper been torn around each point of contact, but the very path of the bullets left its mark in the plaster. The effect was so strikingly lifelike that I jumped for joy. This was one of those happy occurrences that on rare occasions take place during production. I was all the more delighted because I hadn't thought of this very important detail when I wrote the shooting script" (*Vbd*, 149). These remarks are stunning testimony to Carné's fundamental resistance to the unpredictable.

"The aesthetic motion in a closed film can be described," writes Braudy, "as a burrowing inward, an exploration of inner space, an effort to get as far as possible into the invisible heart of things, where all connections are clear."[9] Carné "burrows inward" through lingering close shots and restrained camera movements; distance shots and sweeping camera movements, lateral or vertical, are always the exception. Nowhere is his restraint more evident than in *Le Jour se lève*. In this regard, the film's final sequence is its most representative. Thirteen shots before the end, the lieutenant of the gas brigade emerges from a skylight. As he and his assistant crawl along the roof toward the window of François's room, the camera slowly pans with them in low-angle medium shot. The creeping pace underscores the deliberateness with which destiny moves in upon its victim.[10] After the camera moves past the two men and then down and across to François's window, it holds for a second but does not move into the room; rather, Carné cuts to a medium close-up of François sitting on his bed and looking at the gun, out of view. Carné's cut has double significance. It heightens the viewer's sense of François's isolation—an effect which fluid camera motion would weaken. It also bestows a measure of dignity upon François: at his moment of greatest humiliation, the outside world is denied an opportunity to gape.

The alternation of two close-ups of the gun on the mantelpiece with three medium close-ups of François on the bed intensifies suspense. In the third medium close-up, François rises and the camera pans with him as he walks slowly toward the mantelpiece and looks down at the gun, out of view. Françoise's voice then speaks in a voice-over: "You remember what you said? . . . At Easter we'll pick lilac." The original screenplay called for this voice-over to be followed by a subjective superimposition showing François and Françoise cycling together with bunches of lilac on the handlebars of their bicycles. Carné judiciously removed the superimposition from the final version. To have retained it would have upset the film's perfect equilibrium of past and present. It would also have damaged a mood of absolute solemnity. The film is "burrowing inward" toward François's emotional void. The slightest trace of sentimentality would detract from this intent.

Nonetheless, Carné's final camera movement is not inward but backward. As François places the gun's barrel to his chest, the camera tracks in to a close-up of François's face, which the shooting script specifies as "beaten and hopeless." Carné does not portray the moment of death graphically. Rather, he cuts to a medium shot of the lieutenant sitting on top of the window with his gas grenade primed: reacting defensively to the single gunshot inside the room, the lieutenant immediately hurls his grenade. The film's final shot returns attention to François, and its mise en scène is one of Carné's most remarkable (fig. 37). A medium view of the room discloses François's body lying face down on the ground with the window in the background. Behind him rise plumes of gas. Surrounding him clockwise are many of the objects that acquired metaphysical weight as the film progressed: François's bed, his cigarette pack, bicycle tires, a teddy bear, pieces of shattered mirror, the overturned wooden chair—everyday objects now emptied of privileged meaning because the sole person for whom they bore significance is dead. On a table in the foreground is the alarm clock that François had set to go off at dawn. At the very moment that the clock rings, Carné's camera slowly tracks backward, revealing more of the room, and holds on it in medium shot as the first rays of dawn break through the window. This perfect conjunction of the sun and clock is an ironic one, for both nature and technology are imperiously indifferent to François's defeat. The Wagner-like strains that follow the alarm are likewise ironic: beginning with woodwind trills,

37 A primal image of France's imminent disaster: the final moment
in *Le Jour se lève*

then joined by brass, they rise to a grandiose crescendo that ought
to suggest cosmic fullness. Here, they denote the twilight of human
hope.

The slow backward tracking of Carné's camera renders defeat definitive. It insinuates retreat and withdrawal. Although more of François's
room is disclosed, so are its limits. Rather than have us embrace a reality
that might lie beyond the window, Carné forces us to accept the ironic
value of the sunrise and become as enshrouded in the obscurity resulting
from the gas bomb as is François. Carné's backward tracking is, I suggest, a symbolic anticipation of France's acceptance of defeat in World
War II.

It was perhaps inevitable that Carné and Prévert would be the sole commercial filmmakers of the 1930s to depict successfully the plight of an
ordinary French factoryworker. Feyder's sympathies lay elsewhere. Clair
was the anarchistic son of an *haut* bourgeois, and his fanciful satire of
big business in *A Nous la liberté* (1931) is compromised by a utopian
ending in which factory automation becomes the working class's pana-
cea. Duvivier was too motivated by profit to respond sincerely to the

proletarian cause. His *La Belle Equipe* (1936) depicts the attempt of five unemployed workers to establish a cooperative enterprise. Yet Duvivier and scenarist Charles Spaak contrived two endings: a tragic version for upper-class theaters, in which the cooperative fails, and a happy version for working-class neighborhoods, in which the unemployed become lighthearted proprietors. Renoir's allegiance to the Popular Front was more authentic; he had expressed its aspirations in *Le Crime de Monsieur Lange, La Vie est à nous,* and *La Marseillaise* (1938). But Renoir's personal background and experience inclined him toward portraying interactions among individuals of different social classes. Despite the considerable fame and income they had acquired by the late 1930s, Carné and Prévert's political ties remained with *le peuple.* Unlike Clair and Duvivier, they were committed in earnest to working-class ideals. Unlike Renoir, they were disposed to view issues in terms of clear-cut heroes and villains.

Carné and Prévert were social melodramatists. Their representations of society are imbued with appeals to presumed values of good and evil. Peter Brooks describes literary social melodramatists—Balzac, Dickens, Dostoevsky, James—in terms applicable to prewar Carné and Prévert: "On the one hand, they refuse any metaphysical reduction of experience and refuse to reduce their metaphorical enterprise to the cold symbolism of allegory . . . On the other hand, they insist that life does make reference to a moral occult that is the realm of eventual value . . . The melodramatists refuse to allow that the world has been completely drained of transcendence; and they locate that transcendence in the struggle of the children of light with the children of darkness."[11] In 1939 the children of light were without hope. Neither Clair's whimsy nor Renoir's relativism was appropriate for treating such a subject. It required the blend of nostalgic idealism, unshakable pessimism, and thorough empathy that was unique to Carné and Prévert.

The actor who best embodied the vain struggle against dark forces was Jean Gabin. *Le Jour se lève* provided Gabin with what is probably his greatest screen role. It also brought to culmination his persona as the common working man whose innate dignity is destroyed by social forces beyond his control. Gabin had portrayed workers in *La Belle Equipe, La Bête humaine,* and *La Grande Illusion,* but these roles had an aura of glamour about them. In *Le Jour se lève,* Gabin's factoryworker is shorn of romantic allure. The medium tracking shots that first present him and his co-workmen operating sandblasting machines suggest the exotic: helmeted, wrapped in protective suits and footgear, hooked up to hoses and tubes, these men evoke images of today's spacewalking astronauts. But the élan vital is deceptive. The laborers' identical uniforms, the deafening noise of their equipment, and the sand spray that assails them—all establish the factory as a site of dehumanization.

The primary fruit of François's labors is lung congestion. His inability to conceive of better conditions is one mark of his personal defeat. His co-workers are no more militant or politically enlightened than he. Their disorientation and impotence are emblematic of the fate of the Popular Front. The shout of one comrade from among the crowd—"François! Come down! There's still hope"—rings hollow even for François. From his window François beats his chest, tears at his hair, and delivers a eulogy as much for an era and a class as for himself: "François . . . Who's that? . . . Don't know him . . . never heard of him! It's over, there isn't a François anymore . . . There isn't anything anymore." If the habitual destiny of Gabin's characters was, in Bazin's words, "to be deceived by life,"[12] Gabin here exhibits an awareness so disabused as virtually to guarantee imminent defeat.

Shortly before Prévert and Viot began to write their screenplay, French trade unions suffered a monumental blow. In mid-November 1938 the conservative finance minister Paul Reynaud sought to revive the economy by lifting price controls, reducing overtime pay allowances, and curbing public services. Within weeks the CGT (France's confederation of trade unions) condemned the Reynaud Acts and announced a general strike. Their motive was to serve notice to big business and government that French workers would not endure repression. President Daladier, egged on by Reynaud and the right wing of his party, refused to negotiate. On the day of the strike, Daladier seized control of the public utilities, ordered a military occupation of all major warehouses, and—for the first time in French history—authorized the police to use tear-gas bombs. These measures were so effective that business appeared to proceed as usual. For the unions the episode was disastrous: "With the support of public authority, the heads of business had won their Battle of the Marne: the Popular Front had truly been laid to rest."[13]

There are no representatives of the comfortable classes in *Le Jour se lève*. The film's subject, at least allegorically, is the downfall of the proletariat. But the enemy is conspicuously absent. Although the film's opening credits unfold on a distance shot of the factory at dawn, François is seen at work only for several minutes at the start of the first flashback. These absences and ellipses are telling. François defines his existence by his work, yet his work is so alienating that it occupies almost no place in his subjective life; or if it does, he represses it. Further, communication between employer and employee is nonexistent. The great French historian Marc Bloch analyzed the temper of the prewar bourgeoisie in his account of France's fall, *Strange Defeat*. Many of his remarks elucidate that class's absence from *Le Jour se lève*: "The *bourgeoisie* lived completely separated from the people. Its members made no attempt to reach that understanding which might have led to sympathy. Turn and turn about, either they refused to take the masses seriously, or they trembled before their implied threat. What they did not realize was that, by so doing, they were separating themselves effectively from France." Bloch recognizes that the Popular Front collapsed in large part because of the failings of its leaders and the follies of its supporters. But he indicts "the stupid mulishness" that characterized the greater part of middle-class opinion: "Whatever the faults of which the [Popular Front] movement may have been guilty, there was in that striving of the masses to make a juster world a touching eagerness and sincerity which ought not to have been without effect on any man animated by ordinary human feelings." [14] The gaping void of human feeling in France, suggests Bloch, facilitated the nation's fall.

François confronts two heartless forces in *Le Jour se lève*: the police (in the present) and Valentin (in the past). Viewed ideologically, the two have much in common. In the first edition of *La Vie à belles dents*, Carné makes some revealing comments about the scene in which riot police emerge from a truck and violently shove a crowd of sympathetic onlookers. Referring to this platoon as *gardes mobiles*—state security police—Carné writes: "When I attended public screenings of the film, this particular passage never failed to elicit some sneers. At first astonished by such a reaction, I finally came to understand it. To my mind, the action was supposed to take place in a small provincial town, which I wanted to keep anonymous. But the filmgoers, deceived by I know not what, imagined that it took place in a suburb. In truth, a suburban district would never have had the state security police called in for a matter of this sort; they would simply have appealed to the local police [*la gendarmerie de l'endroit*]. Hence the viewers' confusion—for which I alone must take responsibility. I ought to have sorted this matter out better" (*Vbd*, first edition, 147).

Carné eliminated this anecdote from the second edition of his memoirs. In "sorting out" his own comments, he possibly realized that viewers were not reacting to his oversight but rather were responding viscerally to the depiction of police brutality. It is likely that the film's tear-gas incident evoked associations with France's rightward-moving government. Moreover, the rifle-bearing troops to which Carné refers are decidedly Teutonic in allure. Wearing iron helmets, dark knee-length over-

38 Jules Berry as Valentin in *Le Jour se lève:* a demagogue seduces
the masses

coats, and high black leather boots, they constitute a sinister visual
counterpoint to François's protective factory outfit.

A scene cut from most prints now in circulation accentuates the implication that the police are Fascist henchmen. Berating an officer for
bungling this affair, an inspector remarks: "Have him shot at from the
rooftops, in front of everybody, it's ludicrous! You heard the crowd yourself . . . 'bloodthirsty brutes' . . . Oh, it's a big success . . . And him up
there, he's no longer an assassin, he's a hero . . . a hero! . . . That's the
word. He's acting the hero, alone against the world, saving his last bullet,
the chevalier Bayard . . . the Siege of Beauvais . . . the War of Vendée . . .
A hero." With these lines removed, the viewer's inclination to romanti-
cize François is held in check and the movie refrains from becoming a
film à thèse. But Carné and Prévert's ideological intent is clear: François
is an allegorical figure of France, and the police are emblematic of the
German threat to France.

Jules Berry's Valentin personifies the threat from within (fig. 38). Berry
(1888–1951) was primarily a stage actor, but he played in nearly ninety
films between 1931 and his death. His most memorable screen work was
scripted by Prévert: *Le Crime de Monsieur Lange*, *Le Jour se lève*, and
Les Visiteurs du soir. In all three films Berry plays deceptively charming
manipulators. Projecting neurosis and villainy, he shows a genius for
character construction through rapid-fire delivery of text, nervous gestic-

ulation, and studied inflections of an eyebrow, lip, or word. Berry is an ideal foil for actors as low-key and sympathetic as René Lefèvre, Jean Gabin, and Alain Cuny.

The political dimension of Berry's character in *Le Crime de Monsieur Lange* is overt: a despised publishing-house owner, Batala is the repressive capitalist par excellence. The politics of Valentin, a second-rate vaudevillian, are less obvious. Defined by profession, Valentin is a social marginal whose precise economic profile is undeterminable. Yet Valentin embodies traits that distinguish him clearly from the working classes. His trained-dog routine depends less on manual labor than on disguising it through sleight of hand. His stage attire—top hat, silk-lined cloak, white gloves—goes so far as to suggest the aristocrat; and his flashy street dress—fur-collared overcoat, ample polka-dot tie, wide-brimmed hat tilted over his right eye—evokes American film gangsters. A master of language, Valentin twists words to manipulate people. Clara (Arletty) remarks: "And it's fantastic how he can talk, that man ... All that smooth talk, you'd almost think he pulled it out of his sleeve, like a conjurer. He can tell you all sorts of tales, and you fall for them." Valentin appears not so much a bourgeois per se as a demagogue who flaunts magnified bourgeois values in himself in order to seduce the masses. Holding the proletariat in disregard, Valentin points to François's job as reason for separating him from Françoise: "Think for a minute ... you have no position ... no future ... (*He hesitates*) ... and no health."

In vying with François for possession of Françoise, Valentin acts out a power play that French society was actually experiencing: the bourgeoisie's attempt to restrain the encroachment on their property by the proletariat. "The workers," writes Bloch, "were setting their faces stubbornly against all attempts to reduce wages, with the result that after each recurrent crisis, profits and dividends alike grew smaller ... The aggressive mood of the new-comers to the social scene was already threatening the economics and political power of a group which had long been accustomed to command ... The country was splitting into two opposed groups."[15] Grossly labeled, these two groups were the pro-Fascists and the anti-Fascists. Berry's Devil in *Les Visiteurs du soir* (1942) has often been viewed as a figurative depiction of Hitler. Although less blatant, his Valentin already evokes the Nazi mentality:

CLARA: He trains a dog in three days. Do you want to know how? Well, he shaves off the hairs at the joint of the paw, and burns the skin with a red hot iron ... to make the dog work in front of the audience, he touches the wound—gently—with a little wand.

FRANÇOIS: Shut up . . . how disgusting. Don't talk about that man . . . he's revolting! He's mad.

In granting Valentin the traits and accouterments of a pro-Fascist fanatic without explicitly identifying him as such, Carné and Prévert expose the inauthenticity of France's Fascist movement. One of the film's most pointed moments occurs at the end of François's confrontation with Valentin in the café of Clara's hotel. Valentin has just claimed to be Françoise's father. Losing his temper, François grabs the liar by the collar and lifts him up. Valentin remains speechless as François shouts: "Get out! Get the hell out of here!" It is actually François who leaves the frame, suggesting the futility of his effort. But as the camera holds on Valentin, in medium close-up, the blusterer is caught unawares: in a state of utter terror, he raises his right hand to his face, gnaws at his fingers, and stares ahead with the panic-stricken look of one of his abused dogs. In demystifying the mystifier for these few seconds, Carné, Prévert, and Berry lay bare the sterility and impotence at the core of French Fascism.

The film's women resist the lure of illusion better than its men. Françoise is bedazzled by Valentin's charms. Yet once she declares love for François, she expresses a willingness to cease seeing the older man. It is François who cannot accommodate to life's realities. The lovers' initial encounter has been the object of considerable critical attention. As François sandblasts, he senses the gaze of someone behind him (as did Nelly in her first meeting with Jean in *Le Quai des Brumes*). François turns round and, staring through his visor, looks upon a young brunette carrying a huge potted plant (fig. 39). She is a flower-shop assistant who has lost her way while making a delivery. The two converse and discover that they were both raised in public orphanages and that they are both today celebrating their saint's day. Allen Thiher underscores the degree to which Françoise functions here as a rhetorical figure, "the *femme-fleur*, the woman flower who is the representative of the surrealist love ideal, the object that can bring about the abolition of the distinction between the objective world of reality and the subjective world of desire." [16] By the time this encounter ends, a high-angle close-up reveals that the blossoms of the plant have wilted. The omen is not favorable. But the flowers portend disaster only if they are perceived metaphorically. Raymond Durgnat's analysis is suggestive. For Durgnat, Françoise "is not *reduced* to a bunch of flowers. Their presence *enriches* her, but in no way limits her, as, in itself, a 'like' clause might do. She 'is' as fresh as the flowers, but she is herself too, with all her dramatic possibilities." [17] Indeed, it seems to me that François's personal tragedy results from an inability to separate the woman Françoise from the connotations of purity and in-

39 Carné directing Jacqueline Laurent as Françoise on the foundry set of *Le Jour se lève*

nocence that his first gaze upon her with the flowers imprints on his psyche. He is unable to conceive that Françoise might still be a source of moral and spiritual redemption even if she has been physically involved with Valentin—a fact never firmly established.

François is equally blinded to the affecting humanity of Arletty's Clara. From the moment she lets Valentin's top hat fall and walks off the stage during their act, Clara claims her right to freedom, both economic and physical. She confides to François: "I've had a bellyful of men who are always talking about love. It's true . . . They talk so much about love, they forget to make it." While the laconic, virile worker satisfies Clara's physical needs along with his own, his obsession with female virginity prevents François from viewing Clara as a serious partner in life and love. When he ends their liaison, Clara accepts the disappointment with decorum. When she reveals that Valentin gives an identical brooch "to every woman who sleeps with him" (both Clara and Françoise possess one), the script specifies "a look of triumph in her eyes." But Clara's triumph is less an act of spite than an attempt to demystify François. By the movie's end, it is clear that Clara is the strongest and most generous of the film's characters. When Françoise becomes delirious over François's plight, Clara cares for her rival with compassion: "Don't excite yourself like this . . . Try to sleep." She then turns her head away from Françoise, and with the camera holding on her in close-up, Clara weeps.

In divesting herself of the tutu and black-sequined bodice she sports in Valentin's act, Clara divorces herself from the values they connote: tawdry spectacle and manipulation of the masses. The modest, undistinguished clothing she wears in the remainder of the film situates her more closely in the working class. Yet Arletty characters resist pigeonholing. A scene cut from all prints during the Occupation shows Clara entirely naked (figs. 40 and 41). François, who has just arrived to spend Sunday with her, finds her showering. Seen in full shot, Clara smiles radiantly while applying a cloth to her crotch with one hand and washing her extended right leg with a large spherical sponge held in her other hand. The inclusion of such a shot in a nonpornographic film in 1939 was daring—even in France. Arletty recalls: "At the time it was considered bold. But it was really quite natural. A man is in love with an eighteen-year-old girl. He sees me, a much older woman, in the shower, and thinks, 'Hey, this lady's not too bad.'"[18] Carné remembers that Arletty agreed to do the scene on two conditions—that only a skeleton crew be present and that all still photographers be banned from the set: "And yet, somehow, a photograph was secretly taken, and one week later a magazine printed it. Arletty never mentioned the matter to me, but I was furious. To this day I don't know who did it, but I imagine it was someone positioned near the camera—an assistant cameraman perhaps."[19]

The publicity did not hurt Arletty's career. It rebutted the claim that she was neither young nor beautiful enough to play leading roles. Regrettably, the nude shot has not been restored to prints currently in circulation. In the expurgated version, only Clara's head appears as she holds the shower curtains together to hide the rest of her body. This excision lessens the force of François's rather learned perception: "You look lovely like that, you know. You look like Truth rising out of the well." François's simile (which anticipates Arletty's first pose in Les Enfants du paradis) becomes richer if Clara is seen extending the huge sponge along her leg. With its capacity to bend, absorb, and turn both soft and tough, the sponge epitomizes the "truth" of Clara's character. It contrasts with the ephemeral allure of innocence associated with the potted flower Françoise holds earlier in the film. Standing before Clara,

40 Two-page spread from a press
book for *Le Jour se lève*
featuring the shot of Arletty nude

41 The excised shot of Arletty nude
(detail from fig. 40)

42 Jean Gabin and Jacqueline Laurent in *Le Jour se lève*'s greenhouse
scene: a grandiose projection of François's obsession with female
purity

François ignores the symbolic for the literal (Clara's body). Before François, he so fixates on the symbolic that he loses contact with the real (Françoise's capacity and her right to have relations with others).

The famous greenhouse scene—in which François and Françoise wander among teeming banks of lush flowers—is a grandiose magnification of the *femme-fleur* image that dominates François's subjective life (fig. 42). Languishing strings and woodwinds emphasize the unreality of this paradisiacal vision. The floating pan shots, painterly compositions, and stylized angle shots likewise signal François's immersion in illusion. Carné's admirers note the paradox that "this man who in real life is intimidated by women has succeeded in bringing to the screen many of its most beautiful love scenes."[20] His detractors assert that "there is, in this great director, an incapacity to express cinematically the lyricism of Prévert's love scenes."[21] Assessing the greenhouse episode, Gérard Guillot finds Carné's direction "as cold as the panes of glass on the greenhouse": "Why does he have a long series of close-ups, as if the two lovers were separated, as if they were listening to their partner without seeing and feeling the other's presence, without being stirred by the warmth of the other's body?"[22] Guillot is not entirely fair; the scene includes several tight two-shots, and when Gabin fondles Jacqueline Laurent's breasts, an erotic dimension is undeniably present. Yet Carné's directorial fussiness does detract from the scene's sensuality. It cools and distances. But even if the scene does not correspond to Prévert's intentions (a questionable presumption), it succeeds on other grounds. For Carné's aim here is precisely to underscore the insubstantiality of François's vision of love and to accentuate the distance between romance and reality.

The final flashback depicts the last encounter between François and Valentin, climaxing in the murder. By eliminating a figure of bourgeois repression, François avenges the proletariat. In eradicating a rival for Françoise's affections, he ejects the serpent from his private Eden. The act is triggered when Valentin insinuates that his desire for Françoise was reciprocal: "Since she wanted me, if you see what I mean . . . the child and I . . . I would have been wrong to restrain myself . . . I love youth . . . Are you interested?" But why murder? Why murder by gunshot? Moments earlier, François reacted to Valentin's salacious comments by grabbing him at the throat, pushing him to the open window, and threatening to drop him from its ledge. Photographed in a severe high-angle medium shot that looks vertically down the side of the building from above the window, Valentin's body sways perilously in space. Although François could have let Valentin fall, he restrains himself—possibly from common decency. Nonetheless, this incident could have sufficed to affirm François's physical superiority over Valentin and to frighten the villain away. On the contrary, Valentin continues to provoke François, and the result is murder.

Why murder? For Carné, the answer has more to do with the motives of the victim than with those of the perpetrator: "I know that most people have not interpreted it this way, and I guess it isn't clear enough, but Valentin comes to François's room with the *intention* of being murdered. Of course he says he's coming to kill François. But just think about it. If he kills François, he'll go to prison and probably die there. But he already sees himself as finished. He's lost Clara; he's lost Françoise; life no longer holds interest for him. An alternative would be to kill himself. But how much more efficient to make François kill him, thereby ensuring that François, too (once he has been caught or killed by the police), will be separated from Françoise. Of course Valentin incites François by talking about his taste for adolescent girls. But it's all part of Valentin's elaborate death wish. When Gabin shoots and mutters, 'See where it's got you now,' Valentin replies, as he staggers out, 'And you?' These two last words are the key to the murder. Few people have been attuned to their importance, and I'm afraid it's due to a lapse on my part. Perhaps I should have insisted on a scene of Valentin buying the revolver, or maybe a close-up of his expression at the end to show that he's giving himself up to François quite willingly."[23]

Carné's interpretation brings to light yet another continuity between Berry's roles in *Le Crime de Monsieur Lange* and *Le Jour se lève*. In the Renoir film, Batala tells Lange flippantly, "You should kill me"; within minutes, the protagonist actually does. In *Le Jour se lève*, Valentin offers no verbal invitation to murder, but he renders the act easy for François. After their scuffle by the window, Valentin loses control and murmurs: "It's ridiculous . . . It made me dizzy. I always get dizzy. Clara was right . . . I'm getting old." Valentin then removes a pistol from his coat pocket, declares that he came to kill François but "made a mess of it," and flamboyantly hurls the revolver on the table between them. This act of surrender parallels Edmond's at the end of *Hôtel du Nord*. It is followed by a series of statements that bring to mind the sexual-identity problems of Lucien and Zabel in *Le Quai des Brumes*: "I'm all washed up . . . Clara's right . . . I'm a laughingstock . . . And yet . . . What a man I used to be! (*He sighs heavily.*) If you had only known me when I was young . . . Everyone loved me . . . Repulsive . . . me? . . . Repulsive? And yet, why not? That, too, has its advantages! . . . they don't love me . . . but they want me . . . (*His face lighting up*) . . . And that's everything: to be wanted!" As Carné's comments intimate, Valentin's relinquishing his pistol to François is tantamount to an acknowledgment of his emasculation.

Acknowledgment and evasion, insight and illusion, are the fundamental tensions of the Carné universe. It is not insignificant that the first of *Le Jour se lève*'s characters to perceive that an incident has occurred is an anonymous blind man (fig. 43). Climbing the staircase and hearing a body tumble to the top floor landing, the blind man shouts: "What happened? Did someone fall?" We, the spectators, observe a wounded man stagger and fall dead. We also hear the gunshot that presumably caused the victim's death. But like the blind man, we remain unaware of the meaning and motivation of the crime for almost all of the film. The blind accordionist seen at the very end of *Nogent* held special interest because of his seemingly symbolic relationship to notions of fate, earthly paradise, and Carné's cinematic aesthetic. Insofar as *Le Jour se lève* conforms to the classical dramatic unities, the blind man may be considered, as in *Nogent*, a figure of tragic destiny (just as *Le Jour se lève*'s crowds might be compared to a Greek chorus). His uttering the word "fall" may be taken as an ironic biblical reference, and this, too, links him with *Nogent*'s accordionist. But it is especially the blind man's questioning, his

43 A figure of spectatorial and directorial desire: the blind
man (Georges Douking) in *Le Jour se lève*

effort to probe beyond surfaces and illuminate the invisible, that ties him
to Carné the director and Carné the man.

Carné's art relies upon minute observation of people from whom he
sees himself as standing apart. His distance manifests itself in the
guarded quality of his mise en scène, in the constraint of his editing, and
in an effort to exert total control over his actors. Pursuing his art with
passionate detachment, Carné embodies the director as voyeur. Within
his films the theme of the privileged, transgressive glance recurs almost
obsessively. This is not unique to Carné. Braudy suggests that "voyeurism is a characteristic visual device of the closed film, for it contains the
proper mixture of freedom and compulsion: free to see something dangerous and forbidden, conscious that one wants to see and cannot look
away." [24] What is special in Carné is the appearance in each film of a
variant of the primal scene, a situation in which one character inadver-

44 The voyeur exposed: Valentin (Jules Berry) kneeling at the bedroom keyhole; Clara (Arletty) at right

tently intrudes on the intimacy of two others. In all these instances, the activity of observing is self-consciously underscored and the consequences of the experience bear significantly on the plot and our interpretation of it.

Le Jour se lève offers two versions of the primal scene. One occurs when François visits Clara, finds her naked in the shower, and then cuddles with her in bed. Their intimacy ends when a suspicious Clara tiptoes to the door, opens it abruptly, and, as specified in the script, reveals Valentin "in the embarrassing position of a man listening at a keyhole" (fig. 44). In a sense, this is the most graphic example of primal scene in all of Carné: the couple whose privacy is encroached upon are actually viewed in bed together. (In *Les Enfants du paradis*, Nathalie intrudes on Baptiste and Garance, but only after they have made love.) Yet this scene differs radically from the others in its point of view. The significant disclosure here is not amorous activity but the sight of Valentin kneeling at the keyhole. In a reversal of the basic schema, the voyeur does not intrude but is intruded upon. François and Clara are not "caught in the act" by Valentin; rather, it is they who expose him. Valentin feigns composure: "Ah yes, I listen at keyholes . . . Personally, I'm a man without prejudices. Do you find that shocking?" Compared with François's and Clara's unruffledness, however, Valentin's nonchalance is unconvincing. Opposite their maturity stands Valentin's infantilism—which François and Clara deride through words and glances.

The psychological implications of this variant are intriguing. I have proposed that Carné's films are, in some measure, a projection of private fantasies. I have suggested that the early childhood events that marked Carné for life were the premature death of his mother and his father's frequent visits to bordellos, often accompanied by Marcel. I have also established that Carné admired the rugged masculine image of Jean Gabin because it did not exclude sentiment—a trait he found lacking in his father, who did not remain faithful to his dead wife. Moreover, as of *Hôtel du Nord*, Carné was attempting to transform Arletty's persona from flamboyant streetwalker to ideal maternal presence. It is thus quite likely that the François-Clara relationship reflects Carné's vision of a desirable parental couple. Were it not for François's fixation on Françoise's virginity (which one might equate with Carné's own idealization of his mother's purity), François and Clara would appear to be one of the rare healthy and minimally neurotic couples in Carné's works.

The consequences of such an interpretation are a bit surprising. If François and Clara are Carné's parent figures, then Valentin—at least to some degree—is a figure of Carné. The assertion is not altogether implausible. Like Valentin, the director Carné is a manipulator par excellence. Like Valentin, the man Carné is an outsider incapable of securing the allegiance and love that came easily to Prévert, Renoir, and Gabin. Yet if Valentin the voyeur is taken to be a figure of Carné, this crucial scene in *Le Jour se lève* must also be read as revealing a desire for punishment and humiliation on the part of the director—perhaps still guilty over the moviegoing pleasures he secretly experienced as a boy; perhaps still guilty over having chosen a profession his father disapproved of; or (a more compelling hypothesis) still guilty over a private life deviating from the norm. Most disturbing, however, is the fact that an identification of Valentin with Carné forces us to posit that, at least unconsciously, the overt leftist felt some degree of empathy with the right.

The other version of primal scene in *Le Jour se lève* is as lengthy as the one just examined is brief: it encompasses virtually the entire film. At the movie's start, the camera rises up the staircase and holds outside François's closed door. The final words of a conversation are heard in voice-over, but the men who speak them are unseen. We, the spectators, eventually overcome the door's obtrusiveness by way of the flashback construction. In this regard, the voyeuristic Valentin kneeling at the keyhole is as much a figure of the moviegoer as is the blind man ascending the stairs. Indeed, despite the difference in point of view, the brief instance of primal scene in Clara's hotel reproduces in miniature the film's overall construction of impeded voyeurism followed by disclosure.

Viewing the murder in light of the primal scene schema, we can understand more fully why Carné was so excited by Viot's flashback idea; why he devised to have Gabin and Berry project a level of energy and tension unparalleled in any of his works or theirs; and why he takes enormous pride in the success of the sequence (*Vbd*, 147). The crucial factor is the absence of women. When viewers finally observe the scene, they are intruding upon the privacy of two men—not, of course, in amorous activity, but plainly in sexual combat. Valentin's first words are: "I've absolutely got to talk to you—alone—man to man [*d'homme à homme*]." In truth, this episode is a primal test of sexual prowess in which Gabin (the son/idealized father) seems to triumph over Berry (the father/humiliated child). Their nervous cat-and-mouse maneuvers, their verbal teasing and provocations, are a kind of foreplay to the rough skirmish by the window—all of which constitutes a prelude to the climax in which Berry submits to having Gabin shoot him. The sequence is extraordinary because it allows Carné to place his ideal male, Jean Gabin, in the explicitly heterosexual situation of a man disputing his claim to a woman, but with homosexual overtones.

Le Jour se lève comes to not one but two climaxes: François's suicide follows Valentin's death. In a curious sense, François and Valentin consummate the double suicide pact which Pierre and Renée bungle in *Hôtel du Nord*. For Carné, François's suicide surely had personal significance, since it results from societal repression as embodied explicitly by the police. For the French public, the depiction of Gabin's self-destruction was an event of overwhelming import. It was quite normal for Gabin to come to tragic ends. As Bazin notes, "Gabin [was] the only French actor and almost the only actor worldwide (Chaplin excepted) whom the public expected to finish badly."[25] Yet Gabin's only previous suicides occurred in *Pépé le Moko*, where he played an inveterate gangster, and in *La Bête humaine*, where it was a matter of bizarre psychopathology. In *Le Jour se lève*, Gabin's suicide signified the ultimate destiny of the average, upstanding Frenchman vis-à-vis a society, government, and economy hostile to his well-being. When Carné pulls back and holds on the sight of Gabin, dead, he captures the horror of a people's vitality squelched to nothingness. As the sun rises, the burden of recognition and illumination associated with primal scenes no longer falls on a Carné character, but falls instead on the filmgoing public confronted with a primal image of itself.

*　　*　　*

The initial critical reaction to *Le Jour se lève* was lukewarm and at times hostile. The film's politics elicited strong disfavor and led to its being banned by Daladier in December 1939 and then again by the Germans during the Occupation. In the first edition of *Histoire du cinéma* (1948), the Fascist historians Maurice Bardèche and Robert Brasillach deplored the fact that Carné's "undeniable talent" had been too closely associated in *Le Jour se lève* with "a Jewish-leaning aesthetic [*une esthétique judaï-sante*] with which even the most indulgent persons were starting to get annoyed." "Pimps, whores, and sordid love affairs," they asserted, "were rather unfortunate subjects for French cinema of that period, too similar in fact to the German film prior to 1933, which—for the same reasons—exhibited an equally debased aesthetic."[26] Later versions of their influential history substitute the term "questionable" [*contestable*] for "Jewish-leaning."[27]

Throughout the war the film had vocal supporters, including dramatist Jacques Audiberti, for whom the picture's beauty and power lay precisely in its "terrifying, overstrained, and stifling" qualities.[28] It was not until after the Liberation, however, that the French perception of *Le Jour se lève* as a masterpiece took hold generally. This reversal of opinion owed much to Bazin, who selected the picture to be the first in a series of screenings and discussions held under the auspices of Travail et Culture, a Communist-supported organization of the post-Liberation period that sought to create a proletarian class consciousness.

Le Jour se lève soon disappeared from public view in the United States. RKO bought the rights in 1946, destroyed as many prints of the original as possible, and produced a remake in 1947 entitled *The Long Night*. The film was directed by Anatole Litvak. Its cast featured Henry Fonda and Barbara Bel Geddes in the leading roles, Vincent Price and Ann Dvorak as the supporting players. When news of the remake in progress broke out, British journalist Richard Winnington put the matter baldly: "All the things that make 'Le Jour se lève' a bright confirmation of one's sorely tried faith in the cinema are not to be imitated, certainly not in Hollywood . . . I have written of this film in superlatives before. I have seen it four times and it still seems to have no flaw. It's absolutely national and absolutely universal. Hollywood must hate it a lot."[29]

The cinematic equivalent of a tone poem or Symbolist drama, *Le Jour se lève* makes little compromise for the sake of audience ease. Devoid of *Jenny*'s sentimentality, *Drôle de Drame*'s comic eccentricities, *Hôtel du Nord*'s picturesqueness, and even *Le Quai des Brumes*'s mannered atmosphere, *Le Jour se lève* discloses Carné's specific genius: to give visual coherence to states of mind. *Les Visiteurs du soir* is surely a tour de force of cinematic fantasy. *Les Enfants du paradis* may be, as many have claimed, the greatest French sound film. But these later films advertise their attractiveness by magnifying the sentiment, spectacle, and mannerisms of the earlier works. *Le Jour se lève*, on the contrary, proclaims its severity. It dares spectators to contemplate a portrait of absolute human alienation. The other films are profitably viewed as masterworks of Carné *and* his collaborators. But in his style and handling of theme, Carné reveals himself to be the outstanding creative force behind *Le Jour se lève*. *Le Jour se lève*, one might say, is the most Carnésian of Carné's films.

PART III

The Monumentmaker

CHAPTER 9

The Occupation

Hitler invaded Poland on September 1, 1939, and France declared a state of war with Germany two days later. Toward the end of that week Carné found himself in military uniform at the Gare de l'Est. His destination was Coulommiers, where he was to join the 606th Régiment des Pionniers: "I left, as you can imagine, with neither a smile on my lips nor a flower on my gun. I was simply depressed and resigned. Fatalistic. Moreover, resignation seemed to me to be the general feeling . . . Although the image is cliché, I felt like part of a herd being led unawares to the slaughterhouse" (Vbd, 159).

Carné's unit was moved beyond the Maginot Line. Its less-than-heroic charge was to dig ditches. Months later Carné discovered why, unlike Lieutenant Jean Renoir, he had not been assigned to the military's Section Cinématographique. The head of that organization was Commander Calvet, the Ministry of War's representative to the Commission de Contrôle, who two years earlier had been offended by antimilitarist elements in the synopsis of Le Quai des Brumes. A man of long memory, Calvet was not disposed to easing Carné's wartime burdens. Carné's commanding officer, however, was film producer André Huguet. Although not previously acquainted with Carné, Huguet wanted to protect the director of Drôle de Drame from onerous and potentially dangerous tasks. This beneficent posture aroused envy and scorn among fellow soldiers. When Huguet attempted to promote Carné from caporal to fonctionnaire-caporal, one sergeant protested, calling Carné "defeatist" and "totally unfit for leadership."

That the sergeant was casting a slur upon Carné's manliness is plain in Carné's sarcastic commentary on this incident: "Of course, such virile military courage [cette mâle vertu militaire] was indispensable for ordering a handful of men to fetch juice or sweep the barracks" (Vbd, 164). In truth, during the eight months of inactivity known as the drôle de *guerre*, the French armed forces were characterized by a system of command that was "neither sufficiently rigorous in its hierarchy nor loose enough to encourage independence and initiative."[1] Effective leadership was absent even at the highest levels.

It is not surprising that Carné's sexuality evoked aspersions from insensitive comrades in arms. More remarkable is the frankness with which Carné explains in his memoirs how his affectionate friendship with a younger man, indicated only by the initial "W.," enabled him to be transferred from the German border to General Headquarters at Ferté-sous-Jouarre, a town close to Paris. Carné recounts his having met W. shortly before the war, the *joyeuses soirées* they shared, and W.'s determination to have Carné close to him. Thanks to a sympathetic captain, W. succeeded in arranging Carné's transfer to the office where W. had been assigned. Instead of digging ditches, Carné now sorted mail. Rather than submit to the calumny of fellow soldiers, he lived with dignity—even enjoying weekend sprees in the capital (*Vbd*, 165–67; the words *joyeuses soirées* appear in the first edition, p. 167, but are deleted from the second).

The deceptive calm ended on May 10, 1940. Skirting the northern end of the Maginot Line, German armored divisions accompanied by Stuka dive-bombers began their drive across the Ardennes Forest, cut off British and Belgian forces from the main French armies and from Belgian defenses, forced a massive evacuation of British and French troops from the beaches of Dunkirk, and eventually moved south toward Paris. Within weeks the French army was broken. Carné describes the pandemonium that reigned: "For a few days we had begun to see on the surrounding roads pitiful processions of exhausted men, women, and children . . . Then we, too, received the command to flee—there is no other word to describe it. It is probably not for me to characterize this journey, except to say that everyone was giving orders but no one was really in command . . . Trains, trucks, and buses seemed to follow upon one another as if by chance improvisation, not in any orderly motion but in perpetual zigzags, this way and that" (*Vbd*, 169). If Carné's penchant for total directorial control and stolid mise en scène became more pronounced during the Occupation, it was in part a reaction to his war experience.

The German army entered the City of Light on June 14. Between June 9 and 13, as the enemy approached, the refugee throng from Paris swelled to nearly two million people. On the evening of June 10 President Albert Lebrun and much of his cabinet fled Paris for Tours; on June 15 they moved further south to Bordeaux. Meanwhile, Winston Churchill exhorted the French to assume a stance of resolution and defiance.

Franklin Roosevelt urged that offensive fighting be pursued from North Africa. But despite counsel from leaders in the Senate and the Chamber of Deputies to heed this advice, Lebrun asked Henri Philippe Pétain, the eighty-four-year-old World War I hero, to form a new government on French soil. On the evening of June 18 Charles de Gaulle addressed his compatriots from London over the BBC: "I, General de Gaulle, . . . call on all French officers and men who are at present on British soil, or may be in the future, with or without their arms . . . to get in touch with me. Whatever happens, the flame of French resistance must not and shall not die!" [2] De Gaulle's words were barely heard. One day earlier Marshal Pétain had broadcast his intention to sue for peace, believing that the course for defeated France was to remain on national ground and establish a solid buttress against the invader. An armistice was signed on June 22. It provided for German occupation of most of the northern, eastern, and western regions of France. On July 10 the National Assembly voted to abolish both itself and the Third Republic, and Pétain became chief of a nominally independent southern country known as the French State, whose capital was located at the famous health spa, Vichy.

Still in uniform, Carné spent the last week of June near Toulouse, in a villa requisitioned by the French army. The armistice brought about immediate demobilization. Like many other creative artists, Carné was required to make the weightiest decisions of his career. Should he remain in the Free Zone? Should he return to Paris? Should he leave France altogether? The director's determination not to consider the latter option remains at the heart of much controversy that still surrounds Carné and his career.

Immediately following France's defeat, Julien Duvivier managed, with his wife and son, to embark for New York from Bordeaux. In mid-August 1940, Nazi representatives asked Jean Renoir to work for the New France: the filmmaker decided "it was time to clear out." [3] With help from his friend Robert Flaherty, Renoir and his future wife, Dido Freire, reached Hollywood via North Africa, Lisbon, and New York. Months earlier René Clair, together with his wife and child, had fled to Lisbon. Assisted by playwright Robert E. Sherwood, the Clairs secured an exit visa and went swiftly to Hollywood; from among numerous offers, the director of *Sous Les Toits de Paris* signed a contract with Universal Pictures. After much vacillation Michèle Morgan took advantage of a prior arrangement with RKO to leave France. Her lover, Jean Gabin, reportedly implored, "Leave before *they* make you work for them." [4] Gabin himself, parrying pressure from the German film industry, accepted an offer from Darryl Zanuck. Mistakenly believing that he would serve its propaganda aims in the still ostensibly nonbelligerent United States, the Vichy government granted France's most popular screen star a special eight-month visa. In fact, Gabin did not return to France until 1944, when he participated in the Allied Liberation invasions.

Other members of the French film community fled to southern California because they were Jews. These included directors Robert Siodmak and Max Ophuls, actors Marcel Dalio and Jean-Pierre Aumont, and cinematographer Boris Kaufman. Still other screen luminaries chose to exile themselves in Switzerland, most notably Carné's ersatz parents, Feyder and Rosay. After a brief stay in Switzerland, Louis Jouvet and his theater company toured Latin America for the remainder of the war. Yet the film people who left France for real or apparent political motives constituted a small minority. The Golden Age of French cinema did not cease with the Occupation. Established directors such as Gance, Grémillon, L'Herbier, Christian-Jaque, and Guitry continued to make pictures. Actors and actresses as familiar as Albert Préjean, Fernandel, Raimu, Pierre Renoir, Charles Vanel, Jean-Louis Barrault, Jules Berry, Carette, Danielle Darrieux, Viviane Romance, Ginette Leclerc, Arletty, Gaby Morlay, and Yvonne Printemps all continued to perform. Most French moviegoers of the Occupation period perceived the films associated with these figures as a felicitous prolongation of the robust national cinema industry of the late 1930s.[5]

However, none of the other directors who stayed was as artistically and commercially prominent in 1939 as Marcel Carné. Only Renoir, Feyder, Clair, and Duvivier were his equals, and they had all fled. Their exodus seems to have signaled an unwillingness to participate in France's capitulation to Germany. By not seeking exile, was Carné issuing a political message different from that of his distinguished colleagues? Or had he decided to make a similar statement in an entirely different manner?

Exile was not an attractive possibility for Carné. He has never liked to travel, he is thoroughly monolingual, and if not quite xenophobic, he is fiercely Gallocentric. Unlike Clair and Renoir, Carné did not have Anglo-American acquaintances to facilitate escape and settlement abroad. Further, he was not willing to abandon his craft. Carné's directorial practice required intense interaction with a scenarist, and for him this could occur only in the French language. Prévert's decision to remain in France was therefore overwhelmingly influential for Carné, both professionally and personally. Finally, the eminent French directors who went to Hollywood were married. Carné was not. In France, Carné had become adept at juggling the requirements of an unconventional personal life with public expectations. To venture to Los Angeles alone—its film community's reputation for deviation from norms notwithstanding—would have been an act so daunting for Carné the man as to render Carné the professional largely unproductive.

Carné accepted other challenges. During his early years as a director Carné had striven to assert his artistic identity vis-à-vis mentors and rivals. With Clair, Feyder, and Renoir in exile, conditions were favorable for solidifying his status as the most imposing creative force in French film. Opportunism of a sort was probably at play. But it was not the primary impulse, at least as Carné views the matter retrospectively. Explaining to an American audience in 1981 his reasons for having remained in France, Carné underscored his desire, above all, to demonstrate that French culture could withstand Germany's political victory: "After Pétain signed the provisional armistice there were two possible postures to assume: either go into exile or work in my own country and try to show that France was not entirely vanquished. I chose the second. Was I right or wrong? All I can be sure of is that I do not regret my choice, not because I filmed two of my greatest films in this period, but because I helped prove that France had not lost in spirit what we had lost through arms. I am also grateful to have provided work for so many co-professionals in a time of severe need."[6]

In his memoirs Carné skirts the issue of possible exile. His reluctance to address the matter straightforwardly in print suggests continued defensiveness. Carné treats more directly his equally controversial decision to return to Paris. Initially he anticipated remaining in the south because, like many movie professionals, he viewed the Riviera as a potential Hollywood à la française. In point of fact, the Côte d'Azur hosted thirty-two productions during the Occupation, including *Les Visiteurs du soir* and *Les Enfants du paradis*. But in the early months of the Vichy regime Carné found it impossible to remain in the Free Zone: "The little cash I had with me was dwindling away fast, and despite what people were saying, Victorine Studios were not reopening their gates immediately. I attempted to contact my bank in Paris. But with France cut in two, no transfer of funds was permitted." Unwilling to accept loans from acquaintances, Carné decided that "in spite of my repulsion at the very idea of living in the Occupied Zone, it was necessary for me to return to Paris." Describing his emotion after German officials boarded his train at the Demarcation Line to check papers, Carné writes: "The incident itself was minor, but it sufficed to make my heart feel as if it were caught in a vise that tightened progressively with each turn of the wheel that led me to Paris" (*Vbd*, 170–71). The simile is hackneyed; the sentiment is sincere. Together they highlight the degree to which Carné projects a self-image not unlike that of a character in his films: a victim of events, even when these result from seemingly independent choice.

From the Occupation's outset, the Nazis were attentive to the French film industry.[7] Within weeks of the victory, Joseph Goebbels established in Paris's Hotel Majestic a French Propaganda Department (*Propaganda-abteilung*) that wielded authority over regional Propaganda Sections (*Propagandastaffeln*) and over a Film Control Board (*Filmprüfstelle*). The Propaganda Department's principal function was to police the hiring, production, and distribution practices of all media industries in Occupied France.

Alongside these official agencies of control and censorship stood a mighty force in the reshaping of the French film industry: Continental Films. A German production company run under Goebbels's aegis and headed autocratically by a Nazi named Alfred Greven, Continental produced 30 of the 220 feature fiction films made in France during the Occupation—a number larger than that of any other film company. At a time when the average cost of a French picture was 3.4 million francs, Continental's initial capital worth was 10 million Reichsmarks or 200 million francs. In addition, Continental controlled the Paris-Cinema and Neuilly studios, many labs, and thirty-nine moviehouses—the last acquired in large measure from the confiscation of theater chains owned by two prominent Jewish exhibitors, Siritsky and Haik.

In late fall of 1940 Greven summoned Carné to discuss a possible contract. He led Carné to believe that directors Christian-Jaque, Georges Lacombe, Henri Decoin, Léo Joannon, and Jean-Paul Le Chanois had already consented to work for Continental. Carné acquiesced to Greven's offer. But he insisted that his contract include two provisos: first, that he have full control over choice of subject matter, thereby minimizing the risk of his bolstering the Nazi propaganda effort; second, that his films be made entirely in France, thereby ensuring that French, not German, actors and technicians would gain employment from his endeavors. After some hesitation, Greven agreed to Carné's terms. Carné soon realized that he had nonetheless been "hoodwinked" (*joué*) (*Vbd*, 177). He learned that the directors he believed had already signed with the German company did not do so until Greven showed them Carné's signature on a Continental contract. It is unclear why Carné did not consult personally with these directors in order to verify Greven's claims. But it is certain that Carné had an opportunity to exert anti-German leadership among the French film community and failed to do so.

In fact, Carné never directed a film for Continental. He began a project to adapt Marcel Aymé's novella *Les Bottes de sept lieues*, but he soon concluded, along with the author, that the property was too slight for a feature film. He himself sabotaged the only Carné-Continental project that took on momentum, an adaptation of Jacques Spitz's science fiction novel *Les Evadés de l'an 4000*. Preproduction was almost completed for what was to be a lavish undertaking. Jacques Viot had written the screenplay. Jean Anouilh provided the dialogue. Andrei Andrejew conceived sets so extravagant that Greven proposed to rent the Grand Palais as a studio. But when Greven chose not to sign Jean Cocteau as costume designer, Carné seized the moment to make trouble. Construing Greven's decision as a breach of good faith, Carné renounced his contract. Greven initiated a suit for damages; Carné responded with a countersuit, demanding even higher compensation for damages. Carné knew that he was courting danger. Greven was both Goebbels's deputy and an intimate of Hitler's successor-designate and founder of the Gestapo, Hermann Goering. But Carné wanted his freedom: "*Toutes proportions gardées*, a prisoner of war working on an enemy farm must know this sensation. The farmer he works for is pleasant, treats him like a worker who is of his own kind; he is well kept and fed, and he really has nothing specific to reproach his employer for. Yet there can be no real sympathy for one another. There are no two ways about it. It's visceral. That man is the enemy" (*Vbd*, 179). Carné's comparison is not entirely convincing. *Toutes proportions gardées*, this particular "prisoner of war" could have avoided "capture" by having refused to sign with Continental or by having left France entirely. Nonetheless, Carné's effort to extricate himself from an unbecoming situation gives testimony to his moral unease. Thanks to the intercession of Raoul Ploquin, Carné succeeded in having his contract annulled and the lawsuits dropped.

Greven did exact revenge on the renegade Carné. Following the Continental episode, Carné signed a contract to make three films for the independent producer André Paulvé (b. 1898). The first was to be a remake of *Nana* (Renoir had directed a silent version in 1926). This project was stymied, however, by Paulvé's inability to secure the rights to Zola's novel. Carné then proposed an adaptation of Georges Neveux's fantastical play *Juliette ou la clé des songes*. Viot wrote a complete screenplay. Cocteau penned the dialogue. Christian Bérard sketched sets and costumes. The film was to star Cocteau's protégé Jean Marais in his film début, Micheline Presle, and Fernand Ledoux. But as soon as the project was announced in the trade press, Greven threatened Paulvé with his power to bring about a complete ban on the finished picture. Already doubting the film's commercial viability, Paulvé reluctantly heeded Greven's threats and halted the project. Carné was shattered. He vowed to return to *Juliette ou la clé des songes* at a later time. Realizing that Greven's grudge would make it impossible for a Carné film to be launched in the Occupied Zone, Paulvé urged the director to go to the relatively freer atmosphere of the Côte d'Azur and seek out Prévert.

Paulvé's faith in Carné is impressive, since Carné was not especially favored in Vichy circles either. Pétain's regime had begun as a pluralistic dictatorship of the right. It was, as Stanley Hoffmann observes, "a great revenge of . . . conservative forces who, for at least sixteen years, had been feeling that the Republic was no longer conservative enough." Initially opposed to the totalitarian apparatus of the Fascists, the Vichy leaders naively conceived of a "nightwatchman" state with limited prerogatives to administer a hierarchical society that would correspond to a "natural order of things." Soon disabused, the Vichyites realized that only "generalized, intensive, and permanent use of power could possibly restore the forces of conservatism in society and consolidate their annexation of the state." As Pétain's National Revolution resorted more and more to "improvised abuses," "Vichy caused the scale to weigh in favor of Fascists and crypto-Fascists." [9]

The Pétain regime promoted its goal of national regeneration through an appeal to the values of *travail*, *famille*, and *patrie*. Because youth would bear France's glorious future, procreation was prized: even childless husbands were officially discriminated against in job selection. Not surprisingly, the Vichy government encouraged the canard that France's defeat resulted in large part from the demoralizing effect produced by writers such as Proust, Gide, Cocteau, and Mauriac—all homosexual—and by films such as *Le Quai des Brumes* and *Le Jour se lève*.

To reconstruct the French film industry along "rational" and "solid" lines, Vichy legislation facilitated the establishment of the Comité d'Organisation de l'Industrie Cinématographique (COIC) in December 1940. Headed by Ploquin, the COIC brought direction and order to an industry in chaos. But it was clearly an instrument of Vichy's policies and philosophy. The first Vichy law to deal directly with the cinema was issued on October 26, 1940. It called for all film artists to possess a professional identity card. In enforcing this regulation the COIC was serving Vichy's anti-Semitic strategy: one condition for obtaining a card was that the recipient not be a Jew.

Most of the producers of Carné's prewar films were Jewish. The other major directors whose films Vichy considered morbid and decadent had moved abroad. Carné was therefore a convenient target of scapegoatism. Nowhere was he attacked with more virulence than in a notorious text by Lucien Rebatet:

I am speaking especially of the films which Marcel Carné, Jacques Feyder's former assistant, began to make, one after another, as of 1937: *Jenny, Le Quai des Brumes, Hôtel du Nord, Le Jour se lève.* Marcel Carné is an Aryan. But he has been imbued with many Jewish influences. He owes his success to Jews. Jews have coddled him. All his films have been made under their mark, in particular that of [Arnold] Pressburger [for whom Carné worked only during the preparation of the unrealized *Ecole communale* in 1939]. Carné, who did not lack gifts, became the model of Jewified talent, as had Pabst in postwar Germany. Carné has been, in France, the most complete representative of that Marxist aestheticism which is, everywhere, one of the results of the proliferation of Jews and which is spontaneously engendered by the political, financial, and spiritual deliquescence which always follows the Jewification of a nation. Berlin experienced it from 1919 to 1930. It is rampant today in the theater of the Jewish capital called New York, and it is beginning to penetrate Hollywood. This aestheticism is at once whining and brutal. It finds its subjects in filth and blood. It treats these with systematic naturalism accompanied by heavy social symbols of revolt and hatred—shifty and spineless symbols that evoke for the *goyim* the destructive enterprise of Jews, so willingly nihilistic, rather than the valor of an insurgent who protests proudly with gun in hand . . . I am not a preacher. True artists must be free to depict the worst crimes. But Carné and his Jews have made the French cinema wallow in a degrading fatalistic determinism . . .[10]

Rebatet penned such statements regularly in his capacity as film critic for the weekly *Je Suis Partout*, where he wrote under the pseudonym François Vinneuil. (Following the Liberation, Rebatet received a death sentence for collaboration. The sentence was commuted to life imprisonment and then shortened to ten years of detention.)

Carné thus returned to the southern sector in 1941 with a formidable profile: Jewish sympathizer, sexual outlaw, promoter of France's defeat, and collaborationist pawn *manqué*. Taken seriously by certain parties, any component of this profile could have endangered Carné's freedom and safety. As usual, Carné tried to ignore the labels others ascribed to him. His simple—and simplistic—goal was to make the best films he could.

Like many Left Bank celebrities, Jacques Prévert had taken refuge near Nice, residing sometimes at the Riviera resort of Cap d'Antibes, sometimes at the mountain village of Tourrettes-sur-Loup. Early in 1941 Continental Films attempted to woo Prévert into its service. Greven himself paid a visit to the scenarist's coastal retreat to propose possible Carné-Prévert undertakings. Prévert declined unconditionally. "I would rather write a film for Tino Rossi [the popular singer who starred in a light-weight picture scripted by Prévert in 1941] than work for Continental," he proclaimed.[11] But when Carné severed his ties with the German pro-duction company, Prévert had no qualms about resuming what was being perceived as a legendmaking partnership.

The precise genesis of their fourth joint undertaking, *Les Visiteurs du soir*, is uncertain. Both men agreed that in order to avert censorship problems they would abandon the contemporary themes and settings of their prewar pictures. Carné claims that it was he who proposed the Middle Ages and he who suggested that the film be conceived in the "flamboyant style" of the illustrations in a fifteenth-century book of hours, *Les Très Riches Heures du duc de Berry* (*Vbd*, 189). Carné also affirms that in the wake of the abandoned *Juliette ou la clé des songes*, he made Prévert aware of his desire to pursue the fantastic. Trauner dis-putes this version: "Prévert and I had already begun to plan a film of *Puss in Boots*. We worked out many details, and these served as a nucleus for transforming the fairy tale into the legend of *Les Visiteurs du soir*."[12] Examination of Trauner's preliminary sketches for *Puss in Boots* sup-ports his claim that the concept for *Les Visiteurs du soir* was an out-growth of this prior project. Again, Carné seemingly overemphasizes his role in order to remind the public that he was never simply the executor of Prévert's creative genius. Trauner and Carné's accounts are not, how-ever, incompatible. A salient trait of French Occupation cinema was a predilection for historical and fantastic subjects: at least thirty-six fea-tures are set in periods ranging from the fourteenth century to the Belle Epoque, and at least ten depict the supernatural. It is not unreasonable to suppose that Carné and Prévert were independently thinking along like lines when they discussed ideas for their new venture.

Making a film as ambitious as *Les Visiteurs du soir* entailed uncom-mon perils. The first mass arrests of Jews took place in Paris and the Free Zone in July and August 1942, respectively. Until then, overt sympathy toward Jews under the Vichy regime involved minimal risk. Historians Michael Marrus and Robert Paxton note that at first the Vichy anti-Jewish program "remained just under the emotional horizon for most of the French population, substantial enough to wreak real damage but re-strained enough to leave most people unmoved." But by the summer of 1942—when *Les Visiteurs du soir* was in full production—"assisting Jews in any way was extremely dangerous."[13]

Jacques Prévert enjoyed referring to himself as a *philosémite*.[14] From the start of the Occupation, he and his brother shielded two friends who were especially vulnerable to the Aryanization process because they were Hungarian-born Jews: Trauner, hiding in Tourrettes-sur-Loup, and Kosma, living incognito near Cannes. With Paulvé's approval, both men were hired to work clandestinely on *Les Visiteurs du soir*. Designer Georges Wakhevitch (1907–84), a Gentile Russian emigré, agreed to serve as Trauner's "front" in Paris and Nice, where he oversaw the execution of Trauner's set and costume designs. Maurice Thiriet (1906–72), who composed the film's orchestral score, agreed to accept credit as well for the three ballads written by Kosma. The participation of these outlawed men was apparently an open secret in the industry, and even Louis-Emile Galey, director of Vichy's Cinema Section, was in on the secret.[15] Nonetheless, this bizarre work situation was an act of rebellion against authority. Carné's reflections on the matter are self-congratulatory but true: "I do not know if the danger of the enterprise is understood today. More than Jacques, who as scenarist could claim to ignore the choice of anonymous co-workers whose selection was my responsibility alone, I ran the risk, if the ruse were discovered, of being blacklisted for good, and of even worse. But I didn't hesitate. It seemed the right thing to do" (*Vbd*, 190).

Les Visiteurs du soir depicts an epoch of extravagant court splendor. In this time of scarcity and rationing, materials for suitable costumes and adornments were difficult to obtain. A sufficient amount of silk, velvet, and brocade was gleaned to clothe the leading characters. But the numerous extras (including the then-unknown Simone Signoret and Alain Resnais) had to be dressed in cruder fabrics, which accounts in part for the film's preponderance of distance shots.

Feeding the large company on location in the Provence countryside was also problematic. Black-market sandwiches could be procured in Nice, but at prohibitive cost. In a democratic gesture, Carné pressured his leading actors to refrain from buying sandwiches and to join the crew and himself in lunching on "cold stews" and "shriveled cuts of cheap meat" (*Vbd*, 198). However, when extras began to filch the fruit gracing the table in the lavish banquet sequence, Carné turned draconian: he had each piece of fruit injected with carbolic acid. "Today the procedure may appear monstrous even if, naturally, the actors were forewarned. And it did appear so to me. But my assistants assured me that the extras, alerted, would stop touching the fruit" (*Vbd*, 201). France's famine affected the availability of animals as well. The film's hunt scene called for horses and hounds. Carné's production manager succeeded in renting

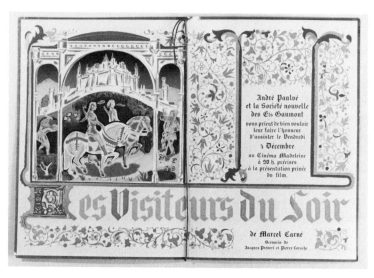

45 Invitation to the Occupation's most imposing cinematic event: the premiere of *Les Visiteurs du soir*

handsome steeds from the Garde Républicaine stationed at Vichy. He was less successful in the matter of canines: Carné had to settle for a pack of scrawny, ailing dogs.

Paulvé's largesse allowed for certain luxuries. Excessive April rains delayed the start of exterior shooting by several weeks. Carné had not completed the fountain scenes in the hills outside Nice when he was compelled to return to Paris to film interior scenes scheduled at the Saint-Maurice Studios. When he went back to the coast in August, he found the lush spring grass and sprouts at the fountain site devastated by the summer's heat. Two ideas came to mind, and both seemed foolish: to reshoot all the fountain scenes in this parched setting, or to relocate the company further north, in the Loire Valley. Instead, Carné decided to retouch Mother Nature herself. He ordered an immense amount of sod and other vegetation from neighboring Grasse, a city renowned for its horticulture. The result was a perfect illusion of April. Although postwar critics chastised Carné for such extravagance, the filmmaker insists that his solution was the most cost-effective.

After a year's effort and an expenditure of twenty million francs, *Les Visiteurs du soir* premiered at Paris's Madeleine Cinema on December 4, 1942 (fig. 45). It was the grandest film event of the Occupation. It enjoyed the longest first run of the period. Reviewers were unanimously rhapsodic. Audiberti opined that "we will never be able to write again

about the cinema without referring back to this masterwork. It transforms our perspective and modifies our scale of judgment." For Roger
Régent, the film presented "Beauty and Grandeur in their pure state."[16]
Even Rebatet considered it "a delicately chiseled piece of jewelry."[17] The
general intensity of emotion is perhaps best conveyed in a letter to Carné
from Charles Spaak: "I saw *Les Visiteurs* last night. It is a magnificent
film. Of all your merits, there is one that touches me particularly: what
a lesson you give us in courage and ambition. (I returned home shame-
faced.) Excuse me for sometimes having made fun of your small size—
you are a great man."[18]

A barely known critic named André Bazin (1918–58) agreed that *Les
Visiteurs du soir* was "the most interesting effort to raise cinema to the
level of poetic expression since the war," and that "it would mark a date,
the beginning of an influence, the origin of a style." By the end of 1943,
however, Bazin began to feel that the first reviewers' unanimity was less
a function of the film itself, which he now saw as having flaws, than of
the gratitude reviewers felt toward Carné for having "restored to French
cinema a grandeur and style which it seemed to have renounced." If *Les
Visiteurs du soir* "exploded from the dreary production of 1941–42 like
a revolutionary event," its popularity at the box office was sustained not
so much by universal approbation but, asserts Bazin, by a justifiable
"snobbism" among those French critics who understood that "from the
militant and historical point of view" the film had to be praised in
print.[19] Occupation conditions prevented Bazin from being more explicit.
But he was interpreting the press's response to *Les Visiteurs du soir* as a
communal gesture of patriotism.

Bazin's allusion to the general public's qualified enthusiasm for the film
was probably justified. It is difficult to imagine typical French moviegoers
attending showings of *Les Visiteurs du soir* and deriving the kind of
middlebrow pleasures inspired by *Hôtel du Nord*. It is likelier that many
viewers attended screenings of *Les Visiteurs du soir* out of a sense of duty,
responding to its alleged artistic value more with boredom than with
excitement. It is also likely that, as Bazin implies, many reviewers who
praised the film in print had reservations which they expressed orally.
Succeeding critics surely have found much to fault in the work.

But of particular interest is Bazin's reluctance to specify unambiguously the purported flaws of *Les Visiteurs du soir*. His most extended
piece on the film appeared in *Revue Jeux et Poésie* in late 1943.[20] Bazin
proposes that since "it is no longer necessary to defend it, we can speak
of Carné's film with more impartiality." He begins by asserting that *Les
Visiteurs du soir* "is not absolutely a 'great' film." An example of a great
film, Bazin claims, is Renoir's *La Grande Illusion*. *Les Visiteurs du soir*

is not equal to *La Grande Illusion* because it lacks "a certain density, an epic élan, an authenticity, that warm—I was going to say charitable— sense of conviction which alone can really do the trick." The film lacks, continues Bazin as he searches for a concept that can subsume all he has stated until now, "faith" (*la foi*). Yet Bazin immediately attenuates his position: "Such as it is, this work nevertheless realizes a high poetic standard, and more generally a *spiritual* one" (my italics). After summarizing the plot, Bazin indicates that the film's originality lies in its technique, specifically, Carné's "turning away from the naturalistic realism of *Quai des Brumes* and *Le Jour se lève*" toward "a poetry and an enchantment that are inherent in cinema." Bazin faults Carné's special cinematic effects for sometimes lacking "the perfection necessary to their complete credibility," and he adds that he finds two of the actors to be miscast. Yet as if embarrassed at criticizing too harshly, Bazin next affirms, "But these very failures are not lacking in intelligence." Moreover, he returns to the matter of special effects to praise Carné for having used these methods "discreetly, rejecting the easy way out offered by spectacular contrivances, fleeing the conventional, and having recourse to the marvelous only where its *spiritual significance* could be expressed in all its force" (my italics).

Bazin's text is a crucial one. It is the first to display the ambivalence commentators over the decades have felt toward *Les Visiteurs du soir*. Bazin's critique is so guarded and apparently contradictory that his "impartiality" reads more like an evasion of an issue raised by the film to which he would like—but is unable—to give a partisan response. In this respect Bazin's reaction is symptomatic of commentary on Carné's oeuvre in general. Elucidation of Bazin's evasiveness in 1943 can lead to fuller comprehension of the peculiar history of Marcel Carné since 1943. Roger Régent was a less astute critic than Bazin, but in 1943 he rightly intuited that considerable passage of time would be necessary to understand *Les Visiteurs du soir*'s initial impact and, by extension, Bazin's atypical indirectness: "As the years cause the dust of age to accumulate on this film, as the criticisms and the praise for it become less dogmatic [*aiguës*], less arrogant, and therefore more profound, we will become aware of the capital importance it had in those long days when the enemy Occupation weighed heavily upon France." [21] It is precisely the relationship between *Les Visiteurs du soir* and France's state of Occupation that Bazin, with good reason, did not wish to acknowledge head-on.

It is May 1485. Gilles (Alain Cuny) and Dominique (Arletty) are agents of the Devil. Dressed as wandering minstrels, they appear one afternoon at the castle of Baron Hugues (Fernand Ledoux), where the betrothal of the Baron's daughter Anne (Marie Déa) and the knight Renaud (Marcel Herrand) is being celebrated. Anne and Renaud do not love each other. At the evening's festivities Gilles sings ballads that provoke feelings of love for him in Anne. By plucking the strings of her mandolin, Dominique miraculously immobilizes the entire company of dancing courtiers and, divested of her disguise as a young man, is revealed to be a ravishing female. She leads Renaud to the garden and proceeds to beguile him. Simultaneously Gilles woos Anne. When the two couples retake their places inside, Dominique plucks her mandolin again and activities resume. Later that night Dominique enters the Baron's bedchamber and entices him, too, with false emotions. Gilles, however, violates the rules of his mission by genuinely falling in love with Anne. To preserve perverse order, the Devil himself (Jules Berry) appears at the castle one stormy night. He causes Gilles to be shackled, and he engineers a joust between the Baron and Renaud over Dominique, in which the young knight is killed.

Dominique's mission completed, she leaves on horseback and is pursued wildly by the Baron, who never returns. Lusting for Anne, the Devil makes advances. At first he is rejected by the girl, who claims not to believe in a Devil and vows to remain faithful to Gilles. But Anne declares that she will become the Devil's companion if he agrees to release Gilles from his pact. The Devil consents but casts a spell that deprives Gilles of memory. Anne asserts that she lied to the Devil in order to save Gilles; she will not accompany the Devil. Through love's power, Gilles wondrously recovers his memory in Anne's presence at the fountain far from the castle where the two first exchanged vows. The enraged Devil metamorphoses the embracing couple into a stone statue. To his utter distress, their unpetrified hearts fuse and beat steadfastly in unison.

According to Carné, one reason why the premiere of *Les Visiteurs du soir* was so stirring an event was that "for some time people had been murmuring off the record that this story from the past was replete with allusions to the situation of the moment, that is, to France under the heel of the Occupier" (*Vbd*, 212). As an allegory of France's plight, *Les Visiteurs du soir* presents a less-than-flattering portrait of the French. If Gilles and Dominique stand for Hitler's forces come to lay claim to France, represented by the Baron's castle, they encounter an atmosphere predisposed to submission. Outside the castle stands the court executioner, who fishes idly for frogs and laments that "my services are barely ever called upon now." By the film's end this fellow willingly becomes an efficient instrument of the Devil. Within the castle reign pomp and ritual bereft of vigor. The knight Renaud bemoans the emasculation of the military ethos: "Love . . . , always love . . . , and then again love with its little moans and mighty tricks . . . In the past, at least, we would sing of war, the pleasure of combat, of killing, and even of death (*sad and embittered*) . . . but now . . . what spinelessness!" Renaud encourages Anne to gaze upon the deformed dwarfs who, in the course of the film, facilitate the envoys' plots. Covered by *cagoules*, or penitents' hoods, these hideous creatures fascinate Renaud, just as the conspiratorial organization known as the Cagoulards appealed to extreme right-wingers of the 1930s who sought to purge the French army of pacifists and Communists. Renaud is so caught up with his warrior mystique that, like France in May 1940, he enters battle with insufficient protection: when he jousts with the Baron, he declines to wear his coat of mail and is killed. Renaud's death at the hands of his prospective father-in-law correlates with the civil dissension plaguing contemporary France. Like Marshal Pétain, Baron Hugues is wedded to a vision incompatible with present-day realities, as underscored by his devotion to a portrait of his dead wife, Berthe. When Dominique begins to seduce him, Hugues declaims piously, "I am a man who lives inwardly . . . in the past . . . in memories." By the film's end, the Baron abdicates authority and capitulates unconditionally to Dominique: "My life belongs to you now . . . Wherever you go, I will go."

In setting their story in 1485, Carné and Prévert did not seek perfect fidelity to either history or legend. But their specification of a year is telling. Situated before Columbus's voyages and before Luther posted his theses on the door of the church at Wittenberg, *Les Visiteurs du soir* depicts medieval France in a state of self-complacent isolation and uncritical adherence to an old order—a situation not unlike France's immediately preceding and during the *drôle de guerre*. Antonioni, who assisted Carné on the film, specifies that Prévert and co-scenarist Laroche sought information and inspiration from historian Johan Huizinga's *Waning of the Middle Ages*.[22] Huizinga's image of the fifteenth century as an epoch of fading and decay parallels remarkably France's decline in the late 1930s and its reluctance, after defeat, to address decline in any way other than by looking backward to past glories. To escape the "sombre melancholy" that weighed on their souls at the close of the Middle Ages, aristocrats cloaked themselves in the fanciful brilliance of a past age, pursuing "the illusion of a heroic being, full of dignity and honour, of wisdom and, at all events, courtesy." At the source of this recourse to spectacle and artificiality lay the nobility's real loss of military prerogatives brought about by the Valois monarchy's ascent as the legitimate form of public power.[23] Although Huizinga does not detail international politics, Prévert and Laroche could not have overlooked one further parallel between the late Middle Ages and the contemporary scene: the German threat of total absorption of Europe. Having become progressively entrenched in central Europe, the Netherlands, Spain, and southern Italy, the Holy Roman Empire—like the Third Reich—promised "a kind of world-state in which no people could preserve its independence."[24]

French commentators have aggressively minimized or denied altogether *Les Visiteurs du soir*'s politico-allegorical dimension. They have disputed Carné's claim that the film is "replete with allusions to the situation of the moment," as well as continuity supervisor Jeanne Witta-Montrobert's assertion that "reference to the era was clear."[25] With the exception of one recent scholar, for whom the film expresses "new social realities . . . within the ideological system of the National Revolution,"[26] forthright acknowledgment of the film as political allegory has come not from the French but from the British. In one of the first articles on the picture to appear in English after the war, Hazel Hackett wrote in *Sight and Sound*, "In the idea of the devil and his creatures who are everywhere, setting each man against his fellow, [the French] saw a reference to the occupying enemy, and, in the triumph of the young girl over evil through her purity and faith, an encouragement to moral resistance."[27] For historian and BBC commentator Eric Rhode, *Les Visiteurs du soir* sat squarely among those Occupation-made films that "insert[ed] clandestine and at times cryptic messages of support for the Free French."[28]

The Gallic antiallegorical stance has hardened over the decades. Sadoul granted that the joint statue "was an image of captive France herself"; but he found the allusion to the Devil as Hitler "barely comprehensible."[29] In 1957 Siclier allowed that "in the night of the Occupation" Anne incarnated hope and freedom: "Anne's heart, continuing to beat, like Gilles's, beneath the stone erected by the Devil, issued a vibrant message which an entire generation picked up on."[30] In 1981, however, Siclier insisted: "The film was even credited with political intentions born of a rumor whose origins I am unaware of: the devil would have been Hitler; the heart of the lovers continuing to beat beneath the stone of the statues would have been the heart of oppressed France. One must not take these crackbrained notions seriously! Jules Berry as Hitler—the idea is raving mad!"[31] Siclier's protestation echoes and supports the views of René Prédal, for whom "this kind of cinema can in no way furnish us with a reflection of the era,"[32] Jean-Pierre Jeancolas, for whom a metaphoric reading of the film is "interpretive delirium,"[33] Raymond Borde, for whom the unbreakable heart of wounded France is "rubbish,"[34] and François Truffaut, who wrote in 1975: "I cannot accept the sometimes espoused patriotic theory that the historical or fantasy films made during this period delivered a courageous message coded in favor of the Resistance." Truffaut preferred to characterize such films as "apolitical and escapist."[35] Although Claude-Jean Philippe claims that the final scene "probably" contained an allusion to France's humiliation and was recognized as such by its first viewers,[36] the most recent French commentator of Carné's complete oeuvre, Michel Pérez, reiterates Truffaut's position.[37]

An explanation of such adamant denials calls for examination of another aspect of the critical debate surrounding *Les Visiteurs du soir*. More than any other component of the film, detractors have found fault with its pace. For Quéval, "the slowness of the rhythm tires one out."[38] Roud finds the film "incredibly slow and amorphous."[39] Siclier laments that "conducted according to such a slow rhythm," Carné's film totally lacks "emotion and life."[40] Bardèche and Brasillach criticize Carné and Prévert for a "terribly slow work" and, in particular, for "the slowness, the coldness, of their medieval reconstructions."[41] Rhode finds that "monumentality stifles this production."[42] And Jeancolas writes, "Jacques Prévert's scenario for *Les Visiteurs du soir* is cut off from the conflictual present which excited the verve of the author of *M. Lange*; too slow, too hampered by the valorization of a décor and costumes which cost money and trouble, it jars with the rest of his oeuvre."[43]

A minority of critics have praised the film's slowness. Soon after its release René Barjavel wrote: "The rhythm is slow, especially at the start, but it is the result of a choice, not an error. The spectator is quickly beguiled by this idling pace and becomes lulled by a triple incantation, by the . . . images, dialogue, and sound."[44] Roger-Marc Thérond admired the pace as "deliberately slow, like a swan on a lake."[45] And Rebatet-Vinneuil insisted that "this film possesses, for those who are capable of perceiving it, a fascinating rhythm, that of an 'andante' whose phrases are harmoniously linked."[46] But the prevailing opinion since at least 1948 faults the film's narrative for getting "bogged down" through "the director's willingness to linger over the magnificence of the spectacle."[47]

The static quality of *Les Visiteurs du soir* is undeniable. Carné's camera movements are restrained, even by his own standards. Shots last longer than convention dictates. The result, to borrow Antonioni's phrase, is "suffocating serenity."[48] But suffocation and serenity are at the

46 Trauner's tapestry-inspired garden: the Baron (Fernand Ledoux, left),
the Devil (Jules Berry), and the knight Renaud (Marcel Herrand)

kernel of the work's intended meaning. To evaluate properly the film's
slowness, one must come to terms with Carné and Prévert's artistic aims.

Les Visiteurs du soir provided Carné with an opportunity to indulge
his penchant for pictorialism on a massive scale. In capturing on film the
painterly aesthetic of the late Middle Ages, Carné pays tribute to Feyder
and *La Kermesse héroïque*. But if exuberance is the hallmark of the seventeenth-century Flemish masters who inspired Carné's mentor, staid
magnificence informs Burgundo-French art in the expiring Middle Ages.
As Huizinga writes, "Decoration and ornament no longer serve to
heighten the natural beauty of a thing; they are overgrowing it and
threaten to stifle it." [49]

The film's garden décor is egregiously extravagant (fig. 46). The mise
en scène of the glittering shrubs, trees, blossoms, trellises, and fountain
makes them as far removed from nature as those represented in the
French and Flemish unicorn tapestries that actually inspired Carné, Trauner, and cinematographer Roger Hubert. Trauner remarks: "We wanted

to return to a plastic two-dimensionality, attenuating normal perspective as much as possible. We certainly did not want conventional photographic or cinematic effects to dominate in the garden scenes. These had to be like the Lady and the Unicorn tapestries, like a fairy tale."[50] One might propose that this sumptuous décor actualizes Saint Thomas's requirements for beauty: "first, integrity or perfection, because what is incomplete is ugly on that account; next, true proportion and consonance; lastly, brightness, because we call beautiful whatever has a brilliant colour."[51] More surely, the garden set marks the summit of Carné's inclination, first shaped by his fascination with the Square des Batignolles and the stage mechanics of the Folies Bergère, to create illusions of nature unsusceptible of real-world blemishes.

The movie's principal source of pictorial inspiration was *Les Très Riches Heures du duc de Berry*. Illuminated by the Limbourg brothers and Jean Colombe, this book of hours is perhaps the most perfect expression of French International Gothic, a mannered representational style characterized by sinuous lines, polished elegance, and very restrained vitality.[52] The book includes twelve full-page miniatures depicting scenes that relate to the seasonal labors of each month. Each is set in front of a precisely rendered castle associated with the Duke's life and time. Several offer parallels with specific scenes in *Les Visiteurs du soir*. January, for example, portrays a magnificent room, probably in the palace of Bourges, during a reception given by the Duke to celebrate the New Year. Seated at table, the Duke is surrounded by the principal members of his court, all ceremonially dressed; behind him is an imposing fireplace. The early feast sequence in *Les Visiteurs du soir* is virtually this painting brought to life. Likewise, the film's cavalcade of lords and ladies leaving for the hunt (fig. 47) mirrors the horseback outing depicted for May. The illustration for July represents peasants tending livestock and working the fields in front of the gleaming white castle of Poitiers. This image is similar in composition to the opening shots of the film's castle, but where the painting displays two farmers and two sheep-shearers, Carné includes only a solitary farmer. In all respects Carné and Trauner's transposition of *Les Très Riches Heures du duc de Berry* accentuates the slowness and stillness of the original.

Another factor that accounts for the film's tempo is Carné and Prévert's effort to convey subconscious time and space. *Les Visiteurs du soir* is not a conventional period piece; its grandiose sets and costumes do not aim to give a full-bodied impression of an era. They serve instead to prepare the viewer for a story that has to do less with real chivalric lords and ladies than with instincts and desires. Dominique and Gilles are as

47 A filmic rendition of the illustration for May in *Les Très Riches Heures du duc de Berry*

much agents of repressed libido as they are agents of the Devil. When Dominique causes the mannered dancers to become locked in a freeze-frame, Anne and Renaud are released from the posturing that society has imposed upon them. The sequence that follows lasts over ten minutes, but it represents that fraction of a second in which one being experiences unlawful desire for another.

The film's very first frames announce its regressive thrust. On a darkened screen, an iris opens in the lower left corner to expose an extreme high-angle view of Gilles and Dominique mounted on dark steeds and moving along a vast, forbidding terrain (fig. 48). This archaic cinematic technique, the iris, imparts a sense that these two characters—who with each successive shot loom larger and advance directly toward the camera—are emerging from a remote time and place. The rugged crags, petrified lava flows, and deep ravines resemble visionary panoramas sketched by Leonardo—who was in his prime in 1485. The landscape also recalls early scientific drawings of the human brain. In short, Gilles and Dominique appear like the embodiment of forces rising out from the inner psyche. These opening shots prime the spectator to construe the entire film as the unfolding of a dream.

In *Profane Mythology: The Savage Mind of the Cinema*, Yvette Biró pursues Susanne Langer's insight that films, like dreams, create an "infi-

48 Gilles (Alain Cuny) and Dominique (Arletty) emerging as if from an objectified psyche

nite present." Biró observes that "the easy ways of mutual reflection and projection, the surprising yet natural combination of events, the expansive flow of continuity in which component elements are not always distinguishable, the fairy tale-like omnipresence . . . these are the principal factors that create the infinite presence." [53] These factors also describe how the fantastic operates in *Les Visiteurs du soir*—naively, primitively, evoking the psychic condition of early childhood when the unconscious is still uninhibited by the ego and when immediate reality is perceived as eternal and ubiquitous. Were *Les Visiteurs du soir* concerned with linear dramatic development and with characters presumed to have realistic depth and substance, its crawling pace might be a flaw. But the film aims to disengage spectators from historical time, to sever their links with the rational, and to plunge them instead into the "infinite present" of a dreamlike fantasy.

An aesthetic that emphasizes static pictorialism and psychological regression is thoroughly appropriate to *Les Visiteurs du soir*. It is therefore curious that so many critics have been unwilling to "explain away" the film's slowness by appealing to the consonance between its tempo and artistic intent—as is often done in treating works of the slow-paced directors Ozu and Bresson. I would suggest that this reluctance to approve of the film's pace is tied to the unwillingness of so many French critics to acknowledge the film as an allegory of current events. To do either is tantamount to conceding the uncomfortable fact that *Les Visiteurs du soir* is an extraordinary expression of the military unpreparedness, political weakness, and, above all, national torpor that contributed to France's defeat by Germany.

Truffaut is correct in asserting that *Les Visiteurs du soir* did not deliver "a courageous message coded in favor of the Resistance." But the film did deliver a message. Over the past five decades no challenge has been greater for the French than confronting the realities of its defeat and capitulation. Given the moral and spiritual devastation caused by the war and its aftermath, it is not surprising that this challenge still remains to be met fully.

One Frenchman did attempt to see through what he called the "mists of ignorance and malice" that had already gathered in the weeks following the debacle. In the summer of 1940 historian Marc Bloch (b. 1886) wrote *Strange Defeat*. Bloch, a veteran of World War I, a captain in charge of oil supplies during the *drôle de guerre*, and a participant in the catastrophic campaign of the Nord, was also a Jew and later a leader in the Resistance movement. *Strange Defeat* was not published until after Bloch was put to death by the Gestapo at Trévoux on June 16, 1944. It is a precious document because of the lucidity Bloch brings to a subject still fresh in his memory.

Bloch's principal thesis centers on the failure of French leadership to recognize that "the whole rhythm of modern warfare had changed its tempo." In contrasting Germany's speed with France's sluggishness, Bloch's text abounds with images of time. As the Germans advanced with incredible rapidity, "the metronome at headquarters was always set at too slow a beat." While the ruling idea of the Germans in the conduct of war was speed, "we, on the other hand, did our thinking in terms of yesterday or the day before." The French, faced with undisputed evidence of Germany's new tactics, ignored "the quickened rhythm of the times ... It was as though two opposed forces belonged, each of them, to an entirely different period of human history." Thus, when the Army of the Meuse had been broken and the enemy became active on the northern front, the French did not establish a properly reorganized defensive line further back; rather, small groups of reinforcements "dribbled into every breach as it occurred" and were cut down: "Our own rate of progress was too slow and our minds were too inelastic for us ever to admit the possibility that the enemy might move with the speed which he actually achieved." For Bloch, the war was "a constant succession of surprises ... The Germans took no account of roads. They were everywhere. They felt their way forward, stopping whenever they ran up against serious resistance. Where, however, the resistance was not serious and they could find a 'soft spot,' they drove ahead, exploiting their gains, and using them as a basis from which to develop the appropriate tactical movement or, rather, as it seemed, to take their choice of a number of alternative possibilities already envisaged in accordance with that methodological opportunism which was so characteristic of Hitler's methods. They relied on action and on improvisation." [54]

Bloch's observations ought to force viewers wary of approaching *Les Visiteurs du soir* as a political allegory to rethink their position. Siclier's assertion that the notion of Jules Berry as Hitler is "raving mad" is undercut by an appreciation of Berry's role in terms of the Germans' perception of time and space. Critics have generally agreed that Berry's broad gestures and rapid speech jar with the delicate bearing and languid delivery of the other principal actors. [55] But no less significant is the fact that the film's special cinematic effects—dissolves, fades, superimpositions, and clever editing—permit the Devil and his envoys to exhibit the very capacity for spontaneity, versatility, and elasticity which Bloch discerned in Hitler's forces. Like the German troops, Gilles and Dominique displace and relocate themselves at miraculous speed. The Devil exults in his ubiquity: to impress Anne, he demonstrates that he can be present at once in her bedroom and in the garden beneath it. Like the Führer, he immobilizes, demobilizes, and literally petrifies those who dare thwart his ambitions. And like Hitler, the Devil fantasizes control over the entire planet: "I who can hold the world (*looking at his agile hands*) . . . in these two hands. (*The Devil, delirious, addresses the girl [Anne] with pride*) . . . It doesn't take much to amuse me . . . the world's unhappiness, for example . . . that amuses me a lot, that warms my heart, that makes me laugh . . . Yes!"

Interpreted as a statement on France's predisposition to subjugation, *Les Visiteurs du soir* unsettles the Gaullist myth of wartime France as a victorious power temporarily defeated in an early battle but soon massively enrolled in the Resistance effort. On the contrary, *Les Visiteurs du soir* exposes a people reveling in the "escapist dream of archaic reaction and sheltered neutrality" which, according to Hoffmann, dominated the French mentality throughout World War II. [56]

In *The Films in My Life*, Truffaut nostalgically recalls that having viewed *Les Visiteurs du soir* twice in one day made him realize, at age ten, "how fascinating it can be to probe deeper and deeper into a work one admires, that the exercise can go so far as to create the illusion of reliving the creation." [57] By trivializing the allegorico-political dimension of *Les Visiteurs du soir*, however, the adult Truffaut represses the lessons which that very film taught him. Truffaut's most successful film in the period before his death, *Le Dernier Métro* (1980), demonstrates the degree to which the director—and the public that enthusiastically greeted the film—remained seduced by the fiction that Occupied France was solidly *résistante*. In a sense, *Le Dernier Métro* fosters a kind of reverse revisionism, reinstating the myth of mass Resistance which Ophuls's *Le Chagrin et la pitié* (*The Sorrow and the Pity*, 1971) had aimed to dismantle once and for all.

Ophuls's documentary on life in the Occupied town of Clermont-Ferrand is a watershed in the history of French public reflection upon the war years. Although it was planned by and for France's government-controlled television network, the ORTF feared its revelations and refused to air it. (The film was not telecast in France until the fall of 1981.) However, when it was exhibited in Paris theaters—thanks in large measure to a campaign triggered by none other than Truffaut—its effect was overwhelming. In its wake came fiction films that also accentuated the responsibility of the French for events that had transpired, such as Pierre Granier-Deferre's *Le Train* (1973), Michel Mitrani's *Les Guichets du Louvre* (1973), Joseph Losey's *Monsieur Klein* (1976), and Costa-Gavras's *Section spéciale* (1975). Writing in *Les Temps Modernes*, François Garçon views these films as having created "a breach in the apparatus of collective repression." But films like Truffaut's *Le Dernier Métro*, fears Garçon, point to French society's need to "reset" (*resouder*) that broken apparatus "in order to facilitate France's acceptance of its history in its entirety." [58]

Truffaut was Carné's unkindest critic in the 1950s. His distaste for Carné had to do with film practice and aesthetics, not politics. Yet I would suggest that Truffaut's disaffection for *Les Visiteurs du soir*'s style is linked inextricably to a disinclination to acknowledge the film's politics. In *Decline or Renewal?: France Since the 1930s*, Stanley Hoffmann asks why the revelation of Vichy's passivity and complicity should make young Frenchmen feel guilty or ashamed; logically, a "generation gap" should shield French youth from feelings of solidarity with their elders. Hoffmann argues that one of Gaullism's assumptions and objectives was precisely to preserve French solidarity, that "the duty of each new generation is to take on—*assumer*—the sum total of French history." [59] These remarks bear on a paradox of Truffaut's career. On one hand, Truffaut conceived of himself as an *enfant terrible* who, with his band of New Wave friends, was going to revolutionize the filmmaking enterprise. On the other hand, probably no practicing filmmaker before Truffaut was more knowledgeable about film history, and none, with the exception of Godard, sought to advertise so self-consciously the continuities between past practice and his own. In the early phase of his career, however, Truffaut chose not to "assume" the sum total of French film history. He "reset" history so that it would extol selected heroes of the older generation, such as Gance, Vigo, Ophuls, and Renoir, and denigrate what he termed *le cinéma de papa* of Claude Autant-Lara, Jean Delannoy, and René Clément—directors whose film practice derived from the man who, to Truffaut's mind, was already a *grand-papa*, Marcel Carné.

Once more, Bloch's analysis of the defeat is illuminating. Exhibiting "a curious form of mental sclerosis," French war leaders were incapable of thinking in new terms. They were confined by regulations, an allegiance to "inflexible tradition," and a "particular type of imagination" that excluded adaptability, spontaneity, and improvisation: "The chief defect of the system lay in the fact that officers had been taught at peacetime lectures to attach too much importance to *manoeuvre* and to theoretical tactics: in other words to *book*-knowledge. Unconsciously they had gotten into the habit of expecting that everything would happen as the manuals said it would. When the Germans refused to play the game according to Staff-College rules, they found themselves as much at sea as the public speaker who is faced by questions to which he has not been taught the answers."[60]

If one substitutes shooting script for military manual, Bloch's remarks describe Carné's filmmaking praxis. Like the aging commanders in 1940 who clung to their memories of 1918 and the lessons about Napoleon learned in military school, Carné's closed-film aesthetic in *Les Visiteurs du soir* exhibits, more intensively than in prior works, the same meticulous attention to formal order and balance (derived from Clair), the same impeccable sense of composition and significant detail (derived from Feyder), the same slow-paced shots and mannered camera movements (derived from Murnau), and the same quest (derived from *Kammerspielfilme* and Lang) to penetrate beneath the surface of people and things already inhabiting a space more mythic than real. For those who sought to rewrite film history in the 1950s, Carné was as much a bogy to be repressed as were the French generals who had led France to defeat. According to the New History, the *Wunderkind* of 1939 was an irrelevant fossil by 1946.

Les Visiteurs du soir's kinship with other Occupation-made films must not obscure its specificity. In its restraint, distance, and literary-pictorial inspiration, *Les Visiteurs du soir* partakes of an emerging Occupation aesthetic which Evelyn Ehrlich felicitously names "the cinema of isolation."[61] This so-called school embraces historical films, such as Baron-celli's *La Duchesse de Langeais* (1942), Delannoy's *Pontcarral, colonel d'empire* (1942), and Autant-Lara's *Douce* (1942); fantasy films, includ-ing Delannoy's *L'Eternel Retour* (1943) and Serge de Poligny's *Le Baron Fantôme* (1943) and *La Fiancée des ténèbres* (1945); and films set in purportedly realistic and contemporary contexts, such as Grémillon's *Lumière d'été* (1943), Bresson's *Les Anges du péché* (1943), and Henri-Georges Clouzot's *Le Corbeau* (1943). A causal relation between France's oppressive political order and the stylization, coldness, and her-meticism of these films is plausible. Yet it is crucial to note that the most distinctive features of this "cinema of isolation" were virtually all present in the prewar Carné-Prévert works.

Both the Germans and Vichyites encouraged artists to turn away from current realities. Vichy, especially, was given to glorifying old national heroes—Joan of Arc, Sully, and Henri IV—in order to legitimate the "roots" (a favored word among Pétainists) of the New Moral Order. In Paris the Germans applauded publisher Bernard Grasset when he launched a series of books entitled *A La Recherche de la France*, in which pro-Nazi writers Jacques Doriot, Drieu la Rochelle, and Georges Suarez proffered sanitized versions of France's past. The extent to which histor-ical films, especially those informed by the aesthetic of isolation, actually upheld Pétainist ideology is unsure.[62] It is certain that Alfred Greven did not use his influence to sabotage or suppress *Les Visiteurs du soir*. But it is also certain that in choosing 1485 as the setting of their film, the cre-ators of *Drôle de Drame*, *Le Quai des Brumes*, and *Le Jour se lève* did not plan their escape to the past in order to extol France's heritage. As in their earlier works, Carné and Prévert sought to capture and indict the failings of a society gone amuck.

Writing in 1948, Roger Régent understood that one of the elements mak-ing *Les Visiteurs du soir* seem in 1943 "the biggest cinematic shock in years" was its unconventional presentation of love: "More than a mere palace revolt, [this film] threatened to assail the cinema's old regime at its deepest foundations . . . all the false gods of movie sex appeal were overturned; all the distorting mirrors that graced the walls of Joinville, Hollywood, and Cinecittà were shattered . . . Marcel Carné's film emit-ted sounds so unusual that the public did not always perceive the mod-ulations . . . Used to the sentimental adventures and psychological work-outs of ordinary film heroes, the public was disconcerted by *Les Visiteurs du soir*'s gift of love in a pure state."[63]

Régent did not specify the nature of this "pure" love. But his assertion that it entails something audiences found menacing and confusing suggests that the ambivalence and negativity still generated by *Les Visiteurs du soir* is tied to the film's gender dynamics. *Les Visiteurs du soir* is a story about freedom of choice in selecting one's partner. It openly disparages the institutions of family and marriage. It tampers with conventional distinctions between masculinity and femininity. Such themes ran counter to Vichy's ideology. But the prejudices that made these themes offensive to the Vichy establishment have outlived Vichy.

Les Visiteurs du soir was the first Carné film to grant Arletty top billing. Her Dominique is one of the great portrayals in the French cinema, yet it is the actress's least sympathetic and most vexing role. Prévert has spoken of Arletty's "chaste beauty."[64] In *Les Visiteurs du soir*, she corresponds more to what her friend Céline describes as "that beauty which, far from bringing souls round to God, leads them astray instead."[65] Carné sketches the role as follows: "Who better than [Arletty], in effect, could play Dominique, an androgynous character but in whom is found all of womankind's trickery, and also all its grace" (*Vbd*, 193). Carné's "but" is significant. As of his directing *Hôtel du Nord*, Carné sought to undo Arletty's showy persona. In *Le Jour se lève*, Arletty's Clara retains a measure of vitality, but of a less obvious kind. In *Les Visiteurs du soir*, her character is altogether lifeless. Dominique fulfills her diabolic duties like an automaton, walking through her assignment with the nonchalance of an actress reciting lines she only barely pretends to believe in. She reminds the Devil, "You know well that I am incapable of suffering, incapable of grief, of joy . . . (*lowering her voice*) . . . of pleasure . . ."

According to Arletty, this *grande tranquillité* is more at one with her genuine personality than the flashiness she exhibited in her stage and screen comedies.[66] This may be so. But Carné was attempting to turn Arletty into an emotionless icon. Disguised as an effeminate boy for a good part of the film, Dominique jostles normal codes of erotic attraction. During the dance, Renaud glances in the direction of Dominique, who is seated (fig. 49). Renaud's fascination with the "boy" is conveyed by a slow, subjective tilt of the camera that moves down, in one shot, from Dominique's head to the base of his/her doublet, and then holds on his/her shapely crossed legs sheathed in dark tights and boots. Dominique thereupon immobilizes the celebrants, assumes a female appearance, and begins to seduce Renaud. No homosexuality occurs, but an ambience of ambiguous erotic desire takes hold. The fear of being thought homosexual shapes a subsequent segment of the film. During the hunt Renaud intrudes upon the Baron and Dominique as Hugues is on

49 Arletty (left) disguised as a male youth

his knees passionately kissing Dominique's hands; the two spring apart as Renaud approaches (fig. 50). The setting is a demolished stone house. The script reads: "In the opening of the door, Renaud looks at Dominique and Hugues. He seeks to hide his mortification [*déconvenue*]." Renaud is mortified that his future father-in-law is dallying with the woman to whom he, too, is attracted. Hugues is likewise stunned, but for another reason: he is unaware that Renaud knows that Dominique, still dressed as a boy, is a woman. "With utmost embarrassment," the Baron assures Renaud of Dominique's gender and speedily arranges a public ceremony at the castle to exhibit Dominique as a beauteous woman.

Despite Carné's use of the term, Dominique is not "androgynous." Androgyny denotes the capacity of a single person of either sex to embody the full range of human character traits, regardless of sociocultural efforts to render some exclusively feminine and some exclusively masculine.[67] Androgyny expands human experience. Dominique, on the

50 Primal confusion: Renaud (Marcel Herrand) having intruded upon an intimate moment between the Baron (Fernand Ledoux) and Dominique (Arletty, dressed as a young man)

contrary, embodies values which, for millennia, have been ascribed specifically to women: treachery, carnality, and the responsibility of humankind's fall from grace. Steeped in biblical and Arthurian traditions, Dominique is a serpentine enchantress who ensnares the Baron while moving a full 360 degrees around him. As a figure of German Occupation, Dominique's success vis-à-vis both Hugues and Renaud underscores once again France's susceptibility to capitulation. Yet Dominique also points to Carné's attitude toward women. Dominique exploits and subjugates, but Carné exploits and subjugates the natural vigor of Arletty. As the woman who most fascinates Carné, Arletty possesses that which most intimidates Carné—a female biology. Rather than capitulate to the mystery of Arletty's femininity, Carné controls it by reducing her to two types: the delicate young man and the invincible femme fatale. Both reduce anxiety because, for Carné, the second is as abstract and unreal as the first is familiar.

Nevertheless, Arletty's face and body transcend Carné's constraints. They enable her to project a persona neither totally defeminized nor awesomely mythic. If the landscape from which she first emerges evokes a Leonardo sketch, Dominique's impassive exterior is as strangely sensuous as the Mona Lisa's. In the cinema, less is often more. Arletty's screen genius lies in her capacity to convey the texture of a past without having to articulate it. Early in the film we learn that Dominique and Gilles are condemned to eternal damnation for having played at love with one another. Each sought to dominate the other and give nothing in return. Dominique recalls: "You would look at me like a cat spying a mouse. But the cat found himself opposite another cat . . . good-bye mouse . . . It's not our fault . . . we each imagined ourselves before a new and tender victim . . . two executioners face to face . . . no one to torture . . . what sadness!" Like Clara in *Le Jour se lève*, Dominique accepts her fate with decorum. But her worldweariness camouflages regret at being unable to love.

Baudelaire defined a beautiful female face as one that induces "simultaneous, though somewhat confused, visions of sensuality and sadness . . . a passionate desire to live as well as a bitterness that seems to stem from deprivation or desperation." Arletty's Dominique embodies Baudelaire's schema. Carné needed to straitjacket Arletty, but Arletty insisted on retaining that "something a little vague" which Baudelaire deemed essential to woman's beauty.[68]

Renaud, by contrast, leaves little uncertain. He begins as a proud warrior for whom Anne is a possession: "Soon you will belong to me entirely . . . Do you understand? . . . All your pleasures, all your desires, and all your pains—if you have any—will be due to me." Scorning Anne's femininity, Renaud prohibits her from dreaming: "Dreams are harmful things . . . and useless . . . Me, I never dream." Whatever he considers unbecoming to men, such as beauty and the capacity to dream, he destroys. The executioner informs Gilles, "The knight Renaud has given me the order to alter your body and face so that no girl will ever again risk falling in love with you." Like Lucien in *Le Quai des Brumes*, Renaud is obsessed by a myth of masculine image. Such men are prime prey for equally rigid femmes fatales. By the film's end Dominique manipulates Renaud to seek out his own death.

Gilles and Anne exist independent of gender expectations. Mainstream filmmaking generally defines women by their "to-be-looked-at-ness" and men by their active, determining gaze.[69] In Carné's oeuvre the bearers of significant erotic glances are often women: for example, Dany in *Jenny* and Margarett in *Drôle de Drame*. Even when the bearer of a significant

51 Alain Cuny as Gilles, shackled by the Devil

erotic glance is a man, the object of the glance tends not to be a woman, but rather a woman and a man together, as in *Hôtel du Nord*; a man alone, as in *Le Quai des Brumes*; or two men together, as at the climax of *Le Jour se lève*. Alain Cuny's Gilles furthers Carné's subversion of common notions of masculinity in film.

Gilles's allure is decidedly passive (fig. 51). Cuny (b. 1913) had recently begun a career on the Paris stage, where he created the role of Orpheus in Anouilh's *Eurydice* (1942). Truffaut recalls that one critic described the slowness of his stage delivery by observing: "Grass springs up between the lines . . . If you want to catch the last Métro, you'd better not go hear Alain Cuny." [70] Cuny's torpor suited *Les Visiteurs du soir*. So did his unusual good looks. Jean Debrix writes: "Alain Cuny was one of this film's revelations. His marble face, closed like a fist and severely chiseled as if by mysterious torments; that mouth which was nothing more than a seam; that thick head of hair; those impenetrable features, entirely closed off like a tombstone—all were singularly eloquent." [71]

52 Gilles (Alain Cuny) as the object in an eroticized spectacle

Handsome leading men, in and of themselves, do not unsettle film conventions. But if a director accentuates the erotic force of male beauty, if
that beauty is photographed so delicately as to seem ethereal, and if that
man appears as a favored object of the camera's gaze, norms are disturbed.

When Gilles sings the Kosma-Prévert ballads "Démons et merveilles"
and "Le Tendre Et Dangereux Visage de l'amour," he is the sexual object
in an erotic spectacle intended to provoke illicit desire in Anne (fig. 52).
The lyrics of "Démons et merveilles" compare the gracefulness of the
poet's beloved to that of seaweed "gently caressed by the wind," and her
eyes to the sea's waves in which he has drowned. But in fact Anne drowns
at the sight of Gilles. It is not so much his song (which Cuny mouths to
a recording by Jacques Jansen) as his body that attracts Anne. Throughout the song Gilles is positioned several feet from the dais at which Anne
is flanked by her father and fiancé. In moving progressively from medium
distance to close-up, the seven shots that alternate between views of
Gilles and Anne communicate Anne's emotional surge toward Gilles.
Anne rises as if in a trance while Gilles intones "Le Tendre Et Dangereux
Visage de l'amour," but she is restrained by the hand of Renaud, ravaged
by jealousy. Renaud, shot in three-quarter profile, casts a proprietary
glance upon Anne. In continuing nevertheless to rivet her gaze upon

Gilles, Anne usurps the masculine prerogative of the aggressive erotic look. Unhinging matters of gender still further, Gilles sings from a woman's point of view. His second song describes the feelings of a woman wounded by the sight of a face and unable to determine if Cupid has taken the form of a dangerous archer or a tender musician. The lyrics mirror Anne's state. But a man, Gilles, articulates that state with tenderness, sensitivity, and empathy—qualities generally deemed feminine.

Inclining toward genuine androgyny, Anne and Gilles are the better because of it. For all his gentleness, Gilles is the only man who defies the Devil. For all her imposed demureness, Anne asserts male-associated traits of rational thought and publicly expressed convictions. Actress Marie Déa's looks correspond to the unthreatening ingénue types Carné chose to play off against Arletty's overt sexuality in *Hôtel du Nord* and *Le Jour se lève*. Yet her actions undo Carné's personal typology, which would relegate Anne to the role of chaste and obedient wife and mother. A figure of incipient rationalism in an epoch imbued with superstition, Anne rejects subordination to her father, her betrothed, and, most important, the Devil. To Berry's "I am the Devil," she responds dispassionately, "If you only knew how little I'm impressed." Emotionally free, she feels no dishonor for loving Gilles: "I don't even know what shame is." Politically astute, she is willing to lie in order to save her lover from the Devil.

The desirability of normalcy and the undesirability of deviation were fundamental tenets of German Nazism, French Fascism, and Vichy's New Moral Order. They led to extreme homophobia and antifeminism. The Occupation saw the strengthening in France of Fascist gangs, such as Jacques Doriot's Parti Populaire Français and Joseph Darnand's Service d'Ordre Légionnaire. These collaborationist bands viewed themselves as "modern *chevaliers* rooting out asocial weeds on behalf of a doctrine of national resurrection."[72] They sought to repudiate, through "tough" and "virile" action, the decadence spawned of Republicanism and democracy. The English historian Richard Cobb has analyzed the pose of virility assumed by collaborationist writers and intellectuals whose fantasies were often realized by these gangs. In the works of Brasillach, Drieu la Rochelle, and Marcel Déat, for example, Cobb notes a fondness for simple verbs of movement and action, a repetition of words associated with mountain climbing, an obsessive emphasis on physical cleanliness and rippling muscles, and a concept of women as objects of masculine conquest: "Montherlant went even further, assigning to

France a feminine role in a sexual relationship with a triumphant and virile Germany: a marriage that was a recurrent theme in collaborationist literature, and that had its parallel in the proposed alliance between a purely rural France and a highly industrialized Germany—the marriage of Ceres and Vulcan."[73]

Les Visiteurs du soir obviously stands counter to this ideology. But paradoxically, its slow tempo, delicate style, and ambiguous gender distinctions lend support to the simplistic Fascist notion that the French lacked the manly strength possessed by the Germans. For those French still unwilling to accept the realities of defeat and Occupation, viewing *Les Visiteurs du soir* is doubly unpleasant. First, by allegorizing the sluggishness and decay that facilitated the Occupation, the film perpetuates the memory of a strain of Fascist propaganda that had some basis in truth. Second, by contesting the primacy of marriage, family, and clear gender distinctions, it forces acknowledgment that certain biases espoused fiercely by Vichy's totalitarian regime continue to prevail in liberal society as well. It seems to me that part of the critical evasiveness and negativity provoked by *Les Visiteurs du soir* has resulted from the film's correspondence in style and content to what still tends to be thought of, deprecatingly, as male "homosexual art": exquisite refinement; subtle allusion and symbol; ambiguous expression of the repressed; a steady consciousness of the dark side of love; heightened awareness of the feelings and assumptions of others; an immediate consciousness of the fragility of the shields that hide human cruelty from general view; a search for transcendent alternatives to ordinary human relations.[74]

Reexamination of his article written for *Revue Jeux et Poésie* suggests that André Bazin was most troubled by the film's dénouement. Commending Carné's use of special effects (which he faulted several sentences earlier), Bazin writes: "We will long remember the moment in which the ball is magically suspended so that Gilles and Dominique can step out of time to exercise their evil charms. We will also remember the spot of blood that clouds the water of the fountain in which Gilles and Anne are watching the tournament."[75] Bazin chooses not to praise the film's most spectacular effect—the Devil's metamorphosis of Anne and Gilles into interlocking statues that emit, to the Devil's chagrin, a joint heartbeat (fig. 53). Bazin's omission is not trivial because, from the time of the film's release, this *coup de cinéma* was viewed generally as its most forceful and memorable image.

The androgynous character of the metamorphosis is clear. Gilles's and Anne's bodies are welded together, and a single heart functions for both.

53 A *coup de cinéma* with psychological and political overtones: the Devil's petrification of Anne and Gilles

The image gives visual expression to Prévert's pet saying, "I am a man; I am a woman; I am plural." It concretizes Carné's view of love as passion at once indulged in and eternally deferred. Additionally, these final moments resonate with the Carnésian motif of the primal intrusive gaze. Early in the picture Anne refuses to look at the hideous dwarfs. Directing her glance toward Gilles, she chooses to recognize only what she perceives as pure and untainted. Hugues and Renaud, by contrast, surrender to desire. They take part in a primal scene that finds Renaud intruding upon Dominique (dressed as a boy) and Hugues in an embarrassing moment of intimacy. This episode may be viewed as the playing out of Carné's fantasy of a son (Renaud) emasculating a father (Hugues) in order to possess a mother (Dominique). As the plot develops, however, the fantasy reverses itself and the father destroys the son (in the joust). A parallel drama transpires among Anne, Gilles, and the Devil. The son (Gilles) defies the father (the Devil) in an attempt to seize the female object of the father's affections (Anne). In this case, the son wins out—

but not until the father (the Devil) unsuccessfully undertakes to emasculate the son by depriving him of memory.

Psychoanalyst Luisa de Urtubey has demonstrated that, for Freud, the devil signified at once the aggregate of unconscious libidinal desires and the father. The father in question is not the parental superego but rather an "archaic father," a "false, seductive, perverse, lawless" father who "coincides very well with the popular image of the devil, capable of all misdeeds . . . he who transgresses God's law." [76] In *Les Visiteurs du soir*, where legitimate authority is absent, the Devil corresponds to the double function elaborated by Freud. In winning out over the Devil, Gilles gains control over the libido. Breaking from the Devil's spell that plunged him into forgetfulness, Gilles acquires heretofore smothered traits of emotional maturity, namely, the capacity for combining autonomy with attachment, and self-determination with affection for another. In short, Gilles becomes a positively-valued father figure wedded to a positively-valued mother figure (Anne). Petrified but alive, Gilles and Anne gaze into one another's eyes for eternity. Reduced to a childish tantrum, the intrusive Devil fades from sight.

At the same time, the petrified couple's beating heart constitutes a compelling image of France's refusal to submit entirely to German subjugation, and Gilles's recovery of memory signifies France's consciousness of its past freedom. Taken together, these two motifs proffer a message of hope. They are also a satirical play on an incident that occurred on June 21, 1940. Hitler insisted that the French receive his peace terms at Rethondes, the spot in the Forest of Compiègne where Generals Foch and Weygand had handed the Allied armistice terms to the defeated Germans twenty-two years earlier. Swastika-ornamented cloths were draped over the monuments commemorating the 1918 signing. But one great granite block was left unsheathed. It bore the inscription: "Here on the eleventh of November 1918 succumbed the criminal pride of the German people." When Hitler saw this, his face lit up with scorn, anger, and hate. Journalist William L. Shirer reported: "[Hitler] steps off the monument and continues to make even this gesture a masterpiece of contempt. He glances back at it, contemptuous, angry—angry, you almost feel, because he cannot wipe out the awful, provoking lettering with one sweep of his high Prussian boot . . . You grasp the depth of his hatred. But there is triumph there, too—revengeful, triumphant hate." [77] Three days later the marble block, upon Hitler's orders, was blown up. When the Devil in *Les Visiteurs du soir* identifies the statue's heartbeat, the Carné-Prévert script reads, "The Devil then brandishes above his head the riding whip he held in hand, and, suddenly seized with a kind of mad fury, begins to beat the stone with his arm, raving ceaselessly." The allusion to Hitler is clear. Thanks to a trick effect, the Devil in *Les Visiteurs du soir* fades away. At the site in Rethondes, Hitler's madness prevailed.

A left-wing Catholic, Bazin was a disciple of Emmanuel Mounier. From Mounier's philosophy of Personalism he learned to value human action over metaphysics. Although the universe may contain mysteries beyond human understanding, individuals, Mounier professed, have the freedom and responsibility to choose and to act. Never a genuine Resister, Bazin wrote for the Resistance journal *Rencontres*. He also helped to organize Pierre-Aimé Touchard's Maison des Lettres, a leftist cultural center on the rue Soufflot that spawned numerous Resistance fighters. Like Teilhard de Chardin, Sartre, and Malraux, Bazin came to conceive of art as an activity by which human beings can remake their world and their situation in it.[78] The final image of *Les Visiteurs du soir* makes action impossible. By situating the metamorphosis at a fountain far from the castle and its garden, now the site of damnation, Carné and Prévert recreate a pristine earthly paradise from which base desire is absent. It is therefore natural that Bazin, a Catholic, would praise the film for realizing "a high poetic standard, and, more generally, a spiritual one." But in their remoteness from the castle, Anne and Gilles are severed from society and realpolitik. It is therefore also fitting that Bazin, the Personalist, would be displeased with what he called the film's lack of "faith"— faith in humanity to effect social change.

From this view came Bazin's statement that *Les Visiteurs du soir* is not as "great" a film as *La Grande Illusion*. To be authentic, convictions must bear deeds. In Renoir's film the goal of the communal effort to escape imprisonment is never in question: to fight and defeat the enemy. In the Carné-Prévert picture, however, the protagonists' state of spiritualized immobility mirrors what Marc Bloch saw as "the appalling situation" of 1940: "that the fate of France no longer depends upon the French."[79] Anne and Gilles's heartbeat is an uplifting symbol of France's ability to endure. But encased within a petrified shell, the symbol cannot generate the "warmth" and "elan" that, for Bazin, infuses *La Grande Illusion*. Vanquished France required more than hearts preserved intact; she required that French blood be shed.

Given censorship restraints, it is implausible that Carné—or any other leading filmmaker—could have produced a film that would have rallied the public to oppose Vichy and the Occupiers. Certain pictures made during the Occupation had politically subversive bite: Louis Daquin's *Nous Les Gosses* (1941), Delannoy's *Pontcarral, colonel d'empire* (1942), and Grémillon's *Le Ciel est à vous* (1944). But the messages of even these movies were veiled. Their political interpretation is still subject to debate.[80] Moreover, Carné and Prévert were pacifists. From *Drôle de Drame* forward, they viewed their films not as instruments to change the world, but as means for conveying the tone of the times. Epitomized by the statue's eternal suspension between transcendence and petrification, *Les Visiteurs du soir* exposes rudely the sentimental core of Prévert's political ethos and the real-world impotence of Carné's yearnings for a more perfect society.

Carné insists that by directing *Les Visiteurs du soir* he served the best interests of France. He provided work for hundreds of compatriots. He demonstrated that France's creative spirit could not be squelched by the Nazis. Carné does not acknowledge, however, that the making of a prestigious French film promoted Germany's propaganda effort and economic strategies as well.[81] If creativity of a high order was possible under Occupation, could France's fate be so dreadful? With war ended and a victorious Germany reigning over a "new Europe," would not films like *Les Visiteurs du soir* be bulwarks against American competition? A letter to producer Paulvé from Georges Franju, then executive secretary of the International Federation of Film Archives, divulges the German tactic. Dated January 26, 1944, it specifies that "thanks to [the] intervention" of the German consul general to Paris, authorization has been granted to send prints of *Les Visiteurs du soir* to foreign French embassies "in the name of French Propaganda." [82]

Carné was not a collaborationist. He never supported Fascism. But his life and work exhibit a fundamental imperviousness to matters beyond his individual sphere of concern. The war exacerbated this trait. For Carné, southern France became Xanadu—a realm in which to exert an artistic voice founded upon the same symbolic systems that characterized his prewar films. His pictures of this period stand as enduring monuments of French civilization. Unquestionably, *Les Visiteurs du soir* is an exquisite work of art. But in sealing himself off from change, Carné was incapable of assessing the full relations between politics and art in a time of war. He was insensitive to the similarities between his cinematic distillation of rarefied truths and Nazism's pursuit of a sanitized reality. He chose not to contemplate that Fascism and filmmaking are both predicated upon collective consent to illusion. He chose not to understand that poetic resistance was no more capable of bringing about change than was poetic realism.

Carné was France's leading young filmmaker in 1939. He took pride in his leftist leanings. He considered himself a voice of the people. He rejoiced when the establishment found his work threatening. For the postwar generation, this early Carné set up expectations that he failed to realize. The war tested the moral convictions of all French citizens. Measured by *Les Visiteurs du soir*, Carné deserves mixed grades at best. The director's postwar decline was due to numerous factors, but it is clear that some people repudiated Carné out of the belief that a celebrity of his stature would have done more good for France by remaining silent than by making *Les Visiteurs du soir*.

CHAPTER 10

The Design of
Children of Paradise

Les Enfants du paradis marks the culmination of France's Golden Age of moviemaking. Never again would the French cinema produce a film so unashamedly literate and lavish. Among postwar fiction features it remains unsurpassed in the quality of its star acting and the richness of its plot, psychology, and period reconstruction. The French regard Marcel Carné as a national institution because of the six motion pictures he directed between 1937 and 1945. Carné's international renown results principally from *Les Enfants du paradis*. Until that unlikely time when movie viewers become unresponsive to impeccably mounted displays of grand feeling and form, *Les Enfants du paradis* will retain a privileged position among film masterworks.

Les Enfants du paradis is also Carné's last great work. It is, at once, a realization of his artistic vision and an indicator of his subsequent inability to revitalize that vision. More forcefully than any of Carné's prior films, *Les Enfants du paradis* discloses the problematic factors associated with the director and his oeuvre: the uncertain attribution of authorship; the ambiguous political implications of his aesthetic; and his unsettling representation of the sexes. Individually and in combination, these factors worked against Carné's professional fortunes from 1946 onward. But with respect to *Les Enfants du paradis*, multiple authorship, political equivocation, and subversive gender depictions benefited the creation of an exceptional work of film art.

In triggering its genesis and shaping large portions of its development, Jean-Louis Barrault is as much the picture's *auteur* as are Carné, Prévert, and Trauner. Barrault was demobilized in Toulouse after France's defeat. Disturbed by Pétain's tenet that the subjugated nation was rightfully atoning for past transgressions, Barrault, like Carné, believed that "above all, France had to safeguard its Spirit." [1] The actor contemplated establishing artistic roots in Aix-en-Provence. But an offer from Jacques

Copeau to join the Comédie Française brought him back to Paris, where he dazzled audiences in 1940 and 1941 in performances of *Phèdre* and *Hamlet*.

In late summer of 1942 Barrault took a vacation on the Riviera to join his wife, actress Madeleine Renaud, who was then working on Grémillon's *Lumière d'été*. This sojourn led to an encounter with Carné and Prévert in Nice, during which Barrault entertained the others with anecdotes about theater life past and present. One story dealt with the legendary nineteenth-century mime Jean-Gaspard Deburau, known as Baptiste (1796–1846). Deburau had revitalized the art of pantomime as performed at the Théâtre des Funambules, one of the numerous theaters located along the Boulevard du Temple. Walking one day with his wife, Deburau was approached by a young scoundrel who insulted the couple repeatedly. At first Deburau attempted to contain his anger, but finally, unable to tolerate the abuse, he brandished his walking stick and hit the knave on the head so violently that the latter collapsed. Within little over an hour the man was pronounced dead. More remarkable than this event was its aftermath. Hordes of Parisians tried to gain admission to the murder trial in order to hear—for the very first time—their great mime speak.[2]

Barrault was toying with the idea of staging a show that would contrast silent acting with talking acting. He had assembled substantial documentation on two historical figures: Deburau, who allegedly transformed the commedia dell'arte's Pedrolino into the Romantic, lovelorn Pierrot; and Frédérick Lemaître (1800–1876), the actor for whom Hugo, Dumas *père*, and Vigny wrote landmark Romantic dramas. Barrault's fascination with this duo stemmed from a personal experience: "At the heart of it all was Charlie Chaplin. When I first learned that Chaplin was going to speak in films, I remember rushing to the theater simply to hear the sound of his voice. This was an exceptional theatrical event for me, and I soon began to associate Charlot with the Deburau anecdote and its implications. Carné and Prévert were looking for a subject. Prévert was like an older brother to me ever since we had both been active in the Groupe Octobre. So I readily offered him my idea and research materials."[3]

Prévert was initially reluctant to consider the subject. According to his brother, "Jacques hated pantomime."[4] Prévert warmed to the subject only when Barrault assured the scenarist that he and his teacher, Etienne Decroux, would take responsibility for elaborating the mime sequences. Trauner offers an additional reason for Prévert's change of heart: "Jacques had already considered writing a screenplay about the poet-assassin Pierre-François Lacenaire [1800–1836], known as the *dandy du crime*." The notion of interlacing that story with those of Deburau and Lemaître posed an irresistible challenge to the scriptwriter with a penchant for intricate plotmaking.[5]

Carné sensed immediately that adherence to the anecdote about Deburau would prove thorny. If Barrault were to play Deburau, the impact of the ending—the mime talks!—would be lost on film audiences already familiar with the voice of an actor swiftly becoming France's leading man of the theater and already a veteran of motion pictures. But Carné was intoxicated by the idea of re-creating on celluloid the acrobatics, side shows, vaudevilles, and dramas performed along the Boulevard du Temple during the regimes of Charles X and Louis-Philippe. Determined to sustain his enthusiasm, he rushed to the Musée Carnavalet in Paris and studied its collections of etchings, costumes, and curios that trace the capital's history. Following Carné's lead, Prévert researched in depth the lives of Deburau, Lemaître, and Lacenaire.

Both the director and scenarist intuited that to do this subject justice their film would have to be longer than usual and possibly more expensive than any in the history of the French cinema. Producer Paulvé was undaunted by such speculation. Elated by the artistic success of *Les Visiteurs du soir*, Paulvé assured Carné that his production company, Discina, and its Italian affiliate, Scalera, were prepared to meet all costs.

No movie made during the Occupation encountered more obstacles than *Les Enfants du paradis*.[6] As had been the case for *Les Visiteurs du soir*, the Jewish members of Carné's team—Trauner and Kosma—were obliged to work clandestinely. Thiriet "fronted" again for Kosma. Kosma's themes, orchestrated by Thiriet, were performed and recorded for the film by the Paris Conservatory Orchestra under the direction of Charles Munch. Léon Barsacq, responsible for the sets in Renoir's *La Marseillaise* (1938), volunteered his name and services to help Trauner. With the assistance of Jeanne Lanvin, painter Antoine Mayo executed Trauner's costume designs.

Prévert had rented rooms in a farmhouse known as Le Prieuré (fig. 54). Located just beyond the mountain village of Tourrettes-sur-Loup, near Nice, this isolated retreat was owned and managed by Madeleine Flamand. Flamand assisted Prévert in shielding Trauner, who resided at Le Prieuré under an assumed identity. Carné decided that preproduction would progress more efficiently if he, too, moved into Le Prieuré. For six months the trio worked on the screenplay. As Prévert wrote, Carné

54 Le Prieuré in 1985: the farmhouse near Tourrettes-sur-Loup in which
Prévert, Carné, and Trauner planned *Les Enfants du paradis*

would comment and Trauner would sketch, and an exhilarating exchange imbued each with the perceptions and sensibilities of the others.

Prévert tailored characterization to conform not only to history but to
the actors he and Carné foresaw playing leading roles: Barrault, Arletty,
Pierre Brasseur, Marcel Herrand, Etienne Decroux, Maria Casarès, Louis
Salou, and Robert Le Vigan. However, Barrault's commitment to direct
Claudel's *Le Soulier de satin* for the Comédie Française imperiled the
film's production. *Le Soulier de satin* turned out to be one of the outstanding theatrical events of 1943. But its preparation placed Barrault—
and Carné—under sizable stress. The actor-director recalls with amusement, "I often had to rush from the film studio to the theater with my
face covered by Pierrot's white grease paint."[7] Carné was so apprehensive
about the feasibility of this work arrangement that he envisaged offering
the role of Baptiste, alternatively, to a relatively unknown music-hall co-
median, Jacques Tati, "whose silhouette actually evoked that depicted by
contemporary engravings of Deburau more than did Barrault's" (*Vbd*,
222). Only after considerable negotiation was a schedule agreed upon
that would permit Barrault to work on both monumental productions
simultaneously.

Filming began on August 17, 1943. The shooting plan called for three
distinct stages. The outdoor Boulevard du Temple sequences and most of
the interior sequences would be shot, in that order, at Victorine Studios

in Nice. Additional scenes would be filmed, near the end of production, at Paris's Joinville and Francoeur Studios. Minor delays in the completion of the elaborate exterior set caused shooting to begin with some of the indoor scenes. Shortly thereafter, Trauner's Boulevard was ready and the crew reverted to its original schedule.

Never again would Carné's passion for fabricating self-contained cityscapes find an outlet so grandiose (fig. 55). Situated near the working-class districts of Saint-Antoine and Saint-Denis, the actual Boulevard du Temple owed its name to the medieval order of Templars, which had been associated with the area in the twelfth and thirteenth centuries. By the Revolution of 1789 the Boulevard had become a popular strolling area, attracting peddlers and showmen who occasionally set up booths. Many of the puppet, acrobat, and pantomime playhouses that sprang up following the Revolution were suppressed during the Empire. But with the Bourbon restoration of 1814, theatrical activity boomed. The most notable theaters included the Gaîté, the Ambigu-Comique, the Variétés Amusantes, the café-théâtre Bosquet, and the Théâtre des Funambules—the last authorized to present acrobatics and pantomime harlequinades. By the 1820s the Boulevard du Temple was dubbed "Boulevard du Crime" because of the sinister deeds that were standard ingredients of the stage melodramas then the rage. The *Almanach des Spectacles* of

55   An imaginary reinstatement of lost Paris life: the Boulevard du Temple as reconstructed in *Les Enfants du paradis*

1823 tallied the "crimes" committed on the Boulevard over a twenty-year period. It disclosed that 151,702 had been shared by six actors alone, "who none the less appear to enjoy excellent health and widespread esteem." [8] During the Second Empire, Baron Haussmann's urban-renovation efforts led to the demolition of the Boulevard's row of theaters on July 15, 1862, making way for the present Place de la République.

For the closed-film director whose earliest efforts at spectaclemaking entailed locking his friends in his father's bedroom to look at one-picture slide shows, the reconstruction of the Boulevard du Temple was a dream come true. It enabled Carné to reinstate a slice of lost Paris life (symbolically resonant with the early childhood years spent with his mother in the working-class district of the Batignolles) and to conjure up, on a magnified yet thoroughly controllable scale, versions of the primitive, childlike pleasures he derived from his first slide shows (symbolic efforts to compensate for a father who had abandoned him emotionally).

The huge set was erected on the lot adjacent to Victorine Studios that had been the site of the gleaming castle in *Les Visiteurs du soir* and that serves today as the studio's parking lot. Because this terrain sloped, 800 cubic meters of earth had to be dug and redistributed before labor could begin. The set's nearly fifty theater and building façades required 35 tons of scaffolding, 350 tons of plaster, and 500 square meters of glass. During a three-month period, an estimated 67,500 man-hours were devoted to construction. Simply laying authentic-looking pavements for the Boulevard and adjacent streets called for eight days of labor. The cost of this single set was five million francs—nearly one tenth of the film's final budget. [9]

After three days of filming the Boulevard scenes, production came to a stunning halt. The invasion of Sicily by American troops in July and August so alarmed the German Occupiers that they ordered cast, crew, and equipment back to Paris immediately. Carné worked feverishly to obtain permission from Louis-Emile Galey, then head of the COIC, to shoot one week longer—the time needed to complete the Boulevard shots. His efforts proved futile: "[Galey] was obeying orders; we had to return" (*Vbd*, 224).

Other events compounded the severity of this setback. In September 1943 Mussolini's successor, Pietro Badoglio, signed an armistice with the Allies. Nice, which had been occupied by Italian forces, fell immediately under German control. Since the Nazis henceforth forbade Franco-Italian co-productions, Paulvé found his financial resources reduced drastically. Moreover, when the authorities determined that a fraction of

Paulvé's ancestry was Jewish, they suspended his right to work. To Carné's mind the inquiry into Paulvé's heritage was the doing of Alfred Greven: the huge success of *Les Visiteurs du soir* had infuriated the director of Continental Films, and this was his way of taking revenge (*Vbd*, 225). In fact, Paulvé was allowed subsequently to produce a film with a lesser director—Pierre Billon's *Mademoiselle X*, which went into production on May 23, 1944.

For two months *Les Enfants du paradis* seemed doomed. Several journalists attempted to raise public consciousness in an effort to ensure that this uncommon production would not perish. In the 5 October 1943 issue of *Le Temps*, Roger Régent wrote: "*Les Enfants du paradis* must be completed . . . It would be rather depressing to imagine that France is free to film a comfortable cargo of lightweight productions but that the authors of *Les Visiteurs du soir*, *Quai des Brumes*, and *Jenny* are constrained either to fold their arms or—if they wish to express themselves in the mode they have made famous—to go into exile."[10]

After complicated negotiations Pathé agreed to take over the production. Shooting resumed in Paris on November 9 and lasted a year. Because of contract extensions, new insurance costs, and indemnification penalties for unused studios, the hiatus added at least ten million to a production budget that would eventually reach the unprecedented figure of fifty-eight million francs or, at the time, the equivalent of one-and-a-quarter million dollars.

When Carné obtained permission to return to the coast in February 1944, he found the Boulevard set damaged severely by a recent storm. Repairs cost nearly one million francs. Worse still were the limitations imposed by the now-stricter curfew regulations. As of August 1943, Nice's curfew was set at seven o'clock. Having planned several night shots of the entire Boulevard du Temple brightly lit, Carné had received permission before the hiatus to deploy scores of spotlights. The authorities now denied his request for an exemption. Two outdoor scenes depicting part of the Boulevard at night do occur in the film: in one, Baptiste arrives at the entrance to the Grand Théâtre while Lemaître's *Othello* is in progress; in an earlier episode, Baptiste and Lemaître drink at a stall in a dark street adjoining the Boulevard. These were shot months later in a Paris studio, using truncated, scaled-down models of Trauner's building façades.

Politics affected the production in still other ways. The theater and street scenes necessitated masses of extras. Each time a casting call took place, German officials accompanied by uniformed soldiers would appear to make certain that a specified percentage of those hired belonged to union locals perceived to be collaborationist. Despite the threat of denunciation, the casting office deceived the Nazis repeatedly by establishing phony personnel lists. When accused of tampering, Carné would intercede with trumped-up artistic justifications to explain why particular sequences demanded particular faces or builds—which, invariably, he could not find among the pool of alleged sympathizers. Less droll was the reality of crew members being hunted down by Gestapo agents. This was the case with the film's original production manager, who, unbeknownst to anyone at the time, was also a Resistance leader. One day, after learning of inquiries being made about him in the front office, he fled the studio through a rear door and never returned (*Vbd*, 227).

More notorious was the disappearance of Robert Le Vigan, for whom Prévert conceived the role of the old clothes man, Jéricho. Throughout the Occupation Le Vigan had publicly voiced racist views that conformed to Fascist ideology. As Germany's defeat became likely, Le Vigan realized that he had to flee France; he eventually joined his friend Céline in Sigmaringen, Germany. Carné replaced him with Pierre Renoir (1885–1952), Jean's elder brother. It remains uncertain, however, exactly when Le Vigan fled and precisely how much of *Les Enfants du paradis* he had filmed. According to Carné, Le Vigan disappeared by the time production resumed in November 1943: "Until that point he had only filmed one scene" (*Vbd*, 226). Yet Arletty insists that he played in "several scenes."[11] Bernard Landry, an early commentator on Carné's oeuvre, and Pol Vandromme, a recent biographer of Le Vigan, both intimate that Le Vigan's participation continued until the events of late spring 1944. "If the Normandy landing had taken place three months later," writes Vandromme, "[Le Vigan's] list of honors would have been enriched by *Les Enfants du paradis* . . . Several scenes shot before the thunder blast of Normandy . . . make clear, according to those privileged persons who have had access to them, that Pierre Renoir's performance, however remarkable, was only an honorable stand-in."[12] Those "privileged persons" remain unidentified, and the footage that includes Le Vigan remains unfound. In light of Le Vigan's postwar conviction and imprisonment for collaboration, it is understandable that Carné would wish to undervalue the perception that he bolstered Le Vigan's prominence during the Occupation. But as we shall see, the antipathetic character Le Vigan was to incarnate in the film constitutes, on its own, a denunciation of collaborationism.

The making of *Les Enfants du paradis* fortified the legend that Carné was France's most demanding, irascible, and invincible film director.

Building materials were scarcer than ever. Film stock was in short supply. Electricity was intermittent. And lives were increasingly entangled in political events that often bore fatal consequences. Yet Marcel Carné persisted in setting extravagant goals and rejecting compromise.

Many co-workers from this period harbor ambivalent feelings about their professional relations with Carné. Casting agent Margot Capelier prefers not to recall the misadventures that befell her when serving as Carné's production secretary: "All I will say is that talent is a sickness; Carné suffered from a massive case of it; and I did not relish staying on as his nurse."[13] Property master Fernand Bernardi, who has been associated with Victorine Studios since his apprenticeship on *Les Visiteurs du soir* and *Les Enfants du paradis*, observes: "Like many in this industry, I owe everything I know to Carné. But he tyrannized me and so many others in a manner I shall never forget. He totally terrorized Maria Casarès, for example, and it shows in her acting." Bernardi points to a related component of Carné's character: "If something went wrong on the set, if a gaffer or rigger made the slightest error, Carné would often stop shooting for the entire day. Worse still, he would refuse to accept responsibility if he himself was in error. With absolute *mauvaise foi*, he would attribute the fault to a member of the crew."[14]

Mauvaise foi—bad faith, or insincerity—is a term numerous film veterans utilize when describing Carné. The director is apparently untroubled by the characterization. Near the end of Christian-Jaque's documentary-homage, *Carné, l'homme à la caméra* (1985), Yves Montand and Carné play at filming a scene. When Carné asks if the actor has comprehended his instructions, the former star of *Les Portes de la nuit* (1946) responds, almost with a sneer, "I have comprehended that you have always been *de mauvaise foi*." Carné's unruffled retort lays bare his priorities: "Well, *mauvaise foi* or not, we are now going to shoot."

The contemporary press, which covered the production of *Les Enfants du paradis* with fierce interest, helped to mythologize Carné's creative gifts. Marveling at the ingenious use of the Schüfftan process to create an impression of height in the interior set of the Grand Théâtre, one reporter described Carné in December 1943 as "a modern-day Merlin," "a master sorcerer . . . whose intelligence and taste can create this miraculous illusion."[15] Distinguished celebrities, including Giraudoux and Sartre, were reported to have visited the sound stage to observe the master at work. But the press did not sufficiently recognize that the sorcerer's "magic" was as much a function of financing as of talent. Like Erich von Stroheim during the 1920s in Hollywood, Carné had become the French cinema's spoiled child. He believed—and wanted others to acknowledge—that quality filmmaking was inseparable from extravagant expense. In an interview with *Ciné-Miroir*, Carné related with pride that when an enormous bouquet of flowers costing twenty thousand francs was needed for retakes the next morning, he instructed his production manager not to refrigerate it overnight, but to order an even larger one: "Contemplating a floral basket whose size was even more imposing than the one from the day before, my face lit up. 'How much?' 'Thirty thousand francs,' answered the zealous manager. I smiled broadly and the scene was shot with utmost serenity." [16]

Carné still thinks that superior filmmaking requires huge production budgets. He is unembarrassed at having operated according to a principle which postwar journalists, parodying Descartes's *cogito*, formulated as *Je dépense, donc je suis*—"I spend, therefore I am" (*Vbd*, 271). Carné admits that his reputation as a difficult and expensive director frightened producers and impeded his postwar career. Nevertheless, without denying that he was a spendthrift, Carné currently prefers to characterize his early professional persona as that of a triumphant surmounter of obstacles.

Shooting at Nice ended shortly before the Allied invasion of Normandy in June 1944. Several weeks of filming remained to be done in Paris, but a shortage of construction workers occasioned delay. Carné now delighted in any incident that might serve as a pretext for slowing down production: "As soon as I learned the news of the Normandy landing, I had but one wish: to make the finishing touches last as long as possible in order that the film be released as the first to appear under our finally regained peace" (*Vbd*, 235). Electric power failures and transportation breakdowns served Carné's purpose splendidly. Shooting, editing, and final cutting were not completed until mid-January 1945. But even this was too soon for Carné: "If two tenths of France were liberated, if Paris, its stomach empty, could at least draw a deep breath, the war was still not over. To release the film now, after the vow I had taken, was tantamount to acknowledging a painful defeat" (*Vbd*, 235). At issue was Carné's conviction that *Les Enfants du paradis* would serve as an antidote to France's military defeat.

Quarrels concerning exhibition further helped to delay the film's release. The three-and-a-quarter-hour length of the final print provoked anxiety among the directors of Gaumont, the company responsible for handling distribution. Gaumont revived an idea Paulvé had proposed at the production's outset—that the film be exhibited in Paris in two parcels, with Part I, "Le Boulevard du Crime," playing at the Madeleine Theater and Part II, "L'Homme blanc," showing simultaneously at the Colisée. Carné and executive producer Raymond Borderie objected vehemently, insisting that the picture be shown in its entirety and without intermission in both theaters. They conceded that even with continuous showings and omission of the customary prefeature newsreels, there could be no more than three screenings per day, instead of the usual four or five. To compensate for the anticipated shortfall of receipts, they advocated a novel scheme. Since the film was the equivalent of two ordinary features in length, the public ought not object to paying a higher entrance fee: the usual forty-franc price would be doubled to eighty. And because entertainment offerings in liberated Paris were still very slim and, consequently, spectators were often obliged to stand in line for nearly two hours only to be told that there were no seats remaining, evening screenings would be run on an advance-booking, reserved-seat basis. Any losses would be offset, reasoned Carné and Borderie, by the public's assurance of seating at an evening performance. Gaumont's officials accepted this strategy reluctantly. Their apprehensions were put to rest, however, when *Les Enfants du paradis* opened on March 15 and played for fifty-four consecutive weeks at the Madeleine Theater alone. Combined receipts from the runs at the Colisée and the Madeleine totaled more than forty-one million francs.

A gala preview took place at the Palais de Chaillot on March 9, 1945. A half hour before the film's end, many invited guests left the auditorium. For a moment the hearts of Carné and Prévert—less confident than those of Anne and Gilles in *Les Visiteurs du soir*—ceased to beat. But they deduced correctly that the cause of this exodus was not the audience's reaction to the film. With taxis and private cars still scarce, spectators were simply hurrying to catch the last metro.

Because of its length, scope, and sharpness of detail and characterization, *Les Enfants du paradis* has repeatedly evoked comparisons to nineteenth-century prose fiction.[17] Assuredly, the film's famous first images prime us to anticipate narrative dynamics akin to those of Hugo, Balzac, and Dickens. The sequence of slowly descending crane shots that track and pan along the teeming Boulevard du Temple is the cinematic correlative of the panorama, a mode of perception that came to the fore in both literary and visual depictions of Paris in the mid-nineteenth century. Celebrated examples include Daguerre's dioramas (dating from 1822), Joseph Niepces's photographs taken from rooftops (in the early 1830s), the opening scene of Hugo's *Notre-Dame de Paris* (1831), and the closing moments of Balzac's *Le Père Goriot* (1834–35), in which the ambitious Rastignac surveys Paris from the heights of Père-Lachaise cemetery and vows to conquer the capital. Like these nineteenth-century antecedents, Carné's panorama demarcates the boundaries of an exuberant yet constrained sphere of concern. It announces a closed-film director's rapacious, Balzacian will to dominate the world within his frame.

The introductory panorama is, in effect, a tidy *mise en abyme*, or miniature model, of *Les Enfants du paradis*'s content. Just as the Boulevard's theater companies offer brief *parades*, or outdoor shows, before beginning the main attraction inside, so the opening panorama displays, in visual shorthand, the substance of the plot to come. Functioning as an omniscient, third-person narrator, Carné's wandering camera focuses attention on eight figures: a tightrope walker, Jéricho, horse-drawn carriages, a weightlifter, a monkey on stilts, a merry-go-round, a booth advertising "Naked Truth in a Well," and the stage door to the Théâtre des Funambules. These eight images may be construed as metaphors for the film's major themes: adventure, evil, fate, power, human vanity, the eternal quest, eroticism, and theatrical art, respectively. The initial impact of these quickly passing images is pictorial, but as the film develops, it transforms these dense figures of meaning into extended narrative strains.

Yet *Les Enfants du paradis* does not exhibit certain narrative properties associated specifically with nineteenth-century novels. In its broadest sense, plot may be viewed as a product of humankind's "refusal to allow temporality to be meaningless." [18] *Les Enfants du paradis* glorifies the capacity of theatrical fictions to confer coherence upon real-life experience. It presents a world in which twin theatrical sources, the commedia dell'arte and *Othello*, thoroughly govern human relations. The film's kaleidoscopic succession of loves, jealousies, infidelities, and acts of vengeance transcend triviality to the degree that they are recognizable as variants of established narrative patterns themselves represented in the film, namely, the parallel adventures of Pierrot, Colombina, Harlequin, and Pantalone (comedy and farce), and Othello, Desdemona, Iago, and Brabantio (tragedy and melodrama). Count Edouard de Montray, for example, moves from being perceived as a mocked Pantalone to a misguided Othello to a tragic Pierrot at the same time that Frédérick Lemaître plays out his offstage life as if he were now Harlequin, now Othello, and as both the Count and Lemaître interact with a woman, Garance, variously and simultaneously viewed as Colombina, Desdemona, and the Greek goddess Phoebe. In this regard *Les Enfants du paradis* is an extraordinarily "plotted" work.

But a rhetorical strategy for making sense of nineteenth-century fictions is the anticipation of retrospection, or the reader's assumption that "we read in a spirit of confidence, and also a state of dependence, that what remains to be read will restructure the provisional meanings of the already read." As classical novelistic plots move forward, they typically recover "markings from the past" that lead to a final solution allowing for a claim to finality.[19] One index of *Les Enfants du paradis*'s refusal to shape such endings is the incompleteness of the dramatic fictions that function as "plays-within-the-film." With the exception of Baptiste's first open-air pantomime, all of the film's staged performances are cut short: we glimpse only fragments of the three pantomimes, *Dangers of the Virgin Forest*, *The Palace of Illusions or the Lover of the Moon*, and *The Old Clothes Man*; of the melodrama-turned-farce, *L'Auberge des Adrets* (*Brigands' Inn*); and of Shakespeare's *Othello*. Even as they buttress viewers' confidence in the effort to make sense of the entire film, these truncated fictions contribute to *Les Enfants du paradis*'s overall aesthetic of indeterminateness.

Highly plotted nineteenth-century novels aim for an illusion of spatio-temporal continuity. *Les Enfants du paradis*, on the contrary, is composed of autonomous sequences that follow casually one upon the other with minimal indication of the time, space, and action separating them. No less than in *Le Quai des Brumes* and *Le Jour se lève*, imperfect cadences and evaporating lines of thought characterize plot units. But while the earlier films culminate in endings so definitive as to make, in retrospect, the whole seem subject to an ineluctable fate, *Les Enfants du paradis* withholds all conclusiveness. Prévert's most elaborate screenplay thus undoes that fundamental trait of classical literary narrative which embraces and comprehends the past "as a panorama leading to realization in the ultimate moment."[20]

Carné's opening panorama—and the symmetrical one that closes the film—constitutes a deceptive narrative frame. (It exists, one might say, in a state of *mauvaise foi*.) Offering an impression of overwhelming plenitude and nearly unbroken spatiotemporal flow, it prepares viewers to anticipate a film whose narrative texture will emulate works such as *Le Père Goriot*, *Les Mystères de Paris*, and *A Tale of Two Cities*. But as the film unfolds, it becomes clear that Prévert and Carné are up to something else. Like their earlier works, *Les Enfants du paradis* is a modern fable of alienation, frustration, and incomprehension. Like them, it requires a narrative form expressive of yearning rather than fulfillment, of absence rather than presence.

Bazin was among the first to note the "elliptical elegance" of *Les Enfants du paradis*.[21] But he lamented the discrepancy between the film's "unusual dimensions" and its "paradoxical impression of meagerness and inadequacy." Expecting the work to exhibit the "precision of psychological analysis" associated with nineteenth-century representational fiction, Bazin was requesting that which the film denies: a built-in anticipation of retrospection that would enable viewers to attribute conclusive meaning to the plot at the film's end. "The auteurs," Bazin wrote, "appear to have had much more to say about their characters but have given up . . . having run out of film and time." Truffaut was better attuned to the film's design. Baptiste's awakening to a vocation, his effort to disengage essence from appearance, his recognition of art as victorious over temporality, and, above all, his effort to recapture the night not spent with Garance indicate, for Truffaut, that "Proust's monumental search for lost time was uppermost in Prévert's mind when he fashioned his screenplay."[22]

It is indeed appropriate and profitable to think of *Les Enfants du paradis* as plotting a trajectory of unfulfilled desire. If we posit that desire for Garance is the story's fundamental motor, the film's narrative form can be seen to reflect the varying intensities of the emotional force that Garance exerts upon four men. Such a view helps to illumine the peculiar shape of the film's overall plot, which begins virtually *in medias res*, has an undepicted middle, and ends inconclusively. Between Parts I and II, Garance travels abroad with the Count. The other men in her life undergo extraordinary external changes. But the film does not record these transformations because the source of the only kind of action that matters genuinely in the work—the emotional—is absent. When Garance disappears into the Carnival crowd at the film's close, the movie ends. But its plot is simply suspended for lack of Garance. In this respect *Les Enfants du paradis* is an interminable film. It deprives spectators of the "lucid repose, desire both come to rest and set in perspective" that Brooks finds characteristic of endings in premodernist storymaking.[23]

Prévert's screenplay originally had Baptiste murder the old clothes man, Jéricho, during the Carnival street sequence that occurs at the film's close. Although it was not shot, this episode has given rise to the belief that Carné and Prévert intended to have the plot continue beyond its current dimensions.[24] Carné insists that such a view is "unfounded."[25] Yet Prévert's friend and archivist André Heinrich observes: "Prévert did in fact conceive a third part that would have depicted Baptiste's and Lacenaire's murder trials. It is certain that Prévert wrote an outline of several pages, but it has been lost."[26] If Heinrich is correct, Garance presumably would have returned to testify in both trials, thereby allowing further plot development and the possibility of a more conclusive ending.

As it stands, *Les Enfants du paradis* is constructed according to a consistent aesthetic of incompletion.

The film's formal tension between plenitude and omission perhaps stems more from pictorial than from literary influences. Like *Jenny* (Monet), *Le Quai des Brumes* (Vlaminck), and *Les Visiteurs du soir* (the Limbourg brothers and Jean Colombe), *Les Enfants du paradis* is a movie that transposes to the screen the style and even the content of specific visual artists. For example, the misty, almost formless setting of the early morning duel that takes place in a forest clearing evokes late Corot landscapes. The images of Garance semi-nude on a curtain-framed bed suggest Ingres's Odalisques. The bearing of Deburau and Lemaître, as well as details of the Boulevard du Temple's buildings and crowds, derive from contemporary drawings, engravings, and lithographs by, among others, Auguste Bouquet, Patrice Dillon, Charles Patémont, and above all Honoré Daumier.[27]

By animating these well-known works, *Les Enfants du paradis* generates viewer confidence: its moving images of what one takes to be a densely textured social reality conform to familiar pictorial representations of nineteenth-century Paris. In turn, these vibrant cinematic images trigger expectations concerning the likelihood of the film's conforming to narrative conventions of nineteenth-century literary works that are also remembered as imparting an impression of social fullness. Yet for all the verisimilitude or surface vitality of individual sequences, the film overall pays minimal attention to concerns typical of nineteenth-century literary fiction: causality and spatiotemporal continuity. The structure of *Les Enfants du paradis* is more closely that of a succession of David-like *grands tableaux*, in which discrete actions tend to become, if not actually frozen in time and space, arrested and disconnected from one another.

In his prewar works Carné always veered toward formal abstraction. But his delicate plays of light and shadow, his search for depth of tone and naturalistic atmosphere, and his intimate feel for commonplace objects made him something like the French cinema's Chardin. In *Les Enfants du paradis* the relative predominance of flat, diffused lighting, impersonal distance shots, and sheer self-proclaimed monumentality make Carné the cinematic inheritor of David's heroic Neoclassicism. The movie does not quote explicitly from the works of David. The overtly political and didactic character of David's major history paintings is inconsistent with *Les Enfants du paradis*'s shunning of direct political reference. But as in, for example, David's *Oath of the Horatii* (1784), *The Intervention of the Sabine Women* (1799), and *Coronation of Napoleon and Josephine* (1805–7), Carné strives for a pictorial grandeur that takes the form of extremely poised, theatrical compositions filmed primarily in long shot by a camera that rarely tracks or pans. Salient examples include all the dramatic performances; the dance at the Rouge-Gorge nightclub; the conclusion to the police investigation in Madame Hermine's office; the mêlée outside Frédérick Lemaître's dressing room; Lacenaire's encounter with the Count in the hallway of the latter's town house; and the Carnival. In opposition to the Romantic passion of *Les Enfants du paradis*'s characters, the director's preoccupation with painstakingly measured composition contributes to the film's aura of frigidity—for which Truffaut would later reproach Carné, just as Eugène Delacroix had censured David.

The picture's most vivacious moments occur either onstage or in the bedroom. But even these are subject almost invariably to interruption, disconnection, or suspension. In fact, the bulk of the movie's essentially melancholy plot takes place in marginal settings—backstage, dressing alcoves, alleys, staircases, balconies, rented boxes, and carriages—that lead to but are not themselves sites of spirited drama. As *Les Enfants du paradis* progresses, Carné and Prévert seem intent, like David, on holding back rather than following through. They truncate scenes before events reach their conclusion. They withhold from view dramatic actions that would most confer an impression of genuine human presence. And perhaps most significant, Carné's camera often holds on the final image of sequences several seconds longer than convention dictates. With remarkably high frequency these final images depict a selfsame subject: one individual, positioned frame center, standing immobile and speechless. More than any other, this composition conveys the existential predicament at the film's core: the inevitable isolation that accompanies the effort to disengage oneself from time's flow.

The tug between, on one hand, cinematic movement and speech, and, on the other, painterly stasis and silence is perhaps the most fundamental determinant of the film's plot design. It corresponds to a psychological dynamic according to which desire for (and memory of) Garance engages in a continuous, unrealized quest to reconnect with lost time and render it eternally fixed. Although presented ostensibly from a detached, third-person point of view, *Les Enfants du paradis*'s narrative is as much embedded within a subjective psychic system—that of its male characters, of Prévert, and above all of Carné—as was *Le Jour se lève*'s. But where the latter came to a full close, the former continues indefinitely, with each of its sequences, or painterly tableaux, constituting successive figurations of desire for an always-inaccessible object named Garance.

In the plot précis that follows, my bracketed commentary highlights some of the ways in which Prévert's scripting and Carné's compositions, camera movements, and editing promote, with simplicity and persistence, *Les Enfants du paradis*'s aesthetic of incompletion, disconnection, and understatement.[28]

[*Long shot of a painted cardboard theater curtain, a proscenium arch, and the pillars and molding framing the arch. Three knocks announce the start of a theatrical performance. The camera tracks in to frame the central portion of the curtain, over which the film's credits unfold.*] The curtain rises to disclose a panoramic daylight view of Paris's bustling Boulevard du Temple, with its acrobats, dancing girls, clowns, animal acts, costumed barkers, peepshows, theaters, and, above all, throngs of spectators. An old clothes man with a bugle hanging round his neck, Jéricho (Pierre Renoir), appears from and disappears into the crowd. Among the Boulevard's attractions is a booth advertising "Naked Truth in a Well": inside, a handful of men view Garance (Arletty) immersed in a rotating tub. At the stage door of the Théâtre des Funambules, an aspiring actor, Frédérick Lemaître (Pierre Brasseur), inquires about a position with the troupe. Distracted by the beauty of Garance, now walking toward a flower vendor's cart, Frédérick dashes off to flirt with her. After some banter, Garance rebuffs him with the coy remark that chance may well bring them together again since, as Frédérick has told her, "Paris is very small for those who love each other with such grand passion." As she vanishes into the crowd, Frédérick espies another pretty woman and proceeds to court her with like sincerity [*a vertical right-left wipe leaves Frédérick's adventure undeveloped*].

Posing as a public scribe, the dandified thief, assassin, and would-be playwright Pierre-François Lacenaire (Marcel Herrand) takes account of the paltry goods stolen by his accomplice Avril (Fabien Loris). When Garance enters the writer's shop, Lacenaire dismisses Avril. Speaking almost in monologue, he reminds Garance, whom he calls his "guardian angel," that he is not like other men and that he anticipates a prodigious destiny for himself. His intense speech ceases with the arrival of Jéricho, who bargains for purchase of the stolen merchandise [*a diagonal right-left wipe leaves inconclusive the details of the deal*].

Meanwhile, on a platform outside the Théâtre des Funambules, an actor dressed as the commedia dell'arte figure Cassandre (Etienne Decroux) physically and verbally abuses a figure who sits motionless on an upturned barrel. The Cassandre is Anselme Deburau, the premier performer at the Funambules; the frightened, white-faced simpleton, sporting a stringy wig and wide-brimmed hat, is his son, Baptiste (Jean-Louis Barrault). Amid the spectators stand Lacenaire and Garance. When Lacenaire filches a pocket watch from a fat burgher who has been making advances toward Garance, the burgher accuses Garance of the theft and insists that a policeman arrest her. Garance is exonerated publicly when Baptiste astounds and delights the crowd by reenacting in pantomime what actually transpired. Out of gratitude, and perhaps already love, Garance removes the rose she has been wearing in her bodice and hurls it to Baptiste, who catches the flower and breathes in its scent. Garance then moves into the crowd and out of sight [*a dissolve on a medium shot of Baptiste, standing immobile frame center, portrays him smiling beatifically*].

Backstage at the Funambules, Jéricho sells props to the stage manager. He also reads the palm of the director's daughter, Nathalie (Maria Casarès), who is in love with Baptiste; Jéricho foresees that Nathalie will marry the man she loves. Onstage, a lively performance of the pantomime *Dangers of the Virgin Forest* [*in progress*] turns chaotic when members of the two reigning families of mime, the Deburaus and the Barrignis, engage in a fistfight. With the curtain brought down, the indignant Barrignis refuse to apologize to the insulted Deburaus, and decide to abandon the Funambules for a theater on the other side of the Boulevard. As the audience clamors for the show to continue, Frédérick seizes the moment: he offers the frenzied director (Marcel Peres) his services as Harlequin; to substitute for Pierrot (also played by a Barrigni), the director chooses Baptiste [*a diagonal right-left wipe on an extreme long shot of the director, standing frame center, cuts short his public announcement of the cast changes*]. Before Baptiste débuts, Nathalie, who is Colombina onstage, coaxes him to admit his love for the unidentified woman who has given him the rose—which serves as a prop in Baptiste's first performance as Pierrot [*unseen; a fade-out is preceded by a left-right pan shot that makes Baptiste and Nathalie, who stare at one another bewilderedly in medium two-shot, progressively disappear from view*].

[*Fade-in.*] That night, Frédérick and Baptiste stop for a drink at a wine stall. Frédérick fantasizes about the great roles he will interpret one day in the legitimate theater—Henry IV, Attila, Julius Caesar. Baptiste expresses a wish to make the crowds in the Funambules' gallery weep as well as laugh. The mime proposes that Frédérick rent a room at the boarding house where he lives, the Grand Relais [*quick dissolve*]. Its proprietor, Madame Hermine (Jane Marken), takes an instant liking to the flirtatious young actor. Despite their difference in age, the two [*presum-*

ably] spend much of the night together [*dissolve on a medium two-shot of Frédérick making amorous overtures to Madame Hermine*]. Baptiste prefers to prowl alone along the outskirts of Belville, near Ménilmontant. He encounters a blind beggar called Fil de Soie (Gaston Modot), who invites him for a drink at the Rouge-Gorge, a dance hall frequented by a sinister crowd and whose name derives from the manner in which its previous owner died: a slit throat [*cut on a medium two-shot of Baptiste and Fil de Soie walking toward the dance hall*].

At the club, the beggar reveals himself to be a sharp-eyed underworld figure; the seemingly ubiquitous Jéricho makes everyone uneasy; and— to Baptiste's rapture—Lacenaire arrives with Garance, Avril, and two other friends. Overwhelmed by this coincidence, Baptiste asks Garance to dance and she accepts. Avril, however—with Lacenaire's sanction— interlopes, grasps Baptiste by the collar of his jacket, and sends him smashing through a window onto the street. The crowd's derisive laughter subsides when Baptiste steps in again, dusts himself off, and bends down to retrieve the rose Garance gave him that afternoon, and which he was wearing in his lapel. Defiantly, Avril swaggers forth. But Baptiste nimbly kicks him hard in the stomach, making him collapse on the floor. Amid laughter now directed at Avril, Baptiste offers to escort Garance home, and the two depart with utmost decorum. Reminding his friends that he is "not one of those who are prepared to complicate their lives for the sake of a woman," Lacenaire proceeds to discuss plans for robbing a debt collector [*a fade-out on a medium-close shot of Lacenaire, frame center, leaves incomplete the discussion of this scheme*].

Walking along the way that overlooks Ménilmontant, Baptiste marvels at Garance's beauty, her eyes, her laughter. Garance insists that she is a woman who is not so much beautiful as alive. When they kiss, Garance proposes, "Love is so simple." Yet it is not so for Baptiste. A brief but violent thunderstorm interrupts their second kiss and causes the couple, observed by Jéricho who is lurking in the shadows, to rush to the Grand Relais [*rapid fade-out/fade-in*], where Madame Hermine provides the homeless Garance with a room—number 10. When Garance begins to remove her soaked dress, Baptiste is embarrassed and turns away. When she offers to have him spend the night with her, he panics. Seated together on the bed, now illuminated only by moonlight, Baptiste articulates a desire for Garance to love him as he loves her. He moves to kiss her but runs away, slamming the door behind him [*cut on the slamming of the door, in long shot, to Garance, in medium shot, frame center, vaguely bemused and disappointed*]. Maintaining composure, Garance sings a few lines of a tune and goes toward the window to lay out her clothes. Hearing a female voice, Frédérick darts to his window, reiterates his conviction that "Paris is very small for those who love each other with such grand passion," and within moments passes to Garance's room [*where he and she presumably enjoy the remainder of the night; fade-out as Frédérick silently enters Garance's room in background long shot and begins to walk toward both the camera and Garance, who is shot from the rear in a foreground medium-close shot*].

[*Fade-in on a high-angle long shot of the open-air show, in progress, outside the Théâtre des Funambules; a visual and audio fade-out cuts short Anselme's patter; fade-in on a long shot of the theater's interior.*] A new attraction has been running [*for about three weeks*] at the Théâtre des Funambules. Written by Baptiste, *The Palace of Illusions or the Lover of the Moon* [*in progress*] depicts the despair of Pierrot (Baptiste), who worships a statue of Phoebe (Garance) that is lured away by the vigorous wooing of Harlequin (Frédérick); Nathalie plays a laundress who unwittingly foils Pierrot's attempts to commit suicide. During this performance Baptiste momentarily loses control and evinces genuine distress when he views Garance and Frédérick together in the wings. Out of jealousy and empathy, Nathalie violates the cardinal rule of pantomime and utters Baptiste's name. Order is soon restored and the show continues [*cut to the wings on Nathalie and Baptiste in medium two-shot as they resume their parts; the remainder of the show goes unseen as the director and Anselme argue in the wings*].

Backstage, Nathalie expresses her hope that Baptiste will someday love her; Garance exhibits fatigue at Frédérick's ceaseless frolicking; and Frédérick informs Garance that in her sleep she mutters the name "Baptiste." With spectacular flair, an unknown admirer named Count Edouard de Montray (Louis Salou) enters Garance's dressing room. He bestows upon her a tremendous bouquet of flowers, an avowal of amorous passion, and an offer to make her Paris's most envied woman of leisure and wealth. Garance makes it clear that she likes her life exactly as it is, and accepts only the Count's calling card. After the Count leaves, Baptiste, as much from self-loathing as jealousy, lashes violently at the Count's oversize bouquet and declares himself dead. As Garance begins to intimate that she loves Baptiste, Nathalie intrudes. Impervious to Baptiste's protestations, Nathalie lays absolute claim to the mime's heart and exits haughtily [*leaving Baptiste and Garance speechless; diagonal right-left wipe on Garance, standing immobile frame center in medium-close shot, her eyes lowered sadly to the ground, avoiding the glance of Baptiste, out of frame*].

Under the pseudonym Monsieur Forestier, Lacenaire has taken an apartment at the Grand Relais, where he and Avril botch their [*unseen*] effort to assassinate a debt collector and rob him of his pouch. Madame Hermine is convinced that Garance stole Frédérick's affections from her. She therefore supports the investigating officer's hunch that Garance is an accomplice to Lacenaire's crime. While interrogating Garance in Madame Hermine's office, an inspector attempts to humiliate her in regard to background (her mother was illegitimate); profession (she calls herself an "artiste" who formerly posed for a Monsieur Ingres); and acquaintances (a policeman identifies her as having been involved with the suspect in the matter of a stolen watch weeks earlier). Pushed to the limit of indignity, Garance removes a calling card from her purse, hands it to the astonished inspector, and with total self-possession makes the request: "Would you be kind enough to let this person know that I am the victim of a judicial error?" The cardboard curtain falls [*on a long shot of the office, with Garance standing in midground medium shot frame center, surrounded by the two officers standing frame left, Madame Hermine seated center background, and the debt collector seated far background—all speechless and immobile except for Garance, whose head turns slightly, causing her heart-shaped earrings to flutter, and whose purse dangles freely from her wrist*].

[*A title superimposed on the cardboard curtain indicates that several years have passed.*] The curtain again rises on a sunlit view of the Boulevard du Temple. Accompanied by two fatuous and infatuated women, Frédérick Lemaître arrives at the stage door of the Grand Théâtre in an elegant carriage. Frédérick has become Paris's most popular dramatic actor, although chronic merrymaking offstage has led him to incur severe financial debts. En route from his dressing room to the stage for a rehearsal of a new melodrama, *L'Auberge des Adrets*, Frédérick is assailed by creditors and jealous husbands. His costume in tatters and his bruised left eye covered by a makeshift patch, Frédérick feels more inclined to play the role of the brigand Robert Macaire, although he finds the play and its three authors thoroughly mediocre. During rehearsal of the final scene, in which the dying Macaire learns that his wife, Marie, has betrayed him to save their son, Frédérick infuriates the authors with his cynical asides and interpolations [*slow dissolve on Frédérick who, in long shot center frame, assumes a defiant, stylized pose as if to reinforce his verbal assault on the play's worth*].

On opening night Frédérick sets the audience roaring with delight when he burlesques the entire final scene of the melodrama [*the rest of the play goes unseen*], improvising lines, contorting the plot, and literally stepping out of his role by moving to a stage box where he flamboyantly declares himself to be Frédérick Lemaître and the real criminals of the piece to be the three authors. The latter do not appreciate Frédérick's triumphant performance. But rather than apologize to such a ridiculous trio, Frédérick arranges for a duel to take place at dawn.

Lacenaire has become France's most notorious criminal. On the pretense of extorting a huge sum from Frédérick, he and Avril take the actor by surprise in his dressing room following the premiere of *L'Auberge des Adrets*. Unintimidated, Frédérick hands over a small sum, establishes a bond with Lacenaire based on their shared scorn for the world's imbeciles, and invites the scoundrels to drink and dine [*a vertical right-left wipe on Frédérick and Lacenaire in medium-close shot, the former pouring champagne, frame left, and the latter unfolding his napkin, frame center, leaves the supper party itself undisclosed*].

Hours later an inebriated Frédérick, still dressed as Robert Macaire, arrives for the duel in a misty forest clearing, with Lacenaire and Avril serving as his seconds. The director of the Grand Théâtre attempts in vain to dissuade Frédérick from participating in the duel [*after Frédérick moves rightward out of frame to begin the duel, unseen, dissolve on a close shot of the exasperated director, frame center, silent*].

That evening Frédérick strolls along the Boulevard du Temple with one arm in a sling: performances of *L'Auberge des Adrets* are suspended temporarily. The show at the Funambules, a four-act pantomime entitled *The Old Clothes Man* [*in progress*] is sold out, but the ticketseller arranges for Frédérick to sit in a box alongside an unknown veiled woman who attends Baptiste's shows each night. To Frédérick's astonishment, the mystery woman is Garance. He makes light of the coincidence, reminding Garance again that "Paris is small for those who love each other as we do." But he admits that her unexplained disappearance wounded his self-esteem. Magnificently attired, Garance indicates that she and the Count have spent the years abroad—first in India, but mostly in England and Scotland; she intimates that she has not been happy. Their attention shifts to the stage.

The curtain rises. Clinging to the rear of the carriage that transports the Duchess (Nathalie) to a party in a stately town house is Pierrot (Baptiste). His attempt to follow his beloved into the house fails: disdainful of his garb, the host's lackeys push him rudely to the ground. A trumpet call signals the appearance of the Old Clothes Man (Baptiste's father, Anselme), and Pierrot's despair changes to joy. He selects a resplendent outfit. But he has no money to pay for it. In response to the Old Clothes Man's insensitivity to his plea for charity, Pierrot pulls from its scabbard a saber that the Old Clothes Man carries under his arm, plunges the blade into the peddler's body, and exits stealthily stage right. The curtain falls.

Frédérick is feverish with jealousy—not from Baptiste's performance, which he finds transcendent, but from his recognition of the depth of Garance's love for the mime. The actor realizes instantly that this newly felt passion can be put to a useful end: at last Frédérick is ready to play Othello, his life's dream. As he leaves the box to pay respects to Baptiste backstage, Garance consents to his informing Baptiste of her presence and of how happy she would be if he came to say hello. When Frédérick and Baptiste meet, they embrace warmly. Nathalie, now Baptiste's wife, glows with a fulfillment reflected in the gentleness of her son, also named Baptiste. The sudden appearance of Jéricho, drunk and furious that his stolen identity is being assassinated on stage every evening, eclipses the general tone. With vindictive intent, he informs Nathalie that Garance has returned and is awaiting Baptiste in box 7. Within moments, a knock is heard on the door to the box. Delivering words composed by his mother, Baptiste *fils* informs Garance that "we all three live very happily together, Mama, Papa, and me." To the child's spontaneous inquiry about whether this beautiful lady is married and has a little boy of her own, Garance replies, "I'm all alone."

The curtain rises, and the next act of Baptiste's pantomime begins. The Duchess is dancing in a large drawing room. In the wings, seconds before Baptiste's entrance, Frédérick confides that the mystery woman in the box is Garance, and that she wishes to see Baptiste. Onstage, Pierrot and the Duchess waltz. But Baptiste cannot continue. He misses a step, stops dancing, and rushes offstage. Amid the audience's deafening calls for "Baptiste! . . . Baptiste!" he arrives at the door to box 7, opens it, and, overcome with disappointment, finds the box empty [*a diagonal right-left wipe on a slightly high-angle, stable medium shot of the vacant box, with Garance's chair positioned midground left and the obstreperous audience visible in background long shot, captures the point of view of Baptiste, paralyzed by loss, out of frame*].

Garance ascends the magnificent staircase of the Count's town house. Seated on the landing is Lacenaire. He expresses disappointment that Garance has remained unchanged by wealth, for she renders imperfect his view of humanity's total corruptibility. He also reveals a perverse desire to have killed both Baptiste and Frédérick; his recent appeal to the latter for money was simply a pretext for what he thought would turn into an assassination—but Frédérick, too, exhibited unexpected generosity of spirit. Lacenaire's obvious hatred is for the Count, with whom he exchanges contemptuous words as the two pass each other on the staircase. In Garance's boudoir the Count expresses torment over his inability to make Garance love him. Garance reveals to the Count that there exists in Paris a man she has loved and continues to love, but who, she senses, no longer loves her. Her sole desire, she declares with muted anguish, is to leave Paris again [*fade-out on close shot of Garance, immobile with eyes bent downward, frame left-of-center*].

[*Fade-in on a nighttime long shot of the Théâtre des Funambules, whose show has been suspended; dissolve to a medium shot of Madame Hermine carrying a tray of food.*] Suffering from depression, Baptiste has taken secret refuge in room 10 at the Grand Relais. Madame Hermine cares for him with compassion. She suggests that Baptiste might forget his troubles by going this evening to see Frédérick in *Othello*; but Baptiste wallows in self-pity and regret. Madame Hermine feels bound to inform Nathalie of Baptiste's whereabouts. Nathalie claims to understand Baptiste's need for solitude [*diagonal right-left wipe on rear view of Madame Hermine, frame left, and front view of Nathalie, frame center, both in medium-close shot*].

At Frédérick's premiere as Othello [*in progress*], Lacenaire is seated in the orchestra; Garance and the Count occupy a box. As Othello and Iago plot Desdemona's fate, Frédérick seems to direct his lines directly at Garance. A sumptuous basket of flowers is delivered to her box, with a note that reads: "Desdemona has come this evening. Othello is no longer jealous. Othello is cured. Thank you." The Count is now convinced that Frédérick is the object of Garance's love. Toward the end of the performance, Baptiste arrives. Standing in the balcony as the curtain falls, he espies Garance and the Count leaving their box. The Count insists upon a confrontation with Frédérick. As Garance reluctantly accompanies him in the direction of the actors' reception area, she and Baptiste meet. Amid the crowd of spectators, they steal away to a terrace where they exchange loving words, looks, and kisses.

Unknown to Garance and Baptiste, Lacenaire has observed the reunion [*as they kiss, in close shot, cut to a long shot of the terrace, with the couple kissing in the background, followed by a slow right-left pan that abandons the couple to themselves, out of frame, and comes to hold on Lacenaire, looking in their direction*]. The dandy-assassin realizes that he can now stage his most sensational real-life *coup de théâtre*. Moving across the reception area, he joins Frédérick in provoking the Count through jibes about infidelity. Responding to the Count's attempt to humiliate him in return, Lacenaire approaches the curtained window that opens onto the balcony, pulls the curtain cord, and reveals Garance and Baptiste embracing. Momentarily paralyzed by the shock, the disgraced

Count pulls the curtains shut. Lacenaire declares the moment to be "one of the rarest . . . of a lifetime." Although the Count insists that this matter is of no concern to Frédérick, the actor provokes a duel; the Count extends his card and declares that he can be found in the morning either at home or at the Turkish baths. In front of the theater, Lacenaire informs Avril of his joy that two men may soon cut each other's throats because of a woman or, rather, because of him. But he hints that he wants still more personal, direct revenge for the insults the Count has made him suffer [*a fade-out on Lacenaire and Avril, in medium-close shot, as they move rightward out of frame, leaves the details of Lacenaire's plot for revenge undisclosed*].

Meanwhile, Garance and Baptiste have gone to room 10 at the Grand Relais [*fade-in as they cross the doorway, in medium shot*]. Garance marvels at how nothing has changed. Even the moon shines through the open window as it did several years earlier. Positioned near the bed, Baptiste and Garance embrace, recline on the bed, and kiss [*a slight backward tracking shot is followed by a rightward pan that holds on a long shot of the open window, frame center, leaving the lovers out of view*]. Baptiste whispers [*out of frame*], "You were right, Garance, love is so simple" [*fade-out*].

[*Fade-in on a sunlit, low-angle medium shot of the cardboard Pierrot advertising* The Old Clothes Man *atop the Théâtre des Funambules.*] Carnival is being celebrated on the Boulevard du Temple. Wending their way through the crowd, Lacenaire and Avril enter the Turkish baths and seek out the Count's private room. Without uttering a word, Lacenaire slits the Count's throat [*out of frame*]. He advises Avril to flee Paris, and with self-satisfied calm he pulls the cord of a bell, sits down, and impassively awaits arrest.

At the Grand Relais, Baptiste awakes to find Garance preparing to leave. The night was beautiful, she explains, but she must prevent the Count from killing Frédérick; if necessary, she will lie to the Count and say she loves him; and she will consent to go away with him, since departures are inevitable. While Baptiste protests, Nathalie and her son arrive at the boarding house. Leaving the boy to wait outdoors, Nathalie knocks on the door to Baptiste's room, opens it, and finds Garance and Baptiste in each other's arms. Garance attempts to leave, but Nathalie obstructs her. Filled with rancor, Nathalie flaunts her wifely loyalty and accuses Garance of an incapacity for sustained emotion. Garance replies quietly but firmly that she has lived with Baptiste for as long as Nathalie has: "Anywhere, everywhere, every day . . . and even at night, all the nights I spent with someone else, all those nights I was with him." Garance slips out as Nathalie attempts vainly to have Baptiste declare in words the truth his silence reveals all too clearly: that he has always been in love with Garance.

Baptiste frees himself from Nathalie's tug and rushes after Garance [*cut on long shot of Nathalie, frame right-of-center, immobile, arms extended, crying out the words "And me Baptiste? What about me?"*]. Taking no notice of his son, the mime plunges into the mass of boisterous merrymakers, many of whom wear facsimiles of the Pierrot costume that Baptiste has made famous. His cries for Garance are mimicked by the drunken Jéricho, who grabs Baptiste's arm and censures him sarcastically for this illicit passion. Baptiste pulls himself free but is unable to reach Garance, who enters a carriage that drives off immediately. Baptiste is progressively swallowed up by the crowd [*cut from a slightly high-angle long shot of Baptiste struggling amid the crowd, frame center, to a medium-close shot of Garance, alone, totally immobile, her eyes slightly lowered, inside the carriage, frame center; cut back to Baptiste standing as if paralyzed amid the masses*]. With the thoroughfare inundated by revelers, the cardboard theater curtain descends slowly on a panoramic view of the Boulevard du Temple [*shot from virtually the same high angle as at the film's opening. The camera then tracks out to a long shot of the make-believe curtains, the proscenium arch, and the pillars and molding that frame the arch*].

CHAPTER 11

Politics and Theater in
Children of Paradise

The Occupation obliged all leftist film artists to couch oppositional inclinations in terms so vague as to make coherent political readings of
their films nearly impossible. But in no instance was the move from politicized assertion to equivocation more conspicuous than in the turn
taken by Carné and Prévert following *Les Visiteurs du soir*. Commentators disagree about the relation between *Les Enfants du paradis*'s content
and contemporary events.[1] Clearly the picture is not an allegorical narrative in the manner of *Les Visiteurs du soir*. It bears no pattern of consistent correspondences between its historical plot and twentieth-century
politics. In fact, although *Les Enfants du paradis* is one of the most elaborate period reconstructions in French cinema, it is devoid of references
to nineteenth-century political affairs. With Part I situated in 1827 and
Part II taking place six years later, the film astonishingly passes over one
of the great events in the history of French democracy: the July Revolution of 1830.[2] Still, *Les Enfants du paradis* often teases us into inferring
that its fabric encodes bold political messages while, simultaneously, it
refrains from actualizing the substance of those messages. In the preceding chapter I identified incompletion and disconnectedness as prime components of the film's formal aesthetic. I now explore how these formal
characteristics bolster a political posture of evasiveness and irresolution.
At issue is not whether *Les Enfants du paradis* is or is not subject
to political interpretation—all films are—but rather the timidity with
which Prévert and Carné approached potentially trenchant political
themes.

The appearances and disappearances of an unattainable woman regulate
Les Enfants du paradis's plot. It is therefore tempting to view Garance as
an extended metaphor for a concept whose overt representation neither

56 Garance (Arletty), conspicuously out of focus, exhibiting a quill pen, symbolically associated with independence; in foreground, Lacenaire (Marcel Herrand)

Vichy nor the Occupiers would have condoned: France's prewar autonomy. Such an interpretation is not implausible. In Part I, Garance (a name rhyming with *la France*) embodies the vitality, self-esteem, and pragmatism associated with the Popular Front spirit. When the Count shamelessly offers to make her the wealthiest kept woman in Paris, Garance responds: "'One word and your whole life can change' . . . I suppose that means that my life is nothing at all! . . . (*She becomes more aggressive.*) And what if I like my life, my own little life?" Throughout Part I Prévert compares Garance to the most insistent symbol of freedom in his verse—birds. She claims to be "gay as a lark"; Frédérick names her "my sweet bird of the evening"; the police inspector calls her "a bird of passage"; and she warbles and recites snatches of the Prévert-Kosma song "Je Suis Comme Je Suis" ("I Am What I Am"), an affirmation of unconstrained liberty. In her first scene with Lacenaire, Carné has her toy with a white quill pen (fig. 56). The result is a visual trope associating Garance's birdlike independence with poetic inspiration.

Like France during the Occupation, Garance becomes, between Parts I and II, the prize possession of a usurper. Having stifled her natural instincts, the Count reduces Garance to a gilded bird either to cage in his town house-cum-prison or to display abroad. "Curious, Garance," the

Count observes in Part II, "when I am not there you sing. But as soon as I arrive you are silent." Yet like France in the minds of Carné and Prévert, Garance transcends enslavement through the constancy of her love for Baptiste, an embodiment of French popular culture. Refusing to collaborate in the Count's delusion of absolute possession, Garance, seated at her dressing table, declares with utmost self-assurance: "You are extraordinary, Edouard. Not only are you rich, but you want to be loved 'as if you were poor'! Be reasonable, my friend, you can't take everything away from the poor! . . . if it would please you, tomorrow the whole of Paris shall know not only that I love you, but that I am crazy about you! . . . I'll shout it from the rooftops. But to you . . . to you alone, my friend, I will tell you this: I have loved a man and I love him still." A moving expression of moral integrity, these lines chime resoundingly with the sentiments of French citizens for whom capitulation to the enemy was unacceptable.

However, if we take Garance as a figure of Occupied France, the Count ought to represent Germany. Nothing in the film substantiates such a claim. To propose, alternatively, that the Count approximates the right-wing opportunists of the Vichy regime is also inadequate: his effete snobbery and irregular personal life run counter to Vichy's social values. At best the Count is a plutocrat ("one of the richest and most brilliant men in France," remarks Lacenaire) whose power is economic and whose murder by an anarchist might be construed as a wishful expression of revenge by the Occupation's have-nots.

More surely the Garance-Count relationship is a dramatization of Prévert's poem "Pour Toi Mon Amour" ("For You My Love"), in which the male narrator goes to a bird market to purchase birds for his beloved; to a flower market to purchase flowers; to an iron market to purchase "heavy chains"; and, finally, "then I went to the slave market / And I looked for you / But I didn't find you / my love."[3] Like *Les Enfants du paradis*, this poem gives voice to a woman's right of autonomy. But its dénouement is more effectively liberating than the film's. In the latter, Garance (unaware that the Count has been murdered) is prepared to return to her protector and, in the hope of avoiding bloodshed, declare that she loves only him. Read as political allegory, this dénouement undercuts the assertive thrust of Garance's earlier position and intimates a posture of further compromise with the enemy. In *Les Visiteurs du soir*, Anne, too, lies for reasons of expediency: to liberate Gilles from the Devil, she informs the latter that she loves only him. But Anne ultimately rescinds her declaration and admits that she lied. *Les Enfants du paradis* furnishes no indication that Garance is inclined to do likewise.

Garance's equivocal final situation corresponds to the uncertain state of France while Carné and Prévert were planning *Les Enfants du paradis*: summer–fall 1942 and winter–spring 1943. On one hand, France's claim to even limited independence collapsed. In response to the Anglo-American invasion of French North Africa, German armed forces occupied France's southern sector on November 11, 1942. Until then, Vichy had accepted Germany's ideological demands while pretending to remain autonomous. But by December 1942 the Third Reich was administering the entire country. A manifestation of what Hoffmann calls "the triumph of forced or enthusiastic masochism," Pétain and Laval condemned themselves to overt collaboration: "an apparently legal government, headed by a national hero and claiming total obedience, [sunk] deeper and deeper into a morass of impotence, absurdity, and crime."[4]

On the other hand, various events taking place at the same time indicated that France's bondage might not be irrevocable. On November 27 resisting crewmen in Toulon thwarted Germany's effort to acquire the remainder of the French fleet by scuttling their own ships. At Stalingrad in January 1943 German troops suffered their first catastrophic defeat. By May, Generals Eisenhower and Montgomery had cleared Africa of Axis forces, and the Free French movement had taken steps to establish headquarters in Algiers. Moreover, guerrilla bands of active resisters known as the *maquis* were organizing in the south as of October 1942, and in the north as of the following January.

When Carné and Prévert conceived and planned *Les Enfants du paradis*, the eventual impact of these isolated events was unclear. On balance, most of the French perceived themselves as being thrust into a "vacuum of political life."[5] The film's final image of Garance, impassively returning to the Count in a carriage that seals her off from the pulsating Carnival crowds, epitomizes France's worsening condition.

Les Enfants du paradis is similarly equivocal in its representation of established authority. As of June 1940 France had become a police state in which the gendarmerie collaborated willingly with the enemy. Paris's Préfecture de Police worked in daily cooperation with the Nazis, carrying out arrests and placing deportees on death trains that departed from detention camps at Drancy. Such collaboration was commonplace throughout France. In 1943 alone, the French police arrested forty thousand compatriots for Gaullist, Communist, or anti-German activity.[6] Shortly before Carné and Prévert began to elaborate the screenplay of *Les Enfants du paradis*, perhaps the most disgraceful of the Paris police actions took place. On the morning of July 16, 1942, a force composed of French "gendarmes, *gardes mobiles*, bailiffs, detectives, patrolmen, and even students from the police school" began to round up Jews. In the course of two days, about half of the 12,884 arrestees were interned in the Vélodrame d'Hiver, a large Paris sports arena. The rest were held at Drancy, from which they were all to be deported to German concentration camps. Known as *La Grande Rafle* or the Great Raid, this event marked a turning point in French public opinion. Until then, anti-Jewish policies could be attributed to the Germans or tolerated as part of Pétain's program of national revival. Now, as roundups occurred throughout France, the French police were conspicuously in charge: "For the first time since the founding of Marshal Pétain's regime, significant numbers of moderate or conventional French people . . . were deeply offended by something it had done. For the first time, voices of opposition arose from establishment figures in positions of power."[7] Such voices notwithstanding, by the time *Les Enfants du paradis* was completed, seventy-five thousand Jews had been deported from France to extermination centers in Poland.

The complete absence of policemen from *Le Quai des Brumes* and their ubiquity in *Le Jour se lève* served as clear-cut commentaries on France's states of internal chaos and repressiveness, respectively. *Les Enfants du paradis*'s view of power relations is more ambiguous. Its depiction of the police is consistently unsympathetic. In Part I a policeman is prepared to arrest Garance on the grounds of a burgher's unconfirmed allegation; a park keeper in the *Lover of the Moon* pantomime chases Pierrot from a public garden; and a police inspector nearly charges the innocent Garance with complicity in an attempted murder. In Part II an officer in *L'Auberge des Adrets* comes to arrest the escaped prisoner Robert Macaire; and guards from the fancy town house in the *Old Clothes Man* pantomime hurl Pierrot to the ground. In most of these instances the targets of police action elude apprehension thanks to superior creative gifts (Baptiste exonerates Garance through pantomime), spontaneous violence (Pierrot gains entry to the party by murdering the old clothes man and stealing a fine suit), or a combination of both (Macaire-Lemaître reverses his imposed role and kills the officer who has come to arrest him). But in no case does a harassed being assault the social structure which grants the police their inordinate authority.

At the end of Part I, Garance resolves her predicament by falling back upon the very establishment she scorns. Toward the end of Part II, Lacenaire, having killed the Count, calmly awaits police arrest. I would suggest that these two episodes emblematize France's political plight under Occupation. With no program for bringing about effective change, even independent and defiant French persons were obliged to acquiesce before an increasingly totalitarian government. *Les Enfants du paradis* prizes recalcitrant individuals, but it gives no hint of alternative systems of power.

The film's grimmest indication of France's adherence to the political status quo lies in Carné and Prévert's treatment of the old clothes man, Jéricho. Jéricho belongs to that line of duly abhorred Carné-Prévert characters that extends from *Jenny*'s L'Albinos to *Les Portes de la nuit*'s Sénéchal: "Nobody ever loved me, nobody, zero, nothing!" The reasons are plain. Unlike the Boulevard du Temple's actors, Jéricho is a hypocrite. Unlike its spectators, he is a spy. Unlike its criminals, he has no loyalties. Jéricho adopts at least twenty aliases: Jupiter, Trumpet, Medusa, the Rat, Sandman, Modest Maiden, and so on. But he is best called, as Lacenaire proposes, "turncoat, twister, Judas, informer."

To the extent that Garance embodies the tragic grandeur of France's captivity, Jéricho incarnates its ordinary shabbiness. As an informer, he personifies the climate of intimidation, witchhunts, and denunciations that flourished in Occupied France. As a hawker of a seemingly inexhaustible supply of mainly stolen goods, he personifies the spirit of collusion that black-market profiteers partook of throughout and beyond the Occupation. German purchasing agencies relied upon French informers to track down hidden materials and produce. While about six thousand Frenchmen originally volunteered for this work, the number increased at least fivefold by the war's end. Constituting a virtual para-Gestapo, these informer-suppliers enabled large agencies, such as the notorious Bureau Otto, to extend their marketing activities into counter-intelligence, "tackling the resistance through the underworld of French agents and informers already on the payroll."[8]

Had it not been for black marketeering, *Les Enfants du paradis* would never have been made. "One must not forget," asserts Alexander Trauner, "that for *Les Enfants du paradis* every nail, every bit of wood had been bought through the black market."[9] In fact, Carné and Prévert are rather indulgent toward petty theft and truck as represented in the film. Lacenaire, Avril, and the sympathetic "blind" beggar, Fil de Soie, all participate in it. But as the latter makes clear to Baptiste during their first encounter, "Informers—we don't like them."

An early draft of Prévert's scenario called for Baptiste to kill Jéricho, just as Pierrot kills Jéricho's look-alike in the *Old Clothes Man* pantomime. Such an ending would have made the film's plot square more firmly with the anecdote that triggered the entire production: the historical Deburau's act of murder and his subsequent trial. It would also have asserted a view that deceit and evil are not inevitable parts of the order of things. Apparently Carné and Prévert were not prepared to issue such a statement. The mimed murder furnishes a catharsis of sorts, but the real Jéricho and the values he represents continue to infiltrate the masses.

In the Old Testament, where the city of Jericho stood as an accursed obstacle that had to be ravaged before earthly salvation could be achieved, the children of Israel succeeded in felling the city's walls to the accompaniment of their priests' trumpets. The Jéricho of *Les Enfants du paradis*, however, remains stubbornly intact. Viewed figuratively, the horn Jéricho wears about his neck and the seven-note motif he plays throughout the film are solemn reminders of the degree to which Occupied France found itself dispossessed of the means to accomplish political salvation.

A political dimension inheres in the film's view of the theater as a privileged site of collective redemption. Carné and Prévert understood the extent to which the Boulevard du Temple provided an arena for common people of the early to mid-nineteenth century to voice their otherwise disregarded will. Its audiences rarely included the upper classes, who generally attended productions of works by "legitimate" dramatists at the Comédie Française or the Théâtre de l'Odéon. Drawn principally from society's lower ranks, the Boulevard's hissing, hooting, and stomping spectators put plays and performers on trial (fig. 57). As a result—and largely without being conscious of it—Boulevard audiences helped to reshape France's theatrical patrimony.

Les Enfants du paradis celebrates the force of these demanding crowds. Before Baptiste takes to the stage, the Théâtre des Funambules is a well-attended theater. Yet its outmoded pantomimes elicit only casual involvement from easily distracted audiences. Baptiste sets out to create a more refined form of pantomime that, without sacrificing popular appeal, will make audiences realize untapped potential. Referring specifically to the occupants of *le paradis*, slang for the theater's highest and least expensive gallery seats, Baptiste tells Frédérick in language redolent of Carné and Prévert's prewar sentimental populism: "They're poor people, but I am like them. I love them, I know them well. Their lives are small, but they have big dreams. And I don't only want to make them laugh, I want to move them, to frighten them, to make them cry." Baptiste succeeds because he addresses the emotional needs of the downtrodden and disenfranchised who, in turn, legitimate his art. Resounding from *le paradis*, this *vox populi* is also a *vox dei*.

The occupants of *le paradis* may well be Carné and Prévert's metaphor for suffering compatriots who, throughout the Occupation, sought relief

57 Intimations of freedom within theatrical confines: occupants of *le paradis,* the uppermost gallery of the Théâtre des Funambules

in plays and movies. Elevated both literally and figuratively, these "children of paradise" enjoy, through performance, a state of integrity denied them since France's fall to Germany. Considered in this light, the film's title is politically charged. But its inherent extendability blunts its edge. Interviewed shortly after the picture's release, Prévert asserted that the title refers not only to the Funambules' "good-natured working-class audience" but to "the actors" as well.[10] This makes perfect sense. The film's thespians emerge from the masses and share their values. They, too, have sought out the theater in order to repossess a state of lost spiritual wholeness. And the success of this shared quest for regeneration depends upon actors' and spectators' identifying and responding reciprocally and totally with one another. Yet the all-too-perfect elaboration of the film's basic conceit—that life and theater are indissoluble—squashes the politically redemptive potential of the theater as an institution.

The first interior view of the Théâtre des Funambules exposes the rarefied character of relations between life and art. As the old-fashioned pantomime *Dangers of the Virgin Forest* proceeds, Carné cuts from the Funambules' audience to showgirls dressed as exotic birds performing what the shooting script specifies as a "flying ballet." The low-angle distance shots of the whistling, fluttering occupants of the balconies establish visual symmetry between, on one hand, the spectators, many of whom are viewed perched, birdlike, on the balconies' edge, and, on the other hand, the actresses as birds. The avian motif announces the Prévertian theme of human freedom. And indeed, both the stage and the hall throb visibly with human energy and movement. Yet the scale, angling, and overall mise en scène of the shots depicting the spectators—inspired by engravings found in Edmond Texier's *Tableau de Paris* (1852–53)[11]—betray Carné's penchant for studied, almost static pictorialism. In content and form this succession of images exhibits the basic tension of the Carné-Prévert oeuvre: a thrust toward liberation (the essential Prévert) held in check by formal constructs (the essential Carné). In the context of *Les Enfants du paradis*, these shots disclose the degree to which freedom exists as a highflying but ultimately hollow symbol that refers only to itself in a theatrical space disengaged from the real world.

Drôle de Drame satirized the sterility of existence more performed than lived. *Les Enfants du paradis* asserts, on the contrary, that human experience takes on texture and depth in direct proportion to its conformity with the patterns and conventions of performance. The film's ever-shifting doubling effects between offstage action and performed commedia dell'arte and melodramatic scenarios are nothing less than dazzling. But in making life and theater not only interchangeable but thoroughly coextensive with their film frame, Carné and Prévert lock *Les Enfants du paradis*'s characters into a world of histrionics no less hermetic than that of *Drôle de Drame*. Although shaped by the trappings of classical melodrama, the film is unable to achieve the moral resolution that the nineteenth-century genre demanded. Villainy cannot be expunged because, like heroism, it is forever inscribed in archetypal theatrical plots that are the sole determinant and measure of real-life behavior.

Lacenaire's murder of the Count exemplifies the filmmakers' reluctance to embrace wholeheartedly the activist potential of theater. Although the film never divulges fully the motivation for Lacenaire's act, the performance of *Othello* seems to provide its explicit cue. After Iago's lines, "Do it not with poison; strangle her in her bed, even the bed she has contaminated," Carné cuts abruptly from the stage to the audience. His camera then tracks in to frame Lacenaire in medium-close shot, the dandy's body seemingly galvanized by Iago's speech. The next morning Lacenaire kills the Count. Does this murder actualize Iago's prescription for dealing with the "contaminated" world? Carné's editing and camera movement lure us into making a connection between Iago's appeal and Lacenaire's act. We are led to posit that Lacenaire, in assuming the role of a hero of melodrama, liberates Garance, a figure of "contaminated" Occupied France, and expunges the Count, her "contaminator." But Lacenaire's act is essentially anarchic. It does not upset the film's established order of perfectly intertwined theater and life. Momentarily a quasi-hero, Lacenaire reassumes his role of society's villain-to-be-punished with a willingness that evokes all too disturbingly the "enthusiastic masochism" Hoffmann found inherent in the self-condemning postures of Pétain and Laval.

Les Enfants du paradis, no less than *Les Visiteurs du soir*, hints at France's incapacity to counteract military subjugation. But where the beating heart of the petrified lovers in *Les Visiteurs du soir* offered a static solution for coping with oppression, *Les Enfants du paradis* proposes a more dynamic program for retaining dignity in the face of defeat. It asserts that the collective élan generated by impassioned theatrical performances and the unassailable prestige of France's dramatic arts heritage can work together to ensure the nation's spiritual survival.

Numerous Occupation-made films took France's artistic legacy as their subject. Among the more successful were Christian-Jaque's biography of Berlioz, *La Symphonie fantastique* (1942); Guitry's homage to French painters from Millet to Derain, *Donne-moi tes yeux* (1943); and Guitry's *La Malibran* (1944), a portrait of the French-born diva. Other films of the period made pointed reference to past cultural glories, such as Delannoy's *Pontcarral, colonel d'empire* (1942), which sings praises to Musset, Sand, and Dumas, and L'Herbier's *La Vie de bohème* (1945), which lionizes Delacroix. These pictures all offered the French public reassurance that, despite present circumstances, new artistic figures were bound to emerge and reaffirm France's cultural prominence.[12]

Yet compared with *Les Enfants du paradis*, the chauvinistic appeal of those movies wilts. While other French films were obliquely asserting the hope of cultural continuity, *Les Enfants du paradis* demonstrated its reality. Where others were enshrining past monuments of French civilization, *Les Enfants du paradis* unveiled its own monumentality. In its backward look at two of France's theatrical giants, Deburau and Lemaître, *Les Enfants du paradis* flaunted the art of two equally brilliant contemporary giants, Barrault and Brasseur. For all its political disconnectedness and evasion, *Les Enfants du paradis* partook of a French humanist tradition extending from Montaigne through Malraux. It affirmed that irrespective of political contingencies a constant resource for social well-being inheres in the potential of each individual to respond creatively to the creative acts of others.

The artistic achievements of the historical Jean-Gaspard Deburau were less imposing than those suggested by the film and less substantial than those attained by Jean-Louis Barrault, even as early in his career as 1944. The real Deburau departed from tradition by replacing Pierrot's frilled collarette and floppy wool hat with a loose, collarless tunic and tight black skullcap. He brought greater composure to the role, paring down the antics of his predecessors and focusing audience attention upon the expressiveness of his whitened face. He usurped Harlequin's preeminence and expanded Pierrot's repertory by portraying wily laborers and tradesmen in contemporary settings. He once even turned explicitly political, lampooning colonialism at a time when the French were occupying and suppressing resistance in Algeria (*Pierrot en Afrique*, 1842). Deburau also distinguished himself as the sole major mime at the Funambules to remain mute throughout his career, despite the July Revolution's repeal of the 1806 legislation that had forbidden speech on that theater's stage.

Deburau's Pierrot was not, however, the elegant and psychologically complex figure which Barrault projects in *Les Enfants du paradis*. His break with convention was not so radical as the glimpse of the ungainly Pierrot in the film's early *Dangers of the Virgin Forest* pantomime suggests. Despite the real Deburau's studied sang-froid, he was still an exponent of the pantomime *sautante*, a type of entertainment that relied upon frenetic action and movement. In all likelihood the innovative *pantomime macabre* inaugurated by Cot d'Ordan's *Le Marrrchand d'habits!* (*The Old Clothes Man*, 1842) was performed not by Deburau but by a younger mime at the Funambules, Paul Legrand. It was probably Legrand, not Deburau, who elaborated the sensitive, lovesick Pierrot persona that Barrault exhibits throughout *Les Enfants du paradis*. In fact, Prévert's proposed title for Part II of the film, "L'Homme blanc," or "The Man in White," was the stage name most associated not with Deburau but with Louis Rouffe (1849–85), founder of the so-called Marseilles school of pantomime.[13]

Carné, Prévert, and Barrault drew heavily upon pseudohistorical sources. Not until 1953 did Tristan Rémy's biography, *Jean-Gaspard Deburau*, debunk the two principal versions of the mime's life: Jules Janin's *Deburau, Histoire du théâtre à quatre sous* (1832) and Louis Péricaud's *Le Théâtre des Funambules* (1897), the second derived largely from the first. Janin was drama critic for the *Journal des Débats*, one of the first French dailies to print reviews of new books and plays. His ulterior motive in promoting the little-known Deburau as "the Talma of the Boulevard" was to highlight, by contrast, the stultification of the Comédie Française.[14] In *Histoire de ma vie*, George Sand claims to have asked Deburau about Janin's biography. The illiterate mime allegedly responded: "Its intention is good for me and its success serves my reputation; but all that is not the art, it is not the idea I have of it. It is not serious, and Monsieur Janin's Deburau is not me. He has not understood me." [15]

By ascribing artistic dimensions to Deburau which the actor himself was unaware of, Janin inaugurated a legend that the Romantics embellished. In a review published by the daily *La Pandore* in 1828, Nodier described Deburau's Pierrot as a character with "infinite nuances." [16] In his *Salon de 1846*, Baudelaire dubbed Deburau "the genuine pierrot of our times, the pierrot of modern history." In his 1855 essay on the comic, *De L'Essence du rire*, Baudelaire compared the robust Pierrot of English pantomime with the more effete Gallic brand epitomized by "the late lamented Deburau"—"this character pale as the moon, mysterious as the silence, supple and mute like the serpent, erect and tall like a bracket, this artificial man activated by strange springs." [17] But it was Théophile Gautier who invested the mime with the full weight of Romantic imagination. In Part II of *Les Enfants du paradis*, Frédérick rants: "I can't stand it! You never hear anything else: 'Baptiste, have you seen Baptiste!' A real bore . . . Even Théophile Gautier has put his oar in: 'Go and see Baptiste! Go and see *Rag and Bone Man* [*Chand d'habits*]! A masterpiece.'" Probably Deburau did not perform the *Marrrchand d'habits!* pantomime which Gautier praised amply and enthusiastically in an article written for the *Revue de Paris* in September 1842. Yet because Gautier labeled Deburau in 1847 "the most perfect actor who ever lived," [18] later readers of his 1842 review presumed erroneously that Gautier was referring to Deburau and not to Paul Legrand, who went unidentified in the critical piece. Thus, when Gautier wrote, apropos *Le Marrrchand d'habits!*, "Pierrot, walking in the street in his white blouse, his white trousers, his floured face, preoccupied with vague desires—is he not the symbol of the human soul still white and innocent, tormented by infinite aspirations toward higher spheres?," he inscribed Deburau within a French literary tradition of personal angst stretching from Rousseau to Claudel. [19]

It is unlikely that Prévert, Carné, and Barrault would have modified their conception of Baptiste had Rémy's erudite biography been available a decade earlier. *Les Enfants du paradis* endeavors to perpetuate theatrical lore, not rectify history. Carné and Prévert might have intended vaguely for Baptiste's emotional anguish to correspond to that of the French populace under Occupation. But more certainly they extolled the reputed dramatic power of the historical Deburau in order to showcase the genuine gifts of Jean-Louis Barrault.

Indeed, Barrault affected the course of French theater in the midtwentieth century as massively as Deburau was alleged to have done in the mid-nineteenth. Upon joining the Théâtre de l'Atelier in 1931, he met actor-mime Etienne Decroux (b. 1898). Together they set out to codify "a new language of the art of gesture" that would replace the late nineteenth century's *pantomime muette* with a more modern *mime silencieux*. Barrault specifies: "If miming only consists in expressing silent speech [*pantomime muette*], its only value lies in the comical and the effete aspect of the incapacity to express oneself silently . . . Yet pantomime is an art which can become as noble and majestic as all the other arts. There can be tragic pantomime [*mime silencieux*]." After two years of collaboration, the two men had a falling out. Decroux was evolving toward what he eventually dubbed *mime statuaire*, a sculptural imagistic art form devoid of narrative context and minimally referential. Barrault was committed to illusion, human psychology, and lyricism. He felt that his mentor was distorting bodily expression rather than making it "truer than truth," and exposing, rather than dissimulating, its intrinsic difficulty. Barrault also believed that Decroux had come to resent his younger colleague's natural gifts: "That's why Decroux pursued me, supported me, and, later, became dead set against me."[20]

Prévert and Carné exploited this troubled relationship by casting Decroux as Baptiste's father, Anselme. During the *parade* outside the Funambules in Part I of the film, Anselme not only humiliates Baptiste through word and gesture but disclaims his paternity: "This one can't do anything . . . the despair of a famous father . . . But when I say, my son . . . luckily I can admit that I'm exaggerating . . . One night . . . when the moon was full . . . he fell down . . . yes, that's all!" After Baptiste unveils his prodigious talent, Anselme's attitude shifts. Yet throughout the film the son displays only disaffection for the father. This rancor reflects partly what Carné and Prévert believed to be facts concerning the historical Deburau family and, in good measure, the actual estrangement between Barrault and Decroux.

Barrault's first independent undertaking exposed three major influences: Decroux's in bodily technique; Charles Dullin's in reverence for literary texts; and Antonin Artaud's in the mystic dimension of performance. An adaptation of Faulkner's *As I Lay Dying*, this self-financed production established Barrault in 1935 as France's premier avant-garde mime. It also disclosed his androgynous potential, upon which Carné and Prévert would later capitalize. Faulkner's plot concerns a dying mother who insists that she witness the construction of her coffin. Barrault intended to play only the illegitimate son, Jewel. But when the actress cast as the mother fell ill two days prior to the opening performance, Barrault chose to take on her role as well: "My idea . . . was to transfigure the mother so as to give her the character of a totem. The mother had an enormous black wig that flowed down her back. Her skirt was made of thin iron sheets of two colors. To top it all off, I appeared barechested." [21]

The four public performances of *Autour d'une mère* (copyright complications precluded using Faulkner's title) marked a date in the history of French theater. Artaud wrote: "I don't know whether this kind of success constitutes a masterpiece; but at any rate it is an event . . . Jean-Louis Barrault performs the antics of an untamed horse and . . . suddenly one is amazed to see him actually turn into a horse. His play brings home the irresistible significance of gesture." [22] Between 1935 and the filming of *Les Enfants du paradis*, Barrault mastered the classics of dramatic literature and was elected *sociétaire* of the Comédie Française. But he never abandoned his commitment to an avant-garde rooted in mime and popular theater. His 1943 production of Claudel's *Le Soulier de Satin* (*The Satin Slipper*, published in 1924 but as yet unmounted) was the realization of a vision of "total theater": "[My production] showed that the French public were prepared to accept a larger field of expression and to give rein henceforth to its imagination." [23]

By making *Les Enfants du paradis*, Barrault provoked a resurgence of interest in pantomime. He also enlarged the field of cinematic expression. Like Chaplin, he understood the natural affinity between the modern medium and its venerable antecedent. Like Chaplin, he believed that the expressivity of the human body in motion was not necessarily at odds with talking pictures. Although Barrault devoted less time to movies than to theater, his screen persona took clear shape following his film début in 1935. About his role as the suicidal lover in Benoît-Lévy's *Hélène* (1936), Maurice Bessy wrote in *Cinémagazine*: "His acting, his glance, his gestures, all express torment and uncertainty. He represents . . . uneasiness, that monstrous uneasiness which all of us among the younger generation are going to die of." [24] In *Les Enfants du paradis* Barrault remains true to this early screen image, but he conveys nonetheless a positive message. His Baptiste demonstrates that personal torment, however persistent, and ardor, however dark, need not lead only to self-destruction. When distilled through a mode of performance accessible to all, individual anguish can serve the collective good.

Pierre Brasseur (1905–72) was as fit to portray the historical Lemaître as Barrault was to depict the Romanticized Deburau. Lemaître infused the French theater with a brand of raw dramatic power hitherto unknown.

Hugo eulogized him in 1876 as "the greatest actor of this century, perhaps the most miraculous stage player of all times."[25] Earlier, Alexandre Dumas had dubbed him "the French Kean, a man of capricious nature, violent and passionate—and therefore very natural in passionate, violent and capricious parts."[26] With regard to his triumph in *Kean*, which the elder Dumas wrote for Lemaître in 1836, Gautier declared, "At this moment Frédérick is truly the world's greatest actor . . . a truly Shakespearean figure, as great, simple, and multiform as nature herself."[27] Never admitted to the Comédie Française because of his supposed brashness and vulgarity, Lemaître was France's Romantic actor-rebel par excellence.

For economy of exposition Prévert took liberties with details of Lemaître's career. Like the film's Frédérick, the historical Lemaître made his theatrical début dressed as a lion. But the play was *Pyramus and Thisbe*, not *Dangers of the Virgin Forest*. The theater was the Variétés Amusantes, not the Funambules. Lemaître's second engagement was at the Funambules, where, for about three years, he mimed numerous Harlequins, possibly to Deburau's Pierrots. The sequence in which Frédérick burlesques *L'Auberge des Adrets* depicts the event that brought Lemaître to the attention of the French press. But it took place in 1823 at the Ambigu-Comique, not at the fictitious Grand Théâtre. The tattered Robert Macaire costume was inspired by a dawdler Lemaître espied one day on the Boulevard du Temple. It was not the result of a backstage scuffle with creditors and jealous husbands. The three authors—Saint-Amand, Benjamin Antier, and Polyanthe—did not, out of outrage, engage Lemaître in a duel. Saint-Amand and Polyanthe were in fact delighted by the uproarious response of the opening-night audience.

Nonetheless, Carné, Prévert, and Brasseur remain true to the spirit of actual events. Finding the melodrama worn and dated, the historical Lemaître plotted in secret to transform the protagonist of *L'Auberge des Adrets* from a sinister villain into a quick-witted rascal much like himself. Lemaître's British biographer, Robert Baldick, relates: "No one performance of the *Auberge* was quite like the next, for every night Frédérick . . . improvised new topical references and hilarious situations. The novelty which found most favour with the public, though not with the authorities, was a scene in which Frédérick pursued a gendarme into one of the boxes, shot him, and tossed the corpse onto the stage."[28] As presented in *Les Enfants du paradis*, the principal thrust of Frédérick's travesty is aesthetic. Dismantling distinctions between actor and spectator, stage and audience, author and creation, Frédérick vividly and hilariously plays out the abstract principle that informs the film's universe:

the breakdown of mutually exclusive artistic categories. But at one point in the sequence Macaire asks his accomplice Bertrand if he should kill the officer who has come to arrest him. Bertrand replies, "Kill a policeman . . . well, there's no harm in wishing." This rapid exchange makes explicit a second, albeit muted, dimension that shapes this episode: the political. Overturning melodrama's axiom that bandits must either be punished or be stricken with remorse, Frédérick-Macaire dislocates society's apparatus for maintaining order.

Given conditions under the Occupation, Prévert and Carné chose not to embellish this theme. They also muffled the political overtones of the film's *Othello* episode. In highlighting the controversial character of Frédérick's performance, Carné, Prévert, and Brasseur seem to assert the Romantic view of Shakespeare as a symbol of popular liberty and rebelliousness. Following Frédérick's premiere as the Moor, the condescending Count and his friends express scorn for "this 'Monsieur Shakespeare'":

COUNT: I have been given to understand that he served his literary apprenticeship . . . (*More and more contemptuous*) . . . chopping meat on a butcher's slab.

FREDERICK (*still smiling*): And why not?

COUNT (*continuing*): Which would explain the bestial and savage character of his plays, and why, when he was alive, he was a great favorite among such people as dockers, carters . . .

FREDERICK (*interrupting ironically*): And kings!

GEORGE (*interrupting in a very affected voice*): Ah! . . . Well, now I understand why the play "dis-pleased" me . . . "shocked" me. (*Smiling.*) Tomorrow evening I will take a seat for my coachman. (*The others laugh.*) It would be an interesting experiment, don't you agree?

FREDERICK (*sure of himself*): I hope you will allow me the pleasure of offering you a box for your horses . . . (*A pause, then imitating the dandy's voice*) . . . It would be an "interesting experiment," don't you agree?

This scene reanimates the zealous aesthetic debate surrounding the birth of French Romantic drama. For the Romantics, and especially Hugo, the ugly and grotesque held as much dramatic interest as the beautiful and sublime. Yet Hugo's plea for breaking with French Neoclassic constraints was meant to apply to all spheres of life: his landmark manifesto, the *Préface de Cromwell* (1827), was, in the words of one political historian, a "revolt against the monarchy as well as against the classical rules of the stage."[29] The subversive, politicized tone of Frédérick's repartee is undeniable: "With consummate elegance [Frédérick] dismisses the entire aristocracy and the bourgeoisie, sending them back to their emptiness and aesthetic incompetence vis-à-vis the theater: for they are neither dockers nor carters (which they do not want to be), nor kings (which they pretend to be)."[30] It is nonetheless essential to note that Prévert's Frédérick is enormously cautious. By invoking positively the authority of "kings" in what is ostensibly the era of Louis-Philippe and Guizot, he softens the truly radical potential for change that Hugo discerned in Shakespeare.

Vigny's 1829 adaptation of *Othello* (*Le More de Venise*) marked an early triumph for the embattled Romantics. But Othello was not one of the historical Lemaître's great roles, and by the mid-1830s he conceded that his talent was better suited to modern drama than to tragedy, be it Elizabethan or French Neoclassic. If Prévert chose to tamper with Lemaître's life history in this instance, it was, first, because *Othello* provided the necessary "lofty" counterpoint to the commedia dell'arte scenarios that regulate the film's melodramatic plot, and, second, because it allowed Pierre Brasseur to brandish his extraordinary gamut of abilities.

By age twenty Brasseur had become a star of light stage comedy. From the 1920s through the 1940s he wrote successful comedies as well as acted in them. A *monstre sacré* of serious French theater following the war, he had his most notable successes as Goetz in Sartre's *Le Diable et le bon Dieu* (1951) and as the title character of Sartre's *Kean* (1953), adapted from the elder Dumas's play specifically for Brasseur and directed by Brasseur himself.

Of his nearly eighty films, many of Brasseur's best were scripted by Prévert. In his autobiography, *Ma Vie en vrac* (*My Life Thrown Together*, 1972), Brasseur recalls with pleasure how the "lightning," "thunder," and "laughter" of Prévert's rapid-fire manner of speaking permeated the roles he wrote for him, "and that was marvelous."[31] Yet *Ma Vie en vrac* intimates that the "lightning" and "laughter" of Brasseur's Prévert roles owe as much to Brasseur as to Prévert. The book reads as if it had been written by the Frédérick Lemaître we know from *Les Enfants du paradis*. To what extent does the film's Frédérick reflect not the real Lemaître but the real Brasseur? To what degree was Brasseur's subsequent life, as well as his view of that life, influenced by the film role? Prévert and Brasseur would have delighted in unanswerable questions like these, for they clash with the standard of truth that *Les Enfants du paradis* deliberately undermines: clear demarcation between the lived and the theatrical, between reality and mask.

Brasseur perhaps most resembled Prévert's Frédérick in his honesty and humility. In Part II of *Les Enfants du paradis*, Frédérick acknowledges that vulgar emotion motivates his noblest endeavor: "I've never felt anything like it. It's heavy, it's unpleasant . . . Do you hear, Garance . . . There, just a moment ago, I was jealous! . . . And with it all, to make sense out of it all, Baptiste, who acts like a god! . . . Thanks to you, thanks to all of you, I shall be able to play Othello!" In *Ma Vie en vrac* Brasseur discloses matter-of-factly his lifelong abuse of alcohol and drugs—a further trait shared with Kean, Lemaître, and Prévert, who were all alcoholics. Hospitalized for pleurisy while on tour in Canada, "I looked at myself in a mirror. That son-of-a-bitch only reflected the image of a cadaver, an unknown man; it was me. And I thought, looking at it, of all the new roles I could play with that face . . . That emaciated image was my true personality, my inner identity, outstripping and annihilating that idiotic and chubby persona I had displayed for years." [32] Earlier perhaps than the actor himself, Prévert discerned and identified with this dark, masochistic side of Brasseur's ordinarily lightsome personality. He had already activated it in *Le Quai des Brumes* and *Lumière d'été*.

My discussion of the relationship between Prévert and Carné portrayed the scenarist as a poet of the sun and the director as a tragedian of the night. A similar contrast holds between Brasseur's Frédérick and Barrault's Baptiste. Prévert sketched his first notions about *Les Enfants du paradis* on a $2\frac{1}{2} \times 3$-foot chart that outlines the film's protagonists in colored pictures and words. [33] In the upper left-hand corner appears "BAPTISTE," followed by a series of phrases that begins "'fallen from the moon,' sensitive, his mother and his childhood in Bohemia." Directly beneath this entry appears "Frédéric" (*sic*), followed by phrases that include "the words" (underscored in orange) and "'The giants of this world' . . . huge freedom." Two drawings dominate Frédérick's entry: a sun and a griffin, in that order. The mythic griffin emblematizes Frédérick's career: in Part I he débuts as a pantomime lion; in Part II he soars eaglelike above all other actors. A creature sacred to Apollo, the griffin also indicates the force of Prévert's initial association of Frédérick-Arlecchino with the sun. Baptiste's Pierrot, on the contrary, forsakes his Italian identity as Pedrolino to seek out the shadowy domain of more northern climes ("Bohemia"). Yet for all their psychological differences (treated in detail in the next two chapters), Baptiste and Frédérick denote the ability of great performers to render the moon and the sun equally appealing.

Barrault's and Brasseur's transcendent depictions of the lives and performances of two historical luminaries, along with the uncanny correspondence between their own accomplishments and those of their nineteenth-century counterparts, demonstrated the capacity of artists to perpetuate and enrich France's cultural identity during the Occupation. By making Barrault's and Brasseur's specifically theatrical talents available to moviegoers throughout France, *Les Enfants du paradis* generated more collective national pride than the theater alone could ever have brought about. In stirring spectators to identify not only with its protagonists but with the theater audiences that identified with these protagonists as they performed on stage, *Les Enfants du paradis* pursued a goal that might best be labeled propagandistic: to ensure a homogeneous community of feeling and identity in relation to the Occupier. *Les Enfants du paradis* was, in a sense, an unauthorized but supreme declaration of the inalienable prerogatives of Gallic culture during a period of war.

The wartime brilliance of French cultural life raises intriguing questions. Entertainment fared well during the Occupation. As early as October 1940 cabarets and music halls reopened in Montmartre and Montparnasse and along the Champs-Elysées. By February 1941 singer Charles Trenet returned in concert to the Avenue Music-Hall, as did Edith Piaf to the Bobino, where she earned up to twenty thousand francs for a night's work. Although Maurice Chevalier chose to limit public appearances, he performed live for Radio-Paris, his bouncy songs continuing to epitomize French joie de vivre. The more elevated performing arts also recovered with notable speed. The Paris Opera reopened on August 24, 1940, with a production of Berlioz's *La Damnation de Faust*. Four days later the Opera's ballet troupe danced *Coppélia*.

Soon after the defeat Cocteau quipped, "Vive la paix honteuse" ("Long live shameful peace"). On December 5 he published an "Address to Young Writers" in the journal *La Gerbe*, advising would-be dramatists: "Put on plays. Trample over us. I am a specialist in destiny and its mysteries, believe me. Seize your chance. It's here."[34] Cocteau did not need to overstate his point. Thanks to distinguished figures of the drama world who worked closely with the *Propagandastaffel*,[35] French theater flourished between 1940 and 1944. Box-office receipts in 1943 were 318 million francs, or three times the total of 1938.[36] The Comédie Française excelled. Boulevard comedy thrived. And among the more lasting serious plays written and mounted during the period were Montherlant's *La Reine morte* (1942), Anouilh's *Eurydice* (1942) and *Antigone* (1944), Giraudoux's *Sodome et Gomorrhe* (1943), and—by newcomers to the theater world—Sartre's *Les Mouches* (1943) and *Huis clos* (1944), and Camus's *Le Malentendu* (1944).

For most Parisians the expense of attending a play, opera, or music-hall extravaganza was prohibitive. French film attendance, however, rose to an annual national average of 250 million spectators during the Occupation years. (In 1938 movie spectatorship numbered 220 million; in 1939, 6 million. But in 1942 French motion-picture theaters sold 310 million tickets.)[37] Of the eighty-one filmmakers responsible for the 220 feature films of the period, nineteen made directorial débuts, including Robert Bresson (*Les Anges du péché*, 1943, and *Les Dames du Bois de Boulogne*, 1945), Jacques Becker (*Dernier Atout*, 1942, *Goupi Mains Rouges*, 1943, and *Falbalas*, 1944), Claude Autant-Lara (*Le Mariage de Chiffon*, 1942, *Lettres d'amour*, 1942, and *Douce*, 1943), and Henri-Georges Clouzot (*L'Assassin habite au 21*, 1942, and *Le Corbeau*, 1943). Among new screen performers to gain lasting celebrity during the Occupation were Marie Déa, Michcline Presle, Odette Joyeux, Madeleine Sologne, and Maria Casarès; Serge Reggiani, Jean Marais, Georges Marchal, and Jean Desailly.

In an arresting book entitled *Chantons sous l'occupation* (*Let's Sing Under the Occupation*, 1976), André Halimi intermingles an exhaustive roster of the period's theatrical events with an inventory of political occurrences marking the progress of totalitarianism and the Aryanization process throughout France. Dedicated to "those who did not sing," Halimi's book purports to present only facts. But the author means to indict those who hampered the nation's Resistance efforts by promoting diversions.

In one of his numerous interviews with important figures who lived through the era, Halimi quotes Edmond Nessler, a politician active in the Liberation movement, as asking: "Why did Hitler, who subjugated us as he did Poland, Norway, Denmark, Holland, and Belgium, grant us an armistice, this kind of fiction of semiliberty? Surely because France still had enormous military resources that could be made inoperative by dividing French public opinion. To return to normalcy under a Pétain regime was the equivalent of forgetting about war. And that is why those who allowed the French to amuse themselves . . . to be deflected from preoccupations that could have coincided with our own, are those who, consciously or unconsciously, participated in a psychological action that was collaboration . . . The more esteem I have [for individual artists], the less indulgent I become. The more talented they were, the more we should be harsh toward them."[38]

By Nessler's and Halimi's standards, we must excoriate *Les Enfants du paradis* doubly. No work of art conceived and executed during the Occupation required a greater investment of time, energy, and talent. And none so compellingly glorified performance as essentially apolitical. But did the making of *Les Enfants du paradis* therefore constitute, as Nessler would have it, a towering act of collaboration?

Les Enfants du paradis premiered less than two months before Germany's surrender on May 8, 1945. Most of France had been liberated by the autumn of 1944. The issue of the film's serving enemy purposes is therefore moot. Indeed, reviewers over the decades have repeatedly endorsed Carné's view of the film as a patriotic antidote to France's military defeat. Press response in March 1945 was unabashedly chauvinistic. *Le Figaro* critic Jean-Jacques Gautier wrote that "a French film of this order eclipses all American and English productions we know." Justifying the film's aesthetic weight in *Libération*, Jeander asserted, "I am not sufficiently 'Americanized' to be unmoved at seeing Carné return to us, arm in arm, our theater of yesterday and our cinema of today." The reviewer in *Fraternité*, "without wishing to insult our friends in Hollywood," extolled the picture's quintessential "French style" and rejoiced in contemplating "the prestige which the screening of this film in Allied countries . . . will bring upon our industry."[39] In 1956 Sadoul rhapsodized, "*Les Enfants du paradis* represented in 1943–44 a prodigious act of faith, a cathedral raised to the glory of French art during the most awful moments of what seemed to be a new Hundred Years' War."[40] And on the occasion of an American rerelease in 1974, Andrew Sarris remarked: "How fitting it is that this movie should have been prepared at the time of the German Occupation, and completed shortly afterward. Hence, out of a period of collective helplessness emerged a poetic tribute to self-expression. Out of evil enslavement came artistic beauty."[41]

But what if Germany had won the war? Such an outcome was not unimaginable when Carné, Prévert, and Barrault conceived and planned their film. In *Cinema of Paradox*, Ehrlich demonstrates that the Nazis deemed it politically and economically self-advantageous to encourage high-quality artistic expression in France, so long as works did not foster an insurrectionary spirit: "The French were now citizens of Europe, and if they produced critically admired films, the prestige these films generated would reflect not on French culture, but on the culture (and prosperity) of [the] 'new Europe.'"[42] One of Germany's long-term goals was in fact to turn the worldwide appeal of French pictures into an economic wedge to force purchase of its own products. *Les Enfants du paradis* would have supported this strategy handsomely.

Even more troubling, *Les Enfants du paradis* would also have bolstered a tenet at the core of Nazi ideology: the supposed racial determination of national cultures. Carné's glorification of a specifically French theatrical tradition lends itself with disturbing ease to the cause of those who would have wished to promulgate the notion of a pure Gallic race. This potentiality of *Les Enfants du paradis* has gone generally unacknowledged because of the timing of the film's release. But the chauvinism that colored the initial press reception is a sure indication of the unsavory purpose to which Fascists, both German and French, could have put the film if France had remained under Occupation.

Carné himself reveals that the film has been construed as racist. During a lecture at Harvard in 1981, he remarked: "I once presented *Les Enfants du paradis* at the Jerusalem Cinémathèque. A question-and-answer period followed, and one viewer rose and said, 'Don't you think you portrayed the old clothes man as having traits that reflected and reinforced anti-Semitic stereotypes?' I was very distressed by this accusation. The notion had never occurred to me." [43] Yet the notion is not entirely unreasonable. Like Michel Simon's Zabel in *Le Quai des Brumes*, Pierre Renoir's impersonation of Jéricho conjures forth a presence decidedly out of place and, by comparison with other players, non-"Gallic." In three of his brother's films, *La Nuit du carrefour* (1932), *Madame Bovary* (1933), and *La Marseillaise* (1937), actor Renoir had distinguished himself in warm, sympathetic, and indubitably unforeign roles: as Inspector Maigret, Charles Bovary, and Louis XVI. But in *Les Enfants du paradis* the bend of his body, the croak of his voice, and the configuration of his facial hair make Renoir's portrayal of the film's only true villain conform all too uncomfortably to the distorted images of Jews propagated in notorious German films such as Fritz Hippler's *Der Ewige Jude* (*The Eternal Jew*, 1940) and Veit Harlan's *Jud Süss* (*Jew Süss*, 1940)—both distributed in France, with the latter breaking 1941 box-office records in Lyons, Toulouse, and Vichy. [44]

Unquestionably, the intentions of those who shaped the making of *Les Enfants du paradis* were honorable. Carné, Prévert, Paulvé, and Barrault sought to sustain the French film industry and bring comfort to the French people. Yet it is equally certain that *Les Enfants du paradis* did not risk provocation. It did not aim to foster active resistance. It did not seek to incite viewers to combat the enemy. Rather, *Les Enfants du paradis* exemplifies what historian Werner Rings names "symbolic resistance." Milder than "offensive," "defensive," and "polemic" resistance, symbolic resistance enhances the self-respect of the Occupied through "solemn, devout, and uplifting displays of national narcissism and self-esteem." Such acts of opposition create no focal points of organized resistance. And as Ring observes, symbolic resistance is "quite compatible with collaboration of all kinds."[45]

Nonetheless, the making of *Les Enfants du paradis* contributed to the French effort to hold fast against Germany's sway. In an essay on dreams, George Steiner relates that after the Nazis came to power in Germany, a *Reichsorganisationsleiter* boasted: "The only person in Germany who still leads a private life is one who is asleep." As a product of sleep, dreams acquire political weight. They become, in Steiner's words, "the last refuge of freedom and the hearth of resistance . . . Up to a certain point, the 'safe houses' of clandestine resistance to totalitarian despotism are those of dreams."[46] *Les Enfants du paradis* demonstrates magnificently that France's theaters—the "safe houses" of those collective dreams that take the form of plays and movies—provided a public site for relief from political oppression.

CHAPTER 12

Androgyny, Masochism, and
Children of Paradise

Les Enfants du paradis raises disturbing ethical issues about quality moviemaking in France during the Occupation. The film compels us to acknowledge the degree to which Carné and Prévert retreated from clear-cut ideological expression and worked, however unwittingly, to the enemy's advantage. But Carné and Prévert did not let Occupation conditions stifle their lasting concern for the conflict between personal freedom and society's dictates. *Les Enfants du paradis* is their most complex statement on the possibility of self-realization in a world hostile to individual difference.

By calling into question the authority of the family, the repression of sexual deviance, rigid gender roles, and the dependence of women on men, *Les Enfants du paradis* assailed the foundation of Vichy's social order. The film did not elaborate an agenda for effecting social change. But through its treatment of the eroticized imagination as a force for unleashing human potential, *Les Enfants du paradis* put forward alternatives not only to Vichy's social values but to patriarchal norms generally. Lacenaire's nonconformity, Frédérick's promiscuity, Baptiste's androgyny, and, above all, Garance's independence threaten the canon of acceptable behavior embodied by Nathalie and espoused sanctimoniously by the Nazi and Vichy regimes.

Chronicling French cinema during the Occupation, Roger Régent wrote: "Under Vichy's nose, *Les Enfants du paradis* expressed certain ideas and a conception of life and love infinitely more seditious than the liberal censors would have allowed before 1939. Unfortunately, we could not take as much pleasure in this subterfuge as we would have wished, since the film appeared only after the Liberation." [1] Régent did not specify the character of this subterfuge, nor has any commentator since then. Such reticence impedes comprehension of the film's enduring capacity to fascinate. It also sidesteps the work's crucial view of the relations between artistic creation and erotic desire.

Lacenaire brings into focus the interplay of art, society, and sexuality. The historical assassin distinguished himself less for his crimes than for his aesthetic attitude toward them. While awaiting trial and execution for two murders, he wrote a Rousseau-like autobiography, *Mémoires de Lacenaire*, and a collection of poems. During the trial he stunned the court with his cynicism, verbal brilliance, and gentlemanly apparel. Like Deburau and Lemaître, Lacenaire inaugurated a legendary persona which others embellished. Hugo, Gautier, and Breton wrote reverently of him.[2] Baudelaire was probably evoking Lacenaire when, among his "heroes of modern life," he singled out "a criminal . . . whose ferocious valor did not lower its head" before the guillotine.[3] In turn, the Lacenaire legend engendered literary characters. Stendhal intended to include an outlaw named Valbeyre, based on (and rhyming with) Lacenaire, in his unfinished novel *Lamiel*.[4] Dostoevsky's interest in the anarchist-assassin gave shape to *Crime and Punishment*'s Raskolnikov (1866). In a piece published in February 1861, the Russian novelist described Lacenaire as "a phenomenal, mysterious, fearful yet interesting individual."[5]

A scene in *Les Enfants du paradis*'s second sequence exemplifies Carné and Prévert's effort to impart the content and tone of Lacenaire's *Mémoires* (see fig. 56). Speaking with Garance in the public scribe's shop, Lacenaire articulates the autobiography's principal themes: his scorn for humanity, his self-perceived exceptionality, his solitude, his taste for creative writing, his miserable childhood, and his obsession with the guillotine. During much of the scene, Lacenaire seems to speak more to himself than to Garance. Positioned in a foreground medium-close shot, his face to the camera, Lacenaire appears in sharp focus, while Garance is noticeably out of focus. This mise en scène conveys the self-centered quality of the posthumous *Mémoires*, captures the misanthrope's physical and spiritual isolation, and announces Lacenaire's relationship to women: unlike Baptiste and Frédérick, the film's Lacenaire does not allow for the consequences of an undiverted gaze upon Garance.

In making Lacenaire their most psychologically opaque character, Carné and Prévert perpetuate the veil of mystery that the historical Lacenaire sought to sustain even as he composed his confessions. Beneath the engraved portrait serving as a frontispiece to the original edition of the *Mémoires*, he wrote: "There is a secret that kills me, / Which I hide from curious eyes, / You will see here only the statue, / The soul is hidden from every eye." [6] On Prévert's chart outlining the film's characters, the entry "Lacenaire" includes the underlined phrase *il est impuissant*.[7] This is an ambiguous statement. It can mean, politically, he is powerless; physiologically, he is impotent; or both. It may or may not unlock "the secret" that the real-life Lacenaire sought to keep hidden. But it suggests that Prévert, Carné, and actor Marcel Herrand conceived the film's dandy-assassin within a context that embraced the political and the sexual.

The historical Lacenaire viewed his powerlessness vis-à-vis society as triggering his criminality: "When, with the best will in the world to earn money by my own talents in an honest way, I found myself rejected and disdained on every side . . . then hatred followed contempt, deep, gnawing hatred, in which eventually I included the whole of humankind . . . It was the social structure I wanted to strike at, in its foundations, in its rich folk, its harsh and egotistical rich." Although he identified with society's poor and wrote a politically brazen song entitled "A Thief's Petition to a King His Neighbor," Lacenaire adhered to no positive philosophy. He never thought of himself as a republican: "I did not meddle in the least with politics . . . a Revolution profits no one but a few intriguers."[8]

Prévert and Carné preserve Lacenaire's anarchistic stance. The film depicts, with some alterations, the two crimes that brought Lacenaire to the guillotine. The attempt to assassinate the debt collector at the end of Part I corresponds to Lacenaire's bungled theft and attempted murder of a bank delivery boy, Louis Genevay, which took place on December 29, 1834. As in the film, Lacenaire rented an apartment for the occasion, and when the act miscarried, he and his accomplice, François Martin, ran from the scene pretending to alert the police. The assassination of the Count at the end of Part II is a transposition of the successful murder of Jean-François Chardon and his widowed mother on December 14, 1834. This event took place not at the Turkish baths on the Boulevard du Temple but in the Chardons' apartment in the Passage du Cheval Rouge. Afterward Lacenaire and Pierre-Victor Avril went to the baths to wash their bloodstained clothes and hands.

The film provides minimal explanation for both events. A fade-out cuts short the discussion of Lacenaire's plan for the incident in Part I. The explicit plot support for the murder in Part II is almost nonexistent. But Lacenaire's assassination of the Count is not gratuitous. It is tied in part, as we have seen, to a dynamic of political subversion that operates weakly throughout the film: revenge exacted by the humiliated upon their oppressors. It is also tied to a much stronger dynamic animating each of the film's male protagonists: the relation of masculine self-consciousness to the feminine.

After Frédérick describes the beauty of feeling "one's heart and the hearts of the audience beating together," Lacenaire retorts: "What promiscuity. As for me, when occasionally my heart begins to beat, it beats so strongly that there is a quite particular sensuality [*volupté*] in knowing that I am the only one to hear it." Lacenaire conforms here to Barbey d'Aurevilly's dictum that "the moment a dandy falls in love, he is no longer a dandy."[9] He also reveals himself as adhering to a tradition of sexual abstinence that originated with "Beau" Brummel (or, more precisely, with Edward Bulwer-Lytton's fictionalized account of Brummel in the novel *Pelham; or, Adventures of a Gentleman*, 1828). To need another emotionally or physically is to concede insufficiency. "I am not one of those who are prepared to complicate their lives for the sake of a woman," declares Lacenaire to his cronies at the Rouge-Gorge. "Women! They barely exist."

During the historical Lacenaire's trial the defendant wore a blue coat with velvet collar and black trousers. His shirt front, collar, and cuffs were clean. And he carried a cambric handkerchief—"the latest thing in 1835."[10] While this apparel distinguished Lacenaire from common criminals, no evidence substantiates the view that Lacenaire was—or had the means to be—as much of a dandy as he appears even in Part I of *Les Enfants du paradis*. In 1835 he was known simply as the "poet-assassin." The nicknames "dandy-assassin" and *dandy du crime* belong to the Lacenaire legend. In the early 1880s Théodore Labourieu penned a fanciful account of Lacenaire's life that describes him as a man "with a face so sweet" and "mannerisms so delicate" that he was often called Demoiselle or Petit-Prêtre.[11] This description influenced subsequent treatments of Lacenaire, including Carné and Prévert's.

When the term "dandy" entered the French vocabulary in 1816, it referred principally to the eccentric dress and impertinent speech typified by Englishmen who identified with Brummel. But by midcentury, Gallic dandies had become associated with the Romantic cult of the individual. For Baudelaire, their lineage included Caesar and Shakespeare as well as Byron.[12] Antibourgeois, elitist, and questing dreamily for power in the post-Napoleonic world, the dandy had an overwhelming passion for asserting his superiority. His principal modes of self-assertion were art, although less as works produced for consumption than the self as art; crime, personally challenging the system with concern neither for the common good nor for changing the status quo; and the flaunting of absolute self-sufficiency, approaching the ideal of a secret society of one. The historical Lacenaire aspired to all of this. By dandifying him sartorially, Carné and Prévert add little to characterization. But they reinforce the theatrically grounded antitheses that structured the persona of the real Lacenaire as well as of nineteenth-century dandies generally: appearance and essence; revelation and concealment; affirmation and denial.[13]

A scene cut from the film suggests that women intimidate Lacenaire. Meant to follow Baptiste's first pantomime, it takes place on the terrace of a café and concludes with the following exchange:

LACENAIRE (*his voice becomes harsher and full of bitterness*): . . . nothing makes me happier than to discover that I'm absolutely right in despising the majority of men (*Close shot. He lowers his voice*) . . . and of women.

GARANCE (*looking at him closely*): Women. Really? What harm have women done to you?

LACENAIRE (*embarrassed and defensive*): None . . . absolutely none at all!

GARANCE (*insisting*): And what have you done to them? To women, Pierre-François . . . (*with an unkind little laugh.*) Not much, I'm sure!

A short pause while GARANCE *watches for* LACENAIRE'S *reaction. Close shot of* LACENAIRE, *hurt; he gives* GARANCE *a look full of hatred. Dissolve.*

At the Rouge-Gorge, another cryptic conversation (uncut) intimates that Lacenaire is willing to consider but unable to engage in more than a platonic relationship with Garance:

LACENAIRE (*suddenly feverish, losing his usual self-control*): Listen, Garance, this is serious. This is something I've never felt for any woman . . .

GARANCE (*interrupting him, gently ironic*): Love, Pierre-François, love!

LACENAIRE (*brutal*): That's got nothing to do with it! (*Lowering his voice.*) I want you, Garance, that's all. But I've got my pride.

GARANCE (*interrupting him again*): . . . and you would like . . . to love . . . (*Lowering her eyes, modest and ironic, but very firm.*) Your head is too hot for me, Pierre-François, and your heart too cold. I'm afraid of draughts. I don't want to lose my health . . . my gaiety . . .

LACENAIRE (*shrugging his shoulders*): It's a pity. We could have done remarkable things together. (*Making an effort to laugh again.*) I would have caused oceans of blood to flow for you! . . . and rivers of diamonds!

These scenes support the view that Prévert's *il est impuissant* referred to physiological impotence as well as political powerlessness. Carné goes further. In an interview published by the journal *Masques* in 1982, Carné asserts, "It is very clear, and historically based, that in *Les Enfants du paradis* Lacenaire is homosexual." [14] According to Arletty, Carné and Prévert had to keep Lacenaire's sexual orientation "ambiguous" for reasons of censorship: "You cannot say for certain that he is homosexual, but he is intended to be." [15]

There is insufficient evidence to make a sure case for either impotence or homosexuality in the historical Lacenaire. He claims in the *Mémoires* to have been "a perfect satyr to the fair sex," but only with prostitutes; to have had a five-year liaison with a married woman he calls Madame Dormeuil, but whose heart, like his, "was stronger than her senses"; and to have attempted to kill a neighborhood wench he had slept with named Javotte. [16] Yet the *Mémoires* are replete with inscrutable remarks such as: "My amorous complexion was of an odd nature"; "My physique was far from being as well-developed . . . as my mind"; "While I adored Madame Dormeuil, my senses were unawakened near her." [17] A landmark phrenological analysis speaks of "the disproportion in the development of his organs" and "the decrepitude in shape and movement of his lower limbs." [18] Moreover, the 1835 police investigation discloses that when serving time earlier in Poissy Prison, Lacenaire had been intimate with a chorus boy from the Ambigu-Comique known as Bâton: "Their relations were of a rather suspicious nature at Poissy with the result that Bâton was accused of having been more than a close friend of Lacenaire." [19] Jean-François Chardon, the man murdered along with his mother by Lacenaire and Avril, was overtly homosexual and known in the underworld as Tante Madeleine. According to Philip J. Stead, "when the crime was first reported in the Press, curious mutilations were referred to which were not mentioned later, possibly in the interests of public decency." [20] One recent commentator speculates that Chardon had been Lacenaire's rival for Bâton's affections in prison. [21] More certain is Lacenaire's exploitation of homosexual men. In the *Mémoires* he relates how he posed as a police officer and employed boys to entrap for profit "men with shameful vices who were caught *in flagrante delicto* in the Champs Elysées." [22]

Carné's comment in *Masques* notwithstanding, *Les Enfants du paradis* does not make "clear" that Lacenaire is homosexual. But it emphasizes his disengagement from women even more than do the *Mémoires*. Lacenaire's sole female acquaintance in the film is Garance. Their rapport is inspired by the real Lacenaire's supposed relationship with Madame Dormeuil. But Prévert and Carné trim the hints of physicality found in the original account and accentuate its platonic character. They also sentimentalize the bond between Lacenaire and Avril. According to the *Mémoires*, the historical Pierre-Victor Avril was a heavy drinker, an habitué of brothels, and a young man who appealed to Lacenaire because "he had no shadow of reasoning power."[23] The film's Avril is doltish, but he prefers hot chocolate to spirits, has no relations with women, and is hypersensitive. Enthralled by "Monsieur Lacenaire" even as the latter treats him with contempt, Avril projects a nonspecific sexuality epitomized by the rosebud he wears unaffectedly behind his left ear and at one point lets dangle from his teeth.

The homoeroticism that colored attachments among underworld men in *Jenny* and *Le Quai des Brumes* culminates in Lacenaire's murder of the Count. The scene reconstructs not the site of the authentic crime, the murder of the homosexual Chardon, but the site where the real Lacenaire and Avril sought to eliminate traces of that crime: the Turkish baths. Carné and Prévert thus suppress the explicitly homosexual component of the historical incident but reinstate it obliquely by situating the Count's murder in an exotically decorated, exclusively male milieu: when the camera tracks swiftly from the bathhouse's entrance to the Count's private cubicle, it discloses men lounging in various states of undress and interaction.

As in *Le Jour se lève*, the climactic murder plays out a primal scene with male homoerotic overtones. But where the interloper in *Le Jour se lève* was the film's audience, presumably made up of men and women, the voyeuristic third party in *Les Enfants du paradis* is Avril, a specifically male audience-surrogate (fig. 58). In fact, the film audience does not see the murder. With near-total silence, the knifing takes place out of frame as the camera moves in toward Avril standing motionless by the door. The published script reads: "He stares, his eyes popping, at what is going on. At the first muffled groan, off, he presses himself even harder against the wall. There is a sound of a body falling into the water. AVRIL jumps, then LACENAIRE comes into shot—slight zoom backward to frame them both in tight close shot. AVRIL admiring and terrified: 'Oh! Monsieur Lacenaire!'"

In terms of conventional realism, the situation is preposterous. Avril, for all his sensitivity, must already have been exposed to violent acts. But in terms of myth, the scene is masterly. Avril's viewing the murder constitutes a young man's rite of initiation to capital crime. Herein lies La-

58 Fabien Loris as Avril witnessing Lacenaire's murder of the Count at the Turkish baths

cenaire's radical difference and his threat to the social order. The murder is the crowning act of a man who perceives reality as a performance shaped and directed solely by himself. In some sense Garance motivates the act: the Count would hold no interest for Lacenaire were he not Garance's protector. But unlike Baptiste and Frédérick's theatrical achievements, Lacenaire's aesthetically fashioned act of murder is not a redirection of desire for a woman. It is a self-willed expression of undefinable passion toward a male object that transpires in the presence of a third male. By ceremoniously exposing Avril to a dark form of physical intimacy infused with horror, Lacenaire celebrates life and death in absolute detachment from female existence. Garance may be, as Lacenaire calls her throughout the film, his "guardian angel," but she is not his creative muse.

Despite his use of the term *impuissant*, it is likely that Prévert, as well as Carné and Herrand, conceived of Lacenaire as homosexual. In choosing not to depict him unambiguously as such, they were exercising, as Arletty suggests, necessary discretion vis-à-vis Occupation censors—and, I would add, general theater audiences of the mid-1940s. But their restraint does not detract from the boldness of the portrayal. The principal impact of homosexuality on modern European society probably has less to do with sexuality per se than with the contestation of prevailing values. "The homosexual," writes novelist and film historian Dominique Fernandez, "is not simply someone who sleeps with men instead of women; he is also (at least the homosexual who reflects upon his destiny, who contributes to 'homosexual culture') someone who feels and thinks differently from the masses, someone who stands apart . . . someone dissatisfied with established order."[24] By denying viewers a ready label for Lacenaire's sexuality (the term "homosexuality" was in fact not employed in France before 1869), Carné and Prévert ensure that Lacenaire's deviance remains nonspecific and hence all the more menacing.

In this regard Lacenaire bears comparison with the homosexual criminal, Vautrin, in Balzac's *La Comédie humaine*. Like Lacenaire, Vautrin manifests sexual difference less through explicit physical acts than through impassioned attempts to undermine social institutions. Like Lacenaire, he inhabits a world in which energetic efforts to transcend the ordinary are extensions of one's natural sexuality, disruptive of society's order, and, for this reason, criminal. But in Balzac passionate souls are compelled to don social masks that disguise their individuality: Vautrin himself is both an underworld boss and chief of the Paris police. The result is a *comédie humaine*, or theatricalization of society, that reduces the true self to calculation, posturing, and controlled emotion. *Les Enfants du paradis*, by contrast, views theater as a realm in which to proclaim one's authentic being. In granting that all of life is a performance and that life's richness derives precisely from the constant, free-flowing bond between enthusiastic performer and equally enthusiastic audience, *Les Enfants du paradis* annuls the Balzacian division between the social and antisocial, between mask and authenticity. Assuredly, *Les Enfants du paradis*'s contrived view of society is anemic in juxtaposition with Balzac's. Its proffered correspondence between reality-as-lived and reality-as-performed is utopian and escapist. But the repression and guilt associated in Balzac with the outsider's need to dissemble give way to pride in *Les Enfants du paradis*. Appearances no longer betoken deception. They are the very source of redemption.

In earlier Carné films, masks are an index of the gap between private desire and public imperatives. *Drôle de Drame*'s Molyneux, *Le Quai des Brumes*'s Zabel, and *Le Jour se lève*'s Valentin exemplify the fragmented personalities such fakery nurtures. Although Carné's heroes and heroines struggle to minimize the breach between mask and authenticity, their efforts result in a deepened sense of social outsiderdom: one thinks of Jenny's final solitude; Kramps's arrest in *Drôle de Drame*; Edmond's murder in *Hôtel du Nord*; and Gilles's petrification in *Les Visiteurs du soir*. *Les Enfants du paradis* reverses this vision. By presenting a world where characterization is grounded explicitly and expressly in theatrical masks, it paradoxically exempts protagonists from having to project false images of themselves. Because their authentic being *is* their image, their individuality and creativity are neither stifled nor marginalized. Onstage and off, they are always "in character." The vitality of their masks—be they Harlequin or Colombina, Iago or Othello—enables them to exhibit, if not an impression of total freedom and spontaneity, at least a sense of fullness and integrity not found in the prior Carné works. Lacenaire's personality is closed and enigmatic. But he is not a hypocrite.

While all Carné protagonists are marginals, his films contain characters whose social outsiderdom correlates especially closely with his own: the blind musician in *Nogent*, standing apart from the masses; the title character of *Jenny*, worn down by bourgeois morality; *Le Quai des Brumes*'s morbid artist, Krauss; and Adrien and Edmond in *Hôtel du Nord*. I have referred to these characters as figures of Carné. But no character in Carné's oeuvre comes closer to mirroring Carné's real-life circumstances than Lacenaire. Like Lacenaire, the young Carné was something of a sartorial dandy. Like Lacenaire, the young Carné was erotically indifferent to women. And like Lacenaire, the young Carné conceived of reality as mise en scène constructed and controlled by himself alone. Inasmuch as Lacenaire becomes, in Mirella Affron's phrase, "the legitimate *auteur* among so many artists,"[25] he is a clear figure of Carné the director.

But Lacenaire is an idealization of Carné the man. In the 1940s Carné still projected a social mask incongruous with his genuine identity. His aggressive, ironhanded comportment on the set was a device intended to deflect the attention of those who would stigmatize him for violating, off the set, prevailing standards of masculinity. Unlike Lacenaire, Carné did not enjoy an existence free of hypocrisy. He did not partake of Lacenaire's impregnable sense of personal worth.

Lacenaire stands as a provocative alternative to common expectations concerning gender, but Carné and Prévert do not present his mode of self-realization as exemplary. For all the dignity infusing his unconventionality, Lacenaire consigns himself to solitude. Neither giving nor receiving love, Lacenaire is incomplete.

Frédérick would seem to represent Lacenaire's opposite. Where the dandy cuts himself off from female existence, the actor vigorously pursues and obtains women's attentions. Yet Frédérick's self-absorption is no less acute than Lacenaire's. His unshakable confidence in accepted forms of manliness prevents him from experiencing sustained intimacy. Unlike Lacenaire, Frédérick is capable of feeling: he regrets Garance's disappearance, and he envies her love for Baptiste. But rather than allow such sentiments to shape a richer self, he enlists them as tools to fortify his Harlequin persona.

By channeling jealousy into art, Frédérick creates his greatest dramatic role, Othello. However, the gender dynamics of Frédérick's *Othello* are thoroughly contrary to Shakespeare's. Frédérick's play ends with the Moor's forbidding Desdemona to say one last prayer, his taking her by the throat, and his strangling her to death. The curtain falls without Emilia's enlightening Othello, without Othello's remorse, and without his stabbing himself "upon a kiss" (V.ii.358). Such foreshortening was typical of nineteenth-century French versions of Shakespeare. But in remaining true to theater history, Carné and Prévert also confirm their view of Frédérick as incapable of emotional expansion.

One study of gender and genre in Shakespeare proposes that the Shakespearean tragic hero's "problem" is a self-conscious concern for his inner life, and that the tragic hero's "privilege" is his capacity to change. Arguing that the masculine self and the nature of the feminine are not mutually exclusive, Linda Bamber suggests that Shakespeare's tragic heroes redefine their idea of manhood by moving from misogyny toward acceptance and, sometimes, even love of women. At the end of *Othello*, *King Lear*, and *Hamlet*, "manliness, self-assertion, and honor are no longer in competition with love and forgiveness." [26] *Les Enfants du paradis*'s truncated *Othello* forecloses the kind of deepened self-awareness Bamber describes.

The mental disposition of the classic Harlequin rejects concepts of morality. Harlequin gets an idea; he gaily applies it; and "no matter what scrape it leads him into, he never gains from his experience: one minute later he will be merrily pursuing another thought." [27] This pattern also characterizes Frédérick's erotic disposition. Early in Part II, Frédérick uncorks a bottle of champagne that spurts rightward across the frame (fig. 59). This shot epitomizes Frédérick's sexuality. A bottle replaces Harlequin's traditional *batte*, or wooden stick. But it similarly connotes carefree promiscuity. Women's absence from this scene (Frédérick is taking supper with Lacenaire and Avril) underscores Frédérick's fundamentally masturbatory relation to the opposite sex. Although a potent stimulant for his imagination, the feminine signifies, at bottom, brisk physical self-gratification.

Proud and uninhibited, the film's Frédérick is more forthright in his attitude toward lovemaking than was the historical Lemaître. As pre-

59 A visual metaphor for brisk sexual gratification: Frédérick (Pierre Brasseur) uncorking a bottle of champagne in the presence of Lacenaire (Marcel Herrand) and Avril (Fabien Loris); superimposed English title reads, "Disagreeable to die on an empty stomach"

sented in his autobiographical *Souvenirs publiés par mon fils*, the private life of the Romantic stage's *enfant terrible* was uneventful: he oriented his fervor exclusively toward his wife, his three children, and his art. Yet Robert Baldick's *Life and Times of Frédérick Lemaître* (1959) furnishes a more reliable and unsanitized account. It documents Lemaître's mismatched marriage, his probable liaison with actress Marie Dorval, and a series of stormy extramarital affairs with lesser known performers—one of whom, Clarisse Miroy, attempted to poison Lemaître in 1855 by pouring laudanum into his Bordeaux. In refusing to whitewash Lemaître's promiscuity, Carné, Prévert, and Brasseur establish a vivid counterpoise to Lacenaire's disengagement from women. They also thumb their noses at Vichy's call for moral order founded on marriage, family, and conjugal fidelity.

The mutual attraction of Carné and Prévert lay, as we have seen, in their shared sense of incompletion. Each saw the other as actualizing potentialities within himself. Inasmuch as Lacenaire and Frédérick jostle conventional mores, they are figures of Carné and Prévert respectively. Yet

60 An exemplar of marriage, family, and conjugal fidelity,
    Maria Casarès as Nathalie finds Baptiste and Garance in
    each other's arms

Lacenaire's misogyny and Frédérick's womanizing point to limitations of
exclusively male- or female-oriented sexuality. Both characters enjoy self-
determination in their private lives, but in rejecting sustained intimacy
with women, neither expands his inner self. The yearning to reconstitute
a primordial unity of the masculine and the feminine finds expression in
Baptiste, the film's sole male character to approach the Carné-Prévert
androgynous ideal.

Baptiste collides with bourgeois morality when he abandons Nathalie
for Garance at the film's end (fig. 60). Playing the laundress who utilizes
the despondent Pierrot as a clothesline pole in the early *Lover of the
Moon* pantomime, Nathalie exposes the values she incarnates throughout the film: domesticity, practicality, and rootedness. Initially Nathalie's
predicament evokes sympathy: a sweet-natured woman finds herself un-
loved. But by accentuating Nathalie's obstinate denial of Baptiste's passion for Garance, Carné and Prévert ultimately equate wifeliness with

suffocation. The mime's flight to Madame Hermine's boarding house in Part II is another instance of a Carné-Prévert protagonist's pursuit of "atmosphere," or emotional liberation.

Carné attributes the "slight quaver" in Nathalie's speech to the fact that this was actress Maria Casarès's screen début (*Vbd*, 223). Others suggest that Casarès's manifest unease resulted from Carné's bent for inspiring fear in young women. Casarès's projection of rancor and defensiveness may well reflect feelings aimed at Carné, a director generally more indulgent toward male newcomers than toward young females. Her portrayal may also reflect personal frustrations. In her autobiography, *Résidente privilégiée*, the Spanish-born Casarès (b. 1922) discloses that while filming *Les Enfants du paradis* she experienced "one of the most devastating secret passions" of her life. She had fallen hopelessly in love with Marcel Herrand, her mentor at the Théâtre des Mathurins. Herrand happened to be homosexual.[28]

Subsequent filmmakers capitalized on Casarès's ability to depict tortured emotion. As the slighted, vindictive Hélène in Bresson's *Les Dames du Bois de Boulogne* (released in September 1945), Casarès plays a symbolic fury pursuing her prey—a posture Nathalie seems primed to assume at the close of *Les Enfants du paradis*. As the netherworldly Princess in Cocteau's *Orphée* (*Orpheus*, 1950), she incarnates the poet's Death. Cocteau, however, alters the self-serving and possessive Casarès persona. In an act of generosity that bears results hardly conceivable within the Carné-Prévert universe, Casarès's Princess returns Orpheus to life and sacrifices her personal love to the poet's glory. Cocteau's Princess also restores Orpheus's bourgeois existence with Eurydice—a domestic situation similar in its ordinariness to Baptiste and Nathalie's.

When Baptiste *fils* inquires of Garance if she is married and has a little boy of her own, Garance answers elegiacally, "I'm all alone." This melancholy response articulates the fundamental condition of Carné's heroes and heroines: a state of loss and alienation deriving from a lack of family ties. Yet *Les Enfants du paradis* does not exalt domesticity. It rejects both the Vichyites' enshrinement of the French *famille* and the Nazi's sanctification of *Kinder, Küche, Kirche*. As in previous Carné films, the challenge of *Les Enfants du paradis*'s adult protagonists is to attain emotional fulfillment outside convention.

Barrault's Baptiste is arguably the most neurotic figure in the Carné-Prévert oeuvre. But the competing forces of society's injunction to marry and the more exotic enticements of the demimonde are not at the core of his private crisis. Rather, Baptiste is torn by the discrepancy between his idealized image of Garance and her reality. The film does not elucidate fully Baptiste's refusal in Part I to make love with Garance. But the *Lover of the Moon* pantomime divulges Baptiste's need to transform Garance into a chaste, unattainable goddess-statue. In this regard Baptiste is no more successful than Lacenaire or Frédérick in communing with the opposite sex. Like the dandy and the thespian, he constructs a solitary emotional space in which woman exists, at best, as a refuge serving specifically male requirements. But while estrangement from the feminine triggers pride in Lacenaire and insouciance in Frédérick, Baptiste is visibly tormented. Barrault has posited an affinity between Baptiste and Hamlet.[29] If Baptiste is ultimately *Les Enfants du paradis*'s leading character, overpowering even Brasseur's Frédérick in dramatic force, it is because, like the Prince of Denmark, Barrault's Baptiste embodies consciousness painfully conscious of itself.

Baptiste's torment explodes following the Count's first meeting with Garance. Wearing his Pierrot costume and make-up, Baptiste enters the dressing room and equates the Count's enormous floral gift with a funeral wreath intended for himself. Shaking his fists and pacing erratically, he next imagines the flowers to be a nuptial bouquet for "a wedding night with the bridegroom all alone, and no bride!" Overcome with rage, he throws some of the flowers on the ground, crushes them with his foot, and destroys the rest of the bouquet by lashing at it with a riding whip. He roars: "I hate these flowers! I hate everybody . . . that man who was here." More quietly he declaims: "I detest myself . . . I loathe myself!" Positioning himself in front of a mirror, he bursts out laughing: "Baptiste? What is he? Baptiste, since the one he loves doesn't love him. A nothing, a will o' the wisp . . . A machine man . . . A werewolf." Sticking his fingers in a pot of make-up, he draws a cross on the mirror and proclaims his death and epitaph: "That's the end of Baptiste. Here lies Baptiste . . . Life gave him only a red flower, a good thrashing, and a wooden overcoat!"

This unsettling scene exposes the paranoia, self-hatred, and morbidity festering beneath the inscrutability of Pierrot's white mask. It plays out Baptiste's urge to appropriate for himself and then demolish and deface that which Prévert and Carné associate most consistently with the feminine principle as embodied by Garance—flowers and mirrors. It suggests that Baptiste's crisis of identity entails a desire to incorporate the feminine into his being and a conflicting urge to deny its presence.

The historical Deburau's personal life was replete with pain, loss, and scandal. His numerous marriages and dalliances left him, in biographer Tristan Rémy's words, "bitter, vindictive, and unhappy."[30] But Prévert,

Carné, and Barrault take inspiration in the dressing room scene not from Deburau's life, nor even from the Deburau legend propagated by Janin, Gautier, and Baudelaire. Instead, they draw upon post-Romantic and early modern literary texts that portray Pierrot as the neurasthenic par excellence, including Paul Margueritte's poetic pantomime *La Peur* (*Fear*), in which the terrified, solitary player "beats the air with his white wings and falls"; Albert Giraud's poem cycle *Pierrot lunaire* (published in 1884 and put to music in German translation by Schönberg in 1912), where "Beautiful verses are great crosses / On which red Poets bleed"; and poet Jules Laforgue's *Les Complaintes* (1885) and *Imitation de Notre-Dame la Lune* (1886), in which a fear of women engenders anguished self-consciousness.[31]

Critics have broached the pertinence of psychoanalytic thought to Carné's oeuvre with appropriate caution. William Hedges speaks of the "unhealthiness" of Baptiste's tenacious belief in absolute female purity, but he probes no further.[32] Raymond Borde views Baptiste's "neurotic" plight as exemplifying a "self-punishing conception of love" prevalent in all of Carné's major films, but he does not explore its ramifications.[33] Expanding upon Borde's insight, I suggest that Baptiste and, by extension, much of the Carné canon partake of a pleasure-pain dynamic that is only one element in a complex literary-psychoanalytic construct best designated as a "masochistic aesthetic."

Gilles Deleuze sets forth the character of the masochistic aesthetic in his post-Freudian rereading of Leopold von Sacher-Masoch (1835–95), the novelist whose name and fiction inspired German sexologist Krafft-Ebing to coin the term "masochism."[34] Recent discourse on film has made use of the concept.[35] According to Deleuze, the basic components of masochistic desire are disavowal, suspense, waiting, fetishism, and fantasy. The masochistic imagination typically elaborates an ideal image of a punishing woman—a cold and distant beauteous object of ritual contemplation—who is at once comforting and cruel. Because erotic pleasure entails sustained submission before this "icy," "supersensuous" image, the masochist freezes desire and defers physical climax—even as nongratification fosters dejection and mental disturbance.[36]

Baptiste's iconization of Garance, his refusal to sleep with her in Part I, his self-abasement in the dressing room scene, and his nervous depression in Part II are consistent with Deleuze's notion of the masochistic aesthetic. But this concept furnishes more than an apt diagnosis of Baptiste's unbalanced comportment. It helps illuminate his profoundly salutary recourse to pantomime.

Baptiste deviates from society's expectation that men are intrinsically aggressive. Exhibiting offstage the delicacy and tenderness that characterize his onstage persona, Baptiste projects what patriarchy scornfully terms effeminacy. Carné and Prévert want viewers to appreciate Baptiste's "softness" as a positive alternative to convention. But as if to avert undue viewer discomfort, they take care to substantiate Baptiste's "manliness" as well. The physical power and one-upmanship inherent in the swift kick he delivers to Avril at the Rouge-Gorge certify Baptiste's assumption of male prerogatives. His marriage to Nathalie and their producing a son place his heterosexuality beyond doubt. Nonetheless, Baptiste's chronic malaise confirms that the coexistence of masculine- and feminine-associated traits does not, ipso facto, result in emotional fulfillment. For Carné and Prévert, self-realization requires overcoming gender categories altogether—an androgynous ideal best cultivated and tolerated not within society but through art.

Confounding gender-based norms of corporeal expression, pantomime—like ballet—fuses physical grace with strength. The mime's body fascinates because, as if liberated from the laws of physics, it seems "wantonly malleable."[37] Barrault demonstrated such polymorphism by playing mother and son in his 1935 adaptation of *As I Lay Dying*. For Barrault, the dramatic arts foster a recovery of "the man-woman unity." He believes that commedia dell'arte best facilitates this recovery because the improvisational mode compels an actor "to get to the pitch of his 'own true personality.'" In Barrault's scheme of things, theatrical performance discloses "the permanent existence of the ternary . . . masculine-feminine-neuter."[38]

Pantomime in *Les Enfants du paradis* does not simply legitimate Baptiste's apparent femininity. Barrault conceived of artistic creation as "a kind of sexual action at the end of which [the artist] gives life to something." He viewed miming, specifically, as "the 'anti-death' art."[39] *Les Enfants du paradis*'s first pantomime is one of the magical moments in French cinema. Swerving radically from the pseudorealism of the film's prior two sequences (the Boulevard panorama and the scenes in Lacenaire's shop), it generates an instantaneous incursion of the miraculous into the quotidian. The pantomime lays bare, simultaneously and paradoxically, art in process and art fully formed. Within 130 seconds it acts out the artist's capacity to give life to himself, occasioning the "re-birth towards self-unity" which Barrault deemed the gift of "natural artists."[40]

The first pantomime builds on Baudelaire's notion that the solitary urban poet enjoys the "incomparable privilege" of "universal communion" with the passing crowd.[41] Just before the pantomime Baptiste epitomizes pariahdom (fig. 61). Sitting motionless on an upturned barrel, he

61 Baptiste (Jean-Louis Barrault) outside the Théâtre des Funambules, alienated, humiliated, and repudiated for his difference by Anselme (Etienne Decroux)

endures Anselme's physical harassment and disavowal of paternity. The fat burgher's taunt likewise derides Baptiste's difference. Targeting his obvious unmanliness, the burgher shouts, "Hey, Baptiste, if you have any little ones, put one aside for me." The first full shot of Baptiste (thirteenth in the sequence) positions him within the Carné mise en scène that repeatedly connotes alienation: he is companionless and immobile, frame center.

The father, the burgher, and the crowd that endorses Baptiste's humiliation through laughter embody society's repudiation of variance. Garance alone responds with compassion, admiration, and attraction. To the burgher's remark, "He looks as mad as a hatter, doesn't he?" she replies, her gaze riveted on Baptiste, "Me? . . . I think he's got beautiful eyes!" Indeed, in the course of the twenty-four-shot prologue to the pantomime, Garance and Baptiste establish a reciprocal gaze. A succession of reverse-angle shots shows each peering intensely from what would be the other's angle of vision and point of view.

While Garance concentrates on Baptiste, Baptiste takes in the drama surrounding Garance: Lacenaire's theft of the burgher's pocket watch and the latter's accusation of Garance. When he reenacts this episode in mime, Baptiste demonstrates a new identity as well as a new art. Both result from his having internalized, through ocular perception, a dramatis personae corresponding to elements of the human psyche as conceived by classic psychoanalytic psychology: the burgher, or the ego; the policeman, or the superego; Lacenaire, or the id; and Garance, or the primordial mother image.

Several elements in this rite of self-reconstruction merit emphasis. The first is the primacy of Garance, whom Baptiste chooses to impersonate before all others. Although he suggests Garance's femaleness via stereotypic hand gestures that outline the curves of her breasts and hips, Baptiste initiates this characterization by tracing the contours of Garance's face and, above all, the prominence of her eyes (fig. 62). For Baptiste, Garance's essence resides in her eyes, not in gender-specific organs. Second, Baptiste turns the tables on the burgher, mocking his obesity and fatuousness and gaining the crowd's approval for it. In an Oedipal triumph of sorts (the burgher had made unreciprocated lustful overtures to Garance), Baptiste shames the burgher into acknowledging publicly his ineffectuality. When he mimics the burgher's search for the stolen watch by running his hands futilely in the region of his private parts, Baptiste affirms the burgher's emasculation (fig. 63). Third, Baptiste's pantomime includes an event that did not actually take place. To underscore the policeman's and the burgher's capacity for violence, he mimes the former leading Garance off to jail and the latter self-complacently dealing her a kick in the rear (fig. 64). For Baptiste, Garance is a victim of male brutality and exclusionism—an untenable state which Baptiste sets right through female-associated traits of tenderness and grace.

Fourth, the pantomime ends with a full shot of Baptiste's body upright yet at total ease (fig. 65). Unlike the earlier presence sitting slouched and sickly on the barrel, Baptiste radiates a bodily health that is the product of his symbolic drama. Fifth, the pantomime depicts Lacenaire's disappearance following his crime. In the remainder of the film Lacenaire interacts with all the leading characters except Baptiste. It is as if the pantomime announces Baptiste's willful exclusion of the id from his psychic framework, thereby foreclosing the possibility of his obtaining satisfaction for instinctual needs in direct accordance with the pleasure principle. Finally, the pantomime's unanticipated coda upsets the state of absolute tranquillity Baptiste achieves at the end of his performance. When Garance moves toward the platform, tosses him a rose, and blows a kiss, she obliges Baptiste to recognize her not simply as an introjected image productive of art and personal identity, but as a real woman (fig. 66). Baptiste's incapacity to do so constitutes much of the drama in the rest of the film, making of the pantomime-plus-coda yet another *mise en abyme* of the work's contents.

I have proposed that *Les Visiteurs du soir* undermines mainstream filmmaking's general principle that defines women by their "to-be-looked-at-ness" and men by their active, determining gaze. *Les Enfants du paradis* tampers further with this convention. To be sure, Garance is the object of Baptiste's gaze in the prologue to the first pantomime. As the film develops, she becomes his icon. But like Anne in *Les Visiteurs du soir*, Garance partakes of the traditionally masculine prerogative of the aggressive erotic look. Having quit the peepshow that displayed her half-naked in a well (the visual inverse of Baptiste seated on the upturned barrel), Garance turns a stalwart gaze upon Baptiste that signals the mime's assumption of the traditionally female role of bodily exhibition-ism. Baptiste's reciprocal gaze (embracing the burgher, the policeman, and Lacenaire as well) does not symbolize sexual possession of Garance. It betokens, instead, psychic submission to Garance's female essence, which Baptiste seeks to incorporate within his self-reconstructed identity. Inasmuch as Baptiste performs specifically for her pleasure (that is, her liberation in the form of exoneration), Garance emerges as a controlling presence and source of power. An imposing example of the consequences of this reversal occurs when Baptiste and Garance share their first kiss, filmed in a close two-shot (fig. 67). To follow custom, the camera ought to focus on Garance. But Carné chooses instead to frame and highlight Baptiste's full face, quivering with expectancy, as Garance, shot from the rear, inclines forward and initiates the kiss.

This shift of gender emphasis conforms to Deleuze's view of the pre-Oedipal, oral mother as the primary determinant of masochistic fantasy. Possessing what the infant lacks—the breast and womb—the powerful, nurturing mother is the child's primordial source of love, its original object of desire, and its first agent of control. Overwhelmed by the narcissistic fear of being abandoned by her, the male masochist fantasizes, at once, complete re-fusion of his infantile ego with the mother's body and a permanent, defensive gap between himself and the mother. Thus Baptiste assimilates Garance's female essence into his onstage being but, from anxiety over rejection, keeps her at a distance offstage. Both postures derive from Baptiste's viewing Garance as the imagined oral mother of plenitude and as the original figure of identification in his construction of a new identity.

All of *Les Enfants du paradis*'s pantomimes reinforce the regressive thrust of Baptiste's first performance. In one respect they are the culmination of Carné's nostalgia for silent movies. The near-immobile camera-work, pasteboard décor, and naive stage effects in the second act of the *Lover of the Moon* pantomime constitute an elegant homage to Georges Méliès and early French cinema (fig. 68). Prévert disliked pantomime.

67 A subtle shift of gender emphasis: Garance initiating their kiss as Baptiste quivers with expectancy

But he, too, felt that movies were strongest when faithful to their unpretentious fairground origins: "Film has become an . . . art, they say. Well, when it was a carnival attraction scorned by the elite, it was all the better for it." [42] Inspired by Chaplin's career, Barrault's first conception of *Les Enfants du paradis* called, as I have noted, for Baptiste to remain mute until the picture's climax—an idea which Carné and Prévert found unworkable. But from a psychoanalytic perspective, one might propose that Baptiste exempts himself from speech through the entire film. The seat of Frédérick's sexual prowess lies as much in his command of language as in his easily excited genitalia: Garance comes to deplore Frédérick's "voice of love." Baptiste, by contrast, reconstitutes for himself an archaic, pre-Oedipal phase of consciousness. He moves in a psychic dimension anterior to both the acquisition of speech and genital primacy. Just as Garance is the masochist's guarantor (in French, *garante* [fem.]) of limitless maternal nurture, so Baptiste substantiates Garance's wistful speculation, made to Frédérick, that "there are, all over the world, lovers who love each other without saying anything."

The deemphasis of genital sexuality in Baptiste must not, however, be construed as a diminution of libidinal energy. Immediately preceding his pantomime, the policeman asks, "Were there any witnesses?" Baptiste asserts: "Yes, me. I am a witness." The French word pronounced by Baptiste and the policeman, *témoin*, derives from the Latin *testis*, "one who gives evidence." It lays bare a primal bonding of knowledge with sexuality: the Latin *testis* also means "testicle." Herein resides the force of Baptiste's declaration, "Je suis témoin." With his testimony taking the unusual form of libidinized corporeal expression, Baptiste exposes the inseparableness of knowledge from the erotic. His arousal as *testis* in both senses of the word generates Garance's exculpation, his new self-identity, and an innovative art form.

Toward the film's end Nathalie compares Baptiste to a somnambulist: "You know, sleepwalkers who walk on roofs, if you call them, they fall down. Baptiste is like them . . . when he wakes up he will come back!" Nathalie misapprehends her husband's plight. Baptiste's awakening from his private dream world would be tantamount to discarding his essence as an artist. Janin's biography describes the historical Deburau's pantomimes as "a sort of waking dream in which . . . you [the spectator] enjoy

68   Filmed pantomime as a celebration of the cinema's silent origins

292 · The Monumentmaker

yourself almost as if you were actually asleep!"[43] In a line cut from the film, Garance exclaims, "Baptiste has no technique; he's not acting; he's inventing dreams." Such correlations among sleep, dream, and panto-mime bear on the regressive character of viewing and performance within *Les Enfants du paradis*. They support Jean Starobinski's specula-tion that images of the circus and popular stage appeal to modern liter-ary and visual sensibilities because, like reflections of a lost world, they are "creatures of regressive desire."[44]

I have suggested that principles of incompletion and disconnectedness shape *Les Enfants du paradis*'s narrative design, and that the work's mel-odramatic themes pertain overwhelmingly to human loss, incomprehen-sion, and alienation. Typically, however, viewers come away from this film with a sense of elation and fulfillment. The probable source of this paradox lies in the parallel regressive pleasures of filmwatching and mas-ochism. Studlar observes: "Masochistic fantasy is dominated by oral pleasure, the desire to return to the nondifferentiated body state of the mother/child, and the fear of abandonment (the state of non-breast, non-plenitude). In a sense, these same wishes are duplicated by the film spec-tator who becomes a child again in response to the dream screen of cin-ema. This dream screen affords spectatorial pleasure in recreating the first fetish—the mother as nurturing environment." Yet the dream screen offers only partial gratification of the re-fusion wish: immobile and im-mersed in darkness, movie spectators are passive receiving objects of a flow of images beyond their control. Indeed, adult viewers know that the cinema cannot provide authentic intimacy or fusion with real objects. Like the masochist, film spectators therefore disavow the absence of re-ality, fetishize its images, and thereby reinstate infantile narcissistic plea-sures founded on fictions of wholeness, omnipotence, and fulfillment.[45]

Considered in this light, *Les Enfants du paradis*'s meticulous recon-struction of a historical period that is nonetheless unspecifiable; its ten-sion between an exceedingly complex plot and a narrative that does not really advance; and the unexpected appearances, disappearances, and reappearances of Garance—all contribute to, rather than detract from, viewer enjoyment. Furnishing a steady mix of near precision and elusive-ness, of pseudopresence and absence, *Les Enfants du paradis*'s imaginary physical environment, spatiotemporal order, and female representations foster an intensely dreamlike—and masochistic—experience.

As a model of cinematic spectatorship, masochism helps account fur-ther for *Les Enfants du paradis*'s most subversive achievement: viewer acceptance of Baptiste's femininity. Post-Freudian thought on infantile narcissism suggests that masochistic regression allows not only for primary identification with the mother but for "the pleasurable possibilities of gender mobility through identification" as well. Thus, Baptiste's internalization of Garance, and our identification with Baptiste (regardless of our gender), reactivate the "urge to restore the wholeness of bisexuality—of having both male and female sexual characteristics." Normally, society works to keep this urge suppressed. But "through the mobility of multiple, fluid identifications, the cinema provides an enunciative apparatus that functions as a protective guise like fantasy or dream to permit the temporary satisfaction of . . . 'one of the deepest tendencies in human nature.'"[46]

In this context Truffaut's association of *Les Enfants du paradis* with Proust's search for lost time deserves renewed attention. Proust drew heavily upon rabbinical and mystic traditions positing that the original child of paradise—Adam—was hermaphroditic. Male-female love in *A la recherche du temps perdu* presents itself repeatedly as a mythlike quest to reunify what was once whole. But like Adam before Eve's creation, male Proustian poets and artists contain within their beings the whole of humanity, including feminine psychosexuality. Their overdetermined, polymorphous personalities make ordinary contact between lover and beloved redundant. Thus, the narrator's love for Albertine is, among other things, desperate and disappointing: Marcel searches outside and beyond himself for a feminine complement to his being that has in fact been within him all along.[47]

An analogous gender economy operates in *Les Enfants du paradis*. By means of the first pantomime, Baptiste restores his primordial androgyny so self-sufficiently that coupling with Garance (the real, as opposed to the imaginary) is superfluous. Baptiste sleeps with Garance in Part II of the film. But this spellbinding event derives less from erotic urgency than from the eminently artistic pleasure of redramatizing a prior event with near-perfect precision. The real Garance is now approachable because she, too, is participating in mythic reenactment. Her unexpected, precarious presence raises the specter of primal absence—a condition the masochist both fears and requires. Baptiste and Garance never indulge in the "uncorked unloosed and overjoyed" love Prévert celebrates in his poem "Lanterne magique de Picasso." They partake, rather, of the more fragile and fugitive Carnésian view of love epitomized in Proust's phrase "True paradises are the paradises we have lost."[48]

By assimilating a feminine principle into the male psyche, Baptiste enriches his inner life, his art, and his audience. Yet as a response to the

Carné-Prévert concern for self-realization within a repressive social order, Baptiste's solution is not optimal. In their lack of attention to the
issue of a woman's incorporating a masculine principle into the female
psyche, Carné, Prévert, and Barrault perpetuate a male-biased tradition
of speculation on androgyny extending from Plato and Midrash through
Jung and Bachelard. Moreover, Baptiste's violation of gender conventions results in extreme self-absorption. Frédérick's frolicsome glances
and Lacenaire's willful disregard exclude them from authentic communion with Garance and women generally. Yet both men are attuned to
others. Baptiste's undiverted gaze upon Garance activates unimagined
emotional resources, but it also produces near psychosis. Like *Drôle de
Drame*'s William Kramps and *Le Jour se lève*'s François, Baptiste over-
romanticizes the woman perceived to be a feminine complement to his
imperfect self and, in the process, renders himself incapable of social
action.

However, insofar as Baptiste, no less than Lacenaire, embodies Marcel
Carné's personal condition and aspirations, these shortcomings are also
signs of a certain success. I have proposed that Carné's films are in some
measure a projection of private fantasies and conflicts. I have observed
that the premature death of his mother, his father's visits to bordellos
often in the company of Marcel, and the father's general lack of sentiment contributed to Carné's self-perception as an exiled child of Eden
yearning to recapture a remnant of lost bliss. I have noted that in adulthood Carné was a loner who, bearing the weight of social pretense, mistrusted demonstrative emotion and was unable to sustain intimacy even
among professional colleagues.

Baptiste represents a resolution of Carné's problems. He demonstrates
that earthly paradise—the state of fullness, equilibrium, and repose that
Carné's film heroes aim to reconstitute from *Nogent* forward—resides
neither in the ersatz gardens of *Drôle de Drame*, *Le Jour se lève*, and *Les
Visiteurs du soir*, nor even in the theaters of *Les Enfants du paradis*,
although theater is its privileged mode of access. Proudly flaunting the
feminine principle symbolic of sustained sentiment, Baptiste reveals *himself* as the paradigm of emotional self-containment and self-sufficiency
for which Eden, Eldorado, and Paradise are simply metaphors. Designating his feminized, creative imagination as the source of self-realization, Baptiste nullifies the dependency generative of the situation at the
root of Carné's personal mythology: irremediable loss of and separation
from the mother. Baptiste and mother are inextricably one. And the
world applauds their union.

In relation to the figures of Carné that I identified in earlier films, Baptiste signifies reversal and enhancement. Xavier's silliness (*Jenny*) converts into poise. Jenny's disrepute transforms into respectability. Kramps's infatuation (*Drôle de Drame*) modulates into devotion. Krauss's quest for death (*Le Quai des Brumes*) becomes perpetual self-renewal. Adrien's homosexuality and Edmond's repressed sensibilities (*Hôtel du Nord*) yield to emotional expansiveness. Valentin's duplicity (*Le Jour se lève*) turns into sincerity. And the marginality of *Nogent*'s blind accordionist—the oeuvre's original Carné figure—changes to centrality and communion with the masses.

Undeniably Baptiste is self-absorbed. But to the degree that it produces popular art, Baptiste's egocentrism is redemptive. The parallels with the director are clear. Baptiste's narcissism mirrors the regressive character of Carné's relation to filmmaking. Through the creation of closed, purportedly self-determined worlds of unreality, Carné, like Baptiste in his pantomimes, asserts a sense of individual harmony, integrity, and worth. The normally hostile world beyond the film studio validates this sense by conferring upon Carné's creations (subjectively viewed as coextensive with himself) attention and enthusiasm symbolically equivalent to the affection his mother's untimely death brought to a stop.

We have seen that each of Carné's films suggests variations on the Oedipus drama. To the extent that regression toward masochism shapes *Les Enfants du paradis*'s psychological subtext, the film would seem to offer a felicitous solution to Carné's preoccupation with father-son rivalries: elimination of the father altogether. Grounded in a primordial alliance between the son and the oral mother, the masochist, in Deleuze's words, "magnifies the mother, by attributing to her the phallus instrumental to rebirth" and "excludes the father, since he has no part in this rebirth." In masochism, the threat of castration normally associated with the father figure in the Freudian Oedipus complex transfers to the image of the pre-Oedipal mother. Neither an obstacle to nor chastisement of incest, the castration threat becomes "the very condition of the success of incest; incest is assimilated by this displacement to a second birth which dispenses with the father's role."[49]

One index of the father figure's expulsion from Baptiste's psychic make-up is the film's recurrent depiction of the mime's unimpeded, reciprocated gaze upon Garance. Salient instances occur during the coda to the first pantomime, the episode of their first kiss on the walkway overlooking Ménilmontant, and the prelude to their night of lovemaking in room 10 of the Grand Relais. The morning after this last event, a close

69 Masochistic regression: Garance as Baptiste's ideal maternal nurturer

two-shot reveals Baptiste resting his head against Garance's left breast (fig. 69). Garance has just declared her intention to depart. But like a Raphael Madonna and Child, the couple radiate serenity, oneness, and absolute disengagement from earthly circumstances. In a film where painterly inspiration generally produces cold, grandiose compositions, this shot stands apart and above for its warmth and tenderness. At no moment in *Les Enfants du paradis* does Baptiste more embody Deleuze's view that the masochist's sexual pleasure is "deprived of its genitality" and transformed into the pleasure of a kind of "parthenogenetic rebirth" in which the father plays no role.[50] This crystalline image discloses Baptiste as the original child of paradise whose mother's purity, like that of the Virgin Mary, remains forever unimpaired. It also confirms the ritual character of Baptiste's first pantomime. Having exorcised himself of the malevolent father, Baptiste is exempt from paternal punishment for his symbolic incest with Garance.

Les Enfants du paradis is nonetheless replete with Oedipal tensions. The initial pantomime entails a humiliation of two father figures, the burgher and the policeman, and deflates the prominence of Baptiste's actual father, Anselme. *The Old Clothes Man* stages a symbolic patricide, with Pierrot-Baptiste murdering the Jéricho look-alike played by Anselme. Garance's enduring love establishes Baptiste's primacy over Frédérick, the Count, and Lacenaire—all real or potential rivals. The

70   Carné (in hat, right of camera) and crew rehearsing the Carnival
sequence; Jean-Louis Barrault (Baptiste) frame center

very insistence with which the film portrays such Oedipal triumphs
points to the insubstantiality of Baptiste's disavowal of paternal presence
and power. The picture's famous closing sequence perhaps best drama-
tizes the fragility of Baptiste's delusion of omnipotence (fig. 70).

In 1948 Antonioni deemed the Carnival sequence "one of the most
astonishing passages the cinema has provided to date." He saw it as "the
probable swan song" of black-and-white moviemaking.[51] From today's
perspective the sequence stands as a spectacular specimen of poetic realism. Devoting unparalleled attention to detail, Carné and Trauner reconstruct the bacchanalian, pre–Ash Wednesday festivities that, until the
Revolution of 1848, took place on the Boulevard du Temple. At the same
time the sequence is a grandiose projection of Baptiste's delirium. Nowhere else in the Carné oeuvre does subjective hallucination coincide so
thoroughly and intensively with a panoramic impression of reality.

Carnival is a prodigious manifestation of *Les Enfants du paradis*'s formal premise: that there can be no clear distinction between performer

and audience. Everyone participates in this all-encompassing play. But by highlighting Baptiste's private drama, the sequence blunts the communal dimension at the root of the Carnivalesque. In Western folk culture through the Renaissance, Carnival played out the masses' symbolic triumph over authority. Ritualized acts of debasement, degradation, and obscenity effected an affirmation of collective growth, productivity, and rebirth. The coolly decorous and almost unfestive character of the revelry in *Les Enfants du paradis* may relate to Occupation realities. Neither Carné nor his two thousand extras seem able to convince viewers that even a metaphoric defeat of established order is truly possible in 1943. More surely, Carné and Prévert situate their Carnival within a Romantic framework that substitutes what Mikhail Bakhtin terms the "interior infinite of the individual" for the "material bodily principle" of popular tradition.[52]

The Carnival sequence brims with irony and pathos. The ebullient throng prevents Baptiste from overtaking Garance. The crowd's high-spiritedness is a vestige of the authentic popular-festive tradition for whose survival Baptiste is himself responsible. Having resuscitated a moribund popular art form, Baptiste enables the multitude, most of whom wear Pierrot-like costumes, to engage with heightened conviction in this rite of collective renewal. Yet Baptiste's own sense of integrity verges on collapse. Still dressed in the undershirt he wore while sleeping with Garance, Baptiste experiences the masochist's nightmare of separation from the oral mother. While the merrymakers luxuriate in Carnival-esque pleasures of kaleidoscopic seeing and being seen, Baptiste loses sight of the one being whose steady, reciprocated gaze guarantees beatitude. For the crowd, the blizzard of confetti symbolizes the joy of fertility and proliferation. For Baptiste, nearly blinded by its fall, the confetti signifies the paternal castration threat attendant upon genital sexuality. The *Old Clothes Man* pantomime enabled Baptiste to "murder" repeatedly, and with impunity, his father, disguised as a Jéricho look-alike. The real Jéricho's appearance amid the crowd (fig. 71) makes manifest the inescapable psychic force of the father, of whom Jéricho is now the double. Six shots depict Jéricho's aggressive effort to keep Baptiste from reaching Garance. They illustrate handsomely the psychoanalytic principle that "an object which has been abolished on the symbolic plane resurges in 'the real' in a hallucinatory form."[53]

Jéricho's apparition bears Christological overtones, too. For the crowd, Carnival is a prelude to the commemoration of the adult Christ's resurrection. For Baptiste, who earlier scrawled the sign of his metaphoric crucifixion on the mirror in the dressing room scene, Carnival

71 An aggressive return of the father in the guise of Jéricho (Pierre Renoir, left center)

occasions an end to his self-perception as the blessed child reborn of an unsullied mother. The return of God the Father in the hostile guise of Jéricho undoes the masochistic fantasy of total communion with the Mother of God. The mutual gaze disintegrates. (Baptiste espies Garance only from behind.) The icon becomes defetishized. (Baptiste's image of Garance merges into that of the crowd.) And language—the sign and prerogative of paternal law—becomes the mime's means of reappropriating that which is no longer a part of himself: "Garance! Garance!" he shouts in vain.

Prévert, as we have seen, intended to have Baptiste murder Jéricho with the old man's walking stick. Carné chose not to film this act. Carné also eliminated Jéricho's most blasphemous line, "You deserve to be flogged, you should both be flogged, you and your whore." During the production of *Les Visiteurs du soir*, Carné omitted the depiction of Baron Hugues's demise and the castle's destruction, as called for by the original screenplay. Carné claims that financial constraints obliged him to make these excisions from *Les Visiteurs du soir*. However, viewed in tandem with those of *Les Enfants du paradis*, where financial concerns were minimally relevant, the cuts suggest that Carné was not eager to bring Oedipal tensions to definitive resolutions.

Inasmuch as his films give expression to unconscious fantasies and conflicts, *Les Enfants du paradis* tells us something about how Carné sought to manage his Oedipus complex. The two deviations from Prévert's screenplay point to a desire to stop short of representing either filial triumph over the father figure or absolute disjuncture from the idealized mother figure. In psychoanalytic terms, Jéricho's survival and Garance's disappearance perpetuate, at once, Baptiste's disavowal of the father's real power and his belief in the eventual return of the pure mother. The Carnival sequence plays out the masochistic fear of maternal abandonment and in the process it reinforces the film's overall masochistic aesthetic.

The work's ambivalence concerning fathers may relate to Carné's personal life in at least two respects. First, as I have posited, Carné's early career stood as a symbolic affirmation of independence from his mentor, Jacques Feyder. In making *Les Enfants du paradis*, Carné knew that he was surpassing Feyder's grandest accomplishments. This certainty probably reactivated a sense of unease. Just as when he directed *Jenny*, Carné felt victorious—but to the detriment of the man whose respect and affection Carné still most desired. Carné's description of Feyder and Rosay's reaction following *Les Enfants du paradis*'s gala premiere exposes his defensiveness: "Knowing they had returned to France from Switzerland, where they spent the entire [*sic*] war, I naturally had them invited. They greeted me rather coldly. Feyder said, 'It's not bad,' in a way that chilled my heart . . . Perhaps they begrudged my having remained in France and having continued to pursue, in spite of all opposition, the craft that was mine" (*Vbd*, 238–39).

Carné's perception of Feyder's disappointment is not unfounded. Shortly following the release of Carné's failed *Les Portes de la nuit*, Feyder wrote a supportive, nostalgic note deploring the "absurd obstacles" facing contemporary filmmakers.[54] But in his published memoirs coauthored with Rosay, *Le Cinéma, notre métier* (1946), Feyder never mentioned the name of his celebrated disciple. For Carné, this omission amounted to a father's publicly repudiating his son. Feyder probably viewed it likewise.[55] (Rosay, too, refrained from mentioning Carné in her posthumous memoirs, *La Traversée d'une vie*, 1974. The actress, who during the latter half of the Occupation left Switzerland to work for the Free French movement in England, referred to neither *Jenny* nor *Drôle de Drame*.)[56]

The second event that possibly bears on Carné's decision not to have Baptiste kill Jéricho is the death of Carné's father in 1944. (Prévert's mother also died that year.) Paul Carné was suffering from cancer while most of *Les Enfants du paradis* was being shot. Reminiscing in 1985, Carné states: "It was a difficult death. I did all I could to help. It was the war, there were very few good hospitals or even available beds, but I did manage to find care for him in an insane asylum, where they were at least able to give him morphine. When he saw the bars on the windows he thought he was a prisoner and got frightened. I invented on the spot the story that this was a convent and that the bars were there to prevent nuns from being molested. He, however, wanted to die at home. And so, without my permission, he managed to leave. He returned home and died that night." [57]

This is an extraordinary account. Ostensibly it asserts Carné's fulfillment of filial obligation toward a man he never cared much for. But I would propose that it masks a story as phantasmagoric as that related to the young Marcel concerning his mother's death in 1911. It tells of a son's desire to incarcerate his father (the barred asylum); to feminize and spiritualize him (the convent nuns); and to undo his sexual aggressivity (the morphine and negative molestation theme). It tells of a father's refusal to conform to the son's desire (the unauthorized escape) and the son's revenge (the death). As in a fairy tale, the ogre-father receives one last chance to do good, fails the test, and suffers extinction. The son's elimination of the father guarantees that which the tale leaves unmentioned, but which the story of Marie Carné's death made explicit for the five-year-old Marcel: the mother's everlasting purity.

Carné's reminiscence suggests that his decision not to have Baptiste murder Jéricho resulted from a wish to avoid an imaginary scenario coinciding all too precisely with an unconscious desire that actual circumstances were bringing to realization: his father's death. It also supports the picture I have drawn of Carné's relation to filmmaking. Initially manifest in the primitive slide shows he gave for friends in his father's locked bedroom (symbolically equivalent to the barred convent), Carné's impulse for moviemaking is rooted in a desire to "lock out" his unfeeling father and restore a semblance of primordial unity with his absent, sanctified mother.

Carné's reminiscence demonstrates the intimate correspondence between his life and his art. Common to both is a masochistic pattern of pleasure, pain, punishment, and guilt. Animating both is a primal story that charts the masochistic enterprise: "the triumph of the oral mother, the abolition of the father's likeness and the consequent birth of the new Man." [58]

CHAPTER 13

Primal Scenes from
Children of Paradise

The most recurrent dramatic situation in Carné's films entails one individual's unexpected discovery of a loved one's intimacy with another person. I have called such moments primal scenes, or variations on the *Urszene* fantasy which Freud considered a critical determinant of human personality and imaginative activity. In *Les Enfants du paradis*, all characters engage in emotion-fraught witnessing, sometimes deliberately, sometimes unintentionally. Jéricho stands leering as Baptiste and Garance share their first kiss. Avril interlopes during their first dance. Hidden behind a screen, Avril overhears Frédérick and Lacenaire's first encounter. He is a privileged spectator when Lacenaire murders the Count. Positioned in the Funambules' wings, the young Frédérick gazes amazedly as the Deburaus and Barrignis scuffle onstage. Gaining access to a private box at the Funambules, Frédérick later encroaches on the site of Garance's nightly communion with Baptiste. Early on, Baptiste espies Frédérick and Garance trifling in the wings and is overcome by dejection. Later, from the balcony of the Grand Théâtre, he glimpses Garance and the Count leaving their box and is infused with hope. In Part I, Baptiste and Garance interrupt Madame Hermine's nocturnal adventure with Frédérick; the Funambules' stage manager intrudes upon the Count's first effort to seduce Garance; and Nathalie intervenes just as Garance is about to declare her love for Baptiste in the dressing room. In Part II, the actor Célestin opens a dressing room door and, embarrassed, finds Frédérick kissing a girlfriend; Lacenaire pulls back the window drape in the Grand Théâtre's reception room and discloses, victoriously, Garance and Baptiste in each other's arms; and, her repeated knocks on the door unheeded, Nathalie enters room 10 of the Grand Relais to discover Baptiste and Garance in tender embrace beside Baptiste's unmade bed.

This profusion of variations on the primal scene is consistent with *Les*

Enfants du paradis's elaboration of a theatricalized world founded upon seeing and being seen. In such a world, demarcations between the public and the private—doors, screens, drapes—exist only to be obliterated. Yet the film's extravagant theatricality may itself be considered a manifestation of a profound psychosexual dynamic. Based on her analyses of children, Melanie Klein proposes that "theaters and concerts, in fact any performance where there is something to be seen or heard, always stand for parental coitus—listening and watching standing for observation in fact or phantasy—while the falling curtain stands for objects which hinder observations, such as bedclothes, the side of a bed, etc." [1]

The cinema is capable of producing an incessant flow of images on a scale commensurate with that of the young child's perspective on the world. It demands that viewers be relatively passive and immobile in a darkened environment. It destabilizes the distinction between one's own body and the exterior world. And it weakens one's ability to separate direct perception from representation. It is, in short, an art form intrinsically disposed to reactivating primal scene fantasies.

By framing their film within the rise and fall of a make-believe theater curtain, and by having the represented audience of each dramatic performance operate as a surrogate for the film's spectators, Carné and Prévert create especially favorable conditions for implicating *Les Enfants du paradis*'s viewers in the work's manifold primal scene transformations. The experience of a motion picture is inherently regressive. *Les Enfants du paradis* makes it emphatically so.

In the primal scene according to Freud, a young child typically misconstrues the real or imagined observation of parental intercourse as the father's act of aggression in a sadomasochistic relationship with the mother. This distortion gives rise to sexual excitement, double and shifting identifications, and castration anxiety. [2] Since Freud, analysts have challenged the conceptual validity of the entity Freud called sadomasochism. (Deleuze's meditation on Sacher-Masoch, for instance, addresses the theoretical flaws of Freud's view that sadism and masochism are inseparable intrasubjective entities.) With respect to the primal scene, much post-Freudian discussion emphasizes its pre-Oedipal and distinctly masochistic character. For example, Ruth Mack Brunswick notes that "the understanding and interest which the child brings to the parental coitus are based on the child's own preoedipal physical experiences with the mother and its resultant desires." [3] Henry Edelheit asserts, "The primal scene schema antedates the oedipal configuration, determines its form,

72 The mêlée between the Deburaus and the Barrignis: a frenetic
projection of anatomical ambiguities

and provides a framework for understanding its distortion by regressive
trends."[4] Exploring primal scene imagery in art, Edelheit discerns a "primary form" of primal scene, in which the child identifies with both parents in the act of copulation, thereby providing a "mental framework for
all forms of male/female ambiguity"; and a "secondary form" that represents "more deeply regressive trends (principally oral projections) and
superimposes upon (or substitutes for) the image of the copulating parents, the combined image of the nursing mother and child."[5] For Jean
Laplanche, the primal scene represents the "essential" regressive fantasy:
"The child, impotent in his crib, is Ulysses tied to the mast or Tantalus,
on whom is imposed the spectacle of parental intercourse." The child's
passive posture is, in Laplanche's words, "not simply a passivity in relation to adult activity, but passivity in relation to the adult fantasy intruding within him."[6]

Frédérick and Baptiste evince two modes of managing primal scene
experience. These might be designated, respectively, as progressive and
regressive, or "Prévertian" and "Carnésian." The mêlée between the Deburaus and the Barrignis is a frenetic projection of the primal scene's
anatomical ambiguities as perceived by the child. A rapid series of multi-
angled close and distance shots depicts an orgylike jumble of out-
stretched, intertwined, and barely identifiable (male) limbs (fig. 72). Terrified, the Funambules' director calls for the curtain to fall. But young
Frédérick, standing in the wings, surveys this pandemonium with wonder
and pleasure. When order returns and the Barrignis depart, Frédérick is

euphoric and volunteers to play Harlequin. Tellingly, the actor whom Frédérick wishes to replace triggered the current turmoil. In a classic Oedipal confrontation, Harlequin had hit Colombina's father, Pantalone, excessively hard on the head with the butt of the latter's own gun.

Frédérick's identification with the original male aggressor, his unproblematic accommodation to a strange erotico-theatrical environment (the pantomime from which the mêlée devolves is entitled "*Dangers* of the *Virgin* Forest"), and his emphatic self-assertion suggest that Frédérick gains mastery over primal scene experience by establishing a strong, masculine—"Prévertian"—ego. Thus, when Frédérick later witnesses Garance observing Baptiste lovingly from her private box at the Funambules, he deals with primal scene feelings of exclusion and jealousy through active retaliation. Frédérick's brusque decision to play Othello provides an adult solution to his infantile, narcissistic need for affection, which he will satisfy via audience adulation. Similarly, by "killing" Desdemona, Frédérick will act out his suppressed anger toward women in accordance with an ideal of male hegemony.

Baptiste's relation to primal scene situations is more complex. My earlier discussion demonstrated that Baptiste-the-artist is emotionally self-sufficient, while Baptiste-the-man seeks forever to reconstitute a primordial mother-son alliance. The artist's self-sufficiency results from having witnessed a primal drama (the theft of the burgher's watch) and having internalized a feminine principle (embodied by Garance). Such artistic plenitude correlates with Edelheit's view that primal scene experience furnishes "a mental framework for all forms of male/female ambiguity." By contrast, Baptiste-the-man's sense of incompletion begets two complementary stances: primal scene terror, as when Baptiste espies Frédérick and Garance flirting in the wings; and primal scene invasion, as when Lacenaire exposes Garance and Baptiste on the terrace, or when Nathalie intrudes into room 10 of the Grand Relais. Both terror and invasion relate to the masochist's simultaneous fear of and need for the threat of maternal abandonment. Both correlate with Edelheit's view that a regressive form of primal scene experience substitutes imagery pertaining to the nursing mother and child for the spectacle of parental intercourse.

Whether self-sufficient or incomplete, terrified by an absence or invaded by a presence, Baptiste distinguishes himself vis-à-vis primal scene experience through literal immobilization and figurative blindness. Primal scenes impel Frédérick to execute bold schemes. They cause Baptiste to freeze gossamer dreams and evade truths. This split between, on one hand, mastery, movement, and speech and, on the other, anxiety, stasis, and silence also describes the tension of sensibilities intrinsic to the Pré-vert-Carné collaboration.

The sequence following the *Othello* performance is *Les Enfants du paradis*'s most intricate elaboration on the primal scene and highlights the Carné-Prévert tug of competing styles. Each of the film's protagonists has just witnessed Othello's strangling Desdemona in her bed. Standing in one of the Grand Théâtre's balconies, Baptiste espies (in a series of high-angle point-of-view shots) Garance and the Count preparing to leave their box. Baptiste rushes from the balcony. Moving toward the reception room where he plans to incite Frédérick to duel, the Count abandons Garance in the corridor behind the boxes. Garance glances about and then rivets her gaze. Five reverse-angle shots, each briefer than the one preceding it, convey the mounting emotion with which Garance and the object of her look, Baptiste, reassert the reciprocal gaze they established in front of the Funambules six years earlier. Conforming to the masochist's fantasy of the oral mother as sole environment, Baptiste begs Garance, "Come!"; she asks, "Where?"; and he responds, "Oh! . . . it doesn't matter where!" This fantasy's delusionary character insinuates itself at once. Baptiste and Garance leave the frame, and the next shot reveals Lacenaire, standing immobile frame center, his eyes fixed on the lovers, whom he proceeds to follow.

Except for some barely perceptible panning and tracking, the camera is virtually immobile throughout this scene. Unobtrusive camerawork and editing are hallmarks of Carné's style. Reflecting upon his oeuvre in 1971, Carné observed: "I directed my films with a good deal of spareness and rigor; there is never any technical ostentation; there is, rather, a certain classical flow . . . To movements of the camera, I prefer movements of the heart . . . What interests me is being on top of characters [*Ce qui m'intéresse c'est d'être sur les gens*], discovering their reactions to certain events. That is precisely Feyder's influence on me."[7]

The camera's relative freedom in the sequence's succeeding shot is in fact atypical for Carné. A lengthy leftward pan embraces the activity in the reception room before holding on a long view of Frédérick and the Count. While lilting panoramas often begin and close Carné's pictures, they occur rarely within the films themselves. Coming after a scene that depicts the restoration of Baptiste's regressive dream world, this mobile shot announces a change of dramatic and psychological emphasis. It prepares us for Frédérick's aggressive confrontation with the Count over matters Shakespearean—a more sophisticated but no less impassioned replay of Frédérick's first stage role as the Oedipus-like Harlequin bent on battering Pantalone.

Given two chains of association—one of them being Prévert, Frédérick, Harlequin, candor; the other, Carné, Baptiste, Pierrot, guardedness—it is tempting to add "forceful camerawork and mise en scène" to the first and "self-effacing camerawork and mise en scène" to the second. Scenes representing Baptiste and Garance tend to be shot with both the camera and its subject immobile, in the manner of Carné. Scenes portraying Frédérick and Garance tend to be shot with the camera and subject in motion, in the spirit of Prévert. Perhaps the film's most un-Carnésian mise en scène precedes Frédérick and Garance's first moments of lovemaking. As if in a Renoir-Prévert film, Frédérick and Garance flirt with each other from separate windows that look out onto a single courtyard. When Garance indicates her willingness to sleep with him, Frédérick leaves his window. The camera positions itself outside Garance's, and, in a single deep-focus shot, captures Frédérick entering her room and moving excitedly toward Garance, who still stands by the window but with her back now to the camera. This fluid mise en scène conforms to Frédérick's—and possibly Jacques Prévert's—playful rapport with the opposite sex: a woman is, simply and inconsequentially, an object of man's proprietary glance and the locus of his self-indulgent penetration.

However, if we return to the sequence under consideration, the equivalences "Prévert-kinetics" and "Carné-stasis" prove inadequate. A brief medium-distance shot discloses Baptiste and Garance standing alone on the Grand Théâtre's terrace. Five reverse-angle medium-close shots and close-ups of the lovers, each (with one exception) lengthier than the preceding one, intensify the aura of intimacy reestablished in the lobby. During the fifth shot, Baptiste verbalizes the masochist's dual fear of possession and rejection, and reemphasizes the primacy of the maternal gaze: "And you, Garance, do you love me? No, don't answer. I ask nothing of you. You are here, that's all that matters . . . No, I ask for nothing. Only the warmth of your body against mine. That mouth that is your mouth. And those eyes that are your eyes."[8] Following these last words, the lovers initiate a kiss photographed in an over-the-shoulder extreme close-up of Baptiste's full face and Garance's rear, left-quarter profile. But before their lips meet, a cut occurs. The resulting shot depicts the kiss itself in rather extreme long shot, with Baptiste and Garance standing immobile, frame center, and resembling a two-figure statue viewed from afar (fig. 73).

This abrupt, unconventional change of scale contradicts Carné's 1971 profession of preference for "classical flow" and for "being on top of characters." It suggests, instead, either a deliberate wish to ensure his subjects' privacy (an aim similarly realized by the editing preceding Fran-

73 A shot whose scale suggests an attempt to desexualize or "freeze" desire

çois's suicide in *Le Jour se lève* and by the camera movement punctuating the start of the actual consummation of Baptiste and Garance's love later on in *Les Enfants du paradis*) or (although one explanation does not exclude the other) a masochistically informed impulse to freeze desire and foreclose on the possibility of complete mother-son fusion. The latter motivation squares with Deleuze's observation that the "masochistic art of phantasy" concerns itself with "frozen" postures and "arrested" movements because it must contain, within the fantasy, "the specific freezing point, the point at which idealism is realized."[9] Such an interpretation lends support to the equivalence "Carné-stasis."

For all its poise, however, the distance view of the statuelike kiss is short-lived. It initiates a lengthy mobile shot that stands as the film's most "technically ostentatious"—to borrow Carné's term for what he claims to have shunned in his pictures. Pivoting virtually 180 degrees leftward from Baptiste and Garance, the camera pans along the Grand Théâtre's exterior wall and holds on a medium shot of Lacenaire, positioned in the doorway leading to the reception room (fig. 74). Lacenaire's eyes are fixed on the lovers as they kiss, and he twirls in his right hand a walking stick that extends nearly perpendicular to the line of his body. The dandy's intrusive glance contaminates the lovers' privacy, which the abrupt cut on the kiss might have sought to guarantee. Desire, which the

74 Resexualized desire: Lacenaire taking pleasure in observing Baptiste and Garance's kiss

cut might have aimed to freeze, is reactivated in the obviously aroused voyeur.

This relay of desire plays out a dynamic inherent to the masochistic aesthetic: "The deeper the coldness of desexualization," asserts Deleuze, "the more powerful and extensive the process of perverse resexualization . . . The crucial point is that resexualization takes place instantaneously, in a sort of leap."[10] In this case, the seat of desire "leaps" from Baptiste to Lacenaire by means of the panning camera which, in spite of its flamboyant movement, is part and parcel of a vision more "Carnésian" than "Prévertian." (An offscreen sound effect coinciding with the pan reinforces the prominence of the Carné imprint: we hear the clippety-clop of horses, presumably drawing a carriage—the motif Carné employs most insistently as a symbol of destiny.)

At no moment in the film is Lacenaire more a figure of Carné, the director as voyeur. The pan translates, at once, the self-distancing, ostensibly desexualized posture that characterizes Carné's portrayal of male-female relations from *Nogent* forward, and that corresponds to his personal estrangement from women; the resexualized, regressive fascination which male-female relations nonetheless hold for Carné, and that connects with his early childhood primal scene experience; and, not least of all, the "progressive," assertive stylistic thrust which Carné, as the director of films determined in significant measure by Jacques Prévert, was obliged to make manifest, even though this thrust was not an innate component of his psychological and artistic make-up. Lacenaire's standing in the doorway—he is neither inside nor outside—symbolizes what I take to be a fundamental split in Carné. The private Carné identifies with the regressive, androgynous, pre-Oedipal world that one can attempt to reconstruct only precariously and on the margins of society—connoted by the lovers on the secluded terrace. The professional Carné adheres to a social imperative that compels men to operate aggressively within a patriarchic, Oedipally structured, strife-torn world—epitomized by the hubbub transpiring in the reception room.

The uncommonly lengthy tracking and panning shot that next accompanies Lacenaire's weaving through the reception room is, therefore, not so much "Prévertian" as "Carnésian in spite of itself," or, more precisely, "Carnésian in deliberate accommodation to the Prévertian"—something quite distinct from "Carnésian in unthinking submission to the Prévertian." In the scene that follows, Lacenaire-Carné becomes, to a certain extent, Frédérick-Prévert's double. The dandy's stupendous execution of a real-life *coup de théâtre* partakes of Frédérick's psychological boldness, effecting a triumph over an Oedipal father figure (the Count), and of Prévert's dramatic daring: "It really doesn't matter what type of play my little piece is, the important thing is that it should be amusing, and that the author should be the first to laugh at it." Nevertheless, Carné's signature prevails (fig. 75). After drawing back the curtain to expose Baptiste and Garance in each other's arms, Lacenaire declares: "Gentlemen, I have just tasted one of the rarest moments of a lifetime." The sentiment might well be Carné's. In technical accomplishment and dramatic power this episode stands, along with *Le Quai des Brumes*'s bumper-car scene and *Le Jour se lève*'s climactic murder, as Carné's finest footage. Viewed psychoanalytically, the scene is especially winning.

Insofar as Lacenaire is victorious in an Oedipal struggle against the Count, the scene's manifest action is progressive, or "Prévertian." Its cinematic technique, however, is decidedly regressive. The five reaction shots that follow the drawing back of the curtain reinstate a silent cinema of melodramatic effect. Devoid of sound, music, and dialogue, a succession of immobile shots depicts the Count paralyzed by the humiliating sight; Baptiste and Garance gazing back with total lack of understanding; Lacenaire exultant; the Count's two friends stunned; and Frédérick looking on with intense interest. Except for the shot of Baptiste and Garance, these reaction views resurrect approximations of what early American filmmakers referred to as "bust pictures," or closely framed shots

75   Lacenaire's real-life *coup de théâtre:* an Oedipally structured primal
scene experience superimposed upon a more regressive one

edited into a scene in order to concentrate viewer attention on actors'
facial expressions.[11] Leaving undepicted the lower parts of bodies, such
shots are an ideal vehicle for conveying symbolic castration. With the site
of the Count's genitals literally cut from sight, the all-powerful nobleman
is leveled, so to speak, with the criminal Lacenaire—whom Prévert first
conceived as impotent, and who, at the start of this very scene, twiddled
his walking stick as if it were a phallic prosthesis.

In contrast to this foregrounded, male-oriented massacre stand Baptiste and Garance, whose entire bodies are visible in a background distance shot. Inasmuch as the classic primal scene has the infant witness
what it misinterprets as bodily harm inflicted on one of its parents, the
true primal scene here does not entail the Count's viewing Baptiste and
Garance, whose integrity is intact, but, rather, the latter's viewing the
Count's emasculation. This episode corroborates Laplanche's capital insight that primal scenes represent, at bottom, adult fantasies intruding
within the child, not vice versa. Carné's directorial tour de force consists
in having literally superimposed an Oedipally structured primal scene
experience (the "Prévertian") upon a second, more regressive form (the
"Carnésian") that exalts the image of the nurturing mother and child.
Otherwise put, Carné does not dutifully execute Prévert's style and vision. Rather, he accommodates them within a film aesthetic distinctly his

own and fundamentally at odds with Prévert's: the masochistic.

In earlier Carné films the primal glance placed a burden of recognition and illumination upon voyeuristic characters. Some confronted disclosure head-on. Others ignored or denied the import of revelation. In *Les Enfants du paradis*, primal divulgences barely alter or enrich protagonists' lives. The film's drift toward willful benightedness is perhaps another manifestation of France's state under Occupation. It is more surely tied to the intractable typology of theatrical personas that governs characterization. Above all, it relates to the Freudian concept of disavowal, a central component of the masochistic aesthetic: "Disavowal," Deleuze specifies, "should perhaps be understood as the point of departure of an operation that consists neither in negating nor even destroying, but rather in radically contesting the validity of that which is: it suspends belief in and neutralizes the given in such a way that a new horizon opens up beyond the given and in place of it."[12]

In the wake of Lacenaire's disclosure, Frédérick attempts to articulate the scandal's significance. But the Count interrupts, pulls the curtain shut, and completes Frédérick's sentence, "What you [Lacenaire] have just done—" with the words "—has nothing to do with you!" More forcefully than its English translation, the French negative phrase "—ne vous regarde pas!" (which the Count utters twice) conveys the discrepancy between the primal scene experience and the Count's interpretation of it. Lacenaire's spectacle literally "looked back" at everyone in attendance, as the French *cela vous regarde*, when formulated positively, implies (*regarder* meaning "to be of concern" and "to look"). But the Count de Montray, whose very name is, ironically, a play on the verb *montrer*, "to show,"[13] squashes this double resonance of *regarder*, just as he terminates the double play of glances in pulling back the curtain. Traumatized, the Count seeks not so much to disavow the incident as to negate and destroy evidence of it.

Baptiste and Garance's response to the primal intrusion approximates disavowal. Positioned as the lovers are behind the glass doors that divide the terrace from the reception room, two discrete panes frame their bewildered faces. This mise en scène imparts the fragility of their union. Its prototype is the two-shot of Jean and Nelly peering at the sunrise through the window of Panama's shack in *Le Quai des Brumes* (fig. 21). Yet where Jean and Nelly strive, however fruitlessly, for enlightenment, Baptiste and Garance retreat to the soothing darkness of disavowal. Baptiste might have attempted to defuse the Oedipal conflict and its potentially fatal consequences for Frédérick and the Count. Garance could have acknowledged her inevitable reseparation from Baptiste. Instead,

76 An ironic play on Sophocles' Tiresias: Gaston Modot, left, as Fil de
Soie; Barrault, right

Garance moves from the terrace door, places herself in a shadowy spot
opposite Baptiste, and gives voice to the masochist's wish to suspend
belief in the real: "But they won't fight before tomorrow . . . No . . . we
have the night in front of us, with us . . . for us . . ."

Fil de Soie, the petty criminal who masquerades as a blind beggar,
assists in Baptiste's evasion of the real (fig. 76). His underworld name
translates literally as Silk Thread. It suggest the cocoonlike environment
Baptiste requires. Fil de Soie is Jéricho's symbolic antithesis. He is the
benevolent, desexualized father figure who perceives the danger inherent
in Baptiste's Oedipal attraction to Garance ("If you want to wake up
tomorrow morning alive, it wouldn't be a bad idea to go home to bed
right now"), but abstains from interfering ("Well, I've got no advice to
give you"). At the Rouge-Gorge he offers Baptiste sustenance ("Wine for
two, and something nice to eat") and engages the mime in a reciprocated
gaze no less intense than that exhibited by Garance and Baptiste. When
Fil de Soie divulges his ability to see, Baptiste's childlike expression is as
wonderstruck as it was while he first observed the woman he idolizes.
Maternal and fatherly, blind and sharp-sighted, submissive and venture-
some, Fil de Soie reinforces Baptiste-the-artist's pre-Oedipal feelings of
omnipotence, plenitude, and self-sufficiency.

Facilitating the convergence of dramatic threads in Part I, Fil de Soie is also an ironic counterpart to Sophocles' blind seer Tiresias—whose blindness, according to ancient legend, was punishment for his "primal" intrusion on Athena bathing, and whose incarnations as man and woman made him an emblem of androgyny. At the start of *Oedipus Tyrannus*, Tiresias states the awful truth which the angered Theban king rejects: "How horrible wisdom is! . . . You have eyes, Oedipus, and do not see your own destruction." Ultimately, Oedipus confronts Tiresias' prophecy—"I see it now! All clear! O Light!"—and destroys his own eyes: "O cloud of darkness! Cruel . . . Assaulting me with no defense to hold you back." [14] In *Les Enfants du paradis*, by contrast, recognition is nonexistent. An accomplice in deception, Fil de Soie encourages Baptiste's defensive withdrawal from injurious truths: "You don't say anything . . . you're a wise man! That's the best way, never say anything."

The entire Rouge-Gorge episode exemplifies Baptiste's "neutralization of the given." While escorting the mime to the dance hall, Fil de Soie gives the history of its name—in English, Red Throat: "It's called that after the man who used to own it. One night, someone slit his throat." Fil de Soie later makes it clear that Lacenaire and his cronies executed the act. Once there, however, and even in Lacenaire's presence, Baptiste is oblivious to the threat of bodily harm. A slit throat, like Oedipus' ripped eyes, may be the symbolic equivalent of castration. But bound to a masochistic regime of pregenital sexuality, Baptiste ignores the possibility of such an outcome. Instead, he fixates on Garance, whose name and perceived essence provide a second, more comforting interpretation of "Rouge-Gorge": in French, *gorge* means "a woman's bust" as well as "throat"; and *rouge*, red, is the color associated with the flowering plant known as a madder or, in French, *garance*—flowers being, for Baptiste, the sign of ideal female purity.

Baptiste's bedroom behavior in Part I is a paradigm of primal scene disavowal. He and Garance enter room 10 of the Grand Relais in perfect silence. Positioned near the closed door, Baptiste looks on as Garance, viewed from the rear, wanders about the room. Because of the sudden storm, Garance has borrowed Baptiste's suit jacket, which she wears draped over her shoulders (fig. 77). Seen in rear full shot, Garance's torso suggests a man, while the dress covering her lower limbs designates a woman. This composite resurrects an infantile perception of copulating parents. It correlates with primal scene derivations in art that exhibit "a proliferation of hybrid images—sirens, centaurs, chimaerae, and other mythological creatures"—and of which the Theban Sphinx is the con-

77 Garance reactivating an archaic state of psychic androgyny

summate expression.[15] In a later sequence Frédérick calls Garance "beautiful Sphinx." Verbalized by the teasing actor, the image is hackneyed. But for Baptiste, nonverbal phenomena retain their primitive charge. Viewing Garance as simultaneously male and female is a serious matter. It reactivates an archaic state of psychic androgyny. And it reasserts a primordial sense of nondifferentiation from the mother's all-powerful, all-sustaining body. If his jacket is also hers, her dress is his.

Chivalry demands that Baptiste display concern for Garance's well-being. He therefore lunges forward, removes the protective jacket, and utters the phrase "How wet you are, Garance." Through gesture and word Baptiste lays the foundation for acknowledging Garance's sexual difference (her "wetness") and physical autonomy (her own clothes). Such a project, however, is at cross-purposes with Baptiste's make-up. Having placed the jacket on a chair, Baptiste turns in Garance's direction. Now photographed with her front to the camera in full shot frame center, Garance undoes her bodice (fig. 78). The moment she reveals her cleavage a medium-close shot displays Baptiste dumbstruck and terrified, his eyes fixed on this sight. Responding to his unease, Garance, in full shot frame center, grasps the nearby bedspread (fig. 79) and informs Baptiste calmly, "Turn round, if you're embarrassed." In the following shot Baptiste makes an about-face, keeping his back to the camera and his hands clasped behind him (fig. 80).

When Garance utters, out of frame, "There—there we are; you can turn round now," Baptiste makes a second about-face. A reverse-angle shot displays Garance in full shot frame center. Draped by the bedcover, which she has transformed into a sort of sari, Garance remarks cheerfully: "Pretty costume, isn't it? One would think one was in India!" Rapid crosscutting reveals Baptiste almost as dumbstruck as when Garance exposed her cleavage. But now Baptiste responds dreamily, "How beautiful you are!" Garance next moves toward the curtained bed, sits down, and extends her bare left leg (fig. 81). Ostensibly, she is demonstrating her qualifications for employment at the Funambules. Tacitly, she is beckoning Baptiste to join her in bed. At first paralyzed, Baptiste rushes forth and cries out: "But Garance, I love you!" Seconds later, he runs out of the room. Filmed in medium-close shot frame center, Garance stands alone, her eyes peering directly at the camera.

Judged by conventional narrative standards, the bedroom scene ends anticlimactically. It is the premier instance of *Les Enfants du paradis*'s overall aesthetic of incompletion. But this virtual coitus interruptus is a necessary consequence of Baptiste's "visus interruptus," that is, his deliberate withdrawal from the sight of Garance's cleavage. In his first pantomime, Baptiste fashioned a transcendent work of art from a banal street incident. Here, his bedroom encounter also produces art. For when Baptiste makes his second about-face, he finds Garance transfigured into a *tableau vivant* inspired by Ingres's Odalisques. Unlike the pantomime, this exceptional work of corporeal art derives not from Baptiste's genius but from Garance's ingenuity. Or rather, it results from Carné's mise en scène and direction of Arletty in an episode called for by Prévert's screenplay. Or more accurately still, it represents Garance's fulfillment of Baptiste's needs, which correspond almost totally to Carné's in relation to Arletty and women generally. The scene's apparent anticlimax is, properly perceived, the culminating expression of masochistic desire. Freezing Garance into a painterly pose makes her an object of sustained contemplation and ever-deferred possession. It renders her less a woman than a fetish or icon.

Facing page:

78   A primal event: Garance about to expose her sexual difference

79   Garance seeking to cover her nudity

80   Baptiste's "visus interruptus": his deliberate withdrawal from the sight of Garance's cleavage

81 Garance iconized into a painterly pose cut to the measure of Baptiste's needs

The bedroom scene plays on the classic view of fetishism. As a clinical entity, adult fetishism entails substituting for the beloved person a bodily part or inanimate object belonging to or associated with that person (long hair, feet, shoes, earrings, undergarments, and so on). Freud considered fetishism exemplary of disavowal generated by castration anxiety.[16] Discovering the primary anatomical distinction between the sexes, a boy child attributes this difference to the woman's penis having been cut off. This discovery actualizes and validates the boy's castration fears. To cope with the traumatic perception of the female lack, the fetishist typically overinvests libidinal energy in the last object seen before becoming aware of the missing penis. By returning compulsively to the object that served as point of departure for the original scandalous sight, the fetishist maintains two apparently inconsistent positions: he both disavows and acknowledges the fact of the female's lack of a penis. Deleuze notes: "The fetish is . . . as it were a frozen, arrested, two-dimensional image, a photograph to which one returns repeatedly to exorcise the dangerous consequences of movement, the harmful discoveries that result from exploration; it represents the last point at which it was still possible to believe." [17]

Two divergences from the prototypal Freudian pattern are notable in *Les Enfants du paradis*'s bedroom scene. First, Baptiste does not see Garance's genitals. His trauma derives instead from the sight of cleavage between her breasts. Second, Baptiste overinvests with erotic energy objects viewed immediately after the momentous disclosure, not before it. Just prior to his first about-face, Baptiste observes Garance extending her right arm and lifting the bedcover. In the subsequent *tableau vivant*, motifs that had been marginal or hidden dominate the image. Concealing Garance's body except for her right shoulder and arm, the bedspread now covers over the fearsome lack. And the briefly glimpsed extended arm, now transformed into the conspicuously exhibited bare leg, is a phallic appendage serving to disavow Garance's sexual difference.

These displacements and substitutions result in an illusion of femininity cut to the measure of Baptiste's needs. The bedroom episode would seem, therefore, to support the view that the filmic representation of woman as icon is grounded in male castration anxiety.[18] Yet Baptiste's passivity, Garance's complicity, and the scene's emphasis upon the undisclosed female breast suggest that "the power of the male protagonist" in a society "split between active/male and passive/female"[19] does not, solely or even predominantly, govern fetishistic scopophilia here. Transpiring in a psychic space devoid of the paternal castration threat, Baptiste's iconization of Garance may be understood, alternatively, as further evidence of the masochist's need for primary identification with an allpowerful, pre-Oedipal mother. In this regard, Baptiste's viewing Garance's cleavage rather than her actual breasts or genitals is a crucial detail.

Much speculative discourse about the nature of cinematic pleasure builds on the "dream screen" concept set forth by American psychoanalyst Bertram D. Lewin in 1946. According to Lewin, the field on which dreams inscribe themselves symbolizes the mother's breast as hallucinated by the infant during the sleep that follows feeding: "When one falls asleep, the breast is taken into one's perceptual world: it flattens out or approaches flatness, and when one wakes up it disappears, reversing the events of its entrance."[20] Writing in 1975, Jean-Louis Baudry takes Lewin's "dream screen" as a model for the "archaic," "oral" manner in which desire, perception, and representation function in film: "The conditions of [cinematic] projection . . . evoke the dialectics internal/external, swallowing/swallowed, eating/being eaten, which is characteristic of what is being structured during the oral phase. But in the case of the cinematographic situation, the visual orifice has replaced the buccal orifice: the absorption of images is at the same time the absorption of the subject in the image, prepared, predigested by his very entering into the dark theater."[21] In his essay "Reflections on the Breast," Robert Eberwein also concludes that film "reverses the process of ego differentiation by plunging us back in memory to the moment of identification with the source of nutrition."[22]

Baptiste's refusal to view Garance's breasts is *Les Enfants du paradis*'s most revelatory gesture. It epitomizes the way in which Carné's masochism shapes the film's overall aesthetic. The bedroom scene plays out the experience of a primal disclosure. For obvious reasons, Carné could not have filmed Arletty's genitals. (The Polish-French painter Moïse Kisling, however, did depict the young Arletty completely nude in a witty reworking of Manet's *Olympia*.)[23] Even the censored shot of her showering in *Le Jour se lève*—breasts fully exposed—included a huge sponge that masked her crotch. Censorship concerns, especially in a time of Occupation, may therefore explain Carné's reluctance to film Arletty's bosom in this and other scenes of *Les Enfants du paradis*. During the Naked Truth peepshow glimpsed at the film's start, the water in which Arletty sits conceals her breasts entirely. When Garance changes clothes behind her dressing screen, Carné accentuates Arletty's bosom covered over, not bared. Operating here is the notion of *pudeur*, or discretion in explicit sexual representation, that prevails in all of Carné's films.

But in *Les Enfants du paradis*'s bedroom scene, more than *pudeur* is at work. The masochist's essence depends upon a simultaneous state of confidence in the maternal breast's presence and anxiety over its disappearance. Garance's cleavage is the sign of this ambivalence. It guarantees the possibility of fusion with the breast, since cleavage implies the breast's actuality. But it also denies possession of the breast, since cleavage designates space unoccupied by the breasts. Baptiste's terror at this primal sight is similar to but not identical with that associated with castration anxiety. Indeed, analysts since Freud have viewed the experience of the breast's withdrawal after suckling as "the prototype of castration": "This *primary castration*, which is repeated at every feed and culminates in the weaning of the child, is considered to be the only real experience capable of accounting for the universal presence of the castration complex. The withdrawal of the mother's nipple . . . is the ultimate unconscious meaning to be found behind the thoughts, fears, and wishes which go to make up this complex."[24]

Baptiste's first about-face constitutes an immediate defensive reaction to the sight of Garance's cleavage: denial. His second about-face constitutes a more calculated defensive maneuver: disavowal. Both movements emblematize the masochist's dual obsession with absence and presence. Both correspond to stylistic dispositions in tension throughout *Les Enfants du paradis*.

On one hand, the psychic force of cleavage-as-absence translates into the ellipses and disconnections between the film's narrative segments. It begets the incompletion of specific episodes and the lack of a definitive overall end. It produces the marginal settings in which most of the movie's unfinished actions transpire. And it governs the very restrained recourse to close-ups. Eberwein posits a symbolic equivalence between the close-up and the "primal metonymy" of nursing, in which "the infant takes the part [of the mother] for the whole": "The face in the close-up is, in essence, the mother's face, the breast, the primal unity of infancy."[25] In 1971 Carné conceded that, in the matter of close-ups, he has remained "a bit behind the times": "The close-up is called for by the crucial importance of a scene. If this scene is not so very important, I see no need to shoot characters in close-up" (*d'être en gros plan sur les gens*).[26] This statement seems to contradict Carné's assertion, quoted earlier, that generally he likes to be "on top of characters" (*d'être sur les gens*). The contradiction is itself illustrative of what I deem to be Carné's struggle, like Baptiste's in the bedroom, between confrontation and withdrawal. *Les Enfants du paradis*'s five extreme close-ups are all erotically charged. Yet except for the two shots of Baptiste and Garance kissing in Parts I and II (the latter interrupted by the cut to a distance shot), these extreme close-ups portray neither people nor parts of people. They depict, instead, inanimate objects that substitute for sexual organs of absent bodies: the rose Garance has given Baptiste; the fan Nathalie-Colombina drops in the *Old Clothes Man* pantomime; and the smoking pipe lying beneath the assassinated Count's hand in the Turkish baths. Less "primal metonymies" than metaphoric renderings of such metonymies, these few images are indicative of an aesthetic posture derived from primal absence and characterized by principles of disconnection, deflection, and distancing.

On the other hand, the psychic force of cleavage-as-implied-presence translates into a stylistic disposition distinguished by principles of abundance, vividness, and relative sweep. It begets the film's impression of historical reality. It generates the attention paid to detail, atmosphere, and harmonious composition. It governs the artistic weightiness each frame tends to advertise. Above all, it regulates Carné's penchant for pictorialism.

Baptiste's second about-face, and his consequent view of Garance as an Ingres-like Odalisque, allegorizes Carné's relation to cinematic creation. Just as Baptiste must transfigure Garance in order to disavow a primal void, so Carné must reconstruct reality through the artifice of motion pictures to disavow the loss of his mother. Masochistic creativity

82   Jean-Auguste-Dominique Ingres's *La Grande Odalisque*

entails an "idealizing neutralization" of the given and the opening up of a "new horizon" beyond the given and in place of it.[27] With respect to Carné, the commanding point is that new horizons always signify refashionings of past images. The manifest conservatism of his filmmaking practice, his requirement of absolute predetermination before shooting, and the compulsive drive to re-create preexistent slices of the material world betoken Carné's profound sense of belatedness vis-à-vis not only master filmmakers (Jacques Feyder being the central reference) but master painters and poets as well (Prévert standing as the nagging symbol of the director's permanent secondariness).

I suggested earlier that *Les Enfants du paradis*'s aura of frigid monumentality derives in part from David's painterly brand of heroic Neoclassicism. The film's autonomous narrative sequences and often arrested actions correspond, I proposed, to the formal character of David's major history tableaux. At its most intensely intimate moment, however, the movie turns for inspiration to David's disciple, Jean-Auguste-Dominique Ingres (1780–1867). The images of Garance Orientalized and positioned seductively on the curtained bed are nothing less than a fanciful appropriation of Ingres's most famous nude, *La Grande Odalisque* (1814) (fig. 82).

If Carné and Prévert make Ingres the film's paramount pictorial reference, it is not only because "Monsieur Ingres" is the name Garance proffers when she informs the inspector at the end of Part I that she "used to pose for painters." Nor is it merely a consequence of Janin's mock-heroic account of the boy Deburau's "unmolested penetration of the [Turkish] Sultan's seraglio" and his "plunged" gaze upon "immobile, semi-nude, reclining . . . odalisques." [28] In significant measure, the recourse to Ingres results from the shared sensibilities of the painter and the film director.

In *Tradition and Desire: From David to Delacroix*, British scholar Norman Bryson explores how the perception of belonging to a tradition threatens an artist's self-definition as a creator. Like Carné, Ingres deemed himself a latecomer. He had to cope, in Bryson's words, with those "monuments of history and culture across whose landscapes [the latecomer artist] moves as exile and wanderer." [29] The *Grande Odalisque* is itself a self-conscious response not only to David's *Mme. Récamier* (1800), on which Ingres had worked as an assistant, but to Raphael's *Madonna of the Chair* (ca. 1514) and Giulio Romano's *La Fornarina* (ca. 1518, formerly attributed to Raphael). By subjecting the female bodies depicted in these prior works to "tropes of displacement," Ingres overcame the weight of tradition and "ma[de] all the precursors his contemporaries in the spring of somatic time." [30]

Animating this reworking of tradition are what Bryson terms "Ingres' highly specialized sexual needs." Baudelaire described Ingres's "love of woman" in language more evocative of Prévert than of Carné: "convincing," "robust," and "rich." But he also discerned a "special taste" in the artist which he was unable to define. [31] Bryson is more explicit. He notes that sexuality in Ingres is "not a positive or *plenary* force" but, as in Carné, "a force of *vacuum*": "The beauty he seeks exists in the terms of his desire, as lack and deferral—if he is in love with the women of his inner pantheon, it is because, in their openness of form and the energy of displacement they arouse, they can never be possessed." [32] It is worth recalling in this context that throughout his career Ingres returned to three subjects, each of which give expression to facets of what I have viewed as the subconscious drama at the core of Carné's oeuvre: Oedipus and the Sphinx, which Ingres first painted in 1808; Antiochus and Stratonice, the story from Plutarch of a son's love for his stepmother and his father's commiseration, first drawn by Ingres in 1807 and painted magisterially in 1840; and the Golden Age as described by Hesiod and Ovid, rendered as a mural begun in 1843 and then replicated in an 1862 oil painting, in which Ingres evokes a lost world of amatory freedom.

The *Grande Odalisque*'s erotic complexity arises from a mix of directness and obliquity. "The prodigious ductility of the line," writes art historian Robert Rosenblum, "suggests a flesh of voluptuous malleability, yet this pliant stuff is polished to a marmoreal firmness, so that it seems alternately warm-blooded and cold, slack and taut." [33] The incongruity between the Odalisque's abstract, impossible anatomy—her seemingly elbowless arm, her apparent extra vertebrae, the precarious torsion of her crossed left leg—and the photographlike precision of its rendering disconcerted first viewers at the Salon of 1819. Decades later, Baudelaire intuited that this clash of the imaginary and the real was the crux of Ingres's style. It resulted in "a powerful sensation . . . of an almost unhealthy nature," having less to do with the direct expression of a "fantasy world" (*un milieu fantasmatique*) than with "a world that is imitating fantasy" (*un milieu qui imite le fantasmatique*).[34]

Baudelaire's distinction bears on the film's quotation from Ingres. The four shots of Garance reclining alone on the draped bed are a direct expression of Baptiste's—and Carné's—"fantasy world." Making Garance a pictorial reference, these images deny the possibility of seduction by an actual woman. But immediately following this "trope of displacement," Garance works to disavow Baptiste's disavowal. She repudiates his effort to freeze her: "Please, Baptiste, don't be so serious. You chill my heart." She contradicts his idealization: "You mustn't be angry with me but I'm not . . . well, not how you dreamed of me." And she blows out the lamp that has lent wings to Baptiste's flight of visual imagination. In effect, Garance plays critic to the pseudopainting of which she is the subject. Like Baudelaire, she unmasks the artifice of "a world that is imitating fantasy." For this woman of Paris, the room's drapes, pillows, curtains, and bed are not permeated with exotic mystery. They are simply quotidian objects in a quasi-reputable boarding house.

The *Grande Odalisque*, writes Bryson, "denies—*undoes*—its reality as authentic presence."[35] *Les Enfants du paradis* complicates this dynamic. The bedroom scene posits Garance consecutively as symbolic absence (the cleavage), as imaginary or displaced presence (the Ingres-like Odalisque), *and* as demystified presence. Garance's attempt at demystification has no impact on Baptiste. Shrouded in darkness, the mime addresses the moon and is oblivious to the real Garance's movements about the room. (The scene's lack of articulation between Baptiste's body and hers, especially their disjointed relay of glances, would seem to echo the formal inconsistencies of Ingres's Odalisque, whose implausible physique had earlier influenced Picasso and the Cubists.) Nevertheless, Garance's demystification effort represents an extraordinary destabilizing element. Insisting upon her bodily reality as a woman, not an icon, Garance makes it impossible for viewers to identify completely with Baptiste's regression through art. Exposing the self-delusion that shapes Baptiste's representation of her, Garance flaunts that which the classical cinema is allegedly designed to disavow: female presence as difference.[36]

I observed earlier that Lacenaire's assassination of the Count expresses a desire for intimacy in an exclusively male milieu. The murder may now

83   The Count (Louis Salou) as a male version of an Ingres Odalisque;
     at left, the bath attendant (Habib Benglia)

be appreciated as a defensive reaction to the sight of woman's difference. Taking place after the scene in which Baptiste and Garance consummate their love, Lacenaire's act allows for an unadulterated repetition of the disavowal mechanism Garance undermines in the first bedroom episode. Lacenaire anticipates the event's "primal" character when, the night before, he tells Avril, "If you aren't witness to a duel there's quite a good chance that you'll witness something else." The pronounced camera movements that cut short direct depiction of the consummation scene also signal a major redeployment of psychic energy. As it pulls back from Baptiste and Garance pressed together on the bed and pans rightward to hold on a view of the open window, the camera translates the call for instantaneous resexualization that the masochistic process of desexualization demands, and which the Turkish baths scene fulfills in displaced fashion. Perhaps the strongest indicator of a correspondence between the erotic character of the murder and of Part I's bedroom scene is the fact that Ingres is again the principal pictorial reference.

The Count, wrapped in an Oriental bathrobe, seated on a curtained divan, with his left leg extended over the other, is a male version of Baptiste's vision of Garance as an Ingres Odalisque (fig. 83). Making this rendition even more "faithful" to the original, the hookah and smoking censer of the *Grande Odalisque* find themselves condensed into the Count's conspicuous pipe. Prior to being seen, the Count is heard humming "I Am What I Am"—the song associated with Garance and whose lyrics she declaims during her effort to demystify Baptiste in the bedroom. Reinforced by the wordlessness in which the murder transpires, the bath scene reconstitutes a psychic state antedating the exercise of speech. Elsewhere in the film such regressive episodes convey masochistic desire for fusion with the pre-Oedipal mother. This one, however, plays out a sadistic need to destroy female difference.

Two currents are operating at once. The aural-visual echoes of Garance and the Odalisque feminize the Count. Lacenaire must defend against this difference—hence the murder. At the same time Ingres's subjects have been decidedly masculinized. The scene alludes not only to the *Grande Odalisque* but to the seraglio settings of Ingres's *Odalisque with the Slave* paintings (1840 and 1842) (fig. 84) and, most conspicuously, to his *Turkish Bath* (1863) (fig. 85). Carné, Prévert, and Trauner have transposed the indolent sensuality of a woman's private world into that of a man's—hence the homoeroticism. (Trauner later designed a Turkish baths setting even more glaringly homoerotic for the episode of Welles's *Othello* in which Iago stabs Cassio and Roderigo.)

During their first encounter on the staircase of the Count's town house, Lacenaire unsettles Garance's protector by intimating that the nobleman is much like himself: "But what [people] really are . . . (*winking with unpleasant familiarity*) . . . really, at the bottom of their hearts, they keep quiet about . . . they hide carefully." In uncovering the Count's androgyny at the baths, the sexually ambiguous criminal confirms their sameness. But in proceeding to kill the Count, Lacenaire suppresses the marks of his own femininity. In the scene's final shot, the assassin assumes a posture on the Oriental divan that bears comparison with the Count's at the start of this scene and with Garance's during the first bedroom episode (fig. 86). Lacenaire evinces no trace of the wavering sexuality associated with the others. Attired in unmistakably male formal wear and tapping the floor with the tip of his ever-visible walking stick, the solitary, smug dandy parades his masculinity. Ingres is still the central reference. But the dandy's haughty pose, tapered silhouette, and walleyed stare paraphrase the elegant, elusive subjects of Ingres's early male portraits, such as *M. Pierre-Louis-Antoine Cordier* (1811) and *Lorenzo Bartolini* (1820) (fig. 87)—themselves reworkings of the coolly virile youths found in Bronzino.[37]

For European and American artists of the past two centuries, the Orient has been, as Edward Said observes, "a sort of surrogate and even underground self" shaped by "a battery of desires, repressions, investments, and projections." Imaginative attention to things Oriental has

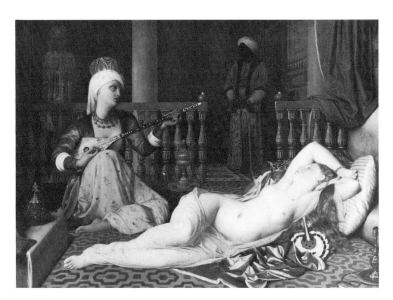

84 Ingres's *Odalisque with the Slave*, 1840

85 Ingres's *Turkish Bath*

86   Lacenaire smugly parading his masculinity

87   Ingres's *Lorenzo Bartolini*

had, in Said's view, less to do with the Orient than with the Western world's need to validate its strength and identity vis-à-vis a putative geographical entity perceived as susceptible of domination.[38] Like Flaubert and Delacroix, Ingres associated the Orient with licentious sexuality and with a repertoire of clichés that included harems, eunuchs, slaves, and omnipotent sultans. Ingres's particular attraction to the seraglio derived, notes Bryson, from an ostensible "interchangeability of the women in the seraglio," permitting the painter to represent desire "in the form of restlessness, of interchangeable images, none of which actually contains desire." Consonant with Said's consideration of Orientalism's real subject, Bryson concludes that "the object of [Ingres's] gaze is less Woman than his own subjectivity, painted in open self-dissection."[39]

Les Enfants du paradis exhibits a similar interplay of desire and the Orientalizing imagination. Disguised as an Odalisque per Baptiste's tacit specifications, Garance vouchsafes, in the bedroom scene, the male bodily integrity which her unconfined difference would otherwise threaten. In the Turkish baths scene, "subjectivity . . . in open self-dissection" discloses itself even more flagrantly than in Ingres's Oriental pictures. The scene's concentrated fusion of destructive and libidinal energies betrays a need—most obviously Carné's, but patriarchy's as well—to glorify male power by expunging female identity altogether. In some measure the extreme close-up of the murdered Count's delicate hand and forearm restates the scene's overall gender ambiguity (fig. 88). It, too, is a quotation, although its reference is poetic, not painterly. After contemplating the historical Lacenaire's preserved hand, Gautier celebrated, in *Emaux et Camées*, "the faunlike fingers" of a member "at once flaccid and fierce."[40] Precisely because the "feminized" Count is Lacenaire's double here, the assassin commits what might be termed an act of Western, male imperialist aggression against the unbearable projection of his suppressed, "Orientalized" self. Paradoxically, by disengaging the hand and forearm from the Count's full physical being, the extreme close-up—shot from Lacenaire's angle of vision—makes of them as much a phallic appendage defending against castration fears as is Garance's extended leg in the first bedroom scene.

The Turkish baths scene is abundantly troublesome. Interpreted as revenge against a plutocratic oppressor, the assassination is a positive political gesture. Yet in terms of gender politics it is an abusive act of male supremacy. Viewed as a transgression against heterosexual hegemony, the murder exalts individual difference. Yet it also denies woman's specificity. In making the iconized Count an object of Lacenaire's possessive gaze, the scene undermines mainstream cinema's axiom that the male figure cannot bear the burden of sexual objectification. Yet—like Bap-

88 The hand, forearm, and pipe of the assassinated Count: a complex
interplay of politics and eroticism

tiste in the bedroom—the scene also binds difference to a symbolic order
in which men live out their fantasies and obsessions by imposing them
on a "silent image" that is "bearer of meaning, not maker of meaning."[41]
In sum, the Turkish baths scene requires acknowledgment that for all its
socially subversive impulse, *Les Enfants du paradis* remains attached to
the ruling ideology and those psychic structures that underpin it. Otherwise stated, the film displays an equivocation with regard to sexuality
similar to its ambivalence in the matter of contemporary politics. *Les
Enfants du paradis* resists capitulation to the status quo, while at the
same time lending it support.

Garance can be considered the focal point of *Les Enfants du paradis*'s
ambiguities, paradoxes, and tensions. Over the decades, commentators
have hailed this demimondaine as a peerless depiction of female—more
specifically, French female—emancipation. John Simon speaks of her
"seering femininity" which, "when fully awakened," becomes "torren-
tial, transcending all dimensions."[42] Roud emphasizes her "intelligent"
and "independent" character.[43] More on target, Manvell identifies an
"enigmatic remoteness" that allows her to be "tender but at the same
time free from entire involvement."[44] Yet even Manvell grants Garance a

89 A dramatic, psychological, and ideological matrix: Garance as a peepshow attraction

hefty measure of independence which the film does not corroborate. The extraordinary "feminine 'presence'" (Manvell's term) which all these critics see as inhering in Arletty's Garance is, more precisely, an accretion of male-contrived stereotypes. From our perspective Garance does represent a version of the "liberated" woman. But her central interest lies in the extent to which her freedom is constrained by a principle that purportedly governs mainstream Western cinema and, radically formulated, entails "the repression of woman as woman and the celebration of her nonexistence."[45]

The inaugural image of Garance as a peepshow attraction epitomizes woman's subordination to male-devised artifice (fig. 89). The two shots of Garance in the tub last only fourteen seconds, but they define *Les Enfants du paradis*'s dramatic, psychological, and ideological matrix. The four patrons inside the booth prefigure Garance's four suitors. The concealed anatomy foreshadows Baptiste's disavowal of female difference. And Garance's impassive participation in an exploitative enterprise adumbrates issues of resistance and collaboration and their relation to the politics of spectaclemaking. Embedded within the opening panorama of the Boulevard du Temple, this image constitutes a point of origin for our perceiving the picture's as-yet-unidentified female protagonist. It replicates Baptiste's original exposure to his feminine ideal—a primal witnessing more seminal than even the momentous drama of the stolen watch. (The mime confides to Nathalie: "I leaned over the edge of a well. There were many of us looking [*regarder*] at her, but I was the only one to see [*voir*] her . . . I saw her again [*je l'ai revue*] today, by chance, and she gave me this flower.") And it symbolizes the popular roots of Arletty's screen personality, which Carné was bent on altering.

Rather than represent Garance lightheartedly as a slightly overripe stripper, Carné, Prévert, and Trauner steep this image in mythologic and iconographic tradition. The water, the tub's rotation, and Garance's hand-held mirror generate impressions of an archaic moon goddess. Her gravitational impact on the men encircling her suggest Mother Earth and the cosmic center. The tub insinuates notions of the universal womb and fountain of life. More specifically, the image draws upon Western art's overlapping representations of Truth and Venus, each tied to motifs of female nakedness, water, and mirrors. Like the barker's prattle, a painted canvas outside the booth promises a lewd viewing of Venus Rising from the Waters (fig. 90). Inside, a tame and not-so-tawdry spectacle depicts Truth Hidden in a Well—a classical literary theme often found in Renaissance and Baroque pictorial allegories.[46]

Throughout the film Garance's clothes assist in sustaining presumed feminine truths. The gingham street dresses she sports in Part I emblematize the Prévertian woman of youth, freshness, and humble origins (fig. 91). Arletty wears them with authority and ease. But the virginal, *jeune fille* quality of their puffed short sleeves, fitted bodices, and full skirts jars with the character's worldliness and the actress's obvious maturity. (Arletty was forty-five when shooting began.) Like Phoebe's classical drapery in the *Lover of the Moon* pantomime and the paisley bedspread transformed into a sari, the gingham dresses unloose Garance from fact and envelop her in myth.

In Part II the overabundant satins, jewels, and headdresses of her two evening costumes transfigure Garance into a Carnésian version of the remote mother-goddess. Half-hidden by a latticed shutter and wearing a sequined veil that obscures her facial features except for her eyes, Garance reappears, serene and shimmering, to observe Baptiste clandestinely from box 7 of the Funambules (fig. 92). (Numerous mythological traditions associate the number seven with the Great Mother, the moon goddess, and the archetypal feminine.)[47] Although Frédérick and then Baptiste *fils* extol her beauty in words, Carné takes pains throughout this sequence to disembody Garance. Filming her in immobile close shots that frame her from the midriff up, he makes Garance's lower limbs seem severed from the rest. Moreover, despite the daring off-the-shoulder

90   A promise of scopophilic pleasure: the painted
     advertisement for the peepshow

neckline, the oversize bejeweled pleats make the contours of her breasts
imperceptible and leave no sign of cleavage.

By comparison, the satin gown Garance wears to the premiere of
Othello seems naturalistic (fig. 93). But it, too, objectifies ambivalent
male desire. Its whiteness suggests ideal purity. Its uncluttered décolle-
tage discloses the shape of Garance's breasts and a soupçon of cleavage.
Yet as if to defend against the revelation of female anatomy that is in fact
imminent, jet flowerlike ornaments trim the gown along its skirt, at its
shoulders, and at a spot just below Garance's cleavage. Contrasting with
the authentic rose she committed to Baptiste at the film's start and reinstating the forbidding darkness associated with her previous gown, these
decorations announce the artificial and menacing character of Garance's
impending "wedding" to Baptiste. They link Garance to Lacenaire and,
more generally, to the Romantic *homme fatal*, for whom black clothing
signaled "austere . . . detachment from female emotive and procreative
life." [48]

91 Arletty wearing a dress that emphasizes the girlish quality of her role in Part I of the film

92 Garance transfigured into a disembodied icon; with Frédérick (Pierre Brasseur) and the doorman (Léon Larive)

93 Arletty modeling the gown worn to the *Othello* premiere

The atmospheric excess and unsettled androgyny that infuse Carné's iconization of Arletty point to Sternberg's handling of Marlene Dietrich in their six Paramount pictures. Yet female imagery in Part II of the film is grounded principally in Ingres's society portraits of the 1840s and 1850s. The movie's most extensive quotation from Ingres occurs when Garance encounters Lacenaire on the first-floor landing of the Count's town house (figs. 94 and 95). Photographed in long shot as she ascends the staircase, Garance seems no more sentient than the life-size statuary that adorns the vestibule. With a full-length velvet cloak embellishing the gown worn to the Funambules, her attire is a figural condensation of the opulent, protective milieus to which she has been relegated for over six years. When she reaches the landing, Garance's actions and bearing allude to three Ingres portraits that dramatize the distillation of human

94 and 95 Garance's reunion with Lacenaire at the Count's town house: the distillation of human presence amid overwhelming material wealth

presence amid overwhelming material wealth. Her imperturbability evokes *Madame Inès Moitessier* (1851) (fig. 96), itself a reworking of Greco-Roman female deities and Byzantine Madonnas. The often unfocused gaze of her heavy-lidded eyes rhymes with that of *The Princesse de Broglie* (1853) (fig. 97), Ingres's great study of female melancholia. And the sustained interplay between Garance as seen and as reflected in mirrors paraphrases Ingres's supreme abstraction of woman, *Madame Inès Moitessier Seated* (1856) (fig. 98).

This last picture is arguably the fullest realization of the fundamental duality of Ingres's art, which, as described by Rosenblum, parallels Carné's in "its constant veering between the most close-eyed record of the data of perception and the imposition of ideal formal order upon these empirical data."[49] The work's influence on twentieth-century painting—most notably Picasso's *Woman with Book* (1932)—derives from its notorious discrepancy between the sitter's "real" and "reflected" image and the consequent undermining of viewer expectation that the painting's subject is in fact a living, corporeal presence. Bryson writes: "To each glance of possession [the picture] responds with a shift in temporality, in register, in viewpoint, in a vertigo of displacements that return the viewer to her or his own desire, to the body in dispossession."[50] In the reunion on the landing, Carné approximates this dynamic cinematically. He has Garance continuously change position, rearrange her clothes, and divert her glance from Lacenaire's. He photographs her standing, leaning, and seated, frontally and from behind, at eye level and at high angle, in full and close shot, at the frame's center and periphery, and twice leaving the frame altogether. The resulting impression is not one of woman's freedom and mobility but, as in Ingres, of a man-made construction drained of human vitality. The naked truth about woman, the scene seems to say, is that she is always reflected, refracted, and covered over.

Les Enfants du paradis leads us to suppose that Garance's truth is her anatomy, and that so long as men remain unable to confront that truth, Garance possesses a powerful resource. But no real deployment of that resource takes place. In appropriating the traditionally male prerogative of the aggressively erotic gaze, Garance unsettles gender conventions. Yet such an assault on the establishment entails, at best, a reversal of custom, not a revelation of fresh possibilities. Alert to the images men project onto her, Garance challenges their attempts to denature her essence. In the first bedroom scene, she demystifies Baptiste's idolatry. In the dressing room sequence, she punctures Frédérick's rhetoric and the Count's impulse to own her. After becoming the latter's mistress, she assures Lacenaire that although "bought . . . I'm still free!" Yet for all her protest

96 Ingres's *Madame Inès Moitessier*

97 Ingres's *The Princesse de Broglie*

98 Ingres's *Madame Inès Moitessier Seated* (above)

Garance barely makes explicit the essence and freedom men seek to eclipse. Phrases such as "I'm not beautiful, I'm alive, that's all" and "I'm simple—very simple" are poetically pleasing. But they are also self-deluding. They obscure the fact that, virtually at all times, Garance is subject to others' desires and deeds.

Garance's first act in the film typifies the scope of her rebelliousness. Less an action than a reaction to circumstance, Garance is forced to quit the peepshow. This event provides an opportunity to deplore the disparity between her reality and the manner in which male exploiters package her. She informs Lacenaire, "'Truth, but not below the shoulders' . . . [the spectators] were disappointed." But with minimal resistance Garance continues through the remainder of the film to be repackaged: as an Oriental concubine, a Greek goddess, a glittering paramour, a Renaissance Madonna, and so forth.

The gap between Garance's self-image and her actual condition is troubling. But her acquiescence to male desire is understandable. Inhabiting a world in which survival hinges on the whim of a charlatan, an assassin,

a womanizer, or a millionaire, Garance forever negotiates delicate entanglements with individuals more powerful than she. Given such circumstances, Garance's relative selflessness, self-esteem, and self-containment are beyond praise. However, in light of the premise that Garance is
a metaphoric representation of France, the preceding assessment demands qualification. Garance eludes police pressure to inform against
Lacenaire, but in the process, she solicits aid from the Count and yields
to his control. In private, she denounces the Count's claim to absolute
possession and makes known the constancy of her love for Baptiste, but
like most of the French during the Occupation, Garance does not move
from sentiment to action. Prepared neither to militate against the Count's
authority nor to struggle and remain with Baptiste, Garance returns to
her protector and leaves Baptiste to his life of convention.

A more moderate interpretation would contend that in returning to
the Count, Garance adheres with honor to an unwritten contract, and
that in forsaking an incorrigible idealist, she evinces good sense. The film
supports such a view. But it is precisely the incongruity between Garance's cool rationality and the values at stake—independence and
love—that scandalizes. *Les Enfants du paradis* is not a perfect allegory
of France under Occupation; no one-to-one correlation exists between
Garance and *la France*. Yet Garance's readiness to accommodate an
enemy and relinquish a lover reverberate disturbingly with the climate of
compromise and collaboration in Occupied France.

The real-life inspiration for Garance is Léonie Maria Julia Bathiat (b.
1898), better known as Arletty. As a fashion model in 1918, Bathiat
adopted a name from Maupassant's *Mont-Oriol*: "Arlette" is the illegitimate daughter of that novel's strong-willed female protagonist. In 1919
Arlette made her stage début at the Théâtre des Capucines. Its director,
Armand Berthez, allegedly took the liberty of Anglicizing the name,
changing the final "e" to "y."

In *Les Enfants du paradis*, Prévert and Carné imagine a mid-
nineteenth-century Léonie Bathiat. The name "Garance" is itself a *nom
de théâtre* for "Claire," daughter of a laundress called "Reine." Like Arletty, Garance takes pride in her working-class origins. Like Arletty, she
matures quickly and experiences a succession of admirers, lovers, and
protectors. Like Arletty, she poses for celebrated artists. (Braque, Ma-
tisse, and Van Dongen were among the many who painted Arletty.) And
like Arletty, Garance gains show-business celebrity that leads to ties with
men from the highest ranks of French society.

Beyond these specific parallels, Prévert and Carné envisioned Garance as embodying Arletty's uncommon individualism. The death of her first boyfriend in World War I triggered Arletty's nonconformity. The actress recalls: "I realized that the only way to avoid becoming a war victim's widow or mother was never to marry or have children. It was a kind of protest against war. I am against all war." From an early age Arletty thought of herself as an outsider: "I am something of a marginal, on the fringe of things. All actors are marginal vis-à-vis society. But I am marginal vis-à-vis actors." Although an impeccable professional, Arletty refused to take herself or her career too seriously. Unlike many stars of her generation, she never sought to conceal her years: "To hide one's age is to suppress one's memories." And she mistrusted raving reviewers: "I prefer constructive negative criticism to unthinking praise. At least you might learn something from the former." Above all, Arletty valued self-determination: "I refuse to have others impose their ideas and rules on me. The song Prévert wrote for Garance ["I Am What I Am"] describes me—a woman who doesn't give a hoot for what others think of her, who wants only to enjoy life to its fullest, to laugh and to love when and how she pleases."[51]

Léonie Bathiat suffered for her pleasures. In December 1940 she met a Luftwaffe colonel named Hans Soehring. Six months later they became lovers. Their affair lasted through much of the Occupation. In the summer of 1944 a Free French tribunal in Algiers responded to this liaison by condemning Arletty, in absentia, to death: "After having been the most fêted woman in Paris, I became its most dreaded."[52] By September self-appointed "purification" committees began targeting for reprisals those who had allegedly abetted the enemy. In the late fall of 1944 Arletty was arrested, placed in Drancy Prison, and sentenced to house arrest in the village of La Houssaye for eighteen months.

Arletty claims to hold no grudges: "Feeling hatred inside only makes you become ugly outside."[53] She sees herself as having been an object of jealousy and scapegoatism. Tens of thousands of Frenchwomen slept with Germans during the Occupation.[54] None but Arletty starred in three films as imposing as Roger Richebé's *Madame Sans-Gêne* (1941), *Les Visiteurs du soir*, and *Les Enfants du paradis*: "I am sure that if I had not been so famous, I would never have been incarcerated."[55] To straighten the record, Arletty makes clear in her memoirs, *La Défense* (1971), that the sole time she solicited aid from a Nazi minister was to help Sacha Guitry secure the release of playwright Tristan Bernard and his wife, arrested by the Gestapo in October 1943. She also observes that she declined to work for Continental Films "not because I feared the consequences, but simply because I would not have enhanced [the films they proposed]." [56]

Arletty's plight prompts further reflection on two issues concerning *Les Enfants du paradis*'s production history. First, Carné claims to have wanted to delay the film's release until all of France was liberated. Might a further motive for gaining time have been his hope that the Arletty scandal would blow over? Second, there exist only vague, contradictory assertions concerning Prévert's projected third part of the picture. Might this uncertainty relate to the likelihood that Arletty would be unavailable to perform? Might Prévert have destroyed his manuscript in order to spare Arletty further humiliation?

These questions will probably never be settled. It is certain, however, that Arletty's ordeal compounds the political ambiguities inhering in *Les Enfants du paradis*. Audiences in 1945 could not fail to construe Garance's final line in Part I—"Would you be kind enough to let this person know that I am the victim of a judicial error?"—in ways Prévert did not foresee when he wrote it. In 1942 Prévert was aware of Arletty's liaison with Soehring. He probably viewed it as a benign affirmation of personal freedom. (Arletty reportedly told her custodians in 1944, "My heart is French, but my ass belongs to the world"—a very Prévert-like conceit.)[57] But as of 1945 the import of Garance's dialogue and action became inseparable from the turn of events in Arletty's life at the Liberation, and from the viewing public's varying perceptions of her misfortunes.

Paradoxically, Arletty's adversity secured her an artistic triumph. It conferred upon Garance a degree of freedom, in the sense of fresh resonance and depth, unpredicted by those who had sought to mold the character and actress to their desires. Ex post facto, Arletty became as much the *auteur* of the film as Carné, Prévert, Trauner, and Barrault. It is fitting that hers is the first name to appear in the opening credit sequence, preceding even Carné's and Prévert's. For Arletty guarantees the movie a contemporary, controversial edge. She incites viewers to grapple with the myths and realities of France's wartime comportment. She obliges reevaluation of the notion of a "liberated" woman.

In one sentence of *La Défense* Arletty describes an extraordinary and generally overlooked occurrence: "By the way, I was in the clink when *Les Enfants* came out." [58] Arletty's absence from the premiere at the Palais de Chaillot probably elicited feelings ranging from glee to compassion to outrage. Feyder's coolness toward Carné that night surely reflected unease over the film's apparent homage to an actress whose real-life activities were currently deemed traitorous. After all, Madame Feyder (Françoise Rosay) had spent much of the Occupation in London broadcasting Resistance messages over the BBC.

Feyder's disfavor wounded Carné. But from the perspective of Carné's private mythology, that evening of March 9, 1945, stands out as a unique accommodation of reality to fantasy. Just as Garance's disappearance at *Les Enfants du paradis*'s end perpetuates Baptiste's desire, so Arletty's absence from the Palais de Chaillot served Carné's need to distance himself from the maternal presence she had come to represent.

Carné concludes his autobiography in a peculiar manner. After evoking Feyder's early prophecy that his disciple would experience the "terrible" sense of solitude inherent to a film director's profession, Carné ends with the assertion that, despite the truth of Feyder's warning, he will continue to make pictures "so long as I have the strength, and so long as I am given the resources to do so" (*Vbd*, 490). Carné then leaves a blank space of about eighteen lines and writes: "I almost forgot . . . Just recently, a friend pointed out to me something I had never realized: rather amused, I thus discovered that the anagram of my name was: [Carné skips another nine lines, and centers in capital letters] ÉCRAN [screen]."

This postscript might translate as follows: "I, Marcel Carné, having reviewed my life in these pages, hereby renounce my paternal lineage ('Carné') and identify instead with the enterprise to which I have devoted my life and being, and of which the movie screen (*écran*) is the material sign." If, as much psychoanalytic film theory contends, the cinematic screen symbolizes the mother's breast, Carné thus ends his memoirs by affirming unconsciously what I have posited as the fundamental stimulus in his life and art: the desire for total, unencumbered reunion with the mother he lost at age five.

More fully than his earlier films, *Les Enfants du paradis* gave expression to Carné's regressive fantasies. More compliantly than his prior leading ladies, Arletty served as a screen onto which Carné projected primal desires. Arletty collaborated with Carné in many senses: as a co-worker on six films; as a friend who refused to pass judgment on his sexual orientation; and as a female who understood the nature and limits of Carné's attraction to her. By remaining "frozen" at La Houssaye on March 9, Arletty collaborated with Carné in yet another way. She allowed him to bask in her screen presence while depriving him of her reality. In short, Arletty played along with Carné's masochism.

Arletty knew the naked truth about Carné, about women, and about France during the Occupation. She knew that Carné's masochism was in some ways also France's. And she knew that her relegation to La Houssaye represented France's desire not to acknowledge truths.

PART IV

The Outsider

CHAPTER 14

In the Afterglow
of Triumph

In mid-August 1944 Carné visited headquarters of the Comité de Libération du Cinéma Français (CLCF). An amalgamation of Resistance film
organizations, the Comité was then coordinating insurrectionary actions
to coincide with the general Liberation uprising in Paris that was to begin
on August 19. Direct participation in such activist maneuvers was of
little interest to Carné. He was eager, however, to partake in the shooting
of *La Libération de Paris*, a documentary on the final days of Occupation
in the capital, whose production the CLCF was overseeing: "I still owned
the hand-held camera that had served me in making *Nogent*. But for lack
of film stock I could not record the battles I was witnessing" (*Vbd*, 243).

The Comité turned down Carné's request on the grounds that no film
was available. Yet even if it had had supplies at its disposal, the CLCF
would probably not have been receptive to Carné's advances. Its prime
movers were Jacques Becker, Louis Daquin, Jean-Pierre Le Chanois, Jean
Painlevé, and André Zwoboda—filmmakers who had all been engaged
in clandestine activities to subvert and eventually replace the system of
film production in operation since the Occupation's start. For them, the
director of *Les Visiteurs du soir* and *Les Enfants du paradis* was glaring
evidence of the accommodating spirit they deemed reprehensible.

Carné maintains that his rejection by the CLCF was a blow to his
professional pride but not to his "personal esteem." He claims to have
interpreted the Comité's lack of sympathy toward him as a response to
his association with Arletty: "I thought I knew what they were reproach-
ing me for: to have shot during the Occupation two films with the cooperation of an actress whom certain parties could not pardon for having
had relations with a German officer! People had often alluded to that
matter in my presence. I would answer these superpatriots of the female
sex in an appropriate fashion, and they would consider the issue settled"
(*Vbd*, 244).

For the CLCF, the issue to be settled in the case of Marcel Carné was not guilt by association with Arletty, but the director's own activities. The Comité's agenda included an *épuration*, or purge, of professionals culpable of misdeeds. As of September 1944 ad hoc *épuration* committees with no official legitimacy were arbitrarily arresting prominent members of the show-business community, including Maurice Chevalier, Pierre Fresnay, Sacha Guitry, Albert Préjean, Tino Rossi, Ginette Leclerc, Mary Marquet, and Arletty. By the spring of 1945 government legislation instituted more licit procedures for dealing with alleged collaborators. Accordingly, *épuration* committees were authorized to pass judgment on relatively minor transgressions within specific professions, while suspected instances of gross collaboration were dealt with by the courts. Among film industry cases handled by the courts were those of critic-novelist Robert Brasillach and director Jean Mamy, who were both executed; critic-novelist Lucien Rebatet, who was condemned to death but eventually freed on parole; and actor Robert Le Vigan, who was imprisoned for four years.[1]

According to the announcement in the 13–14 August 1945 issue of the *Bulletin Municipal Officiel de la Ville de Paris*, Carné was the recipient of a "censure [*blâme*] with posting [of the censure] in the workplace" for having "favored the enemy's designs by signing a contract with Continental."[2] Carné recalls his hearing: "I was brought before a committee composed of riggers, hairdressers, and electricians who had barely worked during the war. I reminded them of the degree to which my own safety had often been jeopardized. I explained how I had been trapped into signing with Continental, and how I managed to break my contract. And I showed them, as required, all relevant documents. They seemed most attentive to those indicating my earnings."[3]

Carné finds it "curious" that "[while] big industrialists who amassed considerable fortunes thanks to their collaboration with the enemy were passed over, the so-called purification effort hounded especially the world of show business" (*Vbd*, first edition, 247; in the second edition, the word "spared" replaces "passed over," 245). He notes also that "whereas certain of my colleagues shot several pictures for the very same company and were left unbothered, *I* was being somehow sanctioned for having made none!" (*Vbd*, 247). Carné believes that "jealousy and petty envy" (*Vbd*, 245) were at the root of the *épurateurs'* inconsistencies: "In reality, what some parties could not forgive me for was having directed two films which, despite the Occupation, had exerted considerable impact" (*Vbd*, 247).

The committee passing judgment on Carné dealt with *artisans du film*, a category that embraced producers and distributors as well as directors and technicians. A separate body investigated *artistes*, or stage and screen performers. Carné's reviewers had twelve sanctions to choose from. The most severe was a "prohibition against occupying a managerial post in the profession and against serving as a director or trustee of any commercial company, as well as against exercising managerial or administrative powers deriving from honorary membership." This penalty was exacted on twenty top executives. The three mildest sanctions, in order of decreasing severity, were "censure with posting in the workplace," "censure without posting," and "transfer of duties." Between fall 1944 and spring 1949, inquiries into 975 *artisans du film* resulted in 504 sanctions, most of which were imposed for a six-month term. "Censure with posting in the workplace" was the verdict for 163 of those sanctioned. Out of fifty-seven directors subjected to inquiry, twenty-four were acquitted, nineteen were censured, and fourteen received sanctions entailing a suspension of work. Of these fifty-seven, only six were directors of feature fiction films. The others had been engaged principally in newsreel and documentary production.[4]

Three of the six feature fiction directors received penalties more severe than Carné's. Prior to the Liberation, the underground film publication *L'Ecran Français* had singled out Henri-Georges Clouzot, Henri Decoin, and Albert Valentin as having made films for Continental that abetted the enemy's propaganda efforts. Following their committee hearings, these three directors were banned from the profession.

Errors of excess as well as of clemency, false denunciations motivated by private vendettas, and the apparent whimsicality of condemnations and acquittals promoted a political climate often as inhumane as that which the *épuration* sought to indict. In the fall of 1944 Albert Camus was convinced that France had "to destroy a still living part of this country in order to save its soul." By August 1945 he saw that the *épuration* was undermining an "elementary concern for clarity and [moral] distinctions" and "poisoning still further an atmosphere in which Frenchmen already find it hard to breathe."[5]

Many film professionals voiced opposition to the purge and its premises. In August 1945 an *épuration* committee specified that the censure of, among others, directors Clouzot, Decoin, Jean de Limur, and Georges Lacombe be publicized in three motion-picture trade journals—*Le Film*, *L'Entr'aide Cinématographique*, and *Vie Cinématographique*.[6] Yet as early as December 22, 1944, J. Bernard Derosme inaugurated a weekly column in *Le Film Français* that offered an alternative view. Entitled "Ces Hommes de bonne volonté" ("These Men of Good Will"), Derosme's column celebrated those who, by having worked during the Occupation, ensured that "amid all that enormous poverty," an industry, a trade, and an art remained "rich" and "edifying."[7]

A sardonic recollection of scenarist-director Michel Audiard perhaps best captures the prevailing temper: "In the wake of the Liberation [we pretended that] only Clouzot had made pictures and only Fresnay had acted; that cleared everyone else's name, and we could all calm down . . . We had to have some scapegoats, so we pointed out Mister So-and-so, calling him a swine [salaud] while placing the rest of us on the other side of the table—that is, the épuration committee's table."[8]

Carné was one of the "swine." But like most others who had been reprimanded, Carné resumed his professional affairs with apparently little loss of vigor and commitment. Along with the 1940 defeat and the four years of Occupation, the épuration soon became an episode most of the French were keen to repress. As early as March 1947 the Ministère de la Jeunesse des Arts et des Lettres initiated moves to name Carné to the Legion of Honor.[9] Carné was unresponsive to these overtures. In November 1952 a second initiative took place. This time it originated with the office of the secretary general of the Syndicat des Techniciens de la Production Cinématographique—none other than Louis Daquin, one of the CLCF's Communist leaders who allegedly had treated Carné with contempt at the time of the Liberation.[10]

A letter written in September 1948 by Jacques Becker, another former CLCF leader, discloses that, appearances to the contrary, Carné was in fact suffering from the censure. The letter intimates that Italian producer Salvo d'Angelo was invoking the sanction to abandon a projected film with Carné. Equally revealing are Becker's explicit references to his role in Carné's épuration: "Whatever you may have thought about the matter, I have always liked you. I did begrudge you at a certain moment for having believed (and I know that you still believe it) that I tried to harm you in connection with the so-called épurations. I reproached you, and I continue to reproach you, for not having sought to see me first at the time. I would have met swiftly, in your presence, those people who were accusing me of having sought to harm you . . . I complained about all this at the time to Pierre and Jacques Prévert."[11]

Becker's magnanimous letter may point to belated unease over his participation in the postwar purges. More certainly, it divulges the degree to which Carné's immediate postwar experience fortified his isolation from and general mistrust of co-professionals.

Carné's annoyance over the épuration was not so acute as to make him leave France and work for British Lion. Alexander Korda proposed that

Carné direct three pictures in London. Negotiations crumbled, however, when the director insisted that one of the films be French-language and another be in Technicolor. Korda objected to Carné's first demand on financial grounds: a French-language project could not guarantee a profit for his newly acquired company. Korda was also uncertain that he could furnish Carné with the materials required for Technicolor shooting. In light of the difficulties that beset him in the years to follow, Carné views his inability to strike a compromise with Korda as "the gravest error" of his career (*Vbd*, 251).

Difficulties arose swiftly. Common opinion holds that the lesser quality of Carné's postwar films derives from the dissolution of his partnership with Prévert in 1949. *Les Portes de la nuit* (1946) gives the lie to that diagnosis. A final attempt to match poetic realism with monumentality, *Les Portes de la nuit* points not only to failures of judgment and invention in Carné and Prévert, but to an exhaustion of the kind of filmmaking they had come to embody. One of the French cinema's costliest productions (its 118-million-franc budget was over twice the size of *Les Enfants du paradis*'s), *Les Portes de la nuit* marks the decadence that bridged the passage from France's Golden Age of moviemaking to its Silver Age.

The odd preproduction history of *Les Portes de la nuit* raises an issue that has never been addressed forthrightly: the relation between the Carné-Prévert decline and the perception of Carné's political profile following the Occupation. Pathé had hired Carné and Prévert to direct and write Jean Gabin's first postwar film. The duo was coaxing Gabin to consider an adaptation of *Le Rendez-vous*, a ballet Prévert and Kosma had conceived for Roland Petit. Performed at the Sarah Bernhardt Theater in June 1945, the ballet concerned a young man who falls in love with "the most beautiful girl in the world" and dies when Destiny carries her away. Gabin was more inclined to film Pierre-René Wolf's novel *Martin Roumagnac*, to which he owned the screen rights. He yielded to Carné and Prévert's wishes—they abhorred Wolf's novel—on one condition: that *Le Rendez-vous* co-star Marlene Dietrich, with whom Gabin had been involved romantically since his exile in Hollywood. Dietrich, too, set conditions. Sensitive to her German accent and sure that the French public had had their fill of *chleuh* (Occupation slang for the German language), Dietrich insisted that her role not be long. Moreover, she demanded that her contract not become binding until she approved the completed script.

When it envisioned the picture as a vehicle for Gabin's return to the

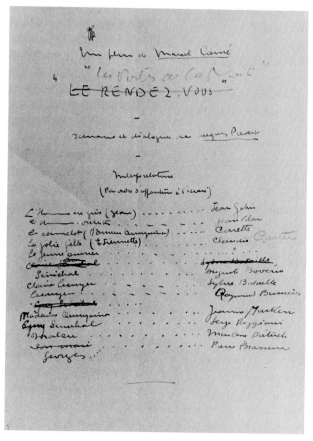

99 The cover page of Carné's handwritten draft of the shooting script for *Les Portes de la nuit,* indicating the original title, "Le Rendez-vous," and the intended cast, including Jean Gabin and Marlene Dietrich

French screen, RKO agreed to co-produce. Informed of Dietrich's participation, RKO withdrew its support. It contended that a sizable segment of American society viewed Gabin and Dietrich's extramarital affair as morally offensive and would boycott the film. Untroubled by such concerns, Alexander Korda shouldered the financing Pathé now required.

As in the past, Carné worked intensively with Prévert, who drafted the screenplay and dialogue at the Colombe d'Or in Saint-Paul-de-Vence (fig. 99). Carné was pleased to wrangle with only one writer, not two, as had been the case with Aurenche and Jeanson for *Hôtel du Nord* and Prévert and Laroche for *Les Visiteurs du soir.* But it was now Dietrich who jeopardized the Carné-Prévert symbiosis: "Marlene . . . examined [the screenplay] scene by scene . . . She clearly intended to become personally involved in the elaboration of the plot, and made a thousand proposals for changes that seemed, to Jacques and me, each one more inept than the rest . . . Naturally we handled these proposals in the manner they deserved" (*Vbd*, 257).

In late December 1945 Dietrich read the completed script of *Les Portes de la nuit.* (To avoid confusion with Lubitsch's *The Shop Around the Corner*, recently released in France as *Rendez-vous*, Prévert retitled the project with a phrase from one of the film's songs.) Dietrich speedily broke her contract. Gabin followed suit. Unlike the actress, Gabin had no control over the picture's content. But when circumstances forced the date of initial shooting to be pushed back (complications associated with Janine Prévert's pregnancy prevented Jacques from writing at normal pace), Gabin maintained that other commitments now took priority. Michel Fourré-Cormeray, head of the Direction Générale du Cinéma, arbitrated the dispute. Following a bitter hearing, Fourré-Cormeray approved the nullification of Gabin's contract.

Characteristically, Carné depicts the matter as Gabin's having opted for Dietrich over himself: "Beaming from the victory he thought he had won, Gabin thus went ahead to realize what had been for years his life's dream: *Martin Roumagnac.* His manifest patience and obstinacy concerning this project brought him a well-deserved bonus. It came in the person of Marlene Dietrich playing the ever-so-plausible part of a Norman farm woman [actually she plays a woman-of-the-world recently returned from Australia]—a role for which she was surely born. I have never seen the film . . . Perhaps *The Blue Angel*'s star was able to demonstrate her talents as a cook and her supposedly exclusive knack for preparing *boeuf gros sel*" (*Vbd*, 260).

Carné's sarcasm indicates the intensity of his anger and frustration. In a real sense Dietrich's withdrawal contributed to Carné's professional decline. Her "defection," as Carné called it at the time,[12] deprived him not only of Gabin but of the most suitable candidate to succeed Arletty in the cinematic project at which Carné excelled: the iconization of mature women. In denying herself to Carné, Dietrich also impaired his sustaining the international prominence acquired in the wake of *Les Enfants du paradis*: whatever failings *Les Portes de la nuit* might have displayed, Dietrich's presence in a Carné film would have guaranteed attention worldwide. In another sense, however, Dietrich was fulfilling Carné's personal destiny. She had worked with three of the principal influences on Carné: Sternberg, Feyder (*Knight Without Armour*, 1937), and Clair (*The Flame of New Orleans*, 1941). Always measuring himself against these models, Carné was bereft of an opportunity to outstrip them all once more. By leaving him with only an image of what might have been, Dietrich was unwittingly perpetuating Carné's masochistic relation to strong women and exacerbating his sense of belatedness vis-à-vis male predecessors.

Hired to direct Gabin, Carné was free to break his contract with Pathé. Instead he went on with the project, rationalizing that the picture's true protagonist was neither the Gabin nor the Dietrich character, but "the image of a working-class neighborhood" (*Vbd*, 261). *Faute de mieux*, he proceeded to hire Yves Montand and Nathalie Nattier for the leading roles (fig. 100). The twenty-five-year-old Montand, who was then Edith Piaf's protégé, had begun to gain notice as a singer, but he had played in only one film. The twenty-one-year-old Nattier had been making pictures for three years, but she had yet to take on a starring role. Neither had the authority to project the world-weariness required by the script. Under Carné's direction, neither was able to activate a credible erotic field that could justify their characters' relationship.

In her 1984 autobiography, *Marlène D.*, Dietrich does not mention either Carné or *Les Portes de la nuit*. She refers only parenthetically to "a picture for which I refused a role."[13] But at the time Dietrich gave several reasons for objecting to the Carné-Prévert script. Interviewed by journalist Gérard Fabrice in February 1946, she claimed: "I no longer want to play in . . . glamour movies. When I worked with Sternberg, you know, people reproached me a lot for that—beautiful, elegant women with feathers, roles in which you don't really do much . . . My character's actions and responses [in *Les Portes de la nuit*] have nothing to do with the picture's plot . . . If I have come to make a picture in France, it's to create a role different from those I have played until now." Asked by Fabrice whether Carné and Prévert could have modified the screenplay to meet her desires, she responded: "It wasn't a question of just changing a few scenes. It was the very essence of my character, her psychological basis that would have had to change."[14]

In a letter written to Pathé in January, Dietrich set forth a more specific and delicate concern: "Several scenes evoking regrettable attitudes under the Occupation create in certain parts of the picture an atmosphere that seems to me to have the potential for constituting harmful propaganda abroad and thereby makes my cooperation distressing." Less circumspect, Gabin informed *Le Canard enchaîné*: "Let me tell you, [Marlene] finds that *Les Portes de la nuit* is immoral, and that it is not the moment

100   Nathalie Nattier and Yves Montand replacing Dietrich
and Gabin in *Les Portes de la nuit*

to take advantage of the period we are in to show things occurring in places around La Chapelle where I wouldn't dare take my mother. Well, the public is my mother! And I respect my mother!"[15]

Dietrich's wish to alter her image might have been authentic. But since she knew from the project's outset that she would portray "the most beautiful girl in the world," her argument about "glamour movies" fails to convince. Her unease over the film's political thrust, reiterated by Gabin, strikes a more compelling note. Although Gabin and Dietrich had agreed to do the film several weeks before the official announcement of Carné's censure, it is unlikely that the censure, in and of itself, predisposed them to break their contracts. Dietrich understood the ambiguities of the moral climate in which the *épuration* was transpiring, and she was one of Maurice Chevalier's firm supporters.[16] Moreover, *Martin Rou-*

magnac's director, Georges Lacombe, had worked for Continental and received a censure more severe than Carné's.[17]

But Gabin and Dietrich did have personal stakes in the way the French would be represented on the postwar screen. Both were perceived as Liberation heroes. Seaman Gabin left Hollywood in April 1943 to enlist in the Free French movement's naval operations. He led his unit in defending against a German air attack off the Algerian coast. Following the Normandy invasion, he joined General Philippe Leclerc's armored division and became the oldest tank combatant in his regiment. At the war's close he was awarded the *croix de guerre*. Dietrich, who had rejected attempts by Nazi officials to woo her into serving the Reich, became an American citizen in June 1939. Beginning in March 1943, she entertained American troops at bases and hospitals in the States and in Europe. Under the Office of War Information's auspices, she made broadcasts in German and French to Europeans under Axis rule. When touring camps with the USO, she performed for German prisoners of war as well as for Allied soldiers in battle zones. In 1947 General Maxwell Taylor presented her with the Medal of Freedom, and in April 1951 she was named to the French Legion of Honor.

Arletty is one of Dietrich's warm admirers. The two actresses have much in common. In their best films they project a nonchalant, androgynous sensuality that gives the impression of their being uncommitted to nearly everything and everyone. Yet just as often their cool façade masks desire and vulnerability. In their most memorable roles Arletty and Dietrich play women who demonstrate that moral integrity and sexual promiscuity need not be mutually exclusive. Moreover, both actresses allowed their most gifted directors—Carné and Sternberg—to delude themselves and the public into believing that these men were entirely responsible for their female creations. Insofar as each challenged social conventions, Arletty and Dietrich were also alike in their private lives. But their postures vis-à-vis world events could not have been further apart. Where Arletty protested war through professions of pacifism, Dietrich risked her life by participating in what she viewed as the just cause. Arletty is fond of saying: "Gabin and I draw from the same suit. He had his *Prussienne*. I had my *Prussien*."[18] But Dietrich was no ordinary *Prussienne*. As Ethan Mordden comments: "This was a woman who made a contribution to the morale of the war effort in dangerous places, a German Army officer's daughter who defied Hitler's orders that she abandon the 'Jew films' in Hollywood . . . Dietrich's life is crowded with public events."[19]

Les Portes de la nuit is crowded with private misdeeds. The film begins with a voice-over: "February 1945. It is the hard, sad winter of Paris's

Liberation. The war is not yet over, but in the north of the city, life has begun again with its miseries, its terrible secrets." The picture then depicts events that transpire between one dusk and dawn. The male protagonist, Diego, is a former Resistance fighter. Unexpectedly he discovers that his buddy Raymond (Raymond Bussières) is alive: both men had been caught and tortured by the Gestapo. As they celebrate their reunion, Diego espies the female protagonist, Malou, with whom he soon falls in love. After many years abroad, Malou has returned from England with the intention of dissolving her marriage to Georges (Pierre Brasseur), a wealthy munitions industrialist. Malou's father, Sénéchal (Saturnin Fabre), is a demolitions contractor who engaged in questionable dealings with the enemy throughout the Occupation. Malou's brother, Guy (Serge Reggiani), is the informant responsible for Raymond's having been captured by the Gestapo. As dawn approaches, Diego identifies Guy. The latter panics and attempts unsuccessfully to kill Diego. Diego intimates that Guy will never survive the wrath of fellow Resisters. Shortly thereafter, Guy commits suicide. Georges, having gone berserk from jealousy over Malou's love for Diego, murders Malou.

Intended partly as a documentation of near-contemporary events, *Les Portes de la nuit* abounds with topical allusions. These include the August 19 insurrection, Drancy Prison and the *épuration*, the "Chant des Partisans," blackouts, black markets, the famine, and the last metro. If the picture emphasizes themes such as denunciation, blackmail, collaboration, torture, and profiteering, it is because these phenomena were among the period's leading concerns. But *Les Portes de la nuit* paints an exorbitantly bleak portrait of the French at the start of what was purportedly a period of national renewal. Its most sympathetic characters—the railroad worker Raymond and his wife (Sylvia Bataille)—are unimposing. The vague hopes of its protagonists, ex-Resistance fighter Diego and seeker-of-lost-innocence Malou, are no less doomed than those of Jean and Nelly in *Le Quai des Brumes*. Absolute goodness takes the guise of Malou and is destroyed. Absolute evil takes the guise of Guy and self-destructs. The film barely hints at the possibility that the future will, or even might, belong to morally responsible members of society.

The scene in which Guy informs his father that he is fleeing to Spain exemplifies the "harmful propaganda" Dietrich probably had in mind when she explained her withdrawal to Pathé:

GUY SENECHAL: People would probably also accuse me of having lent a hand in various interrogations that were a bit . . . "lively" . . . And so on!

SENECHAL (*compassionate*): After all . . . you only did your duty . . . You acted according to your principles . . .

GUY SENECHAL (*insinuating*): Which were also your own . . . at the time . . .

SENECHAL: Oh! I don't deny it, but you understand . . . "dear little one" . . . what good does it do to knock one's head against the wall . . . when the world changes . . . the best thing is simply to evolve with it! . . . Oh, of course . . . I understand that you're a touch demoralized . . .

GUY SENECHAL: Demoralized! . . . (*dreamy*) . . . You know, after all, "dear daddy," a dozen bullets do not necessarily kill a man . . . (*suddenly excited, feverish*) . . . But what I wouldn't want . . . is for the others to get hold of me . . . (*more and more febrile*) . . . Yes . . . for them to interrogate me . . . to judge me . . . to laugh in my face . . . to treat me as garbage . . . even if it's true. . . . and then, after all . . . is it my fault? . . . Did I ask to be born? I didn't stand in line for a license! . . . I'm not responsible . . . I was just born . . . (*shouting*) . . . for no reason, you hear . . . for no reason! . . . Not even for my death, which I can't control! . . .

Martin Roumagnac is hardly uplifting. It concerns a woman with a shadowy past (Dietrich) who is ultimately killed by her lover (Gabin), who is in turn murdered by one of the woman's rejected suitors. But set in prewar provincial France, the picture avoids explicit political reference. By 1947 Billy Wilder was able to convince Dietrich to play the ex-mistress of a former high-ranking Nazi in *A Foreign Affair* (1948), Wilder's satire of Allied corruption in Occupied Berlin. In the immediate wake of France's Liberation, however, Dietrich could not endorse *Les Portes de la nuit*'s savage exposé of a people whose freedom she had struggled to ensure. Carné claims to have ignored Dietrich's criticisms. Yet the script Dietrich had read included sarcastic and self-righteous references to the *Frisés* (Occupation slang for the Germans), right-wingers, concentration camps, anti-Semitism, the good life at the Place Vendôme, and American culture—all of which Carné deleted from the final shooting script.[20]

In 1946 it took courage to portray the unsavory aspects of early postwar France. Although opportunism might have been a motivating factor, Carné and Prévert were exercising again the social consciousness that had imbued their prewar efforts. Reassuming what they viewed to be their proper role as filmmakers, Carné and Prévert believed that a screen depiction of kindly representatives of the proletariat and Resistance gaining revenge over a nasty collaborationist would promote a national catharsis of sorts.

Their expectations were wide of the mark. Premiering on December 3, 1946, *Les Portes de la nuit* was a critical and commercial fiasco. One person in attendance at the press screening recalls: "A third of the audience left before the film's end. Others emitted angry yells. At the screening's close, Carné and Prévert stood outside and not a soul walked over to shake hands with them."[21] Surely, ad hominem prejudices were operating. Many in the film industry were jubilant that the authors of *Les Visiteurs du soir* and *Les Enfants du paradis* gave evidence of an artistic weakening. Many resented the fact that a director and a scenarist who had accommodated so successfully to the Occupation era were now moralizing about the evils of collaboration. Yet irrespective of critics' vindictiveness, Carné and Prévert misjudged their public.

First, audiences were not ready to confront images of themselves and their acquaintances so aggressively condemnatory as *Les Portes de la nuit*'s. The clamor attending Ophuls's *Le Chagrin et la pitié* in 1971 and Serge Mosco's *L'Affaire Manouchian (Terrorists in Retirement)* in 1985 suggests that the French may never come fully to terms with their conduct during the Occupation. On the whole, postwar critics and audiences were receptive to films that exalted the courage of Resisters, such as Yves Allégret's *Les Démons de l'aube* (1946) and Alexandre Esway's *Le Bataillon du ciel* (1946). They were less prepared to embrace pictures dealing with the tormented fate of collaborators, such as Clément's *Les Maudits* (1947) and Clouzot's *Manon* (1949). They were thoroughly baffled by Renoir's American-made *This Land Is Mine* (1943), which attempted to show, in scenarist Dudley Nichols's words, that "there are no villains in life but only human beings embodying elements of good and evil."[22]

Second, *Les Portes de la nuit*'s Manicheanism perpetuated the mindset of numerous *épurateurs* whose accomplishments many of the French, by late 1946, had repudiated. Unlike the Nuremberg trials, the French *épuration* proceeded without examination of the context that had produced alleged criminals and collaborators: "By making the French believe, and far too quickly, that legitimacy could reside only in the Resistance, and that the latter's combat was necessarily the foundation for a new regime, without first examining the social realities of the parenthesized dark years, the leaders [of the *épuration* process] preferred order and efficiency to the duty of civic reflexion."[23] *Les Portes de la nuit* depicts random economic and social phenomena of the Occupation and its aftermath.

But Carné and Prévert do not impart a convincing picture of the overall societal structure. Inveterate social melodramatists, they present individuals whose moral bearings appear as if predetermined by that structure. The film's characters are either good or evil. They are never in between.

Finally, by immersing their portrait of French society within the poeticized atmosphere of their prewar films, Carné and Prévert ensured the disaffection even of those who would have otherwise applauded a documentation of unpleasant realities. The film's lilting opening train shots hark back to *Nogent*. A street singer's melancholic strains recall *Jenny*. Wet pavements, nighttime settings, and chiaroscuro suggest *Le Quai des Brumes*. The lovers' sitting despondently at a cafe evokes *Hôtel du Nord*, as does the Expressionist-inspired mise en scène of Guy's suicide. Diego and Malou's precarious idyll in the warehouse echoes François and Françoise's in *Le Jour se lève*'s greenhouse. The measured reappearances of an enigmatic tramp named Destin (played by Jean Vilar) seem to make the plot move slowly and irrevocably to its tragic end. Reinforcing Destin's grasp on events is the arsenal of symbols for fate found in earlier Carné films: a horse-drawn milk cart, shrieking train whistles, labyrinthine iron-and-steel structures, and a harmonica—on which Destin plays "Les Feuilles mortes" ("Autumn Leaves"), the Prévert-Kosma song intended to be sung by Dietrich and eventually made popular worldwide by, among others, Montand.

Viewed today, *Les Portes de la nuit* can be appreciated as an intense and visually striking dramatization of a theme that remains valid above and beyond social settings: two strangers in the night, ignorant even of each other's names, establish an immediate rapport, have nothing to hide from one another, and imagine a shared future. But in late 1946 audiences could not separate the film's romantic strain from its social context. Nor did Carné and Prévert want them to. Prior Carné-Prévert films had made no pretense to addressing politics head-on. They effectively coupled poetry with purported reality because the latter was conceived as stylized, dreamlike, and atemporal. Through metaphor and allegory those works captured the spirit of their times. *Les Portes de la nuit*, on the contrary, aimed to furnish a social document. With the Occupation ended, Carné and Prévert no longer had to confine themselves to subjects set in the Middle Ages or the nineteenth century; they could again give expression to the temper of their age. Their miscalculation lay in the inherent incompatability between the newer, more direct realism they strove for and the *poésie* they could not abandon.

For many viewers *Les Portes de la nuit* (which some detractors dubbed *Les Portes de l'ennui*) appeared especially effete in juxtaposition with

Italian Neorealist films that were tackling similar themes with apparent vigor and inventiveness.[24] Oddly enough, the term "Neorealism," as applied to film, made one of its first appearances in a 1948 essay by Umberto Barbaro that took *Le Quai des Brumes* as a marker for the direction that Italian cinema ought to be moving in.[25] By underscoring the movement's Neoromantic and fantastical strains, numerous more recent analysts of Neorealism have demonstrated further links with French poetic realism.[26] It is nonetheless clear that Carné and Prévert were incapable of generating the freshness and *bonne foi* which their Italian colleagues were bringing to the attempt to depict a nation's contemporary plight. *Les Portes de la nuit* exhibits the very falsification of reality that, for Barbaro, had set apart Italian pictures of the 1930s and early 1940s from *Le Quai des Brumes*'s inspiring "truth and artistic verisimilitude."

Some French filmmakers were more successful in creating credible depictions of contemporary affairs. Clément based *La Bataille du rail* (1946) on actual stories of Resistance fighters, using unknown and nonprofessional actors to reconstruct events in a documentarylike mode. In *Le Point du jour* (1949), Daquin traced the daily life of coalminers in northern France, shooting his film entirely on location. But the strange interplay of image, silence, and voice-over narration in Melville's *Le Silence de la mer* (1947) intimated that a cinematic probing of the Occupation experience called for radical departures from conventional narrative—a premise Alain Resnais and Marguerite Duras confirmed a decade later with *Hiroshima mon amour* (1958). In 1946 Carné and Prévert's goals might have been in advance of their time. But backward-looking vision and technique flew in the face of their ambition.

CHAPTER 15

Carné sans Prévert

The termination of the Carné-Prévert partnership affected Carné's life and career profoundly. It required him to deal, virtually on his own, with a new era of French filmmaking in which modes of production and public tastes were to change drastically.

Carné attributes the separation to Prévert's displeasure over *Les Portes de la nuit*'s critical reception: "Jacques, especially, was wounded by what the press had written about him, to such an extent that two weeks after the film's release he informed me of his intent to stop working in pictures. 'You understand,' he told me, 'I am tired of slaving for ten months on a screenplay only to be abused in ten lines by some cretin of a critic!'" (*Vbd*, 298, first edition; in the second edition, an apparent printer's error has caused the omission of the entire page on which this passage would have appeared). Pierre Prévert claims that poor press had nothing to do with the split: "On the contrary, Jacques never took the critics to heart. In fact, he loved when they panned him, because that proved he was on the mark." Pierre proposes, somewhat vaguely, that the breakup occurred "because Jacques felt that he no longer had carte blanche in the creative process." [1]

Numerous alternative explanations circulate. Some speak of a power play in which Prévert allegedly refused to write a part for a young would-be actor friend of Carné. Others refer to a dispute in which Carné insisted that Prévert write a treatment for a subject the scenarist loathed: a life of the *belle époque* actress Réjane. Some underscore Jacques's wish to attend more diligently to his brother's directorial projects. Others point to private events that made Prévert long for a calmer, more solitary life: the birth of his daughter, Michèle, in April 1946; and, in 1948, his accidental fall from the second-floor terrace of the Office de la Radiodiffusion Nationale, rendering him comatose for several weeks.

One fact is irrefutable. *Les Enfants du paradis* had drained the Carné-

Prévert collaboration of its creative juice. *Les Portes de la nuit* demonstrated that, ambition and good intentions notwithstanding, further efforts by Carné and Prévert were bound to prove anticlimactic. Irrevocably associated with the prewar era, the Carné-Prévert voice had become an anachronism.

Prévert did not forsake filmmaking after *Les Portes de la nuit*. He wrote dialogue for his brother's slapstick comedy, *Voyage-surprise* (1947). He scripted Cayatte's *Les Amants de Vérone* (1949). He penned screenplays for Christian-Jaque's *Souvenirs perdus* (1950) and Delannoy's *Notre Dame de Paris* (1956). He also wrote numerous teleplays which his brother directed in the 1960s. Nevertheless, motion pictures were not the principal beneficiary of Jacques Prévert's talents following the war. A limited first edition of his collected poems, *Paroles*, had appeared in December 1945. An immediate success, this iconoclastic and witty collection seemed to speak directly to the sensibilities of France's youth, many of whom perceived it as "a therapeutic detoxification of the whole post-Liberation literary climate."[2] *Paroles* enjoyed several printings and established Prévert as France's most popular contemporary poet. Other verse collections followed, including *Histoires* (1946), *Spectacle* (1951), *La Pluie et le beau temps* (1955), *Fatras* (1960), and *Choses et autres* (1972). Prévert also devoted himself to making collages and to writing essays about friends and their paintings, including Miró, Picasso, Chagall, and Ernst.

Carné was not blessed with Prévert's versatility. Fiction cinema was the sole expressive medium at his disposal. Because he sought to perpetuate the Carné-Prévert vision and voice with subsequent scenarists, many of Carné's post-Prévert pictures have a Carné-Prévert feel. But none of his later screenwriters was sufficiently forceful to counterbalance Carné's temperament. As a result, the post-Prévert works tend to exaggerate the earlier films' despairing tone and weighty mise en scène. Compassion is almost nonexistent. Women become progressively more irrelevant. Sexuality turns more juvenile. And as the insularism of Carné's protagonists increases, their capacity to engage spectator interest diminishes. In early 1947 several critics blamed Prévert duly for *Les Portes de la nuit*'s wordiness.[3] But as verbose as Prévert could be, his dialogue, at its best, bestowed sincerity and believability upon characters and situations. The loss of this credibility handicaps Carné's later films.

In point of fact the Carné-Prévert collaboration did not cease with *Les Portes de la nuit*. In the summer of 1946 Carné negotiated terms for filming Prévert's screenplay about reform school escapees, *L'Ile des enfants perdus*, which the censors had banned a decade earlier. Carné had little difficulty in convincing Prévert to complete and update the scenario. First, Prévert felt strongly about the exposé of corruption and oppression in the juvenile correctional system. Second, Carné intended to have the film serve as a vehicle for Arletty's return to the screen. Prévert was eager to help. He abhorred the false piety surrounding the *épuration*, and he hoped that his film would stigmatize all forms of unjust incarceration. Prévert transformed the leading female role, written originally for Danielle Darrieux, to suit the more mature Arletty. And he changed the picture's title to *La Fleur de l'âge* (*In the Prime of Life*) to avoid confusion with *Les Enfants du paradis* and with Léo Joannon's *Le Carrefour des enfants perdus* (1943).

Had it been completed, *La Fleur de l'âge* would have celebrated Arletty's liberation and exculpation. As specified by the shooting script, the viewer's first glimpse of the star would have occurred in a medium-long shot of a luxurious yacht on whose bridge stands a woman, "her hair blowing in the wind, smiling and happy to be alive." Medium-close shots of Arletty showering nude in her cabin would have reaffirmed graphically the actress's prior public claim to do with her body as she pleased. And as the only figure among the wealthy bourgeoisie to pity the young delinquents, Arletty would have spoken lines replete with autobiographical import. Apropos the seventeen-year-old boy (Serge Reggiani) who has fallen in love with her, the heroine tells one of her jaded male friends: "In spite of his misfortunes, he has something which you have never had . . . and which you will never have . . . the joy and the desire to live (*lowering her voice*) . . . and to love!"

Today, most of the French venerate Arletty. La Salle Garance—the screening room in the Centre Georges Pompidou that is named after Arletty's most memorable role—bears witness to the public's affection for this uncommon woman, and to the arts establishment's recognition of Arletty's centrality in French film culture. Following her house arrest, however, producers were wary about Arletty. And Arletty was wary about accepting offers indiscriminately. Her first postwar stage performance was as Blanche DuBois in Cocteau's 1949 adaptation of *A Streetcar Named Desire*. It was a triumphant comeback. Yet Arletty sensed that, delivered by her, a literal translation of Blanche's line "I have always depended on the kindness of strangers" would unsettle Parisian audiences: in French, *étranger* means "foreigner" as well as "stranger." At her request Cocteau changed the line to read, "J'ai toujours dépendu de la gentillesse des *inconnus*," that synonym of *étrangers* having little overt political connotation.[4]

Jeanne Witta-Montrobert speculates that a principal reason for *La Fleur de l'âge*'s being abandoned was its controversial subject: "Was the production company yielding to pressure from the Ministry of Justice, not very eager, as one can imagine, to put on display the horrid state of young convicts detained in a reform school?"[5] Witta-Montrobert is perhaps too discreet to mention a related issue: is it not possible that the film's producers were having second thoughts about investing in a picture that seemed an unofficial vindication of Arletty's alleged wrongdoings during the Occupation? Carné's version of the production's fate is more prosaic (*Vbd*, 279 ff). Prévert's revised screenplay called for considerable location shooting on and around Belle-Isle-en-Mer, a small island off the Brittany coast. The weather's excessive variability; the lack of cooperation from the captain whose yacht was rented for too brief a period; the financial unreliability of the producers, triggering a series of strikes by actors and technicians; and, finally, the producers' insistence that certain scenes be cut—all contributed to *La Fleur de l'âge*'s demise after barely three months of shooting and with only one quarter of the picture completed.

In the wake of two unfinished films—a projected adaptation of Anouilh's *Eurydice* also failed to materialize—Carné knew that Jean Gabin was the one person who could help stabilize his tottering career. Although Pathé-Cinéma had successfully sued Gabin for three million francs in the aftermath of *Les Portes de la nuit*, Gabin's confidence in Carné was unshaken. He therefore persuaded producer Sacha Gordine to engage the director for an adaptation of Georges Simenon's novel *La Marie du port* (*Marie of the Port*, 1938), to which Gabin held the rights. Prévert, however, was less of a mind to undertake the project. Despite Carné's insistence that *La Marie du port* was a full Carné-Prévert effort (*Vbd*, 298), Prévert agreed only to supervise the work of two friends, scenarist Louis Chavance and dialogue writer Georges Ribemont-Dessaignes. In accordance with his wishes, Prévert's name does not appear in the film credits.

La Marie du port put Carné's bankability to the test. A letter from Gordine in February 1949 testifies to the director's near disenfranchisement in the eyes of producers no longer willing to endure his excesses. It denies him a sum of money requested for personal "professional expenses" not specified in his contract, and calls attention to "the importance which the act of directing a picture represents for you, given that circumstances, surely independent of your will, have prevented the two pictures you previously undertook from being brought to a successful conclusion." Gordine's tone is a mix of prudence and condescension. But his letter reveals that however patronizing producers might have become toward Carné, they did not want to preclude their eventually profiting from a prestigious superproduction of the kind he was capable of turning out. Gordine's final paragraph reads, "On the other hand, we agree to envisage, if *La Marie du port*'s production goes well and remains within the limits of what is foreseen, to try to underwrite the production of *Juliette ou la clé des songes*, on which you have set your heart and about which you have spoken to us on many occasions." [6]

Given the stakes, the director *maudit* became an *enfant sage*. Carné adhered to his budget and completed the film in less than a year. *La Marie du port* put to temporary rest the legend of Carné's recklessness. It proved that he could treat modern themes without giving offense. It showed that he could bridle his inclination for abstruse symbolism. And it even gave evidence that *Les Portes de la nuit*'s director had a gift for location shooting. Many had viewed *Les Portes de la nuit*'s reconstruction of the Barbès-Rochechouart metro station as scandalously irresponsible, both financially and artistically. With *La Marie du port* Carné sought to emulate Neorealists by including shots of authentic daily life at Port-en-Bessin, a village near Cherbourg. Indeed, these images have a documentary and poetic feel that evokes Visconti's depiction of Sicilian fishermen in *La Terra trema* (*The Earth Trembles*, 1948). But where Visconti's portrayal of everyday life is his picture's essence, Carné's is peripheral decoration that does not cohere with the film's otherwise conventional dramatic narrative. For the first time in his career the French master of poetic realism consciously restrained his lyricism to produce an unpretentious dramatic comedy of the kind Truffaut would soon denigrate as "psychological realism."

La Marie du port embellishes *La Fleur de l'âge*'s May-December theme. It tells the story of a prosperous Cherbourg restaurateur and movie-house owner, Henri Chatelard (Gabin), who abandons his bored mistress, Odile (Blanchette Brunoy), for Odile's scheming eighteen-year-old sister, Marie (Nicole Courcel). In turn, Marie abandons her young hairdresser beau, Marcel (Claude Romain), for Chatelard, as Marcel becomes the object of Odile's affection. The film also restates *La Fleur de l'âge*'s theme of teenage oppression: Marcel's father, le père Viau (Julien Carette), is an alcoholic who abuses Marcel and forbids him to court Marie. Sensitive and idealistic, Marcel is jealous over Marie's attraction to Chatelard and makes a suicide attempt. But as Odile's maternal concern turns to physical desire, Marcel finds reasons for surviving. In short, *La Marie du port* is a domesticated variation on Murnau's *Tabu* (1931), scenes of which Chatelard projects in his theater. While Murnau's South Seas idyll turns tragic, Carné's provincial tragicomedy ends with all

101 Gabin *embourgeoisé:* as Chatelard in *La Marie du port;* in bed, Blanchette Brunoy as Odile

characters finding, if not happiness, that which they deserve.

The picture's enduring interest lies mainly in its unveiling of a new Gabin persona (fig. 101). *Martin Roumagnac* (1946), Raymond Lamy's *Miroir* (1947), and Clément's *Au-delà des grilles* (1948) were attempts to capitalize on Gabin's prewar outcast image. With *La Marie du port* Carné and Chavance jostled viewers' expectations by making Chatelard conform more closely to the real-life Gabin, now forty-five years old, and to the spirit of economic reconstruction and political conservatism that would shape much of France's history in the early and mid-1950s. The screen destiny of Gabin, gray-haired, stylishly groomed, and a productive member of the capitalist establishment, is no longer violent death from entanglement with a sultry femme fatale, but marriage to a shrewd young social climber. Supplanting the formerly de rigueur outburst of rage is the fit of laughter emitted at finding his mistress in bed with a youth about one third his age. Gabin's laugh clinches the transformation. The cynical young anarchist who discovered love's transcendent potential in *Le Quai des Brumes* is now the aging womanizer philosophically settling for whatever small pleasures and deceits the fair sex may grant him.

La Marie du port's commercial success made Sacha Gordine honor his promise to support *Juliette ou la clef des songes* (*Juliette or the Dream*

Book), the adaptation of Georges Neveux's Surrealist-inspired drama which Carné and Cocteau had sought to bring to the screen in 1942. Carné's last attempt at monumentmaking, the film diverges considerably from both Neveux's play and the screenplay which Cocteau and Jacques Viot drafted during the Occupation. The Carné-Cocteau rapport had always been strained. Despite coinciding interests and tastes, each man was wedded to a distinct milieu and set of values. Carné's artistic industriousness, solemnity, and *pudeur* derived from his identification with the proletariat. Cocteau's facility, frivolity, and exhibitionism bespoke aristocratic pretensions. In a letter written in September 1946, *Le Sang d'un poète*'s author fumes over what he refers to as "muddles which people are trying to put between us": "You will [henceforth] know that anything disturbing which people 'repeat' to you will be false and invented by those who profit from separating us. I place my respect for your enterprise above these imbeciles and I was at fault for believing them sensitive to certain profound nuances of our spirits . . . My dream would be to show you *La Belle* [*et la Bête*] and to see *Les Portes* [*de la nuit*] arm in arm, with no outsiders looking on."[7] An earlier letter, apropos *Les Visiteurs du soir*, delineates aesthetic differences that would probably have made Cocteau's resuming work on *Juliette ou la clef des songes* inauspicious. Cocteau informs Carné: "I regretted certain workings of the supernatural [*mécanismes du mystère*] within a magnificent story—I did not like the Devil, except for the admirable episode of the vase-turned-snakes—(Arletty is prodigious) . . . What I [most] questioned was the poetry—serious problems—that have nothing to do with the way journalists and chatterers speak of works."[8]

In 1950 Neveux opted to take part in an extensive revision of the earlier screenplay. Cocteau yielded graciously. He granted Carné, Viot, and Neveux permission to use his previous contributions gratis: "I will be proud to see one of my lines in an oeuvre I admire."[9] However, the new team stripped the screenplay of elements most redolent of Cocteau: a smiling female mask that takes on a life of its own; mirrors that frame human images with no real-world reference; characters who make themselves invisible; the unearthly aura of statues, candelabra, and seashells.[10] Had Cocteau remained with the project, *Juliette ou la clef des songes* would probably have emphasized the magical interstices between this world and another. Instead, the film treats the competing enticements of two complementary worlds: reality and dream. In the personal obsessions it expresses and in its overall mood and cinematic values, *Juliette ou la clef des songes* owes little to Cocteau and very much to Carné. Indeed, of his twenty feature films, *Juliette ou la clef des songes* is Carné's favorite: "I love *Juliette* as a mother loves a slightly unhealthy child when her others are in better condition."[11]

Making his rounds, a nightwatchman peers through the peepholes on the doors to the cells in La Santé Prison. Among the inmates in the third cell is protagonist Michel Grandier (Gérard Philipe). Michel is incarcerated for having stolen twelve thousand francs from the cash box at the Paris shop where he worked as a salesman. The impulse behind his theft was Michel's desire to spend a weekend at the sea with Juliette (Suzanne Cloutier), a customer with whom he had begun a romance and whom he had tried to impress by misrepresenting himself as the employer's son.

Shortly after falling asleep, Michel dreams. The door to his cell opens, Michel exits blissfully, and he follows a road leading to a village in a land known as Oblivion, where neither time nor memories exist. Michel searches for Juliette with great difficulty. An affable accordionist (Yves Robert) claims to be the sole denizen of this realm who is in touch with the past: "Things come back to me whenever I play." The accordionist urges Michel to curtail his quest: "You will be too unhappy." After viewing what he takes to be Juliette's tomb in the local cemetery, Michel is brutalized by a detective. He then encounters the region's apparent overlord, the Personage (Jean-Roger Caussimon). The Personage, too, is searching for Juliette, and he is also questing for his identity: the library in his castle holds every history book in existence because the Personage is certain that accounts of distinguished men speak of him. One of his rooms contains seven closets: six hold women's used garments; a seventh stores a wedding gown intended for Juliette.

Michel meets Juliette in the forest, and they talk of love. She asks him to buy memories for them from a vendor. The Personage reappears with a pack of Dalmations and whisks Juliette away in an enclosed horse-drawn carriage. As the coach moves forward, Michel runs alongside it. Peering at the Personage and Juliette through a glass window, Michel cries out: "I love you! Remember me!" Michel succeeds in rallying the villagers to storm the Personage's castle. Inside they find the room with seven closets, blood-stained dresses, and a coffer of wedding rings. The Personage and Juliette, who is now dressed as a bride, stand at the top of a steep staircase. Positioned at the foot of the stairs, Michel attempts to intercept the Personage as he moves to slip a ring on Juliette's finger. Michel warns Juliette that this man is Bluebeard. Juliette responds, "Bluebeard, but that is a very pretty name." Michel exhorts the crowd to recount what they have discovered, but the crowd has already forgotten. Juliette almost recalls Michel's identity. However, her thoughts are obscured by the crowd's din, a clanging bell, and Michel's shout, "I'll come back every night, every night. Do you hear me? And every night it will be the first time."

The prison's morning alarm awakens Michel. The warden's office summons him. Michel's employer—identified as Monsieur Bellanger and identical in appearance to the Personage—announces that he has dropped charges and that he plans to marry Juliette. Michel rushes off in an effort to stop the marriage. It is nighttime. Michel breaks into Juliette's apartment by scaling a lamppost and entering through a window. When Juliette arrives, she confirms her plan to marry: "Don't be sad. It would have been impossible. You didn't earn any money. And you will find another girl." Michel responds: "I've already found another. A blonde, like you. With hazel eyes, like yours. And perhaps more beautiful than you. She will never make me suffer."

Michel leaves by the window, and Juliette pursues him as he dashes down precipitous steps leading to the Place Caulaincourt. Michel eludes Juliette by hiding in a doorway. Sobbing, he turns around and espies a sign reading "No Admittance: In Danger of Life." A disembodied female voice whispers: "My beloved . . . I was afraid I would lose you . . . If you had left me, what would I have done?" As in a trance, Michel approaches the door, opens it, and is inundated by a stream of light. Michel then walks through the door and finds himself on the country road that led him to Oblivion in his dream.

Juliette ou la clef des songes is the only Carné work to portray an actual dream. The rapid jumps, incoherent connections, and overdetermined motifs of the dream's content make manifest the archaic, prelogical workings of Michel's mental activity during sleep. Yet the strangeness of the film's nondream sequences is barely less marked. Taken as a whole, *Juliette ou la clef des songes* is Carné's most regressive and self-revelatory work. The nightwatchman's voyeurism at the film's start would seem to allegorize the selfsame drive motivating Michel's quest for an unattainable woman, Carné's pursuit of a career in film, and viewers' attentiveness to films generally: unauthorized and uncensored scopophilia.

Michel's dream is at once a "proleptic dream," a "dream of desire," and an "anxiety dream." [12] In terms of immediate narrative thrust the dream is proleptic, foreshadowing experiences that occur subsequent to it: just as Michel proves incapable of preventing the Personage's marriage, so he fails to impede his employer's real-life wedding. The epic search through a fantastical forest and labyrinthine castle signals a desire to satisfy libidinal attraction to Juliette. Yet as the search progresses the dreamer aims simultaneously to retreat from a situation laden with anxiety: adult heterosexuality. In this respect Oblivion is the world of the deep psyche. Its objects, characters, and situations materialize contradictory forces governing Michel's unconscious. Michel both wants and does not want to assume the role of Juliette's lover. The Personage is at once Michel and Michel's antithesis. He is fear-inspiring and powerless. He craves women and despises them. He embodies lust and lust's interdiction. His pathetic effort to solve the enigma "Who am I?" projects Michel's wish for this redoubtable rival and father figure to become identityless and incapable of inflicting punishment. Yet Michel also desires punishment.

Traditionally, versions of the Bluebeard tale depict a female protagonist who endures the consequences of her curiosity concerning the seventh door. In Carné's variant, Michel, not Juliette, illicitly uncovers the closet's contents. The Personage may well be a figure of displaced homosexual longing. It is not irrelevant that over the course of history the Bluebeard story has become enmeshed with the exploits of Gilles de Rais, the fifteenth-century marshal of France who, after fighting alongside Joan of Arc, supposedly kidnapped, tortured, and murdered children, mostly boys. Indeed, masochistic desire for homosexual pleasure-in-pain receives direct expression in the scene where an exaggeratedly masculine detective drags Michel through a catacomblike passageway, manhandles him, and then gently urges Michel to titillate him by recounting details of his romance with Juliette.

A distillation of the eternal feminine as imagined by a man who fears women, Juliette is emotionless, devoid of sensuality, and capable of cruelty and betrayal (fig. 102). If Michel wakes up from his dream because he does not want to gratify his desire for Juliette, his decision to pass beyond the dangerous threshold at the end of the postdream sequence amounts to a repudiation of women altogether. Reimmersing himself in a regressive state associated as much with death and life in utero as with sleep and dreams, Michel seeks to restore the physiological and psychic wholeness that alone can relieve the trauma of his nightmare.

The primitive meaning of "nightmare" was a female monster—a "night-fiend" or "night-hag"—that settled upon people's chests and suffocated them during sleep. For classical psychoanalysis this archaic meaning translates into "an expression of a mental conflict over an incestuous desire" and entails, most often, "'repression' of the feminine or masochistic component of sexual instinct."[13] Carné's cinematic oeuvre,

102 A version of the eternal feminine: Suzanne Cloutier as the
title character in *Juliette ou la clef des songes*

as we have seen, gives considerable expression to the masochistic component of the human psyche. In this regard his films are defensive responses to the nightmarish experience which *Juliette ou la clef des songes*
exposes graphically: a man's sexual confrontation with a woman.

In *On the Nightmare*, Ernest Jones proposes that the assimilation of
the English term for a female horse, "mare," into the word "nightmare"
mirrors a correspondence between horse mythology in Indo-European
culture and the deep content of nightmares themselves: "In the terror of
the night attack, whether of fiend as such or fiend in equine guise, we
find extensive evidence of the dread of castration and of death, the plain-
est indication of the sensations of coitus and emission, and the characteristic propensity to sex inversion." Emphasizing that "the sex and the
sexual attitude both of the dreamer and of the supposed nightly visitor
are extraordinarily interchangeable," Jones concludes that the importance of horse mythology in its relation to nightmares consists in its "ul-

103 Michel (Gérard Philipe) peering into the horse-drawn carriage that
carries off Juliette (Suzanne Cloutier) and the Personage (Jean-Roger
Caussimon)

timately represent[ing] a huge *compensation* for the fears of 'softening'
and loss."[14]

In light of Jones's analysis and my interpreting Carné's cinematic trans-
figuration of women as a disavowal of sexual difference, we can appreciate better the impulse behind the persistent appearance in the director's
works of draft horses and horse-related motifs, especially at a film's start
(as in *Jenny*, *Le Jour se lève*, *Les Visiteurs du soir*, *Le Pays d'où je viens*,
and *La Merveilleuse Visite*) or at climactic moments (as in *Hôtel du Nord*
and *Les Enfants du paradis*). *Juliette ou la clef des songes* features a
galloping steed that draws the closed coach which joins Juliette with the
Personage and separates them from Michel. In a variation on the primal
scene, Michel peers into the coach and views with frustration the intimacy that is not his to share (fig. 103). But in accordance with the logic
of masochistic desire, Michel's wish to be inside is, as well, a desire to
remain outside, like the steed. No less so than Garance's extended leg in
Les Enfants du paradis's bedroom scene, horses here and elsewhere in
Carné's oeuvre seem to take on the character of fetish objects, serving to
allay fears concerning heterosexuality. In Michel's world of Oblivion, as
in Carné's world of fictionmaking, mares transform themselves invariably into stallions.[15]

*   *   *

Juliette ou la clef des songes was one of France's three main entries in the 1951 Cannes Film Festival. Its reception was devastating. Virtually no applause followed the screening at the Palais du Festival. Carné and Gérard Philipe left the hall amid embarrassed glances and cold shoulders. The French press saw an opportunity to deflate a sacred cow. A *Paris-Presse* headline read: "Surprise at Cannes: Carné's film is a disaster!" That paper's special correspondent went on to say: "We expected . . . a high-quality work . . . he gave us a chaotic, slow, and boring film." [16] The Cannes critics' near-unanimous disfavor prejudiced the film's Paris run, which was very short. It reignited the furor of those who regularly decried the mixing of Art and Mammon at Cannes. And it convinced some members of the French film industry that Carné was the prime target of a new philistinism sweeping the Fourth Republic. [18]

When the brouhaha subsided, Bazin sought to explain why the Cannes episode took on "the proportions of disaster, of national mourning." In "Carné et la désincarnation," an essay written for *Esprit* in September 1951, Bazin describes the postwar Carné as "the bearer of an inordinate and contradictory hope." On one hand, the public expects him to discern and express the myths of 1950 as perfectly and effectively as in the prewar films. On the other, it "more or less consciously" asks him "not to create a new mythology, but to restore life to the old myths, to give us back their obsolete romanticism." Bazin judges the first demand unreasonable because Carné's imagination dovetails with "metaphors of history" prevalent before the war. And he deems the second impracticable because the resurrection of old myths for changed times leads only to failure: "It is no more possible for Carné to remake *Le Jour se lève* than it was for Voltaire to redo Racine." [19]

Although Bazin tries to remain dispassionate in analyzing what he calls the "Marcel Carné case," a barely masked prejudice and regret color his diagnosis. Bazin summarizes nicely the stylistic trajectory of Carné's oeuvre. He notes that from *Le Jour se lève*'s "unique synthesis of symbolism and realism" Carné moved to *Les Visiteurs du soir*'s emphasis on idealism and transcendence over concrete objects and motifs, and then, in *Juliette ou la clef des songes*, objects and motifs underwent a virtual "disincarnation." Bazin loses critical control, however, when he attempts to evaluate this evolution. He begins by refusing to pass judgment: "It remains to be seen whether this development represents progress or decline." Nonetheless, Bazin proceeds to assess *Juliette ou la clef des songes* in accordance with evaluative distinctions taken as axiomatic—although not without some preliminary hedging: "Without even stating as a principle that in art, and particularly in cinema, realism may be a safer poetic path than explicit symbolism, one must admit that the equilibrium of a work like *Le Jour se lève* is a priori superior to the flamboyant symbolism of *Juliette*, as classic is to baroque." Yet with the same guardedness and ambivalence that marked his writing on *Les Visiteurs du soir*, Bazin hastens to add that "baroque, too, is a style" and that the film has "its own beauties." *Juliette ou la clef des songes*, Bazin concludes, is "perhaps a mistake, certainly a mistake, but despite everything a sumptuous mistake that dishonors neither the artist nor his public." [20]

Bazin's equivocation results from his reasonable reluctance to blame Carné for no longer doing what Bazin personally feels films do best: relate explicitly to social realities. Earlier in the essay Bazin posits emphatically that "a work should not be defined only in relation to itself and without reference to its time." [21] But Bazin's regret over Carné's disregard for politics and sociology is, I would suggest, symptomatic of his unstated frustration about contemporary French cinema generally, especially by contrast with the Italian Neorealist school, which Bazin was then applauding vigorously in other essays. In the decade after the Liberation, French film was, as Roy Armes observes, "an inward-looking cinema which turned its back not only on the profound changes undergone by society in metropolitan France but also on events in the French overseas empire. For these were years which saw the end of the French war in Indo-China with the fall of Dien-Bien-Phu and the beginnings of the Algerian revolution—events which the film making of the period totally ignored." [22] In his 1951 essay on Carné, Bazin declines to acknowledge that *Juliette ou la clef des songes* in fact *does* relate to social realities. It is arguably Carné's fullest expression of a proclivity—no less the French nation's than Carné's, and no less characteristic of the 1950s than of the late 1930s and the early 1940s—for selective evasion, delusion, and forgetting.

In all likelihood, social concerns were not paramount in bringing about the Cannes critics' negative appraisal of Carné's movie. It is certain that the Festival's judges were not ill-disposed to fantasy films and filmic dreams. De Sica's *Miracolo a Milano* (*Miracle in Milan*) won the best-picture prize (sharing it with Alf Sjöberg's *Miss Julie*). Buñuel's *Los Olvidados* (*The Young and the Damned*) won the award for best direction. Such pictures, however, make the narcissistic introspection of *Juliette ou la clef des songes* all the more apparent. The supernatural in De Sica's film and the dream sequence in Buñuel's serve to condemn societal injustice. They express the characters' desire to survive, reproduce, and thrive in a more humane community. *Juliette ou la clef des songes* expresses another sort of desire: absolute withdrawal to the imaginary.

The public response to *Juliette ou la clef des songes* demonstrated the risks attending overt expression of what Hans Mayer, in his reflections on Western attitudes toward women, Jews, and homosexual men, calls "the existential particularity of the outsider."[23] In laying bare his most primitive obsessions, Carné showed substantial daring. The consequence, however, was Carné's irreparable alienation both from critics, who were sympathetic neither to his enterprise nor to what it disclosed, and from producers, who could no longer entrust Carné with large budgets. The challenge now facing Carné was to muster up, sans Prévert, sufficient courage to continue asserting his difference, all the while realizing that the film establishment was prepared at best to tolerate him as a fellow traveler.

Thérèse Raquin (1953) gave evidence of Carné's resilience. Produced with extremely limited funds by Robert and Raymond Hakim, this adaptation of Zola's novel was a French entry in the fourteenth Venice Biennial, where it won a Silver Lion. Although the award did not resurrect Carné's mystique as France's premier director, it did revive international interest in his work. The film's success seemed to demonstrate that Carné could remain true to himself without provoking scandal or embarrassment. And it gave evidence of Carné's independence from the old Prévert team: Trauner had begun to design English-language pictures and would soon leave France for the United States; and Kosma's allegiance had shifted entirely to the Prévert brothers and to Jean Renoir, for whom he composed through the 1960s.

Two trends distinguish cinematic adaptations of Zola. One exploits Naturalism's pseudoscientific project of representing social and individual reality via the supposedly objective recording of authentic detail. French examples include Duvivier's *Au Bonheur des dames* (1929) and Christian-Jaque's *Nana* (1955), in which the vivid depiction of ostensibly precise milieus governs directorial choices. A second trend responds to the discordance between Zola's Naturalist theory and practice. Renoir's *Nana* (1926), for example, addresses insistently the problematic relation of observer and object, a preoccupation that corresponds to Zola's own sense of antagonism between his purported assertion of "the 'truth' of factual detail" and that truth's "source in the observations and prejudices of an author."[24]

Carné's film belongs to this second category of adaptation. The movie offers convincing representations of Lyons in the 1950s, Camille's warehouse, and the elder Madame Raquin's dry-goods shop. But it shuns the picturesqueness which Carné's espousal of poetic realism—and gigantic production budgets—engendered in prior works. Less concerned with correspondences between scenic detail and characters' states of being, Carné focuses on the empty spaces between beings. Erotic gazes, accidental glances, intimidating peerings, and petrified stares constitute the film's dramatic essence. In this respect *Thérèse Raquin* is as much about the consequences of seeing and being seen as *Les Enfants du paradis*. But in the earlier film, characters transform painful revelations into art; in *Thérèse Raquin*, witnessings lead only to devastation.

Several factors motivated Carné to undertake *Thérèse Raquin*. First, the project provided another occasion to surpass Jacques Feyder. Three silent screen versions preceded Carné's. The first was by the Danish filmmaker Einar Zangenberg in 1911; the second, by the Italian director Nino Martoglio in 1915; and the third, a Franco-German collaboration by Feyder in 1928. Starring Gina Manès, and one of the rare French pictures of the 1920s to be printed entirely on black-and-white rather than color-tinted film stock, Feyder's three-hour *Thérèse Raquin* drew on Expressionism, *Kammerspielfilme*, and French avant-garde narrative practice. Although historians often refer to it as Feyder's masterpiece, the work was a commercial failure and, apparently, all prints of it have disappeared.[25]

A second motivating factor was Carné's desire to recoup lost opportunities. In 1952 the two pictures Carné most regretted not having directed were *La Bête humaine*, from Zola's 1890 novel, and *The Postman Always Rings Twice*, from James M. Cain's 1934 fiction. Carné claims to have proposed the Zola property to the Hakim brothers before they offered it to Renoir in 1938 (*Vbd*, 119–20). He also claims that "regardless of the success of the picture directed by Renoir," the Hakims "were sorry that I did not shoot *La Bête humaine*" (*Vbd*, 321). In adapting *Thérèse Raquin*, Carné and Charles Spaak seem to have borrowed key elements from *La Bête humaine*: the site of the murder is no longer a canoe on the Seine but, as in *La Bête humaine*, a passenger train heading for Paris; the invention of a witness to the crime, which the original source barely justifies, mirrors *La Bête humaine*'s central situation, that of a stranger who observes a murder and then involves himself intimately with its perpetrators. *Thérèse Raquin* is also a variation on the classic adultery-murder plot of *The Postman Always Rings Twice*. Carné writes (*Vbd*, 153) that prior to *Le Jour se lève*'s release he convinced producers Jack Forester and André Parent to have him direct what would have been the first screen version of the American thriller. The picture was to have starred Viviane Romance and Jean Gabin as the guilt-ridden lovers and Michel Simon as the murdered husband. The project miscarried, however, when Carné failed to secure Romance's services—one of the producers' nonnegotiable requirements. A French film version of Cain's book did appear in 1939. Entitled *Le Dernier Tournant*, it was directed by Pierre Chenal and starred Corinne Luchaire, Fernand Gravet, and Michel Simon. Chenal's picture enjoyed a mild success. But Carné's sustained disappointment over his abortive enterprise derived not from jealousy over Chenal's accomplishment but from the missed opportunity to antedate and rival more distinguished renditions of the novel, notably Visconti's *Ossessione* (1942) and Tay Garnett's *The Postman Always Rings Twice* (1946). *Thérèse Raquin* provided some retroactive consolation.

"The lovers in my film are more idealized than in the novel, and I also wanted the murder to be much less premeditated." [26] Carné's comment succinctly describes the thrust of his adaptation, which many first reviewers interpreted as unfaithful to Zola. [27] In his preface to *Thérèse Raquin*'s second edition (1868), Zola responded to those who "held their noses while speaking of [the story's] filth and stench": "In *Thérèse Raquin* I aimed to study temperaments, not personalities . . . I chose characters extremely dominated by their nerves and their blood, deprived of free will, and led to each act of their lives by the fatalities of their flesh. Thérèse and Laurent are human brutes, nothing more . . . my starting point [was] the study of temperament and the profound modifications which the organism experiences under the pressure of milieus and circumstances." [28]

In Carné, "flesh" regulates the mutual attraction of Thérèse (Simone Signoret) and Laurent (Raf Vallone). But with characteristic *pudeur* Carné declines to indulge in Zola's dissection of "two living bodies." [29] Carné "idealizes" Zola's protagonists by deemphasizing the sordid character of their liaison; by eliminating Laurent's pecuniary motives for murdering Thérèse's husband, Camille; and by transforming Thérèse from a "brute" into a sympathetic victim of bourgeois mores. For all of Carné's desire to emulate Garnett's *The Postman Always Rings Twice*, the distance separating *Thérèse Raquin* from American film noir is evident in Carné and Spaak's refusal to keep Thérèse sexually treacherous and Laurent criminally depraved. "I have not yet learned to lie," Thérèse tells Laurent early in the film. As the plot unfolds, Thérèse's moral fiber remains intact: invariably she opts for silence over telling untruths. Even

Laurent's act of murder is happenstance: when Camille incites him to scuffle ("You will never have her! . . . You foreigners are all alike!"), Laurent does not anticipate that the door to the train's vestibule will fly open and that Camille will tumble out.

In effect, Carné and Spaak turn Zola's "human beasts" into well-intentioned, disenchanted lovers à la Carné-Prévert. Like Jean and Nelly, François and Françoise, and Gilles and Anne, this gentle couple yearns to be released from suffocating surroundings. And like their predecessors, they collide with uncontrollable forces that eradicate every chance for escape.

In Zola, destiny entails the interplay of physiology and environment. In Carné, circumstance alone determines the future. Feyder's adaptation of *Thérèse Raquin* reportedly diverged little from the novel. According to Léon Moussinac, "In the second part, Feyder came to the melodramatic action without trying to fake, and develop[ed] in detail the odious and cruel psychology of his characters." [30] But Carné recalls that while the audience at the premiere of Feyder's picture was enthusiastic about the first part, which ends with Camille's murder, it was indifferent to the second, in which Camille's ghost haunts the lovers: "The second part . . . fatigued everyone by its absence of genuine peripeteia" (*Vbd*, 321). Carné and Spaak decided, therefore, to modify substantially the second half of Zola's plot in order to allow for a less subjective and more explicitly eventful narrative. They introduced a character not found in the literary source: the sailor (Roland Lesaffre) who claims to have witnessed the murder, proceeds to blackmail Laurent and Thérèse, and, through his own accidental death at the film's end, guarantees Thérèse and Laurent's condemnation by the authorities.

This major plot overhaul yields mixed results. On one hand, it allows Carné to embellish the themes of voyeurism and primal viewing. The first shot of the sailor shows him nestled on a seat in Thérèse and Camille's train compartment, apparently asleep, with a pompon hat covering his eyes. This image resonates with earlier shots of Madame Raquin's black cat—whose name is Monsieur Pompon—nestled on Thérèse's bed. In Zola's text, the cat (who is tiger-striped and named François) witnesses Thérèse's adultery and causes Laurent to hallucinate that the dead Camille's spirit has entered the animal's body; Laurent is finally moved to kill the beast. In the film, the cat is also a witness to Thérèse's affair, and its fixed eyes prefigure those of the paralyzed Madame Raquin (played by character actress Sylvie), who is aware of the crime yet incapable of communicating her knowledge. But an equally powerful correlation holds between the cat's spectral aura and the sailor's psychopathic comport-

104 A relay of petrified stares: Laurent (Raf Vallone) and Thérèse (Simone
Signoret) respond to the revelation of the dying sailor (Roland
Lesaffre) at the climax of *Thérèse Raquin*

ment. Carné's sailor first unnerves Thérèse by prowling catlike outside
the Raquin boutique. Thérèse later describes his sneer as that of "a cat
looking at a bird." In brief, the sailor lends a measure of objective plausibility to Thérèse's state of panic.

On the other hand, the staggering series of plot twists which the sailor
precipitates weakens the film's overall credibility. The lovers' plight
seems resolved when they meet the extortionist's demands, passing on
the benefits paid to Thérèse following her husband's "accident." Thérèse
and Laurent plan to depart for Italy that very night. But when the sailor
takes leave of his prey and walks to the spot opposite the Raquin shop
and apartment where he parked his motorcycle, he fails five times to
trigger the ignition. Occurring with the same rapidity as the final events
in *Le Quai des Brumes*, a boy in knee pants passes beyond the curb to
chase his ball; a huge truck races down the narrow street; and, in an
effort to avoid hitting the boy, the truckdriver swerves his vehicle, runs it
into the sailor, and wounds him mortally. Laurent rushes to the sailor's
aid, carries him back to the Raquin premises, and positions him supine
on the shop's counter top (fig. 104). Staring with the same paralytic intensity as Madame Raquin, the sailor manages to emit the words, "The
letter! The letter!" In a flash Thérèse and Laurent sense the meaning of

these words, to which we, the viewers, have been privy: the sailor arranged for a letter revealing the specifics of the murder to be mailed to an examining magistrate in the event that he failed to return to his hotel by a set time. The final close-ups of Thérèse and Laurent convey their stupefaction and powerlessness. The film's next-to-last shots depict the sailor's letter being handed to the postman. As the camera pulls back and surveys the Lyons skyline, a police siren's screech intensifies.

Carné's effort to naturalize Zola's story thus produces a contrary effect. Like Destin in *Les Portes de la nuit*, the sailor is so much a catalyst of the protagonists' fates that he assumes quasi-metaphysical weight. Thérèse and Laurent are neither the collection of nerves, fibers, blood, and bones Zola conceived them to be nor the relatively healthy and honorable beings Carné wanted them to become. Depriving them of responsibility, the sailor's intervention transforms a potentially compelling psychological drama into a schematized tragic fable.

From today's vantage point *Thérèse Raquin*'s principal allure resides in Simone Signoret's and Roland Lesaffre's performances. In *Nostalgia Isn't What It Used to Be*, Signoret (1921–85) relates that her initial reluctance to play Thérèse stemmed from a decision she took after the shooting of Becker's *Casque d'or* (1952). Eager to become a "devoted, unobtrusive and happy wife" to Yves Montand, whom she had married in December 1951, Signoret announced publicly that she was quitting her profession. After eighteen months of wifedom, however, the actress acceded to Montand's urging that she renew her career and accept the Hakims' offer to star in *Thérèse Raquin*.[31]

Signoret looked forward to working with Carné. Her first role as an identifiable, albeit nonspeaking, screen character was in *Les Visiteurs du soir*, where she played one of the four ladies of the castle. But once she read *Thérèse Raquin*'s script Signoret had qualms about the new part. In a letter to Carné she observed: "I continue to regret that the blackmail is not provoked by [Thérèse and Laurent's] anxiety and is, rather, imposed by destiny, which gives their distress more of a 'thriller' slant than a psychological one. But I am perhaps splitting hairs." Signoret was more vexed by what she called Thérèse's "lifeless" dialogue: "Everything [Thérèse] expresses with respect to love or impassioned hate is frightfully banal. The sole moment in which she speaks like a woman in love is in the tiny, charming dining-room scene when the others are playing the table steeplechase game."[32]

Jacques Prévert was Simone Signoret's close friend. (He was her witness at the wedding to Montand.) Had Prévert written *Thérèse Raquin*, Signoret's role would probably have exuded more of the "passion" which

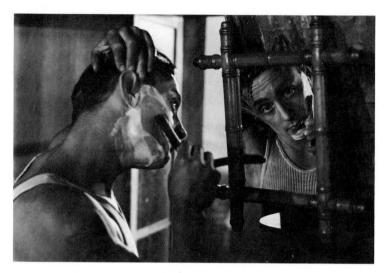

105 Roland Lesaffre in *Thérèse Raquin:* a projection of fearsome narcissism

the actress found lacking in Spaak's dialogue. But Carné was bent on having the film accentuate a woman's repressed desires. *Thérèse Raquin* thus represented a major departure for Signoret. From her first important role as a prostitute in Yves Allégret's *Dédée d'Anvers* (1947) to her portrayal of the heroine in *Casque d'or*, Signoret had established a persona based on feminine warmth, sauciness, and uncomplicated physicality. Obliging her to play a closed and sexually insecure woman, Carné forced Signoret to expand her dramatic range. From her next effort, Clouzot's *Les Diaboliques* (1954), through her Oscar-winning role in Jack Clayton's *Room at the Top* (1958), and even on to late pictures such as Moshe Misrahi's *La Vie devant soi (Madame Rosa*, 1977), Signoret's depictions of outwardly calm but emotionally strained women descend directly from her Thérèse Raquin.

For Roland Lesaffre (b. 1927), *Thérèse Raquin* marked an artistic height. At the film's start, the brawny sensuality projected by Italian actor Raf Vallone makes his Laurent a convincing contrast to Camille's asexuality and a fit complement to Thérèse's repression. But in the film's second half, as the libidinal fiber of the Thérèse-Laurent rapport mollifies, erotic interest shifts to the sailor. Like Pierre Brasseur in *Le Quai des Brumes*, Lesaffre unveils a portrait of perverse narcissism as hypnotic as it is disturbing (fig. 105). By the film's end his performance eclipses both Vallone's and Signoret's. As Bazin noted, the sailor's "unexpected overstepping" of Carné's "traditional Manicheanism" transforms what "a priori ought to have been the most artificial and least pardonable invention of the scenario" into "one of the best, if not the very best, element in the film."[33] Less a criminal than a confused punk unable to readapt to French society after his war experience in Indochina, the sailor is one of the rare Carné villains to elicit authentic compassion.

Carné and Spaak based part of the role on Lesaffre's life. Abandoned in infancy, Roland Lesaffre was a rebel schoolboy who in 1942 became a Resistance fighter in France's Corrèze region. Falsifying his birth date, he joined the Fusiliers Marins in 1943, engaged in combat against the Germans off the North African coast, and fought the Japanese during the liberation of Saigon. Lesaffre relates: "When I say, in the picture, 'My childhood was an endless row of kicks in the rear, my youth a row of gunshot wounds,' it's my personal story that's being told. And believe me, a lot of bourgeois reviewers were very uneasy about our not-too-muffled allusions to the horror of war in Indochina."[34]

The generally accepted account of Lesaffre's introduction to Carné has the storybook quality that colors narratives of Carné's mother's death, his fortuitous encounter with Françoise Rosay, and his first meeting with Jacques Prévert. In September 1949 Lesaffre found himself demobilized and penniless in Paris. One morning he learned that an "old friend" from his fighting days in the Mediterranean was making a motion picture at the studios in Joinville. Lesaffre decided to pay the friend a surprise visit that very day. Passing unnoticed through the studio's front gate, the ex-navy man walked directly onto sound stage B and into the frame of a shot in progress. The picture was *La Marie du port*. The director was Marcel Carné, who, infuriated by this intruder's presence, brusquely pushed him aside. But when Lesaffre rushed to embrace his "old friend"—who was none other than ex-seaman Jean Gabin—Carné's pique diminished. At Gabin's request the director hired Lesaffre as an extra. And on that day Roland Lesaffre became—and has remained—Carné's closest friend.[35]

Carné encouraged the twenty-two-year-old to study acting. He arranged cameo appearances for him in prestigious films, including his own. In *Juliette ou la clef des songes* Lesaffre portrayed the Legionnaire whose fancies of a lofty past crumble when a soothsayer reads his palm and sees "nothing but suffering and fatigue, no friends, no girls, and no pleasure." In *Casque d'or* Lesaffre played Anatole, the blond waiter-turned-police-informant whom Leca (Claude Dauphin) assassinates. His first major role, as *Thérèse Raquin*'s sailor, already exhibited the two facets of what would become the Lesaffre persona: the neurotic criminal and the sympathetic down-and-out. His triumph in *Thérèse Raquin* led to a part in Hitchcock's *To Catch a Thief* (1954) and to supporting roles in more than sixty features. Lesaffre has appeared in every Carné film since 1953 with the exception of *Le Pays d'où je viens*, which was shot during the year he worked in Japanese pictures and married actress Yoko Tani (1956).

To the extent that he served as Lesaffre's mentor and protector, Carné's relationship to the young actor bears comparison with Cocteau's to Jean Marais and Visconti's to Alain Delon. Lesaffre arguably had more raw talent than either Marais or Delon. If he failed to acquire their stature, it was not for lack of beauty, screen charisma, or ambition. It was partly because of Carné's inability to groom a temperament as fiery as his own. As the years passed and stardom eluded him, it was Lesaffre who more and more protected and groomed Carné—or at least the Carné image. Lesaffre became Carné's unofficial manager, agent, publicist, and archivist, and, above all, an indefatigable defender of Carné's professional worth.

In the early 1970s Henri Langlois, co-founder and secretary general of the Cinémathèque Française, wrote to Lesaffre: "I shall never forget the courage and moral force that has enabled you to remain true to yourself while at the same time never failing to rush into combat . . . for and at the side of Carné. I will not say that friendship is rare . . . But true friendship, and everyone knows it, is extremely uncommon. For it consists in sacrificing all that one possesses, as a mother does for her child, and as only two lovers who are willing to die for each other know how to do."[36] Langlois understood that Roland Lesaffre had replaced Jacques Prévert as Carné's principal support and inspiration.

As the films of the Carné-Prévert era gave way to those of the Carné-Lesaffre era, there occurred a shift from women's iconization toward a celebration of the male body. A boxing and track-and-field champion in the navy, Roland Lesaffre had an exquisite physique. Carné exposed and glorified it in their next picture, *L'Air de Paris* (1954). But in *Thérèse Raquin*, too, Lesaffre's screen power results amply from his projection of fearsome, tantalizing sexuality. His cunning rebelliousness, the electric pleasure he takes in taunting Thérèse and Laurent, and his association with tattoos, straight razors, torn underwear, leather jackets, and motorcycles, make the sailor a close cousin to the protagonist of Kenneth Anger's *Fireworks* (1947), to Death's emissaries in Cocteau's *Orphée* (1950), and to the bad boys played by James Dean and the early Marlon

Brando. Injecting a measure of sexual erraticm into *Thérèse Raquin*, Lesaffre reactivates viewer fascination with individual difference and unconventional longings of the kind Zola provoked in readers of his novel. He restores some of the moral murkiness which Carné and Spaak's "idealization" of the central couple sought to eliminate, and he guarantees the picture's film noir quality.

A distinguishing feature of American film noir is what David Bordwell calls "a challenge to the prominence of heterosexual romance."[37] Bordwell is referring to the situation of a sexually alluring but potentially treacherous heroine and the resulting uncertainty of the male protagonist, who typically finds the heroine "barring access to his goal or holding him in her power." From our perspective the commanding point is that in *Thérèse Raquin* Carné reverses this schema with respect to gender: the sexual magnetism of an *homme fatal* generates the film's atmosphere of fear, peril, and uncertainty.

L'Air de Paris shares little with American film noir. But it is Carné's most explicit "challenge to the prominence of heterosexual romance." A long-time prizefight enthusiast, Carné claims to have known the boxing milieu sufficiently well "to avoid the crude errors that disappointed me so in prior [boxing] films" (*Vbd*, 331). The picture's ostensible aim, as he relates in his memoirs, was "to evoke the courageous lives of young amateurs who, having barely finished their often arduous day's work, rush to a gym to 'put on the gloves' and fight with all their heart, clinging to the hope of one day entering a ring" (*Vbd*, 331). Validation of the film's having achieved this goal came two months prior to *L'Air de Paris*'s public release. In July 1954 the jury of the Prix Populistes du Cinéma (established in 1953) bestowed its highest honor on Carné for "*L'Air de Paris* and the entirety of his oeuvre," and awarded the picture's star, Roland Lesaffre, its prize for the year's best male actor.[38]

Yet *L'Air de Paris*'s evocation of a working-class milieu is rather skimpy. As the film progresses, the glittery world of high fashion and interior design receives nearly as much attention as that of laborers, Arab-run hotels, and daily life in Paris's Grenelle district. The picture rings truest in neither its scenic nor its sociological dimensions but, as one reviewer put it, in the trainer's "slightly gruff affection . . . for the kid" and the latter's "violent susceptibility . . . to this unfeigning friendship."[39]

Carné's plot summary in *La Vie à belles dents* is telling. He writes: "The story is as simple as can be. Among the boys who come to train at his gym, the owner [Victor, played by Gabin] takes notice of a young working-class fellow [Dédé, played by Lesaffre] who is particularly

106 A celebration of male homosensuality: Gabin, Lesaffre, and Arletty in
L'Air de Paris

gifted. In the hope of turning him into the champion he never was, he
decides to devote all his efforts to training him. His hope flourishes when
the young trainee's first amateur fight at The Central proves promising.
But just then a woman [Corinne, played by Marie Daems] comes and
spoils everything . . . potentially destroying the hopes which the manager
grounded in his protégé" (*Vbd*, 332–34).

Carné might also have mentioned the trainer's wife, Blanche (Arletty),
and her unhappiness over the attention her husband lavishes on Dédé;
the local grocers' daughter, Maria (Maria-Pia Casilio), who has an unreciprocated crush on the young hopeful; and Chantal (Simone Paris),
the socialite antique dealer who complicates Corinne's liaison with Dédé.
In passing over these characters, however, Carné's plot précis is at one
with the film's gender dynamic: the conflation of all women into a single
force that threatens the integrity of a male environment. Sociologically,
L'Air de Paris is a cautionary tale that pits *le haut monde*'s deceitfulness
against *le petit peuple*'s integrity. Psychologically, *L'Air de Paris* is an
apology for male camaraderie (fig. 106).

Early in the film Victor-Gabin sits on the edge of Dédé-Lesaffre's bed
and confesses: "I've got a kind of bee in my bonnet . . . to create someday
a great boxer . . . With you, I think I have found him . . . So, everything
I do for you could also be because it suits me, too . . . It's an exchange."

Given Lesaffre's real-life closeness to Gabin (the two "old friends" supposedly boxed together during the war), these lines might be interpreted as the elder actor's publicly passing on the early Gabin image to a successor. Indeed, a Lesaffre-Gabin resemblance did not escape *L'Air de Paris*'s first viewers. Bazin wrote: "There is something of the young Gabin in Lesaffre's role, the Gabin of *Gueule d'amour* and *Pépé le Moko*, but without the serious strength, the kind of wisdom-derived-from-misfortune, that now prevails in the older Gabin. Lesaffre makes me think of Gabin in counterpoint, several octaves higher, as if played on the slimmest and tautest string of a violin."[40] The nature of their difference demands greater precision. In *Le Quai des Brumes* Gabin's convincing blend of toughness and sentiment owed much to Prévert's affecting dialogue and to the actor's authentic attraction to Michèle Morgan. In *L'Air de Paris* Lesaffre is most Gabinesque when he fights: his body in combat engenders a masculine lyricism that combines strength with sensitivity. Lesaffre diverges from the Gabin persona, and gives a less credible performance, in the sentimental scenes with Marie Daems: his movements become stilted and his speech turns strained. This awkwardness around women evokes Barrault's Baptiste in *Les Enfants du paradis*. But where the visionary mime chose to substitute a fetish for a genuine woman, the pragmatic pugilist learns that life's rewards are attainable only through total disregard for women.

Dédé is insufficiently self-aware to be labeled a misogynist. Nor is he obviously homosexual. But he and Gabin's Victor are protagonists in a film that extols homosensuality, iconizes the male body, and portrays women as, at best, superfluous and, at worst, impediments to men's self-realization. Arletty's participation in such a film is at once rueful and fascinating. In the picture's opening credit sequence her name appears second, after Gabin's. But the script relegates Arletty to a de facto supporting role. The actress who, in *Les Enfants du paradis*, was the awesome embodiment of female mystery now plays a frumpish housewife nagging at her husband to move south and open a modest health club. Blanche's occasional sarcasms echo Raymonde's in *Hôtel du Nord*. Her patient endurance recalls Clara's in *Le Jour se lève*. But these vestiges of scintillation and nobility of soul have minimal bearing on *L'Air de Paris*'s story. The woman who served as the object of Carné's most complex fantasies no longer commands the director's interest. With the adoring care he once heaped on Arletty, Carné now photographs Lesaffre in erotically charged contexts: showering in the nude, being massaged by Gabin, lounging in silk pajama bottoms. Arletty herself gives expression to the change. While making Dédé's bed, Blanche confides to Maria: "Monsieur is looking for 'young hopefuls'! (*Pointing to the bed and thinking of Dédé*) . . . But when it becomes as serious as this, I think I'd prefer that he get involved with some bitch!"

Blanche's wish goes unsatisfied. The film's final scene finds Victor and Dédé standing together and peering at the Seine. Reminiscent in form and tone of the classic Carné setup for male-female lovers, a series of medium-close two-shots shows Victor grasping Dédé's closed fist and prying it open gently. It contains the gold charm which Corinne left Dédé as a souvenir of their brief romance. Victor hurls the charm into the river. He consoles Dédé by saying, "You don't need a souvenir . . . You have a future." He then places his arm around Dédé's shoulder, and the two men walk slowly beyond the camera's field of vision.

In September 1982, at the close of the fiftieth Venice Biennial, the festival's jury awarded the Gold Lion to Wim Wenders for *The State of Things (Der Stand der Dinge)*. The jury members were Luis Garcia Berlanga, Mario Monicelli, Gillo Pontecorvo, Frank Perry, Satyajit Ray, Andrei Tarkovsky—and Marcel Carné, who served as its president. Following the announcement of prizes Carné delivered a statement to the press: "I would like to add a personal note. As president of the jury, I must express regret at not having convinced my colleagues to place *Querelle*, the film by R. W. Fassbinder, on the list of honors. In effect, I was the only one to defend the film. Nonetheless, I persist in believing that, controversial though it is, R. W. Fassbinder's last work, whether one wishes it to be so or not, whether one deplores it or takes pleasure in it, will one day have its place in the history of the cinema." [41]

Fassbinder's posthumously shown adaptation of Genet's novel *Querelle de Brest* is perhaps the Western cinema's most powerful expression of male homoeroticism. In sharing his opinion with the international press, Carné made a political as well as an aesthetic statement. He declared his difference, his conviction, and his displeasure over an industry in which homophobia continues to prevail.

This remarkable episode illumines the extent to which an understanding of Carné's postwar creative decline must take into account the accident of Carné's chronology. *L'Air de Paris* is not an especially good film. But it points to a new direction which Carné, without Prévert, might have followed had the social climate of the 1950s been different: the cinematic exploration of themes relating to homosexuality. Carné, however, is among the last of a generation of narrative filmmakers—including Eisenstein, Murnau, and Vigo—for whom the expression of homosexual drives and conflicts could occur only through metaphor and allegory. Carné's technique, vision, and values are marked indelibly by the repression and covertness demanded of mainstream film artists in earlier decades of this century. Witnessing the possibilities, if not the fact, of a revolution in sexual expression during the 1970s and 1980s, Carné was nonetheless unprepared and unconditioned to emulate the Pasolinis, Bertoluccis, and Fassbinders he so admires.

L'Air de Paris's oblique treatment of the homoerotic confirms that the emblem for the later Carné style remains *Les Enfants du paradis*'s pulled theater curtain—a device that provides only momentary glimpses onto intimacy. Indeed, the drama of Carné's post-Prévert life and career lies in the competing attractions of the ideal of nakedness and the reality of the mask.

CHAPTER 16

Carné and the New Wave

In January 1980 François Truffaut reflected in private: "I have never really had the opportunity to exchange views with Carné. Frankly, I do not think there would be much point to it. But if I could, I would say to him, 'What we liked among your works has become even better with the years; and what we didn't is really of no importance anymore.'" [1]

Six months before Truffaut's death, he and Carné had their only sustained encounter. On April 14, 1984, the municipality of Romilly, in the Aube region east of Paris, inaugurated a 278-seat "*salle* Marcel Carné" and a 166-seat "*salle* François Truffaut" in its renovated Eden Theater. The occasion did not allow for an extended exchange of words. But during the dedication ceremony Carné's most celebrated detractor of the 1950s invoked jokingly "the statute of limitations" and informed Carné and guests: "I have made twenty-three pictures. Well, I would swap them all for the chance to have made *Les Enfants du paradis*." [2]

Truffaut's public views on Carné had softened prior to this event. In a 1975 radio broadcast he stated: "I do not think that Carné and Prévert's ideas and their way of perceiving life and cinema are old-fashioned. I think that if a film as beautiful as *Les Enfants du paradis* were released now, it would be considered the best film of the year." In the same interview Truffaut asserted: "When we were critics, Marcel Carné was not our favorite target because he was already in trouble with producers and he was not making the films he wanted to do. Our attack against the French cinema was directed at . . . a *cinéma de scénaristes*, which we found conformist. Carné was a bit on the margin of that; and we were also still smitten by the great films he had made before and during the war—so much that we always had a certain respect for him." [3]

Such statements are a far cry from Truffaut's assessment of Carné in the 31 October 1956 issue of the weekly *Arts; lettres; spectacles*. Ostensibly reviewing Carné's *Le Pays d'où je viens*, Truffaut began with an ad hominem assault on the director. He called Carné "a very confused spirit" who "has never known how to evaluate a scenario [and] has never known how to choose a subject. For a long time others performed these tasks for him, and for years we have been offered films created by Jacques Prévert and rendered in images by Marcel Carné. Henceforth Carné is condemned to be 'taken in' by the first screenwriter to come along." [4]

Truffaut's mellowing may reflect his own career trajectory. Like Carné, the maker of *Jules and Jim* suffered a fairly steep fall from critical grace. In both cases the decline related to expectations triggered by brilliant early works. If critics in the ranks of the Parisian intelligentsia often accused the later Truffaut of lacking "substance, purpose, and depth," pundits beyond France remarked frequently that not far short of thirty years after his dogged attacks on *le cinéma de papa*, Truffaut himself had seemed to lapse into cinematic *papa*dom. [5]

In the early 1950s Truffaut wrote regularly for *Cahiers du Cinéma* and *Arts*. One associates Truffaut more with *Cahiers du Cinéma* partly because that monthly's most notable contributors—including future New Wave directors Godard, Chabrol, Rohmer, and Rivette—shared and promulgated many of Truffaut's bold assumptions about film criticism and practice. These assumptions, which eventually became known as the *politique des auteurs*, provided a conceptual framework for the rereading and revision of cinematic history. At its worst the framework cultivated dogmatism, favoritism, and an obsession with hierarchy. At its best it engendered pathbreaking commentary that broadened the range of values and tastes in filmgoers and filmmakers alike. Unfortunately for Marcel Carné, the framework was not conducive to a deep appreciation of his oeuvre.

It is a mistake, however, to take Truffaut's pronouncements as representative of the magazine's stance. Most *Cahiers du Cinéma* writers treated Carné quite fairly. In the June 1951 issue, for example, Frédéric Laclos pointed out the injustice being dealt Carné when fellow journalists gloated over his lesser works while pretending that the masterworks never existed. [6] In 1953 the magazine's editors balanced a hastily penned negative critique of *Thérèse Raquin* in October ("The [picture's] true victim is Thérèse, and Carné is her assassin") with Jacques Doniol-Valcroze's reasoned and generally favorable commentary in December ("One would have to be prejudiced not to recognize the natural mark of a great director"). [7] Jean Desternes, in his November 1954 assessment of *L'Air de Paris*, bent over backward to stress the film's strengths as well as its deficiencies. [8] And the journal's 1957 catalogue of "Sixty French Directors" offered a remarkably balanced profile. [9]

Truffaut, however, relished controversy. In response to Truffaut's vitriolic review of a monograph on Carné in the summer of 1953, the book's
author, Jean Quéval, sent a letter of protest to *Cahiers*. It appeared in the
September issue alongside Truffaut's sarcastic reply. Quéval made clear
that his letter was motivated by a desire to safeguard Carné's good name
from the onslaught of "a venomous iconoclast." [10] In all fairness, it is
notable that tucked among his injurious remarks on Quéval's book and
on its subject, Truffaut refers to Carné as "a filmmaker I admire." [11]
Nonetheless, Truffaut jabbed Carné relentlessly throughout 1954 and
1955.[12] His coup de grâce was the review of *Le Pays d'où je viens* in
Arts. Its ramifications for Carné's reputation are palpable in the effect it
had upon as independent a thinker as Eric Rohmer. In December 1955
Rohmer spoke fondly of how his first viewing of "Marcel Carné's film
[*Le Quai des Brumes*] unveiled the brilliance of a poetry which I had not
known to be within the powers of the seventh art." [13] A year later—and
less than two months after Truffaut's dismissal of Carné as Prévert's *metteur en images*—Rohmer echoed Truffaut by dubbing Carné "a good
illustrator" and by insinuating that in contrast to Clair, Cocteau, Becker,
Bresson, Clément, and Tati, Marcel Carné had "nothing to say." [14]

Truffaut's quip was not original. In April 1945 Henri Jeanson—using
the pen name Huguette ex-MICRO—wrote in *Le Canard enchaîné*:
"Carné does not make actors perform. He photographs them. He is not
a director [*un metteur en scène*]: he is an image renderer [*un metteur en
images*]." [15] In 1951 Claude Mauriac proffered aphorisms that were no
less cutting: "The degree to which Marcel Carné is given free rein is
probably directly proportional to his producing execrable work"; "We
must thus wonder whether his first masterpieces attained such a high
degree of poetry in spite of Carné, and precisely to the extent that his
creations eluded his control"; "It is not Carné who has declined; it is we
who, from the start, overestimated him." [16]

These condemnations were meant to imply that the principal creators
of the Carné canon were his scriptwriters. Yet as the 1950s progressed,
Prévert, too, suffered denigration. A 1957 *Arts* survey of top scenarists
acknowledges him as "a true *auteur*." [17] But for Rohmer in *Cahiers du
Cinéma*, "our generation looks kindly on Prévert only better to demolish
those who imitate him." [18] For Henri Agel, who contributed occasionally
to *Cahiers*, "We can today ask if the partnership enjoyed and, alas, still
enjoys such brilliant acclaim precisely to the extent that Prévert's sham
gold—false poetry, phony psychology, and counterfeit language—was
wedded to Carné's meretricious academicism." [19]

Agel's statement appeared in his 1959 book, *Les Grands Cinéastes*. In
a second edition, published in 1967, Agel chose to eliminate his chapter

on Carné: "Realizing that I changed my ideas concerning a number of filmmakers, I considered that the most honest and *sound* [*saine*] solution . . . was to neither strain nor restrict myself to maintaining in this new edition men who no longer inspired much interest in me" (my italics).[20] In French, the adjective *sain(e)* can mean "healthy" and "wholesome" as well as "sound." Attention to the connotations of Agel's vocabulary in his 1959 commentary on Carné is instructive: "It is extraordinary that from 1938 to 1948 so few critics were sensitive to . . . [Carné's] *monstrous* degradation of Vigo's sublime lyricism . . . [Carné's] set purpose to *discredit life* . . . is not so much what ruffles us today: that matter belongs especially to the domain of *psychoanalysis*. It is rather that the flight into unreality . . . the lyric nihilism . . . is *spineless* and as *sugary* as a set piece. The *mental confusion* evident in all these films (Prévert is responsible for a good part of it) is felt in the *anesthetized flow* of images that make *Les Visiteurs*, for example, despite the appearances that have deceived so many people, the most *antispiritual* film in the world. Here all is *soft, limp, nerveless*—in the clinical sense—and, to put it in a word, *inverted* [*inverti*]. As soon as Prévert's verve or Spaak's craftiness (*Thérèse Raquin*) abandons Carné, as soon as he falls victim to Jacques Sigurd's inconsistencies (*L'Air de Paris, Les Tricheurs*), the sinking of this universe into a sort of *refined malaise* becomes inevitable. It is an *ethic*, but also an aesthetic, of *stagnation* and *rot*"[21] (my italics; in French, the word *inverti*, used as a noun, means "homosexual").

Homophobic overtones color the statements of many of Carné's critics. As is evident in his memoirs, Carné has been alert to heterosexist assaults (*Vbd*, 288, for example). By the end of his directorial career Truffaut felt comfortable treating homosexuality: the awkward representations of homosexual males in *Baisers volés* (*Stolen Kisses*, 1968) and *La Nuit américaine* (*Day for Night*, 1973) give way to humane, matter-of-fact depictions of lesbianism and male homosexuality in *Le Dernier Métro*. Nevertheless, the tenor of Agel's 1959 critique makes one wonder if sexual orientation was a half-hidden item on the agenda of Truffaut's early attack program. In his review of *Le Pays d'où je viens*, the twenty-four-year-old critic dubbed Carné's handling of children "sacrilege" and worthy of investigation by "Paris police headquarters." He also described Carné as having employed singer-actor Gilbert Bécaud in a manner "contrary to his nature."

Carné himself resorted to malicious tactics when retaliation seemed opportune. In an interview with *Le Figaro Littéraire* in February 1965, Carné reflected on the New Wave phenomenon: "It is very simple. We experienced a period in which a new director was born each morning . . . And, out of two hundred of these 'creators,' how many survived? Three or four. Once emerged from their autobiographical stammerings, the others could only demonstrate their incapacity to build a story. They could exhibit only their congenital impotence!"[22]

Had Carné been able to give more explicit, personal expression to the homoerotic in his films, it is possible that the young Truffaut would have supported his enterprise more enthusiastically. Truffaut was an immediate champion of Cocteau, whose oeuvre, filmic and otherwise, is stamped by a homosexual sensibility. Truffaut admired what he has called Cocteau's "cinema of jubilation" because *Le Sang d'un poète*'s maker "exposed himself constantly" and "worked to satisfy himself."[23] In his 1954 manifesto, "A Certain Tendency of the French Cinema," Truffaut decries "the pederastic relationships of characters in [Clouzot's] *Le Salaire de la peur* [*The Wages of Fear*, 1953]."[24] Truffaut's reservation, however, concerns not the theme but its literary, anticinematic treatment. For Truffaut, a director is an *homme de cinéma* only to the degree that, like Cocteau, he eludes the tyranny of *littérateurs*, or professional screenwriters. Only then can he discharge the spontaneous and improvisational impulses that vitalize the works of the French directors Truffaut idolized: Vigo, Gance, Bresson, Ophuls, Tati, and above all Renoir.

Therein lay the principal thrust of Truffaut's antipathy for Carné. Truffaut recognized that Carné's prewar and Occupation films were superior to those belonging to the postwar "tradition of quality," a term coined by Jean-Pierre Barrot in 1953 to describe the success of directors such as Delannoy, Christian-Jaque, Jean Faurez, and Henri Calef.[25] But Carné remained, for Truffaut, the paradigm of a team director as opposed to an *auteur*. Carné's "stubborn overcarefulness, too many hesitations, obsession with detail, too many rehearsals and reshots" made a film like *Le Pays d'où je viens* pale by comparison with Sacha Guitry's self-scripted *Assassins et voleurs* (1956), a picture Truffaut applauded for its being "innocent of any esthetic ambitions."[26]

Truffaut was also uncomfortable with the view of humanity embodied in Carné's oeuvre. He concedes, in "A Certain Tendency of the French Cinema," that Prévert's scripts were implicitly uplifting: "If most of his characters were . . . burdened by all the sins of creation, there was nonetheless always room for a couple on whom, like a new Adam and Eve, history was going to repeat itself." But in lashing all current French films that exhibited "the habitual dose of gloom, nonconformism, and easy daring" and "abject beings . . . [who] when they are not vile are at best inordinately grotesque," Truffaut obliquely indicts Carné and the prewar school of "darkness" that was the model for much post-Liberation cinema.[27]

My discussion of *Les Visiteurs du soir* highlighted the political dimensions of Carné's stolid, closed-film aesthetic. Viewer discomfort with the picture, I suggested, relates in part to its allegorization of the passive and inflexible attitudes that facilitated France's defeat to Germany in 1939–40. We have also seen that Carné's prewar films gave powerful expression to the expiring Third Republic's political paralysis, isolation, and defeatism. At least half of Truffaut's *Cahiers du Cinéma* colleagues were too young to have been called for military service in 1939. But they all lived through the Occupation. Unlike older intellectuals of the Sartre-Camus generation, Truffaut and his contemporaries at *Cahiers* were impatient both with the past that had brought about the present and with those in the present obsessively embittered over the past. As Stanley Kaufmann notes, "These younger men seemingly wanted to wash their hands of the ledger-keeping of history, to put their vigor into fresh visions in a field much less trammeled by the past than were others." [28]

The social vision conveyed by Renoir's prewar films was often less than optimistic. *La Chienne* was as much a forerunner of 1950s *réalisme noir* as was *Le Quai des Brumes*. But Renoir's emigration to America made it convenient for the *Cahiers* group to bracket his films' politics and to focus instead on their aesthetics. Here was a "humanist" with "universal" appeal whose oeuvre transcended a specifically French context. Renoir's two patriotic Hollywood-made pictures, *This Land Is Mine* (1943) and *Salute to France* (1944), constituted reassuring evidence of at least long-distance resistance against the enemy. Moreover, Renoir had confided that his reluctance to return to France was tied to his discomfort over resuming business with producers whose loyalties he found questionable: "I cannot stop believing that the producers who made films during the Occupation did not do so without entering more or less into agreements with the Germans . . . I see their names in the newspapers; they get on with Americans just as they did with Nazis. All that disgusts me a bit, and I would prefer to work in France the day the cinema is in new hands." [29]

Carné's political dossier was more problematic. Having remained in France, having abetted the Occupier's hopes for the French film industry, and, above all, having taken no clear-cut public position on France's plight, Carné typified the everyday French person's response to the Occupation. For those seeking "to wash their hands of the ledger-keeping of history," the dismissal of Marcel Carné on aesthetic grounds was tantamount to exorcising a distasteful part of France's political and historical identity.

Many commentators on the early New Wave and its relation to *Ca-*

hiers du Cinéma have questioned the movement's ostensibly apolitical character. John Hess, for example, argues that *la politique des auteurs* was "a justification, couched in aesthetic terms, of a culturally conservative, politically reactionary attempt to remove film from the realm of social and political concern." [30] Jim Hillier proposes that the *Cahiers* critics' extraordinary predilection for American cinema derived in large measure from a comforting perception that Hollywood pictures were "socially 'critical,' but critical without being directly 'political.'" [31] Perhaps Raymond Durgnat puts the matter most pointedly: "One can understand why Hawks's films mean so much to French intellectuals. His very simplicity can have a tonic, and a real value, as a corrective to various debilitating concomitants of European culture ('confusionism,' snobbery, contempt for decision, action, efficacy, simplicity)." [32]

In 1962 Godard proclaimed: "The Americans, who are much more stupid when it comes to analysis, instinctively bring off very complex scripts. They also have a gift for the kind of simplicity which brings depth . . . The Americans are real and natural. But this attitude means something over there. We in France must find something that means something—find the French attitude as they have found the American attitude." [33]

No corpus of films conveyed a French attitude more consistently than Marcel Carné's did between 1937 and 1951. But that socially drenched, pessimistic vision was precisely what the postwar generation wished to disown. Michel Marie observes that the "ideological concept" shaping the New Wave stressed youth: "young films representing a young country: France at the beginning of the Fifth Republic." [34] I would suggest that the speed, spontaneity, mobility, and informality that characterized most New Wave productions in 1958–59 were a reaction against contrary values associated as much with the superannuated military leaders responsible for France's rout in 1940 as with Marcel Carné's monuments of French film culture. By relegating Carné's oeuvre to a state of critical belittlement and, eventually, near neglect, the New Wave critic-filmmakers were rewriting France's political as well as cinematic history. Perhaps they did not realize at the time that they were themselves thereby perpetuating an escape from moral responsibility and critical accountability.

Superficially, the film that triggered Truffaut's tirade in *Arts* is atypical of Carné. His only musical and his first color picture, *Le Pays d'où je viens* (1956) is a lighthearted divertissement that takes its dramatic and pictorial cues from Hollywood nostalgia musicals, such as Minnelli's *Meet Me in St. Louis* (1944) and Leonard's *In the Good Old Summertime* (1949). The disproportion between the intensity of Truffaut's attack and the occasion's slightness may reflect Truffaut's resentment that the French director most associated with gloom was having a try at an American genre whose intrinsic zest enthralled Truffaut and his *Cahiers du Cinéma* confreres. Ironically, Carné's attempt at diversification bears out auteurist premises. Technically and thematically *Le Pays d'où je viens* is at one with Carné's other works: it is a fable of identity that unfolds within a closed, impeccably crafted world of unreality. But in 1956 the young Truffaut was not prepared to acknowledge, as he did twenty-three years later, that "Carné's team spirit would probably have made him thrive in Hollywood . . . Carné has an instinct for American-style genre direction." [35]

Le Pays d'où je viens was in fact a "package" to which Carné, much like a major-studio American director, was brought in only after the picture's overall concept had been determined and its principal actors had been selected. Producer Clément Duhour envisioned the project as a pre-Christmas vehicle to launch Gilbert Bécaud's film career. Although Carné claims to have "winced" initially at the prospect of such a confining work situation (*Vbd*, 341), the production had manifold appeal. First, like Gabin and Montand, Bécaud was a product of the Paris music hall. Here was Carné's first opportunity to help inaugurate a screen persona that would capitalize on a celebrity's music-hall mystique rather than transfigure it. Second, the producers planned a supporting role for Claude Brasseur (b. 1936) in his movie début. The chance to direct Pierre Brasseur's son would confer an *en famille* character on the undertaking. It would also furnish ammunition against those assailing Carné's remoteness from contemporary experience: Brasseur was to play a teenage tough who defines himself by hot rods, transistor radios, and loden-green coats. Finally, the project would afford Carné an occasion to work in color.

French color featuremaking dates from the productions of Pagnol's *La Belle Meunière* and Tati's *Jour de fête*, both shot in 1948. Until 1955, however, color pictures accounted for less than two percent of commercial production in France. Carné's eagerness to indulge in color was the overriding consideration in his accepting Duhour's offer. Given the picture's festive theme, he and cinematographer Philippe Agostini decided to bathe the screen with "the saturated colored style of holiday greeting cards" (*Vbd*, 342).

The story takes place in a snow-covered Savoie town named Saint-

Parfait. It begins on the afternoon before Christmas and ends twenty-four hours later. Eric Perceval (Gilbert Bécaud), an extravagant bon vivant whom two detectives are pursuing, takes refuge in Saint-Parfait. Eric's wealthy uncle Ludovic (Jean Toulet) has hired these men to bring his profligate nephew home and to his senses. When Eric peers through the window of the local brasserie, he is astonished to discover that the musician at the piano, Julien Barrère (Gilbert Bécaud), is his double. As introverted as Eric is outgoing, Julien loves the brasserie's barmaid, Marinette (Françoise Arnoul), but he is too shy to make his feelings known. Anonymously, Julien has been placing an edelweiss on Marinette's windowsill each day. Marinette patiently awaits the moment when her secret admirer will identify himself. But when the town's young ruffian, Roland (Claude Brasseur), causes her to lose her job, Marinette decides to leave for Grenoble with her orphaned brother, Michel (Jean-Pierre Bremmer), and sister, Sophie (Gaby Basset). These youngsters, however, have already encountered Eric, who convinces them that he is X–27, one of Santa Claus's novice helpers. X–27 promises the children to fulfill their wishes, which include having Marinette meet her dream lover.

As the plot unfolds, Eric woos Marinette under Julien's name and seems almost to fall in love with her; Marinette becomes aroused by Julien's apparently newfound aggressiveness but considers his sentimentality more pleasing; and the detectives seize Julien, who confounds Eric's uncle when he is shown to lack "the Perceval birthmark." By the film's end, Marinette regains her job; the children receive the presents they hoped for; Julien and Marinette marry; and Eric manages yet again to elude the clutches of his uncle's detectives, who still trail him wildly. The picture concludes as it began, with distance shots of Eric walking alone on a mountainous highway beyond the town limits.

Le Pays d'où je viens most distinguishes itself from contemporaneous American color musicals in its lack of dance. Two years earlier Françoise Arnoul unveiled extraordinary dancing capabilities as Nini, the female lead in Renoir's *French Cancan*. Carné shies away from physical abandon, making his film showcase Bécaud's predominantly vocal gifts. Pairing Bécaud in a dance number with Arnoul was feasible, but it would have worked to her advantage, not his. Moreover, the physical intimacy which a dance duo implies would have been out of character for both the inhibited Bécaud-Julien and the loner Bécaud-Eric. During one of his four songs, "Mon Coeur éclate," Bécaud does dance briefly. Tellingly, it is a solo performance.

Much of the picture's brio resides in sight gags reminiscent of René

Clair, such as the car chases and the enter-exit door play in the church. But Carné's camera movements, editing, and mise en scène are no more light-handed here than in his serious films. The essential mobility of *Le Pays d'où je viens* is thematic—Truffaut might have said "literary." It pertains principally to Julien's doubling, that is, his seeming capacity to be himself and another simultaneously. It descends more from comic opera than from modern ballet. With respect to his female protagonist, Carné reverts to iconization. Most obvious in the scene where Marinette dons an evening gown, Carné freezes the actress in poses that preclude a projection of authentic vitality. Nonetheless, *Le Pays d'où je viens* reveals a relatively relaxed and unguarded Carné. The satiric portrayal of Eric's uncle and the two detectives is broad and rollicksome. The music is sportive: a violin and muted trumpet play the voices of unseen partners in telephone conversations; a repeated mambo passage punctuates the conservative uncle's search for his nephew; and the overtures to *William Tell* and *Lakmé*, as performed by a local trio, deflate the seriousness viewers might attach to the plot imbroglio. *Le Pays d'où je viens* also contains the only woman in Carné's oeuvre to exude raw sex appeal. Portrayed by the buxom redhead Madeleine Lebeau, the divorced pharmacist Madame Théron likes virile men and makes them know it.

Perhaps the most revelatory departure from Carné's habitual restraint in matters sexual occurs near the film's start and end. Two accidental slips of the hand—the first Roland's, the second Julien's—cause Marinette to lose her wraparound skirt and expose her bare legs and panties. Truffaut singled out this gag as being "in the worst of taste for a film that pretends to be charming and pleasant."[36] Yet both times the stunt is executed briskly, blithely, and with minimal traces of sexism. In light of the momentousness of primal viewing in Carné, the nonchalance with which this gag takes place is all the more remarkable.

Indeed, *Le Pays d'où je viens* reconciles values that are mutually antagonistic in Carné's more serious films. For all his deviation from stereotypic masculinity, Bécaud-Julien complies with gusto to society's expectation that men must marry and generate families. For all his manly appeal to women, Bécaud-Eric rejects heterosexist dogma. Eric spends the night with the pharmacist. But like Montand in *Les Portes de la nuit*, Philipe in *Juliette ou la clef des songes*, and Lesaffre in *L'Air de Paris*, Bécaud-Eric ultimately repudiates women, romance, and marriage. Like individualist "outlaw heroes" of classic American films who arrive on the scene to involve themselves with fostering the community's values but just as speedily disappear in order to preserve their difference, Bécaud-Eric travels alone at the film's close.

In the picture's shooting script, the department-store manager has a bit of dialogue that was not filmed but is central to the movie's meaning. Guiding Marinette and Eric through the store, he remarks: "Here is the jewel of our showcases: the bedroom . . . As you see, we have adopted the double bed. Twin beds have proved unsuccessful in this region."[37] Leaving to Bécaud-Julien this region where double beds are the norm, Bécaud-Eric returns to (or continues to quest for) another land—the *pays* of the film's title, which translates literally as "the land from which I come." Thanks to the conventions of musical comedy, *Le Pays d'où je viens* exorcises, at once, the panic of being different and the threat of conformity.

The demons of difference reassume a tragic cast in Carné's last popular success, *Les Tricheurs (The Cheaters)*. *Les Tricheurs* won the Grand Prix du Cinéma for 1958. Independent polls conducted by *Le Figaro* and *Cinémonde* designated it as "best French film of the year." *Les Tricheurs* was also the highest-grossing picture of the 1958–59 season. Françoise Giroud, then editor-in-chief of *L'Express*, saw fit to devote the bulk of the October 16 issue to the movie and the social issues it raised. In *Cahiers du Cinéma* Truffaut and Rohmer were depicting Carné as a dinosaur. But in autumn 1958 the mass media seemed to be saying that *Hôtel du Nord*'s director was still a sure barometer of France's social and political mood.

Les Tricheurs was, for *L'Express*, a troubling portrait of the first generation to approach adulthood with the consciousness of a potential nuclear holocaust. Carné concurred with this appraisal and emphasized that youth's disenchantment with politics was symptomatic of the deeper malaise: "What is especially striking among youth is their lack of interest in politics. Before the war . . . students were much more political. There were Action Française students, Communist students, Socialist students. Clearly, students today are less involved, and we tried to show this in the film . . . What I have observed is that [young people] are living with the near certainty of an atomic war by which, sooner or later, humanity is destined to disappear. Not for an instant do they consider that a general 'modus vivendi' can be arranged: therefore, why bother oneself with anything!"[38]

Carné was possibly the first filmmaker of the 1950s to use the expression "New Wave" publicly—although not in reference to the cinema. As of June 26, 1958, *L'Express*'s subtitle became "Le journal de la Nouvelle Vague." *L'Express* profiled young adults in de Gaulle's France and referred to them as a "New Wave" two weeks before its issue devoted to

Les Tricheurs. In his interview with the magazine about the film, Carné acknowledged the "undeniable" similarities between *L'Express*'s portrait of this "New Wave" and his own.[39]

Carné's film practice was easily distinguishable from what Françoise Giroud, Pierre Billard, and other journalists soon dubbed "the New Wave" of French moviemakers.[40] Yet *Les Tricheurs*'s success was in some measure responsible for the ease with which ninety-seven novice directors managed to make their feature débuts between 1958 and 1962. Like the most popular New Wave productions, *Les Tricheurs*'s concern was youth. Its treatment of sex was explicit. Its extras were mainly non-professionals. Its music was the American jazz of, among others, Stan Getz, Dizzy Gillespie, and Coleman Hawkins. Above all, young and relatively unknown actors portrayed its protagonists. Carné perhaps exaggerates when he asserts, "Had it not been for *Les Tricheurs*, the New Wave filmmakers would not have been so encouraged to shoot films without costly stars and on a smaller budget."[41] Yet even Truffaut admits that "the New Wave benefited from *Les Tricheurs*." Producers realized that if the profligate Carné could effect huge receipts for a film costing a "mere" 280 million francs, newcomers might do the same with very modest allowances.[42]

Les Tricheurs's foreshadowing of certain New Wave preoccupations is a matter of coincidence, not revised aesthetics. Jacques Sigurd's well-made plot exposes its old-wave essence. The action takes place in flashback, as Bob Letellier (Jacques Charrier) sits in a Latin Quarter café and recalls the past few weeks' events. A university student and the son of a wealthy industrialist, Bob espies Alain (Laurent Terzieff) in a record shop. Alain is an Ecole Normale dropout who sleeps where he can and whose principal possession is a toothbrush. Spontaneously, Bob shields Alain when the latter filches a record. Alain's anticonformism and post-Existential despair dazzle Bob, and the two young men become friends. That night Clo (Andréa Parisy) hosts a party for the "crowd." The daughter of titled parents, Clo lives for pleasure. In the course of her orgiastic soirée, Clo and Bob make love, but Bob is more attracted to a girl he meets named Mic (Pascale Petit), the daughter of a lower-middle-class family. The next day Mic and Bob make love in her shoddy studio apartment. Each develops feelings for the other but cannot admit to them, since the paramount rule among this set is noncommitment.

Prodded by Alain, Mic and Bob take advantage of a blackmail scheme involving an unseen middle-aged married woman who paid for an affair with Peter (Alfunso Mathis), another member of the crowd. Mic's motivation is to buy a white Jaguar she saw in the mechanic's shop where her

107   An intemperate soirée in *Les Tricheurs;* Jean-Paul Belmondo, second
from left with head lowered; Dany Saval and Andréa Parisy, center

brother, Roger (Roland Lesaffre), and his steady girlfriend, Line (Arlette
Coignet), work. Bob's motivation is to satisfy Mic's expectations of him.
When Bob refuses to join her in following through with the caper, Mic
becomes angry over Bob's "bourgeois" scruples. Mic's disappointment
impels Bob to surprise her by completing the transaction alone. When he
appears at her door with the blackmail money in hand, he finds Mic in
bed with Alain. He hurls the cash on the bed and leaves. Although Mic
proceeds to buy the Jaguar, she discovers that in denying her feelings for
Bob, she feels pain.
    A week passes and Clo hosts another hedonistic gathering, this time at
her parents' country estate (fig. 107). Along with drunkenness and promiscuity, the party features an amusement known as "truth," in which each
player takes a turn at asking personal questions that must be answered
honestly. In Bob's presence, Alain asks Mic if she loves Bob. She replies
in the negative. Mic then asks Bob if he ever loved her. He too replies in
the negative. He also calls Mic a slut and announces his intention to
marry Clo, who is pregnant and rejects her mother's urging to have an
abortion. Mic leaves the party and Bob pursues her, shouting: "I love
you, Mic, I cheated! I cheated!" As the two race their cars down the
country highway, Mic accelerates her Jaguar to maximum speed and

drives directly into an oncoming truck; she dies after unsuccessful surgery. The attending physician asks Mic's brother: "But what is wrong with these kids? For heaven's sake, what is the matter with them?" Roger responds: "A universe that's slipping away . . . Fifty years of mess behind them, and surely fifty more ahead . . . But it's like that everywhere. So there must be a reason for it."

As Bob's thoughts return to the present, he rises and leaves the café, and the camera pans to several younger boys and girls who are passing the word about a "super" party taking place that night.

Carné's films occasionally exhibit the New Wave penchant for allusion to other movies and moviemakers. Ever so lightly *Les Enfants du paradis* evokes Méliès. In *Thérèse Raquin* a touch of ironic self-reference occurs when Madame Raquin insists scornfully that going to the movies is bad, "for all you do is take in other people's germs and watch couples kissing on screen." In *La Marie du port* a clip from Murnau's *Tabu* mirrors Chatelard's aspirations. Calling himself X–27 in *Le Pays d'où je viens*, the Bécaud-Eric figure winks to Dietrich's spy in *Dishonored* (1931). But these instances of cinematic self-consciousness and intertextuality are negligible by comparison with *Les Tricheurs*'s Cinémathèque sequence.

The sequence begins with a close shot of a poster showing images of Rudolph Valentino and James Dean. The caption reads, "Two Eras: Two Legendary Heroes." As Bob enters the screening room, a love scene from Valentino's last picture, *The Son of the Sheik* (1925), is being projected. Composed primarily of youths, the audience howls derisively at the Latin lover's exaggerated brand of kissing and eye movement. These youngsters are more at ease with Dean's inarticulate brooding. Since joining Alain's crowd, Bob, too, has tried to play the disenchanted rebel-loner à la Dean. But like Frédérick watching Baptiste perform at the Funambules, Bob undergoes an epiphany at the Cinémathèque: he realizes that Valentino's effusive emotionalism speaks to a portion of his being as authentic as the alienated side of himself that identifies with Dean.

Asked about his intent in this sequence, Carné replied: "I think that, in part, I was saying something about the vicissitudes of cinematic taste. I also wanted to criticize young people who cannot deal with sentimentality and human commitment. That, after all, is the very subject of *Les Tricheurs*."[43] This assertion speaks to what is, on one hand, most poignant and, on the other, most specious about *Les Tricheurs*. After a decade of rebuke for having lost touch with contemporary life, the fifty-two-year-old Carné (*L'Express* took him for forty-nine) shook the establishment with a fairly convincing exposé of adolescent dissoluteness. The Young Turks' whipping boy proved that his tried-and-true theme—emotional repression and the human misery it fosters—was well suited to modern times.

Yet the film's judgmentalism points to a discordance between Carné's sensibilities and his subject. Roger's final words to the doctor seem to exempt everyone from guilt. But they are a feeble afterthought in a movie that steadily stigmatizes hedonism and exalts the wholesomeness associated with hard labor and monogamy, as epitomized by Roger. Bob's initial infatuation with Alain brings to the surface a certain *nostalgie de la boue* (fig. 108). Carné the man finds this release of instinct attractive because it corresponds to his own experience of self-realization through the flouting of convention. Yet Carné the filmmaker is unable to break with the commonplace notion that love and sexuality best entail definitive pairing and exclusivity. *Les Tricheurs* flirts with but misses a genuinely radical subject. Carné and Sigurd might have focused on Alain, the bisexual loner, or Clo, the nymphomaniac who aspires to motherhood. They might have made a picture about what Robin Wood, with reference to *La Règle du jeu*, has called, quite simply, "people relating freely to one another." By this phrase Wood means "the potential loveliness of genuinely shared relationships, in which none of the participants feels excluded, in which love is recognized as a life-principle that transcends the exclusive romantic attachment." [62] Wood also means to articulate nonpejorative terms that describe how homosexuality challenges society's "dominant ideological norms," and to encourage filmmakers and film critics to be attentive to these terms—even in pictures that do not deal with homosexual characters. Renoir's protagonists do not achieve this state of emotional "generosity," but his film posits it as a potential good. [44]

In *Les Tricheurs*, by contrast, Carné's attitude toward his characters is essentially one of prurience and guilt-ridden voyeurism. Carné laments the direction the younger generation is taking, yet he showcases and glamorizes their manners, language, and rituals. Carné's is a stance that precludes generosity and fosters moralism. His film tells us that Bob and Mic *might* have lived happily ever after were it not for diabolic social forces that make potentially responsible youngsters susceptible to the corrupting influence of the world's Alains and Clos. For all its surface boldness, *Les Tricheurs* is a conservative, if not reactionary, film that leaves unquestioned the prevailing social order. In 1958 *Les Tricheurs* sensationalized a certain slice of contemporary life. Today it is, at best, a quaint documentation of dated mores and fashions.

108 A confrontation between mainstream values as embodied
      by Bob (Jacques Charrier, left) and social deviance as
      found in Alain (Laurent Terzieff)

Les Tricheurs's box-office success makes clear that the film spoke to desires and needs of the French public, old and young alike. But the movie's notoriety was ephemeral and parochial. *Les Tricheurs* was not released in the United States until June 1961—subsequent to *Le Beau Serge, Les 400 Coups*, and *A Bout de Souffle*. By then, Chabrol's, Truffaut's, and Godard's portraits of French youth had revolutionized filmgoers' expectations. As Bosley Crowther observed in the *New York Times*, "However one feels about the license and frankness of the 'new wave,' one has to acknowledge their modernity in being spare with conscience and morals." By comparison, Crowther found *Les Tricheurs* "drenched with the social climate and moral judgment of post–World War I." [45]

Carné brought greater sincerity to *Terrain vague* (1960), his treatment of juvenile delinquency in the then-newly-constructed housing projects outside Paris. Inspired by Hall Ellson's 1950 novel, *Tomboy*, Carné and scenarist Henri-François Rey transposed the story's action from Brooklyn to the Porte Saint-Ouen.[46] Carné's initial attraction to Ellson's book lay in its graphic sketches of violence: "Well before the vogue for violent pictures . . . I wanted to direct a film whereby, deliberately, viewers' nerves would be put to a rough test. Some of the adolescents whose stories the novel recounts suffered from true sadistic derangement . . . For example, a girl wanting to join a gang had to submit to having her nipples burned with the lighted end of a cigarette. If she could withstand this trial stoically, only then would she be admitted to the clan" (*Vbd*, 366).

National politics obliged Carné and Rey to temper their adaptation. While the project was in preproduction André Malraux, then Minister of Cultural Affairs, declared to the Chamber of Deputies that the French cinema must be free from censorship except in one respect: its depiction of youth. Malraux's dictum did not intimidate the director of *Le Quai des Brumes* and *Les Tricheurs*. But producer Louis Dolivet did not share Carné's pluck. Having won a Gold Lion at Venice for Tati's *Mon Oncle* (1958) and a Gold Palm at Cannes for Fellini's *La Dolce Vita* (1960), Dolivet wanted *Terrain vague* to represent France at the next Venice Biennial. This meant not annoying the French government. Carné and Rey reluctantly toned down their script's more lurid scenes in accordance with Dolivet's wishes. Ironically, the black-and-white film was completed too late to compete in Venice.

Terrain vague, unlike *Les Tricheurs*, contains no explicit reference to James Dean. But its affinity with Nicholas Ray's *Rebel Without a Cause* (1955) is palpable throughout. In both pictures juvenile delinquency is essentially a metaphor to articulate anger over adult society's insensitivity to the needs of its young. *Terrain vague* begins with a precredit sequence in which a hard-nosed magistrate sentences a youth to reform school as the boy's mother admits to her helplessness. It closes with a title card that reads: "May adults assume responsibility toward their children." Carné's film lacks an actor equal in impact to Dean. Its unity of tone and vision derives instead from the longings of its diminutive and diffident fifteen-year-old protagonist, Babar (Jean-Louis Bras). In fact, Babar's troubled personality resembles that of Plato, the boy portrayed by Sal Mineo in Ray's film. His plight is no less affecting. Babar joins the neighborhood gang—all of whose members are older than he—in a conscious effort to establish a surrogate family. He breaks with precedent by choosing to mix his blood not with one of the boys in the twenty-four-member gang, but with Dan (Danièle Gaubert), the club's tomboy leader. Dan, who is a victim of her stepfather's sexual abuse, becomes, for Babar, a benign mother-sister-lover figure. Their platonic idyll is intense but doomed. Marcel (Constantin Andrieu), the charismatic and misogynistic older youth who was sent to reform school at the film's start, seizes the club's leadership from Dan. The entire gang turns on Babar when they mistakenly suspect him of foiling their plans to rob an Esso station. The picture's most unsettling scenes depict the gang's twice assaulting Babar and Babar's finding his pet dog, M'sieur, lying at the foot of the door to his apartment, its throat slit. When Babar discovers Dan in bed with his friend Lucky (Maurice Cafarelli), the devastated youth commits suicide (fig. 109).

Unlike *Les Tricheurs*, Carné's subject in *Terrain vague* is not so much the counterculture of the young as the state of being marginal even within that counterculture. Unlike *Les Tricheurs*, *Terrain vague* eschews Manichean simplism. In giving the lie to the premise that love, trust, and hard work, when delivered ex post facto, can undo the effects of early material and emotional deprivation, *Terrain vague* aligns itself with Luis Buñuel's *Los Olvidados* (*The Young and the Damned*, 1950). But where Buñuel is unremitting in his dissection of the atrocious and frightful character of slum society, Carné adopts Babar's vantage point, conferring a quasi-magical aura onto the world of the gang. In the picture's first half, the gang tenders, for Babar, a promise of Eden. Gritty daytime shots of the unattractive housing project give way, in the film's central portion, to Romantic, near-Expressionistic nighttime depictions of the gang's clubhouse and to cheery night shots of their adventures at a carnival. As if in homage to *Nogent* and the proletarian grandparents of this generation of youngsters, Carné and cinematographer Claude Renoir place their camera on rides in motion and produce, for Carné, some uncommonly exhilarant images. The result is a film more delicate in overall feel than *Los Olvidados*. The final images of both pictures, however, are equally brutal. *Los Olvidados* ends with young Pedro's corpse being rolled into a garbage dump. In *Terrain vague* the gang abandons the dead Babar in a *terrain vague*, the "vacant lot" of the film's title and a symbol of the human devastation which this moving, unpretentious film decries.

109 Babar (Jean-Louis Bras) prepares to commit suicide in *Terrain vague*

Terrain vague was not a commercial blockbuster like *Les Tricheurs*, but it was a more honest film. Carné did not pretend to document the intimate lives of people among whom he himself was an outsider. He chose instead to portray something he knew from personal experience: a young person's alienation and the rejection and discrimination that contribute to it.

The press greeted *Terrain vague* lukewarmly. Devoting only several paragraphs to it in *Le Monde*, Jean de Baroncelli called the picture "neither mediocre, vulgar, nor shameful. It is simply a failed film." [47] In *Les Lettres Françaises*, Georges Sadoul regretted its being "for Carné, far from a major success." [48] Yet one spectator, who viewed the film in the southern city of Carcassonne, had enthusiastic thoughts and decided to share them with Carné in writing. Dated Sunday, December 4, 1960, and penned on the back of a picture postcard, the viewer's note read: "*Cher Monsieur*, I went to see Terrain Vague here last evening. The theater was full and announced '*a special continuation of Terrain vague through next week.*' The audience was at first puzzled, then attentive, more and more interested, and finally genuinely moved. I write you this because I reacted exactly like the audience; there are, in this film, some moments of very sharp truth and some moments of very pure fantasy. I have read some very unfair articles. I hope to please you with this card as you have pleased me with this film; I have never belonged to a gang and yet I breathed, in Terrain Vague, whiffs of my own adolescence; thank you." The card was signed, "Admiringly yours, François Truffaut."[49]

CHAPTER 17

Persistence of Vision

Summarizing his fortunes of the early 1960s, Carné writes: "Tossed from producer to producer, all of whom were disoriented by the momentary success of . . . the New Wave, I was floating a bit" (*Vbd*, 389). Carné's statement highlights a constant feature of his career. Unlike Pagnol in the 1930s and Pagnol's New Wave emulators Truffaut and Rohmer, Carné never established his own production company. During his heyday Carné had been, as Signoret puts it, "emperor" of the French cinema.[1] Yet for all the authority he wielded during a production, the emperor's power was always subject to the whims of those he still refers to as *les patrons*—the "bosses" who control salaries and financing. Except when he negotiated a series of films, as he did with André Paulvé and Sacha Gordine, the profits from any one Carné picture were unavailable for reinvestment in another or for recouping losses from a previous one.

During the early 1960s Carné planned four major projects and all failed to materialize. One was an adaptation of Zola's *Germinal*, which Carné co-wrote with Spaak. Filming was to take place in Hungary. But Hungarian state bureaucracy proved too exasperating for Carné, and he abandoned the enterprise during preproduction. A second aborted undertaking was a modernization of *La Dame aux camélias* (*The Lady of the Camelias*), in which Dumas's self-sacrificing heroine was to be a starlet making her way in the Paris movie world. Carné withdrew when the Hakim brothers insisted that Jeanne Moreau play the lead instead of Claudia Cardinale, whom Carné had selected. Carné also planned a period film about Balzac's master criminal, Vautrin. But even when Jack Palance was proposed for the leading role, no producer evinced interest. A similar fate attended his effort to portray the life of Diaghilev, with Orson Welles envisioned as the impresario and Rudolf Nureyev as Nijinsky.

Out of frustration Carné agreed to direct an adaptation of Albert Simonin's 1960 gangster thriller, *Du Mouron pour les petits oiseaux* (*Lots of Trouble over Little Birds*). Rather than treat the property seriously, Carné, scenarist Sigurd, and producer Jules Borkon chose to burlesque the original, aiming to recreate the broad humor that infuses the detective subplot of *Le Pays d'où je viens*. The result was hardly felicitous. Initially the scenario was constructed around a concierge and her interactions with the zany inhabitants of the Paris apartment house she cares for: "a likable, kind, and funny concierge, who would do anything to help her tenants whenever they came upon certain romantic complications" (*Vbd*, 382). Arletty was to play this role. However, shortly before Sigurd and Carné completed a full draft, Arletty suffered a freak accident. Applying left-eye medication to her right eye and vice versa, she so aggravated her glaucoma that she was left almost blind. Deprived of the actress he imagined as the film's "soul" (*Vbd*, 384), Carné instructed Sigurd to retailor the role for actress Suzanne Gabriello and to create additional scenes for the eccentric tenants. Yet the estimable performances of Paul Meurisse, Dany Saval, Franco Citti, and Lesaffre proved insufficient to mask the comedy's muddled narrative.

Carné's subsequent undertaking was an adaptation of Georges Simenon's 1946 novel, *Trois Chambres à Manhattan* (*Three Beds in Manhattan*). A bittersweet love story of two cynical outcasts, François (Maurice Ronet) and Kay (Annie Girardot), the production called for location shooting in New York City. The experience was calamitous. Although Carné had brought a technical team from France, a United States regulation required that an American crew be employed as well. The U.S. crew included a bilingual assistant director named Steve Kesten. Arrogating to himself what Carné construed as inordinate authority, Kesten promptly enraged his Gallic colleague. When Kesten took to ordering the camera to roll, Carné launched a defensive attack: "The next day, in the middle of Central Park where we were located, I burst out, 'We are shooting a *French* film, financed by the *French*, and I intend to work according to *FRENCH* methods!'" (*Vbd*, 396).

This outburst resulted in sustained hostility between the French and American contingents for the remainder of the week-long shoot, which included takes at Dover and Pearl Streets, Forty-second Street and Tenth Avenue, and three Central Park locations. Even when Carné attempted to give orders in English, the Americans were deliberately unresponsive. If he shouted, for example, "See-launce pleeeze!" they would not comply until Kesten uttered, "Quiet, fellas!" In the mid-1960s President de Gaulle fared handsomely at diminishing Americans' affection for the French. Carné's brief stint in the United States did little to remedy the strain. One crew member confided to a *New York World Telegram & Sun* reporter, "He's always yelling."³

Although the Italians seemed to enjoy the film, French critics savaged *Trois Chambres à Manhattan* when it appeared at the Venice Biennial. According to the director, the French assault was the work of an anti-Carné cabal formed to avenge those New Wave filmmakers whom Carné had branded as "congenitally impotent" seven months earlier in his statement to *Le Figaro Littéraire* (*Vbd*, 400). Carné retaliated several weeks later in an interview with Anne Capelle for *Les Nouvelles Littér-aires*. Capelle formulated her remarks and questions to fuel Carné's wrath. Insisting that "an Italian public's judgment . . . is not necessarily a criterion of quality" and wondering why Carné "did not try to escape from conformism and convention," Capelle elicited this response: "It is just such reasoning that is killing the French cinema . . . To youth, genius; to the rest, senility . . . For me it is settled! Finished! I will never film again in France. I've had enough! I surrender!" Asked where he intended to work in the future, Carné replied, "In Italy."³

Carné did not abandon the French film industry. In fact, he became more involved than ever in its struggles. When Malraux attempted to divest Henri Langlois of his authority at the Cinémathèque Française in late winter 1968, Carné was swift to offer help. In addition to his participation in demonstrations and sit-ins, Carné served as one of the twenty board members of the Committee for the Defense of the Cinémathèque Française, working with persons who had hitherto been less than supportive of him and his work, including Jean-Paul Le Chanois, Truffaut, and Godard.⁴ The man who had suffered censure during the *épuration* was now on the "proper" side in a major political controversy whose source was in fact being traced back to Nazi machinations a quarter-century earlier. (The government agency allegedly seeking to turn the Cinémathèque into its vassal was the Centre National de la Cinématographie, an organization that had evolved from the Occupation era's Direction Générale du Cinéma.)⁵ Five days after the resolution of this conflict, Langlois wrote to Carné: "I do not know how to thank you for all you have done. Of course, it is now, more than ever, that the Cinémathèque must be the cement binding all those who love and make Cinema. That is why I am requesting you to grant me permission to ask the Administrative Council to bestow upon you the honorary presidency of the Cinémathèque Française."⁶ Carné acceded to Langlois's request.

The protracted Langlois affair demonstrated that the French could undo the increasingly arbitrary decisions of the de Gaulle regime. It also demonstrated that the French cinema would retain maximum autonomy through cooperation, not factionalism. Following the war, the screenings Langlois programmed in his little theater on the avenue de Messine nurtured the early film sensibilities of Rohmer, Rivette, Truffaut, Godard, and Chabrol. If these critic-directors chose to denigrate or ignore portions of French film history, Langlois's greater genius lay in his respect for the entirety of France's film patrimony—not to mention his equal zest for every other national cinema. His gesture of homage to Carné was at one with a view of French film culture as a continuum. In 1968 no active French director more embodied the continuity of French film than the former *Cinémagazine* journalist-turned-director, Marcel Carné. For all the ill will he was capable of generating, Carné was incontrovertible evidence of what Jacques Rivette was then extolling as "the permanency of the cinema." [7]

Just prior to the Langlois affair, Carné waged his own battle against state autocracy. During July and August 1967, Carné had shot his eighteenth feature, *Les Jeunes Loups (The Young Wolves)* (fig. 110). An updated variation on *Manon Lescaut, Les Jeunes Loups* relates the story of Alain (Christian Hay), a nineteen-year-old bisexual social climber; Sylvie (Haydée Politoff), a young woman who pretends to be free-living but clings to traditional values; and Chris (Yves Beneyton), a hippie who has renounced his upper-middle-class family's way of life. As the plot evolves, Alain and Sylvie acknowledge love for one another; Alain professes to abandon his dissolute ways; but he continues to sell himself to all who can afford the price which his beauty and charm command. A female Des Grieux to Alain's Manon, Sylvie is duped and abused by this *garçon fatal* whom she is powerless to resist.

Having received a government subvention, Carné had to submit his screenplay to the Commission de la Censure before shooting could begin. The Commission characterized the script, co-written with Claude Accursi, as "a monument of immorality and insanity." It warned that if the scenario did not become "considerably tempered," the film would risk being banned in its entirety (*Vbd*, 408). The film's producer, René Pignères, had already been worried about "scenes referring to the protagonist's homosexuality" (*Vbd*, 408). He therefore insisted upon major revisions. Unable to break his contract without suffering legal action, Carné "attempted to console myself with the idea that what I would be unable to show, I would sugggest. But I knew well that, whatever I would do, the game was lost from the start" (*Vbd*, 409).

Pressured by Pignères, Carné suppressed a key sequence in which Syl-

110 Poster for the sole Carné film which the director has
disavowed

vie intuits that Alain has slept with a wealthy male entrepreneur, Ugo
(Maurice Garrel).[8] When a rough cut was ready, the Commission de la
Censure demanded fourteen further excisions, including underwater
shots in which Alain and Sylvie swim nude and exhibit pubic hair. Carné
succeeded in reducing the number of excisions to five after weeks of debate and politicking. Nonetheless, Carné believed that his freedom of
expression had been assaulted grossly. Having declined to attend the premiere of *Les Jeunes Loups* on April 2, 1968, Carné later wrote: "I no
longer recognized the film I had conceived. That is why, today, I formally
renounce its authorship [*paternité*]."[9]

Carné perceived Georges Pompidou's regime as having brought about "a
new gust of liberalism" (*Vbd*, 414). He decided, therefore, to treat yet

111 Jacques Brel as the earnest magistrate decrying police corruption in *Les Assassins de l'ordre*

another explosive subject: French police brutality. *Les Assassins de l'ordre* (*Assassins of the Law*, 1971), adapted from Jean Laborde's 1956 novel, fictionalizes authentic events that transpired in 1951 near Bordeaux. It depicts the heroic efforts of an examining magistrate (Jacques Brel) to indict and try a police commissioner (Michel Lonsdale) and his two aides for having murdered a man (Roland Lesaffre) suspected of a minor offense (fig. 111). Ultimately the magistrate proves helpless in court. The commissioner's financial and political clout enable him to hire the nation's most talented and unscrupulous defense attorney (Charles Denner), thereby ensuring that the criminals are acquitted and that "the system's assassins" win the day.

To Carné's surprise, the Commission de Contrôle found the film unobjectionable. Yet a more insidious form of censorship apparently took place before and upon the picture's release. Carné writes that he learned, "without ever being able to verify the fact," that many provincial police inspectors bullied local exhibitors into canceling bookings of the film (*Vbd*, 427). Moreover, the Paris and national press gave *Les Assassins de l'ordre* exceedingly short shrift: "Thus Alexandre Astruc, who upon leaving a [press] screening was dithyrambic, omitted all mention of the film in *Paris-Match* . . . Others, like [Pierre] Billard or [François] Nourissier of *L'Express*, were unfortunately going on vacation or absorbed by other matters" (*Vbd*, 426). A radio interview scheduled for the morning after the film's premiere "was brusquely canceled without justification" (*Vbd*, 427). Carné also claims that a high state official took reporter Pierre Bouteiller to task for having granted him interview time on France-Inter the preceding day. Carné does not deny that some press coverage occurred. But he attempts to underscore, somewhat disingenuously, the discrepancy between, on one hand, the fact that many critics "shared their enthusiasm with me" at press screenings and, on the other, the media's overall disregard and deprecation for the picture.

Not surprisingly, this film about police brutality was greeted far more warmly in Brezhnev's Russia than on this side of the iron curtain. Russian esteem for Carné dates from his prewar association with Prévert. The German ban on screenings of *Le Quai des Brumes* and *Le Jour se lève* heightened Soviet acclaim for the director and his works. Shortly following the war, filmmaker Serge Youtkevitch ran a major Carné retrospective in Moscow.[10] Reportedly, Stalin was so moved by *Les Enfants du paradis* that he presented Carné with a Pierrot puppet in the image of Jean-Louis Barrault (fig. 112). In July 1971 *Les Assassins de l'ordre* won a Special Prize (*Spetsialny Priz*) from the Union of Soviet Cinematographers at the Seventh Moscow International Film Festival. According to *L'Aurore*, the Soviet news agency Tass asserted that "this film . . . treats a theme that rouses millions of people in the world: the problem of the citizen's security and the defense of his rights . . . Marcel Carné has seen in such a fact a danger that threatens man and his civic freedoms."[11]

Publicly, Carné denies that *Les Assassins de l'ordre* is a thesis film: "I have simply related a story and it is to the viewer that I leave the chore of extracting a moral . . . I do not admit to have attacked 'the police.' I am attacking certain police practices."[12] Yet the picture is a social-protest film that advocates an unambiguously "correct" cause. It anticipates many of the captivating yet politically simplistic films that garnered substantial favor in the late 1970s, such as Tavernier's *Le Juge et l'assassin* (1976), Yannick Bellon's *L'Amour violé* (1977), and Michel Drach's *Le Pullover rouge* (1979). Its fortunes will rest on the value which future generations place upon motion pictures that offer solemn critiques of society's hypocrisy and repressiveness.

In the early 1970s most French critics concurred that Marcel Carné had become an inconsequential force in contemporary cinema. But if the major voices of French critical opinion chose to neglect Carné's overall contribution to the seventh art, such was not the case elsewhere. Several days

112   A Pierrot puppet in the likeness of Jean-Louis Barrault,
       reportedly a gift to Carné from Joseph Stalin; on display
       at the French Library in Boston

following *Les Assassins de l'ordre*'s screening at the Venice Biennial, the
festival's officials presented lifetime achievement awards to three directors: John Ford, Ingmar Bergman, and Marcel Carné. "Of all the international awards granted me," Carné writes in his memoirs, "this was
surely the highest and the one to which I would never have dared to lay
claim. My name joined with those of the authors of *Stagecoach* and *Cries
and Whispers* filled me with both pride and unease" (*Vbd*, 428).

When the night's festivities ended, Carné took to his hotel room and experienced a moment of "depression . . . mixed with rage": "Why was it that I was always being honored and celebrated abroad, while in the country that is my own, in which I was born, I encounter only attacks, sarcasms, and even disdain from those who claim to love an Art to which I have devoted my life? It seems to me that if a Frenchman is honored and placed on equal footing with a John Ford and an Ingmar Bergman, whose renown is worldwide, whoever that Frenchman may be, whether one admires or detests him, the occasion ought to prove gratifying, at least a bit, to [French] national pride . . . But I was surely deceiving myself again . . . With the exception of three half-hidden lines in *Le Monde*, not one newspaper breathed a word about what had happened on that evening in Venice" (*Vbd*, 428–29).

Engraved with the signatures of, among others, Fellini, Visconti, De Sica, and Zeffirelli, Carné's award is on display in one of the rooms constituting Les Salles Carné of the French Library in Boston—the American institution Carné has chosen over the Cinémathèque Française to house his papers, archives, and memorabilia.

In the spring of 1974 Carné completed his last feature, *La Merveilleuse Visite*. A fable of alienation and persecution, this picture is an adaptation of H. G. Wells's 1895 novel, *The Wonderful Visit*. It relates the trials of a mysterious and handsome figure (Gilles Kohler) who is discovered naked and unconscious on a desolate beach in Brittany (fig. 113). An elderly village vicar (Lucien Barjon) and his simpleminded sexton, Ménard (Roland Lesaffre), encounter and care for this stranger. When he regains consciousness, the man asserts that he is an angel fallen from heaven because of a gust of cold wind that upset the highest regions of the sky. Although the vicar remains incredulous, his sexton accepts wholeheartedly the visitor's claim to otherworldliness. A winsome child (Pierre Répécaud), a beautiful young housemaid named Délia (Deborah Berger), and the region's dowager chatelaine, the Duchess of Quéfélec (Mary Marquet), share Ménard's conviction. Others, however, evince only fear and hostility toward this exotic presence and the singular events he engenders: mirrors break when they capture his reflection; the touch of his hand metamorphoses a dead bird into an egg; his glance transmutes a wrecked boat into a perfect floating vessel; and although he has never seen or touched such an instrument, he executes ethereal airs on the vicar's violin. Unwilling to endure the angel's presence, a mob of adult male villagers drives the stranger off the edge of a seaside cliff. With arms extended, the angel falls backward but does not plummet (fig. 114). In-

113 Gilles Kohler as the angel in *La Merveilleuse Visite*

114 The angel metamorphosing into a gull

stead, he turns into a white gull that soars through the sky, impervious to the bullets speeding toward him.

The picture's troublesome production history is a revealing gauge of the establishment's discomfort with Carné's handling of this subject. Only through the intercession of Jacques Duhamel, then Minister of Culture, did the Commission des Avances sur Recettes reverse its decision not to award a preproduction subvention to Carné and producer Jacques Quintard. Only through special pleading did the Office de la Radiodiffusion et Télévision Française (ORTF) agree to co-produce. But even as shooting began, the film's multiple producers, including the ORTF, sought to evade their financial obligations (*Vbd*, 447). This crisis led to strikes by actors and technicians and to a three-month work hiatus. Thanks to eleventh-hour appearances of additional producers, Carné was able to finish *La Merveilleuse Visite* within a very modest total budget. But the hostility Carné endured in the process led the director to declare, yet again, that he planned to abandon France for Italy.[13]

Although poorly publicized, the movie's Paris premiere was a gala benefit for the French Association of Film Critics. This organization's membership, however, showed little enthusiasm for the work. The picture's few supporters, such as Pierre Lherminier, admired Carné's thorough disregard for the modernist notion that "the cinema is dead and, henceforth, only the anti-cinema is filmable": "I marvel . . . that a classical moviemaker like Carné can today, to such an extent, give not a hoot for the modes, taboos, and rules necessary to please; that he has the juvenile impudence to be so deliberately out-of-date."[14] Likewise, Gilles Colpart applauded the "beauty" and "simplicity" of the film's reactionary aesthetic: "One might take it for the first film of a very young director who is still idealistic [*peu roué*] about cinematic expression."[15] But most reviewers scoffed at the picture's alleged ingenuousness. Baroncelli observed that "if innocence is sometimes a source of freshness, it can also be one of affectation and puerility."[16] Chazal found the film's "poetry" to be "rarely convincing" for lack of authentic "instinct" and "inspiration."[17] Carné summarizes aptly the overall critical reception: "This time, they did not insult me. They spoke ironically of my innocence!" (*Vbd*, 456).

For all the effort to portray himself as a victim of the press, Carné in fact manipulated public opinion. At Cannes, where the picture was shown as part of the "Marché du Film," Carné and his publicists declaimed repeatedly that the difficulties encountered in gaining financial backing lay with the property's lack of raw sexuality, and that "in these times, without eroticism, it is difficult to inspire confidence."[18] A week before its Paris opening, Carné told *Le Figaro*, "I am presenting a picture that owes nothing to eroticism and violence." He went on to specify that at special previews "female spectators came to kiss me as thanks for having brought to them 'something else.'" [19] On the day the film premiered in Paris, an article by Carné appeared in *Pariscope*. Lambasting the conniving tendencies of France's three major distribution companies, the director also pondered facetiously: "How . . . could I not have understood that [today's] viewer wants 'blood and ass'? And nothing else . . . Are there today, in this nation, people still capable of *dreaming*?" [20]

The intent of this verbal barrage was to predetermine viewer response and deflect attention from what the film actually is: a tame but nonetheless libidinally charged exaltation of male androgyny. Chazal's commentary typifies the "safe" reaction Carné thought it prudent to promote. Speaking of Gilles Kohler's angel, whom Chazal qualifies simply as "very photogenic," the critic writes, "He asks only to love, in the most disincarnated meaning of the word." In one sense Chazal is correct. When the angel informs Délia of his chaste emotion for her, he says that "love . . . can assume thousands and thousands of colors," and that the one most adequate for describing his feeling for her is "transparency." When Délia's rugged fiancé, François (Jean-Pierre Castaldi), explodes at the knowledge of her having spent a night on the beach with this stranger, Délia replies: "With him, it was different . . . It is impossible to be unfaithful with a boy like that one." However, Chazal's insistence on the angel's ostensible asexuality ignores two essential facts. First, Carné's mise en scène fosters steady viewer fascination with the spectacle of the angel's always semi-naked body. Second, Carné's editing bestows prominence on the angel as the object of an ambivalent male gaze, embodied on one hand by Ménard's desiring stares and on the other by François's contemptuous glances. Assuredly, the angel himself can conceive only of "disincarnated" love. But the film's particular organization of gazes guarantees that his representation is erotically tinged.

Jean-Louis Bory was the sole reviewer to confront this issue, at once respecting and debunking Carné's assertion that the erotic is absent from this film. Writing in *Le Nouvel Observateur*, Bory began his critique by appropriating Carné's public position almost verbatim: "*La Merveilleuse Visite*'s first merit is to have resisted the great commercial tide of blood and ass and to have made a claim for charm and dream." But Bory then exposed the film's homoerotic drift by contrasting it with works of less diffident filmmakers of like orientation: "Marcel Carné, a very clever man, does not repeat the *coup* of Pasolini's *Teorema* [1968]. His angel, as should be, is asexual. That is oh-so-evident. And if he wears a little red heart on his immaculate jeans . . . it is positioned fastidiously to the side of his fly. Turning his back on Brother Pasolini's *aggiornamento*, Marcel Carné fashions his angel in the Saint-Sulpician style, giving him fine blond hair, a celestial glance, a prepossessing smile, and a long delicate hand that knows how to caress the cheeks of tiny tots. And that is how it should be." Insisting that one must also not confuse Carné's angel with Cocteau's Heurtebise, Bory concluded that all connections with Pasolini and Cocteau disappear "behind Carné's smile—a smile not devoid of malice." [21]

In a review that was itself not free of malice, the critic indicted Carné's excessive caution. Bory had little choice but to support Carné's bland, "Saint-Sulpician" expression of homoeroticism. But Bory was convinced that by diverting attention away from the undeniable libidinal impulse shaping the movie, and by packaging a potentially subversive narrative as if it were a child's Christmas entertainment, Carné ultimately rendered a disservice to his film and to a progressive social cause which the film might have fostered.

Future viewers of *La Merveilleuse Visite* may, like Bory, find themselves uncomfortable with the prissy nature of Carné's angel. Yet justification for the angel's primness lies in Wells, who describes the visitor, first, as "a youth with an extremely beautiful face, clad in a robe of saffron and with iridescent wings," and, later, as "slight of figure, scarcely five feet high, and with a beautiful, almost effeminate face, such as an Italian old Master might have painted." Moreover, Wells anticipates Carné by toying coyly with the possibility of a homosexual dynamic between the vicar and his find. Despite the emphatic protestations of Wells's vicar, the worldly Lady Hammergallow (the model for Carné's Duchess) insists knowingly: "Really—I'm not a *narrow* woman—I *respect* you for having him . . . I never suspected you were nearly such an interesting man . . . It is most romantic." [22]

Nonetheless, the film's dislocation of gender expectations derives more from Carné and scenarist Didier Decoin's modifications of Wells's tale. In the novel, the angel's capacity to activate dormant emotions affects primarily the old vicar: "He is stimulated by a sense as of something seen darkly by the indistinct vision of a hitherto unsuspected wonderland lying about his world." [23] Carné and Decoin displace such intimations of otherness onto the childlike sexton Ménard, a character not found in the novel. Through Ménard, the primitive character of eroticized spectatorship asserts itself forcefully. Ménard is the first person to espy the angel lying naked on the beach: the subjective zoom-in that conveys his excitement underscores the momentousness of Ménard's discovery. When the visitor later announces, "I am an angel," an immediate cut to a close-up of Ménard's face reveals his eyes aglow and his expression as beatific as Baptiste's when he learns the truth about Fil de Soie's physical capacities in *Les Enfants du paradis*. Like Baptiste, Ménard endured ridicule as a boy for being a dreamer: the local fishermen deemed him insufficiently manly to follow in the footsteps of his father, a sailor long lost at sea. Like Baptiste, Ménard partakes of weighty primal observations. The film's plot hinges on Ménard's nocturnal peering through iron bars that surround the Duchess's garden and his catching sight of the angel and Délia walking hand in hand toward the beach. Like Dany's discovery of her mother's licentiousness in *Jenny*, this sight crushes Ménard's faith in the being he most idealizes. His presumption that the angel and Délia's bond is carnal leads him, Judas-like, to denounce Délia to her fiancé and thereby intensify the community's animosity toward the angel.

The movie's dénouement diverges radically from the novel. In the latter, the angel rushes to rescue Délia, who is trapped in the vicar's burning house. Wells's final image of the angel suggests a male-female coupling of sorts, describing "two figures with wings, that flashed up and vanished among the flames." [24] In Carné's version women are absent from the closing sequence, which stages a rather unconventional male-male effort to escape into the unknown. Délia has been reconciled with her virile fiancé (another character not found in Wells). Ménard, who has become reassured of the gentle stranger's chastity, now hopes to realize a daydream shared earlier with the angel: that "one day . . . we would take to the sea and we would go far away." The film's next-to-last images depict Ménard running hand in hand with the angel toward the coast as armed vigilantes follow in pursuit. In driving the angel over the cliff, the mob shatters Ménard's fantasy. Yet the angel's transformation into a soaring white bird, and the shots of its flight against a pristine blue sky, constitute the most uplifting ending of the Carné oeuvre. The cut to Ménard, who observes this spectacle with blissful calm, reinforces the sense that something quite extraordinary has taken place. Indeed, for the first and only time in a Carné film, a character's intimations of transcendence strengthen rather than founder.

We have seen that Carné's characters strive to appropriate symbolic remnants of paradise, and that these generally assume the form of landlocked urban gardens. Carné's protagonists also yearn persistently for proximity to the sea: Raymonde fantasizes a trip to the Riviera in *Hôtel du Nord*; François and Françoise dream of the southern coast in *Le Jour* se lève; Diego and Malou imagine a return to Easter Island in *Les Portes de la nuit*; Michel envisions a weekend by the ocean with his girlfriend in *Juliette ou la clef des songes*. The sea bird in *La Merveilleuse Visite* is yet another symbol for escape from society's repressiveness. Evoking the purity of regions uncontaminated by real-world existence, Carné's angel-cum-bird gives expression to the impulse motivating all sympathetic figures in Carné: a return to a state of oneness with nature.

From preproduction onward, Carné spoke intensely and lyrically about the pleasure he took in situating and shooting *La Merveilleuse Visite* in Brittany. At issue was not Carné's desire to demonstrate, once again, that he could film on location. Rather, Carné conceived of his working in Brittany as an opportunity to steep himself in the mystery associated with the region of his mother's ancestry. Typical of his many statements to the press on this matter was his declaration to André Lafargue: "I chose Brittany . . . because it is the region of the miraculous, of dreams, of beauty, of purity. And then, sentimentally, I must admit, my mother was a Breton." [25] Carné proffered an unusually revealing comment to Nicole Jolivet: "I shot *La Merveilleuse Visite* in Brittany, of which I am a native via my mother, and I gave her maiden name, 'Racouët,' to one [sic] of my characters [the man and woman whose house the angel repaints in psychedelic tones]. I felt at home in Saint-Guénole, at La Pointe du Van at Pen-Hir, and in the bird sanctuary at Sizun, amid the sea gulls that play an important role in the film. I breathed there the perfume of my youth. A youth which will never leave me so long as I can feel the steel of a camera between my hands and I can say, 'Motor! Silence! Action!'" [26]

I have suggested that Carné's films are responses to fears about castration and female sexuality, and that both the iconization of certain female figures and the fetishization of objects such as legs and horses are obvious manifestations of these fears. *La Merveilleuse Visite* begins with images that foreground, first, the angel's bare legs as he walks along the beach, and, second, the horse that pulls the vicar's carriage. By the film's midpoint, white jeans cover the angel's legs (while his chest remains bare), and the vehicle that catalyzes the plot is no longer the vicar's horse-drawn carriage but, instead, François's huge delivery truck. It would appear that Carné's fetish objects have yielded to the requirements of modernity, progress, and civilization. But this is not precisely the case. As Carné intimates in his statement to Jolivet, a new and significant object has entered and altered the field of symbolic motifs common to the Carné oeuvre: the sea gull.

In earlier films, privileged objects ensured male bodily integrity vis-à-vis female difference. A denizen of the sea, the gull, on the contrary, denotes identification with a primitive maternal principle. It fosters a symbolic expression of the primordial alliance of son and oral mother whose representation Carné—a masochistic-narcissistic filmmaker par excellence—had been striving for nearly five decades to capture on film. Typically, the Carné protagonist experiences a conflict between the desire to recover an androgynous, pre-Oedipal state of being and the social imperatives that compel men to comport themselves in accordance with patriarchic norms. In *La Merveilleuse Visite*, Carné's hero possesses from the outset the ideal androgyny toward which men in his other films incline precariously. For the angel, self-realization depends neither on heterosexual intimacy with Délia nor on a homosexual alliance with Ménard. For this child of paradise, self-realization requires only freedom from defilement by the inhabitants of the fallen world. In the film's mythopoeic terms such freedom translates into the angel-gull's reintegration with the all-sustaining maternal force represented by the sea.

Approximately ten minutes before the picture's close, masses of white gulls inundate the screen. The angel, having heeded Ménard's bidding to isolate himself, sits at the edge of a cliff and contemplates the sea, the sky, and the swarming gulls. Sound emanates only from the screeching birds and the crashing waves. Positioned in the midground, frame center, the angel is shot from behind, with only his naked rear torso and the back of his head visible to the spectator. In the course of six succeeding shots Carné's camera slowly tracks inward and tilts upward to embrace the vista as perceived by the angel. Like the Carnival sequence in *Les Enfants du paradis*, this lyric flourish intimates blissful abandon. But where the earlier film's surface exuberance underscored, by contrast, its protagonist's alienation, these vibrant images in *La Merveilleuse Visite* announce the actual fusion of an individual with nature.

In *Nogent*, Carné's hand-held camera penetrated a grove of shrubs to disclose, with self-conscious embarrassment, a couple engaged in amorous activity. This self-distancing, voyeuristic posture vis-à-vis adult physical intimacy became a cardinal feature of Carné's cinematic aesthetic. In *La Merveilleuse Visite*, however, Carné triumphs over the scandal and trauma of primal scene experience by effecting a more thorough symbolic regression to pre-Oedipal innocence. The signs of this triumph are the perfect matching of the camera's field of vision with the angel's, and the unthreatening allure of the natural elements.

The six shots depicting the angel's communion with the sea and sky exemplify the "naive" brand of filmmaking which reviewers of *La Merveilleuse Visite* either patronized or excoriated in 1974. Ultimately, such evaluations are beside the point. What matters is the conspicuous degree to which the uncomplicated, almost primitive mise en scène and editing of these shots hark back to Carné's very first spectacles: the one-picture slide shows which the young Marcel mounted for boyhood friends on a tablecloth tacked to the walls of his father's locked bedroom. In both instances the fascination with projected images betrays the director's desire for reincorporation with his prematurely deceased mother.

Epilogue:
A Filmmaker of Sadness

Shortly before *La Merveilleuse Visite* went into production, rumor had it that Marcel Carné was destitute. Press reports maintained that financial favors tendered discreetly by, among others, Françoise Rosay, Michèle Morgan, Roland Lesaffre, and André Malraux alone prevented *Les Enfants du paradis*'s director from seeking out public assistance. One journalist observed that Carné was fulfilling a prophecy made by Jacques Prévert, who had allegedly said: "At the end of his life Méliès sold oranges in railroad stations. It is very possible that the same thing will happen to Marcel." [1]

Such speculation cut Carné to the quick, and he tried to reset the record. To those who claimed that he was "sleeping under bridges," the filmmaker responded: "Let's not exaggerate. I am not a billionaire, but I am not a tramp. When I have very little money, I manage. When I have a lot, I spend it." [2] Today Carné is prone to disavow contrasts between the quality of his life during the Golden Age and now. Looking back on his career, he often quotes Hugo's phrase "To fight is to live" and Gide's aphorism "Art thrives in constraint but dies from liberty." [3] Carné thus perpetuates the persona of an embattled Romantic and a careworn sensualist. These self-assigned epigraphs highlight the mix of pugnaciousness and masochism that have contributed genuinely to Carné's longevity as a director.

Since 1982 Carné has resided in a stately apartment on the rue de l'Abbaye that overlooks Place Saint-Germain-des-Prés (fig. 115). Although he acquired these quarters through the good graces of Mayor Jacques Chirac, [4] Carné does not subsist on public support. From 1974 forward he has worked steadily. In 1977 he completed *La Bible*, a ninety-minute documentary on the mosaics of the Monreale Basilica in Sicily. Since then he has devoted himself to a multimedia mode which he refers

115 Carné in his apartment on the rue de l'Abbaye, 1985; in foreground, the special César awarded in 1979 to honor *Les Enfants du paradis* as "the best French film in the history of talking pictures"

to as *le spectacle audiovisuel*: "Originally devised to meet the needs of businesses wishing to promote their products, *spectacles audiovisuels* started out as simple slide shows. What I have done is to create computer-programmed spectacles in which twenty projectors converge at once on a single giant screen that is twenty meters wide and twelve meters high. By juxtaposing, linking, and superimposing images, and by utilizing a quadraphonic sound system, I can create multiple patterns and unusual effects. This mode lacks the movement of the motion-picture camera. But it is different. It enables me to go beyond reality and achieve some stunning poetic suggestions." [5]

Uncooperativeness on the part of Jack Lang's Ministry of Culture supposedly made it impossible for Carné to complete a *spectacle audiovisuel* on Versailles in 1982.[6] But Carné has brought to fruition four major *spectacles*: the first deals with Saint Bernadette, and premiered at Lourdes in summer 1980; the second is entitled *Martinique, île des fleurs*, and has played year-round on that Caribbean island since 1983; a third illustrates the life and works of Toulouse-Lautrec, and can be seen in the artist's native city of Albi; the most recent, *Rome éternelle*, has proved to be a successful tourist attraction at a site near the Vatican. Currently Carné is finishing a *spectacle* on Paris that will be projected aboard a specially designed *bateau-mouche* anchored in the shadow of the Eiffel

Tower, and he is planning still another on Impressionist painters.

It is perhaps fitting that a director whose cinematic style favored the production of near-frozen tableaux should ultimately preoccupy himself with photographic slides. It is almost uncanny that Carné's final grandiose efforts at spectaclemaking recall so obviously the magic lantern shows he staged as a child in his father's bedroom. In fact, the *spectacle audiovisuel* has enabled Carné to readdress some of his favorite subjects: the miraculous, in *Bernadette de Lourdes*; the intolerance of difference, in *Martinique*; the artist as marginal and voyeur, in *Toulouse-Lautrec*; and the return to one's roots, in the Paris show, which Carné envisages as "a human Paris . . . much like what I revealed in *Hôtel du Nord*." [7]

In statements to the press, Carné has waxed ecstatic over the gratification he derives from this activity; in private, he expresses frustration. These *spectacles audiovisuels* are essentially team-made commercial ventures for which Carné serves as a very limited artistic supervisor. Such undertakings have brought financial security, yet they have barely allowed for the more compelling challenges of fiction filmmaking, which Carné misses deeply.

Carné's final cinematic effort, *La Bible* (1977), marked a reluctant return to documentary. Following the collapse of plans for *La Puissance et l'argent*, a picture that would have starred Jean Gabin as a muckraking newspaper publisher, Carné agreed to direct this low-budget film inspired by the Byzantine mosaics of Sicily's Monreale Basilica. Although financed in part by the ORTF, *La Bible* has yet to enjoy a telecast. It was, however, screened at Cannes, where it won the 1977 Ecumenical Jury Prize. Part travelogue, part educational movie, *La Bible* anticipates Carné's *spectacles audiovisuels* insofar as the director's primary task was to select and reassemble a preexisting corpus of images—in this case, the Basilica's 130 *grands tableaux* depicting Old and New Testament stories. Yet Carné did not let genre conventions stifle idiosyncratic impulse. A major interest of the film lies in the way Carné sustains throughout *La Bible* the expression of blissful abandon achieved only at *La Merveilleuse Visite*'s end.

The documentary begins with swirling aerial views of the Mediterranean as if seen from the vantage point of the gull which, at *La Merveilleuse Visite*'s close, announced humankind's refusion with a primordial maternal principle. In the remainder of the picture Carné's camera stands in relation to the Basilica's enveloping interior as does the infant to its undifferentiated mother. Exhibiting an exuberance not evident in Carné since *Nogent, Eldorado du dimanche*, his panning, tracking, and zooming camera explores, caresses, and magnifies its object of celebration.

With point of view and field of vision coinciding, *La Bible* elicits an oceanic feeling of plenitude and security. Its predictable narrative fortifies this effect. Moving from the Basilica's representations of Chaos and Creation to Eden and the Fall, and from Jesus' birth to the Crucifixion and Resurrection, *La Bible* culminates with exterior high-angle shots of gigantic crashing waves. These images are, at once, a visual echo of the film's opening shots and a symbolic equivalent to the words employed by the unseen narrator to describe the mother-child intimacy at the moment of Jesus' descent from the cross: "It is not with her hands that Mary gave the ultimate caress to her dead child, but with her glance; a glance in which infinite tenderness vied with infinite suffering."

Carné's current project to adapt Maupassant's 1890 story "Mouche" holds the promise of a much less solemn treatment of maternity. In Maupassant's tale five boatmen fancy one woman, whom they nickname Mouche. To avoid strife, the fun-loving friends arrange to sleep with the lady on assigned days of the week. When Mouche gets pregnant, the young men assume joint responsibility and agree to adopt the child communally. When the pregnancy miscarries, they console Mouche by announcing in unison that they will "make her another one." [8]

Carné views *L'Amour de vivre*—the project's working title—as an occasion to indulge, one last time, his inclination for pictorialism and historical reconstruction: "I would like this color film to be to the French Impressionists what Feyder's *La Kermesse héroïque* was to the seventeenth-century Flemish masters. Set mainly along the Seine near Argenteuil, the picture would bring to life paintings such as Monet's *La Grenouillère*, Manet's *Les Canotiers* and *Le Déjeuner sur l'herbe*, and Renoir's *Le Moulin de la Galette*." [9] Maupassant's story also provides a pretext for Carné's recreating on film the kind of innocent male camaraderie he experienced as a boy in the Square des Batignolles. It allows, as well, for the manufacture of still another unintimidating female figure of diffused desire: Maupassant's narrator describes Mouche as "a rough sketch of a woman in which there was everything; one of those silhouettes which an artist pens in three strokes on a café tablecloth after dinner between a brandy and a cigarette. Nature sometimes makes a few like that." [10]

L'Amour de vivre's boldness would lie primarily in its departure from Maupassant's story line. "In my version," Carné explains, "there would be seven friends, each sleeping with Mouche on one night of the week. When an eighth joins this group, one of the original seven gives up his day, saying 'I am not really interested in women.' In fact, that man and the newcomer proceed to have an affair of their own. And when Mouche

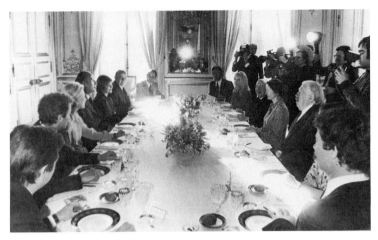

116 At the Elysée Palace, February 1975: left to right, François Périer, Jean-Louis Barrault, Michèle Morgan, Valéry Giscard d'Estaing, Annie Girardot, Bernard Blier, Roland Lesaffre, M. Sauzet (Giscard's *chef du cabinet*), Dany Saval, Marcel Carné, Madame Giscard d'Estaing, Michel Simon, Jacques Charrier

loses her baby, the only person to console her is the bisexual member of the original group of seven friends. It is he who says, generously, 'Don't worry, I'll help you to have another one.'"[11] *L'Amour de vivre* would thereby deploy the Carnésian fantasy of mother-son symbiosis in terms which, by comparison with *Les Enfants du paradis* and *La Merveilleuse Visite*, are remarkably optimistic and humane.

In 1951 Bazin evoked Carné's "knack for crystallizing all the widespread harshness of spoken and written criticism." He observed that "no other French director of the first rank . . . has been slandered so often; a kind of evil legend has sprung up in which he appears as an ogre to producers, a megalomaniac of decor, a sadist in exceeding the budget."[12] In 1974 Maurice Perisset wrote in an open letter to Carné, "Of all the directors of your generation or that which preceded it, I know of not one who, after having been adored, has been so knocked about, ridiculed, reviled, and rejected as you."[13]

Events of the past decade would seem to call for a softening of Bazin's and Perisset's appraisals. In 1975, the year Giscard d'Estaing honored him with a luncheon at the Elysée Palace (fig. 116), Carné was promoted to the rank of Officer in the Legion of Honor. In 1978 Carné was named

117 President François Mitterand (right) conferring upon Carné (far left)
France's highest civil award, the insignia of Commander in the Legion
of Honor, October 22, 1985

Commander in the National Order of Merit, and two years later he became the first film director to hold a seat in the French Institute's Academy of Fine Arts. On September 18, 1982, the city of Saint-Michel-sur-
Orge inaugurated a Place Marcel Carné.[14] A year later, on the occasion
of its fiftieth anniversary, the British Film Institute selected the first six
Institute Fellows: the honorees were David Lean, Michael Powell, Emeric
Pressburger, Satyajit Ray, Orson Welles, and Marcel Carné. In June 1984
the Cannes Film Festival commemorated the fortieth anniversary of *Les
Enfants du paradis* with a gala soirée for Carné and Alexander Trauner
at the newly reopened Victorine Studios. In August and September 1985
Christian-Jaque's film homage, *Carné, l'homme à la caméra*, had a well-
publicized theatrical run in Paris. On October 22, 1985, François
Mitterand granted Carné France's highest civil award, the insignia of
Commander in the Legion of Honor (fig. 117). In August 1986 the radio
network France-Culture turned Carné's eightieth birthday into a national
event by broadcasting five one-hour weekly programs on the director's
life and works.

For Carné, this spate of awards is proper compensation for years of
public denigration. Yet Carné remains disgruntled over the fact that producers and state grant-making agencies are reluctant to support his cur-

rent cinematic projects. As Roland Lesaffre remarked in 1981: "Governments change and they all decorate Maestro Marcel Carné as if he were a Russian general. But they do not give him a foot of film."[15]

Two decades ago, it would have been foolhardy to suggest that Marcel Carné would be perceived once again as a major figure of twentieth-century French culture. Oblivion seemed the likelier destiny for the boy from the Batignolles whose rise to fame coincided with France's political collapse, whose most imposing triumphs took shape during a period of national humiliation, and whose artistic practice appeared antiquated and irrelevant in the wake of the French New Wave. Yet today Marcel Carné is something of a sacred institution in France. Alongside Gance, Vigo, Renoir, and Truffaut, Carné's place within the pantheon of French film directors is—at least for the moment—securer than ever.

The varying critical fortunes which Carné and his films have encountered over the past five decades result from factors as disparate as aesthetic conviction, political inclination, and sexual orientation. Undoubtedly, the appeal of Carné's works will continue to rise and fall in accordance with shifts in prevailing standards of artistic, ideological, and affectional worthiness.

It is nonetheless likely that Carné will always prove troublesome for viewers, critics, and historians. His is an oeuvre of unmitigated sadness. Predicated upon a view of humanity as fallen and irredeemable, his films rarely inspire or console. Equating individualism with abject solitude, they suggest that human fulfillment resides not in maturity, critical consciousness, and emancipation, but in regression, dependence, and disengagement from the material world. Moreover, Carné frustrates one's desire to discern a lifelong flow to his command of the medium. The dense string of early masterworks followed by a lengthy period of qualitatively dubious productions undermines one's expectation that an extraordinary director ought to make extraordinary pictures every so often. In rehashing the story of an outsider's quest for human dignity, many of the later films smack of indignity on the part of their maker. Through repetition, the emotional intensity associated with the original plight loses its cinematic, moral, and psychological power and veers toward banality. Finally, Carné's refusal to modernize his practice in the light of technological innovation points as much to timidity as to tenacity. Carné's best films captured exquisitely the social and cultural climate in which they were made. But they barely gave momentum to what one refers to as the cinema's evolution.

Carné's time-honored achievements are bound to remain uncontested: the immaculate imagery; the consummate technical control; the abundant investment of the everyday world with transcendent meaning. We are only beginning to appraise other factors in Carné's life and works that are equally significant: his destabilization of gender codes; his questionable response to the Occupation; his pictures' often unflattering reflections of French society in crisis. More controversial than the former, these latter aspects guarantee Carné's centrality in future assessments of the French cinema.

It is perhaps inevitable that a film director who portrays life's essential loneliness will fail to command universal assent. But to overlook Carné's cinema of sadness is to misrepresent the past in conformity with a wish for only positive images of human possibility. Carné's films bear out the Baudelairean view of sorrow and melancholy as fundamental components of art. They confirm that an individual's consciousness of loss, exile, and impossibility can engender works of profound beauty.

Filmography

NOGENT, ELDORADO DU DIMANCHE (Marcel Carné, 1929). Assistant director: Michel Sanvoisin; running time: 17 minutes; premiere: March 1929, Studio des Ursulines, Paris; an unauthorized sound print with music by Bernard Gérard was released by L'Avant-Scène in 1961.

JENNY (Réalisations d'Art Cinématographique, 1936). Producer: Albert Pinkéwitch; screenplay: Jacques Prévert and Jacques Constant, from Pierre Rocher's novel *Prison de velours*; assistant director: Pierre Blondy; cinematographer: Roger Hubert; set decoration: Jean d'Eaubonne; music: Joseph Kosma and Lionel Cazeaux; American spiritual sung by The Five Kentucky Singers; editor: Ernest Hajos; cast: Françoise Rosay (Jenny Gautier), Albert Préjean (Lucien Dancret), Lisette Lanvin (Dany), Charles Vanel (Benoît), Margo Lion (Madame Vrack), Sylvia Bataille (Florence), Jean-Louis Barrault (Dromadaire), Roland Toutain (Xavier), Robert Le Vigan (L'Albinos), Joseph Kosma (harmonium player), Marcel Mouloudji (Paris street singer), René Génin (the fisherman in the café), Roger Blin (the friendless patient), Génia Vaury (the woman with the dog), Raymond Segard (Dany's London fiancé); running time: 90 minutes; premiere: September 18, 1936, Madeleine Theater, Paris.

DROLE DE DRAME (BIZARRE, BIZARRE) (Corniglion-Molinier, 1937). Producer: Charles David; screenplay: Jacques Prévert, assisted by Jacques Constant, from Storer Clouston's novel *The Lunatic at Large: His First Offense* (1900); assistant directors: Pierre Prévert, Claude Walter; cinematographer: Eugen Schüfftan, assisted by Louis Page and Henri Alekan; set decoration: Alexander Trauner; costumes: Lou Tchimoukoff; music: Maurice Jaubert; sound: Antoine Archimbaud; editor: Marthe Poncin; cast: Michel Simon (Irwin Molyneux, alias Felix Chapel), Françoise Rosay (Margarett Molyneux), Louis Jouvet (Monseigneur Soper, Bishop of Bedford), Jean-Louis Barrault (William Kramps), Pierre Alcover (Inspector Bray), Jean-Pierre Aumont (Billy), Nadine Vogel (Eva), Annie Carriel (the Bishop's wife), Henri Guisol (Buffington), Jean Sinoël (the prison guard), Jeanne Lory (Auntie Mac

Phearson), Agnès Capri (the street singer), René Génin (the streetsweeper), Ky-Duyen (the Chinese hotelkeeper), Madeleine Suffel (Victory), Max Morise (James, the butler), Jenny Burnay (Madame Pencil, the cook), Francis Korb (the newspaper boy), Marcel Duhamel (a reveler), Jean Marais (the second reveler knocked down in Chinatown); running time: 105 minutes uncut; 87 minutes in most American prints (the latter omit the love scenes between Billy and Eva, episodes involving Auntie Mac Phearson, Molyneux's attempt to caress Eva, and the shot of William Kramps fully nude); premiere: October 20, 1937, Colisée Theater, Paris.

LE QUAI DES BRUMES (PORT OF SHADOWS) (Ciné-Alliance, 1938). Producer: Grégor Rabinovitsch; screenplay: Jacques Prévert, from Pierre Mac Orlan's novel *Le Quai des Brumes* (1927); cinematographer: Eugen Schüfftan, assisted by Louis Page, Henri Alekan, Marc Froissard, and Philippe Agostini; set décoration: Alexander Trauner; costumes: Coco Chanel; music: Maurice Jaubert; sound: Antoine Archimbaud; editor: René Le Hénaff; cast: Jean Gabin (Jean), Michèle Morgan (Nelly), Michel Simon (Zabel), Pierre Brasseur (Lucien), Edouard Delmont (Panama), Raymond Aimos (Quart Vittel, the tramp), Robert Le Vigan (Michel Krauss, the painter), René Génin (the doctor), Jenny Burnay (Lucien's girlfriend), Marcel Peres (the truckdriver), Roger Legris (the hotel waiter), Kiki (the dog); running time: 91 minutes; premiere: May 17, 1938, Marivaux Theater, Paris.

HOTEL DU NORD (SEDIF, 1938). Producer: Jacques Lucachevitch; screenplay: Jean Aurenche and Henri Jeanson, with dialogue by Henri Jeanson, from Eugène Dabit's novel *L'Hôtel du Nord* (1929); assistant directors: Claude Walter, Pierre Blondy; cinematographer: Armand Thirard, assisted by Louis Née; set decoration: Alexander Trauner; costumes: Lou Tchimoukoff; music: Maurice Jaubert; editor: Marthe Gottie; cast: Annabella (Renée), Jean-Pierre Aumont (Pierre), Arletty (Raymonde), Louis Jouvet (Edmond), Bernard Blier (Prosper), Paulette Dubost (Ginette), Jane Marken (Madame Lecouvreur), André Brunot (Emile Lecouvreur), François Périer (Adrien), Henri Bosc (Nazarède), Raymone (Jeanne), René Bergeron (Maltaverne), Andrex (Kenel), Jacques Louvigny (Mimar), Marcel André (the surgeon), Génia Vaury (the nurse); running time: 110 minutes; premiere: December 10, 1938, Marivaux Theater, Paris.

LE JOUR SE LEVE (DAYBREAK) (VOG–Sigma, 1939). Producer: Pierre Frogerais; screenplay: Jacques Viot and Jacques Prévert, with dialogue by Jacques Prévert; assistant directors: Pierre Blondy, Jean Fazy; cinematographer: Curt Courant, assisted by Philippe Agostini, André Bac, and Viquier; set decoration: Alexander Trauner; costumes: Boris Bilinsky; music: Maurice Jaubert; sound: Armand Petitjean; editor: René Le Hénaff; cast: Jean Gabin (François), Jacqueline Laurent (Françoise), Jules Berry (Valentin), Arletty (Clara), René

Génin (the concierge), Mady Berry (the concierge's wife), Bernard Blier (Gaston), Marcel Peres (Paulo), Georges Douking (the blind man), René Bergeron (the café proprietor), Gabrielle Fontan (the old woman on the staircase), Germaine Lix (the music-hall singer), Jacques Baumer (the police inspector); running time: 87 minutes; premiere: June 17, 1939, Madeleine Theater, Paris.

LES VISITEURS DU SOIR (THE DEVIL'S ENVOYS or THE DEVIL'S OWN ENVOY) (Scalera–Discina, 1942). Producer: André Paulvé; screenplay: Jacques Prévert and Pierre Laroche, with dialogue by Jacques Prévert; assistant directors: Pierre Sabas, Bruno Tireux, Michelangelo Antonioni; cinematographer: Roger Hubert, assisted by Maurice Pecqueux and Marc Fossard; set decoration: Alexander Trauner, assisted by Georges Wakhevitch; music: Maurice Thiriet, Joseph Kosma; sound: Jacques Le Breton; editor: Henri Rust; cast: Arletty (Dominique), Alain Cuny (Gilles), Jules Berry (the Devil), Marie Déa (Anne), Marcel Herrand (Renaud), Fernand Ledoux (Baron Hughes), Gabriel Gabrio (the executioner), Roger Blin (exhibitor of the monsters), Jean d'Yd (man with the bear), Piéral (one of three dwarfs), Simone Signoret (a lady of the castle), Alain Resnais (an extra), Jean Carmet (an extra), Georges Sellier (an extra), François Chaumette (a page), Jacques Jansen (the singing voice of Alain Cuny); running time: 120 minutes; premiere: December 4, 1942, Madeleine Theater, Paris.

LES ENFANTS DU PARADIS (CHILDREN OF PARADISE) (Pathé, 1945). Producer: Raymond Borderie; screenplay: Jacques Prévert; assistant directors: Pierre Blondy, Bruno Tireux; cinematographer: Roger Hubert, assisted by Marc Fossard; set decoration: Alexander Trauner, assisted by Léon Barsacq and Raymond Gabutti; costumes: Alexander Trauner, assisted by Antoine Mayo and Jeanne Lanvin; music: Maurice Thiriet, Joseph Kosma; pantomime music by Georges Mouqué; sound: Robert Teisseire; editors: Henri Rust, Madeleine Bonin; cast: Arletty (Garance), Jean-Louis Barrault (Baptiste Deburau), Pierre Brasseur (Frédérick Lemaître), Marcel Herrand (Pierre-François Lacenaire), Maria Casarès (Nathalie), Pierre Renoir (Jéricho), Louis Salou (Count Edouard de Montray), Fabien Loris (Avril), Etienne Decroux (Anselme Deburau), Jane Marken (Madame Hermine), Gaston Modot (Fil de Soie, the "blind" beggar), Marcel Peres (director of the Funambules), Paul Frankeur (the police inspector), Louis Florencie (the policeman), Lucienne Vigier (one of Lemaître's girlfriends), Cynette Quéro (one of Lemaître's girlfriends), Auguste Boverio (first author), Paul Demange (second author), Jean Diener (third author), Jean-Pierre Delmon (Deburau's son), Habib Benglia (the attendant at the Turkish bath), Léon Larive (stage doorman at the Funambules), Pierre Palau (stage manager at the Funambules), Albert Rémy (Scarpia Barrigni), Jacques Castelot (a dandy), Jean Gold (a dandy), Raphael Patorni (a dandy), Maurice Schutz (the bank collector), Gustave Hamilton (stage doorman at the Grand Théâtre), Rognoni (director of the Grand Théâtre), Marcelle Monthil

(Marie), Robert Dhéry (Célestin), Lucien Walter (ticketseller), Jean Lanier (Iago), Jean Carmet (an extra); running time: 195 minutes; premiere: gala performance, March 9, 1945, the Palais de Chaillot, Paris; first run, March 15, 1945, Madeleine and Colisée Theaters.

LES PORTES DE LA NUIT (THE GATES OF THE NIGHT) (Pathé, 1946). Producer: Raymond Borderie; screenplay: Jacques Prévert, from *Le Rendez-vous* (June 1945), a ballet by Jacques Prévert, Joseph Kosma, Roland Petit, and Brassaï; assistant directors: Roger Blanc, Georges Baudoin; cinematographer: Philippe Agostini, assisted by André Bac; set decoration: Alexander Trauner; music: Joseph Kosma; editor: Jean Feyte; cast: Yves Montand (Diego), Nathalie Nattier (Malou), Serge Reggiani (Guy Sénéchal), Pierre Brasseur (Georges), Saturnin Fabre (Monsieur Sénéchal), Julien Carette (Monsieur Quinquina), Jean Vilar (Destin), Raymond Bussières (Raymond Lécuyer), Sylvia Bataille (Claire Lécuyer), Dany Robin (Etiennette Quinquina), Mady Berry (Madame Quinquina), Christian Simon (Cricri), Jane Marken (Madame Gervaise), Fabien Loris (the street singer), Michel Salina (the surgeon); running time: 120 minutes; premiere: December 3, 1946, Marignan and Marivaux Theaters, Paris.

LA MARIE DU PORT (MARIE OF THE PORT) (Corona, 1950). Producer: Sacha Gordine; screenplay: Louis Chavance and Jacques Prévert, from Georges Simenon's novel *La Marie du port* (1938), with dialogue by Georges Ribemont-Dessaignes and Jacques Prévert; cinematographer: Henri Alekan; set decoration: Alexander Trauner, Auguste Capelier; music: Joseph Kosma; sound: Antoine Archimbaud; editor: Léonide Azar; cast: Jean Gabin (Henri Chatelard), Nicole Courcel (Marie Le Flem), Blanchette Brunoy (Odile Le Flem), Claude Romain (Marcel Viau), Julien Carette (le père Viau), Jane Marken (owner of the Café du Port), Louis Seigner (the uncle), René Blancard (the trawler helmsman), Robert Vattier (the rebuffed customer in the brasserie); running time: 88 minutes; premiere: March 17, 1950, Marignan and Marivaux Theaters, Paris.

JULIETTE OU LA CLEF DES SONGES (JULIETTE OR THE DREAM BOOK (Discina, 1951). Producer: Sacha Gordine; screenplay: Jacques Viot and Marcel Carné, from Georges Neveux's play *Juliette ou la clé des songes* (1927), with dialogue by Georges Neveux; assistant directors: Roger Dalcier, Michel Romanoff; cinematographer: Henri Alekan; set decoration: Alexander Trauner, Auguste Capelier; costumes: Antoine Mayo; music: Joseph Kosma; sound: Jacques Le Breton; editor: Léonide Azar; cast: Gérard Philipe (Michel Grandier), Suzanne Cloutier (Juliette), Jean-Roger Caussimon (the Historical Personage and Monsieur Bellanger, Michel's employer), Yves Robert (the accordionist), Roland Lesaffre (the Legionnaire), René Génin (le père La Jeunesse and the bailiff), Max Dejean (the detective and the judge), Arthur Devère (the memory vendor), Edouard Delmont (the village official), Gabrielle Fontan (the grocer), Marcelle Arnold (a shrew), Marion Delbo (a shrew), Claire Olivier (the old woman), Martial Rèbbe (a functionary), Fernand René (the postman), Jean Besnard (the cripple), Paul Bonifas (the cargo captain), Gallet (the notary); running time: 93 minutes; premiere: April 16, 1951, Cannes Film Festival; May 18, 1951, Biarritz and Madeleine Theaters, Paris.

THERESE RAQUIN (THE ADULTERESS) (Paris-Film Production–Lux Films [Rome], 1953). Producers: Robert and Raymond Hakim; screenplay: Charles Spaak and Marcel Carné from Emile Zola's novel *Thérèse Raquin* (1867); assistant directors: Jean Valère, Carlo Lombardini; cinematographer: Roger Hubert; set decoration: Paul Bertrand; costumes: Antoine Mayo; music: Maurice Thiriet; sound: Antoine Archimbaud; editor: Henri Rust; cast: Simone Signoret (Thérèse Raquin), Raf Vallone (Laurent), Roland Lesaffre (the sailor), Jacques Duby (Camille Raquin), Sylvie (Madame Raquin, the elder), Nério Bernardi (the doctor), Marcel André (Michaud), Martial Rèbbe (Grivet), Maria-Pia Casilio (Georgette), Madeleine Barbulée (Madame Noblet), France Vernillat (Françoise), Paul Frankeur (the railroad conductor), Lucien Hubert (the Dijon Station Chief); running time: 108 minutes; premiere: September 3, 1953, Venice Biennial; November 6, 1953, Moulin-Rouge, Normandie, and Rex Theaters, Paris.

L'AIR DE PARIS (THE AIR OF PARIS) (Del Duca Films [Paris]–Galatea [Rome], 1954). Producer: Robert Dorfmann; screenplay: Jacques Viot and Marcel Carné, with dialogue by Jacques Sigurd; assistant directors: Lou Bunin, Pierre Blondy, Pierre Granier-Deferre; cinematographer: Roger Hubert; set decoration: Paul Bertrand; music: Maurice Thiriet; title song by Francis Lemarque and Bob Castella, sung by Yves Montand; sound: Antoine Archimbaud; editor: Henri Rust; cast: Roland Lesaffre (André Ménard, known as Dédé), Jean Gabin (Victor Le Garrec), Arletty (Blanche Le Garrec), Marie Daems (Corinne), Jean Parédès (Jean-Marc, the couturier), Simone Paris (Chantal), Marcelle Praince (the elderly woman), Maria-Pia Casilio (Maria), Folco Lulli (Angelo Posi), Ave Ninchi (Angela Posi), Mathilde Casadessus (the lady at the train station), Séraphin Ferrin (the opponent boxer), Roger Michelot (the opponent's manager), M. Cremer (the referee), Van Campenhoven (the announcer); running time: 100 minutes; premiere: September 24, 1954, Paris Theater, Paris.

LE PAYS D'OU JE VIENS (Duhour, 1956). Producers: Gilbert Bokanowski, Clément Duhour; screenplay: Jacques Emmanuel, Marcel Achard; cinematographer: Philippe Agostini; set decoration: Jean Douarinou, Jean-Denis Malclès; music: Gilbert Bécaud; cast: Gilbert Bécaud (Julien Barrère and Eric Perceval), Françoise Arnoul (Marinette Ardouin), Claude Brasseur (Roland, the tough kid), Madeleine Lebeau (Adrienne Théron, the pharmacist), Gaby Basset (little Sophie), Jean-Pierre Bremmer (little Michel), Jean Toulot (Ludovic, Eric's uncle), Gabriello (Michelet, the brasserie proprietor); running time: 86 minutes; premiere: October 20, 1956, Gaumont-Palace, Paris.

LES TRICHEURS (THE CHEATERS) (Silver Films–Cinétel, 1958). Producer: Robert Dorfmann; screenplay: Jacques Sigurd, from a synopsis, "Les Mains vides," by Charles Spaak and Marcel Carné; cinematographer: Claude Renoir; set decoration: Paul Bertrand; music: excerpts from recordings by Ray Brown, Fats Domino, Roy Eldridge, Herb Ellis, Stan Getz, Dizzy Gillespie, Norman Granz, Coleman Hawkins, Gus Johnson, Oscar Peterson, Buddy Rich, Maxime Saury, Sonny Spitt; editor: Albert Jurgenson; cast: Jacques Charrier (Bob Letellier), Laurent Terzieff (Alain), Pascale Petit (Mic), Andréa Parisy (Clo), Roland Lesaffre (Roger), Dany Saval (Nicole), Denise Vernac (Mic's mother), Jean-Paul Belmondo (Lou), Alfunso Mathis (Peter), Arlette Coignet (Line), Jacques Porteret (Guy), Pierre Brice (Bernard), Roland Armontel (the surgeon), Jacques Perrin (an extra); running time: 123 minutes; premiere: October 10, 1958, Marignan and Marivaux Theaters, Paris.

TERRAIN VAGUE (Gray Films–Films Rive Gauche, 1960). Producer: Louis Dolivet; screenplay: Henri-François Rey and Marcel Carné, from Hal Ellson's novel *Tomboy* (1950); cinematographer: Claude Renoir; set decoration: Paul Bernard; costumes: Mayo; music: Michel Legrand, Francis Lemarque; sound: Jacques Carrère; editors: Henri Rust, Marguerite Renoir; cast: Jean-Louis Bras (Babar), Danièle Gaubert (Dan), Constantin Andrieu (Marcel), Maurice Cafarelli (Lucky), Roland Lesaffre (Big Chief), Alfunso Mathis (Hans), Dominique Dieudonné (Le Râleur), Denise Vernac (the mother); running time: 100 minutes; premiere: November 9, 1960, Berlitz, Paris, and Wepler Theaters, Paris.

DU MOURON POUR LES PETITS OISEAUX (Champs-Elysées Productions–CICC–Films Borderie [Paris]–Variety Films [Rome], 1962). Producer: Jules Borkon; screenplay: Jacques Sigurd and Marcel Carné, from Albert Simonin's novel *Du Mouron pour les petits oiseaux* (1960); assistant director: Jacques Corbel; cinematographer: Jacques Natteau; set decoration: Jacques Saulnier; music: Georges Garvarentz and Charles Aznavour; sound: William Sivel; editor: Albert Jurgenson; cast: Paul Meurisse (Monsieur Armand), Dany Saval (Lucie), Suzy Delair (Antoinette, the butcher's wife), Franco Citti (Renato), Roland Lesaffre (the religious fanatic), Jean Richard (Louis, the butcher), Dany Logan (Jojo), Suzanne Gabriello (Madame Communal, the concierge), Jeanne Fusier-Gir (Mademoiselle Pain), France Anglade (the waitress), Alfunso Mathis (the barman), Jean-Marie Proselier (the hairdresser), Robert Dalban (the inspector), Jean Parédès (Fleurville), Sophie Destrade (the prostitute), Pierre Duncan (Victor), Joëlle Bernard (Gladys); running time: 91 minutes; premiere: February 15, 1963, Paris.

TROIS CHAMBRES A MANHATTAN (Production Montaigne, 1965). Producer: Charles Lumbroso; screenplay: Jacques Sigurd and Marcel Carné, from Georges Simenon's novel *Trois Chambres à Manhattan* (1946); assistant directors: Michel Romanoff (France), Steve Kesten (United States); cinematographer: Eugen Schüfftan; set decoration: Léon Barsacq; music: Mal Waldron; sound: Jacques Le Breton; editor: Henri Rust; cast: Annie Girardot (Kay), Maurice Ronet (François Combe), Roland Lesaffre (Pierre), Geneviève Page (Yolande), O. E. Hasse (Hourvitch), Gabriele Ferzetti (Count Larzi), Margaret Nolan (June), Virginia Lee (the black singer), Robert Hoffmann (Thierry Damiot), Robert De Niro (an extra); running time: 105 minutes; premiere: September 4, 1965, Venice Biennial; November 10, 1965, Triomphe, Danton, Monte-Carlo, Cinévog St.-Lazare, Vedettes, and Atlas Theaters, Paris.

LES JEUNES LOUPS (Société Nouvelle de Cinématographie–Stéphan Films, 1968). Producer: René Pignères; assistant directors: Stéphane Iscovesco, Benoît Jacquot; screenplay: Claude Accursi and Marcel Carné; cinematographer: Jacques Robin; set decoration: Rino Mondolini; music: Jack Arel, Guy Magenta-Cyril; sound: Antoine Bonfanti; editor: René Gillet; cast: Haydée Politoff (Sylvie), Christian Hay (Alain), Roland Lesaffre (Albert), Yves Beneyton (Chris), Maurice Garrel (Ugo Castellini), Elina Labourdette (Madame Sinclair), Gamil Ratib (Prince Linzani), Elisabeth Tessier du Gros (Princess Linzani), Serge Leaman (Jojo), Luc Bongrand (Eddie), Bernard Dhéran (Jean-Noël); running time: 110 minutes; premiere: April 2, 1968, Balzac Theater, Paris.

LES ASSASSINS DE L'ORDRE (Les Productions Belles Rives–West Films, 1971). Producer: Michel Ardan; screenplay: Paul Andréota and Marcel Carné, from Jean Laborde's novel *Les Assassins de l'ordre* (1956); cinematographer: Jean Badal; set decoration: Rino Mondolini; music: Pierre Henry, Pierre Colombier; sound: René Longuet; editor: Henri Rust; cast: Jacques Brel (Bernard Level), Catherine Rouvel (Catherine Lebègue), Paola Pitagora (Laura), Charles Denner (Maître Graziani), Michel Lonsdale (Commissioner Bertrand), Roland Lesaffre (Michel Saugeat), Didier Haudepin (François Level), Harry-Max (Moulard), Françoise Giret (Geneviève Saugeat), François Cadet (Rahut), Serge Sauvion (Bonetti), Jean-Roger Caussimon (the division commissioner), Bobby Lapointe (Louis Casso), Jean Franval (Doctor Sabatier), Luc Méranda (Marco), Jacques Legras (an inspector), Luc Ponette (Maître Rivette); running time: 110 minutes; premiere: May 7, 1971, Balzac, Rio, Opéra, Max-Linder, Paramount Gobelins, Miramar, Paramount Montmartre, and Triomphe Theaters, Paris.

LA MERVEILLEUSE VISITE (THE WONDERFUL VISIT) (Mandala-Film–ORTF–Paris-France-Films [Paris]–Zafes [Rome], 1974). Producers: Jacques Quintard and Roger Delpey; screenplay: Didier Decoin, Robert Valey, and Marcel Carné, from H. G. Wells's novel *The Wonderful Visit* (1895); assistant director: Patrick Brown; cinematographer: Edmond Richard; set decoration: Louis Le Barbenchon and Bernard Evein; music: Alan Stivell; sound: René Longuet; editor: Henri Rust; cast: Gilles Kohler (Jean, the angel), Roland Lesaffre (Ménard), Deborah Berger (Délia), Lucien Barjon (the rector), Jean-Pierre Castaldi (François Mercadier), Mary Marquet (the Duchess of Quéfélec), Tania Busselier (Lucette, the barmaid), Pierre Répécaud (the little boy), Yves Barsacq (Doctor Jeantel), Jacques Debary (Father Léon); running time: 102 minutes; premiere: special screenings on May 15, 1974, Paris Theater, Cannes; and on August 18, 1974, Casino Theater, Deauville; general release on November 27, 1974, the Gaumont Champs-Elysées, Pathé Montparnasse, Cluny Palace, Cambronne, Saint-Lazare Pasquier, and Gramont Theaters.

LA BIBLE (THE BIBLE) (Antenne 2–ARC Films, 1977). Producer: André Tranché; screenplay: Didier Decoin and Marcel Carné, from Don Raffaello Lavagna's text *La Sainte Bible*; cinematographer: Jean Collomb; music: Jean-Marie Benjamin; editor: Maurice Laumain; running time: 90 minutes; premiere: special screening at Cannes, May 25, 1977.

Bibliographical Note

My notes document many of the major critical writings on Carné and his films. Significant texts not referred to in the notes are listed in the following paragraphs.

A thoughtful monograph on Carné is Roberto Nepoti, *Marcel Carné* (Florence: La Nuova Italia, 1979). For an overview of the Golden Age, see Raymond Borde, "'The Golden Age': French Cinema of the '30s," in Mary Lea Bandy, ed., *Rediscovering French Film* (New York: Museum of Modern Art, 1983), pp. 67–81. On poetic realism, see Dudley Andrew, "Poetic Realism," in Bandy, ed., *Rediscovering French Film*, pp. 115–19. Analyses of eroticism in Carné include André Abet, "La Femme chez Marcel Carné," *Les Cahiers de la Cinémathèque*, no. 5 (Winter 1972): 22–23; François and Jeanine Chirpaz, "Carné, ou la rencontre impossible," *Esprit*, no. 244 (November 1956): 716–23; and Ado Kyro, *Amour-érotisme au cinéma* (Paris: Le Terrain Vague, 1957). For commentary on décor, see René Jeanne and Charles Ford, *Paris vu par le cinéma* (Paris: Hachette, 1969), pp. 118–36; and Alexander Trauner, *Cinquante ans de cinéma* (Paris: Editions Jade, 1986). On ideology and the prewar films, see Ginette Vincendeau, "Community, Nostalgia, and the Spectacle of Masculinity: The Jean Gabin Persona in Films from the Popular Front Period," *Screen* 26, no. 6 (November–December 1985): 18–38. On the Occupation period, see "Le Cinéma de Vichy," special issue of *Les Cahiers de la Cinémathèque*, nos. 23–24 (1977); Jean Gili, "La Vie cinématographique à Nice de 1939 à 1945," *Annales de la Faculté des Lettres et Sciences Humaines de Nice*, no. 19 (1973): 173–96; and Stéphane Lévy-Klein, "Sur le cinéma français des années 1940–1944," *Positif*, nos. 168 and 170 (April and June 1975): 21–30 and 35–44.

Further remarks on Prévert's contributions are found in Barthélemy Amengual, "Prevert, du cinéma," *Les Dossiers de la Cinémathèque* (Montreal: La Cinémathèque Québécoise, 1978); Bernard Chardère, "Lettre ouverte ou de toutes les couleurs à un jeune cinéphile à propos de bottes et de Jacques Prévert," *Mémoires d'en France, 1936–1939* (Paris: Association Images des Mémoires Ouvrières, 1986); Danièle Gasiglia-Laster, *Jacques Prévert* (Paris: Librairie Séguier-Vagabondages, 1986); Roger Leenhardt, "Esthétique de Jacques Prévert," *Fontaine*, no. 42 (May 1945); Jean Quéval, *Jacques Prévert* (Paris: Mercure de France, 1955).

Additional essays on *Les Enfants du paradis* include James Agee in his *Agee on Film* (New York: Grosset, 1969), vol. 1, pp. 246–47; Umberto Barbaro in his *Servitú e grandezza del cinema* (Rome: Editori Riuniti, 1962), pp. 360–63; Michel Chion, *La Voix au cinéma* (Paris: Editions de l'Etoile, 1982), pp. 86–89; J. D. Gomery, "Semiology and Film Criticism: *Children of Paradise,*" *Sub-stance,* no. 9 (1974):15–23; Marcel Herrand, "Les Théâtres et leurs personnages (Lacenaire parle," *Conferencia: Journal de l'Université des Annales,* nos. 6–7 (1–15 July 1946): 247–55, 297–302; Dwight Macdonald in his *Dwight Macdonald on Movies* (Englewood Cliffs, N. J.: Prentice-Hall, 1969), pp. 456–57; Pierre Malfille, "Les Enfants du paradis," *IDHEC Fiche Filmographique,* no. 12 (1946); Marcel Martin, "*Les Enfants du paradis*: Fiche culturelle UFOLEIS," *Image et Son,* no. 94 (July 1956); and Nancy Warfield, "Notes on *Les Enfants du paradis,*" *Little Film Gazette of N.D.W.* 2, no. 1 (March 1967): v-xiv, 2–19. On *Juliette ou la clef des songes,* see Gaston Bounoure, "*Juliette ou la clef des songes,*" *IDHEC Fiche Filmographique,* no. 107 (n.d.).

The French Library in Boston is a principal repository of documents relating to Carné's films and career. Its Carné Archives contain mimeographed shooting scripts for nearly all the feature films; handwritten shooting scripts for *Hôtel du Nord, Les Evadés de l'an 4000* (unrealized), *Juliette ou la clef des songes* (both versions, both with pages missing), *Ecole communale* (unrealized), *Les Visiteurs du soir, Les Portes de la nuit, La Marie du port, Thérèse Raquin, Les Tricheurs, Germinal* (unrealized), *Trois Chambres à Manhattan, Les Jeunes Loups,* and *La Bible;* personal memorabilia, including medals, awards, and certificates of honor; and a modest amount of correspondence. The Archives also house over four thousand photographs and production stills; an abundant collection of posters and press books; and files (assembled largely by Roland Lesaffre with the assistance of Tania Busselier) of periodical clippings concerning most of the post-war films.

Notes

Prologue

1. Marcel Carné, *Discours prononcés dans la séance publique tenue par l'Académie des Beaux-Arts le mercredi 14 mai 1980 pour la réception de M. Marcel Carné élu membre de la section des membres libres en remplacement du comte Arnauld Doria* (Paris: Firmin-Didot, 1980), p. 17. All translations of French texts are mine unless otherwise indicated. An excerpt of Carné's address appears in *L'Avant-Scène Cinéma*, nos. 251–52 (1–15 July 1980): p. 121.

2. Louis Sapin, "Marcel Carné: 'Le Cinéma de l'âge d'or. Quelle aventure!'" *Paris-Match*, 28 February 1979, pp. 4–5.

3. Sapin, "Marcel Carné," p. 3.

4. Until his death in November 1981, Abel Gance, Carné's senior by seven years, was the dean of French cinema. But despite his ambition to realize an epic on Christopher Columbus, Gance—unlike Carné—was no longer working actively in film. Moreover, Gance's seminal work occurred during the two decades prior to the Golden Age. The still-active Robert Bresson, born in 1907, is one year younger than Carné. However, Bresson's first feature, *Les Anges du péché*, was not released until 1943; and although he worked shortly as René Clair's assistant before World War II, Bresson's career and works are not associated with the period under consideration here.

5. Among the lesser luminaries, Julien Duvivier (1896–1967) worked in Britain and Hollywood; Jean Grémillon (1901–59) remained in France throughout his career, producing his best works, *Lumière d'été* (1942) and *Le Ciel est à vous* (1943), during the German Occupation; and Marcel Pagnol, too, remained in France, but made only one film during the Occupation, *La Fille du puisatier* (1940).

6. In a poll taken among professionals in the film industry, the ten best films named, in order, were: *Les Enfants du paradis*; Jean Renoir's *La Grande Illusion* (1937); Jacques Becker's *Casque d'or* (1952); Renoir's *La Règle du jeu* (1939); Jacques Feyder's *La Kermesse héroïque* (1935); Jean-Luc Godard's *Pierrot le fou* (1965); Alain Resnais's *Hiroshima mon amour* (1959); René Clément's *Les Jeux interdits* (1952); Carné's *Le Quai des Brumes* (1938); and Henri-Georges Clouzot's *Le Salaire de la peur* (1953).

7. Illness prevented Carné from attending the inauguration of Les Salles Carné

in September 1979; the festivities were repeated on April 29, 1981, in his presence.

8. Pierre Montaigne, "Marcel Carné 'clochard d'honneur' de la culture française," *Le Figaro*, 15 April 1982.

9. In Marcel Carné, *La Vie à belles dents* (Paris: Jean Vuarnet, 1979), p. 486.

1. Intimations of Eden

1. *Carné, l'homme à la caméra* (released 28 August 1985), directed by Christian-Jaque; written by Didier Decoin, Roland Lesaffre, Jacques Robert, and Henri-François Rey; music by Georges Delerue; commentary spoken by Jean-Louis Barrault and Arletty; dialogue spoken by Carné, Yves Montand, and Roland Lesaffre; produced by Paule Sengissen for Les Réalisateurs Associés–Télébulle–Antenne 2–Le Ministère de la Culture. This eighty-minute critical anthology of Carné's works alternates sequences from thirteen of his films with interviews, old documentary footage, and contemporary shots of Carné at home, at work, and at play. *Carné, l'homme à la caméra* is a modified version of Christian-Jaque's two-part documentary telecast in 1980 under the title *Portrait de Marcel Carné, ou La Vie à belles dents*.

2. A first edition of Carné's *La Vie à belles dents* was published in 1975 by Editions Jean-Pierre Ollivier. The 1979 edition, published by Editions Jean Vuarnet, Paris, is revised, corrected, and expanded; it includes many more stills. Unless otherwise indicated, I will quote from the 1979 version.

The title defies literal translation. The expression *à belles dents* is found in at least two French idioms: *manger à belles dents*, "to consume something with great enjoyment and relish"; and *déchirer quelqu'un à belles dents*, "to criticize someone fiercely." In the book, Carné portrays himself as having devoured life with gusto; he also does not hesitate to reprove enemies and critics.

3. Jean Renoir, *My Life and My Films*, trans. Norman Denny (New York: Atheneum, 1974; orig. 1974), p. 282.

4. Spoken in Christian-Jaque's *Carné, l'homme à la caméra*.

5. Virtually all reference books and monographs published before 1986 designate Carné's date of birth erroneously, the most common date proposed being 1909. The *Minutes des actes de naissance du dix-septième arrondissement de Paris*, housed in the *mairie* on the rue des Batignolles, substantiates, however, that Carné was born on "August 18, 1906, at 5 p.m." In a personal interview on 7 September 1985, Carné conceded to me that 1906 is "the correct year."

6. Marcel Carné, personal interview, Paris, 7 January 1980.

7. Alain Hardel, *Strass* (Paris: Jean-Claude Simoën, 1977), pp. 83, 88.

8. Quoted by Marcel Lapierre, *Aux Portes de la nuit* (Paris: La Nouvelle Edition, 1946), p. 10.

9. Carné, personal interview, Boston, 1 May 1981.

10. To commemorate the first half-century of talking pictures, *L'Avant-Scène*

Cinéma has reprinted significant excerpts from *Cinémagazine*. Among articles by Carné are "Rétrospective sur le film policier américain" (nos. 259–60); "A La Recherche des films perdus" (no. 274); and "Films de guerre" (nos. 282–83). Six of Carné's *Cinémagazine* articles, plus his review of Pabst's *Diary of a Lost Girl*, appear in the anthology *Cinémagazine 1930* (Paris: L'Avant-Scène, 1983).

11. Jean Mitry, "La Naissance d'un cinéaste," *L'Avant-Scène Cinéma*, no. 81 (May 1968): 7.
12. Carné, personal interview, Paris, 7 January 1980.
13. See *L'Avant-Scène Cinéma*, no. 81 (May 1968): 9.
14. See Dudley Andrew, "Sound in France: The Origins of a Native School," *Yale French Studies*, no. 60 (1980): 109.
15. From "*Le Jour se lève . . .* Poetic Realism," trans. John Matthews, introduction to the script of *Le Jour se lève* (New York: Simon and Schuster, 1970), passim. Bazin's remarks originally appeared in Jacques Chevalier, *Regards neufs sur le cinéma* (Paris: Peuple et Culture, 1953).
16. René Jeanne, *Le Petit Journal*; Alexandre Arnoux, *Les Nouvelles Littéraires* (March 1929). A wide selection of contemporary reviews is included in *L'Avant-Scène Cinéma*, no. 81.
17. See François Truffaut, "Annuaire biographique du cinéma," *Cahiers du Cinéma* 4, no. 24 (June 1953): 61.

2. Monsieur Feyder's Protégé

1. René Clair, *Cinema Yesterday and Today*, trans. Stanley Appelbaum (New York: Dover, 1972; orig. 1970), p. 126.
2. Fescourt, Grémillon, and Gance are quoted more extensively in Francis Courtade, *Les Malédictions du cinéma français: une histoire du cinéma français parlant (1928–1978)* (Paris: Alain Moreau, 1978), pp. 54 ff. On the technological impact of sound, see Andrew, "Sound in France," pp. 94–103, and Richard Abel, *French Cinema: The First Wave, 1915–1929* (Princeton: Princeton University Press, 1984), pp. 59–65.
3. Quoted in Georges Charensol and Roger Régent, *50 Ans de cinéma avec René Clair* (Paris: La Table Ronde, 1979), p. 74.
4. Marcel Carné, "Quand le cinéma descendra-t-il dans la rue?" *Cinémagazine*, November 1933, reprinted in Robert Chazal, *Marcel Carné* (Paris: Seghers, 1965), pp. 94–96.
5. Marcel Carné, "La Caméra, personnage du drame," *Cinémagazine*, 12 July 1929, reprinted in Chazal, *Marcel Carné*, pp. 87–89.
6. John Russell Taylor, "René Clair," in Richard Roud, ed., *Cinema: A Critical Dictionary* (New York: Viking, 1980), p. 215.
7. Carné, "Quand le cinéma descendra-t-il?"
8. Léon Barsacq, *Caligari's Cabinet and Other Grand Illusions: A History of Film Design*, trans. Michael Bullock (New York: New American Library, 1976; orig. 1970), pp. 131–32.

9. Quoted in Charles Ford, *Jacques Feyder* (Paris: Seghers, 1973), p. 64.

10. Georges Sadoul, *French Film* (New York: Arno Press, 1972), p. 79; trans. of *Le Cinéma français* (Paris: Flammarion, 1962).

11. Barthélemy Amengual, "La Kermesse héroïque," in Jean-Louis Bory and Claude-Michel Cluny, eds., *Dossiers du cinéma* (Paris: Casterman, 1971), Films I, pp. 133–34.

12. Carné, personal interview, Paris, 7 January 1980.

13. Quoted in Lotte Eisner, *Murnau* (Berkeley: University of California Press, 1973), p. 86.

14. With respect to "aestheticized male-gendered characters" in Murnau, see Janet Bergstrom, "Sexuality at a Loss: The Films of F. W. Murnau," in Susan Rubin Suleiman, ed., *The Female Body in Western Culture* (Cambridge, Mass.: Harvard University Press, 1986), pp. 243–61.

15. Leo Braudy, *The World in a Frame: What We See in Films* (Chicago: University of Chicago Press, 1976), especially sec. 1, "Varieties of Visual Coherence."

3. Carné and Jacques Prévert

1. Spoken in rare interview footage shot in March 1966 and included in Christian-Jaque's *Carné, l'homme à la caméra*.

2. Henri-François Rey, "Parole d'homme et de prévert," *Magazine Littéraire*, no. 155 (December 1979): 19; this issue is devoted largely to Prévert.

3. Guy Jacob, "Situation de Jacques Prévert," *Premier Plan*, no. 14 (1960): 6.

4. See, for example, Tristan Renaud, "Marcel Carné," in Bory and Cluny, eds., *Dossiers du cinéma*, Cinéastes I, pp. 49–52.

5. Carné, *Discours*, p. 30.

6. Jacques Prévert, "Il ne faut pas . . . ," in *Paroles* (Paris: Point du Jour, 1947), p. 50.

7. Prévert's distaste for interviews explains the curious format of the book *Hebdromadaires* (Paris: Guy Authier, 1972): rather than grant journalist André Pozner conventional interviews, Prévert chose to comment on diverse newspaper and magazine cuttings—whose text and commentary by both men form the content of the book.

8. Rey, "Parole d'homme," p. 17.

9. Quoted in Sapin, "Marcel Carné," p. 3.

10. Gérard Guillot, *Les Prévert* (Paris: Seghers, 1966), p. 36.

11. Didier Decoin, "Un Jour le cinéma s'est mis à parler Prévert," *Les Nouvelles Littéraires*, no. 2470 (27 January–2 February 1975).

12. Prévert, "Le Jardin," in *Paroles*, p. 233.

13. Guillot, *Les Prévert*, p. 76.

14. See Jacques Siclier, *La Femme dans le cinéma français* (Paris: Les Editions du Cerf, 1957), pp. 74 ff.

15. See Gilles Barbedette and Michel Carassou, *Paris Gay 1925* (Paris: Presses de la Renaissance, 1981), pp. 128–31.

16. Gerald Mast, *A Short History of the Movies* (Indianapolis: Bobbs-Merrill, 1976), p. 259.

17. See *Cahiers du Cinéma*, no. 78 (December 1957): 35. For a fuller discussion of the production of *Le Crime de Monsieur Lange*, see Alexander Sesonske, *Jean Renoir* (Cambridge, Mass.: Harvard University Press, 1980), pp. 184 ff.

18. Marcel Carné, public remarks following a screening of his *Thérèse Raquin*, Massachusetts Institute of Technology, Cambridge, 1 May 1981.

19. See my "Conversation with Arletty," *American Film* 7, no. 2 (November 1981): 68–70.

20. In Truffaut's review of Carné's *Le Pays d'où je viens* in *Arts; lettres; spectacles*, 31 October–6 November 1956, p. 3.

21. Carné, *Discours*, p. 30. See also an interview with Fabrice Rouleau, "De *Jenny* aux *Portes de la nuit*," *Magazine Littéraire*, no. 155 (December 1979): 20–22, in which Carné asserts that "most of the time we succeeded in composing [scenes] only after one of us had yielded to the other. Our working principle was to spurt out whatever came into our heads. Something interesting can often come from silly remarks."

22. See William E. Baker, *Jacques Prévert* (New York: Twayne, 1967), p. 79 and passim; and Marc Mancini, "Prévert: Poetry in Motion Pictures," *Film Comment* 17, no. 6 (1981): 34–37.

23. Prévert, "Fête," in *Spectacle* (Paris: Gallimard, 1951), p. 361.

4. Framing an Identity

1. Pierre Leprohon, *Présences contemporaines: cinéma* (Paris: Debresse, 1957), p. 230. See also Chazal, *Marcel Carné*, pp. 21–22, and Sadoul, *French Film*, p. 82.

2. In Patrick Préjean, *Albert Préjean* (Paris: Editions Candeau, 1979), p. 138.

3. Jean-Louis Barrault, personal interview, Paris, 31 December 1979.

4. Claude Renoir, telephone interview, Troyes-Paris, 1 October 1985.

5. Renoir, telephone interview, Troyes-Paris, 1 October 1985.

6. See Jean Mitry, *Histoire du cinéma* (Paris: Jean-Pierre Delarge, 1980), vol. 4, p. 594. The entire issue of *Cahiers de la Cinémathèque*, Perpignan, no. 8 (October 1979), is devoted to the history, criticism, and theory of film melodrama.

7. Barrault, personal interview, Paris, 31 December 1979.

8. I am referring to the definitive shooting script housed in the Carné Archives, The French Library in Boston. Prévert's original scenario, recently published in *Jenny; Le quai des brumes* (Paris: Gallimard, 1988), places "Danielle" in the dressing room of her mother's lingerie shop-cum-bordello, from which she both sees and hears Jenny's management of illicit affairs, p. 79. (Shortly before filming began, the threat of censorship compelled Prévert's co-scenarist, Jacques Constant, to transform the lingerie shop into a nightclub.)

9. See Max Tessier, "Le Mélodrame, genre ou vision du monde," *Cinéma 71*, no. 150.

10. Mitry, *Histoire du cinéma*, vol. 5, p. 489.
11. Excerpts from the Arnoux and Vinneuil reviews are reprinted in Chazal, *Marcel Carné*, pp. 155–56.

5. The Popular Front

1. For an analysis of the many plot differences between Clouston's novel and Prévert's screenplay, see André G. Brunelin, "Histoire d'un drôle de drame," *Cinéma 61*, nos. 56, 57, 58 (May, June, July 1961): 90–96 and 156–58; 88–96; 90–96 and 152–57. Details of Brunelin's account of the film's production history are questionable. In claiming, for example, that Pierre Prévert played the newspaper boy in the tea salon, Brunelin perpetuates an error found in other accounts and filmographies. Pierre Prévert, in a personal interview, Paris, 8 October 1985, insists that he never acted for Carné.
2. See, for example, Pierre Autre, *Cinérance*, no. 23 (5 November 1937), n.p.; and Frank S. Nugent, *New York Times*, 21 March 1939, p. 27.
3. Herbert Lottman, *The Left Bank* (Boston: Houghton Mifflin, 1982), pp. 12–13.
4. Suzanne Chantal, *Le Ciné-monde* (Paris: Grasset, 1977), p. 301.
5. Jean-Louis Barrault, Introduction to *Drôle de Drame*, Bibliothèque des Classiques du Cinéma (Paris: Balland, 1973), p. 7.
6. Wilfrid Knapp, *France: Partial Collapse, From the Stavisky Riots to the Nazi Conquest* (London: Macdonald St. Giles House, 1972) pp. 84, 96.
7. For a full account, see Henri Noguères, *La Vie quotidienne en France au temps du Front Populaire, 1935–1938* (Paris: Hachette, 1977).
8. See René Prédal, *La Société française à travers le cinéma* (Paris: Armand Colin, 1972), pp. 207 ff; also Goffredo Fofi, "The Cinema of the Popular Front in France (1934–38)," *Screen* 13, no. 4 (Winter 1972–73): 5–57; Elizabeth Grottle Strebel, *French Social Cinema of the Nineteen Thirties: A Cinematographic Expression of Popular Front Consciousness* (New York: Arno Press, 1980), a reprint of a 1973 Ph.D. dissertation (Princeton); R. Escobar and V. Giacci, *Il Cinema del fronte populare: Francia 1934–37* (Milan: Edizione il Formichiere, 1980); François Garçon, *De Blum à Pétain: cinéma et société française (1936–1944)* (Paris: Editions du Cerf, 1984); Jonathan Buchsbaum, "Toward Victory: Left Film in France, 1930–35," *Cinema Journal* 25, no. 3 (Spring 1986): 22–52; Christopher Faulkner, *The Social Cinema of Jean Renoir* (Princeton: Princeton University Press, 1986); and Guillaume Guillaume-Grimaud, *Le Cinéma du Front populaire* (Paris: Lherminier, 1986).
9. Quoted in Sesonske, *Jean Renoir*, p. 232.
10. The use of Carné's clips is recognized in the presentation of *La Vie est à nous* in *L'Avant-Scène Cinéma*, no. 99 (January 1970).
11. Renoir, *My Life*, p. 142.
12. See Gerald Mast, *The Comic Mind: Comedy and the Movies* (Indianapolis: Bobbs-Merrill, 1973), p. 307.

13. Northrop Frye, *Anatomy of Criticism* (Princeton: Princeton University Press, 1952), p. 163.

14. Ibid., p. 178.

15. See Jacques Fansten, *Michel Simon* (Paris: Seghers, 1979); also Claude Gauteur, "Michel Simon," in *L'Avant-Scène Cinéma*, no. 234 (October 1979): 67–96.

16. Quoted in Pierre Leprohon, *Hommes et métiers de cinéma* (Paris: André Bonne, 1967), p. 94.

17. See Maurice Bessy, *Les Passagers du souvenir* (Paris: Albin Michel, 1977), p. 119; and Leprohon, *Hommes et métiers*, p. 100.

18. Cited by Barrault, Introduction to *Drôle de Drame*, p. 9.

19. Dominique Noguez, *Le Cinéma, autrement* (Paris: Union Générale d'Editions, 1977), p. 104.

20. Jean-Pierre Aumont, *Sun and Shadow*, trans. Bruce Benderson (New York: Norton, 1977; orig. 1976), p. 26.

21. Alexander Trauner, personal interview, Boulogne-Billancourt, 21 December 1979.

22. Barsacq, *Caligari's Cabinet*, p. 82.

23. "Interview Marcel Carné," in *Drôle de Drame* (Paris: Balland, 1973), p. 212.

24. Edgardo Cozarinsky, "G. W. Pabst," in Roud, ed., *Cinema*, pp. 757–58.

25. Quoted in Lottman, *Left Bank*, p. 13.

26. Renoir's characterization; quoted in Faulkner, *Social Cinema of Jean Renoir*, p. 109, from Marguerite Bussot's interview with Renoir in *Pour Vous*, 25 January 1939.

27. Mast, *Comic Mind*, p. 234.

28. Renoir, *My Life*, pp. 172–73.

29. Henry Chapier, "*Drôle de Drame*," *Combat*, 11 November 1964; excerpts reprinted in Chazal, *Marcel Carné*, p. 157.

30. Carné, personal interview, Paris, 7 January 1980. For the ending as originally conceived, see Jacques Prévert, *La Fleur de l'âge; Drôle de drame* (Paris: Gallimard, 1988), p. 360.

31. A transcription of this symposium is included in Hélène Climent-Oms, "Carné parle," *Cahiers de la Cinémathèque*, no. 5 (Winter 1972); the entire issue is devoted to Carné; passage quoted, p. 40. In one chapter of Sébastien Chardin, *Ils parlent de leur mère* (Paris: Hachette, 1979), Carné reflects on the loss of his mother and the extent to which his maiden aunt Marguerite (whose name recalls *Drôle de Drame*'s Margarett) sacrificed her life "in order . . . to surround me with tenderness," n.p.

32. See John W. Martin, *The Golden Age of French Cinema, 1929–39* (Boston: Twayne, 1983), pp. 104–11.

6. Poetic Realism

1. The film is commonly referred to in French and English as *Quai des Brumes*. However, the definite article *Le* appears in the film's credit sequence, in the

title of the published shooting script (*L'Avant-Scène Cinéma*, no. 234), in all of Carné's written references to the film, and in the title of Mac Orlan's novel. The precise reference is therefore *Le Quai des Brumes*.

2. For full documentation see André Brunelin, *Gabin* (Paris: Robert Laffont, 1987), pp. 225 ff; and André Heinrich's preface to the original screenplay in Prévert, *Jenny; Le quai des brumes*, pp. 147 ff. Brunelin and Heinrich both aim to correct Carné's account, but their versions of the overall story do not coincide.

3. Clair, *Cinema*, p. 20.

4. Pierre Mac Orlan, *Le Quai des Brumes* (Paris: Gallimard, 1927), pp. 220–21.

5. Ibid., p. 141.

6. Ibid., p. 192.

7. Quoted by Carné in Rouleau, "De *Jenny* aux *Portes de la nuit*," p. 21.

8. Mac Orlan, *Le Quai des Brumes*, p. 159.

9. Barrault, personal interview, Paris, 31 December 1979.

10. Roger Boussinot, *Encyclopédie du cinéma* (Paris: Bordas, 1980), p. 787.

11. See John Baxter, *The Cinema of Josef von Sternberg* (New York: Barnes, 1971), p. 10.

12. Frank S. Nugent, *New York Times*, 30 October 1939, p. 13.

13. Andrew Sarris, *The American Cinema* (New York: Dutton, 1968), p. 76.

14. In his Ph.D. dissertation written for Northwestern University in 1966, "The Content Analysis of Film: A Survey of the Field, an Exhaustive Study of *Quai des Brumes*, and a Functional Description of the Elements of the Film Language," Rod Whitaker determines that "65.9% of the things shown [in *Le Quai des Brumes*] are vehicles or parts thereof," and that "58.9% of the film's 73 sound effects are created by vehicles or parts thereof" (p. 214).

15. Henri Alekan, *Des Lumières et des ombres* (Paris: Le Sycomore [Centre National des Lettres and La Cinémathèque Française], 1984), pp. 150, 144.

16. Mac Orlan, *Le Quai des Brumes*, p. 213.

17. Charles Baudelaire, "Spleen [89(78)]," *Les Fleurs du mal*, in *Oeuvres complètes* (Paris: Seuil, 1968), p. 88. Translations here and following by Richard Howard, *The Flowers of Evil* (Boston: David R. Godine, 1982).

18. See Nichole Ward Jouve, *Baudelaire: A Fire to Conquer Darkness* (London: Macmillan, 1980), p. 281.

19. Truffaut, "Une Certaine Tendance du cinéma français," *Cahiers du Cinéma*, no. 31 (January 1954): 16.

20. Mitry, *Histoire du cinéma*, vol. 4, p. 292.

21. Braudy, *World in a Frame*, pp. 33, 37.

22. Jean Desternes, "Quatre Premiers Entretiens: avec Welles, Pabst, Lattuada, Castellani," *La Revue du Cinéma* 3, no. 18 (October 1948): 54.

23. Climent-Oms, "Carné parle," p. 36.

24. See Roy Armes, *Film and Reality* (New York: Penguin, 1974), chap. 7, "Renoir's Poetic Realism."

25. Sadoul, "Les Films de Carné, expression de notre époque," *Les Lettres Françaises*, 1 March 1956, p. 8.
26. Letter to the Director of the European Film Alliance, Carné Archives, The French Library in Boston.
27. Courtade, *Les Malédictions*, p. 10.
28. Knapp, *France*, p. 107.
29. Girard Chaput, "What's Wrong with France?" *Saturday Evening Post* 210 (18 September 1937): 106.
30. Whitaker, "Content Analysis of Film," p. 248.
31. Quoted in ibid., p. 245.
32. Fofi, "Cinema of the Popular Front," p. 39.
33. Cited by Courtade, *Les Malédictions*, p. 11.
34. Marcel Carné, "Cinéma, vieux frère . . . ," *Aujourd'hui*, 30 September 1940.
35. Marcel Carné, "Rétrospective sur le film policier américain," *Cinémagazine*, no. 6 (June 1930): 93. Portions of this article are reprinted in Chazal, *Marcel Carné*, pp. 90–94. The entire piece appears in *L'Avant-Scène Cinéma*, nos. 259–60, and in *Cinémagazine 1930* (Paris: L'Avant-Scène, 1983), pp. 89–94.
36. See Jorge Luis Borges, *Discusión* (Buenos Aires: Enecé, 1957).
37. François Truffaut, personal interview, Paris, 13 December 1979.
38. Grégor Rabinovitsch, letter to Marcel Carné, 24 March 1938, Carné Archives, The French Library in Boston. Although Carné, in his memoirs, refers consistently to the producer as "Rabinovitch," the spelling on the letterhead of the latter's personal stationery reads "Rabinovitsch."
39. Carlos Clarens, *Crime Movies* (New York: Norton, 1980), passim.
40. Carné, "Rétrospective sur le film policier américain," p. 93.
41. Written in March 1954 to celebrate Gabin's fiftieth birthday and his twenty-five years in the cinema, the poem is entitled "Poème de Jacques Prévert à Jean Gabin" and appeared in *Ciné-Club* (April 1954); it is reprinted in full in Claude Gauteur and André Bernard, *Gabin ou les avatars d'un mythe* (Paris: PAC, 1976), pp. 146–47, and in Brunelin, *Gabin*, pp. 401–2.
42. Renoir, *My Life*, pp. 269, 132.
43. Quoted in Gauteur and Bernard, *Gabin*, p. 138.
44. Jack Edmund Nolan, "Jean Gabin: His Sexual Magnetism Has Served Dubious Sociological Ends," *Films in Review* 14, no. 4 (1963): 193.
45. Cited by Nolan, "Jean Gabin," p. 195.
46. Renoir, *My Life*, pp. 268–69.
47. André Bazin, *What Is Cinema?*, ed. and trans. Hugh Gray (Berkeley: University of California Press, 1971), vol. 2, pp. 176–78.
48. Otis Ferguson, "French and Indians," *New Republic* 22 (November 1939); reprinted in *Film Criticism of Otis Ferguson* (Philadelphia: Temple University Press, 1971).
49. See Denise Tual, *Le Temps dévoré* (Paris: Fayard, 1980), pp. 137–38.
50. Michèle Morgan and Marcelle Routier, *With Those Eyes*, trans. Oliver Coburn (London: W. H. Allen, 1978; orig. 1977), p. 72.

51. Chazal, *Marcel Carné*, p. 29.
52. Morgan and Routier, *With Those Eyes*, p. 104.
53. Ibid., p. 85.
54. Pierre Philippe in *Cinéma 67*, quoted by Mitry, *Histoire du cinéma*, vol. 4, p. 339.
55. See Claude Gauteur, "Michel Simon," pp. 72, 78.
56. In *Le Nouvel Observateur*, 22 November 1976; cited in *L'Avant-Scène Cinéma*, no. 234 (15 October 1979): 73.

7. "Atmosphere, Atmosphere"

1. Eugène Dabit, *L'Hôtel du Nord* (Paris: Denoël et Steele, 1929). The definite article in the novel's title was dropped for the screen adaptation, unlike the case of *Le Quai des Brumes*.
2. Eugène Dabit, *Journal Intime (1928–1936)* (Paris: Gallimard, 1939), p. 352.
3. Chantal, *Le Ciné-monde*, p. 328.
4. Graham Greene, "*Confessions of a Nazi Spy/Hôtel du Nord*," *The Spectator*, 23 June 1939; reprinted in *Graham Greene on Film* (New York: Simon and Schuster, 1972), pp. 229–30.
5. Claude Mauriac, *L'Amour du cinéma* (Paris: Albin Michel, 1954), p. 36.
6. Carné, personal interview, Paris, 26 June 1983.
7. For an extensive study of homosexuality in American movies, see Vito Russo, *The Celluloid Closet* (New York: Harper and Row, 1981). For international perspectives, see Jean-François Garsi, ed., *Cinémas homosexuels*, "Dossier CinémAction" (Paris: Papyrus, 1983), and Bertrand Philbert, *L'Homosexualité à l'écran* (Paris: Henri Veyrier, 1984).
8. Jean Cocteau, *Mes Monstres sacrés* (Paris: Encre, 1979), p. 87.
9. See Charles Affron, *Cinema and Sentiment* (Chicago: University of Chicago Press, 1982), p. 114.
10. John Simon, "Of Paradise and Parasites," *Private Screenings* (New York: Macmillan, 1967), p. 120.
11. Trauner, personal interview, Boulogne-Billancourt, 21 December 1979.
12. Arletty, personal interview, Paris, 6 December 1979.
13. Roger Manvell, *Love Goddesses of the Movies* (New York: Crescent Books, 1975), p. 79.
14. *Paris-Cinéma* yearbook (1946); cited by Siclier, *La Femme*, p. 56.
15. Louise Brooks, *Lulu in Hollywood* (New York: Knopf, 1982), p. 74.
16. Arletty, personal interview, Paris, 6 December 1979.
17. As related by Henri Jeanson in "Mademoiselle Arletty"; quoted in Philippe Ariotti and Philippe de Comes, *Arletty* (Paris: Henri Veyrier, 1978), p. 204.
18. In an unrealized screenplay, *Yvette*, adapted from Maupassant. Quoted in Henri Jeanson, *En Verve*, ed. Nino Frank and Roger Régent (Paris: Pierre Horay, 1971), p. 29.

19. Pierre Serval, "Le rire d'Henri Jeanson," Preface to Henri Jeanson, *Soixante-Dix Ans d'adolescence* (Paris: Stock, 1971), p. 68.
20. Bessy, *Les Passagers du souvenir*, p. 241.
21. Ibid., p. 247.
22. Jeanson, *En Verve*, p. 40.

8. Strange Defeat

1. Jacques Brunius, "Un Des Jalons majeurs de l'histoire du cinéma," *L'Avant-Scène Cinéma*, no. 53 (November 1965): 6. For detailed analyses of the flashback structure in *Le Jour se lève*, see Francis Vanoye, *Récit écrit-récit filmique* (Paris: Editions Cedic, 1979), pp. 182–89; Inez Hedges, "Form and Meaning in French Film, I: Time and Space," *French Review* 14, no. 1 (October 1980): 29–32; and André Bazin's celebrated "Fiche du *Jour se lève*," first published in *Doc* (Paris: Editions Peuple et Culture, 1948). Bazin's piece is reprinted in *Regards neufs sur le cinéma* (Paris: Editions Peuple et Culture, 1963), ed. Jacques Chevalier; and reprinted again in Bazin, *Le Cinéma français de la libération à la nouvelle vague (1945–1958)* (Paris: Editions de L'Etoile, 1983), ed. Jean Narboni, pp. 53–69. Excerpts in English translation appear in the preface to the published script, *Le Jour se lève* (New York: Simon and Schuster, 1970), trans. Dinah Brooke and Nicola Hayden. The attribution of the flashback device to Viot rather than to Prévert is called into question by Brunelin, *Gabin*, p. 259.
2. Jaubert is quoted by Leprohon in *Hommes et métiers*, p. 184.
3. In *Débats*, 4 May 1936; quoted by Annette Insdorf, "Maurice Jaubert and François Truffaut: Musical Continuities from *L'Atalante* to *L'Histoire d'Adèle H.*," *Yale French Studies*, no. 60 (1980): 206.
4. Jaubert, cited by Bazin in "Jaubert et le cinéma français," in *Le Cinéma français*, p. 218.
5. Michelangelo Antonioni, "Marcel Carné, parigino," *Bianco e Nero* 9, no. 10 (December 1948): 32.
6. Claude Debussy, "Letter to the Secretary-General of the Opéra-Comique in Paris (1894)," trans. Ulrich Weisstein, in *The Essence of Opera*, ed. U. Weisstein (New York: Norton, 1964), p. 256.
7. Joseph Kerman, *Opera as Drama* (New York: Vintage, 1956), p. 177.
8. See Jacob, "Situation de Jacques Prévert," p. 8; Allen Thiher, *The Cinematic Muse* (Columbia: University of Missouri Press, 1979), p. 123; and Mitry, *Histoire du cinéma*, vol. 4, p. 344.
9. Braudy, *World in a Frame*, p. 66.
10. See Thiher, *Cinematic Muse*, p. 120.
11. Peter Brooks, *The Melodramatic Imagination* (New Haven: Yale University Press, 1976), p. 22.
12. Bazin, "Mort d'Humphrey Bogart," in *Qu'est-ce que le cinéma?* (Paris: Editions du Cerf, 1958–62), vol. 3, pp. 83–88.

13. Jean-Pierre Azémas, *De Munich à la libération, 1938–1944* (Paris: Editions du Seuil, 1979), p. 26.
14. Marc Bloch, *Strange Defeat: A Statement of Evidence Written in 1940*, trans. Gerard Hopkins (New York: Octagon Books, 1968; orig. 1949), pp. 167, 166.
15. Ibid., pp. 164–65.
16. Thiher, *Cinematic Muse*, p. 122.
17. Raymond Durgnat, *Films and Feelings* (Cambridge, Mass.: MIT Press, 1967), p. 266.
18. Arletty, personal interview, Paris, 6 January 1980.
19. Carné, personal interview, Boston, 1 May 1981. According to actress Edwige Feuillère, Abel Gance "created a national scandal" by making her appear in a bathtub "with my breasts showing," in Gance's *Lucrèce Borgia* (1935); see Bernard Drew, "A Great French Actress Seizes the Limelight at a Major Retrospective," *New York Times*, Arts and Leisure, 2 January 1983, p. 13.
20. Voiced by Jean-Louis Barrault in Christian-Jaque's *Carné, l'homme à la caméra*.
21. Philippe Haudiquet, "Les Frères Prévert," in *Image et Son*, no. 189 (December 1965); quoted by Guillot, *Les Prévert*, p. 62.
22. Guillot, *Les Prévert*, p. 62.
23. Carné, personal interview, Paris, 8 January 1980. Carné restated this view in similar terms to an audience at Harvard University on 30 April 1981.
24. Braudy, *World in a Frame*, p. 49.
25. Bazin, *Le Cinéma français*, p. 68.
26. Excerpts appear in *Le Jour se lève*, *L'Avant-Scène Cinéma*, no. 53 (1965): 42.
27. Maurice Bardèche and Robert Brasillach, *Histoire du cinéma* (Paris: Les Sept Couleurs, 1964), vol. 2, p. 73.
28. Written for *Comoedia* and cited in Ariotti and de Comes, *Arletty*, p. 131.
29. Richard Winnington, "A Slight Case of Murder," 11 May 1946, reprinted in *Drawn and Quartered* (London: Saturn, n.d.), p. 54.

9. The Occupation

1. Knapp, *France*, p. 130.
2. Cited and translated in Tom Schachtman, *The Phony War: 1939–40* (New York: Harper and Row, 1982), p. 249.
3. Renoir, *My Life*, p. 183.
4. Quoted in Gerty Colin, *Jean Gabin* (Paris: Presses de la Cité, 1983), p. 67.
5. See Jacques Siclier, *La France de Pétain et son cinéma* (Paris: Henri Veyrier, 1981), p. 21.
6. Marcel Carné during a presentation at Harvard University, 30 April 1981. Carné expressed similar thoughts in his interview with Louis Sapin, *Paris-Match*, 28 February 1979, p. 7.

7. Major studies of the French film industry during the Occupation include, in French, Courtade, *Les Malédictions*; Jean-Pierre Jeancolas, *15 Ans d'années trente* (Paris: Stock, 1983); Paul Léglise, *Histoire de la politique du cinéma français*, vol. 2, *Le Cinéma entre deux républiques (1940–46)* (Paris: Pierre Lherminier, 1977); Prédal, *La Société française*; Siclier, *La France de Pétain*; and Garçon, *De Blum à Pétain*; and, in English, Evelyn Ehrlich, *Cinema of Paradox: French Filmmaking Under the German Occupation* (New York: Columbia University Press, 1985).

8. See Ehrlich, *Cinema of Paradox*, p. 44; also Jürgen Spiker, *Film und Kapital: Der Weg der Deutschen Filmwirtschaft zum national socialistischen Einheitskonzern* (Berlin: Verlag Volker Spiess, 1975), p. 193.

9. Stanley Hoffmann, *Decline or Renewal?: France Since the 1930s*, 7th ed. (New York: Viking, 1974), pp. 5, 16–20.

10. Lucien Rebatet, *Les Tribus du cinéma et du théâtre* (Paris: Nouvelles Editions Françaises, 1941), pp. 86–87. This book is vol. 4 of the series *Les Juifs en France*. The passage on Carné also appeared in *Le Film*, no. 17 (16 June 1941). It is reproduced *in toto* as an appendix to Siclier's *La France de Pétain*, pp. 459–60.

11. Events and remarks related by André Heinrich, Prévert's friend and archivist of Prévert's screen and screen-connected writings, in a personal interview, Paris, 6 October 1985.

12. Trauner, personal interview, Paris, 4 January 1980. Trauner provides further details on the *Puss in Boots* project, and a sketch of the torture chamber conceived for it but modified for *Les Visiteurs du Soir*, in Michel Ciment and Isabelle Jordan, "Entretien avec Alexandre Trauner (1)," *Positif*, no. 223 (October 1979): 18.

13. Michael R. Marrus and Robert O. Paxton, *Vichy France and the Jews* (New York: Basic Books, 1981) pp. 214, 206.

14. See Michel Rachline, *Jacques Prévert, Drôle de vie* (Paris: Ramsay, 1981), p. 22.

15. See Ehrlich, *Cinema of Paradox*, pp. 68–69, based on interviews with Galey and Pierre Prévert.

16. Jacques Audiberti and Roger Régent are quoted in *L'Avant-Scène Cinéma*, no. 12 (15 February 1962): 6.

17. In Rebatet's review for *Je Suis Partout*, quoted in Ariotti and de Comes, *Arletty*, p. 155.

18. Letter to Marcel Carné from Charles Spaak, 15 December 1942, Carné Archives, The French Library in Boston.

19. André Bazin, *French Cinema of the Occupation and Resistance: The Birth of a Critical Esthetic*, trans. Stanley Hochman, ed. François Truffaut (New York: Ungar, 1981; orig. 1975), pp. 31, 44, 63. Originally published as *Le Cinéma de l'occupation et de la résistance* (Paris: Union Générale d'Editions, 1975).

20. Bazin, "Marcel Carné's *Les Visiteurs du Soir*; Robert Bresson's *Les Anges du*

Péché," in *French Cinema of the Occupation*, pp. 43–51. The article is dated "end of 1943."

21. Roger Régent, *Cinéma de France de "La Fille du Puisatier" aux "Enfants du Paradis"* (Paris: Editions Bellefaye, 1948), p. 90.

22. Antonioni, "Marcel Carné," p. 37.

23. Johan Huizinga, *The Waning of the Middle Ages: A Study of the Forms of Life, Thought and Art in France and the Netherlands in the XIVth and XVth Centuries* (New York: Doubleday, 1954), pp. 31–40. Huizinga's study was first published in Holland in 1919; the first English edition dates from 1924; it was published in France by Payot in the late 1930s.

24. R. R. Palmer and Joel Colton, *A History of the Modern World*, 5th ed. (New York: Knopf, 1978), p. 70.

25. Jeanne Witta-Montrobert, *La Lanterne magique: mémoires d'une scripte* (Paris: Calmann-Lévy, 1980), p. 145. In his booklet *Marcel Carné* (London: British Film Institute, 1950), Jean Quéval asserts that Pierre Laroche claimed, a few years after the film's release, that he and Prévert both intended "a symbolic, patriotic interpretation," p. 17. All subsequent citations from Quéval's *Marcel Carné* refer to his more substantial French-language book of the same title published in 1952 by Editions du Cerf, Paris.

26. Jean-Pierre Bertin-Maghit, *Le Cinéma français sous Vichy* (Paris: Revue du Cinéma–Editions Albatros, 1980), p. 123.

27. Hazel Hackett, "The French Cinema During the Occupation," *Sight and Sound*, no. 57 (Spring 1946): 3.

28. Eric Rhode, *A History of the Cinema from Its Origins to 1970* (New York: Hill and Wang, 1976), p. 424.

29. Sadoul, *French Film*, p. 99. My translation; the original French of the clause about Hitler is *peu compréhensible*.

30. Siclier, *La Femme*, p. 104.

31. Siclier, *La France de Pétain*, p. 144.

32. Prédal, *La Société française*, p. 270.

33. Jeancolas, *15 Ans*, p. 328.

34. Preface to Courtade, *Les Malédictions*, p. 13. In an interview with Evelyn Ehrlich, Pierre Prévert is of the same opinion; see Ehrlich, *Cinema of Paradox*, p. 215, n. 16.

35. François Truffaut, "André Bazin, the Occupation, and I," Introduction to Bazin, *French Cinema of the Occupation*, p. 19.

36. Claude-Jean Philippe, *Le Roman du cinéma* (Paris: Fayard, 1986), vol. 2, p. 282.

37. Michel Pérez, *Les Films de Carné* (Paris: Ramsay, 1986), pp. 70–71.

38. Quéval, *Marcel Carné*, p. 48.

39. Roud, ed., *Cinema*, p. 192.

40. Siclier, *La France de Pétain*, p. 143.

41. Bardèche and Brasillach, *Histoire du cinéma*, vol. 2, p. 153.

42. Rhode, *History of the Cinema*, p. 426.

43. Jeancolas, *15 Ans*, p. 329.

44. In *L'Echo des Etudiants*; cited in *L'Avant-Scène Cinéma*, no. 12: 6.
45. Quoted by Chazal, *Marcel Carné*, p. 41.
46. In *Le Petit Parisien*, 1943; quoted by Chazal, *Marcel Carné*, p. 161.
47. Quéval, *Marcel Carné*, p. 48.
48. Antonioni, "Marcel Carné," p. 39.
49. Huizinga, *Waning of the Middle Ages*, pp. 248–49.
50. Trauner, personal interview, Paris, 4 January 1979.
51. See Huizinga, *Waning of the Middle Ages*, p. 267.
52. See Edmond Pognon, *Les Très Riches Heures du duc de Berry: 15th-Century Manuscript*, trans. David Macrae (New York: Crescent Books, 1979).
53. Yvette Bíró, *Profane Mythology: The Savage Mind of the Cinema*, trans. Imre Goldstein (Bloomington: Indiana University Press, 1982; orig. 1982), p. 103.
54. Marc Bloch, *Strange Defeat: A Statement of Evidence Written in 1940*, trans. Gerard Hopkins (New York: Octagon Books, 1968), pp. 37–75, passim.
55. See, for example, Leprohon, *Présences contemporaines*, p. 289.
56. Hoffmann, *Decline or Renewal?*, p. 56.
57. François Truffaut, *The Films in My Life*, trans. Leonard Mayhew (New York: Simon and Schuster, 1978; orig. 1975), p. 3.
58. François Garçon, "Le Retour d'une inquiétante imposture: *Lili Marleen* et *Le Dernier Métro*," *Les Temps Modernes*, no. 422 (September 1981): 538–48.
59. Hoffmann, *Decline or Renewal?*, p. 52.
60. Bloch, *Strange Defeat*, passim and p. 116.
61. Ehrlich, *Cinema of Paradox*, pp. 97 ff.
62. See ibid., passim. See also Naomi Greene, "Mood and Ideology in the Cinema of Vichy France," *French Review* 19, no. 3 (February 1986): 437–45. For an especially subtle analysis of the continuities between French prewar and Occupation cinema, see Garçon, *De Blum à Pétain*, passim.
63. Régent, *Cinéma de France*, pp. 91–93.
64. Prévert and Pozner, *Hebdromadaires*, p. 149.
65. Louis-Ferdinand Céline, *Arletty, jeune fille dauphinoise* (Paris: La Flûte de Pan, 1983), p. 26; Céline wrote this unrealized screenplay synopsis for Arletty in March 1948.
66. Ariotti and de Comes, *Arletty*, p. 155.
67. See Cynthia Secor, "The Androgyny Papers," *Women's Studies* 2 (1974): 139.
68. Baudelaire, *Mon Coeur mis à nu* (Fusées 10), in *Oeuvres complètes* (Paris: Seuil, 1968), p. 626. When I first visited Arletty on 6 December 1979, two books lay on her coffeetable: Pléiade editions of Rabelais and Baudelaire. Arletty, almost totally blind, says that these are the two writers whose works she most likes to have read to her.
69. See Laura Mulvey, "Visual Pleasure and Narrative Cinema," *Screen*, no. 3 (Autumn 1975): 6–18.
70. Truffaut, "Introduction," in Bazin, *French Cinema of the Occupation*, p. 8.

71. Jean Debrix, *"Les Visiteurs du soir," IDHEC Fiche Filmographique*, no. 39 (1947): 7.

72. Hoffmann, *Decline or Renewal?*, p. 36.

73. Richard Cobb, *French and Germans, Germans and French: A Personal Interpretation of France Under Two Occupations, 1914–1918/1940–1944* (Hanover: University Press of New England, 1983), p. 161.

74. See Introduction to Jeffrey Meyers, *Homosexuality and Literature 1890–1930* (Montreal: McGill-Queens University Press, 1977), and, especially, Benjamin DeMott, "But He's a Homosexual . . . ," in Irving Buchen, ed., *The Perverse Imagination: Sexuality and Literary Culture* (New York: New York University Press, 1970), pp. 147–64.

75. Bazin, *French Cinema of the Occupation*, p. 47.

76. Luisa de Urtubey, *Freud et le diable* (Paris: Presses Universitaires de France, 1983), p. 181.

77. William L. Shirer, *Berlin Diary: The Journal of a Correspondent* (New York: Knopf, 1941), p. 422.

78. See Dudley Andrew, *André Bazin* (New York: Oxford University Press, 1978), chap. 2, "The War Years," and chap. 3, "Birth of a Critic."

79. Bloch, *Strange Defeat*, p. 174.

80. See, for example, Ehrlich, *Cinema of Paradox*, chap. 6; and Jeancolas, *15 Ans*, part 2, chap. 2; and Garçon, *De Blum à Pétain*, chap. 4.

81. This proposition summarizes a major thesis developed in Ehrlich, *Cinema of Paradox*.

82. Georges Franju, letter to André Paulvé, 26 January 1944, Carné Archives, The French Library in Boston.

10. The Design of *Children of Paradise*

1. Jean-Louis Barrault, *Souvenirs pour demain* (Paris: Seuil, 1972), pp. 143–44.

2. For a complete account, see Tristan Rémy, *Jean-Gaspard Deburau* (Paris: L'Arche, 1954), pp. 133 ff.

3. Barrault, personal interview, Paris, 31 December 1979.

4. Pierre Prévert, personal interview, Paris, 8 October 1985.

5. Trauner, personal interview, Paris, 4 January 1980.

6. An abbreviated account of the film's production history is found in my "The Birth of *Children of Paradise*," *American Film* 4, no. 9 (July-August 1979): 42–49.

7. Barrault, personal interview, Paris, 31 December 1979.

8. Quoted in Robert Baldick, *The Life and Times of Frédérick Lemaître* (Fair Lawn, N.J.: Essential Books, 1959), p. 36.

9. See "Petite Histoire d'un grand film," in *L'Avant-Scène Cinéma*, nos. 72–73 (July-September 1967): 106.

10. Cited in *L'Avant-Scène Cinéma*, nos. 72–73: 106.

11. Ariotti and de Comes, *Arletty*, p. 164; also see Ehrlich, *Cinema of Paradox*, p. 166.

12. See Bernard-G. Landry, *Bernard-G. Landry présente Marcel Carné* (Paris: Jacques Vautrain, 1952), p. 32; and Pol Vandromme, *Robert Le Vigan: compagnon et personnage de L.-F. Céline* (Kessel-Lo: La Revue Célinienne, 1980), p. 58.

13. Margot Capelier, personal interview, Paris, 8 October 1985.

14. Fernand Bernardi, personal interview, Nice, 25 September 1985.

15. Arthur Hoérée, *Toute la vie*, 2 December 1943; cited in *L'Avant-Scène Cinéma*, nos. 72–73: 107.

16. In an interview with Jany Casanova for *Ciné-Miroir*, quoted in *L'Avant-Scène Cinéma*, nos. 72–73: 108.

17. See, for example, Georges Sadoul, *Dictionary of Films* (Berkeley: University of California Press, 1965), p. 102; Siclier, *La France de Pétain*, p. 168; and Mast, *Short History of the Movies*, p. 260.

18. Peter Brooks, *Reading for the Plot: Design and Intention in Narrative* (New York: Knopf, 1984), p. 323.

19. See ibid., pp. 23, 28.

20. Ibid., p. 52.

21. André Bazin, "*Les Enfants du Paradis* de Marcel Carné," *Le Parisien Libéré*, 30 March 1945; reprinted in Bazin, *French Cinema of the Occupation and Resistance*, pp. 107–9.

22. Truffaut, personal interview, Paris, 13 September 1979.

23. Brooks, *Reading for the Plot*, p. 61.

24. See, for example, the editors' n. 116 to the published script in *L'Avant-Scène Cinéma*, nos. 72–73: 99.

25. Carné, personal interview, Paris, 7 September 1985.

26. André Heinrich, personal interview, Paris, 6 October 1985.

27. See Judith Wechsler, *A Human Comedy: Physiognomy and Caricature in 19th Century Paris* (Chicago: University of Chicago Press, 1982), chaps. 2 and 3, passim.

28. My summary and bracketed commentary is based upon the British Lion 16 mm release print (Mai Harris title version) as distributed in the United States by Films Incorporated. This print, and hence the summary, divulges occasional slight divergences from the "edition" published by *L'Avant-Scène Cinéma*, nos. 72–73, itself based, in part, upon a close screening of the film—although the print utilized by the unnamed *L'Avant-Scène Cinéma* editors goes unidentified.

11. Politics and Theater in *Children of Paradise*

1. Among those who minimize relations between the film and the Pétain era are Siclier, *La France de Pétain*, p. 168, and Jeancolas, *15 Ans*, p. 330. Those who discern a sure relation include Rhode, *History of the Cinema*, pp. 427–28; and William L. Hedges, "Classics Revisited: Reaching for the Moon," *Film Quarterly* 12, no. 4 (Summer 1959): 29.

2. Many English-subtitled prints of the film, including those distributed by the

American distributor, Films Incorporated, contain a written prologue that situates Part I in "Paris, 1840" and a title prefacing Part II that reads "Several years have passed." Yet the published script in both its French (1967) and English (1968) editions indicates, with respect to Part I, "The period is about 1827 or 1828 . . . it really does not matter," and that between Parts I and II, "Several years have passed." Since 1979 the Ranelagh Theater in Paris's Passy district has been exhibiting *Les Enfants du paradis* uninterruptedly. Stripped of all introductory titles except credits, the print, distributed by Pathé-Consortium-Cinéma, specifies no date for the film's action and restores to what must be considered the movie's definitive print the imprecision of Carné and Prévert's original intentions as indicated by the script's phrase "about 1827 or 1828 . . . it really does not matter."

3. In *Paroles*, p. 50.

4. Hoffmann, *Decline or Renewal?*, pp. 44, 58.

5. David Pryce-Jones, *Paris in the Third Reich: A History of the German Occupation, 1940–1944* (New York: Holt, Reinhart and Winston, 1981), p. 183.

6. Ibid., p. 190.

7. Marrus and Paxton, *Vichy France*, pp. 250, 251, 270.

8. Pryce-Jones, *Paris in the Third Reich*, pp. 148–49.

9. Ciment and Jordan, "Entretien avec Alexandre Trauner (1)," p. 17.

10. Interview with Cécile Agay for *Action*, April 1945; reprinted in *L'Avant-Scène Cinéma*, nos. 72–73: 9–10.

11. Edmond Texier, *Tableau de Paris par Edmond Texier* (Paris: Paulin et Le Chevalier, 1852–53). Reproductions of some engravings are included in Wechsler, *A Human Comedy*; see especially p. 43.

12. See Ehrlich, *Cinema of Paradox*, p. 102; and Garçon, *De Blum à Pétain*, p. 125.

13. See Robert F. Storey, *Pierrot: A Critical History of a Mask* (Princeton: Princeton University Press, 1978), pp. 96, 106, 115–16; and Rémy, *Jean-Gaspard Deburau*, pp. 174–75.

14. Jules Janin, *Deburau*, trans. Winifred Katzin (New York: Robert M. McBride, 1928), p. 44.

15. George Sand, *Histoire de ma vie* (Paris: Michel Lévy Frères, 1856), vol. 8, p. 248.

16. Charles Nodier in *La Pandore*, 19 July 1828; cited and translated by Storey, *Pierrot*, p. 97.

17. Baudelaire, *Oeuvres complètes*, pp. 243, 376.

18. Théophile Gautier, "Funambules. *Pierrot pendu*," 25 January 1847, in *Histoire de l'art dramatique en France depuis vingt-cinq ans* (Paris: Magnin, Blanchard et cie, 1858–59), vol. 5, p. 25.

19. Gautier's review, "Shakspeare aux Funambules," appeared in the *Revue de Paris*, 4 September 1842, and was reprinted in his *Souvenirs de théâtre, d'art et de critique* (Paris: G. Charpentier, 1883), pp. 55–67; lengthy excerpts are

provided in Storey, *Pierrot*, pp. 106–7, and in Guitry, *Deburau: comédie en vers libres* (Paris: Fasquelle, 1918), pp. 17–20. In his more recent monograph, *Pierrots on the Stage of Desire: Nineteenth-Century French Literary Artists and the Comic Pantomime* (Princeton: Princeton University Press, 1985), Storey challenges Rémy's assertion that Legrand, not Deburau, played in *Le Marrrchand d'habits!* and suggests that Gautier's review was in fact a fictitious account that inspired Cot d'Ordan, the Funambules' administrator, to "adapt" for the stage, ex post facto, Gautier's sketch (pp. 41–43).

20. Barrault, *Souvenirs pour demain*, pp. 72–73; and J.-L. Barrault, *The Theater of Jean-Louis Barrault*, trans. Joseph Chiari (New York: Hill and Wang, 1961), p. 30; originally published as *Nouvelles Réflexions sur le théâtre* (Paris: Flammarion, 1959).

21. Barrault, *Souvenirs pour demain*, p. 88.

22. Artaud quoted by Jean-Louis Barrault in the latter's *Reflections on the Theater*, trans. Barbara Wall (London: Rockliff, 1951), p. 40; originally published as J.-L. Barrault, *Réflexions sur le théâtre* (Paris: Jacques Vautrain, 1949).

23. Barrault, *Reflections on the Theater*, pp. 142–43.

24. Maurice Bessy, *Cinémagazine*, 19 October 1936; quoted in Pierre Cadars, *Les Séducteurs du cinéma français (1928–1958)* (Paris: Henri Veyrier, 1982), p. 37.

25. Cited in Frédérick Lemaître, *Souvenirs publiés par son fils*, ed. Frédérick Lemaître, *fils*, 2d ed. (Paris: Paul Ollendorff, 1880), p. 77.

26. Quoted and translated by Baldick, *Frédérick Lemaître*, p. 106; from Alexandre Dumas, *père*, *Mes Mémoires* (Paris: Cadot, 1852–54), vol. 25, pp. 306–8.

27. Gautier, "Porte-Saint-Martin. Reprise de *Kean*," 13 June 1842, in *Histoire de l'art dramatique en France depuis vingt-cinq ans*, vol. 2, p. 250.

28. Baldick, *Frédérick Lemaître*, p. 103.

29. Paul A. Gagnon, *France Since 1789* (New York: Harper and Row, 1964), p. 114.

30. Marcel Oms, "Les Enfants du paradis: la mutation cinématographique du mélodrame," *Les Cahiers de la Cinémathèque*, no. 28 (October 1979): 143.

31. Pierre Brasseur, *Ma Vie en vrac* (Paris: Calmann-Lévy, 1972), p. 316.

32. Ibid., p. 303.

33. I am grateful to Alexander Trauner for showing me his photograph of Prévert's chart. According to Trauner the chart went into the care of Henri Langlois and subsequently disappeared. I am equally indebted to the office of Charles and Ray Eames, Venice, California, for providing me subsequently with a duplicate photograph of the chart for use during the course of my research.

34. Quoted in Pryce-Jones, *Paris in the Third Reich*, p. 26.

35. See André Halimi, *Chantons sous l'occupation* (Paris: Olivier Orban, 1976), p. 45.

36. Pryce-Jones, *Paris in the Third Reich*, p. 166.
37. See Ehrlich, *Cinema of Paradox*, p. 83, and Courtade, *Les Malédictions*, p. 219.
38. Halimi, *Chantons*, pp. 271–74.
39. Jean-Jacques Gautier, *Le Figaro*, 10 March 1945; Jeander, *Libération*, 14 March 1945; Maurice Hilero, *Fraternité*, 23 March 1945. Excerpts of each appear in *L'Avant-Scène Cinéma*, nos. 72–73: 101–3; *L'Avant-Scène* misdates the Jeander review.
40. Sadoul, "Les Films de Carné," p. 8.
41. Andrew Sarris, "Films in Focus," *Village Voice*, 31 January 1974.
42. Ehrlich, *Cinema of Paradox*, p. 145.
43. Marcel Carné, lecture-discussion at Harvard University, Carpenter Center for the Visual Arts, 30 April 1981.
44. See Ehrlich, *Cinema of Paradox*, p. 11.
45. Werner Rings, *Life with the Enemy: Collaboration and Resistance in Hitler's Europe, 1939–1945*, trans. J. Maxwell Brown (Garden City, N.Y.: Doubleday, 1982; orig. 1979), pp. 157–58.
46. George Steiner, "The Historicity of Dreams (Two Questions to Freud)," *Salmagundi*, no. 61 (Fall 1983): 10.

12. Androgyny, Masochism, and *Children of Paradise*

1. Régent, *Cinéma de France*, p. 279.
2. Victor Hugo, "Visite à la Conciergerie," 10 September 1846, in *Choses vues* (Paris: J. Hetzel and Maison Quantin, n.d.), p. 113; Théophile Gautier, "Lacenaire" (1851), in *Emaux et Camées*, "Etudes de mains," II, in *Poésies complètes de Théophile Gautier*, ed. R. Jasinski (Paris: Nizet, 1970), vol. 3, pp. 12–13; André Breton, "Rêves d'un condamné à mort," in *Anthologie de l'humour noir*, 3d ed. (Paris: Jean-Jacques Pauvert, 1966; orig. 1939), pp. 119–20.
3. Baudelaire, "De l'héroïsme de la vie moderne," in *Salon de 1846*, in *Oeuvres complètes*, p. 260.
4. See Philip John Stead, Introduction to Pierre-François Lacenaire, *The Memoirs of Lacenaire*, trans. P. J. Stead (London: Staples Press, 1952), p. 46.
5. See Leonid Gossman, *Dostoevsky: A Biography*, trans. Mary Mackler (Indianapolis: Bobbs-Merrill, 1975), pp. 344–45. Dostoevsky also mentions Lacenaire in *The Idiot* (Part II, chap. 7) and in his notebooks for *A Raw Youth*.
6. See Pierre-François Lacenaire, *Mémoires de Lacenaire avec ses Poèmes et ses Lettres*, ed. Monique Lebailly (Paris: Albin Michel, 1968), p. 4.
7. I am referring to the photograph copies possessed by Alexander Trauner and the office of Charles and Ray Eames.
8. Lacenaire, *Memoirs*, ed. Stead, pp. 146–47, 180.

9. Jules-Amédée Barbey d'Aurevilly, *Disjecta membra* (Paris: La Connaissance, 1925), vol. 2, p. 177.

10. See Stead's Introduction to Lacenaire, *Memoirs*, ed. Stead, p. 21.

11. Théodore Laborieu, *Mémoires de M. Claude* (Paris, 1881–83), as cited in *Mémoires de Lacenaire*, ed. Lebailly, pp. 287–88.

12. See Baudelaire, "Le Dandy," in *Le Peintre de la vie moderne*, in *Oeuvres complètes*, p. 560.

13. See Domna C. Stanton, *The Aristocrat as Art: A Study of the Honnête Homme and the Dandy in Seventeenth- and Nineteenth-Century French Literature* (New York: Columbia University Press, 1980); and Sima Godfrey, "The Dandy as Ironic Figure," *Sub-Stance*, no. 36 (1982): 21–33.

14. Jacques Grant and Jean-Pierre Joecker, "Rencontre avec Marcel Carné, Cinéaste Fantastique," *Masques: revue des homosexualités*, no. 16 (Winter 1982–83): 14.

15. Arletty, personal interview, Paris, 6 January 1980.

16. Lacenaire, *Memoirs*, ed. Stead, pp. 116–18.

17. Ibid., pp. 119, 118, 192.

18. Hippolyte Bonnelier, *Autopsie physiologique de Lacenaire* (Paris: L. Mathias, 1836); excerpts quoted in Lacenaire, *Mémoires*, ed. Lebailly, pp. 251–54, 334–35.

19. Victor Cochinat, *Lacenaire, ses crimes, son procès et sa mort, suivis de ses poésies et chansons*, 1857, quoted in Lacenaire, *Mémoires*, ed. Lebailly, p. 330.

20. Stead, Introduction to Lacenaire, *Memoirs*, ed. Stead, p. 27.

21. Jean-Pierre Mogui, *Lacenaire, assassin romantique* (Paris: La Table Ronde, 1980), p. 131.

22. Lacenaire, *Memoirs*, ed. Stead, p. 175.

23. Ibid., p. 190.

24. Dominique Fernandez, "Grandeur et décadence de la culture homosexuelle," *Masques: revue des homosexualités*, no. 21 (Spring 1984): 81.

25. Mirella Jona Affron, "*Les Enfants du paradis*: Play of Genres," *Cinema Journal* 18, no. 1 (Fall 1978): 51.

26. Linda Bamber, *Comic Women, Tragic Men: A Study of Gender and Genre in Shakespeare* (Stanford: Stanford University Press, 1982), p. 18.

27. Allardyce Nicoll, *The World of Harlequin: A Critical Study of the Commedia dell'Arte* (Cambridge: Cambridge University Press, 1963), p. 3.

28. Maria Casarès, *Résidente privilégiée* (Paris: Arthème Fayard, 1980), p. 207.

29. Barrault, *Theater of Jean-Louis Barrault*, p. 29.

30. See Rémy, *Jean-Gaspard Deburau*, pp. 142–44 and passim.

31. See Paul and Victor Margueritte, *Nos Tréteaux: Charades de Victor Margueritte; Pantomimes de Paul Margueritte* (Paris: Les Bibliophiles Fantaisistes, 1910); Albert Giraud, *Pierrot lunaire; Rondels bergmasques* (Paris: Alphonse Choiseul, 1884); and Jules Laforgue, *Les Complaintes* (Paris: Léon

Vanier, 1885) and *Imitation de Notre-Dame la Lune* (Paris: Léon Vanier, 1886).

32. W. Hedges, "Classics Revisited," p. 30.

33. Raymond Borde, "Marcel Carné et le cinéma social," *Cahiers de la Cinémathèque*, no. 5 (Winter 1972): 14.

34. Gilles Deleuze, *Sacher-Masoch: An Interpretation*, together with the entire text of *Venus in Furs* from a French rendering by Aude Willm, trans. Jean McNeil (London: Faber, 1971; orig. 1967); the American edition is entitled *Masochism: An Interpretation of Coldness and Cruelty* (New York: George Braziller, 1971).

35. See Gaylyn Studlar, "Venus in Furs: Masoch, Deleuze and the Films of von Sternberg," *USC Spectator* 2, no. 2 (Spring 1983): 2–3 and 10; Studlar, "Masochism and the Perverse Pleasures of the Cinema," *Quarterly Review of Film Studies* 9, no. 4 (Fall 1984): 267–82; Studlar, "Visual Pleasure and the Masochistic Aesthetic," *Journal of Film and Video* 37 (Spring 1985): 5–26; and the forthcoming publication by the University of Illinois Press of Studlar's revised University of Southern California Ph.D. dissertation, "Visual Pleasure and the Masochistic Aesthetic: The von Sternberg/Dietrich Paramount Cycle."

36. Deleuze, *Sacher-Masoch*, pp. 63, 45.

37. Patrice Pavis, *Voix et images de la scène: essais de sémiologie théâtrale* (Lille: Presses Universitaires de Lille, 1982), p. 129.

38. Barrault, *Comme je le pense* (Paris: Gallimard, 1975), p. 250; *Theater of Jean-Louis Barrault*, p. 103; *Reflections on the Theater*, p. 57.

39. Barrault, *The Theater of Jean-Louis Barrault*, pp. 2, 59.

40. Barrault, *Reflections on the Theater*, p. 165.

41. Baudelaire, "Les Foules," *Petits poëmes en prose (Le spleen de Paris)*, 12, in *Oeuvres complètes*, p. 155.

42. Guillot, *Les Prévert*, p. 118.

43. Janin, *Deburau*, p. 52.

44. Jean Starobinski, *Portrait de l'artiste en saltimbanque* (Geneva: Albert Skira, 1970), p. 25.

45. See Studlar, "Masochism," pp. 275–76.

46. Studlar, "Masochism," pp. 277–78; Studlar draws on, especially, Hans Loewald, *Papers on Psychoanalysis* (New Haven: Yale University Press, 1980); Lawrence Kubie, "The Drive to Become Both Sexes," in Herbert J. Schlessinger, ed., *Symbols and Neurosis* (New York: International Universities Press, 1978); and Otto Fenichel, "Scopophilic Instinct and Identification," in *Collected Papers of Otto Fenichel, First Series* (New York: Norton, 1953).

47. See J. E. Rivers, *Proust and the Art of Love: The Aesthetics of Sexuality in the Life, Times, and Art of Marcel Proust* (New York: Columbia University Press, 1980), pp. 195, 280.

48. Prévert, "Lanterne magique de Picasso," *Paroles*, p. 289, my translation;

Proust, *Le Temps retrouvé* in *A la recherche du temps perdu* (Paris: Gallimard, 1954), vol. 3, p. 870.

49. Deleuze, *Sacher-Masoch*, pp. 87, 81.

50. Ibid., pp. 87, 108.

51. Antonioni, "Marcel Carné," pp. 43–44.

52. Mikhail Bakhtin, *Rabelais and His World*, trans. Hélène Iswolsky (Bloomington: Indiana University Press, 1984; orig. 1965), pp. 18, 44, 255.

53. Deleuze, *Sacher-Masoch*, p. 56. In connection with the issue raised in the previous chapter concerning Jéricho as a possible incarnation of anti-Semitic sentiment, it is useful to read Béla Grunberger, "The Anti-Semite and the Oedipal Conflict," *International Journal of Psycho-Analysis* 45 (April-July 1964): 380–85.

54. Jacques Feyder, letter to Marcel Carné, 17 May 1947, Carné Archives, The French Library in Boston.

55. See Jacques Feyder and Françoise Rosay, *Le Cinéma, notre métier* (Vésenaz-près-Genève: Paris Cailler, 1946).

56. See Françoise Rosay, *La Traversée d'une vie, souvenirs recueillis par Colette Mars* (Paris: Laffont, 1974).

57. Carné, personal interview, Paris, 7 September 1985.

58. Deleuze, *Sacher-Masoch*, p. 88.

13. Primal Scenes from *Children of Paradise*

1. Melanie Klein, "Infant Analysis (1923)," in *Contributions to Psychoanalysis, 1921–45* (London: Hogarth Press, 1968; orig. 1948), p. 112. For a psychoanalytic approach to primal scene imagery in film, see Daniel Dervin, *Through a Freudian Lens Deeply: A Psychoanalysis of Cinema* (Hillsdale, N.J.: Analytic Press, 1985). See also Noel Bradley, "Primal Scene Experience in Human Evolution and Its Phantasy Derivatives in Art, Proto-Science and Philosophy," in *The Psychoanalytic Study of Society* (New York: International Universities Press, 1967), vol. 4.

2. Freud deals tentatively with the primal scene hypothesis as of letters written to Wilhelm Fliess in 1896 and 1897. His fullest elaboration occurs in *From the History of an Infantile Neurosis* (1918 [1914]) in *The Standard Edition of the Complete Psychological Works of Sigmund Freud*, trans. James Strachey (London: Hogarth, 1953), vol. 17, especially parts 4–8, pp. 29–103. For an overview of the concept's evolution in clinical psychoanalytic literature, see Aaron H. Esman, "The Primal Scene: A Review and a Reconsideration," *Psychoanalytic Study of the Child* 28 (1973): 49–81; and Gerhard Dahl, "Notes on Critical Examinations of the Primal Scene Concept," *Journal of the American Psychoanalytic Association* 30, no. 3 (1982): 657–77. For a discussion of theoretical issues surrounding the reality/fantasy dimension of the hypothesis, see Ned Lukacher, *Primal Scenes: Literature, Phi-*

losophy, Psychoanalysis (Ithaca: Cornell University Press, 1986), chap. 4, "Primal Scenes: Freud and the Wolf-Man," pp. 136–67.

3. Ruth Mack Brunswick, "The Preoedipal Phase of the Libido Development (1940)," in *The Psycho-Analytic Reader* (London: Hogarth Press, 1950), p. 243.

4. Henry Edelheit, "Mythopoesis and the Primal Scene," in *The Psychoanalytic Study of Society* (New York: International Universities Press, 1972), vol. 5, p. 220.

5. Ibid., p. 213.

6. Jean Laplanche, *Life and Death in Psychoanalysis*, trans. Jeffrey Mehlman (Baltimore: Johns Hopkins University Press, 1976; orig. 1970), p. 102.

7. Climent-Oms, "Marcel Carné parle," pp. 44–45.

8. These crucial lines do not appear in the published script. The dialogue of the balcony scene as spoken in the film differs markedly from the published versions, French and English.

9. Deleuze, *Sacher-Masoch*, pp. 30, 49, 62, 64.

10. Ibid., pp. 102–3.

11. See Janet Staiger, "The Eyes Are Really the Focus: Photoplay Acting and Film Form and Style," *Wide Angle* 6, no. 4 (1985): 21.

12. Deleuze, *Sacher-Masoch*, p. 28.

13. The French and English published scripts represent consistently the Count's surname as "Monteray," although the cast list on p. 7 of the French version provides the spelling "Montray." N. 51 of the French version claims that Louis Salou's pronunciation suggests "Mortray," but my hearing does not bear this out.

14. Sophocles, *Oedipus Tyrannus*, trans. Luci Berkowitz and Theodore F. Brunner, 1970, in *World Masterpieces*, ed. Maynard Mack (New York: Norton, 1974), vol. 1, pp. 349–51, 368.

15. See Edelheit, *Mythopoesis*, pp. 229, 232, and passim.

16. Freud, "Fetishism (1927)," in *The Standard Edition*, vol. 21, pp. 152–57; and "Splitting of the Ego in the Process of Defence (1940 [1938])," in *The Standard Edition*, vol. 23, pp. 275–78.

17. Deleuze, *Sacher-Masoch*, p. 28.

18. See Mulvey, "Visual Pleasure," pp. 13–14, 18.

19. Ibid., p. 11.

20. Bertram Lewin, "Sleep, the Mouth, and the Dream Screen," *Psychoanalytic Quarterly* 15, no. 4 (October 1946): 421. See also Lewin's "Inferences from the Dream Screen," *International Journal of Psycho-Analysis* 29, part 4 (1948): 224–31.

21. Jean-Louis Baudry, "The Apparatus," *Camera Obscura: Journal of Feminism and Film Theory*, no. 1 (Fall 1976): 125; originally published as "Le Dispositif: approches métapsychologiques de l'impression de réalité," *Communications*, no. 23 (1975): 56–72.

22. Robert T. Eberwein, "Reflections on the Breast," *Wide Angle* 4, no. 3 (Winter 1980): 52.

23. See Alekan, *Des Lumières*, p. 208.

24. J. Laplanche and J.-B. Pontalis, *The Language of Psycho-Analysis*, trans. Donald Nicholson-Smith (New York: Norton, 1973; orig. 1967), p. 58.

25. Eberwein, "Reflections on the Breast," p. 53.

26. Climent-Oms, "Marcel Carné parle," p. 47.

27. Deleuze, *Sacher-Masoch*, pp. 28–29.

28. Janin, *Deburau*, pp. 15–17, 41.

29. Norman Bryson, *Tradition and Desire* (Cambridge: Cambridge University Press, 1984), p. 131.

30. Ibid., pp. 132–33.

31. Baudelaire, *Salon de 1845*, in *Oeuvres complètes*, p. 226 (text and Baudelaire's footnote).

32. Bryson, *Tradition and Desire*, pp. 133, 136, 150.

33. Robert Rosenblum, *Jean-Auguste-Dominique Ingres* (New York: Harry N. Abrams, 1967), p. 107.

34. Baudelaire, *Exposition universelle 1855: Beaux Arts*, in *Oeuvres complètes*, p. 365.

35. Bryson, *Tradition and Desire*, p. 137.

36. For an overview of film theorists' "obsession with the coherence of the male subject," see Kaja Silverman, "Lost Objects and Mistaken Subjects: Film Theory's Structuring Lack," *Wide Angle* 7, nos. 1–2 (Spring-Summer 1985): 14–29.

37. See Rosenblum, *Ingres*, pp. 36, 88, 114, 120.

38. Edward W. Said, *Orientalism* (New York: Pantheon Books, 1978), pp. 3, 8, and passim.

39. Bryson, *Tradition and Desire*, pp. 144, 170.

40. Théophile Gautier, "Lacenaire," in *Emaux et Camées*, ed. Jasinski, pp. 12–13.

41. Mulvey, "Visual Pleasure," p. 7.

42. John Simon, *Private Screenings* (New York: Berkeley, 1967), p. 120.

43. Roud, "Marcel Carné and Jacques Prévert," in *Cinema*, p. 192.

44. Manvell, *Love Goddesses*, p. 79.

45. See Claire Johnston, "Myths of Women in the Cinema," in Karyn Kay and Gerald Peary, eds., *Women and the Cinema: A Critical Anthology* (New York: Dutton, 1977), p. 410; excerpted from "Women's Cinema as Counter-cinema," in *Notes on Women's Cinema*, ed. Claire Johnston, *Screen*, Pamphlet 2, 1974.

46. See James Hall, *Dictionary of Subjects and Symbolism in Art* (London: Cox and Wyman, 1974); Arthur Henkel and Albrecht Schöne, eds., *Emblemata: Handbuch Zur Sinnbildkunst des XVI. und XVII. Jahrhunderts* (Stuttgart:

J. B. Metzlersche Verlagsbuchhandlung, 1976); and Geoffrey Grigson, *The Goddess of Love* (New York: Stein and Day, 1976).

47. See, for example, Joseph Campbell, *The Masks of God: Occidental Mythology* (New York: Viking, 1964), vol. 3; J. C. Cooper, *An Illustrated Encyclopedia of Traditional Symbols* (London: Thames and Hudson, 1978); and Jean Chevalier and Alain Gheerbrant, *Dictionnaire des symboles* (Paris: Laffont, 1982).

48. See Anne Hollander, *Seeing Through Clothes* (New York: Viking, 1978), p. 376.

49. Rosenblum, *Ingres*, p. 33.

50. Bryson, *Tradition and Desire*, p. 174.

51. Arletty, personal interview, Paris, 6 December 1979.

52. Arletty, *La Défense* (Paris: Editions de la Table Ronde, 1971), p. 158.

53. Arletty, personal interview, Paris, 6 December 1979.

54. See, for example, Pryce-Jones, *Paris in the Third Reich*, p. 160; Cobb, *French and Germans*, p. 66.

55. Arletty, personal interview, Paris, 6 December 1979.

56. Arletty, *La Défense*, pp. 152–53, 182–83, 156.

57. See Halimi, *Chantons*, p. 204.

58. Arletty, *La Défense*, p. 154.

14. In the Afterglow of Triumph

1. See Courtade, *Les Malédictions*, pp. 226 ff; Ehrlich, *Cinema of Paradox*, pp. 173 ff; and Jean-Pierre Bertin-Maghit, "1945, l'épuration du cinéma français. Mythe ou réalité?" in *Film et histoire*, ed. Marc Ferro (Paris: Editions de l'Ecole des Hautes Etudes en Sciences Sociales, 1984), pp. 131–42. Bertin-Maghit's study aims to supersede the relevant sections of Robert Aron's *Histoire de l'épuration*, vol. 2, *Le Monde de la presse, des arts, des lettres* (Paris: Fayard, 1975). See also Herbert R. Lottman, *The Purge* (New York: William Morrow, 1986).

2. "Epuration dans les entreprises: sanctions prononcées: Comité d'organisation de l'industrie cinématographique," *Bulletin Municipal Officiel de la Ville de Paris et Annexe au Recueil des Actes Administratifs de la Préfecture de la Seine et de la Préfecture de Police*, 13–14 August 1945, p. 991.

3. Carné, personal interview, Paris, 7 September 1985.

4. See Bertin-Maghit, "1945, l'épuration du cinéma," pp. 133–35.

5. Albert Camus in *Combat*, 20 October 1944 and 30 August 1945; cited and translated by James D. Wilkinson, *Intellectual Resistance in Europe* (Cambridge, Mass.: Harvard University Press, 1981), pp. 67, 70.

6. See *Bulletin Municipal Officiel*, 13–14 August 1945, p. 991; and 31 August 1945, pp. 1064–65.

7. Cited in Bertin-Maghit, "1945, l'épuration du cinéma," p. 141.

8. In Halimi, *Chantons*, p. 202.

9. The Directeur de Cabinet, signature indecipherable, Ministère de la Jeunesse des Arts et des Lettres, letter to Marcel Carné, 27 March 1947, Carné Archives, The French Library in Boston.

10. Jean-Pierre Marchand, Secrétaire-Administratif for Louis Daquin, Secrétaire Général, Syndicat des Techniciens de la Production Cinématographique, letter to Marcel Carné, 4 November 1952, Carné Archives, The French Library in Boston.

11. Jacques Becker, letter to Marcel Carné, 9 September 1948, Carné Archives, The French Library in Boston.

12. In Michèle Nocolal, "Un grand film se prépare: *Les Portes de la nuit*," *La France Au Combat*, 14 March 1946.

13. Marlene Dietrich, *Marlène D.*, trans. Boris Mattews and François Ducout from an unpublished English manuscript (Paris: Grasset, 1984), p. 136. Dietrich's many biographers and commentators include Charles Higham, *Marlene: The Life of Marlene Dietrich* (New York: Norton, 1977); Alexander Walker, *Dietrich* (New York: Harper & Row, 1984); and Donald Spoto, *Falling in Love Again* (Boston: Little, Brown and Company, 1985).

14. Gérard Fabrice, "Carné tourne le dos à Marlène et Gabin," *Paris-Cinéma*, 20 February 1946.

15. In Huguette ex-Micro [Henri Jeanson], "Marlénade et Gabinerie," *Le Canard enchaîné*, 30 January 1946.

16. See Higham, *Marlene*, p. 217. In *Marlène D.*, Dietrich does not refer to the *épuration*.

17. See "Epuration dans les entreprises," *Bulletin Municipal Officiel*, 31 August 1945, p. 1065.

18. Quoted in Pierre Monnier, *Arletty* (Paris: Stock, 1984), p. 87.

19. Ethan Mordden, *Movie Star: A Look at the Women Who Made Hollywood* (New York: St. Martin's Press, 1983).

20. The original handwritten draft is housed in the Carné Archives, The French Library in Boston. The lines in question occur in shots 13 (the *Frisés*), 108 (right-wingers), 129 ff (concentration camps), 193 and 199 (anti-Semitism), 331 (Place Vendôme), and 377 and 398 (American culture).

21. André Heinrich, personal interview, 6 October 1985.

22. Dudley Nichols, "The Writer and the Film," in J. Gassner and D. Nichols, eds., *Twenty Best Film Plays* (New York: Crown, 1943), p. xxxix.

23. Jean-Pierre Rioux, *La France de la IVe République (1)* (Paris: Seuil, 1980), p. 66.

24. See, for example, Louis Raitière, "Les Portes de la nuit," *Bulletin de l'IDHEC*, no. 8 (March–May 1947); and James Agee's review in *The Nation*, 13 September 1947; rpt. in Agee, *Agee on Film*, vol. 1 (New York: Grosset, 1969), p. 276. For recent commentary on the picture as "a major and early documentation of the evasiveness and the narcissistic gaze that became the dominant signs of post-war French film," see Robert Philip Kolker, "Carné's

Les Portes de la nuit and the Sleep of French Cinema," *Post Script* 7, no. 1 (Fall 1987): 46–59.

25. Umberto Barbaro, "Neo-Realismo," orig. in *Film* 6, no. 23 (5 June 1943); rpt. in Barbaro, *Neorealismo e realismo*, ed. Gian Piero Brunetta (Rome: Editori Riuniti, 1976), vol. 2, pp. 500–504; the quotation, p. 501.

26. For example, Mario Cannella, "Ideology and Aesthetic Hypotheses in the Criticism of Neo-Realism," orig. in *Giovane Critica*, no. 11 (1966); trans. John Mathews and Judith White in *Screen* 14, no. 4 (Winter 1973–74): 34–35; Christopher Williams, "Bazin on Neo-Realism," *Screen* 14, no. 4 (Winter 1973–74): 61–68; and Peter Bondanella, *Italian Cinema from Neorealism to the Present* (New York: Frederick Ungar, 1983), p. 32.

15. Carné sans Prévert

1. Pierre Prévert, personal interviews, Paris, 8 October 1985 and 7 January 1980.

2. René Bertelé, publisher of *Paroles*, as quoted in Michel Rachline, *Jacques Prévert, Drôle de vie*, p. 132.

3. See, for example, J. G. Auriol, "La nuit de quat'sous: *Les Portes de la nuit*," *La Revue du Cinéma* 1, no. 4 (1 January 1947): 67–70.

4. See Monnier, pp. 80–81; and John Kobal, *People Will Talk* (New York: Knopf, 1985), p. 241.

5. Witta-Montrobert, *La Lanterne magique*, p. 181. For other accounts of the production see A. Heinrich's preface to the screenplay in Prévert, *La Fleur de l'âge; Drôle de drame*, pp. 20–25; and Alain and Odette Virmaux, "La Malédiction," *Cinématographe*, no. 123 (October 1986): 39–46.

6. Sacha Gordine, letter to Marcel Carné, 25 February 1949, Carné Archives, The French Library in Boston.

7. Jean Cocteau, letter to Marcel Carné, September 1946 (no day), Carné Archives, The French Library in Boston.

8. Jean Cocteau, letter to Marcel Carné, May 1943 (no day), Carné Archives, The French Library in Boston.

9. Jean Cocteau, letter to Marcel Carné, 26 June 1950, Carné Archives, The French Library in Boston.

10. A mimeographed copy of the Carné-Viot-Cocteau shooting script is housed in the Carné Archives, The French Library in Boston. Centered on the title page are the words "La Clé [*sic*] des songes"; above this title appear, hand-written, the words "Juliette ou." An excerpt from this version is printed in Chazal, *Marcel Carné*, pp. 110–20.

11. Climent-Oms, "Marcel Carné parle," p. 39.

12. See Robert T. Eberwein, *Film and the Dream Screen: A Sleep and a Forgetting* (Princeton: Princeton University Press, 1984), pp. 53ff. For another general approach, see Vlada Petric, "A Theoretical-Historical Survey: Film and Dreams," in *Film and Dreams*, ed. V. Petric (South Salem, N.Y.: Redgrave, 1981), pp. 1–48.

13. See Ernest Jones, *On the Nightmare* (New York: Liveright, 1971; orig. 1951), pp. 44, 53, passim.

14. Ibid., pp. 245, 319, 247, 339.

15. For suggestive comments on actor Gérard Philipe's androgynous appeal and, by extension, his suitability for this role, see Pierre Cadars, *Gérard Philipe* (Paris: Henri Veyrier, 1984), pp. 139–40.

16. Marcel Idzkowski, "Surprise à Cannes: le film de Carné est un échec!" *Paris-Presse*, 17 April 1951.

17. The only major critic to praise the film was Pierre Leprohon in a special issue of *Cinémonde*, "Festival de Cannes 1951."

18. See "Charles Spaak au nom du Syndicat des Scénaristes s'addresse à Marcel Carné" in *L'Ecran Français*, no. 310 (13–19 June 1951); the text of this laudatory speech is reprinted as a preface to the 1979 edition of *La Vie à belles dents*, pp. 8–9.

19. André Bazin, "Carné et la désincarnation," orig. *Esprit*, no. 9 (September 1951): 400–405; rpt. in Bazin, *Le Cinéma français*, pp. 71–75; trans. John Shepley as "The Disincarnation of Carné," in Bandy, ed., *Rediscovering French Film*, pp. 131–35. My quotations are from Shepley's translation.

20. Bazin, "The Disincarnation of Carné," pp. 134–35.

21. Ibid., p. 132.

22. Roy Armes, *French Cinema* (London: Secker & Warburg, 1985), p. 147.

23. Hans Mayer, *Outsiders: A Study in Life and Letters*, trans. Denis M. Sweet (Cambridge, Mass.: MIT Press, 1982; orig. 1975), p. 401.

24. See Leo Braudy, "Zola on Film: The Ambiguities of Naturalism," *Yale French Studies*, no. 42 (1969): 68–88, passim.

25. See Abel, *French Cinema*, pp. 134–36.

26. Spoken by Carné in a presentation following a screening of *Thérèse Raquin* at the Massachusetts Institute of Technology, 1 May 1981.

27. See, for example, André Bazin, Michel Mayoux, and Jean-José Richter, "Trahisons," *Cahiers du Cinéma* 5, no. 27 (October 1953): 23–24; and Jean Fayard, "*Thérèse Raquin*: film de Carné, titre de Zola," *Paris-Comoedia*, no. 41 (11–17 November 1953).

28. Emile Zola, *Thérèse Raquin* (Paris: Fasquelle, 1965), pp. 7, 8, 12.

29. Ibid., pp. 8–9.

30. Quoted by Sadoul, *Dictionary of Films*, p. 371; see also Abel, *French Cinema*, p. 136.

31. Simone Signoret, *Nostalgia Isn't What It Used to Be* (New York: Harper & Row, 1978; orig. 1976), pp. 106, 112–13.

32. Simone Signoret, letter to Marcel Carné, 16 January 1953, Carné Archives, The French Library in Boston.

33. André Bazin, "Marcel Carné: *Thérèse Raquin*; des personnages et des mythes," *L'Observateur*, no. 183 (12 November 1953).

34. Roland Lesaffre, personal interview, Paris, 14 December 1979.

35. For published versions of the account, see *La Vie à belles dents*, pp. 303–4; Jacques Mazeau and Didier Thouart, *Les Grands Seconds Rôles du cinéma*

français (Paris: Editions PAC, 1984), pp. 93–98; and Vincent Réal, "Roland Lesaffre croit de nouveau à sa chance," *Ici-Paris*, no. 2125 (27 March–2 April 1986).

36. Henri Langlois, letter to Roland Lesaffre, undated. I am grateful to R. Lesaffre for sharing the contents of this letter with me in Paris on 9 January 1980.

37. David Bordwell, "The Classical Hollywood Style, 1917–60," in D. Bordwell, Janet Staiger, and Kristin Thompson, *The Classical Hollywood Cinema: Film Style and Mode of Production to 1960* (New York: Columbia University Press, 1985), pp. 74–77; Bordwell's formulation of sexual dynamics in film noir draws on E. Ann Kaplan, "Introduction," *Women in Film Noir* (London: British Film Institute, 1978), and Christine Gledhill, "Klute," in the same book. For stimulating commentary on the relations between Carné's prewar films and American film noir, see Jean-Pierre Chartier, "Les Américains aussi font des films 'noirs,'" *La Revue du Cinéma* 1, no. 2 (1 November 1946): 70.

38. See J.F., "Marcel Carné, Ralph Habib, Roland Lesaffre et Etchika Choureau, lauréats des prix du cinéma populiste," *Libération*, 2 July 1954.

39. Jean Desternes, "Après un bon combat: *L'Air de Paris*," *Cahiers du Cinéma* 7, no. 40 (November 1954): 44.

40. Bazin, *Radio-Télé-Cinéma*, 3 October 1954; cited in Mazeau and Thouart, *Les Grands Seconds Rôles*, p. 96.

41. Marcel Carné, "Déclaration de Marcel Carné aux Journalistes de la 50e Biennale," typescript statement on Hotel Excelsior Venezia Lido letterhead, Carné Archives, The French Library in Boston. See also Robert Katz, "Fear Ate His Soul," *American Film* 10, no. 9 (July–August 1985): 43.

16. Carné and the New Wave

1. Truffaut, personal interview, Paris, 9 January 1980.

2. Reported by Marcel Carné in an interview with J.-P. Hauttecoeur, "Carné au présent," *La Croix*, 3 September 1985. Truffaut's sentence, in French, reads: "J'ai fait 23 films . . . eh bien, je les donnerais tous pour avoir fait *Les Enfants du paradis*." I am grateful to Patrick Lepaul, who was present at the Romilly festivities, for corroborating the content of Truffaut's statement.

3. Truffaut's words were rebroadcast in "Marcel Carné, l'oeil du destin," *Les Mardis du cinéma avec Laurence Drummond*, France-Culture, 27 May 1986.

4. François Truffaut, "*Le Pays d'où je viens* de Marcel Carné: une consternante pochade," *Arts; lettres; spectacles*, 31 October–6 November 1956, p. 3.

5. See Anne Gillain, "The Little Robber Boy as Master Narrator," *Wide Angle* 7, nos. 1–2 (special double issue, 1985): 108; and Nick Roddick, "Doodling: *Vivement dimanche!*" *Sight and Sound* 53, no. 1 (Winter 1983–84): 61.

6. Frédéric Laclos, "Des Clefs pour Marcel Carné: *Juliette ou la clef des songes*," *Cahiers du Cinéma* 1, no. 3 (June 1951): 44–46.

7. André Bazin, Michel Mayoux, and Jean-José Richter, "Trahisons," *Cahiers du Cinéma* 5, no. 27 (October 1953): 23–24; Jacques Doniol-Valcroze, "Le Marin de la malchance: *Thérèse Raquin*," *Cahiers du Cinéma* 5, no. 29 (December 1953): 41–42.

8. Desternes, "Après un bon combat," pp. 43–44.

9. Charles Bitsch, Claude Chabrol, Jacques Doniol-Valcroze, et al., "Soixante metteurs en scène français," *Cahiers du Cinéma* 12, no. 71 (May 1957): 51.

10. Jean Quéval, letter to the editors, *Cahiers du Cinéma* 5, no. 26 (September 1953): 64.

11. François Truffaut, "Annuaire biographique du cinéma," *Cahiers du Cinéma* 4, no. 24 (June 1953): 61–62.

12. See, for example, François Truffaut, "Les Truands sont fatigués: *Touchez pas au grisbi*," *Cahiers du Cinéma* 6, no. 34 (April 1954): 54–57; and "Le Vieillissement des films," *Arts; lettres; spectacles*, 28 September 1955.

13. Eric Rohmer, "Redécouvrir l'Amérique," *Cahiers du Cinéma* 7, no. 54 (December 1955): 11ff.

14. Eric Rohmer, "Livres de cinéma; Jean Quéval: *Jacques Prévert*," *Cahiers du Cinéma* 11, no. 65 (December 1956): 56–58.

15. Huguette ex-MICRO [Henri Jeanson], "Quelques réflexions à propos des *Enfants du paradis*," *Le Canard enchaîné*, 11 April 1945.

16. Claude Mauriac, "'Juliette' ou la clé des songes cinématographiques?" *Le Figaro Littéraire*, 26 May 1951.

17. "Petit lexique des scénaristes usuels," *Arts; littérature; spectacles*, 15–21 May 1957, no indication of author(s).

18. Rohmer, "Livres de cinéma," p. 57.

19. Henri Agel, *Les Grands Cinéastes* (Paris: Editions Universitaires, 1959), p. 172.

20. Henri Agel, Introduction to *Les Grands Cinéastes que je propose* (Paris: Editions du Cerf, 1967), p. 7.

21. Agel, *Les Grands Cinéastes* (1959), pp. 173–74.

22. Maurice Tillier, "Carné en liberté!" *Le Figaro Littéraire*, no. 982 (11–17 February 1965): 25. Carné relates the colorful ramifications of his provocative utterance in *La Vie à belles dents*, pp. 400–401.

23. François Truffaut, "Jean Cocteau: *Le Testament d'Orphée*," in *The Films in My Life*, trans. Leonard Mayhew (New York: Simon and Schuster, 1978; orig. 1975), pp. 204–8.

24. Truffaut, "Une Certaine Tendance," p. 28. This essay appears in English translation in *Cahiers du Cinéma in English*, no. 1 (1966); portions are reprinted in John Caughie, ed., *Theories of Authorship* (London: Routledge & Kegan Paul, 1981). Translations from this essay are my own.

25. Jean-Pierre Barrot, "La tradition de la qualité," in *Sept ans de cinéma* (Paris: Cerf, 1953), p. 27.

26. See Truffaut, *Films in My Life*, p. 215.

27. Truffaut, "Une Certaine Tendance," p. 24.

28. Stanley Kauffmann, "Seeing as Believing," *New Republic*, 30 September 1985, p. 36.
29. Jean Renoir, letter to Louis Guillaume, 2 July 1945, in J. Renoir, *Lettres d'Amérique*, ed. Dido Renoir and Alexander Sesonske (Paris: Presses de la Renaissance, 1984), p. 193.
30. John Hess, "La Politique des auteurs: Part One: World View as Aesthetic," *Jump Cut*, no. 1 (May–June 1974): 19.
31. Jim Hillier, Introduction to *Cahiers du Cinéma: Neo-Realism, Hollywood, New Wave* (Cambridge, Mass.: Harvard University Press, 1985), p. 7.
32. Raymond Durgnat, *Films and Feelings* (London: Faber, 1967), p. 82.
33. "Interview with Godard," in *Godard on Godard: Critical Writings by Jean-Luc Godard*, ed. Jean Narboni and Tom Milne (New York: Viking, 1972; orig. 1968), p. 193.
34. Michel Marie, "The Art of the Film in France Since the 'New Wave,'" trans. Robert Ariew, *Wide Angle* 4, no. 4 (1981): 19; orig. in *Cinéma d'aujourd'hui*, nos. 12–13 (Spring 1977).
35. Truffaut, personal interview, Paris, 13 December 1979.
36. Truffaut, "*Le Pays d'où je viens*," p. 3.
37. Shot 228 of the mimeographed shooting script of *Le Pays d'où je viens*, housed in the Carné Archives, The French Library in Boston.
38. Françoise Giroud, "Marcel Carné: Je n'ai rien inventé," *L'Express*, 16 October 1958, pp. 18–19.
39. Ibid., p. 18.
40. Jean-Luc Douin suggests that Pierre Billard, in *Cinéma 58*, no. 24 (February 1958), was the first journalist to refer to a cinematic "new wave"; see Jean-Luc Douin, ed., *La Nouvelle Vague 25 ans après* (Paris: Les Editions du Cerf, 1983), p. 19. According to Charles Ford, in *Histoire du cinéma français contemporain, 1945–1977* (Paris: France-Empire, 1977), the term was borrowed from the plastic arts, where it had been used to designate new painters of the post–World War I era, p. 156.
41. Marcel Carné in Armand Panigel's documentary series for French television, *Histoire du cinéma français par ceux qui l'ont fait*, part 10, *Tu n'as rien vu à Hiroshima*, orig. telecast 8 July 1975.
42. Truffaut, personal interview, Paris, 13 December 1979; also see Réné Prédal, "De Bonnes Recettes pour faire des économies," in Douin, ed., *La Nouvelle Vague*, pp. 73–86.
43. Carné, personal interview, Paris, 7 January 1980.
44. See Robin Wood, "Responsibilities of a Gay Film Critic," *Film Comment* 14, no. 1 (January–February 1978): 14–15.
45. Bosley Crowther, "Screen: A Study of Parisian Youth," *New York Times*, 5 June 1961.
46. See Hal Ellson, *Tomboy* (New York: Scribner's, 1950).
47. Jean de Baroncelli, "*Terrain Vague* de Marcel Carné," *Le Monde*, 15 November 1960, p. 13.

48. Georges Sadoul, "*Terrain Vague* de Marcel Carné," *Les Lettres Françaises*, 17–23 November 1960, p. 6.
49. François Truffaut, postcard to Marcel Carné, 4 December 1960, in Carné Archives, The French Library in Boston. In a letter accompanying the card and dated 7 December 1960, Truffaut extends apologies for having been unable to mail the postcard until his return to Paris, and states that, in the interval, "I have thought over and over about 'Terrain Vague' and my emotion has grown even stronger." Although Carné claims in *La Vie à belles dents*, p. 372, not to have answered Truffaut, Truffaut informed me, during a personal interview in Paris on 9 January 1980, that Carné did respond, "very kindly."

17. Persistence of Vision

1. Signoret, *Nostalgia*, p. 56.
2. Leonard Harris, "Take 6 in Central Park," *New York World-Telegram & Sun*, 12 May 1965.
3. Anne Capelle, ". . . l'amertume de Marcel Carné," *Les Nouvelles Littéraires*, (7 October 1965).
4. See Richard Roud, *A Passion for Films: Henri Langlois and the Cinémathèque Française* (New York: Viking, 1983); "L'Affaire Langlois," *Cahiers du Cinéma*, no. 199 (March 1968): 31–46; "Vers un livre blanc du cinéma français," *Cahiers du Cinéma*, nos. 200–201 (April–May 1968): 72–93; "Le Retour de Langlois," *Cahiers du Cinéma*, no. 202 (June–July 1968): 68; and Georges P. Langlois and Glenn Myrent, *Henri Langlois: premier citoyen du cinéma* (Paris: Denoël, 1986).
5. See Godard's remarks in "L'Affaire Langlois," p. 34.
6. Henri Langlois, letter to Marcel Carné, 27 April 1968, Carné Archives, The French Library in Boston.
7. Jacques Rivette in "L'Affaire Langlois," p. 37.
8. The sequence, as written, appears in *Les Jeunes Loups*'s published script, *L'Avant-Scène Cinéma*, no. 81 (May 1968): 49.
9. Marcel Carné, in an undated note appended to René Pignères, letter to Marcel Carné, 21 November 1967, Carné Archives, The French Library in Boston.
10. See Serge Youtkevitch, "Lettre ouverte à Marcel Carné," 1 September 1946; rpt. in *Cinéma d'aujourd'hui et de demain* (Moscow: Sovexportfilm, 1946); portions appeared in *L'Ecran Français*, no. 98 (13 May 1947).
11. "*Les Assassins de l'ordre* font sensation au Kremlin," *L'Aurore*, 28 July 1971.
12. Marcel Carné, "Notes pour l'histoire future (1): *Les Assassins de l'ordre de Marcel Carné*," *Les Cahiers de la Cinémathèque*, no. 5 (Winter 1972): 56.
13. See Philippe Bouvard, "Carné abandonne à neuf minutes de l'arrivée," *France-Soir*, 1 December 1973.

14. Pierre Lherminier, "Plaidoirie: Carné et les moulins à vent," *Pariscope*, no. 346 (8–14 January 1975).

15. Gilles Colpart, "La merveilleuse visite," *Revue du Cinéma: Image et Son*, no. 293 (February 1975): 102.

16. Jean de Baroncelli, "'La Merveilleuse Visite' de Marcel Carné," *Le Monde*, 1–2 December 1974.

17. Robert Chazal, "'La Merveilleuse visite': l'enfant du paradis," *France-Soir*, 30 November 1974.

18. André Lafargue, "Le Retour de Marcel Carné," *Le Parisien*, 20 May 1974.

19. Pierre Montaigne, "Marcel Carné à contre-courant: Un film d'après H. G. Wells sans violence ni érotisme," *Le Figaro*, 21 November 1974.

20. Marcel Carné, "Polémique: Un Scandale," *Pariscope*, 27 November–3 December 1974, p. 5.

21. Jean-Louis Bory, "Le Droit au charme et au rêve," *Le Nouvel Observateur*, no. 528 (22–28 December 1974): 52.

22. H. G. Wells, *The Wonderful Visit* (London: J. M. Dent & Co., Aldine House, 1895), pp. 15, 33, 131.

23. Ibid., p. 94.

24. Ibid., p. 247.

25. Lafargue, "Le Retour de Marcel Carné."

26. Nicole Jolivet, "Marcel Carné fera mourir le soleil dans son prochain film," *France-Soir*, 7 May 1974.

Epilogue

1. Quoted in Philippe Bouvard, "Carné sauvé par l'amitié," *France-Soir*, 29–30 April 1973.

2. Jean-Claude Mazeran, "Marcel Carné à coeur ouvert: 'Pourquoi m'en veut-on à ce point?'" *Le Journal du Dimanche*, 8 December 1974.

3. See, for example, Maggie Lewis, "Marcel Carné: 'To Fight Is to Live,'" *Christian Science Monitor*, 14 May 1981, p. B14.

4. See Jacques Chirac, letter to Marcel Carné, 18 June 1982, Carné Archives, The French Library in Boston.

5. Carné, personal interview, Boston, 2 May 1981.

6. See Pierre Montaigne, "Marcel Carné, 'clochard d'honneur' de la culture française," *Le Figaro*, 15 April 1982.

7. Carné, personal interview, Paris, 7 September 1985.

8. Guy de Maupassant, "Mouche," in *Contes et nouvelles*, ed. A.-M. Schmidt and G. Delaisement (Paris: Albin Michel, 1967), p. 1347.

9. Carné, personal interview, Paris, 26 June 1983.

10. Maupassant, "Mouche," p. 1340.

11. Carné, personal interview, Paris, 26 June 1983.

12. Bazin, "Disincarnation of Carné," p. 131.

13. Maurice Perisset, *A Bas Le Cinéma, vive le cinéma* (Paris: Editions PAC, 1974), p. 141.
14. The event, including an interview with Carné conducted by Samuel Lachize, is recorded on film by Daniel Martineau, *Inauguration: Place Carné* (1982; producer, Roland Lesaffre; 20 minutes).
15. Roland Lesaffre, letter to me, 27 June 1981.

Credits

For permission to reproduce pictorial materials, I acknowledge gratefully:

The Carné Archives, The French Library in Boston: 1, 3, 4, 5, 6, 8, 9, 10, 16, 17, 18, 20, 21, 22, 26, 27, 28, 29, 32, 33, 34, 35, 36, 37, 38, 39, 40, 41, 42, 43, 45, 46, 47, 48, 49, 50, 51, 52, 53, 57, 58, 60, 67, 70, 71 (also shown on page ii), 72, 76, 83, 90, 91, 92, 93, 94, 95, 99, 100, 101, 102, 103, 104, 105, 106, 107, 108, 109, 110, 111, 112, 113, 114, 116, 117.

Philip D. Cobb: 2, 30, 40, 41, 45, 54, 99, 110, 112, 115.

The Harvard University Art Museums (Fogg Art Museum); bequest, Grenville L. Winthrop: 84.

The Louvre Museum/Cliché des Musées Nationaux, Paris: 82, 85, 87.

The Metropolitan Museum of Art: 97.

The National Gallery of Art, Washington; Samuel H. Kress Collection: 96.

The National Gallery, London: 98.

For permission to reprint textual materials, I acknowledge with thanks: Marcel Carné, for my translated excerpts from *La Vie à belles dents* (Paris: Jean Vuarnet, 1979); David R. Godine, Publisher, for excerpts from *Les Fleurs du Mal* by Charles Baudelaire, trans. Richard Howard, trans. © 1982 by Richard Howard; Lorrimer Publishing Limited, for excerpts, with punctuation and spelling slightly modified by me, from the screenplays of *Children of Paradise*, trans. Dinah Brooke, © 1968, and *Le Jour se lève*, trans. Dinah Brooke and Nicola Hayden, © 1970; Oxford University Press, for excerpts from Marc Bloch, *Strange Defeat*, trans. Gerard Hopkins (New York: Octagon Books, 1968); Madame Jacques Prévert and Editions Gallimard for my translated excerpts from the poems "Il ne faut pas . . . ," "Pour toi mon amour," and "Le Jardin" in *Paroles*, © 1949, and from the poem "Fête" in *Spectacle*, © 1951; and Madame Jacques Prévert for my translated excerpts from "Poème de Jacques Prévert à Jean Gabin" and from the published screenplays of *Drôle de Drame* (Paris: L'Avant-Scène Cinéma, 1969) and *Le Quai des Brumes* (Paris: L'Avant-Scène Cinéma, 1979).

Index